1775-1830 Revolutions

Edited by Merryn Williams

With 24 illustrations, 12 in full colour

Penguin Books in association with The Open University Press

Penguin Books Ltd, Harmondsworth,
Middlesex, England
Penguin Books Inc, 7110 Ambassador Road,
Baltimore, Md 21207, USA
Penguin Books Australia Ltd,
Ringwood, Victoria, Australia

First published 1971
This selection copyright © The Open University, 1971
Introduction and notes copyright © The Open University, 1971

Made and printed in Great Britain by
Hazell Watson & Viney Ltd,
Aylesbury, Bucks
Set in Linotype Granjon

Penguin Education

Revolutions 1775–1830
The Open University

Faculty of Arts Course
'The Age of Revolutions'

Course Team

Tim Benton
Owain Edwards
Clive Emsley
John Ferguson
Ossie Hanfling
Christopher Harvie
Cicely Havely
Arnold Kettle
Graham Martin
Colin Russell
Aaron Scharf
Godfrey Vesey

Preface

Many of the titles of documents in this book are supplied by the editor rather than the original author. This occurs where an extract has been taken or where no title exists. Italicization of titles indicates that the title is that used by the author and the document is printed in its entirety.

The editor is responsible for those phrases, footnotes and omission points in the documents which are printed in square brackets.

Contents

ix Contents

x Contents

L Scientific Change

M High Art

O Religious Changes

List of Plates

Introduction

'We hold these truths to be self-evident,' wrote the authors of the Declaration of Independence, 'that all men are created equal. . . .' Actually, of course, this was very far from self-evident in the year 1776. Many people still assumed that kings (and most kings in Europe were absolutists), an established church and a class system were the foundations of any civilized state. Equality at that time was a new and startling concept. The principles which the American rebels, at least in the abstract, embraced, were revolutionary. So were the slogans of the French Revolution – 'Liberty, Equality, Fraternity' – in 1789.

It was not that people before that time had never dreamed of freedom. Perhaps these ideas were not quite as new as they seemed. There had been another great revolution in England, almost a century and a half before, and anyone who had studied the ideas of Cromwell, the Levellers and the Diggers would have been familiar with the varieties of republican and radical thought. Throughout the eighteenth century the movement of opinion called the Enlightenment (which embraced men like Locke, Hume, Rousseau and Voltaire) had been questioning the rights of absolutist governments. But there was no *qualitative* change until the American colonists asserted their independence, the French overthrew Louis XVI and the industrial revolution began to change the face of England. Our period is called the Age of Revolutions because so many great changes were happening in so many fields at the same time.

This book is a collection of some historical documents from the period (such as the American Declaration of Independence and the French Declaration of the Rights of Man) together with others (like Stendhal's essays, and extracts from Wordsworth's Preface to *Lyrical Ballads* and Kant's *Critique of Pure Reason*) which illustrate, in one way or another, the mind of the age. There are also a few essays by modern writers. They were selected by members of the Open University's Age of Revolutions Course Team, who have also written brief

introductions to their own sections. The course is
designed to give students some idea of what was happening
during this period (1775–1830), first through a general survey of
its political revolutions and economic changes and then by
studying some of the major creative minds of the time. The
method is to take one, or sometimes two, outstanding
representative figures in the fields of literature, science, music,
the visual arts, philosophy, religion and political thought, and
look in detail at their significance. It is impossible to do more
than this in a course lasting only one year. The book is primarily
for students taking the Age of Revolutions course, because it
contains several texts which are discussed in the correspondence
material and others which relate directly to what they are
studying. It will be most valuable if it is read at the same time as
the course units and set books which place the individual
documents in their context. But while we hope that some
non-students will be inspired to buy our course units – they are
all on sale to the public – we feel that the book is interesting in
its own right, so long as the reader accepts its limitations. These
limitations were imposed firstly by the need to keep the book
down to a reasonable size (as originally planned it was nearly
twice as long as it is now), and secondly by the special needs of
the course. If this is not understood, it is bound to seem a rather
eccentric selection. The reader who is looking for a
comprehensive review of the period will find nothing about
Napoleon, for example, nothing about the Romantic poetry of
Blake, Keats, Byron or Shelley, and very little about the
industrial revolution. Some of them have already been discussed
in the course units and no extra documents were necessary.
Beethoven is omitted because all the relevant documents about
him can be found in the set book for the course. There was no
room, anyway, to do more than discuss a cross-section of the great
men and events of the time. But the book does offer an extremely
wide and varied selection of documents – some famous, others
which will almost certainly be unknown to the general reader –
which should be helpful to anyone who is interested in the 'Age
of Revolutions'. Non-specialists are advised to follow up their
own interests, and not try to read the book right through.

Sections A to F are concerned with the political and economic changes towards the end of the eighteenth century. Several of the constitutions and manifestos drawn up by the rebels in America, France and the Netherlands are reproduced here. In Europe the political revolutions were short-lived. The risings in the Netherlands were crushed; the French Republic was destroyed by Napoleon who was, if possible, an even more absolute ruler than Louis XVI [1] – and after him the Bourbons were brought back and lasted until 1830. In England, traditionally the most liberal and tolerant country in the Old World, there was a violent reaction against 'French ideas'. Joseph Priestley's laboratory was sacked by a Tory mob in Birmingham. Tom Paine, perhaps the greatest popularizer of the new radical ideas, who was honoured by the revolutionaries in both America and France, would have been arrested if he had not left the country at the last moment. It is said that the poet Blake warned him, 'You must not go home, or you are a dead man.' Blake himself was put on trial for sedition in 1804 (he was alleged to have said, 'Damn the King!' to a soldier, and he was certainly capable of it). Many writers – like Wordsworth, Coleridge and Southey – became conservatives as they grew older. The younger generation of Romantic poets – all of them too young to remember the revolutionary dawn of 1789 which Wordsworth had described so ecstatically – grew up in an atmosphere of conformity and oppression. Byron, Shelley and Keats all died in exile and never saw the rebirth of revolutionary ideas in the Chartist movement and the European revolutions of 1848.

Only in America was the movement for freedom successful,[2]

1. But he was also a much more *modern* figure, having become Emperor through his own efforts instead of *inheriting* his power like the kings of the *ancien régime*. The idea of genius rising from obscurity and forcing the world to honour it fits easily into the romantic world view. Napoleon's career was an inspiration to ambitious young men throughout Europe for the rest of the century. Examples of this in literature are Dostoevsky's *Crime and Punishment*, Stendhal's *Le Rouge et le Noir*, and Tolstoy's *War and Peace*.

2. Liberals in Europe tended to see America as a promised land. Shelley in *The Revolt of Islam* (1818) wrote: 'There is a People mighty in its

and this was largely because of the country's isolation from Europe and the revolution's limited aims. Unlike some European thinkers, the Americans never contemplated abolishing property – the whole basis of their national prosperity was that they lived in a vast, unexplored, virgin country where each individual was encouraged to make himself rich. They were also so far from believing in total freedom that Negro slavery was tolerated (although Jefferson would have liked to abolish it). The issue here was much more the nation's freedom to expand and become prosperous than the individual's freedom from persecution. The country was not to tear itself apart until nearly a century later, when the issue of slavery could no longer be shelved.

Section G concentrates on Thomas Jefferson, the third President of the United States and the chief author of the Declaration of Independence. Jefferson was a typical man of the enlightenment – cultivated, sceptical, a humanitarian and a passionate believer in freedom. He was more fortunate than the European revolutionaries in that he saw the triumph of his cause and took a major part in the making of history. In the last letter he wrote, ten days before his death, he looked forward confidently to a new age of freedom:

All eyes are opened, or opening, to the rights of man. The great spread of the light of science has already laid open to every view the palpable truth, that the mass of mankind has not been born with saddles on their backs, nor a favoured few booted and spurred ready to ride them.

Section H is concerned with Goethe, perhaps the greatest writer of the age, and Rousseau, its most influential thinker. Rousseau, who died before the French Revolution, had a central influence on its ideology and was also one of the founding fathers of Romanticism. 'Man is born free,' he opened his famous book *The Social Contract*, 'and everywhere he is in chains.'

---

youth/A land beyond the Oceans of the West/Where tho' with rudest rites, Freedom and Truth/Are worshipped.' He hoped that America would write 'an epitaph of glory for the tomb/Of murdered Europe'. Both Paine and Priestley finally settled in America and died there.

Rousseau taught that human beings were naturally good, but had been corrupted by living in society. He attacked inequality, the artificiality of modern civilization, and even property – 'the fruit of the earth belong to all and the earth itself to no man'. Although not all his followers went as far as this, he did have a very great influence on the makers of the American and French Revolutions. Men who were taking the almost unprecedented step of overthrowing their lawful governments needed to feel that they were justified by some kind of natural law. Their assertions that they had the right as it were to go back to nature, to draw up their own constitutions, and to rebuild society from the foundations, can clearly be traced back to Rousseau's philosophy. But he only became really popular after he was dead; during his lifetime he was persecuted by the French and Swiss governments and threatened with arrest several times.

Rousseau's other great contribution to philosophy was his emphasis on what Keats was later to call 'the holiness of the heart's affections' – the truth and purity of human emotions in their uncorrupted state. In this respect he was flamboyantly opposed to most eighteenth-century philosophers who appealed to reason in their arguments and tended to distrust emotion as an irrational and unpredictable force. It is a familiar Romantic position that the reasoning power cut off from normal human feelings is cold, destructive and sterile. This can become exaggerated, of course, and Rousseau's writings are often marred by their hectoring, sentimental or hysterical tone. But the remarkable thing is that, so far from trying to separate reason and emotion, he insisted that any such separation was unreal and that it was necessary to feel deeply in order to think clearly :

It is by the activity of the passions that our reason is im-proved; for we desire knowledge only because we wish to enjoy; and it is impossible to conceive any reason why a person who has neither fears nor desires should give him-self the trouble of reasoning.

In fact, Rousseau would not have had nearly as much influence as he did if he had not been an extremely cogent and brilliant reasoner. This influence was so widely diffused that it is almost impossible to trace it. We find it in political writers like Paine – 'Government, like dress, is the badge of lost innocence' – and also in poets like Wordsworth, the subject of the next section.

Rousseau's influence on the early Wordsworth (section J) is fairly obvious. They had the same faith in the essential goodness of man, the same interest in childhood and the same concern that the increasing complexity of modern civilization [3] would destroy natural innocence and drive people towards violence and insensibility. Wordsworth, explaining why he had generally chosen to write poems about rural life, said that it was

because in that situation the essential passions of the heart find a better soil in which they can attain their maturity, are less under restraint, and speak a plainer and more emphatic language; because in that situation our elementary feelings exist in a state of greater simplicity.

He went on to define good poetry as 'the spontaneous overflow of powerful feelings' – a clear echo of Rousseau's teaching. But he added immediately that it could only be written by 'a man who, being possessed of more than usual organic sensibility, had also thought long and deeply'. The sober and reasonable Wordsworth was the very antithesis of the popular image of the wild-eyed romantic poet. But only the minor Romantics ever allowed their writing to degenerate into a shapeless outpouring of emotion. In the great Romantics – and Wordsworth was one of the very greatest – the capacity for deep feeling was never separated from a sense of social responsibility. Each of his poems, Wordsworth claimed, had 'a worthy *purpose*', and 'if in this opinion I am mistaken I can have little right to the name of a Poet'. He was contemptuous of critics who 'will converse with us as gravely about a *taste* for Poetry ... as if it were a thing as indifferent as a taste for Rope-dancing, or Frontiniac or Sherry'. The greatest fault of many contemporary writers had been to 'separate themselves from the sympathies of

3. Wordsworth spoke apprehensively in the Preface to *Lyrical Ballads* of 'the increasing accumulation of men in cities, where the uniformity of their occupations produces a craving for extraordinary incident'.

men, and indulge in arbitrary and capricious habits of expression in order to furnish food for fickle tastes and fickle appetites of their own creation'. The purpose of all genuine poets was to remind men of the things that mattered most to them, and in this way to fight against the spiritual degradation threatened by modern life.

Wordsworth's Preface to *Lyrical Ballads* – which we have only been able to quote in part – is one of the most important statements in English literature of the meaning and purpose of poetry. He was well aware that what he was saying was revolutionary, and the poems were ridiculed by several critics when they came out. Some of them were certainly naïve, but most people today would feel that the Preface was more important than all but a few of the poems it introduced. Its central significance lies in its essentially *democratic* conception of poetry and of human nature. It was democratic first in that Wordsworth deliberately concentrated on ordinary people – mostly shepherds and farmers – and on 'the incidents of common life'. It was also deeply democratic in Wordsworth's refusal to see poets or their readers as members of a small elite. For him the poet was simply 'a man speaking to men',[4] in language which must be clear and comprehensible but which would inevitably 'fall far short of that which is uttered by men in real life'.

One of the strongest influences on Wordsworth in his youth was the French Revolution, whose overpowering effect on him he described in the famous line, 'Bliss was it in that dawn to be alive'. In this anthology we can study his early radical views in some less well-known pieces; his descriptions of his visit to France in *The Prelude* and his letter to the reactionary Bishop of Llandaff. Later his views changed; he grew more and more conservative, wrote a series of sonnets supporting capital

4. Wordsworth qualified this by saying that a poet would have 'more lively sensibility, more enthusiasm and tenderness . . . a greater knowledge of human nature, and a more comprehensive soul, than are supposed to be common among mankind'. The younger romantic Keats pushed the argument further in *The Fall of Hyperion*: 'Who alive can say/Thou art no poet – mayst not tell thy dreams?/Since every man whose soul is not a clod/ Hath visions, and would speak, if he had loved/And been well nurtured in his mother tongue.'

punishment and ended up as the Poet Laureate. The younger Romantic poets always felt his defection as a tragedy and Browning mourned it much later in *The Lost Leader*.

Rousseau's influence on his fellow philosophers (section K) is very much less important. The great thinkers of the eighteenth century were generally older than him and belonged to the rationalistic movement with which Rousseau, as a pre-Romantic, had only a limited sympathy. Of the three represented in this course John Locke, who lived before our period, was one of the great founders of the Enlightenment. He argued in favour of religious toleration and against despotic governments, and his ideas have been credited with a great influence on the American and French constitutions. The Scotsman David Hume befriended Rousseau when he was in danger of arrest from the French government in 1766 and sheltered him in England, until the splenetic Jean-Jacques picked a quarrel and left the country. Their ideas, no less than their personalities, were, in the long run, incompatible. Hume had made himself notorious by his apparent atheism and denial that any knowledge was possible outside the realm of sense-experience, whereas Rousseau believed passionately in a benevolent deity and argued the case for natural religion in his great work on education, *Émile*.

Immanuel Kant spent his entire life in the little Prussian town of Königsberg where he was a professor at the university. It is said that his habits were so regular that the citizens used to set their clocks by the time of his afternoon 'constitutional'. He only broke this habit twice, once to read *Émile* and once when he heard about the fall of the Bastille. Kant was a lifelong liberal who welcomed the French Revolution. He himself fell foul of the despotism in his own state in 1794 when the King of Prussia ordered him not to publish anything more on religious matters. For although Kant was morally certain that God existed he tried to re-interpret metaphysics in the light of Hume's sceptical philosophy and was regarded as a very unorthodox thinker. Kant is notoriously difficult to read, and Hume, although his style is smoother, is like him in being an intellectual writing for intellectuals. Perhaps their basic difference from Rousseau is that it was Rousseau's mission, above all, to *popularize* certain ideas.

Section L includes some English scientific documents from our period, with particular reference to Humphry Davy. Davy was a remarkable man, a friend of Coleridge and Southey, who read the proofs of *Lyrical Ballads* and wrote romantic poetry describing his passionate love of nature. Davy's career showed that it was possible for a distinguished thinker to combine being intensely practical with being intensely romantic (the 'two cultures' of our own day would have made no sense to him). He is remembered for his invention of the miners' safety lamp.

Section M deals with the concept of 'High Art' and the reaction to it from contemporary painters and thinkers in England and France. The tradition of 'High Art' defended certain values in painting which go back to Raphael and the Italian Renaissance. In France, the Academy had maintained these standards since the seventeenth century and they can only fully be understood in terms of support by an official Academy. In England, Sir Joshua Reynolds, in our period, tried to formulate the principles which lay behind this tradition. Several passages in this anthology are taken from the Discourses he gave annually for several years to the students of the Royal Academy, which had been founded under the patronage of King George III and of which he was the first president. Reynolds was the most popular portrait painter of his day and may be said to have dominated English painting for a generation. The ideal he taught was a 'grand style' dealing only with lofty subjects (such as those drawn from classical mythology) and he urged students to learn all they could from the great Renaissance painters, and from the art of Greece and Rome. But his reverence for the past imposed severe limitations on his conception of what was possible for the modern artist. 'Search after novelty, in conception or in treating the subject,' he wrote, 'has no place.'

William Blake, whose uniquely beautiful poems and engravings remained almost unknown in his lifetime, was never a member of the Academy. We know, however, what he thought of Reynolds, from the abusive comments he scribbled in the margin of his copy of the *Discourses*. To an outsider like him, Reynolds seemed the personification of smugness. Reynolds's pronouncements, and Blake's comments, form a running dialogue of the greatest interest between two conceptions of art. The debate between traditionalists and those who wished to experiment with new kinds of art was to preoccupy nineteenth-century painters in both England and France, and some of their arguments can be read elsewhere in section M. The complexity of the period can best be understood by looking at a painter like Ingres who is neither completely classical nor completely Romantic but has a whole web of different, strongly held beliefs – which are illustrated in his aphorisms.

The stifling nature of the 1820s in France under the Restoration is described – not without partisanship – in Stendhal's essays in section N. The two chapters from Jacques Droz's book, *Europe Between the Revolutions*, gives the historical background in more detail. This section is part of the background reading for Stendhal's wonderful novel, *Scarlet and Black*, which is a set book for the course. Together with Balzac – they are probably the two greatest French novelists – Stendhal transformed the novel into something entirely new; in fact this may be said to be the period when the modern novel was *created*. This kind of novel focused directly on the problems of man in society – usually of an exceptional man in a corrupt society like contemporary France. Detailed descriptions of institutions, of class relationships and of the struggle for power entered fiction for the first time – as well as a much closer attention to human psychology than had been common in the last century. *Scarlet and Black* is clearly a post-Revolution novel, for, although the old order had been restored in France, it still appeared – and was – possible for a man of genius to overthrow it, as Napoleon had done thirty years before. Social relationships were no longer rigidly stratified; ambitious men could move upwards and downwards in a society which is implicitly compared (in the title) to a game of roulette. It is also in some sense a deeply Romantic novel, or perhaps one should say post-Romantic. Stendhal was too much of a cynic to accept the whole of Romanticism; few writers have described human weakness with more detachment and irony. He had, however, been associated with the Romantic movement in criticism when he published the pamphlet *Racine and Shakespeare*,[5] and many of the attitudes of that movement continued to colour his work. The hero of *Scarlet and Black* is a genius who achieves nothing, a Napoleon who dies on the guillotine without ever having been recognized by the world. He is also (I would argue) an idealist at heart who is forced by the society he lives in to become unscrupulous, calculating and hypocritical. Julien's tragedy is that he cannot *consistently* be either a man of principle or a careerist, and he ultimately throws away his life because his feelings are too deep and powerful to allow him to go on acting a role. Stendhal's novel transforms into great art the dialectic (the term had just been given its modern meaning by Hegel) between the Romanticism which wanted to take the world by storm and the cynicism and venality of French society in his day.

Section O deals with the religious or Evangelical revival in England, which is associated with John Wesley and the Methodists and also with William Wilberforce and the Clapham Sect within the established Church. Perhaps the first thing to note is that in many respects it was definitely hostile to the spirit of the age. The great thinkers of the eighteenth and early nineteenth centuries had rarely been orthodox Christians; the French revolution had been on very hostile terms with the Church. Philosophers tended to be deists. These doctrines, when they were popularized by Tom Paine, seem to have found some response among the working classes; Bishop Porteous wrote:

they have even found their way into the very bowels of the earth, among the miners of Cornwall and the colliers of Newcastle, some of whom are said to have sold their bibles in order to purchase the *Age of Reason*.

It was, however, primarily to this same class that the movement appealed. George Eliot, herself the product of a strict Evangelical home, movingly described in several of her novels

5. The literary establishment of the seventeenth and eighteenth centuries was inclined to dismiss Shakespeare as uncivilized, though a genius, because he wrote irregular blank verse and ignored the 'three unities' of Greek classical drama. The Romantics revered him and in their period there was a great upsurge of interest in Shakespeare.

the need which the working classes felt for a religion that would make sense of their lives. In *The Mill on the Floss* she speaks of

> a wide and arduous national life condensed in unfragrant, deafening factories; cramping itself in mines; sweating at furnaces; grinding, hammering, weaving, under more or less oppression of carbonic acid – or else, spread over sheepwalks, and scattered in lonely houses and huts on the clayey or chalky cornlands, where the rainy days look dreary. This wide national life is based entirely on emphasis – the emphasis of want ... Under such circumstances, there are many among its myriads of souls who have absolutely needed an emphatic belief ... something that good society calls 'enthusiasm'.

The chapter from her first novel, *Adam Bede*, is included because it gives the feeling, as contemporary documents cannot, of what it was actually *like* to be a Methodist at the turn of the century and how the Methodists appeared to other people. Dinah Morris is an ordinary working girl (her mistakes of grammar are carefully transcribed) but Methodism gives her the strength to overcome the traditional restrictions on her class and her sex because of her burning need to communicate the truth that is in her. 'Jesus Christ spoke those words – he said he came *to preach the Gospel to the poor*.' The Evangelical revival was in many ways distinctly radical, though anti-revolutionary. It appealed to large sections of the labouring classes. It spilled over into active social concern, as in Elizabeth Fry's work at Newgate and Wilberforce's campaign against the slave trade. The secret of its appeal to large masses of people lay, clearly, in its 'enthusiasm' – its unashamed appeal to the emotions. Wilberforce tells us, in his defence of 'the place of the affections in religion', that their opponents accused them of 'substituting a set of mere feelings in place of the worship of the understanding' – of being hostile to 'rational' religion. One of the really interesting things about the Evangelical movement is that its language is, in many cases, purely Romantic. Listen to John Newton describing the process of personal conversion which was necessary to each individual before he could be saved:

There is a certain important change takes place in the heart, by the operation of the Spirit of God, before the soundest and most orthodox sentiments can have their proper influence upon us. . . . Till a person has experienced this change, he will be at a loss to form a right conception of it: but it means, not being proselyted to an opinion, but receiving a principle of divine life and light in the soul. . . . At length he begins to *feel* the inward depravity, which before he owned as an opinion. . . . Here reasoning will stand him in no stead. . . . Then he learns that scriptural faith is a very different thing from a rational assent to the Gospel. . . . No other faith will purify the heart, work by love, and overcome the world.

This is related, of course, to the central Protestant teaching of 'justification by faith', but its links with the Romantic assertion that reason without powerful feelings is useless, and the Romantic emphasis on the autonomy of each individual soul, are no less clear and important. Although they denounced the French Revolution as anti-Christian and encouraged the poor to be resigned to their situation, the later Evangelicals were still very much a product of the revolutionary age.

We end this selection with two extracts from Shelley's *A Defence of Poetry* (section P). In many ways this continues the argument of Wordsworth's preface to *Lyrical Ballads*, which had a crucial influence on nearly all of the English Romantics. Shelley was the most overtly 'political' poet of his generation, although Byron had championed the Greek rebels and the Nottingham weavers, and Keats – it is not widely enough recognized – was a very serious and consistent radical. But Shelley, ever since he had been sent down from Oxford for writing *The Necessity of Atheism*, had identified himself passionately with the revolutionary cause in every way possible, both as a poet and as a man. Poems like *The Masque of Anarchy* and *Men of England* are a passionate appeal to the people of England to rise in revolt.

The *Defence* is really a description of the dialectical process whereby the revolutionary in Shelley's nature gradually came to terms with the poet. It is an attempt to reconcile the act of writing poetry with the great aim, which he never abandoned, of doing some good to humanity. At much the same time as the 'unpolitical' Keats was asking himself, in *The Fall of Hyperion*, whether poets were not inferior to those who actively struggled to help others, Shelley was moving towards the position that the poet must not be too deeply involved in politics. When he was, Shelley thought that his poetry usually suffered. He praised 'the exertions of Locke, Hume, Gibbon, Voltaire, Rousseau and their disciples in favour of oppressed and deluded humanity', but saw their achievements as ultimately less than those of the greatest poets. Where they were attacking the negatives of oppression and superstition, the poets were asserting the best in man and thereby creating a new positive morality:

The great secret of morals is love, or a going out of our own nature, and an identification of ourselves with the beautiful which exists in thought, action or person not our own. [...] The great instrument of moral good is the imagination.

The Romantic opposition of imagination to reason resulted, as usual, in the victory of the imagination. Shelley ended his essay on a note of transcendent optimism. He and his kind were the only real legislators. There had been many attempts, over the last fifty years, to bring freedom into existence through constitutions, but it was only the poets, after all, who could create a new world. Reading this essay, and remembering that it was written after the triumph of reaction in Europe and the failure of Shelley's personal attempts to spread enlightened ideas among his contemporaries, it is impossible not to suspect that he was trying to cheer himself up. Yet his emphasis on the infinite value of human creativity – so central to Romanticism – was very important in its own right. And none of the poets – or other artists and thinkers – whom we study here can really be understood in isolation from the Age of Revolutions, for – as Shelley pointed out – what they created showed 'less their spirit than the spirit of the age'.

M.W.

A Worldwide Revolution?

Since the French Revolution people have been tempted to find links between it and the American Revolution, which had preceded it by a decade. French troops had, after all, fought side by side with the colonists. The French commitment in America on the side of the colonists had further weakened the unstable finances of the *ancien régime*. In both upheavals, some of the revolutionaries spoke in terms of liberty, equality and the rights of man. In recent years two historians, Robert R. Palmer and Jacques Godechot, have suggested that there was more than just a link between the American and the French Revolutions. They have noted that as well as the Revolutions in America and France, there were political disturbances and upheavals in Britain, the Low Countries and elsewhere in Europe. Palmer and Godechot have concluded that, towards the end of the eighteenth century a single revolutionary movement spanned the Atlantic Ocean. Palmer considers the aim of this movement was the creation of a more democratic society and he has christened the period the 'Age of Democratic Revolution'.

The first four units in the Open University's Age of Revolutions course are an examination of the Palmer–Godechot thesis. The passages in sections A to E have been selected entirely with reference to the contents of the course units. Most of the passages are to be employed in self-assessment exercises in the course material, or else they are designed to enlarge upon, or add colour to the correspondence and broadcast components. The three French Revolution songs for example (D5 and D6) are to be heard in a television programme dealing with the Terror of 1793–4, and there is a considerable amount of quotation from Tom Paine (B3 and E2) partly because he was an important propagandist during the period but also because one radio broadcast deals with Paine's political career. Consequently the passages which follow should not be taken as a positive statement for or against the Palmer–Godechot thesis, nor should they be taken as sufficient documentation to make any conclusive judgement on the thesis.

This section contains one of Palmer's earliest statements of his thesis of a single revolutionary movement sweeping the 'Western World' towards the end of the eighteenth century. The two passages which follow Palmer's article show his thesis to be not entirely new. The Abbé Barruel and John Robison, who both published their conclusions in 1798, also noted disturbances elsewhere in Europe during the decade of the French Revolution and saw these as part of a single movement. But the movement described by Barruel and Robison was an organized conspiracy of atheists and freemasons to destroy European society, and they were not conscious of any links between the French Revolution and earlier events in America.

C.E.

Further Reading

* Jacques Godechot, *France and the Atlantic Revolution of the Eighteenth Century, 1770–1799*, translated by H. H. Rowen, Macmillan Co., 1971.
* F. L. Ford, *Europe, 1780–1830*, Longman, 1970.
The fullest and best treatment of the Atlantic-Democratic revolution is in R. R. Palmer, *The Age of the Democratic Revolution*, 2 vols, Princeton University Press, vol. 1, 1959, vol. 2, 1964.

* Open University Set Book.

1 R. R. Palmer

The World Revolution of the West: 1763-1801

from *Political Science Quarterly*, vol. 64   1954

In the streets of Paris, on the ninth of Thermidor of the Year Six (27 July 1798), there took place a long and memorable procession. It was in celebration of Liberty Day, as the anniversary of the fall of Robespierre was then officially called. It began at nine o'clock in the morning at the Museum of National History. First came cavalry and a band. They were followed by professors and students from the Museum, marching beside triumphal cars that bore various minerals, exotic plants and some crystals presented by the people of Valais in Switzerland. There were also a live bear from the zoo at Berne, lions from Africa, and two camels and two dromedaries sent by General Bonaparte from Egypt. After more soldiers and more musicians came delegates from the printers of Paris, librarians of the public libraries and professors from the *Polytechnique* and the *Collège de France*. Prize pupils from the new *école centrale* carried manuscripts and rare books. Next appeared teachers and students of the arts, who were followed by Art itself – the treasures captured by victorious armies in Italy: paintings by Titian, Raphael and Paul Veronese, sculpture in stupefying abundance, the Laocoön, the Dying Gladiator, the Discus Thrower and the Apollo Belvedere, to name only the most famous. Most conspicuous of all were the ancient bronze horses from St Mark's in Venice. They bore an inscription: 'Transported from Corinth to Rome, from Rome to Constantinople, from Constantinople to Venice, from Venice to France. They rest at last upon free ground.' Numerous other inscriptions, up and down the procession, explained the assembled wonders to onlookers. One was a quotation from Seneca: 'To live ignorant is to be dead.'

All this plunder, for such most of it literally was, was ceremoniously presented to the Minister of the Interior, who received it at the feet of a statue of liberty. The festivities ended with the ascension of a balloon, or 'aerostat', carrying aloft more inscriptions, together with 'attributes of liberty and the arts', and the tricolour of the Revolution.

The men of the French government who arranged this extraordinary spectacle obviously intended it to have a symbolic meaning. It may serve also as a symbol for us. It may remind us of certain paradoxes, or seeming paradoxes, of the French Revolution: the association of liberty with force, of enlightenment and education with propaganda and histrionics, of a sense of progress with a sense of conquest, of soldiers with professors, of a feeling of attachment to the western tradition with one of angry repudiation of the historic past. And the bears, lions, camels, strange plants and imported statuary may suggest also the idea of a world revolution, of which many people in Paris, and in other countries, believed France to be the centre.

In the summer of 1798 France was bordered by other revolutionary republics in Holland, Switzerland and Italy. Belgium and the Rhineland had been annexed, and unrest spread through Germany. Ireland was in rebellion, and in Great Britain the government of William Pitt, to use the word of various British historians, was resorting to terror. In Sweden, said the British Foreign Secretary, half the people were Jacobins. In the United States, in July 1798, the same fear of Jacobins, that is of democrats, produced the Alien and Sedition laws; nor were such fears allayed when the democrats won the next election. The president of the college at Princeton, shortly thereafter, shuddered at 'those irreligious and demoralizing principles which are tearing the bands of society asunder'.[1]

The idea that these events constituted a world revolution, that is, a revolution of the western world, is a very old one, since it dates from the eighteenth century itself. Recently, both in this country and in Europe, historians have begun to revive it. I need only mention our own Louis Gottschalk, or Georges Lefebvre of the Sorbonne, who, rewriting in 1951 his book of 1930 on the French Revolution, completely recast it to show the supranational implications. It may be that we should try to develop some integrating or unifying conceptions for this whole revolutionary movement in Europe and America taken together. It is

1. From an unpublished letter from Samuel Stanhope Smith to Jedediah Morse in the Princeton University Library. References in the present article are confined to direct quotations and a few other points which seem to be not generally known.

not enough to have a rough semi-Marxist idea of the 'bourgeois revolution', or simply to place different countries side by side for comparison, or to speak vaguely of the 'influence' of France or of America upon a world left otherwise undescribed.

Such a world revolution may be bounded, for convenience, by the dates 1763 and 1800 or 1801. At the hither end, we have a dramatic close in the election of Jefferson to the American presidency, and the personal triumph of Napoleon Bonaparte in Europe. The two events were not exactly alike, to be sure, but both were followed by a decline of political agitation. At the same time, with the Peace of Amiens and the Concordat both the British government and the papacy recognized the consequences of international revolutionary republicanism, at least tentatively and pending further developments.

There are good reasons for beginning about 1763. With the decade of the sixties some of the characteristics of the revolutionary era become apparent – the ideas and issues, the alignments of protagonists on both the domestic and the international fronts, the types of political activity and methods of rebellion against government, with the virtual creation of a public opinion on political questions in many countries. In the realm of ideas, the years 1762 and 1763 see the publication of the main writings of Rousseau, and we have it from Daniel Mornet, the leading authority, that the *philosophe* movement had triumphed by 1770. In 1765 the French Assembly of the Clergy issued its first wholesale condemnation of the *philosophe* literature, which it said would undermine, if unchecked, all churches, states and societies. The same years of the mid-sixties bring, in France, the quarrel of Louis XV's ministers with the more or less united *parlements* of the kingdom. The cry of 'Wilkes and Liberty' is heard in England, and the Sugar Act and the Stamp Act arouse America. No one can read E. S. Morgan's book, *The Stamp Act Crisis*, without sensing what was to come. He himself calls the American agitation of 1765 a revolution nipped in the bud. It anticipated what was soon to happen, in America and elsewhere, both in the ideas employed, that is, the appeal to historic or natural rights against a sovereign authority recognizing no direct dependence on the people, and in the practical tactics devised, that is, gatherings of the merchant and lawyer class into clubs and committees, and their exploiting of mob violence to obtain their ends. At the same time the close of the Seven Years' War marked the triumph of Great Britain and in particular of its parliamentary governing class, the most brilliantly successful of all people under eighteenth-century conditions, and hence the least inclined to see conditions changed. The stage is already set for the solid British conservatism which was in time to be the main support of counter-revolution, and for that British superiority in wealth, and command of the sea, with the consequent anti-British feeling, which were to affect all international relations for many years.

The problem now is to suggest a few unifying themes, running through these years, and more or less common to an Atlantic civilization.

To begin with ideas. To imply that ideas 'caused' the Revolution has long been the signal for controversy, carrying the implication of a conservative approach. Since the Revolution, and indeed before, as in the French Assembly of the Clergy of 1765, there have been warnings that the literature of the Enlightenment made people unruly and filled them with impractical ideas. This is probably true. It is not the whole truth, for the ideas in question were more than mere rebellious opinions. They derived from centuries of European thought, and they applied to the actual conditions of the day. The whole issue as between ideas and circumstances in the causation of the Revolution was set forth with extraordinary clarity, as early as 1799, by Friedrich Gentz.[2] In 1790 a French conservative, Sénac de Meilhan,[3] in his book of that year, remarked that 'the French Revolution seems to be a revolution of the human mind'.

The main idea, if we must single one out, seems to have been a demand for self-determination, a sense of autonomy of the

2. Friedrich Gentz, *Historisches Journal* (1799), immediately translated and published by Mallet du Pan in his *Mercure Brittanique* (London, 1799) which appeared also in English as the *British Mercury*. Both Gentz and Mallet du Pan were writing as journalists in the service of the counter-revolution. Gentz's analysis may be read in English in the *British Mercury* for 30 April and 15 June 1799.

3. G. Sénac de Meilhan, *Des Principes et des causes de la Révolution en France* (London, 1790), as quoted in a hitherto unpublished work on French counter-Revolutionary thought by Professor Paul Biek.

personality, a refusal to accept norms laid down outside the self, leading sometimes to a profound subjectivity, or an insistence on self-expression rather than adjustment to pre-existing authoritative standards. This seems to be the message of Rousseau, in the *Confessions* and the novels as well as in the *Social Contract*. In the latter, it is a collective self that defines the right; and each citizen is triumphantly demonstrated to be subject and sovereign at the same time. The same note of personal autonomy underlies all the practical demands for liberty, political and economic. It may be found in Kant's metaphysics and in his political theory, and in the world-creating Ego of Fichte, who believed himself and his philosophy to be part and parcel of the revolutionary movement. It presumably explains what Hegel meant when he said that Mind became fully free only with the French Revolution. It inspired the educational doctrine of Pestalozzi, who welcomed the revolutionary Helvetic Republic in Switzerland. It has been found, by those versed in music, in the work of that obstreperous republican, Beethoven. It is obviously central to romanticism, and, in the demand for spontaneity and the rejection of artificial restraint, inspires the *Lyrical Ballads* of 1798. Surely there exists here the opportunity for what modern parlance knows as a 'synthesis', bringing together not only many peoples of different language or nationality, but also many different fields of activity and thought.

It might be shown also, in such a synthesis, how the universal impulse to liberty is at least in principle kept in order. Anarchic individualism is avoided, in the political sphere, by the stress on the equality of rights, and by the ideas of fraternity and of law; and all are bound together in the idea of constitutionalism. About fifteen new written constitutions were proclaimed in America, and ten in Europe, in the quarter-century ending in 1801. In economic theory, it is natural law, or the natural harmony, that prevents liberty from degenerating into confusion. In the arts, a generation that revived the sonnet can hardly be charged with looseness. In moral philosophy, with Rousseau and Kant, it is the human conscience that stands between freedom and anarchy. In more recent times, with the ideas of conscience and natural law losing their force, and the drive for emancipation of self-expression as strong as ever, a great deal of trouble

has been attributed to such ideas. Some have sought philosophical composure in the Middle Ages. The matter cannot be
amplified here. Suffice it to say that liberty has always been
known to be dangerous.

A unified conception of world revolution would be the easier
to arrive at if we could point to an organized and centrally
directed revolutionary party, international in its operations. Conservatives in the 1790s, unable to believe that revolutionary sentiment had any real or, so to speak, legitimate foundation, naturally imagined that such an international conspiracy was at work.
The French émigré Barruel, and the Scotsman John Robison,
independently produced large treatises proving its existence. In
this country Jedediah Morse spread the same alarm. There was,
however, no such international organization. Agitators and sub-
versives did exist in all countries, and sometimes French
generals or civil commissioners in neighbouring states employed
secret agents. They had little or no connection with each other,
or with the French government or any super-society in France.
The French Jacobins were never secret, and had no organization
after 1794. Revolutionary secret societies were more the consequence than the cause of the great revolution of the 1790s. The
Italian Carbonari, for example, may be traced to a kind of Jacobin club in Burgundy in 1790. It was in a Paris prison, in 1795,
that Babeuf launched the revolutionary underground of the
nineteenth century. In 1798, when all England was reading the
shocking revelations of Barruel and Robison, the House of Commons appointed a Committee of Secrecy to inquire into subversion. The committee made the strongest possible case to show a
conspiratorial movement in England since 1792. It published
numerous documents and it named names. No French agent is
mentioned in its report, and no foreigner other than Irish.

Class analysis offers another common theme. Carl Becker once
observed of the American Revolution that, with the question of
home rule settled by independence, it remained to be seen who
should rule at home. Thus the establishment of independence
was followed by the heightened democratic agitation of the
1790s. The same pattern can easily be seen in parts of Europe,
especially in regions subject to a sovereignty increasingly felt to
be foreign. Cases in point are the Lombard and Belgian pro-

vinces, under the Hapsburg emperor; or the Swiss territory of
Vaud, which belonged to the canton of Berne. In Belgium the
assertion of independence in 1789 was followed by the strife between Statists, the upper class of the old regime, which wanted
no internal change, and the democratic or 'Vonckist' party,
which demanded new rights for the hitherto unprivileged
classes. The same pattern can be traced even in countries having
native governments, since under the old regime all governments
were in a sense foreign to their populations, the lack of moral
bond between ruler and ruled being precisely the point at issue.
It is now generally agreed that, in France, the Revolution began with a revolt of the nobility against royal absolutism. This
was no mere prelude, but an integral phase of the movement.
If this revolutionary role of the aristocracy is once fixed in mind,
then the attempts of Polish gentry to stage a revolution against
the partitioning Powers, or the uprising of Hungary against
Joseph II, can be brought into a unified conception of a general
revolution. Even in England some of the gentry favoured parliamentary reform; and parliamentary reform, involving equal,
individual, numerical and 'real' representation in the House of
Commons, was rightly felt by conservatives to be a revolutionary
change, both in the vicious practice and in the virtuous theory of
the British Constitution.

In most countries having a middle class a bourgeois phase
soon followed the aristocratic protest, and the sub-bourgeois or
working classes were often heard from also, not only in France,
but in England, Scotland, Holland and elsewhere. A historian
of the city of Manchester, for example, remarks that the United
Englishmen of 1797 offered the first example in that city of
working-class political organization without middle-class leader-
ship or support. In the long run, however, the landed interest
seems to have had the last word, and it was the action of country
people, perhaps more than anything else, that determined what
happened as between one place and another. Only in France
and America did small farmers become really revolutionary,
and only in these countries do we find complete and thoroughly
indigenous revolutions. In Ireland the rural population was dis-
affected, but helpless. In England the 'land' meant a well-con-
tented aristocracy. In eastern Europe the very ownership of rural

land was generally confined to nobles, who were the only political class, so that there was scarcely a tremor of revolution except for the noble opposition to outside powers. In the Kingdom of Naples, the flimsiness of the so-called Parthenopean Republic of 1799 was due to the non-participation of peasants; and Cardinal Ruffo, with his famous Army of the Holy Faith, easily won back the country, not by the forces of clericalism, but because, being the administrative type of churchman he had constructive ideas on land reform and could appeal to peasants.[4]

Class differences manifested themselves constitutionally, in almost every country affected by the revolution, in the question of whether the new state should be unitary or federal. In the Dutch provinces, the Swiss cantons, and the Italian republics, as in France after 1792, we hear the cry for a 'republic one and indivisible'. The same idea is evident in Belgium, in the German Rhineland and in Ireland with its United Irishmen, who believed that Irish Catholics and Presbyterians must combine indivisibly against the English. The idea of a republic 'one and indivisible' was not primarily nationalist; at least, it had no necessary relation to linguistic or ethnic groups. It meant that persons struggling for a democratic revolution must integrate territorially for self-protection, since the old local units of province and town – Brittany and Languedoc, Bologna and Ferrara, Amsterdam and Rotterdam, Brabant and Flanders, Cologne and Mainz, not to mention the twenty-one boroughs of Cornwall – were everywhere the seats of entrenched, exclusive and self-perpetuating oligarchic or privileged families. To insist that these historically-developed corporate entities should retain a separate influence was called 'federalism' in revolutionary parlance, and federalism was with reason regarded as one of the many aspects of counter-revolution. Advanced democrats everywhere demanded the dissolution of such entities into a uniform state built upon individual citizenship. It seems important to note that a contrary situation existed in America. The fact that federalism in America meant the centralized state is a mere difference of words. The significant matter is that, in America, the advanced democrats continued to fear strong government,

4. This is the general thesis of N. Rodolico, *Il popolo agli inizi del Risorgimento nell' Italia meridionale, 1792–1801* (Florence, 1925).

or any central government, and to put their trust in local authorities close to the people. In America it was the democrats who were 'federalist' in the European sense. At a time when big government was even harder to keep under control than now, democracy in America was not committed to big government, as it had to be in Europe to exist at all. The difference is due, like so much else, to the fact that America had no old regime in the true European sense, and hence no such internecine struggle.

Finally, it is in the sphere of international relations, and especially in war, that a unifying conception for the era may be formed. It is the misfortune of our own generation to know something of the interaction between war and revolution, and we should perhaps therefore be able to analyse the corresponding phenomena of the eighteenth century with a dreary wisdom not given to Sorel or Von Sybel. Whether revolution must lead to war we cannot really be certain. It has been both affirmed and denied of the war of 1792. We do know that war can be a great breeder of revolution. We know, too, that war aims change during the stress of fighting; that governments or aroused peoples may crush enemies or seize and hold advantages in a way having little to do with initial ideology or intentions.

The revolutionary struggle, throughout the thirty-odd years, was inseparable from the struggle between England and France. The British government opposed every revolutionary effort – the American, the Irish, the Dutch of 1784 and the Belgian of 1789. It went to war with France in 1793 to maintain the *status quo* in Belgium and Holland, against which many Dutch and Belgians were in rebellion, but which for over a century had been favourable to British naval and mercantile interests. The French, on the other hand, under both the Bourbon and the ensuing republican governments, patronized virtually all revolutionary disturbances.

The French were the only people to make a lasting revolution by their own efforts. All others depended on them. The French shipped 30,000 muskets to America in the year 1777. Nine-tenths of all the gunpowder used by Americans before the battle of Saratoga was from foreign sources, mainly French. It is clear that the success of the American revolt depended on France even before France openly intervened. In this respect the

American Revolution resembles the revolutions twenty years later which produced the Batavian, Cisalpine and other short-lived republics. The difference lies in the fact that the French withdrew from America, leaving the country independent, whereas they did not, could not, or would not withdraw from Holland or Italy except by abandoning their supporters to the counter-revolution.

The fact that the French alone accomplished a revolution with their own resources leads to comparative reflections on the Reign of Terror. There is no simple explanation for the Jacobin Terror of 1793. There is therefore no simple explanation for its absence. Yet the fact is that only in France did revolutionaries not depend on outside aid, and that only France had a real Terror. The Americans in the 1770s, and in the 1790s the Dutch and the Italians, managed to conduct revolutions of some magnitude without going to such lengths as the French in 1793. One reason surely is that they did not depend on their own precarious revolutionary resources – unorganized, unreliable, shifting, opportunistic and virtually ungovernable, as resources of men and material in time of revolution are. They expected and received the aid of France. As a working hypothesis, we may suppose that revolutionaries had three alternatives: either capitulation to the old regime, or terroristic control of the means of defiance, or the acceptance of outside aid. The French did not have the third alternative. Of others, including our own esteemed Founding Fathers, it may be argued that receipt of French aid spared them the unpleasant necessity of terrorizing their fellow countrymen more than they in fact did. The matter is at least worth considering.

It is clear that war aims changed with war itself. The British government under Pitt, late in 1792, declared that it had no interest in the internal government of France, and would go to war only to preserve the existing situation in Belgium and Holland. Within two years, in July 1794, the same Pitt, in a secret cabinet memorandum, was planning to let Austria keep its acquisitions while Great Britain retained all those 'already or yet to be conquered in the East and West Indies'.[5] In five more

5. Great Britain, Historical Manuscripts Commission, *The Manuscripts of J. B. Fortescue Preserved at Dropmore* (London, 1892–1927), vol. 2, p. 599.

years he doubted whether any lasting peace could be made except by restoring the French Bourbons – an opinion not shared by Prussia, Austria, or even the Bourbon monarchy of Spain.

The French went to war in 1792 in a spirit of crusading for liberty, of raising a world revolution against all kings and all nobles. As Brissot wrote, anticipating Lenin, 'we cannot be at ease until all Europe is in flames'.[6] As the Abbé Grégoire put it, in a phrase that would have suited either Metternich or Franklin Roosevelt: 'If my neighbour keeps a nest of vipers I have the right to stamp it out, lest I be its victim.'[7] But as early as 1793 a more national and hard-headed attitude began to prevail in France. There began to be a contemptuous feeling that no people except the French was really suited for liberty. The idea of world revolution gave way to the idea of revolution in one country first. Some writers, like Albert Mathiez, make a great deal of this change, which in a way relieved the Jacobins of responsibility for world turmoil. Actually the change made little practical difference. It is consequences, not intentions, that enter into the crude realm of fact. Since the enemies with whom they were at war were the privileged classes of Europe – the nobilities and town oligarchies and wealthy landowning clergy – the French republicans attacked them by attacking their sources of power, by abolishing their privileges, their laws, their tithes and their feudal rents, by summoning their former dependents to freedom, by granting equal rights to Jews, Protestants, Catholics, freethinkers or whoever it might be that was outside the locally established church – and even by the confiscation of property, the property of hostile ruling classes, be it understood. Such procedure horrified conservatives, especially in England, where it was ascribed to some peculiar perversity in the Jacobin character, or to an excessive belief in abstract ideas. It was not altogether different from what happened to the South during and after our Civil War, or from what governments in general seem historically to have done in pursuing conquest or suppressing opposition. One thinks of the Celtic regions of the British Isles, and the Scottish Highlands as recently as 1745.

The point is that revolution does not have to be caused by

6. J. P. Brissot, *Correspondance* (Paris, 1912), p. 313.
7. *Moniteur*, vol. 14, p. 587, session of 21 November 1792.

revolutionary ideas. It may only be a weapon of war. The distinction is never clear. In France, even under the consulate and empire, there were many who remained attached to revolutionary ideas. They believed in principle in liberating men from feudalism, clericalism or stupidity. Outside of France there were idealistic persons who first welcomed the French, then turned against them, disillusioned. The fact that they turned anti-French does not mean that in all cases they turned against revolutionary ideas, since the revolution was not French alone. They became the spiritual or actual fathers of the European revolutionaries of 1830 or 1840. The case of Michael Venedey is an example. He was a German republican of 1797, his son was a German republican of 1848.

Or again, if we say that revolution need not be caused by revolutionary ideology, we may have in mind that societies collapse for negative reasons, not so much from the strength of revolutionary sentiment as from the absence of any powerful sentiment in favour of the existing order. There were important revolutionary elements in Holland, Belgium, the Rhineland, Switzerland and Italy; but what caused the collapse of old governments and governing classes, in every one of these countries, was the war. More specifically, it was that they would not or could not defend themselves, that their own peoples did not believe in them, that there was no loyalty, faith or conviction on which to build, that they all were permeated by neutralism, and hoped plaintively, and vaguely, to be rescued by British money or the British fleet. In Holland in 1794 the Prince of Orange attempted a levy in mass; he is said to have raised fifty men. In Belgium the authorities were afraid to arm the people. In Italy it had long been unheard of for Italians to be soldiers. The Swiss had not fought in their own cause for generations. All fell before revolutionary republicanism, French and domestic.

The French, being at war, accepted assistance wherever offered. They stirred up the very dregs of society, as we may read in a hundred contemporary accusations. They brought the 'masses', or at least a great many lower-middle-class and working people, into the practical politics of the western world. By a historical irony, the liberal bourgeois awakened his Marxist doom. As for the British, being also at war, they brought into the practical politics of the western world, though it would be premature to call it a Marxist doom, the mammoth power of Imperial Russia. No doubt historical irony can be overdone. Yet as early as 1775 there was talk in England of using Russian mercenaries in America. The Earl of Suffolk jocosely remarked that 20,000 Russians would be 'charming visitors to New York and would civilize that part of America'.[8] Vergennes, alarmed, foresaw that Britain might some day hire Russian troops for operations in Western Europe. In 1796 the British Cabinet agreed to give the island of Corsica to Russia. In 1798 Henry Dundas advised his cabinet colleague, Pitt, to subsidize an army of Russians for British purposes, to attack Holland, defend Switzerland, capture Malta, open the markets of South America, or occupy Brest.[9] In 1799 there was talk of using Russians in Ireland. In that same year Vergennes' fears were realized when Russian troops, paid for by Great Britain, invaded Switzerland and Holland, on their way to France. It seems strangely modern to find Reubell, the former Director, declaring in 1801 that his policy of revolutionizing Switzerland in 1789 had prevented the Cossacks from riding into Paris.

The age of the French Revolution, it may be said in closing, has been used historically for a great many purposes. It has been used to explain the rise of nationalism or of liberalism, of class struggle or the 'perpetual revolution' of Trotsky, to celebrate the freedom of thought, or, contrariwise, to demonstrate that dogmatic Jacobin ideology must lead to totalitarianism. Let us avail ourselves of the privilege of our predecessors, and use the revolutionary era to investigate what is most on our minds, to find out what a world is like that is divided by revolution and war. There is something to be said for leaving the national histories of France, or Italy, or Holland, to persons born or living in those countries. Perhaps we in America are best equipped to be the synthesizers. As that notable revolutionary, Thomas Paine, remarked in a notable revolutionary year, 1776,

---

8. Keith Feiling, *The Second Tory Party* (London, 1938), p. 129. See also the *Parliamentary History*, vol. 19 (1778), p. 1355, where the use of 50,000 Russian troops is mentioned.

9. The 'Dropmore' or 'Fortescue' papers, cited on p. 26, vol. 4, pp. 434–5.

America is 'the colony of all Europe'. We are of all European nationalities, and of none; and so should be the better able to see the whole movement as one common to the Atlantic world. If we do, we shall not be mere innovators, nor be forcing the past to fit the present. We shall be saying what contemporaries before 1800 all but universally believed. We shall be performing the oldest and humblest of all the roles assigned to history – the preservation of memory. Indeed, I am reminded of the very first words of the first book of Herodotus, where he says that the aim of his 'researches' as he calls them, is that the memory of the past may not be blotted out by time, that the actions of Greeks and barbarians may be known, 'and especially that the causes may be remembered for which they waged war with each other'. Each can decide for himself which were the Greeks, and which the barbarians. Or he may think that it was really a civil war in Hellas.

2 Abbé Augustin Barruel
Memoirs Illustrating the History of Jacobinism

from *Preliminary Discourse*, vol. 1 in *Memoirs Illustrating the History of Jacobinism*, translated by the Hon. Robert Clifford, 4 vols 1798

The result of our research, corroborated by proofs drawn from the records of the Jacobins, and of their first masters, has been, that this sect with its conspiracies is in itself no other than the coalition of a triple sect, of a triple conspiracy, in which, long before the revolution, the overthrow of the altar, the ruin of the throne and the dissolution of all civil society had been debated and resolved on.

First. Many years before the French Revolution, men who styled themselves Philosophers conspired against the God of the Gospel, against Christianity, without distinction of worship, whether Protestant or Catholic, Anglican or Presbyterian. The grand object of their conspiracy was to overturn every altar where Christ was adored. It was the conspiracy of the *Sophisters of Impiety*, or the ANTICHRISTIAN CONSPIRACY.

Secondly. This school of impiety soon formed the *Sophisters of Rebellion*: these latter, combining their conspiracy against kings with that of the Sophisters of Impiety, coalesce with that ancient sect whose tenets constituted the whole secret of the *Occult Lodges* of Free-masonry, which long since, imposing on the credulity of its most distinguished adepts, only initiated the chosen of the elect into the secret of their unrelenting hatred for Christ and Kings.

Thirdly. From the Sophisters of Impiety and Rebellion, arose the *Sophisters of Impiety and Anarchy*. These latter conspire not only against Christ and his altars, but against every religion natural or revealed: not only against kings, but against every government, against all civil society, even against all property whatsoever.

This third sect, known by the name of Illuminés, coalesced with the Sophisters conspiring against Christ, coalesced with the Sophisters who, with the Occult Masons, conspired against both Christ and kings. It was the coalition of the adepts of *impiety*, of the adepts of *rebellion*, and the adepts of *anarchy*, which *formed the* CLUB *of the* JACOBINS. Under this name, common to the triple sect (originating from the name of the order, whose convent they had seized upon to hold their sittings), we shall see the adepts following up their triple conspiracy against God, the King and Society. Such was the origin, such the progress of that sect, since become so dreadfully famous under the name of JACOBIN.

3 John Robison

Proofs of a Conspiracy against all the Religions and Governments of Europe

from *Proofs of a Conspiracy against all the Religions and Governments of Europe* 1798

Nothing can more convincingly demonstrate the early intentions of a party, and this a great party, in France to overturn the constitution completely, and plant a democracy or oligarchy on its ruins. The Illuminati had no other object. They accounted all Princes usurpers and tyrants, and all privileged orders as their abettors. They intended to establish a government of Morality, as they called it, (*Sittenregiment*), where talents and character (to be estimated by their own scale and by themselves) should alone lead to preferment. They meant to abolish the laws which protected property accumulated by long continued and successful industry, and to prevent for the future any such accumulation. They intended to establish universal Liberty and Equality, the imprescriptable Rights of Man (at best they pretended all this to those who were neither Magi nor Ragentes). And, as necessary preparations for all this, they intended to root out all religion and ordinary morality, and even to break the bonds of domestic life, by destroying the veneration for marriage-vows, and by taking the education of children out of the hands of the parents. *This was all that the Illuminati could teach*, and THIS WAS PRECISELY WHAT FRANCE HAS DONE. [...]

Hence it has arisen that the French aimed, in the very beginning, at overturning the whole world. In all the revolution of other countries, the schemes and plots have extended no farther than the nation where they took their rise. But there we have seen that they take in the whole world. They have repeatedly declared this in their manifestoes, and they have declared it by their conduct. This is the very aim of the Illuminati. Hence it may be explained how the revolution took place almost in a moment in every part of France. The revolutionary societies were early formed, and were working in secret before the opening of the National Assembly, and the whole nation changed again, and again, as if by beat of drums. Those duly initiated in this mystery of iniquity were ready everywhere at a call. [...]

After all these particulars, can any person have a doubt that the Order of Illuminati formally interfered in the French Revolution, and contributed greatly to its progress? There is no denying the insolence and oppression of the Crown and the Nobles, nor the misery and slavery of the people, nor that there were sufficient provocation and cause for a total change of measures and of principles. But the rapidity with which one opinion was declared in every corner, and that opinion has quickly changed, and the change announced everywhere, and the perfect conformity of the principles, and sameness of the language, even in arbitrary trifles, can hardly be explained in any other way.

B The American Revolution

Any collection of documents illustrating the American
Revolution would naturally need far more material than is set
down in this section. The Proclamation of 1763 (B1) and the
Declaratory Act of 1776 (B2) are only a fraction of the legislation
introduced by the British government concerning the Thirteen
Colonies from the end of the Seven Years' War (1756–63), which
left Britain in control of North America, to the outbreak of
hostilities between Britain and the colonists (1775) and the
subsequent Declaration of Independence (1776). Similarly the
documents quoted here which originated among the colonists
are only part of the story. Paine's *Common Sense* (B3), though
the first pamphlet to call openly for independence, was neither
the first nor the last pamphlet called forth by the conflict and the
birth of the new republic. For a more detailed treatment of the
documents of the Revolution, the reader should turn to the
Commager collection from which these passages have been
taken.

The contrast between Jefferson's first draft of the Declaration
of Independence (B4) and the final draft adopted by Congress at
the beginning of July 1776 (B5) (here printed in parallel) makes
interesting reading in its own right and sheds light on the
problem of unity among the colonists at the beginning of the war.
At least one of Jefferson's liberal principles can be seen to have
been sacrificed in order that the colonies, who were united by little
more than their hostility to Britain, might act together in taking
the monumental step of declaring independence. Another
interesting contrast is to be found between the system of government for the American states as established by the Articles of
Confederation (B7), drafted in 1777 but not ratified by all the
states until 1781, and that system which superseded it as a result
of the Constitution of 1787 (B8) ratified in 1788. The Constitution
was only ratified by the individual states after a close and
hard-fought political struggle between its advocates and those
jealous of the independence and the rights of individual states.

The Bill of Rights (B9), the first ten amendments to the
Constitution adopted in 1791, originated in amendments
proposed by individual states during the struggle for ratification.

C.E.

1 The Proclamation of 1763

from the *Annual Register* 7 October 1763. Reprinted in
H. S. Commager (ed.), *Documents of American History*, 1963

Whereas we have taken into our royal consideration the extensive and valuable acquisitions in America secured to our Crown by the late definitive treaty of peace concluded at Paris the 10th day of February last; and being desirous that all our loving subjects, as well of our kingdom as of our colonies in America, may avail themselves, with all convenient speed, of the great benefits and advantages which must accrue therefrom to their commerce, manufactures, and navigation; we have thought fit, with the advice of our Privy Council, to issue this our Royal Proclamation, hereby to publish and declare to all our loving subjects that we have, with the advice of our said Privy Council, granted our letters patent under our Great Seal of Great Britain, to erect within the countries and islands ceded and confirmed to us by the said treaty, four distinct and separate governments, styled and called by the names of Quebec, East Florida, West Florida, and Grenada, and limited and bounded as follows, viz.:

First, the government of Quebec, bounded on the Labrador coast by the river St John, and from thence by a line drawn from the head of that river, through the lake St John, to the South end of the lake Nipissim; from whence the said line, crossing the river St Lawrence and the Lake Champlain in 45 degrees of North latitude, passes along the High Lands, which divide the rivers that empty themselves into the said river St Lawrence, from those which fall into the sea; and also along the North coast of the Bayes des Chaleurs, and the coast of the Gulph of St Lawrence to Cape Rosieres, and from thence crossing the mouth of the river St Lawrence by the West end of the island of Anticosti, terminates at the aforesaid river St John.

Secondly. The government of East Florida, bounded to the Westward by the Gulph of Mexico and the Apalachicola river; to the Northward, by a line drawn from that part of the said river where the Catahoochee and Flint rivers meet, to the source of St Mary's river, and by the course of the said river to the

Atlantic Ocean; and to the East and South by the Atlantic Ocean, and the Gulph of Florida, including all islands within six leagues of the sea coast.

Thirdly, The government of West Florida, bounded to the Southward by the Gulph of Mexico, including all islands within six leagues of the coast from the river Apalachicola to lake Pontchartrain; to the Westward by the said lake, the lake Maurepas, and the river Mississippi; to the Northward, by a line drawn due East from that part of the river Mississippi which lies in thirty-one degrees North latitude, to the river Apalachicola, or Catahoochee; and to the Eastward by the said river.

Fourthly, The government of Grenada, comprehending the island of that name, together with the Grenadines, and the islands of Dominico, St Vincent and Tobago.

And to the end that the open and free fishery of our subjects may be extended to, and carried on upon the coast of Labrador and the adjacent islands, we have thought fit ... to put all that coast, from the river St John's to Hudson's Streights, together with the islands of Anticosti and Madelane, and all other smaller islands lying upon the said coast, under the care and inspection of our governor of Newfoundland.

We have also [...] thought fit to annex the islands of St John and Cape Breton, or Isle Royale, with the lesser islands adjacent thereto, to our government of Nova Scotia.

We have also [...] annexed to our province of Georgia, all the lands lying between the rivers Atamaha and St Mary's.

And [...] we have [...] given express power and direction to our governors of our said colonies respectively, that so soon as the state and circumstances of the said colonies will admit thereof, they shall, with the advice and consent of the members of our council, summon and call general assemblies within the said governments respectively, in such manner and form as is used and directed in those colonies and provinces in America, which are under our immediate government; and we have also given power to our said governors, with the consent of our said councils, and the representatives of the people, so to be summoned as aforesaid, to make, constitute, and ordain laws, statutes, and ordinances for the public peace, welfare, and good government of our said colonies, and of the people and inhabitants thereof, as near as may be, agreeable to the laws of England, and under such regulations and restrictions as are used in other colonies; and in the mean time, and until such assemblies can be called as aforesaid, all persons inhabiting in, or resorting to, our said colonies, may confide in our royal protection for the enjoyment of the benefit of the laws of our realm of England: for which purpose we have given power under our great seal to the governors of our said colonies respectively, to erect and constitute, with the advice of our said councils respectively, courts of judicature and public justice within our said colonies, for the hearing and determining all causes as well criminal as civil, according to law and equity, and as near as may be, agreeable to the laws of England, with liberty to all persons who may think themselves aggrieved by the sentence of such courts, in all civil cases to appeal, under the usual limitations and restrictions, to us, in our privy council.

And whereas it is just and reasonable, and essential to our interest and the security of our colonies, that the several nations or tribes of Indians with whom we are connected, and who live under our protection, should not be molested or disturbed in the possession of such parts of our dominions and territories as, not having been ceded to or purchased by us, are reserved to them, or any of them, as their hunting-grounds; we do therefore, with the advice of our Privy Council, declare it to be our royal will and pleasure, that no Governor or commander in chief, in any of our colonies of Quebec, East Florida, or West Florida, do presume, upon any pretence whatever, to grant warrants of survey, or pass any patents for lands beyond the bounds of their respective governments, as described in their commissions; as also that no Governor or commander in chief of our other colonies or plantations in America do presume for the present, and until our further pleasure be known, to grant warrants of survey or pass patents for any lands beyond the heads or sources of any of the rivers which fall into the Atlantic Ocean from the west or northwest; or upon any lands whatever, which, not having been ceded to or purchased by us, as aforesaid, are reserved to the said Indians, or any of them.

And we do further declare it to be our royal will and pleasure, for the present as aforesaid, to reserve under our sovereignty, protection, and dominion, for the use of the said Indians all the land and territories not included within the limits of our said three new governments, or within the limits of the territory granted to the Hudson's Bay Company; as also all the land and territories lying to the westward of the sources of the rivers which fall into the sea from the west and northwest as aforesaid; and we do hereby strictly forbid, on pain of our displeasure, all our loving subjects from making any purchases or settlements whatever, or taking possession of any of the lands above reserved, without our special leave and license for that purpose first obtained.

And we do further strictly enjoin and require all persons whatever, who have either wilfully or inadvertently seated themselves upon any lands within the countries above described, or upon any other lands which, not having been ceded to or purchased by us, are still reserved to the said Indians as aforesaid, forthwith to remove themselves from such settlements.

And whereas great frauds and abuses have been committed in the purchasing lands of the Indians, to the great prejudice of our interests, and to the great dissatisfaction of the said Indians; in order, therefore, to prevent such irregularities for the future, and to the end that the Indians may be convinced of our justice and determined resolution to remove all reasonable cause of discontent, we do, with the advice of our Privy Council, strictly enjoin and require, that no private person do presume to make any purchase from the said Indians of any lands reserved to the said Indians within those parts of our colonies where we have thought proper to allow settlement; but that if at any time any of the said Indians should be inclined to dispose of the said lands, the same shall be purchased only for us, in our name, at some public meeting or assembly of the said Indians, to be held for that purpose by the Governor or commander in chief of our colony respectively within which they shall lie: and in case they shall lie within the limits of any proprietary government, they shall be purchased only for the use and in the name of such proprietaries, conformable to such directions and instructions as we or they shall think proper to give for that purpose. And we do, by the advice of our Privy Council, declare and enjoin, that the trade with the said Indians shall be free and open to all our subjects whatever, provided that every person who may incline to trade with the said Indians do take out a license for carrying on such trade, from the Governor or commander in chief of any of our colonies respectively where such person shall reside, and also give security to observe such regulations as we shall at any time think fit, by ourselves or commissaries to be appointed for this purpose, to direct and appoint for the benefit of the said trade. And we do hereby authorize, enjoin, and require the Governors and commanders in chief of all our colonies respectively, as well as those under our immediate government as those under the government and direction of proprietaries, to grant such licenses without fee or reward, taking especial care to insert therein a condition that such license shall be void, and the security forfeited, in case the person to whom the same is granted shall refuse or neglect to observe such regulations as we shall think proper to prescribe as aforesaid.

And we do further expressly enjoin and require all officers whatever, as well military as those employed in the management and direction of Indian affairs within the territories reserved as aforesaid, for the use of the said Indians, to seize and apprehend all persons whatever who, standing charged with treasons, misprisions of treason, murders, or other felonies or misdemeanors, shall fly from justice and take refuge in the said territory, and to send them under a proper guard to the colony where the crime was committed of which they shall stand accused, in order to take their trial for the same.

Given at our Court at St James's, the 7th day of October 1763, in the third year of our reign.

2 The Declaratory Act   18 March 1776

from H. S. Commager (ed.), *Documents of American History* 1963

[...] be it declared [...], That the said colonies and plantations in America have been, are, and of right ought to be, subordinate unto, and dependent upon the imperial crown and parliament of *Great Britain;* and that the King's majesty, by and with the advice and consent of the lords spiritual and temporal, and commons of *Great Britain*, in parliament assembled, had, hath, and of right ought to have, full power and authority to make laws and statutes of sufficient force and validity to bind the colonies and people of *America*, subjects of the crown of *Great Britain*, in all cases whatsoever.

II. And be it further declared [...], That all resolutions, votes, orders, and proceedings, in any of the said colonies or plantations, whereby the power and authority of the parliament of *Great Britain*, to make laws and statutes as aforesaid, is denied, or drawn into question, are, and are hereby declared to be, utterly null and void to all intents and purposes whatsoever.

3 Tom Paine
Common Sense

from *Common Sense* 1776

Society in every state is a blessing, but government even in its best state is but a necessary evil; in its worst state it is an intolerable one. Government, like dress, is the badge of lost innocence; the palaces of kings are built on the ruins of the bowers of paradise. For were the impulses of conscience clear, uniform, and irresistably obeyed, man would need no other law giver. [...]

England, since the conquest, hath known some few good monarchs, but groaned beneath a much larger number of bad ones; yet no man in his senses can say that their claim under William the Conqueror is a very honourable one. A French bastard landing with an armed banditti, and establishing himself King of England against the consent of the natives, is in plain terms a very paltry rascally original. It certainly hath no divinity in it. [...]

We have boasted the protection of Great Britain, without considering, that her motive was interest not attachment; that she did not protect us from our enemies on our account, but from her enemies on her own account, from those who had no quarrel with us on any other account, and who will always be our enemies on the same account. Let Britain waive her protections to the continent, or the continent throw off the dependence, and we should be at peace with France and Spain were they at war with Britain. This new world hath been the asylum for the persecuted lovers of civil and religious liberty from every part of Europe. Hither have they fled, not from the tender embraces of the mother, but from the cruelty of the monster; and it is so far true of England, that the same tyranny which drove the first immigrants from home, pursues their descendants still. [...]

To be always running three or four thousand miles with a tale or a petition, waiting four or five months for an answer, which then obtained requires five or six more to explain it in, will in a few years be looked upon as folly and childishness. [...]

Small islands not capable of protecting themselves, are the proper objects of kingdoms to take under their care; but there is something very absurd, in supposing a continent to be perpetually governed by an island. In no instance hath nature made the satellite larger than its primary planet, and as England and America, with respect to each other, reverse the common order of nature, it is evident they belong to different systems; England to Europe, America to itself. [...]

But where, says some, is the King of America? I will tell you. Friend, he reigns above, and doth not make havoc of mankind like the royal brute of Britain. Yet that we may not appear to be effective even in earthly honours, let a day be solemnly set apart for proclaiming the charter; let it be brought forth placed on the divine law, the word of God; let a crown be placed thereon, by which the world may know, that so far we approve of monarchy, that in America the law is king. For as in absolute governments the king is law, so in free countries the law ought to be king; and there ought to be no other.

4 Thomas Jefferson

First Draft of the Declaration of Independence
(See facing pages for the final version)

*A Declaration by the Representatives of the United States of
America, in General Congress Assembled* 1776. Reprinted
in Carl L. Becker, *The Declaration of Independence*, 1942

When in the course of human events it becomes necessary for a
people to advance from that subordination in which they have
hitherto remained, & to assume among the powers of the earth
the equal & independent station to which the laws of nature & of
nature's god entitle them, a decent respect to the opinions of
mankind requires that they should declare the causes which
impel them to the change.

self-evident;
We hold these truths to be ~~sacred and undeniable~~; that all
men are created equal & independent; that from that equal
creation they derive ~~in~~ rights inherent & inalienable, among
which are the preservation of life, & liberty, & the pursuit of
happiness; that to secure these ends, governments are instituted
among men, deriving their just powers from the consent of the
governed; that whenever any form of government shall become
destructive of these ends, it is the right of the people to alter or
to abolish it, & to institute new government, laying it's foundation on such principles & organizing it's powers in such form,
as to them shall seem most likely to effect their safety & happiness. prudence indeed will dictate that governments long
established should not be changed for light & transient causes:
and accordingly all experience hath shewn that mankind are
more disposed to suffer while evils are sufferable, than to right
themselves by abolishing the forms to which they are accustomed. but when a long train of abuses & usurpations,
begun at a distinguished period, & pursuing invariably the same
object, evinces a design to ~~subject~~ reduce them to arbitrary
power, it is their right, it is their duty, to throw off such
government & to provide new guards for their future security.
such has been the patient sufferance of these colonies; & such is
now the necessity which constrains them to expunge their
former systems of government. the history of his present majesty

5 The Unanimous Declaration of the Thirteen United States of America   4 July 1776

(See facing pages for the first draft)
Final draft adopted by Congress. Reprinted in
H. S. Commager (ed.), *Documents of American History*   1963

When in the Course of human events, it becomes necessary for one people to dissolve the political bands which have connected them with another, and to assume among the Powers of the earth, the separate and equal station to which the Laws of Nature and of Nature's God entitle them, a decent respect to the opinions of mankind requires that they should declare the causes which impel them to the separation.

We hold these truths to be self-evident, that all men are created equal, that they are endowed by their Creator with certain unalienable Rights, that among these are Life, Liberty and the pursuit of Happiness. That to secure these rights, Governments are instituted among Men, deriving their just powers from the consent of the governed, That whenever any Form of Government becomes destructive of these ends, it is the Right of the People to alter or to abolish it, and to institute new Government, laying its foundation on such principles and organizing its powers in such form, as to them shall seem most likely to effect their Safety and Happiness. Prudence, indeed, will dictate that Governments long established should not be changed for light and transient causes; and accordingly all experience hath shown, that mankind are more disposed to suffer, while evils are sufferable, than to right themselves by abolishing the forms to which they are accustomed. But when a long train of abuses and usurpations, pursuing invariably the same Object evinces a design to reduce them under absolute Despotism, it is their right, it is is their duty, to throw off such Government, and to provide new Guards for their future security. – Such has been the patient sufferance of these Colonies; and such is now the necessity which constrains them to alter their former Systems of Government. The history of the present King of Great Britain is a history of repeated injuries and usurpations, all having in direct object the establishment of an absolute Tyranny over these States. To prove this, let Facts be submitted to a candid world.

is a history of unremitting injuries and usurpations, among which no one fact stands single or solitary to contradict the uniform tenor of the rest, all of which have in direct object the establishment of an absolute tyranny over these states. to prove this, let facts be submitted to a candid world, for the truth of which we pledge a faith yet unsullied by falsehood.

he has refused his assent to laws the most wholesome and necessary for the public good:

he has forbidden his governors to pass laws of immediate & pressing importance, unless suspended in their operation till his assent should be obtained; and when so suspended, he has neglected utterly to attend to them:

he has refused 'to pass other laws for the accomodation of large districts of people unless those people would relinquish
the right of representation, a right inestimable to them & formidable to tyrants only:

he has dissolved Representative houses repeatedly & continually, for opposing with manly firmness his invasions on the rights of the people:

he has dissolved, he has refused for a long space of time to cause others to be elected, whereby the legislative powers, incapable of annihilation, have returned to the people at large for their exercise, the state remaining in the meantime exposed to all the dangers of invasion from without, & convulsions within:

he has endeavored to prevent the population of these states; for that purpose obstructing the laws for naturalization of foreigners; refusing to pass others to encourage their migrations hither; & raising the conditions of new appropriations of lands:

he has suffered the administration of justice totally to cease in some of these colonies, refusing his assent to laws for establishing judiciary powers:

he has made our judges dependent on his will alone, for the tenure of their offices, and amount of their salaries:

he has erected a multitude of new offices by a self-assumed power, & sent hither swarms of officers to harrass our people & eat out their substance:

He has refused his Assent to Laws, the most wholesome and necessary for the public good.

He has forbidden his Governors to pass Laws of immediate and pressing importance, unless suspended in their operation until his Assent should be obtained; and when so suspended, he has utterly neglected to attend to them.

He has refused to pass other Laws for the accommodation of large districts of people, unless those people would relinquish the right of Representation in the Legislature, a right inestimable to them and formidable to tyrants only.

He has called together legislative bodies at places unusual, uncomfortable, and distant from the depository of their Public Records, for the sole purpose of fatiguing them into compliance with his measures.

He has dissolved Representative Houses repeatedly, for opposing with manly firmness his invasions on the rights of the people.

He has refused for a long time, after such dissolutions, to cause others to be elected; whereby the Legislative Powers, incapable of Annihilation, have returned to the People at large for their exercise; the State remaining in the mean time exposed to all the dangers of invasion from without, and convulsions within.

He has endeavoured to prevent the population of these States; for that purpose obstructing the Laws of Naturalization of Foreigners; refusing to pass others to encourage their migration hither, and raising the conditions of new Appropriations of Lands.

He has obstructed the Administration of Justice, by refusing his Assent to Laws for establishing Judiciary Powers.

He has made Judges dependent on his Will alone, for the tenure of their offices, and the amount and payment of their salaries.

He has erected a multitude of New Offices, and sent hither swarms of Officers to harass our People, and eat out their substance.

He has kept among us, in times of peace, Standing Armies without the Consent of our legislature.

He has affected to render the Military independent of and superior to the Civil Power.

he has kept among us in times of peace standing armies & ships of war:

he has affected to render the military, independent of & superior to the civil power:

he has combined with others to subject us to a jurisdiction foreign to our constitutions and unacknoleged by our laws; giving his assent to their pretended acts of legislation, for quartering large bodies of armed troops among us;

> for protecting them by a mock-trial from punishment for
>
> any murders ∧ they should commit on the inhabitants of these states;
>
> for cutting off our trade with all parts of the world;
>
> for imposing taxes on us without our consent;
>
> for depriving us of the benefits of trial by jury;
>
> for transporting us beyond seas to be tried for pretended offenses;
>
> for taking away our charters, & altering fundamentally the forms of our governments;
>
> for suspending our own legislatures & declaring themselves invested with power to legislate for us in all cases whatsoever:

he has abdicated government here, withdrawing his governors, & declaring us out of his allegiance & protection:

he has plundered our seas, ravaged our coasts, burnt our towns & destroyed the lives of our people:

he is at this time transporting large armies of foreign mercenaries to compleat the works of death, desolation & tyranny, already begun with circumstances of cruelty & perfidy unworthy the head of a civilized nation:

he has endeavored to bring on the inhabitants of our frontiers the merciless Indian savages, whose known rule of warfare is an undistinguished destruction of all ages, sexes, & conditions of existence:

he has incited treasonable insurrections of our fellow citizens, with the allurements of forfeiture & confiscation of our property:

he has waged cruel war against human nature itself, violating it's most sacred rights of life & liberty in the persons of a

He has combined with others to subject us to a jurisdiction foreign to our constitution, and unacknowledged by our laws; giving his Assent to their acts of pretended legislation:

For quartering large bodies of armed troops among us:

For protecting them, by a mock Trial, from Punishment for any Murders which they should commit on the Inhabitants of these States:

For cutting off our Trade with all parts of the world:

For imposing taxes on us without our Consent:

For depriving us in many cases, of the benefits of Trial by Jury:

For transporting us beyond Seas to be tried for pretended offences:

For abolishing the free System of English Laws in a neighbouring Province, establishing therein an Arbitrary government, and enlarging its Boundaries so as to render it at once an example and fit instrument for introducing the same absolute rule into these Colonies:

For taking away our Charters, abolishing our most valuable Laws, and altering fundamentally the Forms of our Governments:

For suspending our own Legislature, and declaring themselves invested with Power to legislate for us in all cases whatsoever.

He has abdicated Government here, by declaring us out of his Protection and waging War against us.

He has plundered our seas, ravaged our Coasts, burnt our towns, and destroyed the lives of our people.

He is at this time transporting large armies of foreign mercenaries to compleat the works of death, desolation and tyranny, already begun with circumstances of Cruelty & perfidy scarcely paralleled in the most barbarous ages, and totally unworthy the Head of a civilized nation.

He has constrained our fellow Citizens taken Captive on the high Seas to bear Arms against their Country, to become the executioners of their friends and Brethren, or to fall themselves by their Hands.

He has excited domestic insurrections amongst us, and has endeavoured to bring on the inhabitants of our frontiers, the distant people who never offended him, captivating & carrying them into slavery in another hemisphere, or to incur miserable death in their transportation thither. this piratical warfare, the opprobrium of *infidel* powers, is the warfare of the *Christian* king of Great Britain. [determined to keep open a market where MEN should be bought & sold,] he has prostituted his negative for suppressing every legislative determining to keep open a market where MEN should be bought & sold: attempt to prohibit or to restrain this execrable commerce: and that this assemblage of horrors might want no fact of distinguished die, he is now exciting those very people to rise in arms among us, and to purchase that liberty of which *he* had deprived them, by murdering the people upon whom *he* also obtruded them: thus paying off former crimes committed against the *liberties* of one people, with crimes which he urges them to commit against the *lives* of another.

in every stage of these oppressions we have petitioned for redress in the most humble terms; our repeated petitions have been answered by repeated injury. a prince whose character is thus marked by every act which may define a tyrant, is unfit to be the rule of a people who mean to be free. future ages will scarce believe that the hardiness of one man, adventured within the short compass of twelve years only, on so many acts of tyranny without a mask, over a people fostered & fixed in principles of liberty.

Nor have we been wanting in attentions to our British brethren. we have warned them from time to time of attempts by their legislature to extend a jurisdiction over these our states. we have reminded them of the circumstances of our emigration & settlement here, no one of which could warrant so strange a pretension: that these were effected at the expence of our own blood & treasure, unassisted by the wealth or the strength of Great Britain: that in constituting indeed our several forms of government, we had adopted one common king, thereby laying a foundation for perpetual league & amity with them: but that submission to their parliament was no part of our constitution, nor ever in idea, if history may be credited: and we appealed to their native justice & magnanimity, as well as to the ties of our merciless Indian Savages, whose known rule of warfare, is an undistinguished destruction of all ages, sexes and conditions.

In every stage of these Oppressions We have Petitioned for Redress in the most humble terms: Our repeated Petitions have been answered only by repeated injury. A Prince, whose character is thus marked by every act which may define a Tyrant, is unfit to be the ruler of a free People.

Nor have We been wanting in attention to our British brethren. We have warned them from time to time of attempts by their legislature to extend an unwarrantable jurisdiction over us. We have reminded them of the circumstances of our emigration and settlement here. We have appealed to their native justice and magnanimity, and we have conjured them by the ties of our common kindred to disavow these usurpations, which would inevitably interrupt our connections and correspondence. They too have been deaf to the voice of justice and of consanguinity. We must, therefore, acquiesce in the necessity, which denounces our Separation, and hold them, as we hold the rest of mankind, Enemies in War, in Peace Friends.

We, therefore, the Representatives of the united States of America, in General Congress, Assembled, appealing to the Supreme Judge of the world for the rectitude of our intentions, do, in the Name, and by Authority of the good People of these Colonies, solemnly publish and declare That these United Colonies are, and of Right ought to be Free and Independent States; that they are Absolved from all Allegiance to the British Crown, and that all political connection between them and the State of Great Britain, is and ought to be totally dissolved; and that as Free and Independent States, they have full Power to levy War, conclude Peace, contract Alliances, establish Commerce, and to do all other Acts and Things which Independent States may of right do. And for the support of this Declaration, with a firm reliance on the Protection of Divine Providence, we mutually pledge to each other our Lives, our Fortunes and our sacred Honor.

common kindred to disavow these usurpations which were likely to interrupt our correspondence & connection. they too have been deaf to the voice of justice & and of consanguinity, & when occasions have been given them, by the regular course of their laws, of removing from their councils the disturbers of our harmony, they have by their free election re-established them in power. at this very time too they are permitting their chief magistrate to send over not only soldiers of our common blood, but Scotch & foreign mercenaries to invade & deluge us in blood. these facts have given the last stab to agonizing affection, and manly spirit bids us to renounce forever these unfeeling brethren. we must endeavor to forget our former love for them, and to hold them as we hold the rest of mankind, enemies in war, in peace friends. we might have been a free & a great people together; but a communication of grandeur & of freedom it seems is below their dignity. be it so, since they will have it: the road to ~~glory &~~ happiness is open to us too; we will climb it

               & to glory

road to ~~glory &~~ happiness ∧ is open to us too; we will climb it

apart from them,

∧ ~~in a separately state,~~ and acquiesce in the necessity which

de

∧ ~~pronounces our everlasting Adieu!~~ eternal separation!

We therefore the representatives of the United States of America in General Congress assembled do, in the name & by authority of the good people of these states, reject and renounce all allegiance & subjection to the kings of Great Britain & all others who may hereafter claim by, through, or under them; we utterly dissolve and break off all political connection which may have heretofore subsisted between us & the people of parliament of Great Britain; and finally we do assert and declare these colonies to be free and independent states, and that as free & independent states they shall hereafter have ∧full power to levy war, conclude peace, contract alliances, establish commerce, & to do all other acts and things which independent states may of right do. And for the support of this declaration we mutually pledge to each other our lives, our fortunes, & our sacred honour.

6 Thomas Jefferson
Recalling the Declaration of Independence

Letter to Henry Lee 8 May 1825. Reprinted in Philip S. Foner (ed.), *Basic Writings of Thomas Jefferson*, 1944

Monticello, 8 May 1825

Dear Sir, –

That George Mason was author of the bill of rights, and of the constitution founded on it, the evidence of the day established fully in my mind. Of the paper you mention, purporting to be instructions to the Virginia delegation in Congress, I have no recollection. If it were anything more than a project of some private hand, that is to say, had any such instructions been ever given by the convention, they would appear in the journals, which we possess entire. But with respect to our rights, and the acts of the British government contravening those rights, there was but one opinion on this side of the water. All American whigs thought alike on these subjects. When forced, therefore, to resort to arms for redress, an appeal to the tribunal of the world was deemed proper for our justification. This was the object of the Declaration of Independence. Not to find out new principles, or new arguments, never before thought of, not merely to say things which had never been said before; but to place before mankind the common sense of the subject, in terms so plain and firm as to command their assent, and to justify ourselves in the independent stand we are compelled to take. Neither aiming at originality of principle or sentiment, nor yet copied from any particular and previous writing, it was intended to be an expression of the American mind, and to give to that expression the proper tone and spirit called for by the occasion. All its authority rests then on the harmonizing sentiments of the day, whether expressed in conversation, in letters, printed essays, or in the elementary books of public right, as Aristotle, Cicero, Locke, Sidney, &c. The historical documents which you mention as in your possession, ought all to be found, and I am persuaded you will find, to be corroborative of the facts and principles advanced in that Declaration. Be pleased to accept assurances of my great esteem and respect.

7 The Articles of Confederation 1777

in H. S. Commager (ed.), *Documents of American History*
1963

To all to whom these Presents shall come, we the undersigned Delegates of the States affixed to our Names send greeting. Whereas the Delegates of the United States of America in Congress assembled did on the fifteenth day of November in the Year of our Lord One thousand Seven Hundred and Seventy seven, and in the Second Year of the Independence of America agree to certain articles of Confederation and perpetual Union between the States of Newhampshire, Massachusetts-bay, Rhodeisland and Providence Plantations, Connecticut, New York, New Jersey, Pennsylvania, Delaware, Maryland, Virginia, North-Carolina, South-Carolina and Georgia in the Words following, viz. Articles of Confederation and perpetual Union between the states of Newhampshire, Massachusetts-bay, Rhodeisland and Providence Plantations, Connecticut, New York, New Jersey, Pennsylvania, Delaware, Maryland, Virginia, North-Carolina, South-Carolina and Georgia.

Art. I. The Stile of this confederacy shall be 'The United States of America'.

Art. II. Each state retains its sovereignty, freedom and independence, and every Power, Jurisdiction and right, which is not by this confederation expressly delegated to the United States, in Congress assembled.

Art. III. The said states hereby severally enter into a firm league of friendship with each other, for their common defence, the security of their Liberties, and their mutual and general welfare, binding themselves to assist each other, against all force offered to, or attacks made upon them, or any of them, on account of religion, sovereignty, trade, or any other pretence whatever.

Art. IV. The better to secure and perpetuate mutual friendship and intercourse among the people of the different states in this union, the free inhabitants of each of these states, paupers, vagabonds and fugitives from Justice excepted, shall be entitled to all privileges and immunities of free citizens in the several states; and the people of each state shall have free ingress and regress to and from any other state, and shall enjoy therein all the privileges of trade and commerce, subject to the same duties, impositions and restrictions as the inhabitants thereof respectively, provided that such restriction shall not extend so far as to prevent the removal of property imported into any state, to any other state of which the owner is an inhabitant; provided also that no imposition, duties or restriction shall be laid by any state, on the property of the united states, or either of them.

If any Person guilty of, or charged with treason, felony, or other high misdemeanor in any state, shall flee from Justice, and be found in any of the united states, he shall upon demand of the Governor or executive power, of the state from which he fled, be delivered up and removed to the state having jurisdiction of his offence.

Full faith and credit shall be given in each of these states to the records, acts and judicial proceedings of the courts and magistrates of every other state.

Art V. For the more convenient management of the general interests of the united states, delegates shall be annually appointed in such manner as the legislature of each state shall direct, to meet in Congress on the first Monday in November, in every year, with a power reserved to each state, to recal its delegates, or any of them, at any time within the year, and to send others in their stead, for the remainder of the Year.

No state shall be represented in Congress by less than two, nor by more than seven Members; and no person shall be capable of being a delegate for more than three years in any term of six years; nor shall any person, being a delegate, be capable of holding any office under the united states, for which he, or another for his benefit receives any salary, fees or emolument of any kind.

Each state shall maintain its own delegates in a meeting of the states, and while they act as members of the committee of the states.

In determining questions in the united states, in Congress assembled, each state shall have one vote.

Freedom of speech and debate in Congress shall not be impeached or questioned in any Court, or place out of Congress, and the members of congress shall be protected in their persons from arrests and imprisonments, during the time of their going to and from, and attendance on congress, except for treason, felony, or breach of the peace.

Art. VI. No state without the Consent of the united states in congress assembled, shall send any embassy to, or receive any embassy from, or enter into any conference, agreement, or alliance or treaty with any King, prince or state; nor shall any person holding any office of profit or trust under the united states, or any of them, accept of any present, emolument, office or title of any kind whatever from any king, prince or foreign state; nor shall the united states in congress assembled, or any of them, grant any title of nobility.

No two or more states shall enter into any treaty, confederation or alliance whatever between them, without the consent of the united states in congress assembled, specifying accurately the purposes for which the same is to be entered into, and how long it shall continue.

No state shall lay any imposts or duties which may interfere with any stipulations in treaties, entered into by the united states in congress assembled, with any king, prince or state, in pursuance of any treaties already proposed by congress, to the courts of France and Spain.

No vessels of war shall be kept up in time of peace by any state, except such number only, as shall be deemed necessary by the united states in congress assembled, for the defence of such state, or its trade; nor shall any body of forces be kept up by any state, in time of peace, except such number only, as in the judgment of the united states, in congress assembled, shall be deemed requisite to garrison the forts necessary for the defence of such state; but every state shall always keep up a well regulated and disciplined militia, sufficiently armed and accoutred, and shall provide and constantly have ready for use, in public stores, a due number of field pieces and tents, and a proper quantity of arms, ammunition and camp equipage.

No state shall engage in any war without the consent of the united states in congress assembled, unless such state be actually invaded by enemies, or shall have received certain advice of a resolution being formed by some nation of Indians to invade such state, and the danger is so imminent as not to admit of a delay, till the united states in congress assembled can be consulted: nor shall any state grant commissions to any ships or vessels of war, nor letters of marque or reprisal, except it be after a declaration of war by the united states in congress assembled, and then only against the kingdom or state and the subjects thereof, against which war has been so declared, and under such regulations as shall be established by the united states in congress assembled, unless such state be infested by pirates, in which case vessels of war may be fitted out for that occasion, and kept so long as the danger shall continue, or until the united states in congress assembled shall determine otherwise.

Art. VII. When land-forces are raised by any state for the common defence, all officers of or under the rank of colonel, shall be appointed by the legislature of each state respectively by whom such forces shall be raised, or in such manner as such state shall direct, and all vacancies shall be filled up by the state which first made the appointment.

Art. VIII. All charges of war, and all other expences that shall be incurred for the common defence or general welfare, and allowed by the united states in congress assembled, shall be defrayed out of a common treasury, which shall be supplied by the several states, in proportion to the value of all land within each state, granted to or surveyed for any Person, as such land and buildings and improvements thereon shall be estimated according to such mode as the united states in congress assembled, shall from time to time direct and appoint. The taxes for paying that proportion shall be laid and levied by the authority and direction of the legislatures of the several states within the time agreed upon by the united states in congress assembled.

Art. IX. The united states in congress assembled, shall have the sole and exclusive right and power of determining on peace and war, except in the cases mentioned in the sixth article – of sending and receiving ambassadors – entering into treaties and alliances, provided that no treaty of commerce shall be made whereby the legislative power of the respective states shall be restrained from imposing such imposts and duties on foreigners, as their own people are subjected to, or from prohibiting the exportation or importation of any species of goods or commodities whatsoever – of establishing rules for deciding in all cases, what captures on land or water shall be legal, and in what manner prizes taken by land or naval forces in the service of the united states shall be divided or appropriated. – of granting letters of marque and reprisal in times of peace – appointing courts for the trial of piracies and felonies committed on the high seas and establishing courts for receiving and determining finally appeals in all cases of captures, provided that no member of congress shall be appointed a judge of any of the said courts.

The united states in congress assembled shall also be the last resort on appeal in all disputes and differences now subsisting or that hereafter may arise between two or more states concerning boundary, jurisdiction or any other cause whatever; which authority shall always be exercised in the manner following. Whenever the legislative or executive authority or lawful agent of any state in controversy with another shall present a petition to congress, stating the matter in question and praying for a hearing, notice thereof shall be given by order of congress to the legislative or executive authority of the other state in controversy, and a day assigned for the appearance of the parties by their lawful agents, who shall then be directed to appoint by joint consent, commissioners or judges to constitute a court for hearing and determining the matter in question : but if they cannot agree, congress shall name three persons out of each of the united states, and from the list of such persons each party shall alternately strike out one, the petitioners beginning, until the number shall be reduced to thirteen; and from that number not less than seven, nor more than nine names as congress shall direct, shall in the presence of congress be drawn out by lot, and the persons whose names shall be so drawn or any five of them, shall be commissioners or judges, to hear and finally determine the controversy, so always as a major part of the judges who shall hear the cause shall agree in the determination : and if either party shall neglect to attend at the day appointed, without shewing reasons, which congress shall judge sufficient, or being present shall refuse to strike, the congress shall proceed to nominate three persons out of each state, and the secretary of congress shall strike in behalf of such party absent or refusing; and the judgment and sentence of the court to be appointed, in the manner before prescribed, shall be final and conclusive; and if any of the parties shall refuse to submit to the authority of such court, or to appear to defend their claim or cause, the court shall nevertheless proceed to pronounce sentence, or judgment, which shall in like manner be final and decisive, the judgment or sentence and other proceedings being in either case transmitted to congress, and lodged among the acts of congress for the security of the parties concerned : provided that every commissioner, before he sits in judgment, shall take an oath to be administered by one of the judges of the supreme or superior court of the state, where the cause shall be tried, 'well and truly to hear and determine the matter in question, according to the best of his judgment, without favour, affection or hope of reward' : provided also that no state shall be deprived of territory for the benefit of the united states.

All controversies concerning the private right of soil claimed under different grants of two or more states, whose jurisdictions as they may respect such lands, and the states which passed such grants are adjusted, the said grants or either of them being at the same time claimed to have originated antecedent to such settlement of jurisdiction, shall on the petition of either party to the congress of the united states, be finally determined as near as may be in the same manner as is before prescribed for deciding disputes respecting territorial jurisdiction between different states.

The united states in congress assembled shall also have the sole and exclusive right and power of regulating the alloy and value of coin struck by their own authority, or by that of the respective states – fixing the standard of weights and measures throughout the united states. – regulating the trade and managing all affairs with the Indians, not members of any of the states, provided that the legislative right of any state within its own limits be not infringed or violated – establishing and regulating post-offices from one state to another, throughout all the united states, and exacting such postage on the papers passing thro' the same as may be requisite to defray the expences of the said office – appointing all officers of the land forces, in the service of the united states, excepting regimental officers. – appointing all the officers of the naval forces, and commissioning all officers whatever in the service of the united states – making rules for the government and regulation of the said land and naval forces, and directing their operations.

The united states in congress assembled shall have authority to appoint a committee, to sit in the recess of congress, to be denominated 'A Committee of the States', and to consist of one delegate from each state; and to appoint such other committees and civil officers as may be necessary for managing the general affairs of the united states under their direction – to appoint one of their number to preside, provided that no person be allowed to serve in the office of president more than one year in any term of three years; to ascertain the necessary sums of Money to be raised for the service of the united states, and to appropriate and apply the same for defraying the public expences – to borrow money, or emit bills on the credit of the united states, transmitting every half year to the respective states an account of the sums of money so borrowed or emitted, – to build and equip a navy – to agree upon the number of land forces, and to make requisitions from each state for its quota, in proportion to the number of white inhabitants in such state; which requisition shall be binding, and thereupon the legislature of each state shall appoint the regimental officers, raise the men and cloath, arm and equip them in a soldier like manner, at the expence of the united states, and the officers and men so cloathed, armed and equipped shall march to the place appointed, and within the time agreed on by the united states in congress assembled : But if the united states in congress assembled shall, on consideration of circumstances judge proper that any state should not raise men, or should raise a smaller number than its quota, and that any other state should raise a greater number of men than the quota thereof, such extra number shall be raised, officered, cloathed, armed and equipped in the same manner as the quota of such state, unless the legislature of such state shall judge that such extra number cannot be safely spared out of the same, in which case they shall raise officer, cloath, arm and equip as many of such extra number as they judge can be safely spared. And the officers and men so cloathed, armed and equipped, shall march to the place appointed, and within the time agreed on by the united states in congress assembled.

The united states in congress assembled shall never engage in a war, nor grant letters of marque and reprisal in time of peace, nor enter into any treaties or alliances, nor coin money, nor regulate the value thereof, nor ascertain the sums and expences necessary for the defence and welfare of the united states, or any of them, nor emit bills, nor borrow money on the credit of the united states, nor appropriate money, nor agree upon the number of vessels of war, to be built or purchased, or the number of land or sea forces to be raised, nor appoint a commander in chief of the army or navy, unless nine states assent to the same: nor shall a question on any other point, except for adjourning from day to day be determined, unless by the votes of a majority of the united states in congress assembled.

The congress of the united states shall have power to adjourn to any time within the year, and to any place within the united states, so that no period of adjournment be for a longer duration than the space of six Months, and shall publish the Journal of their proceedings monthly except such parts thereof relating to treaties, alliances or military operations as in their judgment require secresy; and the yeas and nays of the delegates of each state on any question shall be entered on the Journal, when it is desired by any delegate; and the delegates of a state, or any of them, at his or their request shall be furnished with a transcript of the said Journal, except such parts as are above excepted, to lay before the legislatures of the several states.

Art. X. The committee of the states, or any nine of them, shall be authorised to execute, in the recess of congress, such of the powers of congress as the united states in congress assembled, by the consent of nine states, shall from time to time think expedient to vest them with; provided that no power be delegated to the said committee, for the exercise of which, by the articles of confederation, the voice of nine states in the congress of the united states assembled is requisite.

Art. XI. Canada acceding to this confederation, and joining in the measures of the united states, shall be admitted into, and entitled to all the advantages of this union: but no other colony shall be admitted into the same, unless such admission be agreed to by nine states.

Art. XII. All bills of credit emitted, monies borrowed and debts contracted by, or under the authority of congress, before the assembling of the united states, in pursuance of the present confederation, shall be deemed and considered as a charge against the united states, for payment and satisfaction whereof the said united states, and the public faith are hereby solemnly pledged.

Art. XIII. Every state shall abide by the determinations of the united states in congress assembled, on all questions which by this confederation are submitted to them. And the Articles of this confederation shall be inviolably observed by every state, and the union shall be perpetual, nor shall any alteration at any time hereafter be made in any of them; unless such alteration be agreed to in a congress of the united states, and be afterwards confirmed by the legislatures of every state.

And whereas it hath pleased the Great Governor of the World to incline the hearts of the legislatures we respectively represent in congress, to approve of, and to authorize us to ratify the said articles of confederation and perpetual union. Know Ye that we the under-signed delegates, by virtue of the power and authority to us given for that purpose, do by these presents, in the name and in behalf of our respective constituents, fully and entirely ratify and confirm each and every of the said articles of confederation and perpetual union, and all and singular the matters and things therein contained: And we do further solemnly plight and engage the faith of our respective constituents, that they shall abide by the determinations of the united states in congress assembled, on all questions, which by the said confederation are submitted to them. And that the articles thereof shall be inviolably observed by the states we respectively represent, and that the union shall be perpetual. In Witness whereof we have hereunto set our hands in Congress. Done at Philadelphia in the state of Pennsylvania the ninth Day of July in the Year of our Lord one Thousand seven Hundred and Seventy-eight, and in the third year of the independence of America.

8 The Constitution of the United States   1787

in H. S. Commager (ed.), *Documents of American History*   1963

We the People of the United States, in Order to form a more perfect Union, establish Justice, insure domestic Tranquility, provide for the common defence, promote the general Welfare, and secure the Blessings of Liberty to ourselves and our Posterity, do ordain and establish this Constitution for the United States of America.

ART. I

Sec. 1. All legislative Powers herein granted shall be vested in a Congress of the United States, which shall consist of a Senate and House of Representatives.

Sec. 2. The House of Representatives shall be composed of Members chosen every second Year by the People of the several States, and the Electors in each State shall have the Qualifications requisite for Electors of the most numerous Branch of the State Legislature.

No Person shall be a Representative who shall not have attained to the Age of twenty five Years, and been seven Years a Citizen of the United States, and who shall not, when elected, be an Inhabitant of that State in which he shall be chosen.

Representatives and direct Taxes shall be apportioned among the several States which may be included within this Union, according to their respective Numbers, which shall be determined by adding to the whole Number of free Persons, including those bound to Service for a Term of Years, and excluding Indians not taxed, three fifths of all other Persons. The actual Enumeration shall be made within three Years after the first Meeting of the Congress of the United States, and within every subsequent Term of ten Years, in such Manner as they shall by Law direct. The Number of Representatives shall not exceed one for every thirty Thousand, but each State shall have at

Least one Representative; and until such enumeration shall be made, the State of New Hampshire shall be entitled to chuse three, Massachusetts eight, Rhode-Island and Providence Plantations one, Connecticut five, New-York six, New Jersey four, Pennsylvania, eight, Delaware one, Maryland six, Virginia ten, North Carolina five, South Carolina five, and Georgia three.

When vacancies happen in the Representation from any State, the Executive Authority thereof shall issue Writs of Election to fill such Vacancies.

The House of Representatives shall chuse their Speaker and other Officers; and shall have the sole Power of Impeachment.

Sec. 3. The Senate of the United States shall be composed of two Senators from each State, chosen by the Legislature thereof, for six Years; and each Senator shall have one Vote.

Immediately after they shall be assembled in Consequence of the first Election, they shall be divided as equally as may be into three Classes. The Seats of the Senators of the first Class shall be vacated at the Expiration of the second Year, of the second Class at the Expiration of the fourth Year, and of the third Class at the Expiration of the sixth Year, so that one third may be chosen every second Year; and if Vacancies happen by Resignation, or otherwise, during the Recess of the Legislature of any State, the Executive thereof may make temporary Appointments until the next Meeting of the Legislature, which shall then fill such Vacancies.

No Person shall be a Senator who shall not have attained to the Age of thirty Years, and been nine Years a Citizen of the United States, and who shall not, when elected, be an Inhabitant of that State for which he shall be chosen.

The Vice President of the United States shall be President of the Senate, but shall have no Vote, unless they be equally divided.

The Senate shall chuse their other Officers, and also a President pro tempore, in the Absence of the Vice President, or when he shall exercise the Office of President of the United States.

The Senate shall have the sole Power to try all Impeachments. When sitting for that Purpose, they shall be on Oath or Affirmation. When the President of the United States is tried, the Chief

Justice shall preside: And no Person shall be convicted without the Concurrence of two thirds of the Members present.

Judgment in Cases of Impeachment shall not extend further than to removal from Office, and disqualification to hold and enjoy any Office of honor, Trust or Profit under the United States: but the Party convicted shall nevertheless be liable and subject to Indictment, Trial, Judgment and Punishment, according to Law.

Sec. 4. The Times, Places and Manner of holding Elections for Senators and Representatives, shall be prescribed in each State by the Legislature thereof; but the Congress may at any time by Law make or alter such Regulations, except as to the Places of chusing Senators.

The Congress shall assemble at least once in every Year, and such Meeting shall be on the first Monday in December, unless they shall by Law appoint a different Day.

Sec. 5. Each House shall be the Judge of the Elections, Returns and Qualifications of its own Members, and a Majority of each shall constitute a Quorum to do Business; but a smaller Number may adjourn from day to day, and may be authorized to compel the Attendance of absent Members, in such Manner, and under such Penalties as each House may provide.

Each House may determine the Rules of its Proceedings, punish its Members for disorderly Behaviour, and, with the Concurrence of two thirds, expel a Member.

Each House shall keep a Journal of its Proceedings, and from time to time publish the same, excepting such Parts as may in their Judgment require Secrecy; and the Yeas and Nays of the Members of either House on any question shall, at the Desire of one fifth of those Present, be entered on the Journal.

Neither House, during the Session of Congress, shall, without the Consent of the other, adjourn for more than three days, nor to any other Place than that in which the two Houses shall be sitting.

Sec. 6. The Senators and Representatives shall receive a Compensation for their Services, to be ascertained by Law, and paid out of the Treasury of the United States. They shall in all Cases, except Treason, Felony and Breach of the Peace, be privileged from Arrest during their Attendance at the Session of their respective Houses, and in going to and returning from the same; and for any Speech or Debate in either House, they shall not be questioned in any other Place.

No Senator or Representative shall, during the Time for which he was elected, be appointed to any civil Office under the Authority of the United States which shall have been created, or the Emoluments whereof shall have been encreased during such time; and no Person holding any Office under the United States, shall be a Member of either House during his Continuance in Office.

Sec. 7. All Bills for raising Revenue shall originate in the House of Representatives; but the Senate may propose or concur with Amendments as on other Bills.

Every Bill which shall have passed the House of Representatives and the Senate, shall, before it become a Law, be presented to the President of the United States; If he approve he shall sign it, but if not he shall return it, with his Objections to that House in which it shall have originated, who shall enter the Objections at large on their Journal, and proceed to reconsider it. If after such Reconsideration two thirds of that House shall agree to pass the Bill, it shall be sent, together with the Objections, to the other House, by which it shall likewise be reconsidered, and if approved by two thirds of that House, it shall become a Law. But in all such Cases the Votes of both Houses shall be determined by yeas and Nays, and the Names of the Persons voting for and against the Bill shall be entered on the Journal of each House respectively. If any Bill shall not be returned by the President within ten Days (Sundays excepted) after it shall have been presented to him, the Same shall be a Law, in like Manner as if he had signed it, unless the Congress by their Adjournment prevent its Return, in which Case it shall not be a Law.

Every Order, Resolution, or Vote to which the Concurrence of the Senate and House of Representatives may be necessary (except on a question of Adjournment) shall be presented to the President of the United States; and before the Same shall take Effect, shall be approved by him, or being disapproved by him, shall be repassed by two thirds of the Senate and House of

Representatives, according to the Rules and Limitations prescribed in the Case of a Bill.

Sec. 8. The Congress shall have Power To Lay and collect Taxes, Duties, Imposts and Excises, to pay the Debts and provide for the common Defence and general Welfare of the United States; but all Duties, Imposts and Excises shall be uniform throughout the United States;

To borrow Money on the credit of the United States ;

To regulate Commerce with foreign Nations, and among the several States, and with the Indian Tribes;

To establish an uniform Rule of Naturalization, and uniform Laws on the subject of Bankruptcies throughout the United States;

To coin Money, regulate the Value thereof, and of foreign Coin, and fix the Standard of Weights and Measures;

To provide for the Punishment of counterfeiting the Securities and current Coin of the United States;

To establish Post Offices and post Roads;

To promote the Progress of Science and useful Arts, by securing for limited Times to Authors and Inventors the exclusive Right to their respective Writings and Discoveries;

To constitute Tribunals inferior to the supreme Court;

To define and punish Piracies and Felonies committed on the high Seas, and Offences against the Law of Nations;

To declare War, grant Letters of Marque and Reprisal, and make Rules concerning Captures on Land and Water;

To raise and support Armies, but no Appropriation of Money to that Use shall be for a longer Term than two Years;

To provide and maintain a Navy;

To make Rules for the Government and Regulation of the land and naval Forces;

To provide for calling forth the Militia to execute the Laws of the Union, suppress Insurrections and repel Invasions;

To provide for organizing, arming, and disciplining, the Militia, and for governing such Part of them as may be employed in the Service of the United States, reserving to the States respectively, the Appointment of the Officers, and the Authority of training the Militia according to the discipline prescribed by Congress;

To exercise exclusive Legislation in all Cases whatsoever, over such District (not exceeding ten Miles square) as may, by Cession of particular States, and the Acceptance of Congress, become the Seat of the Government of the United States, and to exercise like Authority over all Places purchased by the Consent of the Legislature of the State which the Same shall be, for the Erection of Forts, Magazines, Arsenals, dock-Yards, and other needful Buildings; – And

To make all Laws which shall be necessary and proper for carrying into Execution the foregoing Powers, and all other Powers vested by this Constitution in the Government of the United States, or in any Department or Office thereof.

Sec. 9. The Migration or Importation of such Persons as any of the States now existing shall think proper to admit, shall not be prohibited by the Congress prior to the Year one thousand eight hundred and eight, but a Tax or duty may be imposed on such Importation, not exceeding ten dollars for each Person.

The Privilege of the Writ of Habeas Corpus shall not be suspended, unless when in Cases of Rebellion or Invasion the public Safety may require it.

No Bill of Attainder or ex post facto Law shall be passed.

No Capitation, or other direct, Tax shall be laid, unless in Proportion to the Census or Enumeration herein before directed to be taken.

No Tax or Duty shall be laid on Articles exported from any State.

No Preference shall be given by any Regulation of Commerce or Revenue to the Ports of one State over those of another: nor shall Vessels bound to, or from, one State, be obliged to enter, clear, or pay Duties in another.

No Money shall be drawn from the Treasury, but in Consequence of Appropriations made by Law; and a regular Statement and Account of the Receipts and Expenditures of all public Money shall be published from time to time.

No Title of Nobility shall be granted by the United States: And no Person holding any Office of Profit or Trust under them, shall, without the Consent of the Congress, accept of any present, Emolument, Office, or Title, of any kind whatever, from any King, Prince or foreign State.

Sec. 10. No State shall enter into any Treaty, Alliance, or Confederation; grant Letters of Marque and Reprisal; coin Money; emit Bills of Credit; make any Thing but gold and silver Coin a Tender in Payment of Debts; pass any Bill of Attainder, ex post facto Law, or Law impairing the Obligation of Contracts, or grant any Title of Nobility.

No State shall, without the Consent of the Congress, lay any Imposts or Duties on Imports or Exports, except what may be absolutely necessary for executing it's inspection Laws: and the net Produce of all Duties and Imposts, laid by any State on Imports or Exports, shall be for the Use of the Treasury of the United States; and all such Laws shall be subject to the Revision and Controul of the Congress.

No State shall, without the Consent of Congress, lay any Duty of Tonnage, keep Troops, or Ships of War in time of Peace, enter into any Agreement or Compact with another State, or with a foreign Power, or engage in War, unless actually invaded, or in such imminent Danger as will not admit of delay.

Art. II

Sec. 1. The executive Power shall be vested in a President of the United States of America. He shall hold his Office during the Term of four Years, and, together with the Vice President, chosen for the same Term, be elected, as follows:

Each State shall appoint, in such Manner as the Legislature thereof may direct, a Number of Electors, equal to the whole Number of Senators and Representatives to which the State may be entitled in the Congress: but no Senator or Representative, or Person holding an Office of Trust or Profit under the United States, shall be appointed an Elector.

The Electors shall meet in their respective States, and vote by Ballot for two Persons, of whom one at least shall not be an Inhabitant of the same State with themselves. And they shall make a List of all the Persons voted for, and of the Number of Votes for each; which List they shall sign and certify, and transmit sealed to the Seat of the Government of the United States, directed to the President of the Senate. The President of the Senate shall, in the Presence of the Senate and House of Representatives, open all the Certificates, and the Votes shall then be counted. The Person having the greatest Number of Votes shall be the President, if such Number be a Majority of the whole Number of Electors appointed; and if there be more than one who have such Majority, and have an equal Number of Votes, then the House of Representatives shall immediately chuse by Ballot one of them for President; and if no person have a Majority, then from the five highest on the List the said House shall in like Manner chuse the President. But in chusing the President, the Votes shall be taken by States, the Representation from each State having one Vote; a quorum for this Purpose shall consist of a Member or Members from two thirds of the States, and a Majority of all the States shall be necessary to a Choice. In every Case, after the Choice of the President, the Person having the greatest Number of Votes of the Electors shall be the Vice President. But if there should remain two or more who have equal Votes, the Senate shall chuse from them by Ballot the Vice President.

The Congress may determine the Time of chusing the Electors, and the Day on which they shall give their Votes; which Day shall be the same throughout the United States.

No Person except a natural born Citizen, or a Citizen of the United States, at the time of the Adoption of this Constitution, shall be eligible to the Office of President; neither shall any Person be eligible to that Office who shall not have attained to the Age of thirty five Years, and been fourteen Years a Resident within the United States.

In Case of the Removal of the President from Office, or of his Death, Resignation, or Inability to discharge the Powers and Duties of the said Office, the Same shall devolve on the Vice President, and the Congress may by Law provide for the Case of Removal, Death, Resignation or Inability, both of the President and Vice President, declaring what Officer shall then act as President, and such Officer shall act accordingly, until the Disability be removed, or a President shall be elected.

The President shall, at stated Times, receive for his Services, a Compensation, which shall neither be encreased nor diminished during the Period for which he shall have been elected, and he shall not receive within that Period any other Emolument from the United States, or any of them.

Before he enter on the Execution of his Office, he shall take the following Oath or Affirmation : – 'I do solemnly swear (or affirm) that I will faithfully execute the Office of President of the United States, and will to the best of my Ability, preserve, protect and defend the Constitution of the United States.'

Sec. 2. The President shall be Commander in Chief of the Army and Navy of the United States, and of the Militia of the several States, when called into the actual Service of the United States; he may require the Opinion, in writing, of the principal Officer in each of the executive Departments, upon any Subject relating to the Duties of their respective Offices, and he shall have Power to grant Reprieves and Pardons for Offences against the United States, except in Cases of Impeachment.

He shall have Power, by and with the Advice and Consent of the Senate, to make Treaties, provided two thirds of the Senators present concur; and he shall nominate, and by and with the Advice and Consent of the Senate, shall appoint Ambassadors, other public Ministers and Consuls, Judges of the supreme Court, and all other Officers of the United States, whose Appointments are not herein otherwise provided for, and which shall be established by Law : but the Congress may by Law vest the Appointment of such inferior Officers, as they think proper, in the President alone, in the Courts of Law, or in the Heads of Departments.

The President shall have Power to fill up all Vacancies that may happen during the Recess of the Senate, by granting Commissions which shall expire at the End of their next Session.

Sec. 3. He shall from time to time give to the Congress Information of the State of the Union, and recommend to their Consideration such Measures as he shall judge necessary and expedient; he may, on extraordinary Occasions, convene both Houses, or either of them, and in Case of Disagreement between them, with Respect to the Time of Adjournment, he may adjourn them to such Time as he shall think proper; he shall receive Ambassadors and other public Ministers; he shall take Care that the Laws be faithfully executed, and shall Commission all the Officers of the United States.

Sec. 4. The President, Vice President and all civil Officers of the United States, shall be removed from Office on Impeachment for, and Conviction of, Treason, Bribery, or other high Crimes and Misdemeanors.

Art. III

Sec. 1. The judicial Power of the United States, shall be vested in one supreme Court, and in such inferior Courts as the Congress may from time to time ordain and establish. The Judges, both of the supreme and inferior Courts, shall hold their Offices during good Behaviour, and shall, at stated Times, receive for their Services, a Compensation, which shall not be diminished during their Continuance in Office.

Sec. 2. The judicial Power shall extend to all Cases, in Law and Equity, arising under this Constitution, the Laws of the United States, and Treaties made, or which shall be made, under their Authority; – to all Cases affecting Ambassadors, other public Ministers and Consuls; – to all Cases of admiralty and maritime Jurisdiction; – to Controversies to which the United States shall be a Party; – to Controversies between two or more States; – between a State and Citizens of another State; – between Citizens of different States, – between Citizens of the same State claiming Lands under Grants of different States, and between a State, or the Citizens thereof, and foreign States, Citizens or Subjects.

In all Cases affecting Ambassadors, other public Ministers and Consuls, and those in which a State shall be Party, the supreme Court shall have original Jurisdiction. In all the other Cases before mentioned, the supreme Court shall have appellate Jurisdiction, both as to Law and Fact, with such Exceptions, and under such Regulations as the Congress shall make.

The Trial of all Crimes, except in Cases of Impeachment, shall be by Jury; and such Trial shall be held in the State where the said Crimes shall have been committed; but when not committed within any State, the Trial shall be at such Place or Places as the Congress may by Law have directed.

Sec. 3. Treason against the United States, shall consist only in levying War against them, or in adhering to their Enemies, giving them Aid and Comfort. No Person shall be convicted of Treason unless on the Testimony of two Witnesses to the same overt Act, or on Confession in open Court.

The Congress shall have Power to declare the Punishment of Treason, but no Attainder of Treason shall work Corruption of Blood, or Forfeiture except during the Life of the Person attainted.

Art. IV

Sec. 1. Full Faith and Credit shall be given in each State to the Public Acts, Records, and judicial Proceedings of every other State. And the Congress may by general Laws prescribe the Manner in which such Acts, Records and Proceedings shall be proved, and the Effect thereof.

Sec. 2. The Citizens of each State shall be entitled to all Privileges and Immunities of Citizens in the several States.

A Person charged in any State with Treason, Felony, or other Crime, who shall flee from Justice, and be found in another State, shall on Demand of the executive Authority of the State from which he fled, be delivered up, to be removed to the State having Jurisdiction of the Crime.

No Person held to Service or Labour in one State, under the Laws thereof, escaping into another, shall, in Consequence of any Law or Regulation therein, be discharged from such Service or Labour, but shall be delivered up on Claim of the Party to whom such Service or Labour may be due.

Sec. 3. New States may be admitted by the Congress into this Union; but no new States shall be formed or erected within the Jurisdiction of any other State; nor any State be formed by the Junction of two or more States, or Parts of States, without the Consent of the Legislatures of the States concerned as well as of the Congress.

The Congress shall have Power to dispose of and make all needful Rules and Regulations respecting the Territory or other Property belonging to the United States; and nothing in this Constitution shall be so construed as to Prejudice any Claims of the United States, or of any particular State.

Sec. 4. The United States shall guarantee to every State in this Union a Republican Form of Government, and shall protect each of them against Invasion; and on Application of the Legislature, or of the Executive (when the Legislature cannot be convened) against domestic Violence.

Art. V

The Congress, whenever two thirds of both Houses shall deem it necessary, shall propose Amendments to this Constitution, or, on the Application of the Legislatures of two thirds of the several States, shall call a Convention for proposing Amendments, which, in either Case, shall be valid to all Intents and Purposes, as Part of this Constitution, when ratified by the Legislatures of three fourths of the several States, or by Conventions in three fourths thereof, as the one or the other Mode of Ratification may be proposed by the Congress; Provided that no Amendment which may be made prior to the Year One thousand eight hundred and eight shall in any Manner affect the first and fourth Clauses in the Ninth Section of the first Article; and that no State, without its Consent, shall be deprived of it's equal Suffrage in the Senate.

Art. VI

All Debts contracted and Engagements entered into, before the Adoption of this Constitution, shall be as valid against the United States under this Constitution, as under the Confederation.

This Constitution, and the Laws of the United States which shall be made in Pursuance thereof; and all Treaties made, or which shall be made, under the Authority of the United States, shall be the supreme Law of the Land; and the Judges in every State shall be bound thereby, any Thing in the Constitution or Laws of any State to the Contrary notwithstanding.

The Senators and Representatives before mentioned, and the Members of the several State Legislatures, and all executive and judicial Officers, both of the United States and of the several States, shall be bound by Oath or Affirmation, to support this Constitution; but no religious Test shall ever be required as a Qualification to any Office or public Trust under the United States.

ART. VII

The Ratification of the Conventions of nine States, shall be sufficient for the Establishment of this Constitution between the States so ratifying the Same.

Done in Convention by the Unanimous Consent of the States present the Seventeenth Day of September in the Year of our Lord one thousand seven hundred and Eighty seven and of the Independence of the United States of America the Twelfth. In witness whereof We have hereunto subscribed our Names,

9 The Bill of Rights 1791

from H. S. Commager (ed.), *Documents of American History* 1963

[The first ten amendments to the Constitution, 1791.]

ART. I

Congress shall make no law respecting an establishment of religion, or prohibiting the free exercise thereof; or abridging the freedom of speech, or of the press; or the right of the people peaceably to assemble, and to petition the government for a redress of grievances.

ART. II

A well regulated Militia, being necessary to the security of a free State, the right of the people to keep and bear Arms, shall not be infringed.

ART. III

No Soldier shall, in time of peace be quartered in any house, without the consent of the Owner, nor in time of war, but in a manner to be prescribed by law.

ART. IV

The right of the people to be secure in their persons, houses, papers, and effects, against unreasonable searches and seizures, shall not be violated, and no Warrants shall issue, but upon probable cause, supported by Oath or affirmation, and particularly describing the place to be searched, and the persons or things to be seized.

ART. V

No person shall be held to answer for a capital, or otherwise infamous crime, unless on a presentment or indictment of a Grand Jury, except in cases arising in the land or naval forces, or in the Militia, when in actual service in time of War or public danger; nor shall any person be subject for the same offence to be twice put in jeopardy of life or limb; nor shall be compelled in any criminal case to be a witness against himself, nor be deprived of life, liberty, or property, without due process of law; nor shall private property be taken for public use, without just compensation.

ART. VI

In all criminal prosecutions, the accused shall enjoy the right to a speedy and public trial, by an impartial jury of the State and district wherein the crime shall have been committed, which district shall have been previously ascertained by law, and to be informed of the nature and cause of the accusation; to be confronted with the witnesses against him; to have compulsory process for obtaining witnesses in his favor, and to have the Assistance of Counsel for his defence.

ART. VII

In Suits at common law, where the value in controversy shall exceed twenty dollars, the right of trial by jury shall be preserved and no fact tried by a jury, shall be otherwise reexamined in any Court of the United States, than according to the rules of the common law.

Art. VIII

Excessive bail shall not be required, nor excessive fines imposed, nor cruel and unusual punishments inflicted.

Art. IX

The enumeration in the Constitution, of certain rights, shall not be construed to deny or disparage others retained by the people.

Art. X

The powers not delegated to the United States by the Constitution, nor prohibited by it to the States, are reserved to the States respectively, or to the people.

C Disturbances before the French Revolution

The documents in this section should give some idea of the ideas
and motives behind three of the political disturbances in Europe
during the 1780s which the Atlantic–Democratic Revolution
thesis links together. The Association Movement in Britain had
its origins in Yorkshire in 1779. The initial aims of the
Movement are outlined in the Yorkshire Petition (C5). Some of
its more moderate aims were achieved, or appeared to be
achieved at the time, through action in parliament by MPs
sympathetic to, or simply using, the Movement. But division
within the Movement about the extent to which reform was
necessary resulted in eventual failure and dissolution. The
disturbances in Holland during the 1780s, which resulted in an
insurrection in 1787, were directed against the Stadtholder, the
hereditary ruling prince from the house of Orange. In answer to
the rising the Stadtholder requested aid from his brother-in-law,
the King of Prussia, and his father-in-law, the King of England,
and with the assistance of Prussian troops and British seamen the
rising was suppressed within the year. The rising of the Belgians
in 1789 was directed against the Emperor Joseph II who ruled
Belgium (then known as the Austrian Netherlands) as part of
the Austrian Empire. Faction divided the Belgian rebels between
the 'Statists' who sought the preservation of the existing order
of society but independent of Austria, and the followers of Vonck
who hoped for a new and more democratic order. The issue was
eventually settled by the weight of the Austrian army.

C.E.

1 Joan Derck Van der Capellen tot de Pol

Discourse to the People of the Low Countries on the Present Alarming and very Perilous Situation of the Republic of Holland   3 September 1781

from J. Godechot (ed.), *La Pensée révolutionnaire en France et en Europe*   1964. This translation from R. C. Bridges, P. Dukes, J. D. Hargreaves and W. Scott (eds.), *Nations and Empires: Documents on the History of Europe and on its Relations with the World since 1648*, 1969

Ah, my compatriots! Arm yourselves again, and defend the interest of the republic, yours, in a word. The republic is your weal, not at all solely that of the Prince and his court, who consider us all, the Dutch nation in its entirety, the descendants of the free Batavians, as their hereditary vassals, their sheep and cattle, which they have the right to clip or slaughter as their avarice and resentment inspire in them. Such a conception dictates their conduct towards us. The inhabitants of a country, landed proprietors, bourgeois and villeins, poor and rich, great and small, constitute together the proprietors, the lords and the true masters of their country; here are those who should nominate the governors and create the laws. A nation is a great society grouped in a political association; the leaders, the chiefs, the magistrates, the Prince, briefly, those who constitute the effective sovereignty are merely the directors, the commanders and the treasurers of this society; and in their individual worth, or taken together, they are less important than the members of society themselves, that is to say than the body of the nation. Thus the Company of the Indies is a great association of merchants joined in the aim of carrying on commerce with the Indies. They are too numerous, and live too far from one another to meet together constantly, if need be, and to direct in person the affairs of their company; moreover these necessitate more art and science than the members possess separately; that is why they nominate with great wisdom, directors, commanders and treasurers, whom they remunerate for their trouble, and to whom they do not accord powers wider than the conduct of the affairs for which they are employed demands. The directors naturally enjoy a greater authority in the conduct of current business than a single member or a great number assembled together not constituting a *majority*; but if all the members or a clear majority insist on obtaining a modification to the administration or to the direction of the affairs of the company, that is to say of their own affairs, it is incumbent then upon the directors who are entirely at the service of the members, to obey the orders of the latter, of whom a majority represents the true proprietors, masters and lords of the company.

It is the same for the great society that constitutes the nation. The Grandee who reigns over you, the Prince or whoever holds a power in the public domain, exercises this power in your name, and draws his authority from *you*. It is you who are the members, the proprietors and the masters of the national society that bears the title of United Provinces of the Low Countries. The grandees, on the contrary, are no more than the directors and treasurers of this society. To remunerate them, you draw on your own purse, that is to say on the public purse. They are thus at your service, they are your servants; they are responsible before the greatest number and bound by their duty to obey your orders.

Now, all men are born free; nobody, by nature, is subservient to the authority of another. Although certain people possess brilliant aptitudes, physical strength, or a considerable fortune, those who are intelligent, strong and rich do not receive through these accidents any right over simple, weak and poor people. God, our universal father, created man to be happy and commanded everybody without exception to favour as far as possible the happiness of his fellows. In order to realize this grand design of the Creator, that is to say to build the happiness of all, men have recognized the necessity of joining great societies and to associate themselves together even in millions. Note that in these societies, all the members are naturally equal; no member is subordinated to another. In these great societies, commonly called civil societies, the members join together to construct their mutual happiness, to defend their goods and the other rights that they have legitimately acquired. Thus you can realize that if harm threatens the rights and goods of the members of a society – as the English have done for many years to our merchants and seamen – the whole civil society is then bound to resist this violence and to fight with all its force to obtain indemnity and to guarantee the future security of the citizens. ...

Command your delegates to communicate from time to time a report on their actions, in the public journals. Take care of the liberty of the press, for it is the sole support of your national liberty. If we lose the freedom to speak without restraint to our fellow-citizens, or to bestow on them good counsel, it will then be very easy for our oppressors to play their sinister role; and it is for this reason that those who cannot bear to learn that their conduct is being reported never cease to rise up against the liberty of expression and the liberty of the press, and would welcome nothing being printed or sold without their permission.

Arm yourselves; choose leaders; follow the example of the American people where not a drop of blood was spilt, as long as the English had not struck the first blow – and act with prudence, wisdom and moderation; thus Jehovah, God of liberty, who led the Israelites from their servitude, and made of them a free nation, will sustain without any doubt your good and just cause.

I am, people of the Low Countries, dear fellow-citizens, your faithful fellow-citizen.

2 Brabant Declaration of Independence   1789

from J. Godechot (ed.), *Le Pensée révolutionnaire en France et en Europe*   1964. Translated by Clive Emsley

The People of Brabant, through the instrument of the Ecclesiastical Estate, the Third Estate of the three principle towns, joined with several members of the nobility.

To all those who see or hear these words, greetings.

Those political writers who enjoy the highest reputation today and who write with the most brilliance, put the following maxims like so many incontestable truths. It is well-known, they say, that originally the citizens of nations conferred the right to govern them for their proper happiness. Whatever the form of government, the rights of sovereignty must be founded on the consent of the people to make it legitimate. All power is essentially limited by the simple goal which the society has in view; ceaselessly aiming to look after the people, to keep them vigorous and to make their lot happy and agreeable, society can only consent to that which fulfils these aims. Good sense will prove even to those who justify the power of Kings on divine wishes, or who are convinced of the Divine Right of Kings, that however the government was established, the sovereigns stay submissive to such rules as are sufficiently indicated by the interests of society, which ought to be the supreme law for the kings; they are not permitted to substitute their will for this law, or their personal interests to the general interest [...] whether the consent of peoples or whether the Divinity has established the power of the sovereign, whether the nations have granted him the greatest leeway or whether they have confined him by express laws, there remains always in the body of the nation a supreme will, in ineffaceable character, an inalienable right, a right which preceded all others. Vainly sovereigns justified their rights on the grounds of ancient uninterrupted possession, of the silence of the peoples, of the exercise of power undisputed for a great number of centuries, of the prerogatives granted by the body of the Nation; violence, fear, credulity, prejudices, good nature and imprudence often succeed in numbing peoples, in bewildering their understanding, in crushing in them the resort to nature; but when favourable circumstances open the eyes of the people, when they hear the voice of reason, when necessity forces them to quit their lethargy, they blush at their feebleness and their blindness. They see then that the alleged rights of their tyrants are only the effects of injustice, of seduction and force, which are not able to destroy the eternal rights of man: it is then that nations recall their dignity, remembering that it was they themselves who established the authority, that they only submitted to become more happy: that the law is only made to represent their wishes, and that when the sovereign's power departs from their plans, *they return to their natural independence and can revoke the powers unworthily abused* : so the argument goes today.

These maxims acquire great weight in the regard of the people of the Austrian Netherlands since these people have ceded or granted to their respective sovereigns a limited power, a circumscribed authority. [. . .]

No one can disagree that when the laws are harmful, or contrary to fundamental laws, to the constitution and to the wishes of the nation, the nation has the right to contradict them, to revoke them and to oppose this breach of trust. The will of the nation is always the supreme law for the sovereign as well as for the subject. It is the unalterable measure of the power of the one and the obedience of the other; it is the common bond which unites the nation to its rulers and these latter to the nation, this bond is reciprocal, and when the sovereign breaks it, his subjects are no longer bound.

It is [. . .] notorious throughout Europe that his Majesty the King and Emperor [1] has exercised the most frightful despotism over the Belgians, which has broken his most sacred engagements, which has contravened not only his promise, his word, but even his oath on the observation and keeping of his inaugural pact.[2] [. . .]

For all these reasons, seeing the unalterable determination of the Emperor to tyrannize the Belgian people, and to reduce them to slavery in contradiction of his inaugural pact and his own engagements, seeing our obligation to defend and maintain our liberty, our religion, our rights, our privileges, our customs, freedoms, and to transmit them intact to our children as they have been transmitted to us by our forebears, we find ourselves in the hard necessity of removing the tyranny and the domination of the aforesaid Emperor and sovereign.

Consequently, knowing this [. . .] we have declared and declare by this the Emperor Joseph II, Duke of Brabant, etc., *ipso jure* lapsed from the sovereignty, domains, rights and prerogatives of the aforesaid duchy and the dependent lands, and

1. Joseph II.

[2.] The inaugural pact which Joseph II was accused of breaking was the historic charter of Brabant, known as the 'Joyous Entry', issued to the province by the Duke of Brabant in 1355.

henceforth no longer to recognize him in any fashion or manner as such. [...]

We instruct and order that these words be printed and displayed in the province of Brabant and the dependent lands [...] so that no one will be able to claim ignorance.

3 The Belgian Treaty of Union 1790

from J. Godechot (ed.), *La Pensée révolutionnaire en France et en Europe* 1964. Translated by Clive Emsley

The estates of Belgium, after having confined their ancient bonds into a close union and a lasting friendship have resolved on the following points and articles:

I All the provinces are united and confederated under the name of the United Belgian States (États-Belgiques unis).

II These provinces hold in common, united and concentrated the sovereign power; which, however, they limit and restrain to the following objects: a common defence; the power to declare war and make peace ...; to enter into alliances both offensive and defensive with foreign powers; to nominate, to send and receive residents, ambassadors or other such agents. [...]

III To exercise this sovereign power they create and establish a congress of deputies from each of the provinces under the name of the Sovereign Congress of the United Belgian States.

IV The aforesaid provinces profess and will profess forever the Apostolic Roman Catholic religion, and will preserve inviobly the unity of the Church, the Congress will observe and maintain the ancient connections with the Holy See. [...]

V The Congress alone reserves the right to mint the money of the United Belgian States and to settle its title and value.

VI The provinces of the Union will furnish what is necessary for the exercise of the sovereign powers vested in the congress, according to the proportion observed under the former sovereign.

VII Each province retains and keeps to itself all the other rights of sovereignty, its own legislation, its own liberty, its own independence; all the powers finally, jurisdictions and such like rights, which are not expressly held in common and delegated to the sovereign congress.

VIII It is irrevocably agreed, moreover, with regard to such difficulties as might arise [...] [that] each province will nominate a person to the requisition of one or other of the parties: before whom the cause will be summarily read and who will decide upon it. And the Congress will have the right of execution : and if the verdict is carried against the Congress, this latter will be obliged to yield.

IX The United States are bound closely to aid each other; and as soon as one province is attacked by an enemy from outside, they will make a common cause, and together, with all their strength, will defend the attacked province.

X It will not be permitted for any province to make an alliance, or any such treaty with another power without the consent of Congress.

XI This union will be firm, perpetual, irrevocable. It will not be permitted for one province, or for several, or even for the majority, to break this union or to separate themselves. [...]

XII It is also irrevocably agreed that power, both civil and military, or one portion of one or the other will never be conferred on the same person; and that no one having a seat or a voice in the Congress will be considered for military service, and that conversely no one in the military service will be considered to be a deputy to the Congress, to have either a seat or a voice therein. In the same way all those deriving employment or pensions of whatever denomination will not be admitted to Congress. All those who, after the ratification of this treaty of union shall accept any military order or such-like decoration are also excluded.

This concluded, made and decreed at Brussells, 11 January 1790 at 10 a.m.

[There follow signatures of the representatives of the provinces of Brabant, Gueldres, Flanders, West-Flanders, Hainaut, Namur, Tourney, Tournésis, Malines.]

4 J. F. Vonck
Impartial Considerations on the Situation of Brabant

from *Impartial Considerations on the Situation of Brabant* 1790.
Reprinted in J. Godechot (ed.), *La Pensée révolutionnaire en
France et en Europe,* 1964. Translated by Clive Emsley

Since the conquest of the Franks in the fifth century until
today, the political constitution of Brabant has consisted of a
Monarchy where the Prince's authority has been limited by
certain fundamental laws which, on his accession he has sworn
to be inviolable. [...]

If [...] today one claims that the people have been subjected
to the sovereignty of the Estates, how had this come about?
Thus they will have passed from the yoke of a *limited monarchy*
to that of an *aristocracy*. [...] It is quite clear [...] that today
the people have shaken off the yoke of the Monarchy, in other
words the only kind of government to which they ever submitted, after this they have necessarily recovered all their primary
and natural liberties, and consequently also the liberty to choose
for themselves the new kind of government which seems to
them the most proper and the most advantageous.

I will give to the Estates legislative power, to the Council of
State, executive power, as for the judicial power, I will leave it
with those tribunals which exercise it at the moment.

5 The Petition of the County of York 1780

from the *Annual Register* 1780

To the Honourable the Commons of Great-Britain, in Parliament assembled:

The Petition of the Gentlemen, Clergy, and Freeholders of
the County of York, sheweth that this nation hath been engaged
for several years in a most expensive and unfortunate war; that
many of our valuable colonies, having actually declared themselves independent, have formed a strict confederacy with
France and Spain the dangerous and inveterate enemies of Great-

Britain, that the consequence of those combined misfortunes hath been a large addition to the nation's debt, a heavy accumulation on taxes, a rapid decline of the trade, manufactures, and land-rents of the kingdom.

Alarmed at the diminished resources and growing burthens of this country, and convinced that rigid frugality is now indispensably necessary in every department of the state, your petitioners observe with grief, that notwithstanding the calamitous and impoverished condition of the nation, much public money has been improvidently squandered, and that many individuals enjoy sinecure places, efficient places with exorbitent emoluments, and pensions unmerited by public-service, to a large and still increasing amount; whence the crown has acquired a great and unconstitutional influence, which, if not checked, may soon prove fatal to the liberties of this country.

Your petitioners conceiving that the true end of every legitimate government is not the emolument of an individual, but the welfare of the community; and considering that by the constitution of this realm the national purse is intrusted in a peculiar manner to the custody of this honourable house; beg leave further to represent, that until effectual measures be taken to redress the oppressive grievances herein stated, the grant of any additional sum of public money, beyond the produce of the present taxes, will be injurious to the rights and property of the people, and derogatory from the honour and dignity of parliament.

Your petitioners therefore, appealing to the justice of this honourable house, do most earnestly request that, before any new burthens are laid upon this country, effectual measures may be taken by this house to enquire into and correct the gross abuses in the expenditure of public money; to reduce all exorbitent emoluments, to rescind and abolish all sinecure places and unmerited pensions; and to appropriate the produce to the necessities of the state in such manner as to the wisdom of parliament shall seem meet.

And your petitioners shall ever pray, &c. &c.

The following counties presented petitions nearly in the same words:

Middlesex	Dorset
Chester	Devon
Hants.	Norfolk
Hertford	Berks.
Sussex	Bucks.
Huntingdon	Nottingham
Surrey	Kent
Cumberland	Northumberland
Bedford	Suffolk
Essex	Hereford
Gloucester	Cambridge
Somerset	Derby
Wilts.	

Also the cities of London, Westminster, York, Bristol, and the towns of Cambridge, Nottingham, Newcastle, Reading and Bridgewater. The county of Northampton agreed to instruct their members on the points of the petition.

D The French Revolution

The only example in this section of the abundance of legislation passed by the various revolutionary assemblies is the Declaration of the Rights of Man and of Citizens (D2) passed by the National Assembly in August 1789 after the overthrow of despotism and privilege. In the eyes of the historian Georges Lefebvre, the Declaration was 'the symbol of the Revolution of 1798'. It was planned to revise the Declaration after the completion of a new constitution, but when the new constitution was finished in 1791 the National Assembly considered it prudent not to touch the Declaration because of the reverence with which it was already regarded in France.

The only example here of the lively pamphleteering of the Revolution is a chapter from Sieyès's *What is the Third Estate?* (D1). This document was of crucial importance when it was published early in 1789; it articulated the sentiments of the Third Estate and strengthened its resolve for when the Estates General met at Versailles in May 1789. Sieyès's pamphlet had little relevance to the direction the Revolution took after 1791. The *sans-culotte* documents and the revolutionary songs belong to this later period of the Revolution. They should give an idea of the mentality of the popular revolutionary movement during the period surrounding the fall of the monarchy and the early months of the republic and the war.

The documents in this section in no way cover the complexity of events and issues during the French Revolution, and in no way represent the mass of documentation which has been passed down from the Revolution.

C.E.

1 Abbé Sieyès

What is the Third Estate?

from *What is the Third Estate?* 1789. Translated by M. Blondel, 1963

The Third Estate is a Complete Nation

What does a nation require to survive and prosper? It needs *private* activities and *public* services.

These private activities can all be comprised within four classes of persons:

1. Since land and water provide the basic materials for human needs, the first class, in logical order, includes all the families connected with work on the land.

2. Between the initial sale of goods and the moment when they reach the consumer or user, goods acquire an increased value of a more or less compound nature through the incorporation of varying amounts of labour. In this way human industry manages to improve the gifts of nature and the value of the raw material may be multiplied twice, or ten-fold, or a hundred-fold. Such are the activities of the second class of persons.

3. Between production and consumption, as also between the various stages of production, a variety of intermediary agents intervene, to help producers as well as consumers; these are the dealers and the merchants. Merchants continually compare needs according to place and time and estimate the profits to be obtained from warehousing and transportation; dealers undertake, in the final stage, to deliver the goods on the wholesale and retail markets. Such is the function of the third class of persons.

4. Besides these three classes of useful and industrious citizens who deal with *things* fit to be consumed or used, society also requires a vast number of special activities and of services *directly* useful or pleasant to the *person*. This fourth class embraces all sorts of occupations, from the most distinguished liberal and scientific professions to the lowest of menial tasks.

Such are the activities which support society. But who performs them? The Third Estate.

Public services can also, at present, be divided into four known categories, the army, the law, the Church and the bureaucracy. It needs no detailed analysis to show that the Third Estate everywhere constitutes nineteen-twentieths of them, except that it is loaded with all the really arduous work, all the tasks which the privileged order refuses to perform. Only the well-paid and honorific posts are filled by members of the privileged order. Are we to give them credit for this? We could do so only if the Third Estate was unable or unwilling to fill these posts. We know the answer. Nevertheless, the privileged have dared to preclude the Third Estate. 'No matter how useful you are', they said, 'no matter how able you are, you can go so far and no further. Honours are not for the like of you.' The rare exceptions, noticeable as they are bound to be, are mere mockery, and the sort of language allowed on such occasions is an additional insult.

If this exclusion is a social crime, a veritable act of war against the Third Estate, can it be said at least to be useful to the commonwealth? Ah! Do we not understand the consequences of monopoly? While discouraging those it excludes, does it not destroy the skill of those it favours? Are we unaware that any work from which free competition is excluded will be performed less well and more expensively?

When any function is made the prerogative of a separate order among the citizens, has nobody remarked how a salary has to be paid not only to the man who actually does the work, but to all those of the same caste who do not, and also to the entire families of both the workers and the non-workers? Has nobody observed that as soon as the government becomes the property of a separate class, it starts to grow out of all proportion and that posts are created not to meet the needs of the governed but of those who govern them? Has nobody noticed that while on the one hand, we basely and I dare say *stupidly* accept this situation of ours, on the other hand, when we read the history of Egypt or stories of travels in India, we describe the same kind of conditions as despicable, monstrous, destructive of all industry, as inimical to social progress, and above all as debasing to the human race in general and intolerable to Europeans in particular [...]? But here we must leave considerations which, however much they might broaden and clarify the problem, would nevertheless slow our pace.

It suffices to have made the point that the so-called usefulness of a privileged order to the public service is a fallacy; that, without help from this order, all the arduous tasks in the service are performed by the Third Estate; that without this order the higher posts could be infinitely better filled; that they ought to be the natural prize and reward of recognized ability and service; and that if the privileged have succeeded in usurping all well-paid and honorific posts, this is both a hateful iniquity towards the generality of citizens and an act of treason to the commonwealth.

Who is bold enough to maintain that the Third Estate does not contain within itself everything needful to constitute a complete nation? It is like a strong and robust man with one arm still in chains. If the privileged order were removed, the nation would not be something less but something more. What then is the Third Estate? All; but an 'all' that is fettered and oppressed. What would it be without the privileged order? It would be all; but free and flourishing. Nothing will go well without the Third Estate; everything would go considerably better without the two others.

It is not enough to have shown that the privileged, far from being useful to the nation, can only weaken and injure it; we must prove further that the nobility is not part of our society at all: it may be a *burden* for the nation, but it cannot be part of it.

First, it is impossible to find what place to assign to the caste of nobles among all the elements of a nation. I know that there are many people, all too many, who, from infirmity, incapacity, incurable idleness or a collapse of morality, perform no functions at all in society. Exceptions and abuses always exist alongside the rule, and particularly in a large commonwealth. But all will agree that the fewer these abuses, the better organized a state is supposed to be. The most ill-organized state of all would be the one where not just isolated individuals but a complete class of citizens would glory in inactivity amidst the general movement and contrive to consume the best part of the product without having in any way helped to produce it. Such a class, surely, is foreign to the nation because of its *idleness*.

The nobility, however, is also a foreigner in our midst because of its *civil and political* prerogatives.

What is a nation? A body of associates living under *common* laws and represented by the same *legislative assembly*, etc.

Is it not obvious that the nobility possesses privileges and exemptions which it brazenly calls its rights and which stand distinct from the rights of the great body of citizens? Because of these special rights, the nobility does not belong to the common order, nor is it subjected to the common laws. Thus its private rights make it a people apart in the great nation. It is truly *imperium in imperio*.

As for its *political* rights, it also exercises these separately from the nation. It has its own representatives who are charged with no mandate from the People. Its deputies sit separately, and even if they sat in the same chamber as the deputies of ordinary citizens they would still constitute a different and separate representation. They are foreign to the nation first because of their origin, since they do not owe their powers to the People; and secondly because of their aim, since this consists in defending, not the general interest, but the private one.

The Third Estate then contains everything that pertains to the nation while nobody outside the Third Estate can be considered as part of the nation. What is the Third Estate? *Everything*.

2 Declaration of the Rights of Man and of Citizens 1789

Reprinted in Part I of Tom Paine, *Rights of Man* 1791

The representatives of the people of France, formed into a National Assembly, considering that ignorance, neglect, or contempt of human rights, are the sole causes of public misfortunes and corruptions of Government, have resolved to set forth in a solemn declaration, these natural, imprescriptible, and inalienable rights; that this declaration being constantly present to the minds of the members of the body social, they may be ever kept attentive to their rights and their duties; that the acts of the legislative and executive powers of Government, being capable of being every moment compared with the end of political institutions, may be more respected; and also, that the future claims of the citizens, being directed by simple and incontestable principles, may always tend to the maintenance of the Constitution, and the general happiness.

For these reasons the National Assembly doth recognise and declare, in the presence of the Supreme Being, and with the hope of his blessing and favour, the following *sacred* rights of men and of citizens:

I Men are born, and always continue, free and equal in respect of their rights. Civil distinctions, therefore, can be founded only on public utility.

II The end of all political associations is the preservation of the natural and imprescriptible rights of man; and these rights are Liberty, Property, Security, and Resistance of Oppression.

III The Nation is essentially the source of all sovereignty; nor can any individual, or any body of men, be entitled to any authority which is not expressly derived from it.

IV Political Liberty consists in the power of doing whatever does not injure another. The exercise of the natural rights of every man, has no other limits than those which are necessary to secure to every *other* man the free exercise of the same rights; and these limits are determinable only by the law.

V The law ought to prohibit only actions hurtful to society. What is not prohibited by the law should not be hindered; nor should any one be compelled to that which the law does not require.

VI The law is an expression of the will of the community. All citizens have a right to concur, either personally or by their representatives, in its formation. It should be the same to all, whether it protects or punishes; and all being equal in its sight, are equally eligible to all honours, places, and employments, according to their different abilities, without any other distinctions than that created by their virtues and talents.

VII No man should be accused, arrested, or held in confinement, except in cases determined by the law, and according to the forms which it has prescribed. All who promote, solicit, execute, or cause to be executed, arbitrary orders, ought to be punished, and every citizen called upon, or apprehended by virtue of the law, ought immediately to obey, and renders himself culpable by resistance.

VIII The law ought to impose no other penalties but such as are absolutely and evidently necessary; and no one ought to be punished, but in virtue of a law promulgated before the offence, and legally applied.

IX Every man being presumed innocent till he has been convicted, whenever his detention becomes indispensable, all rigour to him, more than is necessary to secure his person, ought to be provided against by the law.

X No man ought to be molested on account of his opinions, not even on account of his religious opinions, provided his avowal of them does not disturb the public order established by the law.

XI The unrestrained communication of thoughts and opinions being one of the most precious Rights of Man, every citizen may speak, write, and publish freely, provided he is responsible for the abuse of this liberty, in cases determined by the law.

XII A public force being necessary to give security to the Rights of Men and of citizens, that force is instituted for the benefit of the community and not for the particular benefit of the persons with whom it is intrusted.

XIII A common contribution being necessary for the support of the public force, and for defraying the other expenses of Government, it ought to be divided equally among the members of the community, according to their abilities.

XIV Every citizen has a right, either by himself or his representative, to a free voice in determining the necessity of public contributions, the appropriation of them, and their amount, mode of assessment, and duration.

XV Every community has a right to demand of all its agents an account of their conduct.

XVI Every community in which a separation of powers and a security of rights is not provided for, wants a Constitution.

XVII The right to property being inviolable and sacred, no one ought to be deprived of it, except in cases of evident public necessity, legally ascertained, and on condition of a previous just indemnity.

3 Definition of a Moderate

from 'Definition of a moderate'   May 1793. Reprinted in Walter Markov and Albert Soboul (eds.), *Die Sansculotten von Paris*, 1957. Translated by Clive Emsley

Definition of a moderate, a Feuillent, and an Aristocrat. In short what is to be understood under that class of citizens from whom the millions have to be taken which are to be raised throughout the whole Republic. (The Guardian Angel of the Liberty and Equality of the Republic one and indivisible to the Citizens who form the Committee of petitions.)

The aristocrat is one who because of his scorn or indifference hasn't been listed on the register of National Guards and who hasn't taken the citizen's oath. [...] One who by his conduct, his activities, his speeches, his writings, and by his connections has given proof that he regrets the passing of the old regime, and despises the revolution in everything. One who, by his conduct has implied he would send money to the *emigrés* or join the enemy's army; if he only had the resources to do the one and the occasion to do the other. One who has ever doubted the triumph of the revolution. One who has announced distressing news which is obviously false. One who by bad management has left land uncultivated without letting any out or selling any at a just price. One who didn't buy national goods when given the occasion and the resources. And above all one who has declared he wouldn't buy them; and has advised against this act of civic duty. One who, having the ability and the occasion, hasn't provided work for workmen and journeymen at a wage adequate to the cost of foodstuffs. One who hasn't subscribed to the volunteers, and especially one who hasn't given as much as he could.

One who because of his arrogance doesn't visit the civil clergy, and especially one who has advised others not to do so. One who hasn't eased the burden of indigent, but patriotic men, while clearly having the means. One who, because of his wickedness doesn't wear a cocade of three inches circumference. One who has bought clothes other than national dress, and especially one who doesn't glory in the title and the clothing of a *sans-culotte*. The Guardian Angel of the Republic assures you that its definition is quite just, and that the true patriot has done the opposite for the general good, and desires that this will be realized.

4 What is a *Sans-Culotte*?

'Reply to an impertinent question: what is a *sans-culotte*?' April 1793. Reprinted in Walter Markov and Albert Soboul (eds.), *Die Sansculotten von Paris*, 1957. Translated by Clive Emsley

A *Sans-Culotte* you rogues? He is someone who always goes on foot, who has no millions as you would all like to have, no *chateaux*, no valets to serve him, and who lives simply with his wife and children, if he has any, on a fourth or fifth storey.

He is useful, because he knows how to work in the field, to forge iron, to use a saw, to use a file, to roof a house, to make shoes and to shed his last drop of blood for the safety of the Republic.

And because he works, you are sure not to meet his person in the Café de Chartres, or in the gaming houses where others conspire and game, nor at the National theatre where *The Friend of the Law* is performed, nor at the Vaudeville theatre at a performance of *Chaste Suzanne*, nor in the literary clubs where for two sous, which are so precious to him, you are offered the filth of Gorsas,[1] the *Chronicle* and the *Patriot Français*.

In the evening he goes to his Section, not powdered or perfumed, or smartly booted in the hope of catching the eye of the

[1.] A pamphleteer tending to the Girondins.

citizenesses in the galleries, but ready to support good proposals with all his might, and to crush those which come from the abominable faction of politicians.

Finally, a *Sans-Culotte* adwaysalways has his sabre sharp ,to cut off the ears of all enemies of the Revolution; sometimes he even goes out with his pike; but at the first sound of the drum he is ready to leave for the Vendée, for the army of the Alps or for the army of the North.

God Save the people. God-dam the Aristocrates! [2] is lately the shout of a true English *Sans-Culotte* and a friend of the famous Dr Priestley, whose house and papers were burnt on 14 July 1791 by the aristocrates of Birmingham as all the world knows. Here is the conclusion of the speech he makes having drunk his part of some bowls of punch.

'Brethren and friends, will you to assure the revolution? Knock down the Snake Brissot, the Vipère Gaudet, the reptil Vergniand, the rascal Barbaroux, the Sweet Pétion, the Dog and hypocritical Rolland and all others *Scélérates* of the Clique Gensonné, Boyer-foufrède, Rabaud, Buzet, etca, etca, etca, etca, and that'il do' !

This Englishman hasn't received any guineas from Pitt.

5 The *Ça Ira* and *Carmagnole*

Traditional French song   1792. Translated by Clive Emsley

Madame Véto [1] has made her promise
To cut the throat of all Paris
But her blow has failed
Thanks to our gunners.

We'll dance the Carmagnole
Long live the sound, long live the sound,
We'll dance the Carmagnole

[2.] This, and the concluding paragraph are in English, then repeated in French. I have kept the original, curious English version.

[1.] Monsieur and Madame Véto are Louis XVI and Marie Antoinette. The nickname refers to the royal power of veto given by the Constitution in 1791, a power which popular radicals thought was grossly abused.

Long live the sound of cannons.
  Ah ça ira [2]
  To the lantern with the aristocrats [3]
  Ah ça ira
  We're going to string up the aristocrats.

Monsieur Véto has promised
To be faithful to his country
But he has failed in this
No more excuses!
  We'll dance the Carmagnole
  Long live the sound etc.

What does a republic demand?
The equality of the human race
No longer the poor on their knees
No longer the rich over them
  To the victors of the war
  Long live the sound etc.

What does a republican need?
Iron, lead, and also bread
Iron to work
Lead for his vengeance
  And bread for his brothers
  Long live the sound etc.

Yes we'll remember forever
The sans-culottes of the faubourgs
Drink to their health
Long live these gallant fellows!
  We'll dance the Carmagnole
  Long live the sound etc.

[2.] *Ça ira* is almost untranslatable. It means 'that will go' literally. Some dictionaries translate it as 'we'll manage'.

[3.] Before the guillotine some enemies of the Revolution were hanged from lamp-posts.

6 Marie-Joseph Chénier
The Song of Departure

c. 1793. Traditional French song translated by Clive Emsley

Singing Victory opens the way for us,
Liberty guides our steps,
And from the North and the South, the warlike trumpet
Has sounded the hour of battle.
Tremble enemies of France!
Kings, drunk on blood and pride!
The sovereign people advance!
  Tyrants, sink into your coffins!

The Republic calls us,
We will conquer – or we will die,
A Frenchman must live for her,
For her a Frenchman must die.

Bara, Viala,[1] how we are envious of their fate!
They died, but they vanquished.
The coward overwhelmed with years just doesn't know life;
Who dies for the people has conquered.
You are valiant, so are we all,
Guide us against the tyrants!
Republicans are men,
Slaves are children!

The Republic calls us.

[1.] Joseph Bara and Joseph Viala were republican boy soldiers killed in
the Vendée.

E The English Reaction

The documents in this section deal with the political turbulence in Britain during the 1790s. Again the section is brief and not fully representative of the wealth of documentation which survives.

Burke and Paine represent the opposite extremes of opinion in Britain about the French Revolution. Burke had been a supporter of the American colonists, but could see no similarities between their goals and those of the revolutionaries in France. He violently condemned the French Revolution from its outset. The *Reflections on the Revolution in France* (E1), published in November 1790, brought forth a crop of outraged replies. Paine's *The Rights of Man* (E2) was one of the most successful of these replies. The radical second part of this pamphlet led to the prosecution of the author in 1792 for a seditious libel. *The Rights of Man* became a principal text for the political societies which began organizing themselves in Britain from about the end of 1791. The aims of the most famous of these popular radical societies, the London Corresponding Society formed in January 1792, are set out in their Resolutions printed here as E3.

The last two documents in this section (E4 and 5) come from the Nore Mutiny of 1797. This mutiny at Nore Anchorage in the Thames was the more serious of a series of mutinies in the home fleet during this year, occasioned by the appalling conditions in which the seamen served on eighteenth-century war ships. The mutinies were particularly serious in that they occurred when invasion by the French appeared a very serious possibility.

C.E.

1 Edmund Burke
Reflections on the Revolution in France

from *Reflections on the Revolution in France* 1790

All circumstances taken together, the French Revolution is the most astonishing that has hitherto happened in the world. The most wonderful things are brought about in many instances by means the most absurd and ridiculous; in the most ridiculous modes; and, apparently, by the most contemptible instruments. Everything seems out of nature in this strange chaos of levity and ferocity, and of all sorts of crimes jumbled together with all sorts of follies. In viewing this tragicomic scene, the most opposite passions necessarily succeed, and sometimes mix with each other in the mind; alternate contempt and indignation; alternate laughter and tears; alternate scorn and horror. [...]

France has bought undisguised calamities at a higher price than any nation has purchased the most unequivocal blessing! France has bought poverty by crime! France has not sacrificed to her interest, but she has abandoned her interest, that she might prostitute her virtue. We have seen the French rebel against a mild and lawful monarch with more fury, outrage, and insult, than any people has been known to rise against the most illegal usurper, or the most sanguinary tyrant. [...]

The vanity, restlessness, petulance, and spirit of intrigue, of several petty cabals, who attempt to hide their total want of consequence in bustle and noise, and puffing, and mutual quotation of each other, makes you imagine that our contemptuous neglect of their abilities is a mark of general acquiescence in their opinions. No such thing, I assure you. Because half a dozen grasshoppers under a fern make the field ring with their importunate chink, whilst thousands of great cattle, reposed beneath the shadow of the British oak, chew the cud and are silent, pray do not imagine that those who make the noise are the only inhabitants of the field; that, of course, they are many in number; or that, after all, they are other than the little, shrivelled, meagre, hopping, though loud and troublesome, insects of the hour.

I almost venture to affirm, that not one in a hundred amongst us participates in the 'triumph' of the Revolution Society. If the king and queen of France and their children, were to fall into our hands by the chance of war, in the most acrimonious of all hostilities, (I deprecate such an event, I deprecate such hostility,) they would be treated with another sort of triumphal entry into London. We formerly have had a king of France in that situation; you have read how he was treated by the victor in the field; and in what manner he was afterwards received in England. Four hundred years have gone over us; but I believe we are not materially changed since that period. Thanks to our sullen resistance to innovation, thanks to the cold sluggishness of our national character, we still bear the stamp of our forefathers. We have not (as I conceive) lost the generosity and dignity of thinking of the fourteenth century; nor as yet have we subtilized ourselves into savages. We are not the converts of Rousseau; we are not the disciples of Voltaire; Helvetius has made no progress amongst us. Atheists are not our preachers; madmen are not our lawgivers. We know that *we* have made no discoveries, and we think that no discoveries are to be made, in morality; nor many in the great principles of government, nor in the ideas of liberty, which were understood long before we were born, altogether as well as they will be after the grave has heaped its mould upon our presumption, and the silent tomb shall have imposed its law on our pert loquacity. In England we have not yet been completely embowelled of our natural entrails; we still feel within us, and we cherish and cultivate, those inbred sentiments which are the faithful guardians, the active monitors of our duty, the true supporters of all liberal and manly morals. We have not been drawn and trussed, in order that we may be filled, like stuffed birds in a museum, with chaff and rags and paltry blurred shreds of paper about the rights of man. We preserve the whole of our feelings still native and entire, unsophisticated by pedantry and infidelity. We have real hearts of flesh and blood beating in our bosoms. We fear God; we look up with awe to kings; with affection to parliaments; with duty to magistrates; with reverence to priests; and with respect to nobility.[1] Why? Because when such ideas are brought before our minds, it is *natural* to be so affected; because all other feelings are false and spurious, and tend to corrupt our minds, to vitiate our primary morals, to render us unfit for rational liberty; and by teaching us a servile, licentious, and abandoned insolence, to be our low sport for a few holidays, to make us perfectly fit for, and justly deserving of, slavery, through the whole course of our lives.

You see, Sir, that in this enlightened age I am bold enough to confess, that we are generally men of untaught feelings; that instead of casting away all our old prejudices, we cherish them to a very considerable degree, and, to take more shame to ourselves, we cherish them because they are prejudices; and the longer they have lasted, and the more generally they have prevailed, the more we cherish them. We are afraid to put men to live and trade each on his own private stock of reason; because we suspect that this stock in each man is small, and that the individuals would do better to avail themselves of the general bank and capital of nations and of ages. Many of our men of speculation, instead of exploding general prejudices, employ their sagacity to discover the latent wisdom which prevails in them. If they find what they seek, and they seldom fail, they think it more wise to continue the prejudice, with the reason involved, than to cast away the coat of prejudice, and to leave nothing but the naked reason; because prejudice, with its reason, has a motive to give action to that reason, and an affection which will give it permanence. Prejudice is of ready application in the emergency; it previously engages the mind in a steady course of wisdom and virtue, and does not leave the man hesitating in the moment of decision, sceptical, puzzled, and unresolved. Pre-

1. The English are, I conceive, misrepresented in a letter published in one of the papers, by a gentleman thought to be a dissenting minister. When writing to Dr Price of the spirit which prevails at Paris, he says, 'The spirit of the people in this place has abolished all the proud *distinctions* which the *kings and nobles* had usurped in their minds; whether they talk of *the king, the noble, or their priest*, their whole language is that of the most *enlightened and liberal amongst the English*.' If this gentleman means to confine the terms *enlightened and liberal* to one set of men in England, it may be true. It is not generally so.

judice renders a man's virtue his habit; and not a series of un-connected acts. Through just prejudice, his duty becomes a part of his nature.

2 Tom Paine
The Rights of Man

from *The Rights of Man* Part I   1791   Part II   1792

I

Every history of the creation, and every traditionary account, whether from the lettered or unlettered world, however they may vary in their opinion or belief of certain particulars, all agree in establishing one point, *the unity of man*; by which I mean that men are all of *one degree*, and consequently that all men are born equal, and with equal natural rights, in the same manner as if posterity had been continued by *creation* instead of *generation*, the latter being only the mode by which the former is car-ried forward; and consequently every child born into the world must be considered as deriving its existence from God. The world is as new to him as it was to the first man that existed, and his natural right in it is of the same kind.

The Mosaic account of the creation, whether taken as divine authority or merely historical, is fully up to this point, *the unity or equality of man*. The expressions admit of no controversy. 'And God said, Let us make man in our own image. In the image of God created he him; male and female created he them.' The distinction of sexes is pointed out, but no other distinction is even implied. If this be not divine authority, it is at least his-torical authority, and shows that the equality of man, so far from being a modern doctrine, is the oldest upon record.

It is also to be observed that all the religions known in the world are founded, so far as they relate to man, on the *unity of man*, as being all of one degree. Whether in heaven or in hell, or in whatever state man may be supposed to exist hereafter, the good and the bad are the only distinctions. Nay, even the laws of Governments are obliged to slide into this principle, by mak-ing degrees to consist in crimes and not in persons.

It is one of the greatest of all truths, and of the highest advantage to cultivate. By considering man in this light, and by instructing him to consider himself in this light, it places him in a close connection with all his duties, whether to his Creator or to the creation, of which he is a part; and it is only when he forgets his origin, or, to use a more fashionable phrase, his *birth and family*, that he becomes dissolute. It is not among the least of the evils of the present existing Governments in all parts of Europe that man, considered as man, is thrown back to a vast distance from his Maker, and the artificial chasm filled up by a succession of barriers, or sort of turnpike gates, through which he has to pass. I will quote Mr Burke's catalogue of barriers that he has set up between Man and his Maker. Putting himself in the character of a herald, he says: *We fear God – we look with* AWE *to kings – with affection to Parliaments – with duty to magistrates – with reverence to priests, and with respect to nobility.* Mr Burke has forgotten to put in 'chivalry'. He has also forgotten to put in Peter.

The duty of man is not a wilderness of turnpike gates, through which he is to pass by tickets from one to the other. It is plain and simple, and consists but of two points. His duty to God, which every man must feel; and with respect to his neighbour, to do as he would be done by. If those to whom power is delegated do well, they will be respected; if not, they will be despised; and with regard to those to whom no power is delegated, but who assume it, the rational world can know nothing of them.

Hitherto we have spoken only (and that but in part) of the natural rights of man. We have now to consider the civil rights of man, and to show how the one originates from the other. Man did not enter into society to become *worse* than he was before, not to have fewer rights than he had before, but to have those rights better secured. His natural rights are the foundation of all his civil rights. But in order to pursue this distinction with more precision, it will be necessary to mark the different qualities of natural and civil rights.

A few words will explain this. Natural rights are those which appertain to man in right of his existence. Of this kind are all the intellectual rights, or rights of the mind, and also all those rights of acting as an individual for his own comfort and happiness, which are not injurious to the natural rights of others. Civil rights are those which appertain to man in right of his being a member of society. Every civil right has for its foundation some natural right pre-existing in the individual, but to the enjoyment of which his individual power is not, in all cases, sufficiently competent. Of this kind are all those which relate to security and protection.

From this short view it will be easy to distinguish between that class of natural rights which man retains after entering into society and those which he throws into the common stock as a member of society.

The natural rights which he retains are all those in which the *power* to execute it is as perfect in the individual as the right itself. Among this class, as is before mentioned, are all the intellectual rights, or rights of the mind; consequently religion is one of those rights. The natural rights which are not retained, are all those in which, though the right is perfect in the individual, the power to execute them is defective. They answer not his purpose. A man, by natural right, has a right to judge in his own cause; and so far as the right of the mind is concerned, he never surrenders it. But what availeth it him to judge, if he has not power to redress? He therefore deposits this right in the common stock of society, and takes the arm of society, of which he is a part, in preference and in addition to his own. Society *grants* him nothing. Every man is a proprietor in society, and draws on the capital as a matter of right.

From these premises two or three certain conclusions will follow:

First, *That every civil right grows out of a natural right; or, in other words, is a natural right exchanged.*

Secondly, *That civil power properly considered as such is made up of the aggregate of that class of the natural rights of man, which becomes defective in the individual in point of power, and answers not his purpose, but when collected to a focus becomes competent to the purpose of every one.*

Thirdly, *That the power produced from the aggregate of natural rights, imperfect in power in the individual, cannot be applied to invade the natural rights which are retained in the individual, and in which the power to execute is as perfect as the right itself.*

We have now, in a few words, traced man from a natural individual to a member of society, and shown, or endeavoured to show, the quality of the natural rights retained, and of those which are exchanged for civil rights. Let us now apply these principles to Governments.

In casting our eyes over the world, it is extremely easy to distinguish the Governments which have arisen out of society, or out of the social compact, from those which have not; but to place this in a clearer light than what a single glance may afford, it will be proper to take a review of the several sources from which Governments have arisen and on which they have been founded.

They may be all comprehended under three heads.

First, *Superstition.*

Secondly, *Power.*

Thirdly, *The common interest of society and the common rights of man.*

The first was a Government of Priestcraft, the second of Conquerors, and the third of Reason.

When a set of artful men pretended, through the medium of oracles, to hold intercourse with the Deity, as familiarly as they now march up the back-stairs in European Courts, the world was completely under the government of superstition. The oracles were consulted, and whatever they were made to say became the law; and this sort of Government lasted as long as this sort of superstition lasted.

After these a race of conquerors arose, whose Government, like that of William the Conqueror, was founded in power, and the sword assumed the name of a sceptre. Governments thus established last as long as the power to support them lasts; but that they might avail themselves of every engine in their favour, they united fraud to force, and set up an idol which they called *Divine Right*, and which, in imitation of the Pope, who affects to be spiritual and temporal, and in contradiction to the Founder of the Christian religion, twisted itself afterwards into an idol of another shape, called *Church and State*. The key of St Peter and the key of the Treasury became quartered on one another, and the wondering cheated multitude worshipped the invention.

When I contemplate the natural dignity of man, when I feel (for Nature has not been kind enough to me to blunt my feelings) for the honour and happiness of its character, I become irritated at the attempt to govern mankind by force and fraud, as if they were all knaves and fools, and can scarcely avoid disgust at those who are thus imposed upon.

(from Part I, 1791)

II

Though it might be proved that the system of Government now called the NEW is the most ancient in principle of all that have existed, being founded on the original inherent Rights of Man; yet, as tyranny and the sword have suspended the exercise of those rights for many centuries past, it serves better the purpose of distinction to call it the *new* than to claim the right of calling it the old.

The first general distinction between those two systems is that the one now called the old is *hereditary*, either in whole or in part; and the new is entirely *representative*. It rejects all hereditary Government:

First, As being an imposition on mankind.

Secondly, As inadequate to the purposes for which Government is necessary.

With respect to the first of these heads – It cannot be proved by what right hereditary Government could begin; neither does there exist within the compass of mortal power a right to establish it. Man has no authority over posterity in matters of personal right; and, therefore, no man or body of men had, or can have, a right to set up hereditary Government. Were even ourselves to come again into existence, instead of being succeeded by posterity, we have not now the right of taking from ourselves the rights which would then be ours. On what ground, then, do we pretend to take them from others?

All hereditary Government is in its nature tyranny. An heritable crown, or an heritable throne, or by what other fanciful name such things may be called, have no other significant explanation than that mankind are heritable property. To inherit a Government, is to inherit the people, as if they were flocks and herds.

With respect to the second head, that of being inadequate to the purposes for which Government is necessary, we have only to consider what Government essentially is, and compare it with the circumstances to which hereditary succession is subject.

Government ought to be a thing always in full maturity. It ought to be so constructed as to be superior to all the accidents to which individual man is subject; and, therefore, hereditary succession, by being *subject to them all*, is the most irregular and imperfect of all the systems of Government.

We have heard the *Rights of Man* called a *levelling* system; but the only system to which the word *levelling* is truly applicable, is the hereditary monarchical system. It is a system of *mental levelling*. It indiscriminately admits every species of character to the same authority. Vice and virtue, ignorance and wisdom, in short, every quality, good or bad, is put on the same level. Kings succeed each other, not as rationals, but as animals. It signifies not what their mental or moral characters are. Can we then be surprised at the abject state of the human mind in monarchical countries, when the Government itself is formed on such an abject levelling system? It has no fixed character. To-day it is one thing; tomorrow it is something else. It changes with the temper of every succeeding individual, and is subject to all the varieties of each. It is Government through the medium of passions and accidents. It appears under all the various characters of childhood, decrepitude, dotage; a thing at nurse, in leading-strings, or in crutches. It reverses the wholesome order of nature. It ocasionally puts children over men, and the conceits of nonage over wisdom and experience. In short, we cannot conceive a more ridiculous figure of Government, than hereditary succession, in all its cases, presents.

Could it be made a decree in nature, or an edict registered in heaven, and man could know it, that virtue and wisdom should invariably appertain to hereditary succession, the objections to it would be removed; but when we see that nature acts as if she disowned and sported with the hereditary system; that the mental characters of successors, in all countries, are below the average of human understanding; that one is a tyrant, another an idiot, a third insane, and some all three together, it is impossible to attach confidence to it, when reason in man has power to act.

It is not to the Abbé Sieyès that I need apply this reasoning; he has already saved me that trouble by giving his own opinion upon the case. 'If it be asked,' says he, 'what is my opinion with respect to hereditary right, I answer, without hesitation, that, in good theory, an hereditary transmission of any power or office, can never accord with the laws of a true representation. Hereditaryship is, in this sense, as much an attaint upon principle, as an outrage upon society. But let us,' continues he, 'refer to the history of all elective monarchies and principalities: is there one in which the elective mode is not worse than the hereditary succession?'

As to debating on which is the worse of the two, it is admitting both to be bad: and herein we are agreed. The preference which the Abbé has given is a condemnation of the thing that he prefers. Such a mode of reasoning on such a subject is inadmissible, because it finally amounts to an accusation upon Providence, as if she had left to man no other choice with respect to Government than between two evils the best of which he admits to be 'an attaint upon principle, and an outrage upon society'.

Passing over for the present all the evils and mischiefs which monarchy has occasioned in the world, nothing can more effectually prove its uselessness in a state of *civil government*, than making it hereditary. Would we make any office hereditary that required wisdom and abilities to fill it? and where wisdom and abilities are not necessary, such an office, whatever it may be, is superfluous or insignificant.

Hereditary succession is a burlesque upon monarchy. It puts it in the most ridiculous light, by presenting it as an office which any child or idiot may fill. It requires some talents to be a common mechanic; but to be a King requires only the animal figure of man – a sort of breathing automaton. This sort of superstition may last a few years more, but it cannot long resist the awakened reason and interest of man.

As to Mr Burke, he is a stickler for monarchy, not altogether as a pensioner, if he is one, which I believe, but as a political man. He has taken up a contemptible opinion of mankind, who, in their turn, are taking up the same of him. He considers them as a herd of beings that must be governed by fraud, effigy, and show; and an idol would be as good a figure of monarchy with him as a man. I will, however, do him the justice to say that, with respect to America, he has been very complimentary. He always contended, at least in my hearing, that the people of America were more enlightened than those of England, or of any country in Europe; and that therefore the imposition of shew was not necessary in their Governments.

Though the comparison between hereditary and elective monarchy, which the Abbé has made, is unnecessary to the case, because the representative system rejects both; yet, were I to make the comparison, I should decide contrary to what he has done.

The civil wars which have originated from contested hereditary claims are more numerous, and have been more dreadful, and of longer continuance, than those which have been occasioned by election. All the civil wars in France arose from the hereditary system; they were either produced by hereditary claims, or by the imperfection of the hereditary form, which admits of regencies, or monarchy at nurse. With respect to England, its history is full of the same misfortunes. The contests for succession between the houses of York and Lancaster, lasted a whole century; and others of a similar nature have renewed themselves since that period. Those of 1715 and 1745 were of the same kind. The succession war for the crown of Spain embroiled almost half Europe. The disturbances in Holland are generated from the hereditaryship of the Stadtholder. A Government calling itself free, with an hereditary office, is like a thorn in the flesh, that produces a fermentation which endeavours to discharge it.

But I might go further, and place also foreign wars, of whatever kind, to the same cause. It is by adding the evil of hereditary succession to that of monarchy, that a permanent family interest is created, whose constant objects are dominion and revenue. Poland, though an elective monarchy, has had fewer wars than those which are hereditary; and it is the only Government that has made a voluntary essay, though but a small one, to reform the condition of the country.

Having thus glanced at a few of the defects of the old or hereditary systems of Government, let us compare it with the new, or representative system.

The representative system takes society and civilisation for its basis; nature, reason, and experience for its guide.

Experience, in all ages and in all countries, has demonstrated that it is impossible to controul nature in her distribution of mental powers. She gives them as she pleases. Whatever is the rule by which she, apparently to us, scatters them among mankind, that rule remains a secret to man. It would be as ridiculous to attempt to fix the hereditaryship of human beauty as of wisdom. Whatever wisdom constituently is, it is like a seedless plant; it may be reared when it appears, but it cannot be voluntarily produced. There is always a sufficiency somewhere in the general mass of society for all purposes; but with respect to the parts of society, it is continually changing its place. It rises in one today, in another tomorrow, and has most probably visited in rotation every family of the earth, and again withdrawn.

As this is in the order of nature, the order of Government must necessarily follow it, or Government will, as we see it does, degenerate into ignorance. The hereditary system, therefore, is as repugnant to human wisdom as to human rights; and is as absurd as it is unjust.

As the republic of letters brings forward the best literary productions, by giving to genius a fair and universal chance; so the representative system of Government is calculated to produce the wisest laws, by collecting wisdom from where it can be found. I smile to myself when I contemplate the ridiculous insignificance into which literature and all the sciences would sink, were they made hereditary; and I carry the same idea into Governments. An hereditary governor is as inconsistent as an hereditary author. I know not whether Homer or Euclid had sons; but I will venture an opinion that if they had, and had left their works unfinished, those sons could not have completed them.

(from Part II, 1792)

III

In the present state of things a labouring man, with a wife and two or three children, does not pay less than between seven and eight pounds a year in taxes. He is not sensible of this, because it is disguised to him in the articles which he buys, and he thinks only of their dearness; but as the taxes take from him, at least, a fourth of his yearly earnings, he is consequently disabled from providing for a family, especially if himself or any of them are afflicted with sickness.

The first step of practical relief, would be to abolish the poor-rates entirely, and in lieu thereof, to make a remission of taxes to the poor of double the amount of the present poor-rates, viz., four millions annually, out of the surplus taxes. By this measure the poor will be benefited two millions, and the house-keepers two millions. This alone would be equal to a reduction of one hundred and twenty millions of the National Debt, and consequently equal to the whole expence of the American War.

It will then remain to be considered, which is the most effectual mode of distributing this remission of four millions.

It is easily seen, that the poor are generally composed of large families of children, and old people past their labour. If these two classes are provided for, the remedy will so far reach to the full extent of the case, that what remains will be incidental, and in a great measure, fall within the compass of benefit clubs, which, though of humble invention, merit to be ranked among the best of modern institutions.

Admitting England to contain seven millions of souls; if one-fifth thereof are of that class of poor which need support, the number will be one million four hundred thousand. Of this number, one hundred and forty thousand will be aged poor, as will be hereafter shown, and for which a distinct provision will be proposed.

There will remain one million two hundred and sixty thousand which, at five souls to each family, amount to two hundred and fifty-two thousand families, rendered poor from the expense of children and the weight of taxes.

The number of children under fourteen years of age, in each of those families, will be found to be about five to every two families; some having two, and others three; some one, and others four: some none, and others five; but it rarely happens that more than five are under fourteen years of age, and after this age they are capable of service or of being apprenticed.

Allowing five children (under fourteen years) to every two families,

The number of children would be   630,000
The number of parents, were they all living, would be   504,000

It is certain, that if the children are provided for, the parents are relieved of consequence, because it is from the expense of bringing up children that their poverty arises.

Having thus ascertained the greatest number that can be supposed to need support on account of young families I proceed to the mode of relief or distribution, which is:

To pay as a remission of taxes to every poor family out of the surplus taxes, and in room of poor-rates, four pounds a-year for every child under fourteen years of age; enjoining the parents of such children to send them to school, to learn reading, writing, and common arithmetic; the ministers of every parish, of every denomination to certify jointly to an office, for that purpose, that this duty is performed. The amount of this expense will be,

For six hundred and thirty thousand children
at £4 per annum each   £2,520,000

By adopting this method, not only the poverty of the parents will be relieved, but ignorance will be banished from the rising generation, and the number of poor will hereafter become less, because their abilities, by the aid of education, will be greater. Many a youth, with good natural genius, who is apprenticed to a mechanical trade such as a carpenter, joiner, millwright, shipwright, blacksmith, etc., is prevented getting forward the whole of his life from the want of a little common education when a boy.

I now proceed to the case of the aged.

I divide age into two classes. First, the approach of age, beginning at fifty. Secondly, old age commencing at sixty.

At fifty, though the mental faculties of man are in full vigour, and his judgement better than at any preceding date, the bodily powers for laborious life are on the decline. He cannot bear the same quantity of fatigue as at an earlier period. He begins to earn less, and is less capable of enduring wind and weather; and in those retired employments where much sight is required, he fails apace, and sees himself, like an old horse, beginning to be turned adrift.

At sixty his labour ought to be over, at least from direct necessity. It is painful to see old age working itself to death, in what are called civilized countries, for daily bread.

To form some judgement of the number of those above fifty years of age, I have several times counted the persons I met in the streets of London, men, women, and children, and have generally found that the average is about one in sixteen or seventeen. If it be said that aged persons do not come much in the streets, so neither do infants; and a great proportion of grown children are in schools and in workshops as apprentices. Taking, then, sixteen for a divisor, the whole number of persons in England of fifty years and upwards, of both sexes, rich and poor, will be four hundred and twenty thousand.

The persons to be provided for out of this gross number will be husbandmen, common labourers, journeymen of every trade and their wives, sailors, and disbanded soldiers, worn out servants of both sexes, and poor widows.

There will be also a considerable number of middling tradesmen, who having lived decently in the former part of life, begin, as age approaches, to lose their business, and at last fall to decay.

Besides these there will be constantly thrown off from the revolutions of that wheel which no man can stop nor regulate, a number from every class of life connected with commerce and adventure.

To provide for all those accidents, and whatever else may befall, I take the number of persons who, at one time or other of their lives, after fifty years of age, may feel it necessary or comfortable to be better supported than they can support themselves, and that not as a matter of grace and favour, but of right, at one-third of the whole number, which is one hundred and forty thousand, and for whom a distinct provision was proposed to be made. If there be more, society, notwithstanding the show and pomposity of Government, is in a deplorable condition in England.

Of this one hundred and forty thousand, I take one half, seventy thousand, to be of the age of fifty and under sixty, and the other half to be sixty years and upwards. Having thus ascertained the probable proportion of the number of aged persons, I proceed to the mode of rendering their condition comfortable, which is:

To pay every such person of the age of fifty years, and until he shall arrive at the age of sixty, the sum of six pounds per annum out of the surplus taxes, and ten pounds per annum during life after the age of sixty. The expense of which will be,

Seventy thousand persons, at £6 per annum	£420,000
Seventy thousand ditto, at £10 per annum	700,000
	£1,120,000

This support, as already remarked, is not of the nature of a charity but of a right. Every person in England, male and female, pays on an average in taxes two pounds eight shillings and sixpence per annum from the day of his (or her) birth; and if the expense of collection be added, he pays two pounds eleven shillings and sixpence, consequently, at the end of fifty years he has paid one hundred and twenty-eight pounds fifteen shillings, and at sixty one hundred and fifty-four pounds ten shillings. Converting, therefore, his (or her) individual tax into a tontine, the money he shall receive after fifty years is but little more than the legal interest of the nett money he has paid; the rest is made up from those whose circumstances do not require them to draw such support, and the capital in both cases defrays the expenses of Government. It is on this ground that I have extended the probable claims to one-third of the number of aged persons in the Nation. Is it, then, better that the lives of one hundred and forty thousand aged persons be rendered comfortable, or that a million a year of public money be expended on any one individual, and him often of the most worthless or insignificant character? Let reason and justice, let honour and humanity, let even hypocrisy, sycophancy and Mr Burke, let George, let Louis, Leopold, Frederic, Catherine, Cornwallis, or Tippoo Saib, answer the question.

The sum thus remitted to the poor will be,

To two hundred and fifty-two thousand poor families, containing six hundred and thirty thousand children	£2,520,000
To one hundred and forty thousand aged persons	1,120,000
	£3,640,000

(from Part II, 1792)

3 Resolutions of the London Corresponding Society adopted at The Bell, Exeter Street, Strand, 2 April 1792

from Resolutions in the Minute Book of the London Corresponding Society, 2 April 1792

Man as an individual is entitled to liberty, it is his Birth-right.

As a member of society the preservation of that liberty becomes his indispensable duty.

When he associated he gave up certain rights, in order to secure the possession of the remainder;

But, he voluntarily yielded up only as much as was necessary for the common good:

He still preserved a right of sharing the government of his country; – without it no man can, with truth call himself *free*.

Fraud or force, sanctioned by custom, with-holds the right from (by far) the greater number of the inhabitants of this country.

The few with whom the right of election and representation remains abuse it, and the strong temptations held out to electors, sufficiently prove that the representatives of this country seldom procure a seat in parliament from the unbought suffrages of a free People.

The nation, at length, perceives it, and testifies an ardent desire of remedying the evil.

The only difficulty then, at present, is, the ascertaining the true method of proceeding.

To this end, different, and numerous Societies have been formed in different parts of the nation.

Several likewise have arisen in the Metropolis, and among them, (though as yet in its infant state), the Corresponding Society, with modesty intrudes itself and opinions, on the attention of the public in the following resolutions:

Resolved, – That every individual has a right to share in the government of that society of which he is a member – unless incapacitated.

Resolved, – That nothing but non-age, privation of reason, or an offence against the general rules of society can incapacitate him.

Resolved, – That it is no less the *right* than the *duty* of every Citizen, to keep a watchful eye on the government of his country; that the laws, by being multiplied, do not degenerate into *oppression*, and that those who are entrusted with the government, do not substitute private interest for public advantage.

Resolved, – That the people of Great Britain are not effectually represented in Parliament.

Resolved, – That in consequence of a partial, unequal, and therefore inadequate representation, together with the corrupt method in which representatives are elected; oppressive taxes, unjust laws, restrictions of liberty, and wasting the public money have ensued.

Resolved, – That the only remedy for those evils is a fair, equal and impartial representation of the People in Parliament.

Resolved, – That a fair, equal, and impartial representation of the People in Parliament can never take place until all partial privileges are abolished.

Resolved, – That this Society to express their *abhorrence* of tumults and violence, and that, as they aim at reform, not anarchy, but reason, firmness, and unanimity, are the only arms they themselves will employ, or persuade their fellow Citizens to exert against the Abuse of Power.

Ordered, – That the Secretary of this Society do transmit a copy of the above to the Societies.

4 Nore Seamen's Song   1797

from R. W. Postgate (ed.), *Revolution from 1789–1906*
1962

All hail, brother seamen, that plough on the main,
Likewise to well-wishers of seamen of fame,
May providence watch over brave British tars,
And guide them with care from the dangers of wars.

Good Providence long looked with pity at last
For to see Honest Jack so shamefully thrashed,
But still held his arm for to let Jack subdue
The pride of those masters whose hearts were not true.

At Spithead Jack from a long silence was roused,
Which waked other brothers, who did not refuse
To assist in the plan that good Providence taught
In the hearts of brave seamen, that add long been forgot.

Old Neptune made haste; to the Nore he did come,
To waken his sons who had slept far too long.
His thundering loud voice made us start with surprise,
To hear his sweet words, and he bid us arise.

'Your brothers,' says he, 'his all firmly resolved,
To banish all tyrants that long did uphold,
Their crewel intentions to scourge when they please,
Sutch a set of bace villians you must instantly seize.

So away, tell your brothers, near Yarmouth they lie,
To embark in the cause they will never deny.
Their hearts are all good, their like lyons I say,
I've furnished there minds and they all will obey.

And when they arrive, which I trust they soon will,
Be steady and cautious, let wrangling lay still,
And love one another, my favour you'll keep,
Suckcess to King George and his glorious fleet.'

Manifesto of the Delegates to their Countrymen, The Delegates of the Different Ships of the Nore Assembled in Council, to their Fellow-Subjects 1797

from R. W. Postgate (ed.), *Revolution from 1798–1906* 1962

COUNTRYMEN,

It is to you particularly that we owe an explanation of our conduct. His Majesty's Ministers too well know our intentions, which are founded on the laws of humanity, honour and national safety – long since trampled underfoot by those who ought to have been friends to us – the sole protectors of your laws and property. The public prints teem with falsehoods and misrepresentations to induce you to credit things as far from our design as the conduct of those at the helm of national affairs is from honesty or common decorum.

Shall we who have endured the toils of a tedious, disgraceful war, be the victims of tyranny and oppression which vile, gilded, pampered knaves, wallowing in the lap of luxury, choose to load us with? Shall we, who amid the rage of the tempest and the war of jarring elements, undaunted climb the unsteady cordage and totter on the topmast's dreadful height, suffer ourselves to be treated worse than the dogs of London Streets? Shall we, who in the battle's sanguinary rage, confound, terrify and subdue your proudest foe, guard your coasts from invasion, your children from slaughter, and your lands from pillage – be the footballs and shuttlecocks of a set of tyrants who derive from us alone their honours, their titles and their fortunes? No, the Age of Reason has at length revolved. Long have we been endeavouring to find ourselves men. We now find ourselves so. We will be treated as such. Far, very far, from us is the idea of subverting the government of our beloved country. We have the highest opinion of our Most Gracious Sovereign, and we hope none of those measures taken to deprive us of the common rights of men have been instigated by him.

You cannot, countrymen, form the most distant idea of the slavery under which we have for many years laboured. Rome had her Neros and Caligulas, but how many characters of their description might we not mention in the British Fleet – men

without the least tincture of humanity, without the faintest spark of virtue, education or abilities, exercising the most wanton acts of cruelty over those whom dire misfortune or patriotic zeal may have placed in their power – basking in the sunshine of prosperity, whilst we (need we repeat who we are?) labour under every distress which the breast of inhumanity can suggest. The British seaman has often with justice been compared to the lion – gentle, generous and humane – no one would certainly wish to hurt such an animal. Hitherto we have laboured for our sovereign and you. We are now obliged to think for ourselves, for there are many (nay, most of us) in the Fleet who have been prisoners since the commencement of the War, without receiving a single farthing. Have we not a right to complain? Let His Majesty but order us to be paid and the little grievances we have made known redressed, we shall enter with alacrity upon any employment for the defence of our country; but until that is complied with we are determined to stop all commerce and intercept all provisions, for our own subsistence. The military have had their pay augmented, to insult as well as to enslave you. Be not appalled. We will adopt the words of a celebrated motto and defy all attempts to deceive us. We do not wish to adopt the plan of a neighbouring nation, however it may have been suggested; but we sell our lives dearly to maintain what we have demanded. Nay, countrymen, more: We have already discovered the tricks of Government in supplying our enemies with different commodities, and a few days will probably lead to something more. In the meantime,

We remain, Dear Countrymen,
Yours affectionately

F Economic Changes

The relevance of this article by the distinguished French economic historian, François Crouzet, to our treatment of the industrial revolution in Britain is that it integrates it into the industrial history of the continent, in setting out to answer the basic question : why was there no comparable movement in the economy of Britain's most powerful political rival?

The content of the article is the chief reason for its inclusion. However, it is also representative – if somewhat wider in scope than most – of the range of minutely detailed articles published in academic journals. It was first published in the French social history review *Annales*, by whose solid footnotes the army of economic history researchers relentlessly marches on.

C.T.H.

Further Reading

* T. S. Ashton, *The Industrial Revolution, 1760–1830*, Oxford University Press, 1948.
* E. J. Hobsbawm, *The Age of Revolution, 1789–1848*, Weidenfeld & Nicolson, 1962.
Peter Mathias, *The First Industrial Nation*, Methuen, 1969.

* Open University Set Book.

1 F. Crouzet

England and France in the Eighteenth Century : A Comparative Analysis of Two Economic Growths

from R. W. Hartwell (ed.), *The Causes of the Industrial Revolution* 1967. First appeared in *Annales*, vol. 21, no. 2, 1966. Translated by J. Sondheimer

The economic historian interested in the key problem of growth is bound to find the comparative approach particularly fruitful. A systematic comparison of the eighteenth-century English economy with that of another country – and France as the leading continental power at that time seems the obvious choice – should bring out more clearly what factors were peculiar to England and might therefore have determined what is a unique phenomenon, the English industrial revolution of the eighteenth-century.

The first point to be made is that the forwardness of England and the backwardness of France, clearly noticeable on the eve of the French Revolution, were not of sudden or recent appearance; this disparity between the two countries had already been evident early in the century, say at the death of Louis XIV. Moreover, to find any explanation for the contrasts between the social and economic structures of France and England we should have to look at the problem over a long period (going well back into the Middle Ages). That task cannot be attempted here, but it must at least be stressed that developments during the seventeenth century had a different effect on the two economies, which partly accounts for the time-lag between them at the beginning of the eighteenth century.

As is well known, a similar point was made some thirty years ago by J. U. Nef, who pressed it very hard with his assertion that the reason why England was the first country to undergo the eighteenth-century industrial revolution was simply that, unlike other countries and particularly France, she had already undergone a first industrial revolution in the late sixteenth and early seventeenth centuries, which meant that her lead had been established some two centuries earlier than was generally thought (Nef, 1936, pp. 289–317, 505–33, 643–66; see also 1934, pp. 3–24; 1937, pp. 155–85; 1941, pp. 21–53, 193–231). But this thesis had been strongly criticized from the British side, and little of it remains intact today (see particularly Coleman, 1956, pp. 345–7; 1959, pp. 506–7, 509–10, 512; Supple, 1959, pp. 2–8; Fisher, 1961, pp. 6–7; Brenner, 1962, pp. 271–3). The 'first English industrial revolution' existed chiefly in Nef's imagination: he attached far too much importance to a few technical innovations, to the understandably fast growth of a handful of new industries (coal excepted, their role was a very minor one – yet he ignored the slow growth in the major woollen industry), and lastly to a few non-representative cases of entrepreneurial giantism.[1]

Nevertheless, Nef deserves our thanks for having stressed the importance of the fast rise in English coal production and consumption during the century after 1540, and its influence on technological progress through stimulating the development and adoption of some completely new techniques, such as furnaces fired by coal or coke, which were quite unknown on the continent. This early adoption of mineral fuels gave English inventiveness an impetus which proved to be lasting and which in France was lacking (Chaloner and Musson, 1960, p. 76; 1963, pp. 20–21, 24–5, 29). Again, it seems that Nef was right in maintaining that between 1540 and 1640 England had an absolute lead over France in mining and metal production and also had a higher output per head for products such as woollen goods and glass, and possibly for industrial output as a whole (Nef, 1936, p. 663).

However, it was after 1640 rather than before that significant disparities between the economic evolution of the two countries appeared. As is well known, recent research has produced a black picture of French economic history in the 'tragic seventeenth century'. This work has shown that after a relatively prosperous start to the century, the 1630s saw the beginning of a long period of stagnation and decline – turning in

1. On the other hand, Nef overstated the stagnation of French industry during the same period, in that he ignored the textile industries on the French side of the channel, above all linen and wool. He also went much too far when he spoke of 'phenomenal acceleration' in English industrial output between 1540 and 1640.

mid-century during the Fronde into collapse – which lasted up to the 1720s. Prices – and especially food prices – over the century show a downward trend, and more significantly, extreme instability; there were frequent and violent economic and demographic crises, attended by terrible mortalities; there was monetary famine and 'tightness of money', which crippled business activity and brought down rents and industrial and commercial profits; there was unemployment and pauperism. In view of all this, it is no wonder that industrial production stagnated and even declined (see Goubert, 1960, pp. 585–91, 595–6, graphs 126–30, supplement pp. 116–19; Deyon, 1963, pp. 947, 950–53; Baehrel, 1961). Colbert's policy of industrialization was really nothing but a desperate effort to counteract this declining trend; it was undertaken in the highly unfavourable conditions of deflation, falling prices, incomes, and consumption, and ended in semi-failure.[2] Although some of his new industrial undertakings survived and developed later, many others declined and quickly disappeared; and on the whole, if there was any increase in total industrial output under Colbert's government, which is not certain, it was not very pronounced. It is true that recent research has shown that despite two great wars, several famines and protestant emigration, there were signs of recovery in the French economy during the latter part of the reign of Louis XIV, long thought to have been catastrophic. This may well reveal a rising underlying trend, a sign heralding the post-1715 growth, but any such recovery was largely counteracted by the bad effects of wars and famines (Léon, 1956a, pp. 132–7; Deyon, 1963, pp. 953–5).[3] Therefore, even if there are a few positive items to enter on the French balance sheet for the seventeenth century, the general picture remains most unfavourable, and nowadays it is accepted that the population of France in 1715 and 1720 was lower than it had been in 1640 (Goubert, 1966, p. 622; Labrousse, 1962, p. 13).

On the English side of the Channel the picture is certainly

2. See Goubert's pessimistic estimate of the resuts of Colbert's policy at Beauvais (1960, pp. 584, 596–7; also pp. 619, 621–4).

3. P. Goubert, in his *Louis XIV et vingt millions de Français* (1966) and *L'Avènement du Roi-soleil 1661* (1967), has somewhat revised his pessimistic picture of the seventeenth-century French economy.

different, and English historians are on the whole moderately optimistic in their estimation of England's economic performance during the seventeenth century. England was not, of course, totally unaffected by the adverse economic climate of the seventeenth century; there were periods of difficulty and stagnation, for example in the 1620s, during the Civil War and at moments in the wars against Louis XIV; England's main industry, woollen manufacture, went through a series of crises and its growth over the century as a whole was relatively modest; chronic poverty and underemployment were serious problems (see Coleman, 1956a, pp. 280–95). But there is nothing to compare with the recurrent violent crises or the deep and lasting depression to be seen in France after 1630. The reversal in the trend of price movements and of the economy in general reached England later than France, about 1650, and in England the subsequent fall in prices was smaller, while short-term price fluctuations seem to have been less violent, less irregular, and hence less injurious to economic activity (Meuvret, 1952, p. 69; Chaunu, pp. 238–40, 251–2; Brenner, 1962, pp. 276, 281–2; Clark, 1946, pp. 108–10; Phelps Brown and Hopkins, 1956, pp. 299–301, 305, 312–13). F. J. Fisher was able to conclude that the global output of agriculture and industry increased slowly but appreciably during the century, and that despite the rise in population, average income per head probably rose (Fisher, 1961, p. 3; 1957, pp. 6–9, 12, 15, 16).

There are also other signs of economic progress, especially after 1660, for which there is no parallel in France: for example, the expansion of the English home market, due principally to the growth of London, which far exceeded that of Paris; the 'frontier-like' development of the northern and western counties (Fisher, 1957, pp. 10–11); and the fast and prolonged growth during the seventeenth century of English foreign trade, largely thanks to early colonial expansion, which meant that from the 1660s England had an important trade in the re-export of exotic products, a trade which continued to rise and was the chief factor in the growth of English trade as a whole, at a time when French colonies and colonial trade were still relatively insignificant (Davis, 1954, pp. 150–54, 159–63; 1962, p. 285; and Farnie, 1962, p. 206).

Thanks to this slow but quite steady growth, at the beginning of the eighteenth century England already had a definite lead over France in several important fields (Fisher, 1957, pp. 17–18). First, in agriculture: various technical improvements were now in use over a large part of the country, productivity was higher and more regular than in France, a fact which, together with England's geographical advantages, helps to explain why bad crops were less disastrous in their effects. Secondly, in industrial technology: the earlier innovations which resulted from the use of coal as a fuel had been supplemented by the great burst of inventive activity of the late seventeenth and early eighteenth centuries, which threw up among others the major inventions of Savery, Newcomen and Derby (Chaloner and Musson, 1963, p. 33).[4] Thirdly, England was also leading in the commercial field, with a higher volume of trade, both in relation to the population and in absolute terms (Levasseur, 1911, p. 405), with a much larger merchant navy, and with a faster accumulation of merchant capital. Lastly, England's superiority was also very evident in the financial field, where the establishment of the National Debt and the Bank of England were signs of a political and economic structure well in advance of France: attempts by Louis XIV to set up a National Bank foundered on the objections of the bankers who thought it incompatible with a 'pure monarchy', and John Law's attempt a few years later to transplant English financial institutions to France ended in disaster (Lüthy, 1959, vol. 1, pp. 94–7, 290–91, 414; Monsieur, 1954, p. 299).

In 1688 Gregory King asserted that England had reached a higher level of wealth than any other country, Holland alone excepted, and estimated the French average income per head at 20 per cent lower than the English; a generation later, just after the Treaty of Utrecht, Daniel Defoe was writing of England as 'the most flourishing and opulent country in the world' (Deane and Cole, 1962, p. 38; Ashley, 1952, p. 230). These opinions were certainly not unjustified, in view of England's modest but growing prosperity in the seventeenth century, when

4. According to Coleman in Chaloner and Musson (1960, pp. 71–2), it might be possible to speak of an industrial revolution at the end of the seventeenth century.

France was stagnant and even declining. Whatever the causes of this disparity – different socio-economic structures, political circumstances – once the unfavourable economic climate of the seventeenth and early eighteenth centuries had lifted and the French economy started to grow, it was already behind the English and began with a serious handicap. If it is accepted that the industrial revolution was merely the crown stage of a long process of growth and change, it is important to our understanding of the British 'take-off' in the last third of the eighteenth century that it came after about two centuries of growth – admittedly broken at times, but never for very long – whereas the growth of the French economy at the same period dated back less than half a century and followed a century of stagnation. It was in fact during this 'tragic' post-1630 seventeenth century that France was clearly outdistanced by England, and despite her relatively fast growth during the eighteenth century she was never able to catch up.

We have seen that the economic developments of France and England during the seventeenth century are in clear contrast; but for the three-quarters of a century between the end of the War of the Spanish Succession and the French Revolution the picture is quite different. In both countries this was a period of growth, and the available statistical data points to the somewhat surprising conclusion that the rates of growth were not at all dissimilar.[5]

Let us start with what is best known, foreign trade, which is also the sector where French growth was fastest – faster in fact than the British. The total foreign trade of England and Wales (imports + exports + re-exports) had an average yearly official value of £13 million for the five years 1716–20 and £31 million for the five years 1784–88, which means it multiplied by 2·4.[6] On the other hand, the average yearly value of France's foreign trade was 215 million livres tournois for 1716–20 and 1 billion 62 millions for 1784–88, which means a fivefold increase

5. Naturally, statistics from the eighteenth century can give only rough orders of magnitude or very approximate indexes of development, and they should be used with caution.

6. E. B. Schumpeter (1960, pp. 15–16, Tables I–IV). Inclusion of Scotland and use of the net imports would not alter this proportion.

(Arnould, vol. 3, Table 10; Levasseur, 1911, p. 512). However, the English official values were calculated at more or less constant prices, so that in fact they give a rough index of the volume of trade, while the French figures are at current prices. Since prices rose about 60 per cent between the 1730s and the 1780s, the comparison is only valid if we deflate the figures for 1784–88 to constant prices. But this would still leave an increase in the *volume* of French trade which at lowest is of the order of 1 to 3, and even so is higher than the English. In any case, the value of French foreign trade, which in 1716–20 was barely more than half that of the English, by the eve of the revolution had reached about the same level (though the value per head of the population was naturally still much lower).[7]

We must, of course, take into account the very low level to which French trade had fallen at the end of the War of the Spanish Succession, but it nevertheless grew faster than the English up to the time of the French Revolution. Moreover, there were several branches of international trade in which the French secured or maintained a dominant position; they continued to be the main suppliers of manufactured goods to Spain, and through Cadiz to Spain's American Empire, while the British had the monopoly of the smaller Portuguese and Brazilian markets; they dominated the markets of Italy and the Levant. Thanks to spectacular progress in sugar and coffee cultivation in San Domingo and to the low prices of these products, which competed successfully with those of the British West Indies where soils were becoming exhausted and production costs were higher, the French snatched most of the entrepôt trade in colonial produce from the English merchants and developed a large and fast-growing re-export trade to Northern Europe (Davis, 1962, p. 294). The British on the whole did not do well in the European markets, where they came up against protective tariffs and French competition. In absolute terms, the increase in English exports to Europe was slow; they did not

7. Moreover, the trade of the great ports such as Bordeaux, Marseilles, and Rouen, grew faster than that of the country as a whole; cf. E. Levasseur (1911, pp. 457, 459); P. Dardel (1963, pp. 548–51).

8. Exports to British possessions (including Ireland and the Thirteen Colonies) increased sixfold between 1716–20 and 1786–90.

double between the beginning of the century and the 1780s, and it was only after about 1785 that the products of 'modernized' British industries started to invade the continent; Europe's share in English total exports also diminished, falling from about four-fifths to under a half. English commercial expansion was due almost entirely to the fast growth of her colonial trade and especially of trade with the American possessions, which up to the revolt of the Thirteen Colonies provided English industry with an almost fully protected market (Davis, 1962, p. 298; Farnie, 1962, p. 214; Deane and Cole, 1962, p. 34; Schumpeter, 1960 pp. 10–11). This 'Americanization' of foreign trade is also noticeable, though less marked, in France; French colonial trade, despite losses of territory due to the Seven Years' War, grew tenfold between 1716–20 and 1784–88, when trade with countries outside Europe made 38 per cent of total trade. French trade, then, was still more orientated on Europe than the English, and this European trade was growing almost as fast as total trade, certainly faster than that of England with the Continent (Levasseur, 1911, pp. 487, 512; Arnould, vol. 1, pp. 326–7, vol. 2, Table 2, vol. 3, Table 12).[9]

This optimistic picture of French foreign trade needs, however, to be qualified on several points. In particular, its relative position seems to have been more favourable during the first half of the period under review, that is before the Seven Years' War. Up to the end of the 1740s, in fact, the development of English trade was 'painfully slow', because of the stagnation in the export of woollen goods and in the re-export; fast growth came only after 1748, with an annual rate of growth of 3·9 per cent between 1745 and 1760. At first, French trade, despite the whiplash of the 'Système', grew at a rate similar to the English, but after about 1735 it accelerated sooner and faster, doubling in value in under twenty years (between 1736–39 and 1749–55). But this spurt was cut short by the Seven Years' War, during which French trade was driven off the seas by the Royal Navy and fell 50 per cent, while English trade continued to grow.

9. It is true that the main growth in French trade with Europe was made by re-exports (of colonial products) which increased eightfold, while exports of French products barely trebled.

Between 1763 and 1771 there was a sharp recovery, whose chief effect, however, was to recover lost ground, and this was followed by distinct stagnation in the 1770s and then an outright recession during the American war. It was only on the very eve of the Revolution that French trade again became buoyant and reached a record level, before collapsing in 1793. English trade on the other hand, despite some slowing down during the 1770s and despite the American crisis, seems to have increased at a slightly faster rate than the French from the time of the Seven Years' War and after the peace of 1783 to have picked up very sharply, to make a rapid and sustained growth until the end of the century. There are also signs that the competitive position of French products deteriorated after 1770 and that they were losing ground in the Levant, in Spain (where the protectionist policy of Charles III was a further obstacle) and in Spanish America (Davis, 1962, pp. 285–8, 294–5; Schumpeter, 1960, pp. 13–14; Deane and Cole, 1962, pp. 29–30, 42–9, 310–11; Levasseur, 1911, pp. 511, 521, 523; Dardel, 1963, pp. 49, 51–2, 101–2, 105, 247; Labrousse, 1943, pp. xxxvi–xxxix). In addition, the course of British trade was much less irregular, because it did not suffer as much from the wars.[10]

Another weakness of French trade was its great dependence on San Domingo, which in the 1780s was responsible for three-quarters of the trade with the French colonies and also supplied most of the re-exports, which themselves made about one-third of total exports (Levasseur, 1900, vol. 2, pp. 556–7). The proportion of re-exports was almost as great in English trade, but the British colonial empire was larger and more various than the French so that British colonial trade was more diversified; moreover, until 1776 it included as one of its chief markets the Thirteen Colonies, with their fast-rising European populations, their relatively high standard of living and expanding demand for manufactured goods of all sorts. Further, the percentage of manufactured goods to total exports was higher in British than

10. But there are also some striking parallels in its development, with alternating phases of fast growth (between the War of the Austrian Succession and the Seven Years' War) and of slow growth or stagnation (after 1713, during the 1770s).

in French trade – about two-thirds as against two-fifths in the 1780s; the leading French exports were coffee, sugar, and wines, linen and silk goods taking second place (Levasseur, 1911, pp. 515, 518, 521).

However, in France, as in England, commercial expansion was a strategic factor in the growth of industry. This is a more difficult question to discuss, because of the shortage of really satisfactory quantitative materials and the highly conjectural character of the structures which have recently been erected on the shaky foundations of those we possess. For England, W. Hoffmann's index shows that industrial production just trebled between 1700 and 1799; the more recent index of real output in commerce and industry established by Phyllis Deane and W. A. Cole goes up from 100 in 1700 to 285 in 1790, which means an average rate of growth of 1·17 per cent per year; an index of the same type, but for export industries only, rises more sharply during this period, from 100 to 383.[11] For French industry, Jean Marczewski has so far published only some provisional results; according to these, the gross physical product of French industry and handicraft at current prices rose from a yearly average of 385 million livres for the decade 1701–10 to 1573 million for 1781–90, which means its volume increased fourfold, in fact at a mean average rate of growth of 1·91 per cent per year (1961, Tables 1 and 3). But it seems that fuller and more precise calculations are likely to modify these conclusions, reducing the rate of growth to little more than 1 per cent per year, which would be very close to the figure Deane and Cole obtained for English production. The idea that English and French industrial production increased at much the same pace between the early eighteenth century and the French Revolution may appear surprising, but comparison of the evolution of the main industries in each country appears to bear it out.

As regards the woollen industry, Deane considers that in England its output rose about 150 per cent in the eighteenth century taken as a whole. For France, Pierre Léon puts the in-

11. W. G. Hoffman (1955, Table 54, Part A); Deane and Cole (1962, p. 78, Table 19). The index given by these authors refers to the ten-year averages centred on the year quoted.

crease between the early eighteenth century and 1789 at a mere 60 per cent. But 1789 was a very bad year, and moreover there was a distinct rise in English production during the last decade of the century, so that the disparity in growth between the two industries cannot be as large as the figures might at first suggest. In France the linen industry was very important, in terms of labour force and value of output perhaps bigger than the woollen industry; according to Pierre Léon, its evolution during the eighteenth century went parallel to that of wool. In Britain, linen manufacture was of little importance at the beginning of the eighteenth century and though it later grew fast in Scotland, particularly at mid-century, by national standards it remained a relatively minor activity, and its growth, though sharp, can have had little consequence for industrial output as a whole. As for the silk industry, imports of raw silk into England slightly more than doubled between the beginning of the century and the 1780s, but the English silk industry remained small in comparison with the French, which was growing altogether faster : according to Léon, the number of looms at work in Lyons increased 185 per cent between 1720 and 1788 (Deane and Cole, 1962, pp. 52–3, 61, 203, 207; Léon, 1960, pp. 175–6, 178–9).[12]

For cotton, the picture is of course different – but not as different as one would think. There is no need to dwell on its phenomenal growth in Britain. Net imports of raw cotton rose from just over 1 million pounds weight in the early eighteenth century to a yearly figure of over 15 million in 1780–89 (and in this last year to 30 million). However, in France the cotton industry was also growing fast. J. Marczewski has calculated that its rate of growth between the first and the ninth decades averaged 3·8 per cent per annum; this was similar to the English growth rate but starting initially at a lower level. Thus in 1786 English net imports of cotton were 18 million pounds weight, French only 11 million. This shows the English cotton industry with a definite superiority, but the margin is not so

12. Professor Léon has very kindly supplied additional information, showing in particular that there was a very fast growth in the linen industry at St Quentin and in Mayenne (at a time when in Normandy the industry was stagnant).

great as it became later. And it must be remembered that until the very last years of the century cotton's contribution to the British national income remained relatively small (Deane and Cole, 1962, pp. 50–52, 163; Léon, 1960, p. 178; Levasseur, 1900, pp. 524–6, 545, 690; Marczewski, 1961, Table 7; Bairoch, 1963, pp. 235–6, 305–7; Ballot, 1923, p. 120; Lüthy, 1959, vol. 2, pp. 663–5; Dardel, 1963, pp. 203, 214, 561).

For the mining and metal industries the quantitative data are very unsatisfactory. French coal production was of course much lower than British, but in the eighteenth century it started to grow very fast and by the time of the Revolution had some national importance. As for the iron industry, although there is still much that is obscure and controversial about its evolution in England during the first part of the century, its growth up to about 1760, in fact up to the time of Henry Cort's invention, was certainly slow; it was only as a result of Cort's inventions that iron production showed dramatic increase, doubling in ten years. Some figures suggest that until the 1780s output in France grew faster. At all events, on the eve of the Revolution, France probably had an output of from 130,000 to 140,000 tons of pig-iron, as against only 60,000 in England (Léon, 1960, pp. 177, 179; 1956, p. 223; Gille, 1964, p. 156; d'Herouville, 1958, p. 997; Heckscher, 1932, p. 132; Levasseur, 1900, vol. 2, p. 675; Marczewski, 1961, Table 8; Bairoch, 1963, pp. 238, 247–8, 313–4; Dean and Cole, 1962, pp. 55, 221; Ashton, 1955, p. 124; Mitchell, 1962, p. 221; Flinn, 1958, pp. 151–2).

This brief survey thus does not contradict the impression left by estimates of global industrial output, and as regards *volume* of output, French industrial performance up to the Revolution compares not unfavourably with the English. France was producing less coal, non-ferrous metals, ships and cotton goods than Britain, but more woollens, linens and silks, as well as more iron. French total industrial production was appreciably higher than the English, but production per head remained smaller, as it had already been in the seventeenth century.

It is true that in industry, as in foreign trade, French performance seems to have been relatively better in the first half of the period under review than the second. Recovery in output after the depression of the later years of Louis XIV occurred before 1720 in some sectors (Dauphiné, Amiens), after this date in others (Beauvais for example). The recovery was sharp: output of woollens seems to have doubled at Amiens between 1715 and 1750 and trebled at Beauvais between 1724 and 1755. In any case, after 1730 growth was general and quite fast (Goubert, 1960, pp. 586, 589; Deyon, 1962, pp. 204, 207; Léon, 1954, vol. 1, pp. 118 *et seq.*) English industrial growth at this period was somewhat sluggish: Deane and Cole observed a faster pace only in the 1740s and 1750s, and even this movement slackened after 1760. Not everyone will agree with this interpretation, but there is no doubt whatever about the violent acceleration during the 1780s in all manufacturing output, which signifies that England had entered on the decisive phase of the industrial revolution (Deane and Cole, 1962, p. 78, Table 19; Ashton, 1955, p. 125; John, 1961, pp. 176–90). Ernest Labrousse has shown that in France there was a slackening in industrial growth from mid-century and after 1770 prolonged stagnation. The old textile industries stopped growing and in some districts – for example Amiens, Normandy, Brittany and Languedoc – even declined. The agricultural depression around 1780, the worsening lot of the poorer classes, made the difficulties of industry more acute and were a preface to its collapse in 1788–89. These difficulties should not, however, be overestimated since the stagnation of the old industries (also noticeable in England, where competition from cotton damaged wool and linen) was in part compensated by the fast rise of new industries – cotton in particular, but also coal, iron, glass and chemical products (Labrousse, 1933, pp. 506–8, 548, 555, 557; 1943, pp. viii, x, xxii–xxiii, xxxii–xxxvii, 177; Deyon, 1962, pp. 207–8; Levasseur, 1900, pp. 527, 602; Lüthy, 1961, vol. 2, p. 594). However this may be, during the eighteenth century, French industry certainly displayed considerable vitality and buoyancy (Léon, 1960, p. 179).

There remains agriculture, a thorny question which cannot be gone into here except to refer to the recent study by J. Toutain which shows for France a 60 per cent increase of the deflated agricultural product between 1701–10 and 1781–90; this growth, somewhat higher than the rise in population, fits in with the disappearance during the eighteenth century of the famines and mass mortalities which had been so frequent in the seventeenth. On the other hand, Deane and Cole have estimated the growth in real output of British agriculture between 1700 and 1790 at 35 per cent. These figures are not exactly comparable, but they point, as in the preceding cases, to a roughly parallel growth. Admittedly, English agricultural techniques underwent great improvements during the eighteenth century, for which there is no equivalent in France, but French agriculture was not so conservative as is often thought (Toutain, 1961, vol. 1, pp. 213, 215, vol. 2, pp. 128, 133, 136, 139, 204, 276; Deane and Cole, 1962, p. 78; Labrousse, 1962, pp. 47–50, 94).

As regards the global growth of the two economies, for Britain the Dean and Cole index of total output rises from 100 in 1700 to 190 in 1970, for France an index of the gross physical product at constant prices, as computed by Marczewski, rises from 100 to 260 between the first and ninth decades of the century, though the last figure may be thought too high (Deane and Cole, 1962, pp. 78–9; Marczewski, 1961, Table 4).[13] And between 1700 and 1781 the population of France apparently increased 35 per cent (from 19.5 or 20 millions to 26 millions), that of England and Wales only 29 per cent (from 5.8 to 7.5 millions). The growth in average real output and income per head might therefore have been roughly of the same order of magnitude in both countries (Toutain, 1963, vol. 3, pp. 9, 160, Deane and Cole, 1962, p. 6, Table 2).

As we have seen, however, at the beginning of the eighteenth century France was behind England, especially as regards the level of average industrial output, foreign trade and incomes; as both economies grew at about the same rate in the next three-quarters of a century, France could not overtake her rival (although some ground was no doubt made up during the second third of the century), and the close similarity in the rates of

13. In establishing this index, use has been made of some figures of Marczewski which take into account the prevailing relationship between food and manufacturing prices – figures which he considers preferable. On the other hand, Bairoch (1963, p. 346, diagram 63) has adopted other figures of Marczewski which give only 69 per cent increase in the total physical output.

growth, which in this paper is deliberately stressed because it has often not been recognized, ought not to disguise the differences between them. In the 1770s England was still the more 'developed', the richer country, with certainly a higher average income per head. England was more urbanized, more industrialized, more involved in international trade; industry employed a higher percentage of the active population and contributed more to national income, roughly over one-quarter, as against one-fifth in France. Moreover, the subsistence sector had virtually disappeared from England as early as the seventeenth century (Deane and Cole, 1962, pp. 3, 256), ousted everywhere by the mercantile and monetary economy; in France the quasi-autarchic subsistence sector was still important and prevailed in extensive areas, acting as a brake on the growth of the economy as a whole.

The fundamental difference between the two economies, however, is in the technological field. The relatively fast expansion of French industry during the eighteenth century took place within a framework which was still, as regards organization and methods, largely the traditional one. Some changes can be observed, for example the tendency towards concentration and growth of commercial capitalism, the migration of industry from the towns to the countryside, the appearance of new products or even of new industries such as cotton, but in general the traditional structures held. On the eve of the Revolution, the French economy was not basically different from what it had been under Louis XIV: it was merely producing much more. In England, on the other hand, where growth during the first half of the century was of the 'French' type, that is, within the traditional framework, after 1760 some revolutionary changes appeared and economic structures were modified in depth by a series of technical inventions which heralded a general revolution.

This is the heart of the matter: Britain was the place where all the basic inventions which created industry – the spinning machine, the flying shuttle, the mechanical loom, the printing drum, the coke furnace, puddling, and most revolutionary of all, the steam engine – were made, perfected and introduced into industry. In France inventions were far fewer and restricted to improvements for the silk industry (Vaucanson and later Jacquard) and the chemical industry (Berthollet and Leblanc). Eighteenth-century France had some excellent technicians in fields like shipbuilding, ordnance (Gribeauval), and public works, not to mention many marvellous craftsmen, but their talent was not applied to the improvement of industrial techniques. French industry only developed on the technical side through taking up foreign machines and techniques, and to assimilate them usually required the help of foreign technicians, most of them British, though some were Swiss or German (see Léon, 1955, pp. 5–14; 1956).

England experienced a real outburst of inventiveness, which in France was almost completely lacking, and this decisive British superiority in ingenuity and willingness to innovate is the basic fact which has accentuated the structural discrepancy between the two economies during the second part of the eighteenth century, and which we must now try to explain.

This is a difficult task, all the more so because the foregoing analysis has removed one convenient explanation: if, as is sometimes believed, British output had increased much faster than the French, British inventiveness could then very easily be explained as a function, a by-product, of growth. But as things are the parallel growth in output in the two countries makes the British superiority harder to understand, since there seems nothing specific or unique about the development of the English economy, or at least of a large part of it. And in so far as individual genius remains something of a mystery, it will never be fully explained why England had so many great inventors in the eighteenth century. All the historian can hope for is to understand the environment which favoured the making of inventions and which made manufacturers eager to take them up.

The earliest economic historians, when they considered this question, attached great importance to the English institutional framework. Efforts by the State to control and regulate industry had been abandoned as early as the seventeenth century, and though the relevant laws were still theoretically in force, they were never applied; at the same time, the guild system had fallen into decay (Ashton, 1948, pp. 11–12). Eighteenth-century England was thus a country of *laissez-faire*, in which the field was left free for individual initiative. In France, on the other hand, the guilds survived and their members resisted the development of large-scale enterprises and the introduction of new techniques. Moreover, Colbertist regulations, by prescribing detailed standards of workmanship, discouraged innovations. And in England, such vestiges of corporate regulation and public control as did survive, as for example in the woollen industry, had precisely the effect of encouraging routinism.

Historians like Levasseur, however, went too far in envisaging eighteenth-century French industry as imprisoned in the double straight-jacket of guilds and regulations, which they saw as an insuperable barrier to progress and the reason why French inventions were so few (Levasseur, 1900, vol. 2, p. 305).[14] Nowadays, it is accepted that the guild system was never general in France and in fact did not apply to the greater part of industry; it was unknown in the economic life of many towns, for example Lyons, in royal manufactures, in rural domestic industries, and in new industries such as cotton.[15] Moreover, the system went into rapid decline in the second half of the century, as did Colbertist regulations, which had always been evaded and which from mid-century were less and less strictly enforced, as governmental circles were converted to *laissez-faire* policies. The contrast between French 'dirigism' and English liberalism should thus not be overestimated and it seems that the influence of the institutional framework, though real, was limited.

Some recent historians have stressed the importance of sociopsychological factors, involving a distinct contrast between the English and French social structures and 'scales of value' to explain British superiority in inventiveness and the entrepreneurial spirit (Ashton, 1955, pp. 20–21; Landes, 1961, p. 7). These writers have shown, with justice, that there was greater vertical social mobility in eighteenth-century England than in France, but it is odd that they should emphasize an aspect of the problem which seems both disputable and of secondary importance. They maintain that in England the social barrier separating the

14. A. Toynbee and W. Cunningham also overestimated the influence of *laissez-faire* on the English side.

15. But the rise of this industry was certainly delayed by the prohibitions against printed cottons which remained in force until 1759.

great landed classes from industry and commerce, the barrier, that is, between the aristocracy and the business world, was relatively low. But this can have very little bearing on the problem, since the industrial revolution was certainly not the work of the British aristocracy nor even of the gentry. As we know, England had the Duke of Bridgewater and his canal and some great landowners who took an interest in business, but on the whole active participation and investment in industry by the nobility and gentry seems to have actually declined during the eighteenth century, notably in metallurgy. Moreover, despite the contrary assertions of some English-speaking sociologists, the French nobility was not a close caste, nor was it totally uninterested in business. It controlled a good part of the metallurgical and glass industries and the coal-mines; it invested in foreign trading ventures and West Indian plantations, and on the eve of the Revolution a number of *grands seigneurs* like the Duke of Orleans and the Count of Artois were active in enterprises concerned to introduce English technology into France.

No one, however, will deny that the social prestige of business was lower in France than in England, that the ideal of *vivre noblement* (that is of doing nothing) was stronger there, contempt for work more widespread. But here, too, caution is necessary. For example, writers have often stressed that the French bourgeois who got rich in business retired from it as soon as possible to buy land or public office. And the sale of offices has been rightly criticized as an important factor in diverting capital and talents away from productive activities (tax-farming and financial deals with a government perpetually hard up played the same role). But this factor was much less important in the eighteenth than in the seventeenth century, as the State was no longer resorting to mass creation and sales of offices. As for the diversion of capital to land, this was also a marked feature in England, where it was the dream of every merchant who got rich to become a country gentleman; and though he himself often retained an interest in the business which had made his fortune, it very rarely survived into the next generation.

As regards our present problem, vertical mobility and scales of values may well be less important than differences between the two countries in the mentality of the men actually engaged in business. In English society there was a more 'capitalist', a more commercial, a more acquisitive spirit; and according to contemporary accounts there was in England a harshness, a ruthlessness, a concentration on the pursuit of gain, which was absent in the more easy-going France of the Ancien Régime. Yet the French social and psychological environment was not basically hostile to innovation, and many manufacturers were quite ready to take up foreign inventions (although they often had difficulty in making them work). French merchants too, displayed plenty of initiative and daring in overseas ventures. In any case, such observations are primarily descriptive and quite superficial, leaving the differences in the two mentalities unaccounted for.

Basically, the problem is still obscure and new research is needed into the relationship between the English and French social structures on the one hand and the entrepreneurial mentalities and attitudes on the other. What is most needed is a close analysis at the local or regional level, since to speak of English society and French society as a whole only leaves one with dubious generalities. After all, the industrial revolution was not made in England but in a few small districts of England – south Lancashire, some sectors of the East Midlands and Yorkshire, Birmingham and the Black Country. The inventors and innovators were recruited from the middle class of these industrial districts, from the merchant-manufacturers and the skilled, well-to-do artisans, and England's wealth in qualified cadres of this type was certainly an important factor.[16] A detailed comparison between these English nurseries of the Industrial Revolution and some French industrial centres would be very instructive. Another pointer is the fact that most of the English discoveries were the product of joint effort, as for example with the notable collaboration of Black, Watt, Boulton and Wilkinson over the steam engine (Ashton, 1948, pp. 14, 69; 1955, p. 105); in France, a larger and more rural country, an element of isolation may have hampered this type of co-operation and cross-stimulus.

16. See the excellent comments of John (1961, p. 188–9) on the increase of their numbers because of the prosperity prevailing in the first half of the century.

Another difficult question is the influence of the Enlightenment. The relationship between the industrial revolution and the English philosophical and scientific movement of the late seventeenth century and the eighteenth century is well known. Recent research has stressed the importance of the belief, which goes back to Newton, that industrial progress was possible through observation and experiment; it has shown that most of the inventions (although largely the work of practical men with little education) were backed by systematic thinking, that British scientists and manufacturers were often in close contact, for example in bodies such as the Birmingham Lunar Society, and that scientific knowledge had penetrated industrial society down to a very modest level (Ashton, 1948, pp. 14, 16; Musson and Robinson, 1960, pp. 222–44). But the philosophical and scientific movement was at least as powerful in France, which had plenty of scientists, some of whom, like Buffon and Réaumur, tried their hand at industrial research; scientific societies and academies existed there in profusion and numbered businessmen among their members; belief in progress and the wish to improve man's material condition were at least as widespread as in England, and Diderot's *Encyclopédie* is striking proof of the interest cultivated people took in technology. But unlike what happened in England, all this intellectual activity had very little practical result; discussions in learned societies remained theoretical in character and those who took part lacked a sense of the concrete.[17] A study of this question which also took education into account would again be very useful. In Britain, dissenters and Scotsmen played a major role in the industrial revolution because, thanks to the dissenting academies and the much more advanced Scottish educational system (Ashton, 1948, pp. 17, 19, 20), they were the best-educated section of the middle class. French businessmen had either a very elementary or a purely classical education. This difference may have had important consequences.

To sum up, although neither the differences in social structure and mentality between the two countries in the eighteenth century nor the features of the English social environment

17. I am grateful to my friend and colleague Louis Trénard for useful suggestions on this point.

which favoured the entrepreneurial spirit should be minimized, the contrast does not appear to be as sharp as is often said. Moreover, the real influence of such concrete differences as did exist is still obscure, and though they may in some respects account for British technical superiority, they can only be a secondary factor in comparison with strictly economic forces. After all, technical progress is closely bound up with economic phenomena, and the explanation we are looking for must be first and foremost an economic one (Schmookler, 1962, pp. 1–2). The contention is that the French did not innovate because, unlike the British, they were not made to do so by the strong pressure of economic forces.

Did this pressure arise from demand? Several writers have maintained that a fast growth in the demand for manufactured goods from both the home and the export markets presented British industry with a challenge it could meet only by a technical revolution. This is an attractive hypothesis, but its major premise, that there was an abnormally fast growth in demand in eighteenth-century England, is still unproved, and in any case there seems no reason why effective global demand should have grown much faster in England than in France.

Population growth in the two countries was of the same order, and anyway there was a comparable upsurge in population throughout western Europe around mid-century. Recently there has been much debate about the relationship between the industrial and demographic revolutions, but some of the contributors are surely right in stressing that while population growth was doubtless a necessary condition for the industrial revolution, it was by no means a sufficient or decisive one, since it was general throughout western Europe.

Turning to average real incomes per head, they certainly rose in England during the first half of the eighteenth century, when the population was almost stationary, food prices falling, and money wages rising; the internal market therefore expanded, consumption of many articles increased, there was a broadening in range and improvement in quality; A. H. John has pointed out that this permanently affected the level of consumption in most classes and even aroused an appetite for mass consumption. This progress, however, did not last, for from mid-century the expansion of the economy was absorbed by the upsurge in population, and average output per head only started to grow again in the 1780s (Ashton, 1955, p. 232; John, 1961, pp. 180–83; Deane and Cole, 1962, pp. 18–19, 21, 41, 80–81). But development in France seems to have been roughly parallel, with a rise in average incomes during the first half of the century followed by a degree of stagnation. Labrousse has shown that from the 1760s food prices and rents were certainly rising faster than money wages, which means a fall in real wages, affecting not only the urban wage-earner and the landless rural proletariat but also many poor peasants with some land of their own, who derived part of their income from wages; a large section of the population therefore became poorer, and this must have meant a fall in its average consumption of manufactured goods. However, the rise in rents and agricultural profits was at the same time enriching a not insignificant part of the population, not only the 'feudal' landlords but also the well-to-do peasants. This was a stimulus to trade, and in particular trade in colonial products, and to industry and urban development, and produced a rise in non-agricultural incomes. There is therefore no reason why average effective demand for manufactured goods should have decreased, except possibly during the late 1770s and the 1780s when according to Labrousse the fall in food prices brought about a general stagnation (1933, vol. 2, pp. 379, 382–3, 444, 497, 598–9, 610–11; 1943, pp. xxv–xxviii, xxxi; 1962, pp. 4–5, 66, 78 et seq., 86, 91, 97). But, and this is the important point, the slowing down in French demand would have come only after the English had made their great innovations, which were put into effect during a period of prosperity on both sides of the Channel.

There is also the demand from foreign markets to consider. In both countries it was more elastic and increased much faster than internal consumption (although it absorbed a much smaller proportion of output); but as we have already seen, British exports of manufactures increased no faster than French, with the important exception of cotton goods.[18] In addition it must

18. Schumpeter (1960, p. 12); Deane and Cole (1962, p. 59); see also Chaloner and Musson (1960, p. 74) and Berrill (1960, p. 358).

be said, against a currently held opinion, that French losses of colonial territories as a result of the Seven Years' War had little effect on exports, since few French goods were taken up by the Canadian and Indian markets, which were only of potential value; nor did England derive much immediate advantage from her conquests (Deane and Cole, 1962, p. 85).

In fact, the important differences between the English and French markets for manufactured goods are to be observed in their structure rather than their evolution.

In the first place, the British home market – unlike the French – was a truly national market, since the country was an economic unity and there were no internal customs or tolls. This factor should not be overstressed, since the principal French customs unit – the 'Five big Farms' – covered a population about as large as Britain. Nevertheless, as K. Berrill has rightly stressed, during the eighteenth century Britain and her colonies formed the largest 'free trade area' in the world. Furthermore, the small size of the country, its configuration, and the early improvement to its transport, contributed to making this national market a reality and internal circulation much more active than in France (Berrill, 1960, p. 358; John, 1961, pp. 185–8).

Again, demand within this market was more intense, because as we have already seen, from the beginning of the eighteenth century Britain had a higher average income per head and a higher standard of living. There is no doubt at all that the British masses were better fed, better clothed, better shod than their French counterparts; the percentage of really poor in the total population may have been smaller and that of well-to-do middle-class people greater. In consequence, if average demand for manufactured goods did not grow faster than in France, it still kept to a higher level for the whole of the period under review.[19]

Lastly, the pattern of consumption was also different, though not in the sense often claimed. Some English-speaking writers maintain that France had only luxury industries such as silk, crystals, porcelain, cabinet-making, which were unsuited to machine production, while England specialized early in making

19. Landes (1961, p. 6). Some absurd objections included in the discussion of Landes's paper may safely be ignored.

cheap goods for a mass market, which could be mass-produced by machinery in factories (Challoner and Musson, 1960, pp. 79–80; Clark, 1946, pp. 169–70). France certainly had luxury or semi-luxury industries which catered for the upper classes; their relative importance was greater than in England and they were little suited to mechanization. But in addition France had large industries which catered for popular consumption, turning out coarse woollens and linens for the peasantry, for West Indian slaves and for the Spanish colonies. Now this production for the masses was not large-scale mass production, since the market was fragmented and the places of manufacture dispersed; moreover, it catered for an unfastidious clientele and used very cheap rural labour, so there was no pressing need to make technical improvements. On the other hand, it appears that British superiority in the eighteenth century was in the manufacture of good quality products suitable for middle-class consumption; and when Frenchmen complained (at any rate before the 1780s) about British competition, they stressed the superior quality, finish and appearance of the goods manufactured in Britain. In part the contrast was a reflection of the differing social structures of the two countries and the colonies: England, relatively speaking, had a larger middle class and the fast-growing population of the Thirteen Colonies had a standard of living close to that of the middle classes in Europe. English industry was therefore not catering for a true 'mass market' – this appeared only in the nineteenth century – but only for a mass market in embryo, among above all the middle classes. But in the result output had to be both somewhat standardized and of good quality, which undoubtedly encouraged increased division of labour and technical improvements in order to keep prices low, and also the concentration of work in factories, to maintain quality by better supervision.[20]

We may also wonder whether the growth in demand for manufactured goods was not more regular in England than in France, where recurrent crises and wars were more serious interruptions. T. S. Ashton has pointed out that in England the

20. The pattern of English consumption was also undoubtedly more 'advanced', textiles having less predominance and metal goods, pottery, etc. greater relative importance.

number of patents rose during periods of expansion and optimism and decreased during depressions or wars. Therefore if economic fluctuations were much more violent in France, this could have had a discouraging effect on innovation. Since it is generally agreed that short-term fluctuations in eighteenth-century industrial output were due mainly to variations in harvest yields, a comparison of fluctuations in grain prices on both sides of the Channel would undoubtedly be of interest. We have nothing for England to set beside the great work of Labrousse, so comparison can only be summary and superficial, based on price series which are not truly comparable. One has the impression, however, that in the eighteenth century, unlike the seventeenth, the amplitude of such fluctuations was not noticeably more violent in France than in England.[21]

As for fluctuations in output, it is known that in some centres in France production fell about 50 per cent in the course of a cycle, but such cases are exceptional. In England two reasonably well-founded manufacturing series, one for printed goods and the other for West Riding cloth, show that in several cases output fell 20 per cent or even 25 per cent in the course of a given cycle (Labrousse, 1933, vol. 2, p. 549; 1943, p. xl; Deyon, 1962, p. 211; Ashton, 1955, pp. 248–9). As a hypothesis, we might conclude that fluctuations were less violent than in France, probably because a larger proportion of output was intended for export, so that in a year of bad harvest the foreign, and especially the non-European, demand was more likely to compensate for the fall on the home market.

The impact of the wars of the eighteenth century has recently stimulated some interesting debates among British historians: for them the problem centres on whether their favourable effects – such as encouraging output and technical innovation in the metal industries – were outweighed by their depressive effects on other branches of the economy (John, 1955, pp. 329–44; Ashton, 1948, pp. 90–91; 1955, pp. 126–7; 1959, pp. 69–83). For France

21. The divergence between average minimum and maximum yearly prices within one cycle is in the worse cases of the order of 1 to 2 – while in seventeenth-century France it was 1 to 3 or 4. But in most of the cycles the amplitude of the movement was much less.

the question hardly arises, since there is no doubt that the balance was unfavourable in view of the very serious interruption to seaborne trade during hostilities. Admittedly, out of the three wars the only really disastrous one for France was the Seven Years' War. But whatever the outcome of particular battles and the conditions of peace, in time of war the Royal Navy was always in command of the seas, leaving France, despite the use of neutral ships, to a large extent cut off from overseas countries and particularly her colonies. The British sea lanes, on the other hand, were kept open and British commerce, despite French privateering, had real protection. French trade thus fell sharply during each of the wars, though the worst collapse was naturally during the Seven Years' War, when its annual average was barely half that of the preceding years; even so, the situation was little better during the American war; only the War of the Austrian Succession was without really adverse effects. The fall in French exports caused a decline in industrial activity but from Labrousse's figures, the recession was not so great as in foreign trade, which is normal since the greater part of industrial output was distributed on the home market. The adverse influence of the wars should therefore not be overstressed, and indeed H. Lüthy and A. Rémond have maintained that on the whole France was fairly prosperous during the Seven Years' War (Labrousse, 1933, vol. 2, p. 548; Levasseur, 1900, vol. 2, p. 551; Lüthy 1961, vol. 2, pp. 12, 42–4, 357–8; Dardel, 1963, pp. 49–50, 249–51, 257, 516; Rémond, 1957, pp. 420–21). On the other hand, while English foreign trade rose significantly during the Seven Years' War, it fell during the War of the Austrian Succession and fell badly (although less than the French) during the American war. A relationship might be seen between the innovations of the 1760s and the optimism, the confidence in expansion, aroused by England's crushing victories; yet the disaster of American independence was immediately followed by acceleration in the rate of economic growth. On the whole, British maritime and colonial victories do not appear to have been important factors in British technical superiority; it was only during the revolutionary and Napoleonic wars that complete command of the seas gave Britain the monopoly of overseas markets as a powerful stimulus to growth.[22]

There are, then, a number of interesting divergences to be noted between the character and evolution of demand for manufactures in France and England; but these appear less important than those to be observed on the supply side of industry, in the analysis of productive factors.

The industrial revolution was not something gratuitous, a triumph of technical progress for its own sake, but a determined effort to solve some concrete problems facing British industry; the character of the most significant inventions reveals what those problems were. The inventions were designed to make possible the replacement of relatively scarce and expensive resources, such as wood, water power and labour by others which were relatively plentiful and cheap, such as coal, steam power and capital, the last in the form of labour-saving machines and processes (Ashton, 1955, pp. 108–9; 1948, p. 91). This underlying character reflects the fact that English industry in the eighteenth century suffered from relative shortages, particularly of fuel in the iron industry and of labour in textile manufactures, and that such bottlenecks were hampering expansion in output. In other words, unless a technical breakthrough was achieved the available productive factors were inadequate (except through an excessive rise in prices) to meet the relatively fast increase in demand which started in mid-century when the population growth made itself felt. The contention is that these shortages and bottle-necks, which in England exerted strong pressure in favour of innovation, did not exist in France.

In the primary iron industry the contrast is quite evident. Admittedly, we must not overestimate the wood 'famine' which some writers say existed in England as early as the seventeenth century. Michael Flinn has shown recently that between 1550 and 1750 charcoal prices rose little higher than prices in general, and that ironmasters could secure a fuel supply either by systematic copse 'cultivation' or by moving their works to remote and wooded districts. Even so, in any region, every attempt to

22. Habakkuk (1962, pp. 185–6). However, there is need for a study in depth of the role of the navy as an outlet for industry and eventually as a stimulus to technical progress.

increase output meant a fast rise in marginal costs, so that prospects for expansion were limited. On the other hand, from the sixteenth century coal had been cheaper than charcoal in terms of heat output per unit. The ironmasters were aware of the economic advantages of coal, and they also knew that vast reerves of it lay hidden underground. There was therefore a strong incentive to look for methods allowing the substitution of coal for charcoal in blast furnaces, a search which began in the sixteenth century. When it had been successful, by the early eighteenth century, ironmasters who wished to take advantage of the growing demand for iron, were induced increasingly to replace charcoal, which was expensive and limited in supply, by coke, which was a cheaper and much more elastic source; eventually, in the last quarter of the century, ironmasters found they either had to go over to coke smelting or close down. Technical progress therefore resulted from the pressure of growing demand on inadequate wood resources, and this explains why coke smelting was discovered and taken up in England rather than in countries where supplies of wood were cheaper and more elastic (Flinn, 1959, pp. 109–20). In France, where large forests were still extant, the situation was quite different, and though there was some pressure on wood resources during the eighteenth century and prices rose sharply[23] such shortage as developed remained purely local and French ironmasters were never faced with the choice between innovation or extinction; and in France coal was scarce and expensive.

Moreover, in England the growing demand for coal for both industrial and domestic purposes during the eighteenth century led to deeper working of the mines, which created the need for more efficient pumping devices; and this of course was a powerful incentive in the development of the steam engines, which was in fact a by-product of the rise of the British coal industry. The same incentive was lacking in France, because of the different balance between wood and coal resources.

23. According to Labrousse (1933, vol. 2, pp. 346–7) the price of wood for burning increased 91 per cent between 1726–41 and 1785–9; but the substantial rise occurred after 1770; this had to do with wood intended for domestic use, and in any case the price of wood represented only a small part of the cost price of iron, whose prices certainly did not follow the rise in wood prices.

A contrast between France and England is also evident in the textile industry, but here it is in the supply of labour. The putting-out system (domestic labour allied with commercial capitalism) which prevailed in the industry had many advantages, but also the disadvantage that expansion of output was hampered by rising marginal costs. Once the development of an industrial centre had passed a certain limit, to increase production work had to be put out over an ever-widening area, and at a period when communications were slow this meant increased distribution costs, which were soon exceeding profits; the worker spent too much time going to and fro; supervision of the work was becoming impossible and the risks of bad workmanship and of embezzlement of the raw materials were growing. Putting-out could, of course, be concentrated on a restricted area where the workers could be made to work longer and faster, but such attempts were thwarted by a regressive labour supply, since the bait of increased earnings was not enough to lure the worker away from his traditional way of life, with its leisure hours and convivial drinking sessions.

There is plentiful evidence of the appearance of this kind of situation during the first half of the eighteenth century in a number of English industrial districts where the putting-out system had developed early and was widespread, with the result that all available labour within reasonable reach of each centre was used up. Nor was there an unlimited supply of mobile labour: the innovations in agriculture, far from creating unemployment, were stimulating demand for labour, which contradicts the older view that England was at this period suffering from large-scale rural under-employment and that there was a mass exodus from the countryside to the industrial centres. We must also remember that up to mid-century the population grew only very slowly. Although it then started growing fast, a number of years had to pass before a large supply was available for the labour market, and by this time demand was again increasing. There was therefore a relative shortage of labour in industrial districts, as is proved by the quite sharp rise in money wages there (not found in the south of England) during the first half of the eighteenth century.

Manufactures were therefore faced with high and rising

labour costs, which was particularly embarrassing in a young industry like cotton, which in practice had to build up its labour force at the expense of the older industries. There must therefore have been great difficulty during the 1750s in meeting the fast-growing demand for cottons, particularly for export to the colonies. But in the 1760s and 1770s, when there was some slackening in demand, the rise in manufacturing costs was really dangerous. It was now imperative to reduce labour costs and therefore to invent and take up labour-saving machinery. The relative shortage of labour which affected English industry seems therefore to have been one of the most powerful incentives to innovation, not only in the cotton industry but in several others as well.

In France the situation is again obviously different. The countryside was relatively less industrialized, the relaxation of the regulations against rural manufactures (especially after the suspension of 1762) freed vast reserves of labour, and this meant it was possible to put work out in a wider area around the industrial centres without unduly increasing labour costs. Moreover, since the rise in the French population was due solely to a fall in deaths (whereas in England there was also an increase in births) in France the number of people of working age may have grown faster. Lastly, and most important, there was in the French countryside a large pool of semi-employed proletarians which putters-out could use without bringing pressure on wages (Labrousse, 1933, vol. 2, pp. 491–2, 598–9; 1943, pp. xxix–xxxi). Labrousse has shown that this proletariat increased fast during the eighteenth century, outpacing the agricultural demand for labour and glutting the labour market.

In sum, during the first half of the eighteenth century, industrial growth in England had reached limits not to be crossed without a technological breakthrough, which the increase in population and in demand from the 1740s made imperative. In France, on the other hand, there was no shortage of labour, output could be increased to meet demand without looking for drastic innovations. This may rank as the most important of the differences to be observed between England and France, but it was in part due to England's earlier and more intense industrialization, and hence to the situation in the seventeenth century.

There remains the question of capital resources. In eighteenth-century England capital was relatively abundant, as is shown by the fall in interest rates over a long period; Ashton saw this as the deciding factor in the Industrial Revolution, but most British historians have not followed him (Ashton, 1948, pp. 11, 58, 94). In any case, there was the same fall in interest rates in France. From what little we know about the financing of French industry in the eighteenth century there is nothing to suggest that its development was hampered by a shortage of capital resources [24] – especially at a time when industrial investment had a very low threshold and the earliest spinning jennies, for example, could be got for a few pounds sterling. We know, of course, that the English banking system was much more advanced than the French, but the banks played only a minor and indirect part in financing the industrial revolution: industries for the most part financed themselves, through ploughing back profits (Crouzet, 1965a, vol. 2, pp. 598 *et seq*.). However, in England capital accumulation was at a faster rate than the growth of other factors in production, especially labour supplies, and this was a powerful incentive to innovation. Things may have been different in France, but this could only be proved by research into the problem, which has not yet been done.

This analysis, which could be accused of being both too long and too general, may appear inconclusive because in many cases it has tried to play down the 'sharp contrasts' between the French and English economies dear to the textbooks, contrasts which have been given too readily as the explanation for Britain's superior inventiveness and economic lead. There is no wish to deny that differences existed between the two countries, though many seem to have been less pronounced than is generally thought, and a matter of degree rather than kind. What is important is that these differences nearly all point in the same direction: in all the various fields investigated, in England the conditions for innovation seem to have been more favourable

24. For a different view see Lüthy (1961, vol 2, p. 41) and C. Fohlen in his Introduction to the French edition of Ashton (1955, pp. xvi–xviii).

than in France.[25] The accumulation of these relative differences, many of them small but very important as regards factors such as fuel and labour supplies, seems to have been sufficient to set in motion a cumulative and self-sustaining process of technical advance; in France there was no such movement, because there was no need for it. In a paper read in Paris in 1961, David Landes used an illuminating metaphor borrowed from nuclear physics: he spoke of a 'critical mass', a piling up of various factors favouring England's growth which triggered off a chain reaction – the industrial revolution (Landes, 1961, p. 6). In France, on the other hand, there was no such critical mass, which is why France did not start spontaneously an industrial revolution. The external stimulus of serious competition from cheaper English goods, first in foreign markets and after the treaty of 1786 in France itself, was needed to set in train a number of French efforts, intensified during the 1780s, which aimed at introducing the new English technology into France. At this date English industry had a clear superiority, but was only just entering the stage of fast growth and widespread revolutionary changes; France was not disastrously behind, and the industrial revolution might have taken off there with only a few years' delay in relation to England. But the 'national catastrophe' which the French Revolution and the twenty years war meant to the French economy would intensify the discrepancy and make it irremediable (Lévy-Leboyer, 1964, p. 29). In 1815 it would be more pronounced than in 1789, because during this quarter of a century, despite a delaying effect due to the wars, the British economy had continued to change and to make rapid growth (see Crouzet, 1958, vol. 2, pp. 863–72; 1962, pp. 182–217, 336–62; 1964, pp. 567–88; 1965, pp. 71–110).

25. Of course, many of these differences had deep historical roots, and for example, the contrast between the English and French colonial markets has its origin in the settlement of the English in Virginia and Massachusetts and of the French in Canada and San Domingo.

References

Arnould, A.M., *De la Balance du Commerce et des Relations commercials extérierues de la France dans toutes les Parties du Globe particulièrement à la fin du Règne de Louis XIV et au Moment de la Revolution*, 3 vols, Paris, 2nd edn.

Ashley, M. (1952), *England in the Seventeenth Century (1603–1714)*, Penguin.

Ashton, T.S. (1948), *The Industrial Revolution*, Oxford University Press.

Ashton, T.S. (1955), *An Economy of England; The 18th Century*, Methuen.

Ashton, T.S. (1959), *Economic Fluctuations in England*, Oxford University Press.

Baehrel, R. (1961), *Une Croissance: Le Basse-Provence Rurale. Essai d'Économie Historique Statistique*, Paris.

Bairoch, P. (1963), *Révolution Industrielle et son développement*, Paris.

Ballot, C. (1923), *L'Introduction du Machinisme dans L'Industrie Française*, Paris.

Berrill, K. (1960), 'International trade and the rate of economic growth', *Econ. Hist. Rev.*, 2nd s., vol. 12.

Brenner, Y.S. (1962), 'The inflation of prices in England, 1551–1650', *Econ. Hist. Rev.*, 2nd s., vol. 15.

Chaloner, W.H., and Musson, A.E. (eds.) (1960), 'The origins of the Industrial Revolution', *Past and Present*, vol. 17.

Chaloner, W.H., and Musson, A.E. (1963), *Industry and Technology*, Studio Vista.

Chaunu, P., Le renversement de la tendence majeure des prix et des activités au XVIIe siècle. Problèmes de fait et de methode', *Studi in Onore di Amintore Fanfani*, vol. 4.

Clark, G.N. (1946), *The Wealth of England from 1496 to 1760*, Oxford University Press.

Coleman, D.C. (1956), 'Industrial growth and industrial revolutions', *Economica*, n.s., vol. 23. Reprinted in E.M. Carus-Wilson (ed.) (1962), *Essays in Economic History*, vol. 3, Edward Arnold.

Coleman, D.C. (1956a), 'Labour in the English economy of the seventeenth century', *Econ. Hist. Rev.*, 2nd s., vol. 8.

Coleman, D.C. (1959), 'Technology and economic history, 1500–1750', *Econ. Hist. Rev.*, 2nd s., vol. 11.

Crouzet, F. (1958), *L'Economie Britannique et le Blocus Continental 1806–1813*, 2 vols., Paris.

Crouzet, F. (1962), 'Les conséquences économiques de la Révolution. À propos d'un inédit de Sir Francis d'Invernois', *Annales historiques de la Révolution française*, nos. 168 and 169.

Crouzet, F. (1964), 'Wars, blockade and economic change in Europe, 1792–1815', *J. econ. Hist.*, vol. 24.

Crouzet, F (1965), 'Bilan de l'économie britannique pendant les guerres de la Révolution et de l'Empire', *Rev. hist.*, no. 475, July–September.

Crouzet, F. (1965a), 'La formation du capital en Grande-Bretagne pendant la Révolution Industrielle', *Deuxième Conférence internationale d'histoire économique. Aix-en-Provence*, 1962, 2 vols. Paris and The Hague.

Dardel, P. (1963), *Navires et Marchandises dans les Ports du Rouen et du Havre au XVIIIe Siècle*, Paris.

Davis, R. (1954), 'English foreign trade, 1660 to 1700', *Econ Hist. Rev.*, 2nd s., vol. 7.

Davis, R. (1962), 'English foreign trade, 1700–1774', *Econ. Hist. Rev.*, 2nd s., vol. 15.

Deane, J., and Cole, W.A. (1962), *British Economic Growth, 1688–1959. Trends and Structure*, Cambridge University Press.

Deyon, P. (1962), 'Le mouvement de la production textile à Amiens au XVIIIe siècle', *Revue du Nord*, vol. 44.

Deyon, P. (1963), 'Variations de la production textile aux XVIe et XVIIe siècles : sources et premiers résultats', *Annales ESC*, vol. 18.

Farnie, D.A. (1962), 'The commercial empire of the Atlantic, 1607–1783', *Econ. Hist. Rev.*, 2nd s., vol. 15.

Fisher, F.J, (1957), 'The sixteenth and seventeenth centuries. The Dark Ages in English economic history?', *Economica*, n.s., vol. 24.

Fisher, F.J. (ed.) (1961), *Essays in the Economic and Social History of Tudor and Stuart England in Honour of R.H. Tawney*, Cambridge University Press.

Flinn, M.W. (1958), 'The growth of the English iron industry, 1660–1760', *Econ. Hist. Rev.*, 2nd s., vol. 11.

Flinn, M.W. (1959), 'Timber and the advance of technology: a reconsideration', *Ann. Sci.*, vol. 15.

Gille, B. (1964), 'La métallurgie française d'Ancien Régime', *Revue d'Histoire de la Sidérurgie*, vol. 5.

Goubert, P. (1960), 'Beauvais et le Beauvaisis de 1600 à 1730. *Contribution à l'Histoire Sociale de la France du XVIIIe Siècle*, Paris.

Goubert, P. (1966), *Louis XIV et vingt millions de Français*, Paris. Published as *Louis XIV and Twenty Million Frenchmen*, Allen Lane The Penguin Press, 1970.

Gougert, P. (1967), *L'Avènement du Roi-Soleil 1661*, Paris.

Habakkuk, H.J. (1962), *American and British Technology in the Nineteenth Century*, Cambridge University Press.

Heckscher, E.F. (1932), 'Un grand chapitre de l'histoire du fer : le monopole suédois', *Annales d'Histoire économique et sociale*, vol. 4.

d'Herouville, H. (1958), 'Reflexions sur la croissance', *Études et Conjoncture*, vol. 13.

Hoffman, W.G. (1955), *British Industry, 1700–1950*, Oxford University Press.

John, A.H. (1955), 'Wars and the English economy', *Econ. Hist. Rev.*, 2nd s., vol. 7.

John, A.H. (1961), 'Aspects of English economic growth in the first half of the eighteenth century', *Economica*, n.s., vol. 28.

Labrousse, C.E. (1933), *Esquisse du Mouvement des Prix et des Revenus en France au XVIIIᵉ Siècle*, 2 vols., Paris.

Labrousse, E. (1943), *Le Crise de L'économie Française à la fin de l'Ancien Régime et au debut de la Révolution, Paris*.

Labrousse, E. (1962), *Le Paysan Français des Physiocrates à nos Jours*, Paris, Cours de Sorbonne.

Landes, D.S. (1961), 'Encore le problème de la Révolution industrielle en Angleterre', *Bulletin de la société d'histoire moderne*, 12th s., vol. 18.

Léon, P. (1954), *La Naissance de la Grande Industrie en Dauphiné (fin du XVIIIᵉ Siècle – 1860)*, 2 vols., Paris.

Léon, P. (1955), 'Tradition et machinisme dans la France du XVIIIᵉ siècle', *Information historique*, vol. 17.

Léon, P. (1956), *Le Fer à Travers les Ages. Hommes et Techniques*, Nancy.

Léon, P. (1956a), 'La crise de l'économie française à la fin du règne de Louis XIV (1685–1715), *Information historique*, vol. 18.

Léon, P. (1960), 'L'industrialisation en France en tant que facteur de croissance économique de début du XVIIIᵉ siècle à nos jours', *Première Conférence internationale d'Histoire économique. Stockholm, 1960*, Paris and The Hague.

Levasseur, E. (1900), *Histoire des Classes ouvrières et de l'Industrie en France avant 1789*, 2 vols., Paris, 2nd edn.

Levasseur, E. (1911), *Histoire du Commerce de la France. Première Partie: avant 1789*, Paris.

Lévy-Leboyer, M. (1964), *Les Banques Européennes et l'Industrialisation internationale dans la première moitié du XIXe Siècle*, Paris.

Lüthy, H. (1959 and 1961), *La Banque Protestante en France, de la Révocation de l'Edit de Nantes à la Révolution*, 2 vols., Paris.

Marczewski, J. (1961), 'Some aspects of the economic growth of France, 1660–1958', *Econ. Development soc. Change*, vol. 9.

Meuvret, J. (1952), 'La géographie des prix des céréales et les anciennes économies européennes : prix méditerranéens, prix continentaux, prix atlantiques à la fin du XVIIe siècle', *Rivista di Economia*, no. 2.

Mitchell, B.R. (1962), *Abstract of British Historical Statistics*, Cambridge University Press.

Mousnier, R. (1954), *Les XVIe et XVIIe Siècles*, Paris.

Musson, A.E., and Robinson, E. (1960), 'Science and industry in the late eighteenth century', *Econ. Hist. Rev.*, 2nd s., vol. 13.

Nef, J.U. (1934), 'The progress of technology and the growth of large-scale industry in Great Britain, 1540–1640', *Econ. Hist. Rev.*, vol. 5.

Nef, J.U. (1936), 'A comparison of industrial growth in France and England from 1540 to 1640', *J. polit. Econ.*, vol. 44.

Nef, J.U. (1937), 'Prices and industrial capitalism in France and England, 1540–1640', *Econ. Hist. Rev.*, vol. 7.

Nef, J.U. (1941), 'L'industrie et l'état en France et en Angleterre (1540–1640)', *Revue historique*, vol. 191.

Phelps Brown, E.H., and Hopkins, S.V. (1956), 'Seven centuries of the prices of consumables, compared with builders' wage-rates', *Economica*, n.s., vol. 23.

Rémond, A. (1957), 'Trois bilans de l'économie française au temps des théories physiocratiques', *Revue d'Histoire économique et sociale*, vol. 35.

Schmookler, J. (1962), 'Economic sources of inventive activity'.

Schumpeter, E.B. (1960), *English Overseas Trade Statistics, 1697–1808*, Oxford University Press.

Supple, B.E. (1959), *Commercial Crisis and Change in England, 1600–1642*, Cambridge University Press.

Toutain, J.C. (1961–3), *Histoire Quantitative de L'Économie Française*, 3 vols., Paris.

G Thomas Jefferson

Thomas Jefferson, President of the United States from 1801 to
1809, may stand before us as the many-sided mind of the late
eighteenth century. He was statesman, scholar, lawyer,
educationalist, scientist, inventor, architect. The passages
quoted here are principally concerned with his work as statesman
and educationalist, though in the attacks and lampoons upon
him we can see the impact of his scientific enthusiasm upon his
contemporaries. How he wished to be remembered we can see
from the epitaph he wrote for himself:

> Here was buried
> Thomas Jefferson
> Author of the Declaration of American Independence
> Of the Statute of Virginia for religious freedom
> And Father of the University of Virginia.

J.F.

1 Virginia Statute of Religious Liberty   16 January 1786

Reprinted in H. S. Commager (ed.), *Documents of American History* 1963

I

Whereas Almighty God hath created the mind free; that all attempts to influence it by temporal punishments or burthens, or by civil incapacitations, tend only to beget habits of hypocrisy and meanness, and are a departure from the plan of the Holy author of our religion, who being Lord both of body and mind, yet chose not to propagate it by coercions on either, as was in his Almighty power to do; that the impious presumption of legislators and rulers, civil as well as ecclesiastical, who being themselves but fallible and uninspired men, have assumed dominion over the faith of others, setting up their own opinions and modes of thinking as the only true and infallible, and as such endeavouring to impose them on others, hath established and maintained false religions over the greatest part of the world, and through all time; that to compel a man to furnish contributions of money for the propagation of opinions which he disbelieves, is sinful and tyrannical; that even the forcing him to support this or that teacher of his own religious persuasion, is depriving him of the comfortable liberty of giving his contributions to the particular pastor whose morals he would make his pattern, and whose powers he feels most persuasive to righteousness, and is withdrawing from the ministry those temporary rewards, which proceeding from an approbation of their personal conduct, are an additional incitement to earnest and unremitting labours for the instruction of mankind; that our civil rights have no dependence on our religious opinions, any more than our opinions in physics or geometry; that therefore the proscribing any citizen as unworthy the public confidence by laying upon him an incapacity of being called to offices of trust and emolument, unless he profess or renounce this or that religious opinion, is depriving him injuriously of those privileges and advantages to which in common with his fellow-citizens he has a natural right, that it tends only to corrupt the principles of that religion it is meant to encourage, by bribing with a monopoly of worldly honours and emoluments, those who will externally profess and conform to it; that though indeed these are criminal who do not withstand such temptation, yet neither are those innocent who lay the bait in their way; that to suffer the civil magistrates to intrude his powers into the field of opinion, and to restrain the profession or propagation of principles on supposition of their ill tendency, is a dangerous fallacy, which at once destroys all religious liberty, because he being of course judge of that tendency will make his opinions the rule of judgment, and approve or condemn the sentiments of others only as they shall square with or differ from his own; that it is time enough for the rightful purposes of civil government, for its officers to interfere when principles break out into overt acts against peace and good order; and finally, that truth is great and will prevail if left to herself, that she is the proper and sufficient antagonist to error, and has nothing to fear from the conflict, unless by human interposition disarmed of her natural weapons, free argument and debate, errors ceasing to be dangerous when it is permitted freely to contradict them.

II

Be it enacted by the General Assembly, that no man shall be compelled to frequent or support any religious worship, place or ministry whatsoever, nor shall be enforced, restrained, molested, or burthened in his body or goods, nor shall otherwise suffer on account of his religious opinions or belief; but that all men shall be free to profess, and by argument to maintain, their opinion in matters of religion, and that the same shall in no wise diminish, enlarge or affect their civil capacities.

III

And though we well know that this assembly, elected by the people for the ordinary purposes of legislation only, have no power to restrain the acts of succeeding assemblies constituted with powers equal to our own, and that therefore to declare this act to be irrevocable would be of no effect in law; yet as we are free to declare, and do declare, that the rights hereby asserted are of the natural rights of mankind, and that if any act shall hereafter be passed to repeal the present, or to narrow its operation, such act will be an infringement of natural right.

2 Virginia Bill of Rights   12 June 1776

Reprinted in H. S. Commager (ed.) *Documents of American History* 1963

A declaration of rights made by the representatives of the good people of Virginia, assembled in full and free convention; which rights do pertain to them and their posterity, as the basis and foundation of government.

1. That all men are by nature equally free and independent, and have certain inherent rights, of which, when they enter into a state of society, they cannot by any compact deprive or divest their posterity; namely, the enjoyment of life and liberty, with the means of acquiring and possessing property, and pursuing and obtaining happiness and safety.

2. That all power is vested in, and consequently derived from, the people; that magistrates are their trustees and servants, and at all times amenable to them.

3. That government is, or ought to be, instituted for the common benefit, protection, and security of the people, nation, or community; of all the various modes and forms of government, that is best which is capable of producing the greatest degree of happiness and safety and is most effectually secured against the danger of maladministration; and that when any government shall be found inadequate or contrary to these purposes, a majority of the community hath an indubitable, unalienable and indefeasible right to reform, alter or abolish it, in such manner as shall be judged most conducive to the public weal.

4. That no man, or set of men, are entitled to exclusive or separate emoluments or privileges from the community, but in consideration of publick services; which, not being descendible, neither ought the offices of magistrate, legislator or judge to be hereditary.

5. That the legislative and executive powers of the state should

be separate and distinct from the judiciary; and that the members of the two first may be restrained from oppression, by feeling and participating the burthens of the people, they should, at fixed periods, be reduced to a private station, return into that body from which they were originally taken, and the vacancies be supplied by frequent, certain, and regular elections, in which all, or any part of the former members to be again eligible or ineligible, as the laws shall direct.

6. That elections of members to serve as representatives of the people in assembly, ought to be free; and that all men having sufficient evidence of permanent common interest with, and attachment to the community, have the right of suffrage, and cannot be taxed or deprived of their property for publick uses, without their own consent, or that of their representatives so elected, nor bound by any law to which they have not, in like manner, assented for the public good.

7. That all power of suspending laws, or the execution of laws, by any authority without consent of the representatives of the people, is injurious to their rights, and ought not to be exercised.

8. That in all capital or criminal prosecutions a man hath a right to demand the cause and nature of his accusation, to be confronted with the accusers and witnesses, to call for evidence in his favour, and to a speedy trial by an impartial jury of his vicinage, without whose unanimous consent he cannot be found guilty; nor can he be compelled to give evidence against himself; that no man be deprived of his liberty, except by the law of the land or the judgment of his peers.

9. That excessive bail ought not to be required, nor excessive fines imposed, nor cruel and unusual punishments inflicted.

10. That general warrants, whereby an officer or messenger may be commanded to search suspected places without evidence of a fact committed, or to seize any person or persons not named, or whose offence is not particularly described and supported by evidence, are grievous and oppressive, and ought not to be granted.

11. That in controversies respecting property, and in suits between man and man, the ancient trial by jury is preferable to any other, and ought to be held sacred.

12. That the freedom of the press is one of the great bulwarks of liberty, and can never be restrained but by despotick governments.

13. That a well-regulated militia, composed of the body of the people trained to arms, is the proper, natural and safe defence of a free state; that standing armies in time of peace should be avoided as dangerous to liberty; and that in all cases the military should be under strict subordination to, and governed by, the civil power.

14. That the people have a right to uniform government; and, therefore, that no government separate from, or independent of, the government of Virginia, ought to be erected or established within the limits thereof.

15. That no free government, or the blessings of liberty, can be preserved to any people, but by a firm adherence to justice, moderation, temperance, frugality and virtue, and by frequent recurrence to fundamental principles.

16. That religion, or the duty which we owe to our Creator, and the manner of discharging it, can be directed only by reason and conviction, not by force or violence; and therefore all men are equally entitled to the free exercise of religion, according to the dictates of conscience; and that it is the mutual duty of all to practise Christian forbearance, love, and charity towards each other.

3 Thomas Jefferson
Jefferson's Revised Penal Code

from 'Notes on the State of Virginia'   1782. Reprinted in
P. L. Ford (ed.), The *Writings of Thomas Jefferson*, vol. 3, 1894

I   Crimes whose punishment extends to *Life*.
   1. High treason. Death by hanging.
                         Forfeiture of lands and goods to the commonwealth.
   2. Petty treason. Death by hanging.   Dissection.
                         Forfeiture of half the lands and goods to the representatives of the party slain.

3. Murder.	1. By poison.	Death by poison. Forfeiture of one-half, as before.
	2. In duel.	Death by hanging. Gibbeting, if the challenger. Forfeiture of one-half as before, unless it be the party challenged, then the forfeiture is to the commonwealth.
	3. In any other way.	Death by hanging. Forfeiture of one-half as before.

4. Manslaughter. The second offence is murder.

II Crimes whose punishment goes to *Limb*.

1. Rape
2. Sodomy   } Dismemberment.
3. Maiming   } Retaliation, and the forfeiture of half of the lands and
4. Disfiguring   } goods to the sufferer.

III Crimes punishable by *Labor*.

1. Manslaughter, 1st offence.	Labor VII years for the public.	Forfeiture of half, as in murder.
2. Counterfeiting money.	Labor VI years.	Forfeiture of lands and goods to the commonwealth.
3. Arson. 4. Asportation of vessels.	} Labor V years.	Reparation threefold.
5. Robbery. 6. Burglary.	} Labor IV years.	Reparation double.
7. House-breaking. 8. Horse-stealing.	} Labor III years.	Reparation.
9. Grand larceny.	Labor II years.	Reparation. Pillory.
10. Petty larceny.	Labor I year.	Reparation. Pillory.
11. Pretensions to witch-craft, &c.	Ducking.	Stripes.
12. Excusable homicide. 13. Suicide. 14. Apostacy. Heresy.	} To be pitied, not punished.	

4 Thomas Jefferson

Hymn to the Husbandman

from Merrill D. Peterson, *Thomas Jefferson and the New Nation* 1970

Those who labor in the earth are the chosen people of God, if ever He had a chosen people, whose breasts He has made His peculiar deposit for substantial and genuine virtue. It is the focus in which He keeps alive that sacred fire, which otherwise might escape from the face of the earth. Corruption of morals in the mass of cultivators is a phenomenon of which no age nor nation has furnished an example. It is the mark set on those who, not looking up to heaven, to their own soil and industry, as does the husbandman, for their subsistence, depend for it on casualties and caprice of customers. Dependence begets subservience and venality, suffocates the germ of virtue, and prepares fit tools for the designs of ambition. This, the natural progress and consequence of the arts, has sometimes perhaps been retarded by accidental circumstances; but, generally speaking, the proportion which the aggregate of the other classes of citizens bears in any State to that of its husbandmen, is the proportion of its unsound to its healthy parts, and is a good enough barometer whereby to measure its degree of corruption. While we have land to labor then, let us never wish to see our citizens occupied at a work-bench, or twirling a distaff.

5 Anonymous

Satire on Jefferson written while he was Vice-President
1798

from Merrill D. Peterson, *Thomas Jefferson and the New Nation* 1970

Now each Jacobinic face
Redden'd with guilt, with fear, disgrace,
While thro' the land, with keenest ire,
Kindles the patriotic fire!
See Jefferson with deep dismay,
Shrink from the piercing eye of day,
Lest from the tottering chair of state,
The storm should hurl him to his fate!
Great Sire of stories past belief!
Historian of the Mingo Chief! [1]
Philosopher of Indian's hair!
Inventor of a rocking chair!
The Correspondent of Mazze'! [2]
And Banneker [3] less black than he!

[1.] Mingo Chief; the story was told in Jefferson's *Notes on Virginia*.
[2.] Mazzei was a Florentine, to whom Jefferson wrote a private letter critical of the US government: the letter was published without permission.
[3.] Banneker: a contemporary Negro astronomer.

With joy we find these rise from coguing
With Judge M'Kean,[4] and 'foolish Logan',[5]
And reeling down the factious dance,
Send Deborah's husband off to France,
To tell the Frenchmen, to their cost,
They reckon'd here without their host;
Whilst thou, to smooth the ills of life,
Held sweet communion with the wife.

6 Anonymous
A Satire on Jefferson

from the *Boston Gazette*   1798

A Song
supposed to have been written by the
Sage of Monticello
(to the tune of Yankee Doodle)

Of all the damsels on the green
    On mountain, or in valley,
A lass so luscious ne'er was seen
    As Monticellian Sally.[1]

Yankee doodle, who's the noodle?
    What wife were half so handy?
To breed a flock of slaves for stock,
    A blackamoor's the dandy.

Search every town and city through,
    Search market street and alley;
No dance at dusk shall meet your view,
    So yielding as my Sally.

[4.] M'Kean was a Republican leader from Pennsylvania.
[5.] George and Deborah Logan were Quakers and admirers of the French Revolution. Jefferson gave Logan a certificate of good character before he went off to France.
[1.] 'Sally' was Sally Hemings, a mulatto girl. Jefferson was accused of fathering a number of her children; his detractors nicknamed her 'The African Venus'.

177 A Satirical Bequest

Verse
When pressed by loads of state affairs,
    I seek to sport and dally,
The sweetest solace of my cares
    Is in the lap of Sally.

Verse
Let Yankee parsons preach the worst –
    Let Tory Wittlings rally!
You men of morals! and be curst,
    You would snap like sharks for Sally.

7 Anonymous
A Satirical Bequest

from *Porcupine's Gazette*   1797

To Thomas Jefferson, philosopher, I leave a curious Norway spider, with a hundred legs and nine pair of eyes; likewise the first black cutthroat general he can catch hold of, to be flayed alive, in order to determine with more certainty the real cause of the dark colour of his skin.

8 Anonymous
The Grand Question Stated

from *Gazette of the United States*   1800

At the present solemn moment the only question to be asked by every American, laying his hand on his heart, is 'Shall I continue in allegiance to
GOD – AND A RELIGIOUS PRESIDENT;
or impiously declare for
JEFFERSON – AND NO GOD!!!'

9 Anonymous

Republican Election Song   1800

Reprinted in Merrill D. Peterson, *Thomas Jefferson and the New Nation*   1970

Rejoice, Columbia's sons, rejoice
To tyrants never bend the knee
But join with heart and soul and voice
For Jefferson and Liberty.

10 Thomas Jefferson

First Inaugural Address   4 March 1801

Reprinted in H. S. Commager (ed.) *Documents of American History*   1963

Friends and Fellow Citizens:

Called upon to undertake the duties of the first executive office of our country, I avail myself of the presence of that portion of my fellow-citizens which is here assembled to express my grateful thanks for the favor with which they have been pleased to look toward me, to declare a sincere consciousness that the task is above my talents, and that I approach it with those anxious and awful presentiments which the greatness of the charge and the weakness of my powers so justly inspire. A rising nation, spread over a wide and fruitful land, traversing all the seas with the rich productions of their industry, engaged in commerce with nations who feel power and forget right, advancing rapidly to destinies beyond the reach of mortal eye – when I contemplate these transcendent objects, and see the honor, the happiness, and the hopes of this beloved country committed to the issue and the auspices of this day, I shrink from the contemplation, and humble myself before the magnitude of the undertaking. Utterly, indeed, should I despair did not the presence of many whom I here see remind me that in the other high authorities provided by our Constitution I shall find resources of wisdom, of virtue, and of zeal on which to rely under all difficulties. To you, then, gentlemen, who are charged with the sovereign functions of legislation, and to those associated with you, I look with encouragement for that guidance and support which may enable us to steer with safety the vessel in which we are all embarked amidst the conflicting elements of a troubled world.

During the contest of opinion through which we have passed the animation of discussions and of exertions has sometimes worn an aspect which might impose on strangers unused to think freely and to speak and to write what they think; but this being now decided by the voice of the nation, announced according to the rules of the Constitution, all will, of course, arrange themselves under the will of the law, and unite in common efforts for the common good. All, too, will bear in mind this sacred principle, that though the will of the majority is in all cases to prevail, that will to be rightful must be reasonable; that the minority possess their equal rights, which equal law must protect, and to violate would be oppression. Let us, then, fellow-citizens, unite with one heart and mind. Let us restore to social intercourse that harmony and affection without which liberty and even life itself are but dreary things. And let us reflect that, having banished from our land that religious intolerance under which mankind so long bled and suffered, we have yet gained little if we countenance a political intolerance as despotic, as wicked, and capable of as bitter and bloody persecutions. During the throes and convulsions of the ancient world, during the agonizing spasms of infuriated man, seeking through blood and slaughter his long-lost liberty, it was not wonderful that the agitation of the billows should reach even this distant and peaceful shore; that this should be more felt and feared by some and less by others, and should divide opinions as to measures of safety. But every difference of opinion is not a difference of principle. We have called by different names brethren of the same principle. We are all Republicans, we are all Federalists. If there be any among us who would wish to dissolve this Union or to change its republican form, let them stand undisturbed as monuments of the safety with which error of opinion may be tolerated where reason is left free to combat it. I know, indeed, that some honest men fear that a republican government can not be strong, that this Government is not strong enough; but would the honest patriot, in the full tide of successful experiment, abandon a government which has so far kept us free and firm on the theoretic and visionary fear that this Government, the world's best hope, may by possibility want energy to preserve itself? I trust not. I believe this, on the contrary, the strongest Government on earth. I believe it the only one where every man, at the call of the law, would fly to the standard of the law, and would meet invasions of the public order as his own personal concern. Sometimes it is said that man can not be trusted with the government of himself. Can he, then, be trusted with the government of others? Or have we found angels in the forms of kings to govern him? Let history answer this question.

Let us, then, with courage and confidence pursue our own Federal and Republican principles, our attachment to union and representative government. Kindly separated by nature and a wide ocean from the exterminating havoc of one quarter of the globe; too high-minded to endure the degradations of the others; possessing a chosen country, with room enough for our descendants to the thousandth and thousandth generation; entertaining a due sense of our equal right to the use of our own faculties, to the acquisitions of our own industry, to honor and confidence from our fellow-citizens, resulting not from birth, but from our actions and their sense of them; enlightened by a benign religion, professed, indeed, and practiced in various forms, yet all of them inculcating honesty, truth, temperance, gratitude, and the love of man; acknowledging and adoring an overruling Providence, which by all its dispensations proves that it delights in the happiness of man here and his greater happiness hereafter – with all these blessings, what more is necessary to make us a happy and a prosperous people? Still one thing more, fellow-citizens – a wise and frugal Government, which shall restrain men from injuring one another, shall leave them otherwise free to regulate their own pursuits of industry and improvement, and shall not take from the mouth of labor the bread it has earned. This is the sum of good government, and this is necessary to close the circle of our felicities.

About to enter, fellow-citizens, on the exercise of duties which comprehend everything dear and valuable to you, it is proper you should understand what I deem the essential principles of our Government, and consequently those which ought to shape its Administration. I will compress them within the narrowest compass they will bear, stating the general principle, but not all its limitations. Equal and exact justice to all men, of whatever state or persuasion, religious or political; peace, commerce and honest friendship with all nations, entangling alliances with none; the support of the State governments in all their rights, as the most competent administrations for our domestic concerns and the surest bulwarks against antirepublican tendencies; the preservation of the General Government in its whole constitutional vigor, as the sheet anchor of our peace at home and safety abroad; a jealous care of the right of election by the people – a mild and safe corrective of abuses which are lopped by the sword of revolution where peaceable remedies are unprovided; absolute acquiescence in the decisions of the majority, the vital principle of republics, from which is no appeal but to force, the vital principle and immediate parent of despotism; a well-disciplined militia, our best reliance in peace and for the first moments of war, till regulars may relieve them; the supremacy of the civil over the military authority; economy in the public expense, that labor may be lightly burthened; the honest payment of our debts and sacred preservation of the public faith; encouragement of agriculture, and of commerce as its handmaid; the diffusion of information and arraignment of all abuses at the bar of the public reason; freedom of religion; freedom of the press, and freedom of person under the protection of the habeas corpus, and trial by juries impartially selected. These principles form the bright constellation which has gone before us and guided our steps through an age of revolution and reformation. The wisdom of our sages and blood of our heroes have been devoted to their attainment. They should be the creed of our political faith, the text of civic instruction, the touchstone by which to try the services of those we trust; and should we wander from them in moments of error or of alarm, let us hasten to retrace our steps and to regain the road which alone leads to peace, liberty and safety.

I repair, then, fellow-citizens, to the post you have assigned me. With experience enough in subordinate offices to have seen the difficulties of this the greatest of all, I have learnt to expect that it will rarely fall to the lot of imperfect man to retire from this station with the reputation and the favor which bring him into it. Without pretensions to that high confidence you reposed in our first and greatest revolutionary character, whose preeminent services had entitled him to the first place in his country's love and destined for him the fairest page in the volume of faithful history, I ask so much confidence only as may give firmness and effect to the legal administration of your affairs. I shall often go wrong through defect of judgment. When right, I shall often be thought wrong by those whose positions will not command a view of the whole ground. I ask your indulgence for my own errors, which will never be intentional, and your support against the errors of others, who may condemn what they would not if seen in all its parts. The approbation implied by your suffrage is a great consolation to me for the past, and my future solicitude will be to retain the good opinion of those who have bestowed it in advance, to conciliate that of others by doing them all the good in my power, and to be instrumental to the happiness and freedom of all.

Relying, then, on the patronage of your good will, I advance with obedience to the work, ready to retire from it whenever you become sensible how much better choice it is in your power to make. And may that Infinite Power which rules the destinies of the universe lead our councils to what is best, and give them a favorable issue for your peace and prosperity.

11 William Cullen Bryant[1]
The Embargo

from 'The Embargo: A Satire' 1809

> But quit the lesser game, indignant Muse,
> And to thy country turn thy nobler views.
> Ill-fated clime! condemn'd to feel th' extremes
> Of a weak ruler's philosophic dreams;
> Driv'n headlong on to ruin's fateful brink,
> When will thy Country feel, when will she think!

[1.] William Cullen Bryant was only thirteen when he wrote this.

Wake Muse of Satire, in the cause of trade,
Thou scourge of miscreants who the laws evade!
Dart thy keen glances, knit thy threat'ning brows,
And hurl thine arrows at fair Commerce's foes!

Much injur'd Commerce! 'tis thy falling cause,
Which, from obscurity, a stripling draws;
And were his powers but equal to his zeal,
Thy dastard foes his keen reproach should feel.
Curse of our Nation, source of countless woes,
From whose dark womb unreckon'd misery flows;
Th' embargo rages like a sweeping wind,
Fear low'rs before, and famine stalks behind.
What words, oh, Muse! can paint the mournful scene,
The saddening street, the desolated green;
How hungry labourers leave their toil and sigh,
And sorrow droops in each desponding eye!

See the bold sailor from the ocean torn,
His element, sink friendless and forlorn!
His suffering spouse the tear of anguish shed
His starving children cry in vain for bread!

The farmer, since supporting trade is fled,
Leaves the rude joke, and cheerless hangs his head;
Misfortunes fall, an unremitting shower,
Debts follow debts, on taxes, taxes pour.

See in his stores his hoarded produce rot,
Or sheriff sales his profits bring to naught;
Disheartening cares in thronging myriads flow,
Till down he sinks to poverty and woe! . . .²

[2.] In the second edition he added after 'poverty and woe!'
　　　Ye, who rely on Jeffersonism still;
　　　And say that fancy paints ideal ill;
　　　Go, on the wings of observation fly,
　　　States, counties, towns, remark with keen review,
　　　Let *facts* convince and own the picture true!

We, who seven years erst brav'd Britannia's power,
By Heaven supported in the gloomiest hour;
For whom our Sages plann'd, our Heroes bled,
Whom WASHINGTON, our pride and glory led;
Till Heaven, propitious did our efforts crown,
With freedom, commerce, plenty, and renown!

When shall this land, some courteous angel say,
Throw off a weak, and erring ruler's sway?
Rise, injur'd people, vindicate your cause!
And prove your love of Liberty and laws;
Oh wrest, sole refuge of a sinking land,
The sceptre from the slave's imbecile hand!
Oh ne'er consent, obsequious, to advance
The *willing vassal* of imperious France!
Correct that suffrage you misus'd before,
And lift your voice above a Congress' roar!
And thou, the scorn of every patriot name,
Thy country's ruin, and her council's shame!
Poor servile thing! derision of the brave!
Who erst from Tarleton fled to Carter's cave;[3]
Thou, who, when menac'd by perfidious Gaul,
Didst prostrate to her whisker'd minion fall;[4]
And when our cash her empty bags supplied,
Didst meanly strive the foul disgrace to hide;
Go, wretch, resign the presidential chair,
Disclose thy secret measures foul or fair,
Go, search, with curious eye, for horned frogs,[5]
Mongst the wild wastes of Louisianian bogs;
Or where Ohio rolls his turbid stream,
Dig for huge bones, thy glory and thy theme;

[3.] The flight to Carter's cave is a renewal of the charge of cowardice before the British advance when Jefferson was Governor of Virginia in 1781.

[4.] The 'whisker'd minion' is probably M. Marbos, France's Minister of Finance, who negotiated the sale of Louisiana.

[5.] Jefferson was interested in natural history and in the discovery of the remains of prehistoric animals.

Go scan, Philosophist; thy ****** charms,[6]
And sink supinely in her sable arms;
But quit to abler hands, the helm of state,
Nor image ruin on thy country's fate!

But vain are reason, eloquence and art,
And vain the warm effusions of the heart.
Ev'n while I sing, see, *faction* urge her claim,
Mislead with falsehood, and with zeal inflame,
Lift her broad banner, spread her empire wide,
And stalk triumphant, with a fury's stride.
She blows her brazen trump, and at the sound,
A motley throng obedient flock around;
A mist of changing hue o'er all she flings,
And darkness perches on her dragon wings!

As Johnson deep, as Addison refin'd,
And skill'd to pour conviction o'er the mind,
Oh might some Patriot rise! the gloom dispel,
Chase error's mist, and break her magic spell!

But vain the wish, for hark! the murmuring meed,
Of hoarse applause, from yonder shed proceed;
Enter, and view the thronging concourse there,
Intent, with gaping mouth, and stupid stare,
While in the midst their supple leader stands,
Harangues aloud, and flourishes his hands;
To adulation tunes his servile throat,
And sues, successful, for each blockhead's vote.

'Oh, were I made a ruler in the land!
Your rights, no man can better understand;
For the dear people, how my bowels yearn!
That *such* may govern, be your chief concern:
Then federal tyranny shall flee away,

[6.] The asterisks conceal nothing more formidable than 'Sally's' – the
Negro woman whom Jefferson was accused of taking to his bed.

And *mild democracy* confirm her sway.' [7]
The powerful influence of the knaves address,
In capers droll, the foolish dupes confess,
With *horrid* shouts the affrighted sky is rent,
And high in air their tatter'd hats are sent.

But should truth shine, distinguishingly bright,
And lay his falsehoods naked to the fight;
He tries new arts to blind their willing eyes,
Feeds with new flatteries, hammers out new lies;
Exerts his influence, urges all his weight,
To blast the laurels of the good and great;
Till reconfirm'd the fools uphold him still,
Their creed, his *dictum*, and their law, his will.

12 Thomas Jefferson

Letter to Peter Carr   7 September 1814

Reprinted in Philip S. Foner (ed.), *Basic Writings of Thomas Jefferson*   1944

Dear Sir: On the subject of the academy or college proposed to be established in our neighbourhood, I promised the trustees that I would prepare for them a plan, adapted, in the first instance, to our slender funds, but susceptible of being enlarged, either by their own growth or by accession from other quarters.

I have long entertained the hope that this, our native State,

[7.] Jefferson's appeal is satirically intensified in the second edition:
　　　　'The advocate of *liberty* I stand –
　　　　Oh were I made a ruler in the land!
　　　　Your interests none more cherishes than I,
　　　　In your sweet service, may I live and die!
　　　　For the dear *people*, how my bowels yearn! –
　　　　That *such* may govern be your chief concern;
　　　　Then *federalism*, and all its lordling train,
　　　　Shall fall disgrac'd before our *equal* reign;
　　　　Dismay'd, diminish'd, our fair presence shun,
　　　　As shadows shorten to the rising sun;
　　　　Spontaneous banquets shall succeed to want,
　　　　No tax shall vex you, and no sheriff haunt.'

would take up the subject of education, and make an establishment, either with or without incorporation, into that of William and Mary, where every branch of science, deemed useful at this day, should be taught in its highest degree. With this view, I have lost no occasion of making myself acquainted with the organization of the best seminaries in other countries, and with the opinions of the most enlightened individuals, on the subject of the sciences worthy of a place in such an institution. In order to prepare what I have promised our trustees, I have lately revised these several plans with attention; and I am struck with the diversity of arrangement observable in them — no two alike. Yet, I have no doubt that these several arrangements have been the subject of mature reflection, by wise and learned men, who, contemplating local circumstances, have adapted them to the conditions of the section of society for which they have been framed. I am strengthened in this conclusion by an examination of each separately, and a conviction that no one of them, if adopted without change, would be suited to the circumstances and pursuit of our country. The example they set, then, is authority for us to select from their different institutions the materials which are good for us, and, with them, to erect a structure, whose arrangement shall correspond with our own social condition, and shall admit of enlargement in proportion to the encouragement it may merit and receive. As I may not be able to attend the meetings of the trustees, I will make you the depository of my ideas on the subject, which may be corrected, as you proceed, by the better view of others, and adapted, from time to time, to the prospects which open upon us, and which cannot be specifically seen and provided for.

In the first place, we must ascertain with precision the object of our institution, by taking a survey of the general field of science, and marking out the portion we mean to occupy at first, and the ultimate extension of our views beyond that, should we be enabled to render it, in the end, as comprehensive as we would wish.

1 Elementary Schools

It is highly interesting to our country, and it is the duty of its functionaries, to provide that every citizen in it should receive an education proportioned to the condition and pursuits of his life. The mass of our citizens may be divided into two classes – the laboring and the learned. The laboring will need the first grade of education to qualify them for their pursuits and duties; the learned will need it as a foundation for further acquirements. A plan was formerly proposed to the Legislature of this State for laying off every county into hundreds or wards of five or six miles square, within each of which should be a school for the education of the children of the ward, wherein they should receive three years' instruction gratis, in reading, writing, arithmetic as far as fractions, the roots and ratios, and geography. The Legislature at one time tried an ineffectual expedient for introducing this plan, which having failed, it is hoped they will some day resume it in a more promising form.

2 General Schools

At the discharging of the pupils from the elementary schools, the two classes separate – those destined for labor will engage in the business of agriculture, or enter into apprenticeships to such handicraft art as may be their choice; their companions, destined to the pursuits of science, will proceed to the college, which will consist, 1st of general schools; and, 2d, of professional schools. The general schools will constitute the second grade of education.

The learned class may still be subdivided into two sections: 1, Those who are destined for learned professions, as means of livelihood; and, 2, The wealthy, who, possessing independent fortunes, may aspire to share in conducting the affairs of the nation, or to live with usefulness and respect in the private ranks of life. Both of these sections will require instruction in all the higher branches of science; the wealthy to qualify them for either public or private life; the professional section will need those branches, especially, which are the basis of their future profession, and a general knowledge of the others, as auxiliary to that, and necessary to their standing and association with the scientific class. All the branches, then, of useful science, ought to be taught in the general schools, to a competent degree, in the first instance. These sciences may be arranged into three departments, not rigorously scientific, indeed, but sufficiently so for our purposes. These are, I Language; II Mathematics; III Philosophy.

I Language

In the first department, I would arrange a distinct science.
1, Languages and History, ancient and modern; 2, Grammar; 3, Belles Lettres; 4, Rhetoric and Oratory; 5, A school for the deaf, dumb and blind. History is here associated with languages, not as a kindred subject, but on the principle of economy, because both may be attained by the same course of reading, if books are selected with that view.

II Mathematics

In the department of Mathematics, I should give place distinctly: 1, Mathematics pure; 2, Physico-Mathematics; 3, Physics; 4, Chemistry; 5, Natural History, *to wit*: Mineralogy; 6, Botany; and 7, Zoology; 8, Anatomy; 9, the Theory of Medicine.

III Philosophy

In the Philosophical department, I should distinguish: 1, Ideology; 2, Ethics; 3, the Law of Nature and Nations; 4, Government; 5, Political Economy.

But, some of these terms being used by different writers, in different degrees of extension, I shall define exactly what I mean to comprehend in each of them.

I 3. Within the term of Belles Lettres I include poetry and composition generally, and criticism.

II 1. I consider pure mathematics as the science of, 1, Numbers, and 2, Measure in the abstract; that of numbers comprehending Arithmetic, Algebra and Fluxions; that of Measure (under the general appellation of Geometry), comprehending Trigonometry, plane and spherical, conic sections, and transcendental curves.

II 2. Physico-Mathematics treat of physical subjects by the aid of mathematical calculation. These are Mechanics, Statics, Hydrostatics, Hydrodynamics, Navigation, Astronomy, Geography, Optics, Pneumatics, Acoustics.

II 3. Physics, or Natural Philosophy (not entering the limits of Chemistry), treat of natural substances, their properties, mutual relations and action. They particularly examine the subjects of motion, action, magnetism, electricity, galvanism, light, meteorology, with an etc. not easily enumerated. These definitions and specifications render immaterial the question whether I use the generic terms in the exact degree of comprehension in which others use them; to be understood is all that is necessary to the present object.

3 Professional Schools

At the close of this course the students separate; the wealthy retiring, with a sufficient stock of knowledge, to improve themselves to any degree to which their views may lead them, and the professional section to the professional schools, constituting the third grade of education, and teaching the particular sciences which the individuals of this section mean to pursue, with more minuteness and detail than was within the scope of the general schools for the second grade of instruction. In these professional schools each science is to be taught in the highest degree it has yet attained. They are to be the

1st *Department*, the fine arts, to wit: Civil Architecture, Gardening, Painting, Sculpture, and the Theory of Music; the

2d *Department*, Architecture, Military and Naval; Projectiles, Rural Economy (comprehending Agriculture, Horticulture and Veterinary), Technical Philosophy, the Practice of Medicine, Materia Medica, Pharmacy and Surgery. In the

3d *Department*, Theology and Ecclesiastical History; Law, Municipal and Foreign.

To these professional schools will come those who separated at the close of their first elementary course, to wit:

The lawyer to the school of law.

The ecclesiastic to that of theology and ecclesiastical history.

The physician to those of medicine, materia medica, pharmacy and surgery.

The military man to that of military and naval architecture and projectiles.

The agricultor to that of rural economy.

The gentleman, the architect, the pleasure gardener, painter and musician to the school of fine arts.

And to that of technical philosophy will come the mariner,

carpenter, shipwright, pumpmaker, clockmaker, machinist, optician, metallurgist, founder, cutler, druggist, brewer, vintner, distiller, dyer, painter, bleacher, soapmaker, tanner, powdermaker, saltmaker, glassmaker, to learn as much as shall be necessary to pursue their art understandingly, of the sciences of geometry, mechanics, statics, hydrostatics, hydraulics, hydrodynamics, navigation, astronomy, geography, optics, pneumatics, physics, chemistry, natural history, botany, mineralogy and pharmacy.

The school of technical philosophy will differ essentially in its functions from the other professional schools. The others are instituted to ramify and dilate the particular sciences taught in the schools of the second grade on a general scale only. The technical school is to abridge those which were taught there too much *in extenso* for the limited wants of the artificer or practical man. These artificers must be grouped together, according to the particular branch of science in which they need elementary and practical instruction; and a special lecture or lectures should be prepared for each group. And these lectures should be given in the evening, so as not to interrupt the labors of the day. The school, particularly, should be maintained wholly at the public expense, on the same principles with that of the ward schools. Through the whole of the collegiate course, at the hours of recreation on certain days, all the students should be taught the manual exercise; military evolutions and manoeuvers should be under a standing organization as a military corps, and with proper officers to train and command them.

A tabular statement of this distribution of the sciences will place the system of instruction more particularly in view:

1st or Elementary Grade in the Ward Schools.
Reading, Writing, Arithmetic, Geography.

2d, or General Grade.
1. Language and History, ancient and modern.
2. Mathematics, *viz.*: Mathematics pure, Physico-Mathematics, Physics, Chemistry, Anatomy, Theory of Medicine, Zoology, Botany and Mineralogy.
3. Philosophy, *viz.*: Ideology, and Ethics, Law of Nature and Nations, Government, Political Economy.

3d, or Professional Grades.

Theology and Ecclesiastical History; Law, Municipal and Foreign; Practice of Medicine; Materia Medica and Pharmacy; Surgery; Architecture, Military and Naval, and Projectiles; Technical Philosophy; Rural Economy; Fine Arts.

On this survey of the field of science, I recur to the question, what portion of it we mark out for the occupation of our institution? With the first grade of education we shall have nothing to do. The sciences of the second grade are our first object; and, to adapt them to our slender beginnings, we must separate them into groups, comprehending many sciences each, and greatly more, in the first instance, than ought to be imposed on, or can be competently conducted by a single professor permanently. They must be subdivided from time to time, as our means increase, until each professor shall have no more under his care than he can attend to with advantage to his pupils and ease to himself. For the present, we may group the sciences into professorships, as follows, subject, however, to be changed, according to the qualifications of the persons we may be able to engage.

I *Professorship*
    Language and History, ancient and modern.
    Belles Lettres, Rhetoric and Oratory.

II *Professorship*
    Mathematics pure, Physico-Mathematics,
    Physics, Anatomy, Medicine, Theory.

III *Professorship*
    Chemistry, Zoology, Botany, Mineralogy.

IV *Professorship*
    Philosophy.

The organization of the branch of the institution which respects its government, police and economy, depending on principles which have no affinity with those of its institution, may be the subject of separate and subsequent consideration.

13 **Thomas Jefferson**
The Rockfish Gap Report

from 'The Rockfish Gap Report to the Legislature of Virginia
Relative to the University of Virginia 1–14 August 1818',
Analectic Magazine, vol. 13   February 1819

In proceeding to the third and fourth duties prescribed by the
Legislature, of reporting 'the branches of learning, which should
be taught in the University, and the number and description of
the professorships they will require', the Commissioners were
first to consider at what point it was understood that university
education should commence. Certainly not with the alphabet,
for reasons of expediency and impracticability, as well from the
obvious sense of the Legislature, who, in the same act, make
other provision for the primary instruction of the poor children,
expecting, doubtless, that in other cases it would be provided
by the parent, or become, perhaps, subject of future and further
attention of the Legislature. The objects of this primary education determine its character and limits. These objects would be,

To give to every citizen the information he needs for the
transaction of his own business;

To enable him to calculate for himself, and to express and
preserve his ideas, his contracts and accounts, in writing;

To improve, by reading, his morals and faculties;

To understand his duties to his neighbours and country, and
to discharge with competence the functions confided to him by
either;

To know his rights; to exercise with order and justice those
he retains; to choose with discretion the fiduciary of those he
delegates; and to notice their conduct with diligence, with can-
dor, and judgement;

And, in general, to observe with intelligence and faithfulness
all the social relations under which he shall be placed.

To instruct the mass of our citizens in these, their rights,
interests and duties, as men and citizens, being then the objects
of education in the primary schools, whether private or public,
in them should be taught reading, writing and numerical arith-

metic, the elements of mensuration (useful in so many callings), and the outlines of geography and history.

And this brings us to the point at which are to commence the higher branches of education, of which the Legislature require the development; those, for example, which are,

To form the statesmen, legislators and judges, on whom public prosperity and individual happiness are so much to depend;

To expound the principles and structure of government, the laws which regulate the intercourse of nations, those formed municipally for our own government, and a sound spirit of legislation, which, banishing all arbitrary and unnecessary restraint on individual action, shall leave us free to do whatever does not violate the equal rights of another;

To harmonize and promote the interests of agriculture, manufactures and commerce, and by well informed views of political economy to give a free scope to the public industry;

To develop the reasoning faculties of our youth, enlarge their minds, cultivate their morals, and instill into them the precepts of virtue and order;

To enlighten them with mathematical and physical sciences, which advance the arts, and administer to the health, the subsistence, and comforts of human life;

And, generally, to form them to habits of reflection and correct action, rendering them examples of virtue to others, and of happiness within themselves.

These are the objects of that higher grade of education, the benefits and blessings of which the Legislature now propose to provide for the good and ornament of their country, the gratification and happiness of their fellow-citizens, of the parent especially, and his progeny, on which all his affections are concentrated.

In entering on this field, the Commissioners are aware that they have to encounter much difference of opinion as to the extent which it is expedient that this institution should occupy. Some good men, and even of respectable information, consider the learned sciences as useless acquirements; some think they do not better the condition of man; and others that education, like private and individual concerns, should be left to private individual effort; not reflecting that an establishment embracing all the sciences which may be useful and even necessary in the various vocations of life, with the buildings and apparatus belonging to each, are far beyond the reach of individual means, and must either derive existence from public patronage, or not exist at all. This would leave us, then, without those callings which depend on education, or send us to other countries to seek the instruction they require. But the Commissioners are happy in considering the statute under which they are assembled as proof that the Legislature is far from the abandonment of objects so interesting. They are sensible that the advantages of well-directed education, moral, political and economical, are truly above all estimate. Education generates habits of application, of order, and the love of virtue; and controls, by the force of habit, any innate obliquities in our moral organization. We should be far, too, from the discouraging persuasion that man is fixed, by the law of his nature, at a given point; that his improvement is a chimera, and the hope delusive of rendering ourselves wiser, happier or better than our forefathers were. As well might it be urged that the wild and uncultivated tree, hitherto yielding sour and bitter fruit only, can never be made to yield better; yet we know that the grafting art implants a new tree on the savage stock, producing what is most estimable both in kind and degree. Education, in like manner, engrafts a new man on the native stock, and improves what in his nature was vicious and perverse into qualities of virtue and social worth. And it cannot be but that each generation succeeding to the knowledge acquired by all those who preceded it, adding to it their own acquisitions and discoveries, and handing the mass down for successive and constant accumulation, must advance the knowledge and well-being of mankind, not *infinitely*, as some have said, but *indefinitely*, and to a term which no one can fix and foresee. Indeed, we need look back half a century, to times which many now living remember well, and see the wonderful advances in the sciences and arts which have been made within that period. Some of these have rendered the elements themselves subservient to the purposes of man, have harnessed them to the yoke of his labours, and effected the great blessings of moderating his own, of accomplishing what was beyond his feeble force, and extending the comforts of life to a much enlarged circle, to those who had before known its necessaries only. That these are not the vain dreams of sanguine hope, we have before our eyes real and living examples. What, but education, has advanced us beyond the condition of our indigenous neighbours? And what chains them to their present state of barbarism and wretchedness, but a bigoted veneration for the supposed superlative wisdom of their fathers, and the preposterous idea that they are to look backward for better things, and not forward, longing, as it should seem, to return to the days of eating acorns and roots, rather than indulge in the degeneracies of civilization? And how much more encouraging to the achievements of science and improvement is this, than the desponding view that the condition of man cannot be ameliorated, that what has been must ever be, and that to secure ourselves where we are, we must tread with awful reverence in the footsteps of our fathers. This doctrine is the genuine fruit of the alliance between Church and State; the tenants of which, finding themselves but too well in their present condition, oppose all advances which might unmask their usurpations, and monopolies of honours, wealth, and power, and fear every change, as endangering the comforts they now hold. Nor must we omit to mention, among the benefits of education, the incalculable advantage of training up able counsellors to administer the affairs of our country in all its departments, legislative, executive and judiciary, and to bear their proper share in the councils of our national government; nothing more than education advancing the prosperity, the power, and the happiness of a nation.

Encouraged, therefore, by the sentiments of the Legislature, manifested in this statute, we present the following tabular statement of the branches of learning which we think should be taught in the University, forming them into groups, each of which are within the powers of a single professor:

I Languages, ancient:
  Latin
  Greek
  Hebrew

II Languages, modern:
  Anglo-Saxon
  French
  Spanish
  Italian
  German

III Mathematics, pure:
  Algebra
  Fluxions
  Geometry,
    Elementary
    Transcendental
  Architecture,
    Military
    Naval

IV Physico-Mathematics:
  Mechanics
  Statics
  Dynamics
  Pneumatics
  Acoustics
  Optics
  Astronomy
  Geography

V Physics, or Natural
  Philosophy:
  Chemistry
  Mineralogy

VI Botany:
  Zoology

VII Anatomy:
  Medicine

VIII Government:
  Political Economy
  Law of Nature and
  Nations History, being
  interwoven with
  Politics and Law

IX Law, municipal

X Ideology:
  General Grammar
  Ethics
  Rhetoric
  Belles Lettres and the
  Fine Arts

Some of the terms used in this table being subject to a difference of acceptation, it is proper to define the meaning and comprehension intended to be given them here:

Geometry, Elementary, is that of straight lines and of the circle.

Transcendental, is that of all other curves; it includes, of course, *Projectiles*, a leading branch of military art.

Military Architecture includes Fortification, another branch of that art.

Statics respect matter generally, in a state of rest, and include
    Hydrostatics, or the laws of fluids particularly, at rest
    or in equilibrio.

Dynamics, used as a general term, include
    Dynamics proper, or the laws of *solids* in motion; and
    Hydrodynamics, or Hydraulics, those of *fluids* in motion.

Pneumatics teach the theory of air, its weight, motion, con-
    densation, rarefaction &c.

Acoustics, or Phonics, the theory of sound.

Optics, the laws of light and vision.

Physics, or Physiology, in a general sense, mean the doctrine
    of the physical objects of our senses.

Chemistry is meant, with its other usual branches, to com-
    prehend the theory of agriculture.

Mineralogy, in addition to its peculiar subjects, is here under-
    stood to embrace what is real in geology.

Ideology is the doctrine of thought.

General Grammar explains the construction of language.

Some articles in this distribution of sciences will need observation. A professor is proposed for ancient languages, the
Latin, Greek, and Hebrew, particularly; but these languages
being the foundation common to all the sciences, it is difficult
to foresee what may be the extent of this school. At the same
time, no greater obstruction to industrious study could be proposed than the presence, the intrusions and the noisy turbulence
of a multitude of small boys; and if they are to be placed here
for the rudiments of the languages, they may be so numerous
that its character and value as an University will be merged in
those of a Grammar school. It is, therefore, greatly to be wished,
that preliminary schools, either on private or public establishment, could be distributed in districts through the State, as preparatory to the entrance of students into the University. The
tender age at which this part of education commences, generally
about the tenth year, would weigh heavily with parents in sending their sons to a school so distant as the central establishment
would be from most of them. Districts of such extent as that
every parent should be within a day's journey of his son at school,
would be desirable in cases of sickness, and convenient for

supplying their ordinary wants, and might be made to lessen sensibly the expense of this part of their education. And where a sparse population would not, within such a compass, furnish subjects sufficient to maintain a school, a competent enlargement of district must, of necessity, there be submitted to. At these district schools or colleges, boys should be rendered able to read the easier authors, Latin and Greek. This would be useful and sufficient for many not intended for an University education. At these, too, might be taught English grammar, the higher branches of numerical arithmetic, the geometry of straight lines and of the circle, the elements of navigation, and geography to a sufficient degree, and thus afford to greater numbers the means of being qualified for the various vocations of life, needing more instruction than merely menial or praedial labour, and the same advantages to youths whose education may have been neglected until too late to lay a foundation in the learned languages. These institutions, intermediate between the primary schools and University, might then be the passage of entrance for youths into the University, where their classical learning might be critically completed, by a study of the authors of highest degree; and it is at this stage only that they should be received at the University. Giving then a portion of their time to a finished knowledge of the Latin and Greek, the rest might be appropriated to the modern languages, or to the commencement of the course of science for which they should be destined. This would generally be about the fifteenth year of their age, when they might go with more safety and contentment to that distance from their parents. Until this preparatory provision shall be made, either the University will be overwhelmed with the grammar school, or a separate establishment, under one or more ushers, for its lower classes, will be advisable, at a mile or two distant from the general one; where, too, may be exercised the stricter government necessary for young boys, but unsuitable for youths arrived at years of discretion.

The considerations which have governed the specification of languages to be taught by the professor of modern languages were, that the French is the language of general intercourse among nations, and as a depository of human science, is unsurpassed by any other language, living or dead; that the

Spanish is highly interesting to us, as the language spoken by so great a portion of the inhabitants of our continents, with whom we shall probably have great intercourse ere long, and is that also in which is written the greater part of the earlier history of America. The Italian abounds with works of very superior order, valuable for their matter, and still more distinguished as models of the finest taste in style and composition. And the German now stands in a line with that of the most learned nations in richness and erudition and advance in the sciences. It is too of common descent with the language of our own country, a branch of the same original Gothic stock, and furnishes valuable illustrations for us. But in this point of view, the Anglo-Saxon is of peculiar value. We have placed it among the modern languages, because it is in fact that which we speak, in the earliest form in which we have knowledge of it. It has been undergoing, with time, those gradual changes which all languages, ancient and modern, have experienced; and even now needs only to be printed in the modern character and orthography to be intelligible, in a considerable degree, to an English reader. It has this value, too, above the Greek and Latin, that while it gives the radix of the mass of our language, they explain its innovations only. Obvious proofs of this have been presented to the modern reader in the disquisitions of Horn Tooke; and Fortescue Aland has well explained the great instruction which may be derived from it to a full understanding of our ancient common law, on which, as a stock, our whole system of law is engrafted. It will form the first link in the chain of an historical review of our language through all its successive changes to the present day, will constitute the foundation of that critical instruction in it which ought to be found in a seminary of general learning, and thus reward amply the few weeks of attention which would alone be requisite for its attainment; a language already fraught with all the eminent science of our parent country, the future vehicle of whatever we may ourselves achieve, and destined to occupy so much space on the globe, claims distinguished attention in American education.

Medicine, where fully taught, is usually subdivided into several professorships, but this cannot well be without the accessory of an hospital, where the student can have the benefit of attending clinical lectures, and of assisting at operations of surgery. With this accessory, the seat of our University is not yet prepared, either by its population or by the numbers of poor who would leave their own houses, and accept of the charities of an hospital. For the present, therefore, we propose but a single professor for both medicine and anatomy. By him the medical science may be taught, with a history and explanations of all its successive theories from Hippocrates to the present day; and anatomy may be fully treated. Vegetable pharmacy will make a part of the botanical course, and mineral and chemical pharmacy of those of mineralogy and chemistry. This degree of medical information is such as the mass of scientific students would wish to possess, as enabling them in their course through life, to estimate with satisfaction the extent and limits of the aid to human life and health, which they may understandingly expect from that art; and it constitutes such a foundation for those intended for the profession, that the finishing course of practice at the bed-sides of the sick, and at the operations of surgery in a hospital, can neither be long nor expensive. To seek this finishing elsewhere, must therefore be submitted to for a while.

In conformity with the principles of our Constitution, which places all sects of religion on an equal footing, with the jealousies of the different sects in guarding that equality from encroachment and surprise, and with the sentiments of the Legislature in favour of freedom of religion, manifested on former occasions, we have proposed no professor of divinity; and the rather as the proofs of the being of a God, the creator, preserver, and supreme ruler of the universe, the author of all the relations of morality, and of the laws and obligations these infer, will be within the province of the professor of ethics; to which adding the developments of these moral obligations, of those in which all sects agree, with a knowledge of the languages, Hebrew, Greek, and Latin, a basis will be formed common to all sects. Proceeding thus far without offence to the Constitution, we have thought it proper at this point to leave every sect to provide, as they think fittest, the means of further instruction in their own peculiar tenets.

We are further of opinion, that after declaring by law that

certain sciences shall be taught in the University, fixing the number of professors they require, which we think should, at present, be ten, limiting (except as to the professors who shall be first engaged in each branch) a maximum for their salaries (which should be a certain but moderate subsistence, to be made up by liberal tuition fees, as an excitement to assiduity), it will be best to leave to the discretion of the visitors, the grouping of these sciences together, according to the accidental qualifications of the professors; and the introduction also of other branches of science, when enabled by private donations, or by public provision, and called for by the increase of population, or other change of circumstances; to establish beginnings, in short, to be developed by time, as those who come after us shall find expedient. They will be more advanced than we are in science and in useful arts, and will know best what will suit the circumstances of their day.

We have proposed no formal provision for the gymnastics of the school, although a proper object of attention for every institution of youth. These exercises with ancient nations, constituted the principal part of the education of their youth. Their arms and mode of warfare rendered them severe in the extreme; ours, on the same correct principle, should be adapted to our arms and warfare; and the manual exercise, military manoeuvres, and tactics generally, should be the frequent exercise of the students, in their hours of recreation. It is at that age of aptness, docility, and emulation of the practices of manhood, that such things are soonest learnt and longest remembered. The use of tools too in the manual arts is worthy of encouragement, by facilitating to such as choose it, an admission into the neighboring workshops. To these should be added the arts which embellish life, dancing, music, and drawing; the last more especially, as an important part of military education. These innocent arts furnish amusement and happiness to those who, having time on their hands, might less inoffensively employ it. Needing, at the same time, no regular incorporation with the institution, they may be left to accessory teachers, who will be paid by the individuals employing them, the University only providing proper apartments for their exercise.

The fifth duty prescribed to the Commissioners, is to propose such general provisions as may be properly enacted by the Legislature, for the better organizing and governing the University.

In the education of youth, provision is to be made for, 1, tuition; 2, diet; 3, lodging; 4, government; and 5, honorary excitements. The first of these constitutes the proper functions of the professors; 2, the dieting of the students should be left to private boarding houses of their own choice, and at their own expense; to be regulated by the Visitors from time to time, the house only being provided by the University within its own precincts, and thereby of course subjected to the general regimen, moral or sumptuary, which they shall prescribe. 3. They should be lodged in dormitories, making a part of the general system of buildings. 4. The best mode of government for youth, in large collections, is certainly a desideratum not yet attained with us. It may be well questioned whether *fear* after a certain age, is a motive to which we should have ordinary recourse. The human character is susceptible of other incitements to correct conduct, more worthy of employ, and of better effect. Pride of character, laudable ambition, and moral dispositions are innate correctives of the indiscretions of that lively age; and when strengthened by habitual appeal and exercise, have a happier effect on future character than the degrading motive of fear. Hardening them to disgrace, to corporal punishments, and servile humiliations cannot be the best process for producing erect character. The affectionate deportment between father and son, offers in truth the best example for that of tutor and pupil; and the experience and practice of other countries, in this respect, may be worthy of enquiry and consideration with us. It will then be for the wisdom and discretion of the Visitors to devise and perfect a proper system of government, which, if it be founded in reason and comity, will be more likely to nourish in the minds of our youth the combined spirit of order and self-respect, so congenial with our political institutions, and so important to be woven into the American character.

14 Washington Irving
Knickerbocker's History of New York

from *Knickerbocker's History of New York*   1812

Wilhelmus Kieft,[1] who, in 1634, ascended the gubernatorial chair (to borrow a favourite though clumsy appellation of modern phraseologists), was of a lofty descent, his father being inspector of wind-mills in the ancient town of Saardam; and our hero, we are told, when a boy, made very curious investigations into the nature and operation of these machines, which was one reason why he afterwards came to be so ingenious a governor. His name, according to the most authentic etymologists, was a corruption of Kyver; that is to say, a *wrangler* or *scolder*; and expressed the characteristic of his family, which, for nearly two centuries, had kept the windy town of Saardam in hot water, and produced more tartars and brimstones than any ten families in the place; and so truly did he inherit this family peculiarity, that he had not been a year in the government of the province, before he was universally denominated William the Testy. His appearance answered to his name. He was a brisk, wiry, waspish little old gentleman; such a one as may now and then be seen stumping about our city in a broad-skirted coat with huge buttons, a cocked hat stuck on the back of his head, and a cane as high as his chin. His face was broad, but his features were sharp; his cheeks were scorched into a dusty red, by two fiery little grey eyes; his nose turned up, and the corners of his mouth turned down, pretty much like the muzzle of an irritable pugdog.

I have heard it observed by a profound adept in human physiology, that if a woman waxes fat with the progress of years, her tenure of life is somewhat precarious, but if haply she withers as she grows old, she lives for ever. Such promised to be the case with William the Testy, who grew tough in proportion as he dried. He had withered, in fact, not through the process of years, but through the tropical fervour of his soul, which burnt like a vehement rush-light in his bosom, inciting him to inces-

[1.] Wilhelmus Kieft is a caricature of Thomas Jefferson.

sant broils and bickerings. Ancient traditions speak much of his learning, and of the gallant inroads he had made into the dead languages, in which he had made captive a host of Greek nouns and Latin verbs; and brought off rich booty in ancient saws and apophthegms, which he was wont to parade in his public harangues, as a triumphant general of yore, his *spolia opima*. Of metaphysics he knew enough to confound all hearers and himself into the bargain. In logic, he knew the whole family of syllogisms and dilemmas, and was so proud of his skill that he never suffered even a self-evident fact to pass unargued. It was observed, however, that he seldom got into an argument without getting into a perplexity, and then into a passion with his adversary for not being convinced gratis.

He had, moreover, skirmished smartly on the frontiers of several of the sciences, was fond of experimental philosophy, and prided himself upon inventions of all kinds. His abode, which he had fixed at a bowery, or country-seat, at a short distance from the city, just at what is now called Dutch Street, soon abounded with proofs of his ingenuity: patent smoke-jacks that required a horse to work them; Dutch ovens that roasted meat without fire; carts that went before the horses; weathercocks that turned against the wind; and other wrong-headed contrivances that astonished and confounded all beholders. The house, too, was beset with paralytic cats and dogs, the subjects of his experimental philosophy; and the yelling and yelping of the latter unhappy victims of science, while aiding in the pursuit of knowledge, soon gained for the place the name of 'Dog's Misery', by which it continues to be known even at the present day.

It is in knowledge as in swimming, he who flounders and splashes on the surface, makes more noise and attracts more attention than the pearl-diver who quietly dives in quest of treasures to the bottom. The vast acquirements of the new governor were the theme of marvel among the simple burghers of New Amsterdam; he figured about the place as learned a man as a Bonze at Pekin, who has mastered one-half of the Chinese alphabet: and was unanimously pronounced a 'universal genius!'

I have known in my time many a genius of this stamp; but, to speak my mind freely, I never knew one who, for the ordinary purposes of life, was worth his weight in straw. In this respect, a little sound judgement and plain common sense is worth all the sparkling genius that ever wrote poetry or invented theories. Let us see how the universal acquirements of William the Testy aided him in the affairs of government.

No sooner had this bustling little potentate been blown by a whiff of fortune into the seat of government, than he called his council together to make them a speech on the state of affairs.

Caius Gracchus, it is said, when he harangued the Roman populace, modulated his tone by an oratorical flute or pitch-pipe; Wilhelmus Kieft, not having such an instrument at hand, availed himself of that musical organ or trump which nature has implanted in the midst of a man's face; in other words, he preluded his address by a sonorous blast of the nose; a preliminary flourish much in vogue among public orators.

He then commenced by expressing his humble sense of his utter unworthiness of the high post to which he had been appointed, which made some of the simple burghers wonder why he undertook it, not knowing that it is a point of etiquette with a public orator never to enter upon office without declaring himself unworthy to cross the threshold. He then proceeded in a manner highly classic and erudite to speak of government generally, and of the governments of ancient Greece in particular; together with the wars of Rome and Carthage, and the rise and fall of sundry outlandish empires which the worthy burghers had never read nor heard of. Having thus, after the manner of your learned orators, treated of things in general, he came, by a natural roundabout transition, to the matter in hand, namely, the daring aggressions of the Yankees.

As my readers are well aware of the advantage a potentate has of handling his enemies as he pleases in his speeches and bulletins, where he has the talk all on his own side, they may rest assured that William the Testy did not let such an opportunity escape of giving the Yankees what is called 'a taste of his quality'. In speaking of their inroads into the territories of their High Mightinesses, he compared them to the Gauls, who desolated Rome; the Goths and Vandals, who overran the fairest plains of Europe; but when he came to speak of the unparalleled audacity with which they of Weathersfield had advanced their patches up to the very walls of Fort Goed Hoop, and threatened to smother the garrison in onions, tears of rage started into his eyes, as though he nosed the very offence in question.

Having thus wrought up his tale to a climax, he assumed a most belligerent look, and assured the council that he had devised an instrument, potent in its effects, and which he trusted would soon drive the Yankees from the land. So saying, he thrust his hand into one of the deep pockets of his broad-skirted coat and drew forth, not an infernal machine, but an instrument in writing, which he laid with great emphasis upon the table.

The burghers gazed at it for a time in silent awe, as a wary housewife does at a gun, fearful it may go off half-cocked. The document in question had a sinister look, it is true; it was crabbed in text, and from a broad red ribbon dangled the great seal of the province, about the size of a buckwheat pancake. Still, after all, it was but an instrument in writing. Herein, however, existed the wonder of the invention. The document in question was a PROCLAMATION, ordering the Yankees to depart instantly from the territories of their High Mightinesses, under pain of suffering all the forfeitures and punishments in such case made and provided. It was on the moral effect of this formidable instrument that Wilhelmus Kieft calculated; pledging his valour as a governor that, once fulminated against the Yankees, it would, in less than two months, drive every mother's son of them across the borders.

The council broke up in perfect wonder, and nothing was talked of for some time among the old men and women of New-Amsterdam but the vast genius of the governor, and his new and cheap mode of fighting by proclamation.

As to Wilhelmus Kieft, having dispatched his proclamation

to the frontiers, he put on his cocked hat and corduroy small-clothes, and, mounting a tall raw-boned charger, trotted out to his rural retreat of Dog's Misery. Here, like the good Numa, he reposed from the toils of state, taking lessons in government, not from the nymph Egeria, but from the honoured wife of his bosom, who was one of that class of females sent upon the earth a little after the Flood, as a punishment for the sins of mankind, and commonly known by the appellation of *knowing women*. In fact, my duty as an historian obliges me to make known a circumstance which was a great secret at the time, and, consequently, was not a subject of scandal at more than half the tea-tables in New-Amsterdam, but which, like many other great secrets, has leaked out in the lapse of years; and this was, that Wilhelmus the Testy, though one of the most potent little men that ever breathed, yet submitted at home to a species of government, neither laid down in Aristotle nor Plato; in short, it partook of the nature of a pure, unmixed tyranny, and is familiarly denominated *petticoat government*. An absolute sway, which, although exceedingly common in these modern days, was very rare among the ancients, if we may judge from the rout made about the domestic economy of honest Socrates, which is the only ancient case on record.

The great Kieft, however, warded off all the sneers and sarcasms of his particular friends, who are ever ready to joke with a man on sore points of the kind, by alleging that it was a government of his own election, to which he submitted through choice; adding, at the same time, a profound maxim which he had found in an ancient author, that 'he who would aspire to *govern* should first learn to *obey*'.

15 Thomas Jefferson
Death-Bed Adieu[1]

from Saul K. Padover, *Jefferson* 1942

Life's visions are vanished, its dreams are no more;
    Dear friends of my bosom, why bathed in tears?
I go to my fathers; I welcome the shore
    Which crowns all my hopes or which buries my cares.

Then farewell my dear, my loved daughter, adieu!
The last pang of life is in parting from you!
Two seraphs await me long shrouded in death;
I will bear them your love on my last parting breath!

[1.] This was written on his death-bed to console his daughter Martha:
the two seraphs are his wife and another daughter already dead. It is appalling doggerel, but it shows that Jefferson had a general belief in survival after
death.

H Rousseau and Goethe

Towering in the background of the 'Romantic' movement are two figures from the continent, one from France, one from Germany.

Jean-Jacques Rousseau (1712–78) was in fact born in Geneva, but from about 1750 he was a prominent figure in the French intellectual scene. *La Nouvelle Héloise* fostered the emergence of the Romantic novel; *Émile* influenced educational theory; *Du Contrat Social* is one of the few seminal political works, while the posthumously published *Confessions* ushered in a mood of self-conscious introspection. Rousseau's idealization of the 'noble savage' and the simple life and his denunciation of the corrupting effects of society were perhaps his most influential concepts.

Johann Wolfgang von Goethe (1749–1832) stands as a Colossus across the turn of the century. Goethe believed, like his own Faust, in human development through experience. Some of his early works had a strong influence on the development of Romanticism, notably *Die Leiden des jungen Werthers* (usually translated *The Sorrows of Werther*) and he was a leading figure in the 'storm and stress' movement. He preferred to regard himself as a classicist, and he poured Romantic attitudes (arising not least from his own innumerable love affairs) into firmly classical moulds. Poet, novelist, dramatist, critic, scientist and scholar, he became something of an Olympian deity.

To understand the intellectual and literary developments of the period from 1780 to 1830 we must first explore Rousseau and Goethe.

J.F.

Further Reading

Jean Guéhenno, *Jean-Jacques Rousseau*, translated by J. and D. Weightman, Routledge & Kegan Paul, 1966.

Alfred Cobban, *Rousseau and the Modern State*, Allen & Unwin, 1968.

Irving Babbitt, *Rousseau and Romanticism*, Meridian Books, 1955.

J.H. Broome, *Rousseau, A Study of his Thought*, Edward Arnold, 1963.

J.P. Plamenatz, *Man and Society*, Longman, 1963, pp. 364–442.

Jean-Jacques Rousseau, *The Social Contract* and *Discourses*, translated by G. D. H. Cole, Dent, 1913.

* Jean-Jacques Rousseau, *Confessions*, translated by J. M. Cohen, Penguin, 1967.

L. MacNeice, *Goethe's 'Faust'*, Oxford University Press, 1961.

Johann Wolfgang Goethe, *Italian Journey*, Penguin, 1970.

* Stephen Spender (ed.), *Great Writings of Goethe*, Mentor Books, 1970

* Open University Set Book.

1 Jean-Jacques Rousseau

A Discourse on the Origin of Inequality

from 'A Discourse on the Origin of Inequality', *The Social Contract* and *Discourses* 1762. Translated by G. D. H. Cole, 1913, pp 144–229

The First Part

A

Important as it may be, in order to judge rightly of the natural state of man, to consider him from his origin, and to examine him, as it were, in the embryo of his species, I shall not follow his organization through its successive developments, nor shall I stay to inquire what his animal system must have been at the beginning, in order to become at length what it actually is. I shall not ask whether his long nails were at first, as Aristotle supposes, only crooked talons; whether his whole body, like that of a bear, was not covered with hair; or whether the fact that he walked upon all fours, with his looks directed toward the earth, confined to a horizon of a few paces, did not at once point out the nature and limits of his ideas. On this subject I could form none but vague and almost imaginary conjectures. Comparative anatomy has as yet made too little progress, and the observations of naturalists are too uncertain, to afford an adequate basis for any solid reasoning. So that, without having recourse to the supernatural information given us on this head, or paying any regard to the changes which must have taken place in the internal, as well as the external, conformation of man, as he applied his limbs to new uses, and fed himself on new kinds of food, I shall suppose his conformation to have been at all times what it appears to us at this day; that he always walked on two legs, made use of his hands as we do, directed his looks over all nature, and measured with his eyes the vast expanse of Heaven.

If we strip this being, thus constituted, of all the supernatural gifts he may have received, and all the artificial faculties he can have acquired only by a long process; if we consider him, in a word, just as he must have come from the hands of nature, we behold in him an animal weaker than some, and less agile than others; but taking him all round, the most advantageously organized of any. I see him satisfying his hunger at the first oak, and slaking his thirst at the first brook; finding his bed at the foot of the tree which afforded him a repast; and, with that, all his wants supplied.

While the earth was left to its natural fertility and covered with immense forests, whose trees were never mutilated by the axe, it would present on every side both sustenance and shelter for every species of animal. Men, dispersed up and down among the rest, would observe and imitate their industry, and thus attain even to the instinct of the beasts, with the advantage that, whereas every species of brutes was confined to one particular instinct, man, who perhaps has not any one peculiar to himself, would appropriate them all, and live upon most of those different foods, which other animals shared among themselves; and thus would find his subsistence much more easily than any of the rest.

Accustomed from their infancy to the inclemencies of the weather and the rigour of the seasons, inured to fatigue, and forced, naked and unarmed, to defend themselves and their prey from other ferocious animals, or to escape them by flight, men would acquire a robust and almost unalterable constitution. The children, bringing with them into the world the excellent constitution of their parents, and fortifying it by the very exercises which first produced it, would thus acquire all the vigour of which the human frame is capable. Nature in this case treats them exactly as Sparta treated the children of her citizens: those who come well formed into the world she renders strong and robust, and all the rest she destroys; differing in this respect from our modern communities, in which the State, by making children a burden to their parents, kills them indiscriminately before they are born. [...]

B

I see nothing in any animal but an ingenious machine, to which nature hath given senses to wind itself up, and to guard itself, to a certain degree, against anything that might tend to disorder or destroy it. I perceive exactly the same things in the human machine, with this difference, that in the operations of the brute, nature is the sole agent, whereas man has some share in his own operations, in his character as a free agent. The one chooses and refuses by instinct, the other from an act of free will: hence the brute cannot deviate from the rule prescribed to it, even when it would be advantageous for it to do so; and, on the contrary, man frequently deviates from such rules to his own prejudice. Thus a pigeon would be starved to death by the side of a dish of the choicest meats, and a cat on a heap of fruit or grain; though it is certain that either might find nourishment in the foods which it thus rejects with disdain, did it think of trying them. Hence it is that dissolute men run into excesses which bring on fevers and death; because the mind depraves the senses, and the will continues to speak when nature is silent.

Every animal has ideas, since it has senses; it even combines those ideas in a certain degree; and it is only in degree that man differs, in this respect, from the brute. Some philosophers have even maintained that there is a greater difference between one man and another than between some men and some beasts. It is not, therefore, so much the understanding that constitutes the specific difference between the man and the brute, as the human quality of free agency. Nature lays her commands on every animal, and the brute obeys her voice. Man receives the same impulsion, but at the same time knows himself at liberty to acquiesce or resist: and it is particularly in his consciousness of this liberty that the spirituality of his soul is displayed. For physics may explain, in some measure, the mechanism of the senses and the formation of ideas; but in the power of willing or rather of choosing, and in the feeling of this power, nothing is to be found but acts which are purely spiritual and wholly inexplicable by the laws of mechanism.

However, even if the difficulties attending all these questions should still leave room for difference in this respect between men and brutes, there is another very specific quality which distinguishes them, and which will admit of no dispute. This is the faculty of self-improvement, which, by the help of circumstances, gradually develops all the rest of our faculties, and is inherent in the species as in the individual: whereas a brute is, at the end of a few months, all he will ever be during his whole life, and his species, at the end of a thousand years, exactly what it was the first year of that thousand. Why is man alone liable to grow into a dotard? It is not because he returns, in this, to his primitive state; and that, while the brute, which has acquired nothing and has therefore nothing to lose, still retains the force of instinct, man, who loses, by age or accident, all that his *perfectibility* had enabled him to gain, falls by this means lower than the brutes themselves? It would be melancholy, were we forced to admit that this distinctive and almost unlimited faculty is the source of all human misfortunes; that it is this which, in time, draws man out of his original state, in which he would have spent his days insensibly in peace and innocence; that it is this faculty, which, successively producing in different ages his discoveries and his errors, his vices and his virtues, makes him at length a tyrant both over himself and over nature. It would be shocking to be obliged to regard as a benefactor the man who first suggested to the Oroonoko Indians the use of the boards they apply to the temples of their children, which secure to them some part at least of their imbecility and original happiness.

Savage man, left by nature solely to the direction of instinct, or rather indemnified for what he may lack by faculties capable at first of supplying its place, and afterwards of raising him much above it, must accordingly begin with purely animal functions: thus seeing and feeling must be his first condition, which would be common to him and all other animals. To will, and not to will, to desire and to fear, must be the first, and almost the only operations of his soul, till new circumstances occasion new developments of his faculties.

Whatever moralists may hold, the human understanding is greatly indebted to the passions, which, it is universally allowed, are also much indebted to the understanding. It is by the activity of the passions that our reason is improved; for we desire knowledge only because we wish to enjoy; and it is impossible to conceive any reason why a person who has neither fears nor desires should give himself the trouble of reasoning. The passions, again, originate in our wants, and their progress depends on that of our knowledge; for we cannot desire or fear anything, except from the idea we have of it, or from the simple impulse of nature. Now savage man, being destitute of every species of intelligence, can have no passions save those of the latter kind: his desires never go beyond his physical wants. The only goods he recognizes in the universe are food, a female, and sleep: the only evils he fears are pain and hunger. I say pain, and not death: for no animal can know what it is to die; the knowledge of death and its terrors being one of the first acquisitions made by man in departing from an animal state.

It would be easy, were it necessary, to support this opinion by facts, and to show that, in all the nations of the world, the progress of the understanding has been exactly proportionate to the wants which the peoples had received from nature, or been subjected to by circumstances, and in consequence to the passions that induced them to provide for those necessities. I might instance the arts, rising up in Egypt and expanding with the inundation of the Nile. I might follow their progress into Greece, where they took root afresh, grew up and towered to the skies, among the rocks and sands of Attica, without being able to germinate on the fertile banks of the Eurotas: I might observe that in general, the people of the North are more industrious than those of the South, because they cannot get on so well without being so: as if nature wanted to equalize matters by giving their understandings the fertility she had refused to their soil.

But who does not see, without recurring to the uncertain testimony of history, that everything seems to remove from savage man both the temptation and the means of changing his condition? His imagination paints no pictures; his heart makes no demands on him. His few wants are so readily supplied, and he is so far from having the knowledge which is needful to make him want more, that he can have neither foresight nor curiosity. The face of nature becomes indifferent to him as it grows familiar. He sees in it always the same order, the same successions: he has not understanding enough to wonder at the greatest miracles; nor is it in his mind that we can expect to find that philosophy man needs, if he is to know how to notice for once what he sees every day. His soul, which nothing disturbs, is wholly wrapped up in the feeling of its present existence, without any idea of the future, however near at hand; while his projects, as limited as his views, hardly extend to the close of day. Such, even at present, is the extent of the native Caribbean's foresight: he will improvidently sell you his cotton-bed in the morning, and come crying in the evening to buy it again, not having foreseen he would want it again the next night. [...]

C

It appears, at first view, that men in a state of nature, having no moral relations or determinate obligations one with another, could not be either good or bad, virtuous or vicious; unless we take these terms in a physical sense, and call, in an individual, those qualities vices which may be injurious to his preservation, and those virtues which contribute to it; in which case, he would have to be accounted most virtuous, who put least check on the pure impulses of nature. But without deviating from the ordinary sense of the words, it will be proper to suspend the judgment we might be led to form on such a state, and be on our guard against our prejudices, till we have weighed the matter in the scales of impartiality, and seen whether virtues or vices preponderate among civilized men: and whether their virtues do them more good than their vices do harm; till we have discovered whether the progress of the sciences sufficiently indemnifies them for the mischiefs they do one another, in proportion as they are better informed of the good they ought to do; or whether they would not be, on the whole, in a much happier condition if they had nothing to fear or to hope from any one, than as they are, subjected to universal dependence, and obliged to take everything from those who engage to give them nothing in return.

Above all, let us not conclude, with Hobbes, that because man has no idea of goodness, he must be naturally wicked; that he is vicious because he does not know virtue; that he always refuses to do his fellow-creatures services which he does not think they have a right to demand; or that by virtue of the right he truly claims everything he needs, he foolishly imagines himself the sole proprietor of the whole universe. Hobbes had seen clearly the defects of all the modern definitions of natural right: but the consequences which he deduces from his own show that he understands it in an equally false sense. In reasoning on the principles he lays down, he ought to have said that the state of nature, being that in which the care for our own preservation is the least prejudicial to that of others, was consequently the best calculated to promote peace, and the most suitable for mankind. He does say the exact opposite, in consequence of having improperly admitted, as a part of savage man's care for self-preservation, the gratification of a multitude of passions which are the work of society, and have made laws necessary. A bad man, he says, is a robust child. But it remains to be proved whether man in a state of nature is this robust child: and, should we grant that he is, what would he infer? Why truly, that if this man, when robust and strong, were dependent on others as he is when feeble, there is no extravagance he would not be guilty of; that he would beat his mother when she was too slow in giving him her breast; that he would strangle one of his younger brothers, if he should be troublesome to him, or bite the arm of another, if he put him to any inconvenience. But that man in the state of nature is both strong and dependent involves two contrary suppositions. Man is weak when he is dependent, and is his own master before he comes to be strong. Hobbes did not reflect that the same cause, which prevents a savage from making use of his reason, as our jurists hold, prevents him also from abusing his faculties, as Hobbes himself allows: so that it may be justly said that savages are not bad merely because they do not know what it is to be good: for it is neither the development of the understanding nor the restraint of law that hinders them from doing ill; but the peacefulness of their passions, and their ignorance of vice: *tanto plus in illis proficit vitiorum ignoratio, quam in his cognitio virtutis*.[1] There is another principle which has escaped Hobbes; which, having been bestowed on mankind, to moderate, on certain occasions, the impetuosity of egoism, or, before its birth, the desire of self-preservation, tempers the ardour with which he pursues his own welfare, by an innate repugnance at seeing a fellow-creature suffer. I think I need not fear contradiction in holding man to be possessed of the only natural virtue, which could not be denied him by the most violent detractor of human virtue. I am speaking of compassion, which is a disposition suitable to creatures so weak and subject

1. So much the more does the ignorance of vice profit the one sort, than the knowledge of virtue the other.

to so many evils as we certainly are: by so much the more universal and useful to mankind, as it comes before any kind of reflection; and at the same time so natural, that the very brutes themselves sometimes give evident proofs of it. [. . .]

The Second Part

D

The first man who, having enclosed a piece of ground, bethought himself of saying 'This is mine', and found people simple enough to believe him, was the real founder of civil society. From how many crimes, wars, and murders, from how many horrors and misfortunes might not any one have saved mankind, by pulling up the stakes, or filling up the ditch, and crying to his fellows: 'Beware of listening to this impostor; you are undone if you once forget that the fruits of the earth belong to us all, and the earth itself to nobody.' But there is great probability that things had then already come to such a pitch, that they could no longer continue as they were; for the idea of property depends on many prior ideas, which could only be acquired successively, and cannot have been formed all at once in the human mind. Mankind must have made very considerable progress, and acquired considerable knowledge and industry which they must also have transmitted and increased from age to age, before they arrived at this last point of the state of nature. Let us then go farther back, and endeavour to unify under a single point of view that slow succession of events and discoveries in the most natural order. [. . .]

E

Matters once at this pitch, it is easy to imagine the rest. I shall not detain the reader with a description of the successive invention of other arts, the development of language, the trial and utilization of talents, the inequality of fortunes, the use and abuse of riches, and all the details connected with them which the reader can easily supply for himself. I shall confine myself to a glance at mankind in this new situation.

Behold then all human faculties developed; memory and imagination in full play, egoism interested, reason active, and the mind almost at the highest point of its perfection. Behold all the natural qualities in action, the rank and condition of every man assigned him; not merely his share of property and his power to serve or injure others, but also his wit, beauty, strength or skill, merit or talents: and these being the only qualities capable of commanding respect, it soon became necessary to possess or to affect them.

It now became the interest of men to appear what they really were not. To be and to seem became two totally different things; and from this distinction sprang insolent pomp and cheating trickery, with all the numerous vices that go in their train. On the other hand, free and independent as men were before, they were now, in consequence of a multiplicity of new wants, brought into subjection, as it were, to all nature, and particularly to one another; and each became in some degree a slave even in becoming the master of other men: if rich, they stood in need of the services of others; if poor, of their assistance; and even a middle condition did not enable them to do without one another. Man must now, therefore, have been perpetually employed in getting others to interest themselves in his lot, and in making them, apparently at least, if not really, find their advantage in promoting his own. Thus he must have been sly and artful in his behaviour to some, and imperious and cruel to others; being under a kind of necessity to ill-use all the persons of whom he stood in need, when he could not frighten them into compliance, and did not judge it his interest to be useful to them. Insatiable ambition, the thirst of raising their respective fortunes, not so much from real want as from the desire to surpass others, inspired all men with a vile propensity to injure one another, and with a secret jealousy, which is the more dangerous, as it puts on the mask of benevolence, to carry its point with greater security. In a word, there arose rivalry and competition on the one hand, and conflicting interests on the other, together with a secret desire on both of profiting at the expense of others. All these evils were the first effects of property, and the inseparable attendants of growing inequality.

Before the invention of signs to represent riches, wealth could hardly consist in anything but lands and cattle, the only real possessions men can have. But, when inheritances so increased in number and extent as to occupy the whole of the land, and to border on one another, one man could aggrandize himself only at the expense of another; at the same time the supernumeraries, who had been too weak or too indolent to make such acquisitions, and had grown poor without sustaining any loss, because, while they saw everything change around them, they remained still the same, were obliged to receive their subsistence, or steal it, from the rich; and this soon bred, according to their different characters, dominion and slavery, or violence and rapine. The wealthy, on their part, had no sooner begun to taste the pleasure of command, than they disdained all others, and, using their old slaves to acquire new, thought of nothing but subduing and enslaving their neighbours; like ravenous wolves, which, having once tasted human flesh, despise every other food and thenceforth seek only men to devour. [...]

F

With this view, after having represented to his neighbours the horror of a situation which armed every man against the rest, and made their possessions as burdensome to them as their wants, and in which no safety could be expected either in riches or in poverty, he readily devised plausible arguments to make them close with his design. 'Let us join,' said he, 'to guard the weak from oppression, to restrain the ambitious, and secure to every man the possession of what belongs to him: let us institute rules of justice and peace, to which all without exception may be obliged to conform; rules that may in some measure make amends for the caprices of fortune, by subjecting equally the powerful and the weak to the observance of reciprocal obligations. Let us, in a word, instead of turning our forces against ourselves, collect them in a supreme power which may govern us by wise laws, protect and defend all the members of the association, repulse their common enemies, and maintain eternal harmony among us.'

Far fewer words to this purpose would have been enough to impose on men so barbarous and easily seduced; especially as they had too many disputes among themselves to do without arbitrators, and too much ambition and avarice to go long without masters. All ran headlong to their chains, in hopes of securing their liberty; for they had just wit enough to perceive the advantages of political institutions, without experience enough to enable them to foresee the dangers. The most capable of fore-seeing the dangers were the very persons who expected to bene-fit by them; and even the most prudent judged it not inexpe-dient to sacrifice one part of their freedom to ensure the rest; as a wounded man has his arm cut off to save the rest of his body.

Such was, or may well have been, the origin of society and law, which bound new fetters on the poor, and gave new powers to the rich; which irretrievably destroyed natural liberty, eternally fixed the law of property and inequality, converted clever usurpa-tion into unalterable right, and, for the advantage of a few ambitious individuals, subjected all mankind to perpetual labour, slavery, and wretchedness. [...]

G

Without entering at present upon the investigations which still remain to be made into the nature of the fundamental com-pact underlying all government, I content myself with adopt-ing the common opinion concerning it, and regard the estab-lishment of the political body as a real contract between the people and the chiefs chosen by them: a contract by which both parties bind themselves to observe the laws therein expressed, which form the ties of their union. The people having in respect of their social relations concentrated all their wills in one, the several articles, concerning which this will is explained, become so many fundamental laws, obligatory on all the members of the State without exception, and one of these articles regulates the choice and power of the magistrates appointed to watch over the execution of the rest. This power extends to everything which may maintain the constitution, without going so far as to alter it. It is accompanied by honours, in order to bring the laws and their administrators into respect. The ministers are also dis-tinguished by personal prerogatives, in order to recompense them for the cares and labour which good administration in-volves. The magistrate, on his side, binds himself to use the power he is entrusted with only in conformity with the inten-tion of his constituents, to maintain them all in the peaceable possession of what belongs to them, and to prefer on every occasion the public interest to his own. [. . .]

H

If the reader thus discovers and retraces the lost and forgotten road, by which man must have passed from the state of nature to the state of society; if he carefully restores, along with the intermediate situations which I have just described, those which want of time has compelled me to suppress, or my imagination has failed to suggest, he cannot fail to be struck by the vast distance which separates the two states. It is in tracing this slow succession that he will find the solution of a number of problems of politics and morals, which philosophers cannot settle. He will feel that, men being different in different ages, the reason why Diogenes could not find a man was that he sought among his contemporaries a man of an earlier period. He will see that Cato died with Rome and liberty, because he did not fit the age in which he lived; the greatest of men served only to astonish a world which he would certainly have ruled, had he lived five hundred years sooner. In a word, he will explain how the soul and the passions of man insensibly change their very nature; why our wants and pleasures in the end seek new objects; and why, the original man having vanished by degrees, society offers to us only an assembly of artificial men and factitious passions, which are the work of all these new relations, and without any real foundation in nature. We are taught nothing on this subject, by reflection, that is not entirely confirmed by observation. The savage and the civilized man differ so much in the bottom of their hearts and in their inclinations, that what constitutes the supreme happiness of one would reduce the other to despair. The former breathes only peace and liberty; he desires only to live and be free from labour; even the *ataraxia* of the Stoic falls far short of his profound indifference to every other object. Civilized man, on the other hand, is always moving, sweating, toiling, and racking his brains to find still more laborious occupations: he goes on in drudgery to his last moment, and even seeks death to put himself in a position to live, or renounces life to acquire immortality. He pays his court to men in power, whom he hates, and to the wealthy, whom he despises; he stops at nothing to have the honour of serving them; he is not ashamed to value himself on his own meanness and their protection; and, proud of his slavery, he speaks with disdain of those, who have not the honour of sharing it. What a sight would the perplexing and envied labours of a European minister of State present to the eyes of a Caribbean! How many cruel deaths would not this indolent savage prefer to the horrors of such a life, which is seldom even sweetened by the pleasure of doing good! But, for him to see into the motives of all this solicitude the words 'power' and 'reputation' would have to bear some meaning in his mind; he would have to know that there are men who set a value on the opinion of the rest of the world; who can be made happy and satisfied with themselves rather on the testimony of other people than on their own. In reality, the source of all these differences is, that the savage lives within himself, while social man lives constantly outside himself, and only knows how to live in the opinion of others, so that he seems to receive the consciousness of his own existence merely from the judgement of others concerning him.

2 Jean-Jacques Rousseau
Émile

from *Émile* 1762. Translated by Barbara Foxley, 1911

A

Let us not forget what befits our present state in the pursuit of vain fancies. Mankind has its place in the sequence of things; childhood has its place in the sequence of human life; the man must be treated as a man and the child as a child. Give each his place, and keep him there. Control human passions according to man's nature; that is all we can do for his welfare. The rest depends on external forces, which are beyond our control.

Absolute good and evil are unknown to us. In this life they are blended together; we never enjoy any perfectly pure feeling, nor do we remain for more than a moment in the same state. The feelings of our minds, like the changes in our bodies, are in a continual flux. Good and ill are common to all, but in varying proportions. The happiest is he who suffers least; the most miserable is he who enjoys least. Ever more sorrow than joy — this is the lot of all of us. Man's happiness in this world is but a negative state; it must be reckoned by the fewness of his ills.

Every feeling of hardship is inseparable from the desire to escape from it; every idea of pleasure from the desire to enjoy it. All desire implies a want, and all wants are painful; hence our wretchedness consists in the disproportion between our desires and our powers. A conscious being whose powers were equal to his desires would be perfectly happy.

What then is human wisdom? Where is the path of true happiness? The mere limitation of our desires is not enough, for if they were less than our powers, part of our faculties would be idle, and we should not enjoy our whole being; neither is the mere extension of our powers enough, for if our desires were also increased we should only be the more miserable. True happiness consists in decreasing the difference between our desires and our powers, in establishing a perfect equilibrium between the power and the will. Then only, when all its forces are employed, will the soul be at rest and man will find himself in his true position.

In this condition, nature, who does everything for the best, has placed him from the first. To begin with, she gives him only such desires as are necessary for self-preservation and such powers as are sufficient for their satisfaction. All the rest she has stored in his mind as a sort of reserve, to be drawn upon at need. It is only in this primitive condition that we find the equilibrium between desire and power, and then alone man is not unhappy. As soon as his potential powers of mind begin to function, imagination, more powerful than all the rest, awakes, and precedes all the rest. It is imagination which enlarges the bounds of possibility for us, whether for good or ill, and therefore stimulates and feeds desires by the hope of satisfying them. But the object which seemed within our grasp flies quicker than we can follow; when we think we have grasped it, it transforms itself and is again far ahead of us. We no longer perceive the country we have traversed, and we think nothing of it; that which lies before us becomes vaster and stretches still before us. Thus we exhaust our strength, yet never reach our goal, and the nearer we are to pleasure, the further we are from happiness.

On the other hand, the more nearly a man's condition approximates to this state of nature the less difference is there between his desires and his powers, and happiness is therefore less remote. Lacking everything, he is never less miserable; for misery consists, not in the lack of things, but in the needs which they inspire.

The world of reality has its bounds, the world of imagination is boundless; as we cannot enlarge the one, let us restrict the other; for all the sufferings which really make us miserable arise from the difference between the real and the imaginary. Health, strength, and a good conscience excepted, all the good things of life are a matter of opinion; except bodily suffering and remorse, all our woes are imaginary. You will tell me this is a commonplace; I admit it, but its practical application is no commonplace, and it is with practice only that we are now concerned.

What do you mean when you say, 'Man is weak'? The term weak implies a relation, a relation of the creature to whom it is applied. An insect or a worm whose strength exceeds its needs is strong; an elephant, a lion, a conqueror, a hero, a god himself, whose needs exceed his strength is weak. The rebellious angel who fought against his own nature was weaker than the happy mortal who is living at peace according to nature. When man is content to be himself he is strong indeed; when he strives to be more than man he is weak indeed. But do not imagine that you can increase your strength by increasing your powers. Not so; if your pride increases more rapidly your strength is diminished. Let us measure the extent of our sphere and remain in its centre like the spider in its web; we shall have strength sufficient for our needs, we shall have no cause to lament our weakness, for we shall never be aware of it.

B

I will go further and maintain that virtue is no less favourable to love than to other rights of nature, and that it adds as much to the power of the beloved as to that of the wife or mother. There is no real love without enthusiasm, and no enthusiasm without an object of perfection real or supposed, but always present in the imagination. What is there to kindle the hearts of lovers for whom this perfection is nothing, for whom the loved one is merely the means to sensual pleasure? Nay, not thus is the heart kindled, not thus does it abandon itself to those sublime transports which form the rapture of lovers and the charm of love. Love is an illusion, I grant you, but its reality consists in the feelings it awakes, in the love of true beauty which it inspires. That beauty is not to be found in the object of our affections, it is the creation of our illusions. What matter! do we not still sacrifice all those baser feelings to the imaginary model? and we still feed our hearts on the virtues we attribute to the beloved, we still withdraw ourselves from the baseness of human nature. What lover is there who would not give his life for his mistress? What gross and sensual passion is there in a man who is willing to die? We scoff at the knights of old; they knew the meaning of love; we know nothing but debauchery. When the teachings of romance began to seem ridiculous, it was not so much the work of reason as of immorality.

C

'How unhappy I am!' said she to her mother; 'I am compelled to love and yet I am dissatisfied with every one. My heart rejects every one who appeals to my senses. Every one of them stirs my passions and all alike revolt them; a liking unaccompanied by respect cannot last. That is not the sort of man for your Sophy; the delightful image of her ideal is too deeply graven in her heart. She can love no other; she can make no one happy but him, and she cannot be happy without him. She would rather consume herself in ceaseless conflicts, she would rather die free and wretched, than driven desperate by the company of a man she did not love, a man she would make as unhappy as herself; she would rather die than live to suffer.'

Amazed at these strange ideas, her mother found them so peculiar that she could not fail to suspect some mystery. Sophy was neither affected nor absurd. How could such exaggerated delicacy exist in one who had been so carefully taught from her childhood to adapt herself to those with whom she must live, and to make a virtue of necessity? This ideal of the delightful man with which she was so enchanted, who appeared so often in her conversation, made her mother suspect that there was some foundation for her caprices which was still unknown to her, and that Sophy had not told her all. The unhappy girl, overwhelmed with her secret grief, was only too eager to confide it to another. Her mother urged her to speak; she hesitated, she yielded, and leaving the room without a word, she presently returned with a book in her hand. 'Have pity on your unhappy daughter, there is no remedy for her grief, her tears cannot be dried. You would know the cause: well, here it is,' said she, flinging the book on the table. Her mother took the book and opened it; it was *The Adventures of Telemachus*. At first she could make nothing of this riddle; by dint of questions and vague replies, she discovered to her great surprise that her daughter was the rival of Eucharis.

Sophy was in love with Telemachus, and loved him with a passion which nothing could cure. When her father and mother became aware of her infatuation, they laughed at it and tried to cure her by reasoning with her. They were mistaken, reason was not altogether on their side; Sophy had her own reason and knew how to use it. Many a time did she reduce them to silence by turning their own arguments against them, by showing them that it was all their own fault for not having trained her to suit the men of that century; that she would be compelled to adopt her husband's way of thinking or he must adopt hers, that they had made the former course impossible by the way she had been brought up, and that the latter was just what she wanted. 'Give me,' said she, 'a man who holds the same opinions as I do, or one who will be willing to learn them from me, and I will marry him; but until then, why do you scold me? Pity me; I am miserable, but not mad. Is the heart controlled by the will? Did my father not ask that very question? Is it my fault if I love what has no existence? I am no visionary; I desire no prince, I seek no Telemachus, I know he is only an imaginary person; I seek some one like him. And why should there be no such person, since there is such a person as I, I who feel that my heart is like his? No, let us not wrong humanity so greatly, let us not think that an amiable and virtuous man is a figment of the imagination. He exists, he lives, perhaps he is seeking me; he is seeking a soul who is capable of love for him. But who is he, where is he? I know not; he is not among those I have seen; and no doubt I shall never see him. Oh! mother, why did you make virtue too attractive? If I can love nothing less, you are more to blame than I.'

Must I continue this sad story to its close? Must I describe the long struggles which preceded it? Must I show an impatient mother exchanging her former caresses for severity? Must I paint an angry father forgetting his former promises, and treating the most virtuous of daughters as a mad woman? Must I portray the unhappy girl, more than ever devoted to her imaginary hero, because of the persecution brought upon her by that devotion, drawing nearer step by step to her death, and descending into the grave when they were about to force her to the altar? No; I will not dwell upon these gloomy scenes; I have no need to go so far to show, by what I consider a sufficiently striking example, that in spite of the prejudices arising from the manners of our age, the enthusiasm for the good and the beautiful is no more foreign to women than to men, and that there is nothing which, under nature's guidance, cannot be obtained from them as well as from us.

You stop me here to inquire whether it is nature which teaches us to take such pains to repress our immoderate desires. No, I reply, but neither is it nature who gives us these immoderate desires. Now, all that is not from nature is contrary to nature, as I have proved again and again.

Let us give Émile his Sophy; let us restore this sweet girl to life and provide her with a less vivid imagination and a happier fate. I desired to paint an ordinary woman, but by endowing her with a great soul, I have disturbed her reason. I have gone astray. Let us retrace our steps. Sophy has only a good disposition and an ordinary heart; her education is responsible for everything in which she excels other women.

D

'Would you live in wisdom and happiness, fix your heart on the beauty that is eternal: let your desires be limited by your position, let your duties take precedence of your wishes; extend the law of necessity into the region of morals; learn to lose what may be taken from you; learn to forsake all things at the command of virtue, to set yourself above the chances of life, to detach your heart before it is torn in pieces, to be brave in adversity so that you may never be wretched, to be steadfast in duty that you may never be guilty of a crime. Then you will be happy in spite of fortune, and good in spite of your passions. You will find a pleasure that cannot be destroyed, even in the possession of the most fragile things; you will possess them, they will not possess you, and you will realize that the man who loses everything, only enjoys what he knows how to resign. It is true you will not enjoy the illusions of imaginary pleasures, neither will you feel the sufferings which are their result. You will profit greatly by this exchange, for the sufferings are real and frequent, the pleasures are rare and empty. Victor over so many deceitful ideas, you will also vanquish the idea that attaches such an excessive value to life. You will spend your life in peace, and you will leave it without terror; you will detach yourself from life as from other things. Let others, horror-struck, believe that when this life is ended they cease to be; conscious of the nothingness of life, you will think that you are but entering upon the true life. To the wicked, death is the close of life; to the just it is its dawn.'

3 Thomas Mann
Goethe's *Faust*

from 'Goethe's *Faust*', in *Essays* 1918. Translated by H. T. Lowe-Porter, 1918

In the sixteenth century, after the coming of the printing-press, there was a great need for matter to feed the presses and exploit the popular possibilities of the new invention. Almost any sort of material would do; and the printer, in order to be able to keep on turning it out, often became his own author. Thus the oldest Faust-book, of the year 1587, was probably compiled in Frankfurt by the printer, Spies. It was a collection of popular legends of the black art, up to then circulated by word of mouth; they grouped themselves round the figure of a Dr Johannes Faustus, a charlatan who had lived some fifty years before and now embodied in the popular fancy the conception of the invoker of evil spirits. His name, it seems, was Georg Helmstätter, but he assumed the highsounding cognomen of Sabellicus, and later, for a definite reason, the name of Faustus. On the Easter Sunday walk, Goethe makes Faust discourse to Wagner in brilliant verse, disclosing various characteristic and probable-sounding things about his antecedents and origins and about his father, the alchemist and quack physician, that '*dunkler Ehrenmann*'.

I mention this old book because it has a chapter, copied down by the printer from some source or other, in which Helena appears. Dr Faustus summons up the most beautiful woman in the world before the eyes of his fortunate students; but then he falls in love with her himself and demands her as bedfellow from the devil who serves him, whose name is already Mephistopheles. The description of Helena's famous or infamous person is amorous, though somewhat conventional. It has elements from the Trojan tales of various literatures; and all the epithets used by Byzantine, medieval and troubadour poets to characterize the European ideal of female beauty are lavished with somewhat mechanical enthusiasm upon it. [...]

Thus it came about that the name of Helena, the legendary queen of antiquity, remained bound up with that of the sixteenth-century witch-doctor. Nor had Goethe, in the beginning, any other intention than to bring his Helena at once on the stage with his Faustus. But the autobiographical triumphed temporarily over the legend. In Frankfurt there had been an early-loved Gretchen, in Alsace there was a Friederike, basely left; and these two flesh-and-blood memories put the classic shade so far in the background that the sweet and sorrowful Gretchen dominates the whole first part of *Faust*. Gretchen put Helena in the shade – yet not quite, and not even altogether in the *Faust Erster Teil*. Thanks to the folk-character of Goethe's genius, Faust and Gretchen rank among the famous lovers of literature. They are as secure a possession of our imagination as are Romeo and Juliet, Hero and Leander, Petrarch and Laura, Paolo and Francesca, Abélard and Héloïse – or Goethe's own Werther and Lotte. But in Goethe's masterpiece the pair of lovers has an interchangeable female half. Faust-Gretchen, Faust-Helena –

there is an extraordinary combination indeed! Not alone because the magnificent Helena episode in the second part is, in its highly developed, highly literary way, as full of genius as are the priceless Gretchen scenes in the first part. No; I mean that in the first part itself there are dreamlike transferences. In the scene in the witches' kitchen, written in Rome, Faust, before he drinks the magic draught, beholds in the magic mirror Woman in all the splendour of her supreme loveliness, and enraptured sees in that recumbent form the summary and brief abstract of heaven itself. Whom does he there see? Obviously no individual woman, rather a wish-picture of sensual loveliness – the pattern of the female kind, as Mephistopheles says, while promising Faust that he shall soon see that pattern before him in the flesh. But she whom he will actually see – that is not Helena, it is sweet Gretchen, for whom 'the pattern of the female kind' is certainly rather a high-flown description. If Faust finds her that, then the only explanation is that given in Mephisto's words:

With this drink inside you, presently
Helen in every female you will see.

There, for the first time in the play, the name of Helena appears; in anticipation, and as a symbol of all that feminine beauty and delight which the sweet, simple German burgher-maid is shortly to embody. Yet it is strange to see that Goethe, in that rapturous outburst of Faust after the first meeting with Gretchen, remains faithful to the description of Helena in the old Faust-book:

Heavens, but that child was fair!
Her like I've not seen anywhere!

cries the Faust of the poem.

So red her lips, her cheek so bright,
Ne'er shall I forget the sight!

And in the Faust-book it says of Helena: *'Ihre Leffzen rot wie Kirschen, rote Bäcklein wie ein Rösslin'* ('Her lips as cherries red, her cheeks like rosebuds'). And her face is described as *'überaus schön gleissend'* ('so shining fair'), of which there is a clear reminiscence in the striking phrase of Goethe: '*der Wange Licht*'. And '*etwas schnippisch doch zugleich*' ('rather tart withal') is the demure Gretchen:

Her pretty, shrewish speech —
It was enchanting!

That, I would wager, is a memory, in a more charmingly turned phrase, of the 'pert and roguish face' given to Helena in the Faust-book.

In short, Gretchen betrays traits, half-obliterated, of Helena. She was originally Helena, and Helena, in some small degree, she is still. Yet what an infinitely more lifelike figure the young poet created when he turned the luxurious beauty of the legend into the sweet and hapless little daughter of the pawn-broker! Infinitely more lifelike than if he had followed the old legend, instead of drawing on his own. '*Bewundert viel und viel gescholten*', 'much admired and censured much', Helena will duly appear in the second part. But her phantasmagorical figure is far from having the vivid emotional appeal of Gretchen's. She remains an episode. When Faust has dreamed to the end his enchanted dream with her — laden as that is with all the weight of Goethe's mind and art — when that is over she disappears, she vanishes from Faust's sight and memory. Gretchen it is, *una pœnitentium*, who in the fullness of time becomes the instrument by which the end of Faust's story and of his life are linked to their beginning:

Bend down, bend down,
Incomp'rable one,
Thy radiant face
Upon my bliss, in grace!
My early lover,
No more in sorrow,
Comes back to me.

The lines, with their parallelism to those of his early years:

Bend down, bend down,
Thou suffering one,

round out the great circle of the poet's life. A life so abundant and manifold that there was ever present danger of its being squandered, here asserts, by the power of memory, its essential unity. *Faust* is the representative achievement, the symbol of Goethe's whole life. He himself said of it:

Man's life's a poem similar to this;
It has, of course, beginning, has an end too –
But yet a whole it does not come to.

It is touching to see how his mind, in the later, elder time, reaches back to give to the fragmentary and illimitable work the unity that in his deepest heart he craved. 'He is,' he said, 'the most fortunate man who can bring the end of his life round to its beginning again.'

It is always a pleasure to speak to the young, to beginning students of Goethe's great poem. For it belongs to their age, it is the conception of one like-minded to them. Originally it was nothing more than the work of a highly gifted student, wherein the author calls faculties and professors over the coals and amuses himself enormously with playing the clever mentor, in diabolic disguise, to the timid freshman newly come up. A contemporary critic – the man's name was Pustkuchen, as one might say Popover – remarked peevishly: 'Faust's attack on all human knowledge is not precisely that of an Alexander standing at the known limits of the world and sighing for more to conquer. It is more like that of a student making fun of his professor – however, it was enough for the needs of the majority of his readers.' And the hard-pushed critic continues: 'But as it goes on, it follows the course of all the Goethian poetry. The great sinner, the titanic figure who outbids the powers of the Devil himself ... he becomes in the writer's hands a hero like all his other heroes. A love-story unfolds, like a thousand others ... there is a good hearted, limited middle-class girl, like Clärchen in *Egmont*. ...'

Yes, really, the man, in his good-hearted, limited way, is quite right in inveighing against a poetic realism which must have seemed to him like a derogation into intimate personalities of material in itself very lofty. The critic is always on the side of the material, against the poet who irreverently deals with it as an instrument, a pretext for his own personal ends. But what such critics fail to see is the remarkable phenomenon displayed in *Faust*: the genius of student youth here usurps the role of humanity itself, and the whole Western world has accepted this valuation and recognized in the symbolism of the Faust-figure its own deepest essence. Much honour is done to youth by this poem and the greatness it achieved. Its uncompromising-ness, its spirit of untamed revolt, its scorn of limitations, of peace and quiet, its yearning and heaven-storming soul, are precisely the expression of what age likes to call 'youthful immaturity'. But, thanks to the power of genius, this immaturity becomes the representative of humanity; youth stands for the human being at large; what was youthful storm and stress becomes ageless and typical.

Of course, in the play it is not a youth but a reverend and learned doctor whom we see at his desk in the dark vault. The filthy brewage of the witches' kitchen is to take thirty years from his age, and he must be a man some thirty years old when he first addresses Gretchen; so at the beginning of the play he would be not less than sixty years old, and as such he is repre-sented on the stage. Yet of this sixty-year-old man Mephisto-pheles says to God:

Indeed, he serves you in the strangest fashion!
Not earthly food or drink do feed his passion.
His inner ferment drives him far,
Of his own frenzy he is half aware;
From heaven he demands the fairest star,
From earth all bliss supremely rare –
And yet not near nor far
Can he find easement for his anguished breast.

Those are not words that fit a man on the threshold of old age. The poet transplants his youthful urgency into the breast of a man at the same time of life as Goethe's own when he wrote the *Elective Affinities*. His Faust is humanity itself, object at once of the divine solicitude and of the lust for conquest of the powers of darkness. But the young poet who so facilely sketched this cosmic figure gave it his own traits, his own nature; and thus the youth became a man, the man a youth.

But this particular youth strives for, and achieves, critical detachment even from his own youngness, from his unbounded urge for freedom and the Absolute Detachment implies irony; and his need of irony just as strongly demands poetic expression as do his other cravings. Irony is his 'second soul'; and Goethe makes Faust speak with a sigh of the two souls within his breast: the one the lusty hunger for love, the clinging sensuality; the other his longing for the pure and spiritual. The sigh he breathes is half-hypocritical: as well might he lament the duality of irony and enthusiasm, for well he knows that dualism is the soil and the mystery of creative fruitfulness. Enthusiasm – that is fullness with God; and what then is irony? The author of *Faust* is youth enough to see in that urge for the Absolute the divine in man; and in irony the diabolic. But this diabolism of his does not stand on such a bad footing with the divine. The Lord God says of it:

Hatred for your sort I have never felt.
Of all the spirits that deny
I find the thorough rascal least offensive.

The diabolism is of an amusing, witty kind, and God has tolerant understanding of it. It is acidulous, unprejudiced worldly sense, unapt for the emotions of the angels but not without sympathy for ordinary human need: 'I feel a pity for the pains of men,' says Mephisto. It makes superior mock of youthful enthusiasm; it is creative inventiveness and conscious anticipation of maturity and experience, fanaticism and worldly good sense; these are the contradiction, the 'two souls' that Goethe likes to project into the dramatic form. Later he will divide himself into Tasso and Antonio; here, on a grander scale, he divides himself into Faust and Mephistopheles. Mephistopheles is the ironic self-corrective to Goethe's youthful titanism.

Mephistopheles is the most vital figure of a devil in all literature; the clearest-cut, the most animated by creative genius. He has not the emotional appeal of Klopstock's and Milton's devils; yet the characterization is so fresh and amusing, so sharply outlined and yet so various, that despite its spirit of ironic self-abrogation it made a permanent conquest of the human imagination for all time. The name Mephistopheles comes from the old Faust-book and the literature of demonology. Has it to do with mephitic? Does it signify sulphurous, pestilential? At any rate, it has the right sound, for the fellow is foul, foul in the grand style, with a sense of humour about his own foulness. He is presiding genius of all vermin – rats, mice, frogs, bugs, lice and so on. But his protection of the more repulsive manifestations of creation is really an expression of his nihilism, his denial of creation and of life altogether.

He says so straight out, and his words have become proverbial:

I am the spirit that ever denies!
And rightly so; for all that's born on earth
Merits destruction from its birth
And better 'twere it had not seen the light.

And much later on, in the second part of the tragedy, when Faust dies, he shrugs his shoulders at the angel's word 'Over!' and mocks at life's lament over its own transitoriness:

Over! A silly word.
Why over?
Over, and sheerest nothing, quite the same!
Then what's the use, eternally to strive,
When all that's made at nothing does arrive?
Over it is! What shall we learn from that?
It is as good as though it never were,
Runs round and round, the same old end to see –
The eternal void is good enough for me.

The grey-haired poet makes his devil speak just as the audacious youth had made him do, in the self-same accents. And we must not think that the devil's nihilism, his critique of life as it is and just because it is, was remote from the poet and foreign to his soul. Through the mouth of Faust he stands up for life, 'the healing, creative force', to which Mephisto opposes the 'cold devil's fist'. But what Mephisto says springs just as much from Goethe's own nature and feelings as does his apologia for life. Goethe, like Mephisto, is no angelic flatterer of creation; and he invents a devil in order to have a mouthpiece for all the rebellion, denial and critical bitterness he feels in himself.

But Mephistopheles is not only the presiding genius of all the vermin. Above all he is the genius of *fire*, he has reserved to himself that destructive, sterilizing, annihilating element. The red waistcoat and the cock's feather are the outward signs of his infernal nature. It is true that the witch misses in him the other classic attributes, the cloven hoof, the two ravens, which the Christian Devil inherited from the pagan Wotan. But in Mephisto the devil of the myth is tamed down in accordance with the cosmopolitan pose which he humorously finds more appropriate to the times. The cloven hoof is replaced by a slight limp. Wotan's ravens do indeed appear in the second part ('I see my raven pair, what message do they bear?'); but they are as a rule invisible. Mephisto regards himself as a cultural product, and seeks to dissociate himself from the legendary 'northern phantom'. He lays aside horns, claws, and tail; as for the cloven hoof, that, he feels, would do him harm in society. He refuses to be addressed as Squire Satan, and prefers the title of Herr Baron, as a gentleman among other gentlemen. Satan, he feels, has become a fable; he accepts the man-of-the-world version of him; though at the same time he asserts that mankind has not gained very much by doing away with the Devil. 'They are rid of the Evil One, the evils remain.' He completely departs from the role, turns his scepticism upon himself, and quite in the spirit of the Enlightenment regards his own existence as a superstition, or at most as so moderated by enlightenment as to fit the new age. The drollest implications arise, as for instance that scene, in only four verses, wherein Faust and Mephistopheles pass by a crucifix. 'Mephisto, why so fast?' says Faust. 'And why cast down your eyes before the Cross?' His companion replies:

I realize it is a prejudice –
Anyhow, there it is: I do not like it.

The fear of the crucifix was a mark of the medieval Devil. But when Mephisto speaks of prejudice, that is good eighteenth-century, and a proper modernized Satan to match. His enlightenment is not religious, it is not the crucifix that he speaks of as a prejudice, it is his own medieval, traditional fear to which he refers, and he excuses it as a weakness and caprice which, despite all his modern culture, he has been unable to overcome.

We see how the poet plays with his conception of the Evil

One, limiting at moments its reality, making it display at times a satiric abrogation of its own identity. But after all it is actually there, actually a devil, who comes when called, and is subject to the laws of demonology. 'I make my homage to the learned man: you certainly have made me sweat quite soundly,' he acknowledges to Faust. Sometimes one might suspect that he is only playing his part in the game; in the witches' kitchen he behaves with good-humoured, sceptical condescension towards the magic claptrap and objectionable humbug which so offend Faust's humanistic feeling.

Oh, suchlike little games – one laughs
At them! My good sir, don't be such an ass!
She is the doctor, she must do her stuff.

He defends the nonsensical Einmaleins (one times one) incantation by an attack on the pious absurdity of the Holy Trinity, in a sarcastic line or so. Yet Mephisto seems to be caught by the pentagram and subject to it; also the signature in blood, to Faust a meaningless gesture, he appears actually to need in order to execute the pact in good medieval demonological style.

Thus we see the artist playing with the traditional figure; making it hover in changeful light or even avaunt and void the right of its own identity. It is even uncertain, for instance, and is deliberately left uncertain, whether this is actually *the* Devil or only *a* devil; only a representative of the infernal powers (*ein Teil von jener Kraft*) or the Evil One himself in person. In the Prologue in Heaven he is plainly the Satan of the Book of Job; for why should a lesser one than he ask permission of God to try a human soul? And at the very end, when Faust's immortal soul is in question, he cannot well be other than Satan himself, the thwarted Devil of legend. But in between he functions, so to speak, as a limited liability company; refers to 'us' and 'folk like us'; says: 'Bethink thee well, for we shall not forget,' and 'Did we force ourselves on you, or you on us?' Goethe even wrote for the Walpurgisnacht a scene in which Satanus himself, Herr Urian, sits on the peak of the Brocken and holds his horrid court. But this was to introduce confusion: to include the scene would have condemned Mephisto to second place in the hierarchy, and Goethe left it out, so that the Prince of Hell, the Whole, might not derogate from the importance of the part.

Mephisto's language is sharply contrasted with the earnest, emotional, passionate key in which Faust speaks. The devil's line is brisk and worldly; it has a careless wit; is eminently critical and contemptuous, spiced with foreign words, altogether diverting. He speaks as it were *en passant*; the result is happy, casual, and most effective:

Yes, my good sir, you look at things
Precisely as in fact one does;
From now on we must manage better —

and so on. That is the tone. It is the superiority of the man of the world (and Mephisto is at bottom nothing but a worldling) who shrugs his shoulders over the man with the deep and troubled emotional nature. Faust, in worldly matters, is Mephisto's pupil; he lets himself be led; and in despair over his own striving for the highest things, even strikes a bargain with the devil. Mephisto's relation to Faust is that of the experienced travelling-companion and tutor who knows his way about; he is courier, *maître des plaisirs*; again he is simply the resourceful servant who Lothario-like makes opportunities for his master. He is all these things by turns, with versatility and wit. In the Paralipomenon, one of the numerous rejected drafts, the devil pictures himself as the corrupt tutor of a young eighteenth-century nobleman:

True, my young master is a trifle wilful,
But birds like that aren't hard to tame.
A tutor's job has made me skilful,
Naught he can do puts me to shame.
Go where he will, I follow with due meekness,
Since for my own ways I still have a weakness,
I preach a lot — and let him have his way.
And when some extra-stupid prank he'll play,
Then my good sense it is my turn to show,
And drag him out of harm's way by the hair:
Leaving him, while the damage we repair,
Always an opening for some new folly.

Goethe continually rhymes *zeigen* and *streichen, neigen* and *reichen*, as though his Frankfurt pronunciation *zeichen* and *neichen* were the universal one. It is certainly a hard pill to swallow, from the greatest lyric poet of Germany. It shows a naïve persistence in local tradition – we have simply to put up with it, and console ourselves with the thought that it is nice to hear how Goethe spoke. The rejected verses just quoted are a good illustration of the wit and variety in Goethe's portrayal of the devil: how it makes itself large and then small, expanding from the satirical human being into the magnificently diabolic and back again at will.

But in the end Mephistopheles is the personification of the hatred of light and life; he is primal night and Chaos' son, the emissary of the void – after his own kind he is on a very grand scale. 'Thou vile abortion, born of filth and fire!' – thus Faust once rails at him, and it is a splendid description. Something about it, we realize, corresponds to the human intellectual elements which both impress and offend us. The filth, that is the cynicism, the obscene wit, launched by the fires of his infernal will to destruction. The essence of his nature is the profoundest lovelessness. Hatred fairly scintillates in the creature's slanting yellow tiger-eyes. 'The bottomless rage that leads thee to destroy.' Faust says to him: 'thy tig'rish glare, thy all-compelling face...'. Here the humorous side fades out, and the devil emerges in all his specific majesty; not without a certain admiration the poet sees and feels it.

Goethe's own attitude towards evil is not uniform; it hovers between recognition and contempt. He says, in one of the Proverbs:

I still remain quite unconvinced
That it's good sense to paint the devil small:
There must be something in a chap
Who's hated so by all.

But in portraying Mephistopheles as the embodiment of evil, Goethe sometimes injects into the character a trace of self-contempt, a hang-dog note: Mephistopheles will sometimes betray his suspicion that the devil is no great shakes when all is said and done:

Let nobody ask me on my oath
Whether I shame me for my kind;
But you, when you speak the words 'the devil' –
You've something big in mind.

When you say 'the devil', you really are not saying much; in other words, evil is a poor thing after all. The poet could scarcely make the idea more impressive than by putting it in the Evil One's own mouth! And in the Prologue, Mephisto feels flattered by the fact that God condescends to converse with him, the old nihilist:

It's very handsome of so great a lord
To talk with the devil as man to man!

Not for nothing have these two light-hearted lines become so famous. Their humour is complex and subtle. Here is the Divine Absolute, in the role of the Grand Seigneur who is human enough to discuss with the Opposition; and here is the Opposition, flattered by the complaisance and recognizing its own inferiority – truly a cosmic jest, a regular poet's joke, and very characteristic of this particular poet; for when in the presence of opposition and negation, Goethe always thought of himself as the grand seigneur and representative of the government. 'If I had had the *misfortune* to be in the Opposition,' he once said in conversation. And yet it was precisely Goethe who created, and invested with lyric meaning, the figure of the arch-nihilist, Mephistopheles.

And further: what character in this play – racked, it is true, by disillusionment, bitterness, yearning and despair – utters the most crushing, nihilistic words in the whole poem: the great malediction upon life, its joys and its seduction; the great curse upon spirit and sense, fame and possessions, love, hope, faith, endurance – so that the chorus of spirits must lament:

Woe! Woe!
Thou hast laid low
With violent blow
The beautiful world –
It totters, it falls,
A demigod hath struck it.

We have borne
Its ruins in the void
And we mourn
For the beauty destroyed!

Which character is it? Mephisto? He could never have summoned the pity or pain for such an anathema against life and joy. No, it is the anguished human being, it is Goethe-Faust who utters the frightful words. Here the roles are reversed, and the nihilistic devil becomes the practical and worldly advocate for life against the desperate and rebellious human spirit.

Do stop playing with your sorrows,
That like vultures feed upon your breast!
Even from the lowest company one borrows
A sense that one's a man like all the rest.

The character of Faust in the poem is no simpler, no more uniform, than that of his diabolic mentor. It varies in the same way. Or rather the whole poem in which they play their parts possesses this variability of the Time-Spirit; since the scene, ostensibly, is laid in the sixteenth century, but continually plays over into the eighteenth, the poet's own. Wagner, the famulus, speaks the language of the age of enlightenment, praises the periods of Gottsched, and feels that science and mankind have made glorious progress. Faust-Goethe, on the contrary, stands for Herder's ideas about the 'age of genius'. The nature-mysticism of his soliloquies, and the religious feeling he shows to Gretchen – all that is inspired by Swedenborg, Ossian, and Lavater, in particular by the northern mystic, who died in 1772, and whose name Goethe replaced by that of Nostradamus in order to preserve the historical perspective. I spoke of Faust's humanism, the intellectual attitude that makes him fundamentally despise magic as despicable rigmarole, although he surrenders to it, that 'through the spirit's mouth and might, mysteries might see the light'. As a matter of fact, he remained, as Mephisto's patron, addicted to it up to his old age and made use of it in all his adventures, first with Gretchen, and then in the world, at the Kaiser's court, in battle, in the affair with Helena, whom he wins only by enchantment and illusion.

Not till very late does there stir in him the desire 'magic from out his path to pat away'. Yet even so, his attitude towards it from the beginning is highly fastidious – or at least towards its practicants and technicians and their obscene trafficking. He inveighs against the witches' kitchen as a *'Wust von Raserei'* (crazy rubbish). 'Why just that old hag?' he asks in disgust. He finds the whole thing as unappetizing as anything he ever saw. Bad taste, offensive – that is his humanistic judgement on the whole of magic art: 'frantic stuff, wild goings-on, disgusting humbug' – he knows and despises it already. The blood-pact – vital to Mephisto because after all, in God's name, he really *is* the devil – Faust knows about that too, it is as familiar as repulsive to him; he refers to the pact with contempt, as a piece of tomfoolery. Why must they have such a superstitious flourish as the signature in blood, when after all, in the eternal flux of things, there can be no such thing as a binding promise, however much a high-minded man would wish to cling to the delusion of truth? Mephisto duly utters his medieval patter, just as it stands in the legend:

Here I bind myself unto your service,
Ever at your beck and call to be;
When we find ourselves in the hereafter,
Then you shall do the same for me.

He speaks of the hereafter as an actuality in the popular mind and his own – in the Prologue, indeed, he stands before God among the heavenly host. But Faust answers him as a humanist and earth-bound human spirit, who does not believe in a hereafter, or at least is not interested in one:

My joys all spring from earthly sources,
My griefs are shined on by this very sun;
When I can sever me from earthly courses,
Let come what can and will; my race is run.
I'll hear no more of it.

Neither understands the other – either temporally or morally. The bargain is struck on the basis of two different conceptions: one primitive and diabolic, the other more evolved and with some knowledge of human dignity. '*Was willst du, armer Teufel, geben?*' asks Faust. ('And what, poor devil, can you give at best?')

When was the human spirit's striving
E'er understanded of a thing like thee?

He makes his pact with the devil out of the same high and human aspiration that mind, science, knowledge had been unable to satisfy; with the same absolute and insatiable passion that made him despair of thought he gives himself to pleasure. And all the while he knows but too well that it will be as impotent as knowledge to still his craving for infinity.

If ever on bed of idleness I lay me,
May I that moment die!
When thou by flattery canst wile me
In self-complacency to rest,
Or e'er with pleasant lusts beguile me –
Then may that moment be my last!

'Beguile with pleasant lusts.' Thus no voluptuary speaks. Rather he who takes up with pleasure as earlier he did with things of the mind, and recognizes but one kind of slavery: inertia and ease.

All threads of thought I sever.
Knowledge abjure forever,
And in the senses deep
My glowing passions steep. . . .
Plunged in time's whirling surge,
Rolled round in life's unending urge,
Let success or failure come,
Alternates of joy and woe
Mingle together how they can;
But let man only striving know.

Thus no voluptuary speaks. Thus speaks an activist, who seeks not pleasure but life, and binds himself to the devil only so far as a man of intellect does who gives himself to life. The formal bond he despises as pedantic and futile, there being no reason to doubt his complete surrender.

There needs no fear this promise shall be broken:
The uttermost of all my powers
Is bent to keep what I have spoken.

One asks oneself, indeed, what does actually come of that
plumbing of the depths of sense, of the intoxications of life and
time, of that furious masculine activity of Faust during his com-
panionship with Mephistopheles. I will not extend the question
to the second part of the poem. There it is only after a multitude
of involved adventures in magic that Faust engages in any kind
of activity that could be called unresting or masculine. As for
the first part, we must admit that Goethe has not gone very far
towards poetic realization of the depths of sensuality or the life
of action, fluctuating between success and failure, to which his
hero would devote himself. What does Mephisto do for his hopeful pupil? He takes him to Auerbach's cellar, where the two
perform conjuring tricks before bawling philistines just as in the
chapbook. Well, at least that is by way of illustration to the
lines:

Even from the lowest company one borrows
A sense that one's a man like all the rest –

though it is hardly even that, for Faust does not succeed in being
hail-fellow-well-met with his brother topers in the cellar. He and
the devil behave more like high-born travelling foreigners, very
spoilt and capricious at that, and with a smack of the charlatan
that would make them suspect to middle-class minds. We hear
that they have just got back from Spain; if that is true, what
have they been doing there? We do not learn. We are equally
puzzled by Faust's remark at the beginning of the Gretchen episode, when he demands that Mephisto deliver the little one
straight into his arms:

If I had only seven hours free,
I should not need to call the Devil in
To teach that little creature how to sin.

If that is only said in order to excuse him for not being able to
seduce the poor child by his own efforts, but needing the powers
of hell to help him to do it, then we must deduce that he is occu-

pied indeed – and with what, and how? We remain in the dark. None of the deceased charlatan's famous deeds or misdeeds come into the first part; the Gretchen story stands alone, for nothing stronger had the young poet to give! He magnified it into his own tragedy, he reduced all the rest of the Faustian programme to this one exploration of the life of passion. And who would regret the fact? For the result was the loveliest, sincerest, saddest love-story in the German language, perhaps in any language, told in the simplest, most natural, convincing, and moving accents in the world.

We must repeat what has so often been said already: this little Gretchen, the pawnbroker's daughter, as we see her move before our mind's eye, in her grief, her humanness and femininity, her childlike purity, her love and devotion, her vicarious, pitiful fate, is a figure of immortal beauty. We see her in the little German imperial city, a small, idyllic setting, with spinning-wheel and fountain, christening feast and gossiping neighbours. But how the young creature, so simple, yet so warm with life, is lifted out of her lowliness and transfigured by the masculine guilt and remorse! At the end she is nothing less than the spirit of love itself, watching from above over the struggles of the erring one and preparing his welcome and redemption. Like Mignon in Goethe's great novel, she has two of her creator's most marvellous lyrics put in her mouth: 'Meine Ruh ist hin,' and 'Es war ein König in Thule.' But she is herself a 'Lied', a folk-song refined by the most personal art. At the end, in desolation and madness, in her prison cell, her soul and her song slip away into the most wonderous, awesome sphere of all folk-poesy:

My mother the whore,
She did me to death!
My father the knave,
My flesh eaten hath! .
My sister so small
My bones gathered all
And laid them to cool.
And then I was turned to a sweet wood bird –
Fly away, fly away!

Such simple, native accents of uncanny fantasy are unknown to
Clärchen in *Egmont*. Yet the two are sisters, Clärchen and Gretchen, unmistakably visualized and created by their author to
live through varying tragic destinies. One becomes the heroine,
the other the martyr of her sex. And just as they are sisters, so
their lovers, Faust and Egmont, are brothers, true sons of Goethe
both, representing the characteristic Goethian eroticism, a little
narcissistic; which finds its peculiar ecstasy in the beguilement
of simple innocence, of the little maid of the people by a lordly
masculinity stooping down from loftier spheres, and in her utter
surrender to her blissful fate. Egmont shows himself to the
virtuous Clärchen in Spanish court dress; nothing could be more
characteristic of Goethe's own wish-dream world than this scene.
In *Faust*, the court dress and the golden fleece are of a metaphysical kind. An elegant, fastidious traveller, from an intellectual sphere unknown to Gretchen's bourgeois simplicity and
most impressive; half nobleman, half scholar, Faust appears as
from another world, and dreaming of him she says:

How much I'd give if I could say
Who that gallant was today!
He looked so very fine and proud,
And I could tell, from some high family:
A nobleman, 'twas plain to see,
So forward else he had not been with me.

Delightful lines. Gretchen betrays in them her profound curiosity and emotion after the first meeting. She is flattered that he
approached her, yet feels her modesty offended and, having
given no occasion for his boldness, explains it by his high rank,
The childlike words betray the specific charm which lay for the
poet in such a situation – as does also the later dialogue:

MARGARETE:
I realize, the gentleman is kind,
And lowers himself, it puts me quite to shame;
For travellers are not to blame
For simply taking up with what they find.
I know too well, my simple chatter,
To such a man as you are, could not matter.

FAUST:
One look from thee, one word is more to me
Than all the wisdom of this world can be.

In this everyday fragment of talk there lies great richness of
feeling. It is so typical of student life; it is so typically the love-
story of the university man, the academic, the Herr Doctor, and
the little girl of the people, who cannot think what the clever
gentleman sees in her. *In abstracto*, it is beauty, poor in spirit,
blushing before the wooing of the intellect. Beauty and 'wisdom'; and the sensual abrogation of the one before the other,
with all the dangers of seduction and ruin which lie for innocence and beauty in this appeal of intellect and sensuality combined. Thus intellect becomes guilty before beauty, and thus
Faust became guilty before Gretchen. Certainly the Gretchen
story is the tragedy of intellect becoming mortally guilty to
beauty, with the cynical connivance of the devil. And here, more
than anywhere else, does Goethe betray himself a revolutionary, in that he would stir our emotions against the cruelty of
human society, which punishes the beauty that falls victim to
the beguilement of the superior mind. This once, and never
again, Goethe, owing to his own tragic sense of guilt, becomes
an accuser and rebel against society. In the prose scene: 'Grey
day, a field' taken bodily out of the *Urfaust* and put unchanged
into the fragment as well as the finished poem, Faust, after the
repulsive distractions of the Blocksburg and the Walpurgisnacht dream, learns that Gretchen is in prison and has been
handed over to the justice of cruel, unthinking men. Mephistopheles flings at him his cynical 'She is not the first'.

'Not the first! Oh, horror, horror! How can any human being understand that the writhing death-agony of the first was
not enough to atone for the guilt of the rest, in the eyes of the
All-Merciful! The agony of this single one pierces me to the
heart – and you can stand there and grin at the fate of thousands!'

The scene is written in rough, savage, almost clumsy prose,
devoid of irony; it scarcely seems to belong to a poem that
otherwise, in all its inward significance, its profound human

symbolism, moves with such light-footed creative objectivity. Shall we call it uncharacteristic? Certainly Goethe seems to have found it so. When the *Faust* was performed at Weimar, he left this scene out. And it is said that as a member of the government he gave society its due by signing the death sentence upon a young girl accused of child murder, although the Duke himself would have shown her mercy.

If this story be true, it bears witness to a stern self-disciplining of his own kindliness and pity, and their suppression in favour of established order. For the mature Goethe held order in such honour that he openly declared it to be better to commit injustice than to tolerate disorder. That too has its fine side; but more youthfully beautiful, certainly, is the rebellion against order, grounded on the remorseful feelings of Friederike Brion's unfaithful lover, and mounting in the Faust poem almost to destructive heights. Gretchen's destruction is almost the ruin of Faust as well. Nowhere else does he, the human being, fall so foul of his companion as here; nowhere does he fling the scorn of his anguished heart so furiously in the grinning face of the demon who mocks at man's double nature: *'Hund! Abscheuliches Untier!'* ('Dog! Detestable monster!')

'Hab' ich doch meine Freude dran!' ('I get my fun out of it too.')

Goethe, in *Faust*, has depicted love as a regular devil's holiday: the 'high intuition' whose conclusion and consummation Mephisto indicates with an obscene gesture. It begins so tenderly, with such extravagant soulfulness, and reaches its end in guilty despair. *'Doch, alles was mich dazu trieb, Gott! war so gut, ach! war so lieb!'* ('And all that drove me thereunto, God! was so dear, ah! was so true'). So poor Gretchen sighs; and her seducer will not have it at any price that he is betraying her when he whispers her eternal loyalty and love. Faust replies to the mockery of his companion:

... when for my feeling,
When for the tumult in my breast,
I seek a name, and find no healing,
When through the world I range and try

With all my senses to express
This ecstasy with which I burn,
And call eternal, infinite —
Is that a devilish lie?

And the Evil One replies: 'And yet I'm right!' For youthful
love, the most human thing in the world, wherein the spirit
and the body, the natural and the divine, mingle in a way so
symbolic and so exemplary for all humanity, is truly the devil's
playground, the theatre of his most prized triumphs. There he
most easily performs his traditional task of betraying the highest
in man to the basest. There truly is his immemorial striving: to
seize on that higher part of man, so mingled with his baser
self, and in the baser swallow up the higher. And he would
triumph, were it not that the Eternal Goodness, with whom in
the Prologue the devil is so cringingly conversable, and who sees
the highest in the lowest, not, as the devil does, the lowest in the
highest, opposes his will to destruction.

The whole Faust-poem is based on the Prologue in Heaven.
Or rather the Prologue was afterwards shoved underneath the
youthful, light-heartedly conceived composition, to prop it up.
For it is in the Prologue that the figure of Faust becomes the
protagonist and symbol of man, in whom the Eternal Goodness
had a share, as he in it. Faust's human trait, which makes him
strive after the universally human, is his noble side, the goodness which is at the same time godliness in him. So it comes
about that he and the devil, who has no understanding of the
painstaking spirit of man, misunderstand each other when they
make their pact. When Faust says: 'Let us still our glowing
passions in the depth of sense,' he means something quite different from what the devil thinks; he means even the sensuality with a difference: as something nobler, deeper, more
serious and fervent. Despairing of thought, he turns to the
world and to life. But of joy, he says, there can be no thought.

To tumult I am vowed, and ecstasy of pain....
My bosom, now of wisdom's craving healed,
Shall to no sorrows from this day be sealed,
But all the pangs that human lot befall,

In my own heart henceforth I'll know them all,
And with my spirit grasp their depth and height.
Their weal and woe my breast shall know,
And so my own self to their self shall grow.

The Mephistophelian 'world' (the devil is only a worldling) becomes for Faust life, with its tortures and desires; but surrender
to it takes on at once a human character; he wishes to live, in
the fullest, most human sense, he would be a son of man, would
take upon himself and exhaust, as representative and sacrifice,
all the joys and sorrows of mankind. And we recall those words,
spoken as in a dream, which Goethe murmured to himself on a
moonlight night in his youth, mounting out of the Ilm:

All do the gods give, the eternal,
To their favourites, wholly:
All the joys, the eternal,
All the pangs, the eternal,
Wholly.

To take the joys and sufferings of mankind upon himself, in
giving himself to life – nothing else is it that Faust promises
the devil. But this 'striving to attain man's utmost height', infinite as it always is, and sinful in the sense that it is presump-
tuous titanism, is after all more allied to God than to the devil;
it is generous, upright, and good, and despite all the perils it
entails, it never from the first holds out any great hopes to the
devil.

In a poem written at the time of his betrothal to Lili Schöne-
mann, we hear Goethe call himself *'ein guter Junge'* ('a good
lad'). 'Why,' he asks:

Ah, why dost thou so resistless draw me
To thy splendour bright?
Was I not, *good lad*, so happy,
In the lonely night?

'Ich guter Junge.' It is touching to hear Goethe so address himself; and whatever the intellectual heights he reached, however
reverend he became to himself, it remained to the end a good description. We know how mild he was, how tolerant, what uni-

versal benevolence he possessed. We know his lifelong wish, 'to do good to men', 'to teach them to live'; we know his confession, that after every flight into solitude he needed but to see a human face 'to love again'. And the man of the Faustian strivings and efforts, he too is 'a good boy'. Just as he means well by himself, and feels that he can be saved, so also he means well by humanity: he wants its good, would have it assisted, positively, lovingly, reasonably; would not have it bewildered, would have it satisfied. In a Paralipomenon Faust says to Mephistopheles:

So hearken now, if thou hast never heard:
The human hearing's very keen,
And glorious deeds can follow one clear word.
Man knows only too sore his human need,
And gladly counsel he will heed.

And again:

Nothing of all is granted thee.
Then how canst thou men's longing read?
Thy warped nature, bitter, curst,
What can it know of human need?

Nothing could be more Goethian, nothing more Faustian. Its conception of man, its attitude towards the human being, are a part of the Everlasting Goodness; and no differently speaks the eternal Goodness itself, God the Lord, in the Prologue, whose characterization of man is young Goethe's characterization of himself; in it self-love grows till it embraces humanity:

Though still he serve me with a darkened mind,
Soon to the light of truth I'll lead his feet.
Knows not the gardener when the tree is green
That flower and fruit the coming year shall greet?

And then that primal word of the Eternal Goodness:

For man must err, so long as man must strive.

And that final pronouncement of God, which in its lofty and trusting mildness has become proverbial for all mankind:

And stand abashed, when you at last must say,
The good man, howsoever dark his striving,
Is ever mindful of the better way.

4 William Makepeace Thackeray
The Sorrows of Werther

from *Miscellanies*, vol. 1   1855

Werther had a love for Charlotte
    Such as words could never utter;
Would you know how first he met her?
    She was cutting bread and butter.

Charlotte was a married lady,
    And a moral man was Werther,
And for all the wealth of Indies,
    Would do nothing for to hurt her.

So he sigh'd and pined and ogled,
    And his passion boil'd and bubbled,
Till he blew his silly brains out,
    And no more was by it troubled.

Charlotte, having seen his body
    Borne before her on a shutter,
Like a well-conducted person,
    Went on cutting bread and butter.

J William Wordsworth

This selection is chosen primarily to augment *The Poetry of Wordsworth* – the anthology used by Open University students of the Age of Revolutions Course. But whilst these are not the poems which one would choose to introduce Wordsworth to a new reader, they can be said to be of real interest to those who wish to see the poet as part of the age he lived in.

In his autobiographical poem, *The Prelude*, Wordsworth records how his early love of nature led him to love and respect humanity. The first men he valued were not eminent or nobly born, but humble and enduring men, the hill-shepherds of his native country. These early sympathies helped to make a Republican of him and he greeted the French Revolution with radical fervour:

Bliss was it in that dawn to be alive.
But to be young was very heaven.

Like many young radicals of the 1790s he was strongly influenced by William Godwin's *Political Justice*. His most explicit statement of republicanism was his reply to a sermon preached by the Bishop of Llandaff on 'The Wisdom and Goodness of God in having made both Rich and Poor'. But such radical views were considered dangerous, and so his letter was never sent and never published. Perhaps the course of the revolution had already begun to disillusion him. Certainly by 1796 Godwin's political solutions and his rationalism had come to seem incommensurate with Wordsworth's own experience of human behaviour and he began to look on the poor (especially the rural poor) not through the eyes of a social reformer but as one who had lived close to them. For Godwin a beggar was merely a useless product of an evil society; Wordsworth took a more compassionate view. Godwin believed that lying is not natural to children but the product of an evil society; Wordsworth's instance is both more simple and more complex than this.

He was no longer a revolutionary but he continued in some sense a radical. The principles stated in the Preface to *Lyrical Ballads* are behind the simple (some would say naïve) poems he wrote until the end of his life: poems about simple people, unspectacular events, small pleasures and humble tragedies, expressed briefly in unpretentious language.

But this is only one side of Wordsworth. Indeed he is often thought of more as a poet of nature than of humanity. What he wrote about nature is not simply descriptive, rhapsodic or emotionally tendentious, as nature poetry of the late eighteenth century was apt to be (I have included two necessarily brief extracts for comparison); it was deeply philosophical. Wordsworth was no philosopher; he had no consistent philosophy of man's relation to his surroundings and his attitude to the German metaphysicians was scathing, but his continuous study of that relationship shows that he was exploring many of the areas examined by the principal philosophers of his time.

C. H.

Further Reading

*T. Crehan (ed.), *The Poetry of Wordsworth*, University of London Press, 1965.

Helen Darbishire (ed.), *The Prelude*, Oxford University Press, 1969. Revised edition.

E. de Selincourt (ed.), *William Wordsworth: Poetical Works*, 5 vols., Oxford University Press, 1940–54.

E. de Selincourt (ed.), *William Wordsworth: Poetical Works*, Oxford University Press, 1969. Revised edition.

* Open University Set Book.

1 William Wordsworth

Love of Nature and Love of Mankind 1804

from *The Prelude*, Book VIII, *Retrospect* 1805–6

With deep devotion, Nature, did I feel
In that great City what I owed to thee,
High thoughts of God and Man, and love of Man,
Triumphant over all those loathsome sights
Of wretchedness and vice; a watchful eye,
Which with the outside of our human life
Not satisfied, must read the inner mind;
For I already had been taught to love
My Fellow-beings, to such habits train'd
Among the woods and mountains, where I found
In thee a gracious Guide, to lead me forth
Beyond the bosom of my Family,
My Friends and youthful Playmates. 'Twas thy power
That rais'd the first complacency in me,
And noticeable kindliness of heart,
Love human to the Creature in himself
As he appear'd, a stranger in my path,
Before my eyes a Brother of this world;
Thou first didst with those motions of delight
Inspire me – I remember, far from home
Once having stray'd, while yet a very Child,
I saw a sight, and with what joy and love!
It was a day of exhalations, spread
Upon the mountains, mists and steam-like fogs
Redounding everywhere, not vehement,
But calm and mild, gentle and beautiful,
With gleams of sunshine on the eyelet spots
And loop-holes of the hills, wherever seen,
Hidden by quiet process, and as soon
Unfolded, to be huddled up again:
Along a narrow Valley and profound
I journey'd, when, aloft above my head,
Emerging from the silvery vapours, lo!
A Shepherd and his Dog! in open day:

Girt round with mists they stood and look'd about
From that enclosure small, inhabitants
Of an aerial Island floating on,
As seem'd, with that Abode in which they were,
A little pendant area of grey rocks,
By the soft wind breath'd forward. With delight
As bland almost, one Evening I beheld,
And at as early age (the spectacle
Is common, but by me was then first seen)
A Shepherd in the bottom of a Vale
Towards the centre standing, who with voice,
And hand waved to and fro as need required
Gave signal to his Dog, thus teaching him
To chace along the mazes of steep crags
The Flock he could not see : and so the Brute
Dear Creature! with a Man's intelligence
Advancing, or retreating on his steps,
Through every pervious strait, to right or left,
Tridded a way unbaffled; while the Flock
Fled upwards from the terror of his Bark
Through rocks and seams of turf with liquid gold
Irradiate, that deep farewell light by which
The setting sun proclaims the love he bears
To mountain regions.
               Beauteous the domain
Where to the sense of beauty first my heart
Was open'd, tract more exquisitely fair
Than is that Paradise of ten thousand Trees,
Or Gehol's famous Gardens, in a Clime
Chosen from widest Empire, for delight
Of the Tartarian Dynasty composed;
(Beyond that mighty Wall, not fabulous,
China's stupendous mound!) by patient skill
Of myriads, and boon Nature's lavish help;
Scene link'd to scene, an evergrowing change,
Soft, grand, or gay! with Palaces and Domes
Of Pleasure spangled over, shady Dells
For Eastern Monasteries, sunny Mounds
With Temples crested, Bridges, Gondolas,

Rocks, Dens, and Groves of foliage taught to melt
Into each other their obsequious hues
Going and gone again, in subtile chace,
Too fine to be pursued; or standing forth
In no discordant opposition, strong
And gorgeous as the colours side by side
Bedded among rich plumes of Tropic Birds;
And mountains over all embracing all;
And all the landscape endlessly enrich'd
With waters running, falling, or asleep.

But lovelier far than this the Paradise
Where I was rear'd; in Nature's primitive gifts
Favor'd no less, and more to every sense
Delicious, seeing that the sun and sky,
The elements and seasons in their change
Do find their dearest Fellow-labourer there,
The heart of Man, a district on all sides
The fragrance breathing of humanity,
Man free, man working for himself, with choice
Of time, and place, and object; by his wants,
His comforts, native occupations, cares,
Conducted on to individual ends
Or social, and still followed by a train
Unwoo'd, unthought-of even, simplicity,
And beauty, and inevitable grace.

Yea, doubtless, at an age when but a glimpse
Of those resplendent Gardens, with their frame
Imperial, and elaborate ornaments,
Would to a child be transport over-great,
When but a half-hour's roam through such a place
Would leave behind a dance of images
That shall break in upon his sleep for weeks;
Even then the common haunts of the green earth,
With the ordinary human interests
Which they embosom, all without regard
As both may seem, are fastening on the heart
Insensibly, each with the other's help,

So that we love, not knowing that we love,
And feel, not knowing whence our feeling comes.

2 William Wordsworth
France in 1790   1804

from *The Prelude*, Book VI, *Cambridge and the Alps*   1805–6

'twas a time when Europe was rejoiced,
France standing on the top of golden hours
And human nature seeming born again.
Bound, as I said, to the Alps, it was our lot
To land at Calais on the very Eve
Of that great federal Day; and there we saw,
In a mean City, and among a few,
How bright a face is worn when joy of one
Is joy of tens of millions. Southward thence
We took our way direct through Hamlets, Towns,
Gaudy with reliques of that Festival,
Flowers left to wither on triumphal Arcs,
And window-Garlands. On the public roads,
And, once, three days successively, through paths,
By which our toilsome journey was abridg'd,
Among sequester'd villages we walked,
And found benevolence and blessedness
Spread like a fragrance everywhere, like Spring
That leaves no corner of the land untouch'd.

Where Elms, for many and many a league, in files
With their thin umbrage on the stately roads
Of that great kingdom, rustled o'er our heads,
For ever near us as we paced along;
'Twas sweet at such a time, with such delights
On every side, in prime of youthful strength,
To feed a poet's tender melancholy
And fond conceit of sadness, to the noise
And gentle undulation which they made.
Unhous'd, beneath the Evening Star we saw

Dances of Liberty, and in late hours
Of darkness, dances in the open air.[1]

Among the vine-clad Hills of Burgundy,
Upon the bosom of the gentle Soane
We glided forward with the flowing stream:
Swift Rhone, thou wert the wings on which we cut
Between thy lofty rocks! Enchanting show
Those woods, and farms, and orchards did present,
And single Cottages, and lurking Towns,
Reach after reach, procession without end
Of deep and stately Vales. A lonely Pair
Of Englishmen we were, and sail'd along
Cluster'd together with a merry crowd
Of those emancipated, with a host
Of Travellers, chiefly Delegates, returning
From the great Spousals newly solemniz'd
At their chief City in the sight of Heaven.
Like bees they swarm'd, gaudy and gay as bees;
Some vapour'd in the unruliness of joy
And flourish'd with their swords, as if to fight
The saucy air. In this blithe Company
We landed, took with them our evening Meal,
Guests welcome almost as the Angels were
To Abraham of old. The Supper done,
With flowing cups elate, and happy thoughts,
We rose at signal giv'n, and form'd a ring
And, hand in hand, danced round and round the Board;
All hearts were open, every tongue was loud
With amity and glee; we bore a name
Honour'd in France, the name of Englishmen,
And hospitably did they give us hail
As their forerunners in a glorious course,
And round, and round the Board they danced again.
With this same Throng our voyage we pursu'd

1. 1850 text reads:

> dances in the open air
> Deftly prolonged, though grey-haired lookers on
> Might waste their breath in chiding.

At early dawn; the Monastery Bells
Made a sweet jingling in our youthful ears;
The rapid River flowing without noise,
And every Spire we saw among the rocks
Spake with a sense of peace, at intervals
Touching the heart amid the boisterous Crew
With which we were environ'd.

3 William Wordsworth
Reply to the Bishop of Llandaff

from Wordsworth's reply to a sermon by the Bishop of
Landaff 1793 Reprinted in Alexander Grosart (ed.), *The Prose
Works of William Wordsworth*, 3 vols. 1876

[The Bishop's sermon was called 'The Wisdom and Goodness
of God having made both Rich and Poor. Its text was Proverbs, xxii, 2: 'The rich and the poor meet together, the Lord is
the Maker of them all.']

You say: 'I fly with terror and abhorrence even from the altar
of Liberty, when I see it stained with the blood of the aged, of
the innocent, of the defenceless sex, of the ministers of religion,
and of the faithful adherents of a fallen monarch.' What! have
you so little knowledge of the nature of man as to be ignorant
that a time of revolution is not the season of true Liberty? Alas,
the obstinacy and perversion of man is such that she is too often
obliged to borrow the very arms of Despotism to overthrow him,
and, in order to reign in peace, must establish herself by violence.
She deplores such stern necessity, but the safety of the people, her
supreme law, is her consolation. This apparent contradiction
between the principles of liberty and the march of revolutions; this spirit of jealousy, of severity, of disquietude, of vexation, indispensable from a state of war between the oppressors
and oppressed, must of necessity confuse the ideas of morality,
and contract the benign exertion of the best affections of the
human heart. Political virtues are developed at the expense of
moral ones; and the sweet emotions of compassion, evidently

dangerous when traitors are to be punished, are too often altogether smothered. But is this a sufficient reason to reprobate a convulsion from which is to spring a fairer order of things? It is the province of education to rectify the erroneous notions which a habit of repression, and even of resistance, may have created, and to soften this ferocity of character, proceeding from a necessary suspension of the mild and social virtues; it belongs to her to create a race of men who, truly free, will look upon their fathers as only enfranchised. [...]

As to your arguments, by which you pretend to justify your anathemas of a Republic – if arguments they may be called – they are so concise, that I cannot but transcribe them. 'I dislike a Republic for this reason, because of all forms of government, scarcely excepting the most despotic, I think a Republic the most oppressive to the bulk of the people: they are deceived in it with a show of liberty, but they live in it under the most odious of tyrannies – the tyranny of their equals.' [...]

Your Lordship will scarcely question that much of human misery, that the great evils which desolate States, proceed from the governors having an interest distinct from that of the governed. It should seem a natural deduction, that whatever has a tendency to identify the two must also in the same degree promote the general welfare. As the magnitude of almost all states prevents the possibility of their enjoying a pure democracy, philosophers – from a wish, as far as is in their power, to make the governors and the governed one – will turn their thoughts to a system of universal representation, and will annex an equal importance to the suffrage of every individual. Jealous of giving up no more of the authority of the people than is necessary, they will be solicitous of finding out some method by which the office of their delegates may be confined as much as is practicable to the proposing and deliberating upon laws rather than to enacting them; reserving to the people the power of finally inscribing them in the national code. Unless this is attended to, as soon as the people has chosen representatives it no longer has a political existence, except as it is understood to retain the privilege of annihilating the trust when it shall think proper, and of resuming its original power. Sensible that at the moment of election an interest distinct from that of the general body is created, an enlightened legislator will endeavour by every possible method to diminish the operation of such interest. The first and most natural mode that presents itself is that of shortening the regular duration of this trust, in order that the man who has betrayed it may soon be superceded by a more worthy successor. But this is not enough; aware of the possibility of imposition, and of the natural tendency of power to corrupt the heart of man, a sensible Republican will think it essential that the office of legislator be not entrusted to the same man for a succession of years. He will also be induced to this wise restraint by the grand principle of identification; he will be more sure of the virtue of the legislator by knowing that, in the capacity of private citizen, tomorrow he must either smart under the oppression or bless the justice of the law which he has enacted today. [. . .]

In the choice of its representatives a people will not immorally hold out wealth as a criterion of integrity, nor lay down as a fundamental rule, that to be qualified for the trying duties of legislation a citizen should be possessed of a certain fixed property. Virtues, talents, and acquirements are all that it will look for. [. . .]

Your Lordship respects 'peasants and mechanics when they intrude not themselves into concerns for which their education has not fitted them'.

Setting aside the idea of a peasant or mechanic being a legislator, what vast education is requisite to enable him to judge among his neighbours which is most qualified by his industry and integrity to be intrusted with the care of the interests of himself and his fellow-citizens? But leaving this ground, as governments formed on such a plan proceed in a plain and open manner, their administration would require much less of what is usually called talents and experience, that is, of disciplined treachery and hoary Machiavelism; and at the same time, as it would no longer be their interest to keep the mass of the nation in ignorance, a moderate portion of useful knowledge would be universally disseminated. [. . .]

The history of all ages has demonstrated that wealth [. . .] includes [. . .] an oppressive principle. Aware of this, and that the extremes of poverty and riches have a necessary tendency to corrupt the human heart, [a Republican legislator] will banish from his code all laws such as the unnatural monster of primogeniture, such as encourage associations against labour in the form of corporate bodies, and indeed all that monopolising system of legislation, whose baleful influence is shown in the depopulation of the country and in the necessity which reduces the sad relicks to owe their very existence to the ostentatious bounty of their oppressors. If it is true in common life, it is still more true in governments, that we should be just before we are generous; but our legislators seem to have forgotten or despised this homely maxim. They have unjustly left unprotected that most important part of property, not less real because it has no material existence, that which ought to enable the labourer to provide food for himself and his family. I appeal to innumerable statutes, whose constant and professed object it is to lower the price of labour, to compel the workman to be *content* with arbitrary wages, evidently too small from the necessity of legal enforcement of the acceptance of them. [...]

You ask with triumphant confidence, to what other law are the people of England subject than the general will of the society to which they belong? Is your lordship to be told that acquiescence is not choice, and that obedience is not freedom? If there is a single man in Great Britain who has no suffrage in the election of a representative, the will of the society of which he is a member is not generally expressed. [...] The fact is that the Kings and Lords and Commons, by what is termed the omnipotence of Parliament, have constitutionally the right of enacting whatever laws they please, in defiance of the petitions or remonstrances of the nation. They have the power of doubling our enormous debt of 240 millions, and *may* pursue measures which could never be supposed the emanation of the general will without concluding the people stripped of reason, of sentiment, and even of that first instinct which prompts them to preserve their own existence.

4 William Wordsworth

Old Man Travelling; Animal Tranquillity and Decay,
A Sketch   c. 1795

in *Lyrical Ballads*   1798

The little hedge-row birds,
That peck along the road, regard him not.
He travels on, and in his face, his step,
His gait, is one expression; every limb,
His look and bending figure, all bespeak
A man who does not move with pain, but moves
With thought – He is insensibly subdued
To settled quiet : he is one by whom
All effort seems forgotten, one to whom
Long patience has such mild composure given,
That patience now doth seem a thing, of which
He hath no need. He is by nature led
To peace so perfect, that the young behold
With envy, what the old man hardly feels.
– I asked him whither he was bound, and what
The object of his journey; he replied
'Sir ! I am going many miles to take
A last leave of my son, a mariner,
Who from a sea-fight has been brought to Falmouth,
And there is dying in an hospital.'

5 William Wordsworth

Anecdote for Fathers, Shewing how the Art of Lying
may be Taught

in *Lyrical Ballads*   1798

I have a boy of five years old,
His face is fair and fresh to see;
His limbs are cast in beauty's mould,
And dearly he loves me.

One morn we stroll'd on our dry walk,
Our quiet house all full in view,
And held such intermitted talk
As we are wont to do.

My thoughts on former pleasures ran;
I thought of Kilve's delightful shore,
My pleasant home, when spring began,
A long, long year before.

A day it was when I could bear
To think, and think, and think again;
With so much happiness to spare,
I could not feel a pain.

My boy was by my side, so slim
And graceful in his rustic dress!
And oftentimes I talked to him,
In very idleness.

The young lambs ran a pretty race;
The morning sun shone bright and warm;
'Kilve,' said I, 'was a pleasant place,
And so is Liswyn farm.

My little boy, which like you more,'
I said and took him by the arm –
'Our home by Kilve's delightful shore,
Or here at Liswyn farm?

And tell me, had you rather be,'
I said and held him by the arm,
'At Kilve's smooth shore by the green sea,
Or here at Liswyn farm?'

In careless mood he looked at me,
While still I held him by the arm,
And said, 'At Kilve I'd rather be
Than here at Liswyn farm.'

'Now, little Edward, say why so;
My little Edward, tell me why;'
'I cannot tell, I do not know.'
'Why this is strange,' said I.

'For, here are woods and green-hills warm;
There surely must some reason be
Why you would change sweet Liswyn farm
For Kilve by the green sea.'

At this, my boy, so fair and slim,
Hung down his head, nor made reply;
And five times did I say to him,
'Why? Edward, tell me why?'

His head he raised – there was in sight,
It caught his eye, he saw it plain –
Upon the house-top, glittering bright,
A broad and gilded vane.

Then did the boy his tongue unlock,
And thus to me he made reply;
'At Kilve there was no weather-cock,
And that's the reason why.'

Oh dearest, dearest boy ! my heart
For better lore would seldom yearn,
Could I but teach the hundredth part
Of what from thee I learn.

6 William Wordsworth
The Two April Mornings 1799

in *Lyrical Ballads*, vol. 2   1800

We walk'd along, while bright and red
Uprose the morning sun,
And Matthew stopp'd, he look'd, and said,
'The will of God be done !'

A village Schoolmaster was he,
With hair of glittering grey;
As blithe a man as you could see
On a spring holiday.

And on that morning, through the grass,
And by the streaming rills,
We travell'd merrily to pass
A day among the hills.

'Our work,' said I, 'was well begun;'
Then, from thy breast what thought,
Beneath so beautiful a sun,
So sad a sigh has brought?

A second time did Matthew stop,
And fixing still his eye
Upon the eastern mountain top
To me he made reply.

'Yon cloud with that long purple cleft
Brings fresh into my mind
A day like this which I have left
Full thirty years behind.

And on that slope of springing corn
The self-same crimson hue
Fell from the sky that April morn,
The same which now I view!

With rod and line my silent sport
I plied by Derwent's wave,
And, coming to the church, stopp'd short
Beside my Daughter's grave.

Nine summers had she scarcely seen
The pride of all the vale;
And when she sang! – she would have been
A very nightingale.

Six feet in earth my Emma lay,
And yet I loved her more,
For so it seem'd, than till that day
I e'er had lov'd before.

And, turning, from her grave, I met
Beside the church-yard Yew
A blooming Girl, whose hair was wet
With points of morning dew.

A basket on her head she bare,
Her brow was smooth and white,
To see a Child so very fair,
It was a pure delight.

No fountain from its rocky cave,
E'er tripp'd with foot so free,
She seem'd as happy as a wave
That dances on the sea.

There came from me a sigh of pain
Which I could ill confine;
I look'd at her and look'd again;
– And did not wish her mine.'

Matthew is in his grave, yet now
Methinks I see him stand,
As at that moment, with his bough
Of wilding in his hand.

7 William Wordsworth
Stepping Westward 1805

reprinted in E. de Selincourt (ed.), *Poetical Works* 1967

While my Fellow-traveller and I were walking by the side of
Loch Ketterine, one fine evening after sunset, in our road to a
Hut where, in the course of our Tour, we had been hospitably

entertained some weeks before, we met, in one of the loneliest
parts of that solitary region, two well-dressed Women, one of
whom said to us by way of greeting, 'What, you are stepping
westward?'

'What, you are stepping westward?' – 'Yea,'
– 'Twould be a *wildish* destiny,
If we, who thus together roam
In a strange Land, and far from home,
Were in this place the guests of Chance:
Yet who would stop, or fear to advance,
Though home or shelter he had none,
With such a sky to lead him on?

The dewy ground was dark and cold;
Behind, all gloomy to behold;
And stepping westward seemed to be
A kind of *heavenly* destiny;
I liked the greeting; 'twas a sound
Of something without place or bound;
And seemed to give me spiritual right
To travel through that region bright.

The voice was soft, and she who spake
Was walking by her native lake:
The salutation had to me
The very sound of courtesy:
Its power was felt; and while my eye
Was fixed upon the glowing Sky,
The echo of the voice enwrought
A human sweetness with the thought
Of travelling through the world that lay
Before me in my endless way.

8 William Wordsworth
The Glow-Worm 1802

reprinted in E. de Selincourt (ed.), *Poetical Works* 1967

Among all lovely things my Love had been;
Had noted well the stars, all flowers that grew
About her home; but she had never seen
A Glow-worm, never one, and this I knew.

While riding near her home one stormy night
A single Glow-worm did I chance to espy;
I gave a fervent welcome to the sight,
And from my Horse I leapt; great joy had I.

Upon a leaf the Glow-worm did I lay,
To bear it with me through the stormy night:
And, as before, it shone without dismay;
Albeit putting forth a fainter light.

When to the Dwelling of my Love I came,
I went into the Orchard quietly;
And left the Glow-worm, blessing it by name,
Laid safely by itself, beneath a Tree.

The whole next day, I hoped, and hoped with fear;
At night the Glow-worm shone beneath the Tree:
I led my Lucy to the spot, 'Look here!'
Oh! joy it was for her, and joy for me!

9 William Wordsworth
The Language of Poetry

from the preface to *Lyrical Ballads* 1802

The principal object [...] which I proposed to myself in these
Poems was to make the incidents of common life interesting by
tracing in them, truly though not ostentatiously, the primary

laws of our nature: chiefly as far as regards the manner in which we associate ideas in a state of excitement. Low and rustic life was generally chosen because in that situation the essential passions of the heart find a better soil in which they can attain their maturity, are less under restraint, and speak a plainer and more emphatic language; because in that situation our elementary feelings exist in a state of greater simplicity and consequently may be more accurately contemplated and more forcibly communicated; because the manners of rural life germinate from those elementary feelings; and from the necessary character of rural occupations are more easily comprehended; and are more durable; and lastly, because in that situation the passions of men are incorporated with the beautiful and permanent forms of nature. The language too of these men is adopted [...] because such men hourly communicate with the best objects from which the best part of language is originally derived; and because, from their rank in society and the sameness and narrow circle of their intercourse, being less under the action of social vanity they convey their feelings and notions in simple and unelaborated expressions. Accordingly such a language arising out of repeated experience and regular feelings is a more permanent and a far more philosophical language than that which is frequently substituted for it by Poets, who think that they are conferring honour upon themselves and upon their art in proportion as they separate themselves from the sympathies of men, and indulge in arbitrary and capricious habits of expression in order to furnish food for fickle tastes and fickle appetites of their own creation.

I cannot be insensible of the present outcry against the triviality and meanness both of thought and language, which some of my contemporaries have occasionally introduced into their metrical compositions; and I acknowledge that this defect where it exists, is more dishonourable to the Writer's own character than false refinement or arbitrary innovation, though I should contend at the same time that it is far less pernicious in the sum of its consequences. From such verses the Poems in these volumes will be found distinguished by at least one mark of difference, that each of them has a worthy *purpose*. Not that I mean to say, that I always began to write with a distinct purpose formally conceived; but I believe that my habits of meditation have so formed my feelings, as that my descriptions of such objects as strongly excite these feelings, will be found to carry along with them a *purpose*. If in this opinion I am mistaken I can have little right to the name of a Poet. For all good poetry is the spontaneous overflow of powerful feeling; but though this be true, Poems to which any value can be attached, were never produced on any variety of subjects but by a man who being possessed of more than usual organic sensibility had also thought long and deeply. For our continued influxes of feeling are modified and directed by our thoughts, which are indeed the representatives of all our past feelings; and as by contemplating the relation of these general representatives to each other, we discover what is really important to men, so by the repetition and continuance of this act feelings connected with important subjects will be nourished, till at length, if we be originally possessed of much organic sensibility, such habits of mind will be produced that by obeying blindly and mechanically the impulses of those habits we shall describe objects and utter sentiments of such a nature and in such connection with each other, that the understanding of the being to whom we address ourselves, if he be in a healthful state of association, must necessarily be in some degree enlightened, his taste exalted, and his affections ameliorated.

I have said that each of these poems has a purpose [...] namely to illustrate the manner in which our feelings and ideas are associated in a state of excitement. But speaking in less general language, it is to follow the fluxes and refluxes of the mind when agitated by the great and simple affections of our nature. [...] I will not abuse the indulgence of my Reader by dwelling longer upon this subject; but it is proper that I should mention one other circumstance which distinguishes these Poems from the popular Poetry of the day; it is this, that the feelings therein developed give importance to the action and situation and not the action and situation to the feeling. [...]

I will not suffer a sense of false modesty to prevent me from asserting, that I point my Reader's attention to this mark of distinction far less for the sake of these particular Poems than from the general importance of the subject. The subject is indeed important! For the human mind is capable of excitement without the application of gross and violent stimulants; and he must have a very faint perception of its beauty and dignity who does not know this, and who does not further know that one being is elevated above another in proportion as he possesses this capability. It has therefore appeared to me that to endeavour to produce or enlarge this capability is one of the best services, in which, at any period, a Writer can be engaged; but this service, excellent at all times, is especially so at the present day. For a multitude of causes unknown to former times are now acting with a combined force to blunt the discriminating powers of the mind and unfitting it for all voluntary exertion to reduce it to a state of almost savage torpor. The most effective of these causes are the great national events which are daily taking place, and the increasing accumulation of men in cities, where the uniformity of their occupations produces a craving for extraordinary incident which the rapid communication of intelligence hourly gratifies. [. . .]

There will [. . .] be found in these volumes little of what is usually called poetic diction; I have taken as much pains to avoid it as others ordinarily take to produce it; this I have done for the reason already alleged, to bring my language near to the language of men, and further, because the pleasure which I have proposed to myself to impart is of a kind very different from that which is supposed by many persons to be the proper object of poetry. I do not know how without being culpably particular I can give my Reader a more exact notion of the style in which I wished these poems to be written than by informing him that I have at all times endeavoured to look steadily at my subject, consequently I hope it will be found that there is in these Poems little falsehood of description, and that my ideas are expressed in language fitted to their respective importance.

10 William Wordsworth
What is a Poet?

from a passage added to the preface to *Lyrical Ballads*   1802

What is a Poet? To whom does he address himself? And what
language is to be expected from him? He is a man speaking to
men: a man, it is true, endued with more lively sensibility,
more enthusiasm and tenderness, who has a greater knowledge
of human nature, and a more comprehensive soul, than are
supposed to be common among mankind; a man pleased with
his own passions and volitions, and who rejoices more than
other men in the spirit of life that is in him; delighting to contemplate similar volitions and passions as manifested in the
goings-on of the Universe, and habitually impelled to create
them where he does not find them. To these qualities he has
added a disposition to be affected more than other men by
absent things as if they were present; an ability of conjuring up
in himself passions, which are indeed far from being the same
as those produced by real events, yet (especially in those parts
of the general sympathy which are pleasing and delightful) do
more nearly resemble the passions produced by real events, than
anything which, from the motions of their own minds merely,
other men are accustomed to feel in themselves; whence, and
from practice, he has acquired a greater readiness and power in
expressing what he thinks and feels, and especially those
thoughts and feelings which, by his own choice, or from the
structure of his own mind, arise in him without immediate
external excitement. [...]

  It will be the wish of the Poet to bring his feelings near to
those of the persons whose feelings he describes, nay, for short
spaces of time perhaps, to let himself slip into an entire delusion,
and even confound and identify his own feelings with theirs;
modifying only the language which is thus suggested to him,
by a consideration that he describes for a particular purpose,
that of giving pleasure. Here [...] he will apply the principle
[...] of selection; on this he will depend for removing what
would otherwise be painful or disgusting in the passion; he will

feel that there is no necessity to trick out or to elevate nature; and, the more industriously he applies this principle, the deeper will be his faith that no words, which his fancy or imagination can suggest, will be to be compared with those which are the emanations of reality and truth.

11 William Wordsworth

Prospectus to 'The Recluse'   1802

reprinted in E. de Selincourt (ed.), *Poetical Works*   1967

On Man, on Nature, and on Human Life,
Musing in solitude, I oft perceive
Fair trains of imagery before me rise,
Accompanied by feelings of delight
Pure, or with no unpleasing sadness mixed;
And I am conscious of affecting thoughts
And dear remembrances, whose presence soothes
Or elevates the Mind, intent to weigh
The good and evil of our mortal state.
– To these emotions, whencesoe'er they come,
Whether from breath of outward circumstance,
Or from the Soul – an impulse to herself –
I would give utterance in numerous verse.
Of Truth, of Grandeur, Beauty, Love, and Hope,
And melancholy Fear subdued by Faith;
Of blessèd consolations in distress;
Of moral strength, and intellectual Power;
Of joy in widest commonalty spread;
Of the individual Mind that keeps her own
Inviolate retirement, subject there
To Conscience only, and the law supreme
Of that Intelligence which governs all –
I sing: – 'fit audience let me find though few!'

So prayed, more gaining than he asked, the Bard –
In holiest mood. Urania, I shall need
Thy guidance or a greater Muse, if such

Descend to earth or dwell in highest heaven !
Deep – and, aloft ascending, breathe in worlds
To which the heaven of heavens is but a veil.
All strength – all terror, single or in bands,
That ever was put forth in personal form –
Jehovah – with his thunder, and the choir
Of shouting Angels, and the empyreal thrones –
I pass them unalarmed. Not Chaos, not
The darkest pit of lowest Erebus,
Nor aught of blinder vacancy, scooped out
By help of dreams – can breed such fear and awe
As fall upon us often when we look
Into our Minds, into the Mind of Man –
My haunt, and the main region of my song.
– Beauty – a living Presence of the earth,
Surpassing the most fair ideal Forms
Which craft of delicate Spirits hath composed
From earth's materials – waits upon my steps;
Pitches her tents before me as I move,
An hourly neighbour. Paradise, and groves
Elysian, Fortunate Fields – like those of old
Sought in the Atlantic Main – why should they be
A history only of departed things,
Or a mere fiction of what never was?
For the discerning intellect of Man,
When wedded to this goodly universe
In love and holy passion, shall find these
A simple produce of the common day.
– I, long before the blissful hour arrives,
Would chant, in lonely peace, the spousal verse

Of this great consummation : – and, by words
Which speak of nothing more than what we are,
Would I arouse the sensual from their sleep
Of Death, and win the vacant and the vain
To noble raptures; while my voice proclaims
How exquisitely the individual Mind
(And the progressive powers perhaps no less
Of the whole species) to the external World

Is fitted: – and how exquisitely, too –
Theme this but little heard of among men –
The external World is fitted to the Mind;
And the creation (by no lower name
Can it be called) which they with blended might
Accomplish: – this is our argument.
– Such grateful haunts foregoing, if I oft
Must turn elsewhere – to travel near the tribes
And fellowships of men, and see ill sights
Of madding passions mutually inflamed;
Must hear Humanity in fields and groves
Pipe solitary anguish; or must hang
Brooding above the fierce confederate storm
Of sorrow, barricadoed evermore
Within the walls of cities – may these sounds
Have their authentic comment; that even these
Hearing, I be not downcast or forlorn! –
Descend, prophetic Spirit! that inspir'st
The human Soul of universal earth,
Dreaming on things to come; and dost possess
A metropolitan temple in the hearts
Of mighty Poets: upon me bestow
A gift of genuine insight; that my Song
With star-like virtue in its place may shine,
Shedding benignant influence, and secure,
Itself, from all malevolent effect
Of those mutations that extend their sway
Throughout the nether sphere! – And if with this
I mix more lowly matter; with the thing
Contemplated, describe the Mind and Man
Contemplating; and who, and what he was –
The transitory Being that beheld
This Vision; when and where, and how he lived; –
Be not this labour useless. If such theme
May sort with highest objects, then – dread Power!
Whose gracious favour is the primal source
Of all illumination, – may my Life
Express the image of a better time,
More wise desires, and simpler manners; – nurse

My Heart in genuine freedom : — all pure thoughts
Be with me; — so shall thy unfailing love
Guide, and support, and cheer me to the end !

12 **Oliver Goldsmith**
The Deserted Village

from 'The Deserted Village'   1770. Reprinted in Austin Dobson
(ed.), *Poetical Works of Oliver Goldsmith*, 1908

   Sweet smiling village, loveliest of the lawn,
Thy sports are fled, and all thy charms withdrawn;
Amidst thy bowers the tyrant's hand is seen,
And desolation saddens all the green :
One only master grasps the whole domain,
And half a tillage stints thy smiling plain;
No more thy glassy brook reflects the day,
But choaked with sedges, works its weedy way;
Along thy glades, a solitary guest,
The hollow sounding bittern guards its nest;
Amidst thy desert walks the lapwing flies,
And tires their echoes with unvaried cries.
Sunk are thy bowers, in shapeless ruin all,
And the long grass o'ertops the mouldering wall;
And trembling, shrinking from the spoiler's hand,
Far, far away thy children leave the land. [...]

   Sweet was the sound, when oft at evening's close
Up yonder hill the village murmur rose;
There, as I pass'd with careless steps and slow,
The mingling notes came soften'd from below;
The swain responsive as the milk-maid sung,
The sober herd that low'd to meet their young;
The noisy geese that gabbled o'er the pool,
The playful children just let loose from school;
The watchdog's voice that bay'd the whispering wind,
And the loud laugh that spoke the vacant mind;
These all in sweet confusion sought the shade,

And fill'd each pause the nightingale had made.
But now the sounds of population fail,
No cheerful murmurs fluctuate in the gale,
No busy steps the grass-grown foot-way tread,
For all the bloomy flush of life is fled.
All but yon widow'd, solitary thing
That feebly bends beside the plashy spring;
She, wretched matron, forc'd, in age, for bread,
To strip the brook with mantling cresses spread,
To pick her wintry faggot from the thorn,
To seek her nightly shed, and weep till morn;
She only left of all the harmless train,
The sad historian of the pensive plain.

13 George Crabbe
The Village

from 'The Village'   1783. Reprinted in A. J. Carlyle and
R. M. Carlyle (eds.), *Poetical Works of George Crabbe*,
1908

Lo ! where the heath, with withering brake grown o'er,
Lends the light turf that warms the neighbouring poor;
From thence a length of burning sand appears,
Where the thin harvest waves its wither'd ears;
Rank weeds, that every art and care defy,
Reign o'er the land, and rob the blighted rye;
There thistles stretch their prickly arms afar,
And to the ragged infant threaten war;
There poppies nodding, mock the hope of toil;
There the blue bugloss paints the sterile soil;
Hardy and high, above the slender sheaf,
The slimy mallow waves her silky leaf;
O'er the young shoot the charlock throws a shade,
And clasping tares cling round the sickly blade;
With mingled tints the rocky coasts abound,
And a sad splendour vainly shines around.
Here joyless roam a wild amphibious race,
With sullen woe display'd in every face;

Who, far from civil arts and social fly,
And scowl at strangers with suspicious eye.

14 William Hazlitt
Godwin

from *The Spirit of the Age* 1825

The Spirit of the Age was never more fully shown than in its treatment of this writer – its love of paradox and change, its dastard submission to prejudice and to the fashion of the day. Five-and-twenty years ago he was in the very zenith of a sultry and unwholesome popularity; he blazed as a sun in the firmament of reputation; no one was more talked of, more looked up to, more sought after, and wherever liberty, truth, justice was the theme, his name was not far off. Now he has sunk below the horizon, and enjoys the serene twilight of a doubtful immortality. Mr Godwin, during his lifetime, has secured to himself the triumphs and the mortifications of an extreme notoriety and of a sort of posthumous fame. His bark, after being tossed in the revolutionary tempest, now raised to heaven by all the fury of popular breath, now almost dashed in pieces, and buried in the quicksands of ignorance, or scorched with the lightning of momentary indignation, at length floats on the calm wave that is to bear it down the streams of time.

Mr Godwin's person is not known, he is not pointed out in the street, his conversation is not courted, his opinions are not asked, he is at the head of no cabal, he belongs to no party in the State, he has no train of admirers, no one thinks it worth his while even to traduce and vilify him, he has scarcely friend or foe, the world make a point (as Goldsmith used to say) of taking no more notice of him than if such an individual had never existed; he is to all ordinary intents and purposes dead and buried. But the author of *Political Justice*[1] and of *Caleb Williams*[2] can never die; his name is an abstraction in letters; his works are standard in the history

1. First printed in 1793.
2. First printed in 1794.

of intellect. He is thought of now like any eminent writer of a hundred-and-fifty years ago, or just as he will be a hundred-and-fifty years hence. He knows this, and smiles in silent mockery of himself, reposing on the monument of his fame

Sedet, æternumque sedebit
Infelix Theseus.

No work in our time gave such a blow to the philosophical mind of the country as the celebrated *Enquiry concerning Political Justice*. Tom Paine was considered for the time as a Tom Fool to him, Paley an old woman, Edmund Burke a flashy sophist. Truth, moral truth, it was supposed, had here taken up its abode; and these were the oracles of thought.

'Throw aside your books of chemistry,' said Wordsworth to a young man, a student in the Temple, 'and read Godwin on Necessity.' Sad necessity! Fatal reverse! Is truth then so variable? Is it one thing at twenty and another at forty? Is it at a burning heat in 1793, and below *zero* in 1814? Not so, in the name of manhood and of common sense! Let us pause here a little. Mr Godwin indulged in extreme opinions, and carried with him all the most sanguine and fearless understandings of the time. What then? Because those opinions were overcharged, were they therefore altogether groundless? Is the very God of our idolatry all of a sudden to become an abomination and an anathema? Could so many young men of talent, of education, and of principle have been hurried away by what had neither truth nor nature, not one particle of honest feeling nor the least show of reason in it? Is the *Modern Philosophy* (as it has been called) at one moment a youthful bride and the next a withered beldame, like the false Duessa in Spenser? Or is the vaunted edifice of Reason, like his House of Pride, gorgeous in front, and dazzling to approach, while 'its hinder parts are ruinous, decayed, and old'? Has the main prop, which supported the mighty fabric, been shaken, and given way under the strong grasp of some Samson; or has it not rather been undermined by rats and vermin? At one time, it almost seemed, that 'if this failed,

The pillar'd firmament was rottenness,
And earth's base built of stubble.'

Now scarce a shadow of it remains; it is crumbled to dust, nor is it even talked of! 'What, then, went ye forth for to see, a reed shaken with the wind?' Was it for this that our young gownsmen of the greatest expectation and promise, versed in classic lore, steeped in dialectics, armed at all points for the foe, well read, well nurtured, well provided for, left the University and the prospect of lawn sleeves, tearing asunder the shackles of the free-born spirit and the cobwebs of school-divinity, to throw themselves at the feet of the new Gamaliel, and learn wisdom from him? Was it for this, that students at the bar, acute, inquisitive, sceptical (here only wild enthusiasts) neglected for a while the paths of preferment and the law as too narrow, tortuous, and unseemly to bear the pure and broad light of reason? Was it for this, that students in medicine missed their way to Lectureships and the top of their profession, deeming lightly of the health of the body, and dreaming only of the renovation of society and the march of mind? Was it to this that Mr Southey's *Inscriptions* pointed? to this that Mr Coleridge's *Religious Musings* tended? Was it for this, that Mr Godwin himself sat with arms folded, and, 'like Cato, gave his little senate laws'? Or rather, like another Prospero, uttered syllables that with their enchanted breath were to change the world, and might almost stop the stars in their courses?

Oh! and is all forgot? Is this sun of intellect blotted from the sky? Or has it suffered total eclipse? Or is it we who make the fancied gloom, by looking at it through the paltry, broken, stained fragments of our own interests and prejudices? Were we fools then, or are we dishonest now? Or was the impulse of the mind less likely to be true and sound when it arose from high thought and warm feeling, than afterwards, when it was warped and debased by the example, the vices, and follies of the world?

The fault, then, of Mr Godwin's philosophy, in one word, was too much ambition – 'by that sin fell the angels!' He conceived too nobly of his fellows (the most unpardonable crime against them, for there is nothing that annoys our self-love so much as being complimented on imaginary achievements, to which we are wholly unequal) – he raised the standard of morality above the reach of humanity, and by directing virtue to the most airy and romantic heights, made her path dangerous, solitary, and impracticable. The author of the *Political Justice* took abstract reason for the rule of conduct and abstract good for its end. He places the human mind on an elevation, from which it commands a view of the whole line of moral consequences; and requires it to conform its acts to the larger and more enlightened conscience which it has thus acquired. He absolves man from the gross and narrow ties of sense, custom, authority, private and local attachment, in order that he may devote himself to the boundless pursuit of universal benevolence.

Mr Godwin gives no quarter to the amiable weaknesses of our nature, nor does he stoop to avail himself of the supplementary aids of an imperfect virtue. Gratitude, promises, friendship, family affection give way, not that they may be merged in the opposite vices or in want of principle, but that the void may be filled up by the disinterested love of good and the dictates of inflexible justice, which is 'the law of laws, and sovereign of sovereigns'. All minor considerations yield, in his system, to the stern sense of duty, as they do, in the ordinary and established ones, to the voice of necessity. Mr Godwin's theory, and that of more approved reasoners, differ only in this, that what are with them the exceptions, the extreme cases, he makes the every-day rule. No one denies that on great occasions, in moments of fearful excitement, or when a mighty object is at stake, the lesser and merely instrumental points of duty are to be sacrificed without remorse at the shrine of patriotism, of honour, and of conscience.

But the disciples of the *New School* (no wonder it found so many impugners even in its own bosom!) is to be always the hero of duty; the law to which he has bound himself never swerves nor relaxes; his feeling of what is right is to be at all times wrought up to a pitch of enthusiastic self-devotion; he must become the unshrinking martyr and confessor of the public good. If it be said that this scheme is chimerical and impracticable on ordinary occasions, and to the generality of mankind, well and good; but those who accuse the author of having trampled on the common feelings and prejudices of mankind in wantonness or insult, or without wishing to substitute something better (and only unattainable, because it is better) in their stead, accuse him wrongfully. We may not be able to launch the bark of our affections on the ocean-tide of humanity, we may be forced to paddle along its

shores, or shelter in its creeks and rivulets: but we have no right
to reproach the bold and adventurous pilot, who dared us to
tempt the uncertain abyss, with our own want of courage or of
skill, or with the jealousies and impatience, which deter us from
undertaking, or might prevent us from accomplishing, the
voyage!

The *Enquiry concerning Political Justice* (it was urged by its
favourers and defenders at the time, and may still be so, without
either profaneness or levity) is a metaphysical and logical commentary on some of the most beautiful and striking texts of
Scripture. Mr Godwin is a mixture of the Stoic and of the
Christian philosopher. To break the force of the vulgar objections and outcry that have been raised against the Modern
Philosophy, as if it were a new and monstrous birth in morals, it
may be worth noticing, that volumes of sermons have been written to excuse the founder of Christianity for not including friendship and private affection among its golden rules, but rather excluding them.[3] Moreover, the answer to the question, 'Who
is thy neighbour?' added to the divine precept, 'Thou shalt love
thy neighbour as thyself', is the same as in the exploded pages of
our author – 'he to whom we can do most good'. In determining
this point, we were not to be influenced by any extrinsic or col-
lateral considerations, by our own predilections, or the expectations of others, by our obligations to them or any services they
might be able to render us, by the climate they were born in, by
the house they lived in, by rank, or religion, or party, or personal
ties, but by the abstract merits, the pure and unbiassed justice of
the case.

The artificial helps and checks to moral conduct were set aside
as spurious and unnecessary, and we came at once to the grand
and simple question – 'In what manner we could best contribute
to the greatest possible good?' This was the paramount obligation in all cases whatever, from which we had no right to free
ourselves upon any idle or formal pretext, and of which each person was to judge for himself, under the infallible authority of his

3. Shaftesbury made this an objection to Christianity, which was
answered by Foster, Leland, and other eminent divines, on the ground
that Christianity had a higher object in view, namely, general philanthropy.

own opinion and the inviolable sanction of his self-approbation. 'There was the rub that made *philosophy* of so short life!' Mr Godwin's definition of morals was the same as the admired one of law, *reason without passion*; but with the unlimited scope of private opinion, and in a boundless field of speculation (for nothing less would satisfy the pretensions of the New School), there was danger that the unseasoned novice might substitute some pragmatical conceit of his own for the rule of right reason, and mistake a heartless indifference for a superiority to more natural and generous feelings. Our ardent and dauntless reformer followed out the moral of the parable of the Good Samaritan into its most rigid and repulsive consequences with a pen of steel, and let fall his 'trenchant blade' on every vulnerable point of human infirmity; but there is a want in his system of the mild and persuasive tone of the Gospel, where 'all is conscience and tender heart'.

Man was indeed screwed up by mood and figure into a logical machine, that was to forward the public good with the utmost punctuality and effect, and it might go very well on smooth ground and under favourable circumstances; but would it work up-hill or *against the grain*? It was to be feared that the proud Temple of Reason, which at a distance and in stately supposition shone like the palaces of the New Jerusalem, might (when placed on actual ground) be broken up into the sordid styes of sensuality and the petty huckster's shops of self-interest! Every man (it was proposed – 'so ran the tenour of the bond') was to be a Regulus, a Codrus, a Cato, or a Brutus – every woman a Mother of the Gracchi.

> It was well said,
> And 'tis a kind of good deed to say well.

But heroes on paper might degenerate into vagabonds in practice, Corinnas into courtezans. Thus a refined and permanent individual attachment is intended to supply the place and avoid the inconveniences of marriage; but vows of eternal constancy, without church security, are found to be fragile.

A member of the *ideal* and perfect commonwealth of letters lends another a hundred pounds for immediate and pressing use; and when he applies for it again, the borrower has still more need of it than he, and retains it for his own especial, which is tantamount to the public, good.

The Exchequer of pure reason, like that of the State, never refunds. The political as well as the religious fanatic appeals from the overweening opinion and claims of others to the highest and most impartial tribunal, namely, his own breast. Two persons agree to live together in Chambers on principles of pure equality and mutual assistance – but when it comes to the push, one of them finds that the other always insist on his fetching water from the pump in Hare-court, and cleaning his shoes for him. A modest assurance was not the least indispensable virtue in the new perfectibility code; and it was hence discovered to be a scheme, like other schemes where there are all prizes and no blanks, for the accommodation of the enterprizing and cunning, at the expense of the credulous and honest. This broke up the system, and left no good odour behind it! Reason has become a sort of byeword, and philosophy has 'fallen first into a fasting, then into a sadness, then into a decline, and last, into the dissolution of which we all complain!' This is a worse error than the former: we may be said to have 'lost the immortal part of ourselves, and what remains is beastly!'

The point of view from which this matter may be fairly considered is two-fold, and may be stated thus: – in the first place, it by no means follows, because reason is found not to be the only infallible or safe rule of conduct, that it is no rule at all; or that we are to discard it altogether with derision and ignominy. On the contrary, if not the sole, it is the principal ground of action; it is 'the guide, the stay, and anchor of our purest thoughts, and soul of all our moral being'. In proportion as we strengthen and expand this principle, and bring our affections and subordinate, but perhaps more powerful motives of action into harmony with it, it will not admit of a doubt that we advance to the goal of perfection, and answer the ends of our creation, those ends which not only morality enjoins, but which religion sanctions. If with the utmost stretch of reason, man cannot (as some seemed inclined to suppose) soar up to God, and quit the ground of human frailty, yet, stripped wholly of it, he sinks at once into the brute. If it cannot stand alone in its naked simplicity, but requires other props to buttress it up, or ornaments to set it off; yet without it the moral structure would fall flat and dishonoured to the ground.

Private reason is that which raises the individual above his mere animal instincts, appetites, and passions : public reason in its gradual progress separates the savage from the civilized state. Without the one, men would resemble wild beasts in their dens; without the other, they would be speedily converted into hordes of barbarians or banditti. Sir Walter Scott, in his zeal to restore the spirit of loyalty, of passive obedience and non-resistance as an acknowledgment for his having been created a Baronet by a Prince of the House of Brunswick, may think it a fine thing to return in imagination to the good old times, 'when in Auvergne alone there were three hundred nobles whose most ordinary actions were robbery, rape, and murder', when the castle of each Norman baron was a stronghold from which the lordly proprietor issued to oppress and plunder the neighbouring districts, and when the Saxon peasantry were treated by their gay and gallant tyrants as a herd of loathsome swine – but, for our own parts, we beg to be excused; we had rather live in the same age with the author of *Waverley* and *Blackwood's Magazine*.

Reason is the meter and alnager in civil intercourse, by which each person's upstart and contradictory pretensions are weighed and approved or found wanting, and without which it could not subsist, any more than traffic or the exchange of commodities could be carried on without weights and measures. It is the medium of knowledge and the polisher of manners, by creating common interests and ideas. Or, in the words of a contemparary writer, 'Reason is the queen of the moral world, the soul of the universe, the lamp of human life, the pillar of society, the foundation of law, the beacon of nations, the golden chain let down from heaven, which links all accountable and all intelligent natures in one common system – and, in the vain strife between fanatic innovation and fanatic prejudice, we are exhorted to dethrone the queen of the world, to blot out this light of the mind, to deface this fair column, to break in pieces this golden chain !

'We are to discard and throw from us with loud taunts and bitter execrations that reason, which has been the lofty theme of the philosopher, the poet, the moralist, and the divine, whose name was not first named to be abused by the enthusiasts of the French Revolution, or to be blasphemed by the madder enthusiasts, the

advocates of Divine Right, but which is coeval with, and inseparable from the nature and faculties of man – is the image of his
Maker stamped upon him at his birth, the understanding
breathed into him with the breath of life, and in the participation and improvement of which alone he is raised above the brute
creation and his own physical nature!' – The overstrained and
ridiculous pretensions of monks and ascetics were never thought
to justify a return to unbridled licence of manners or the throwing
aside of all decency. The hypocrisy, cruelty, and fanaticism, often
attendant on peculiar professions of sanctity, have not banished
the name of religion from the world. Neither can 'the unreason-
ableness of the reason' of some modern sciolists so 'unreason our
reason', as to debar us of the benefit of this principle in future,
or to disfranchise us of the highest privilege of our nature.

In the second place, if it is admitted that Reason alone is not
the sole and self-sufficient ground of morals, it is to Mr Godwin
that we are indebted for having settled the point. No one denied
or distrusted this principle (before his time) as the absolute judge
and interpreter in all questions of difficulty; and if this is no
longer the case, it is because he has taken this principle, and followed it into its remotest consequences with more keenness of eye
and steadiness of hand than any other expounder of ethics. His
grand work is (at least) an *experimentum crucis* to show the weak
sides and imperfections of human reason as the sole law of human
action. By overshooting the mark or by 'flying an eagle flight,
forth and right on', he has pointed out the limit or line of separation, between what is practicable and what is barely conceivable;
by imposing impossible tasks on the naked strength of the will, he
has discovered how far it is or is not in our power to dispense with
the illusions of sense, to resist the calls of affection, to emancipate
ourselves from the force of habit, and thus, though he has not
said it himself, has enabled others to say to the towering aspirations after good and to the over-bearing pride of human intellect:
'Thus far shalt thou come, and no farther!'

Captain Parry would be thought to have rendered a service to
navigation and his country, no less by proving that there is no
North-West Passage, than if he had ascertained that there is one:
so Mr Godwin has rendered an essential service to moral science,
by attempting (in vain) to pass the Arctic Circle and Frozen

Regions, where the understanding is no longer warmed by the affections, nor fanned by the breeze of fancy! This is the effect of all bold, original, and powerful thinking, that it either discovers the truth or detects where error lies; and the only crime with which Mr Godwin can be charged as a political and moral reasoner is, that he has displayed a more ardent spirit and a more independent activity of thought than others, in establishing the fallacy (if fallacy it be) of an old popular prejudice that *the Just and True were one,* by 'championing it to the Outrance', and in the final result placing the Gothic structure of human virtue on an humbler, but a wider and safer, foundation than it had hitherto occupied in the volumes and systems of the learned.

   Mr Godwin is an inventor in the regions of romance, as well as a skilful and hardy explorer of those of moral truth. *Caleb Williams* and *St Leon* are two of the most splendid and impressive works of the imagination that have appeared in our times. It is not merely that these novels are very well for a philosopher to have produced – they are admirable and complete in themselves, and would not lead you to suppose that the author, who is so entirely at home in human character and dramatic situation, had ever dabbled in logic or metaphysics. The first of these, particularly, is a masterpiece, both as to invention and execution. The romantic and chivalrous principle of the love of personal fame is embodied in the finest possible manner in the character of Falkland;[4] as in Caleb Williams (who is not the first, but the second character in the piece) we see the very demon of curiosity personified. Perhaps the art, with which these two characters are contrived to relieve and set off each other, has never been surpassed in any work of fiction, with the exception of the immortal satire of Cervantes. The restless and inquisitive spirit of Caleb Williams, in search and in possession of his patron's fatal secret, haunts the latter like a second conscience, plants stings in his tortured mind, fans the flame of his jealous ambition, struggling with agonized remorse; and the hapless but noble-minded Falk-

4. Mr Fuseli used to object to this striking delineation a want of historical correctness, inasmuch as the animating principle of the true chivalrous character was the sense of honour, ot the mere regard to, or saving of, appearances. This, we think, must be an hypercriticism, from all we remember of books of chivalry and heroes of romance.

land at length falls a martyr to the persecution of that morbid and overpowering interest, of which his mingled virtues and vices have rendered him the object.

We conceive no one ever began *Caleb Williams* that did not read it through: no one that ever read it could possibly forget it, or speak of it after any length of time but with an impression as if the events and feelings had been personal to himself. This is the case also with the story of *St Leon* which, with less dramatic interest and intensity of purpose, is set off by a more gorgeous and flowing eloquence and by a crown of preternatural imagery, that waves over it like a palm-tree! Such is the beauty and the charm of Mr Godwin's descriptions that the reader identifies himself with the author; and the secret of this is, that the author has identified himself with his personages. Indeed, he has created them. They are the proper issue of his brain, lawfully begot, not foundlings, nor the 'bastards of his art'. He is not an indifferent, callous spectator of the scenes which he himself portrays, but without seeming to feel them. There is no look of patch-work and plagiarism, the beggarly copiousness of borrowed wealth; no tracery-work from worm-eaten manuscripts, from forgotten chronicles, nor piecing out of vague traditions with fragments and snatches of old ballads, so that the result resembles a gaudy, staring transparency, in which you cannot distingush the daubing of the painter from the light that shines through the flimsy colours, and gives them brilliancy.

Here all is clearly made out with strokes of the pencil, by fair, not by factitious means. Our author takes a given subject from nature or from books, and then fills it up with the ardent workings of his own mind, with the teeming and audible pulses of his own heart.

K Philosophy

There are questions – such as 'Does God exist?', 'Has man free will?', 'Had the world a beginning in time?' – that do not seem to be answerable by employing the methods of the natural sciences. Traditionally, philosophers have tried to answer them by the exercise of pure reason, that is, reason unaided by observation and experiment. Immanuel Kant's *Critique of Pure Reason* is, as the title may suggest, an inquiry into the capabilities of pure reason to answer such questions.

In brief, the outcome of Kant's inquiry is that the exercise of pure reason cannot yield the desired knowledge. But it is his manner of arriving at this outcome for which he is renowned among philosophers. It involved his making what he described as an 'experiment' in metaphysics similar to that of Copernicus in astronomy. He invited his readers to suppose that, instead of our knowledge conforming to objects, objects must conform to our knowledge. By 'objects' he meant such things as 'that every event has a cause'. His revolutionary idea was that the experienced world is one in which everything is causally determined because, in a sense, we make the experienced world what it is, and the construction process involves positing the principle of causality.

Having built determinism into the experienced world in this way, Kant was faced with the problem of explaining how man can yet be 'free', and thus morally responsible for what he does.

In what he said about causality Kant was reacting against the empiricism of Locke and Hume. This section begins with relevant extracts from the writings of these philosophers. These are followed by extracts from Kant's *Prolegomena* and *Critique*. Finally there are extracts from the work of two twentieth-century philosophers. Kant described his own work as being 'dry', 'obscure', and 'contrary to all ordinary ideas'. Readers may find the last two extracts help to make him seem less dry and obscure. But that his thought is 'contrary to all ordinary ideas' is what qualifies him for a leader's role in the age of revolutions.

G. V.

1 John Locke

An Essay Concerning Human Understanding

from *An Essay concerning Human Understanding* 1690

OF POWER

This idea how got. The mind being every day informed, by the senses, of the alteration of those simple ideas it observes in things without; and taking notice how one comes to an end and ceases to be, and another begins to exist which was not before; reflecting also, on what passes within itself, and observing a constant change of its ideas, sometimes by the impression of outward objects on the senses, and sometimes by the determination of its own choice; and concluding from what it has so constantly observed to have been, that the like changes will for the future be made in the same things by like agents, and by the like ways; considers in one thing the possibility of having any of its simple ideas changed, and in another the possibility of making that change; and so comes by that idea which we call *power*. Thus we say, fire has a power to melt gold, i.e., to destroy the consistency of its insensible parts, and consequently its hardness, and make it fluid; and gold has a power to be melted; that the sun has a power to blanch wax; and wax a power to be blanched by the sun, whereby the yellowness is destroyed, and whiteness made to exist in its room. In which and the like cases, the power we consider is in reference to the change of perceivable ideas. For we cannot observe any alteration to be made in, or operation upon, anything, but by the observable change of its sensible ideas: nor conceive any alteration to be made, but by conceiving a change of some of its ideas.

Power active and passive. Power thus considered is two-fold, viz., as able to make, or able to receive, any change: the one may be called *active*, and the other *passive*, power. Whether matter be not wholly destitute of active power, as its author, God, is truly above all passive power; and whether the intermediate state of created spirits be not that alone which is capable of both active and passive power, may be worth consideration. I shall not now enter into that enquiry: my present business being not to search into the original of power, but how we come by the idea of it. But since active powers make so great a part of our complex ideas of natural substances (as we shall see hereafter), yet they being not, perhaps, so truly active powers as our hasty thoughts are apt to represent them, I judge it not amiss, by this intimation, to direct our minds to the consideration of God and spirits, for the clearest idea of active power.

The clearest idea of active power had from spirit. We are abundantly furnished with the idea of passive power, by almost all sorts of sensible things. In most of them we cannot avoid observing their sensible qualities, nay, their very substances, to be in a continual flux: and therefore with reason we look on them as liable still to the same change. Nor have we of active power (which is the more proper signification of the word power) fewer instances. Since whatever change is observed, the mind must collect a power somewhere, able to make that change, as well as a possibility in the thing itself to receive it. But yet, if we will consider it attentively, bodies by our senses do not afford us so clear and distinct an idea of active power as we have from reflection on the operations of our minds. For all power relating to action, and there being but two sorts of action whereof we have any idea, viz., thinking and motion, let us consider whence we have the clearest ideas of the powers which produce these actions. (1) Of thinking, body affords us no idea at all: it is only from reflection that we have that. (2) Neither have we from body any idea of the beginning of motion. A body at rest affords us no idea of any active power to move; and when it is set in motion itself, that motion is rather a passion than an action in it. For when the ball obeys the stroke of a billiard-stick, it is not any action of the ball, but bare passion: also when by impulse it sets another ball in motion that lay in its way, it only communicates the motion it had received from another, and loses in itself so much as the other received; which gives us but a very obscure idea of an active power of moving in body, whilst we observe it only to transfer but not produce any motion. The idea of the beginning of motion we have only from reflection on what passes in ourselves, where we find by experience, that, barely by willing it, barely by a thought of the mind, we can move the parts of our bodies which were before at rest. So that it seems to me, we have, from the observation of the operation of bodies by our senses, but a very imperfect, obscure idea of active power, since they afford us not any idea in themselves of the power to begin any action, either motion or thought. But if, from the impulse bodies are observed to make one upon another, any one thinks he has a clear idea of power, it serves as well to my purpose, sensation being one of those ways whereby the mind comes by its ideas: only I thought it worth while to consider here by the way, whether the mind doth not receive its idea of active power clearer from reflection on its own operations, than it doth from any external sensation.

OF CAUSE AND EFFECT, AND OTHER RELATION

Whence their ideas got. In the notice that our senses take of the constant vicissitude of things, we cannot but observe that several particular both qualities and substances begin to exist; and that they receive this their existence from the due application and operation of some other being. From this observation we get our ideas of *cause* and *effect*. That which produces any simple or complex idea, we denote by the general name *cause*; and that which is produced, *effect*. Thus finding that in that substance which we call wax fluidity, which is a simple idea that was not in it before, is constantly produced by the application of a certain degree of heat, we call the simple idea of heat, in relation to fluidity in wax, *the cause* of it, and fluidity, *the effect*.

Creation, generation, making, alteration. Having thus, from what our senses are able to discover in the operations of bodies on one another, got the notion of cause and effect, the mind finds no great difficulty to distinguish the several originals of things into two sorts:

First, When the thing is wholly made new, so that no part thereof did ever exist before; as when a new particle of matter doth begin to exist, *in rerum naturâ,* which had before no being: and this we call *creation.*

Secondly, When a thing is made up of particles which did all of them before they exist, but that very thing, so constituted of pre-existing particles, had not any existence before, as this man, this egg, rose, or cherry, &c. And this, when referred to a substance produced in the ordinary course of nature by an internal principle, but set on work by, and received from, some external agent or cause, and working by insensible ways which we perceive not, we call *generation*. When the cause is extrinsical, and the effect produced by a sensible separation or juxtaposition of discernible parts, we call it *making*; and such are all artificial things. When any simple idea is produced which was not in that subject before, we call it *alteration*. Thus a man is generated, a picture made, and either of them altered, when any new sensible quality or simple idea is produced in either of them, which was not there before. In which, and all other cases, we may observe, that the notion of cause and effect has its rise from ideas received by sensation or reflection; and that this relation, how comprehensive soever, terminates at last in them.

2 David Hume
A Treatise of Human Nature

from *A Treatise of Human Nature* 1739

There are seven different kinds of philosophical relation, *viz. resemblance, identity, relations of time and place, proportion in quantity or number, degrees in any quality, contrariety, and causation*. These relations may be divided into two classes; into such as depend entirely on the ideas, which we compare together, and such as may be chang'd without any change in the ideas. 'Tis from the idea of a triangle, that we discover the relation of equality, which its three angles bear to two right ones; and this relation is invariable, as long as our idea remains the same. On the contrary, the relations of *contiguity* and *distance* betwixt two objects may be chang'd merely by an alteration of their place, without any change on the objects themselves or on their ideas; and the place depends on a hundred different accidents, which cannot be foreseen by the mind. 'Tis the same case with *identity* and *causation*. Two objects, tho' perfectly resembling each other, and even appearing in the same place at different times, may be numerically different: And as the power, by which one object produces another, is never discoverable merely from their idea, 'tis evident *cause* and *effect* are relations, of which we receive information from experience, and not from any abstract reasoning or reflexion. There is no single phænomenon, even the most simple, which can be accounted for from the qualities of the objects, as they appear to us; or which we cou'd foresee without the help of our memory and experience.

All kinds of reasoning consist in nothing but a *comparison*, and a discovery of those relations, either constant or inconstant, which two or more objects bear to each other. This comparison we may make, either when both the objects are present to the senses, or when neither of them is present, or when only one. When both the objects are present to the senses along with the relation, we call *this* perception rather than reasoning; nor is there in this case any exercise of the thought, or any action, properly speaking, but a mere passive admission of the impressions thro' the organs of sensation. According to this way of thinking, we ought not to receive as reasoning any of the observations we may make concerning *identity*, and the *relations* of *time* and *place*; since in none of them the mind can go beyond what is immediately present to the senses, either to discover the real existence or the relations of objects. 'Tis only *causation*, which produces such a connexion, as to give us assurance from the existence or action of one object, that 'twas follow'd or preceded by any other existence or action; nor can the other two relations be ever made use of in reasoning, except so far as they either affect or are affected by it. There is nothing in any objects to perswade us, that they are either always *remote* or always *contiguous*; and when from experience and observation we discover, that their relation in this particular is invariable, we always conclude there is some secret *cause*, which separates or unites them. The same reasoning extends to *identity*. We readily suppose an object may continue individually the same, tho' several times absent from and present to the senses; and ascribe to it an identity, notwithstanding the interruption of the perception, whenever we conclude, that if we had kept our eye or hand constantly upon it, it wou'd have convey'd an invariable and uninterrupted perception. But this conclusion beyond the impressions of our senses can be founded only on the connexion of *cause and effect*; nor can we otherwise have any security, that the object is not chang'd upon us, however much the new object may resemble that which was formerly present to the senses. Whenever we discover such a perfect resemblance, we consider, whether it be common in that species of objects; whether possibly or probably any cause cou'd operate in producing the change and resemblance; and according as we determine concerning these causes and effects, we form our judgment concerning the identity of the object.

Here then it appears, that of those three relations, which depend not upon the mere ideas, the only one, that can be trac'd beyond our senses, and informs us of existences and objects, which we do not see or feel, is causation. This relation therefore, we shall endeavour to explain fully before we leave the subject of the understanding.

To begin regularly, we must consider the idea of *causation*, and see from what origin it is deriv'd. 'Tis impossible to reason justly, without understanding perfectly the idea concerning which we reason; and 'tis impossible perfectly to understand any idea, without tracing it up to its origin, and examining that primary impression, from which it arises. The examination of the impression bestows a clearness on the idea; and the examination of the idea bestows a like clearness on all our reasoning.

Let us therefore cast our eye on any two objects, which we call cause and effect, and turn them on all sides, in order to find that impression, which produces an idea of such prodigious consequence. At first sight I perceive, that I must not search for it in any of the particular *qualities* of the objects; since, which-ever of these qualities I pitch on, I find some object, that is not possest of it, and yet falls under the denomination of cause or effect. And indeed there is nothing existent, either externally or internally, which is not to be consider'd either as a cause or an effect; tho' 'tis plain there is no one quality, which universally belongs to all beings, and gives them a title to that denomination.

The idea, then, of causation must be derived from some *relation* among objects; and that relation we must now endeavour to discover. I find in the first place, that whatever objects are consider'd as causes or effects, are *contiguous*; and that nothing can operate in a time or place, which is ever so little remov'd from those of its existence. Tho' distant objects may sometimes seem productive of each other, they are commonly found upon examination to be link'd by a chain of causes, which are contiguous

Plate 1

Johann Zoffany RA
(1734/5–1810)
**The Life School at the
Royal Academy**
1772 99 × 146 cm
Her Majesty the Queen,
Windsor

Zoffany, who was a founder
member of the Royal
Academy, painted this group
portrait of his fellow
Academicians for George III.
It is more than an assembly
of portraits. It is a statement
of the Royal Academy's
devotion to the procedures
of the grand style, based on
studies from the nude in the
poses of ancient sculpture.

Plate 2
Raphael (1483–1520)
Parnassus
1509–11
Vatican, Rome
This is the fresco, measuring
about 15ft across the base,
which Raphael dedicated to
the Beauty of Poetry. It
represents in a perfect form
what Reynolds and others
called 'the grand style' of
painting (see M2).

Plate 3

Titian (1487/90–1576)
Bacchus and Ariadne
1522–3   175 × 190 cm
National Gallery, London

'The conduct of Titian in the
picture of Bacchus and
Ariadne has been much
celebrated, and justly, for the
harmony of colouring'
(Reynolds, *Discourse VIII*).
Reynolds cited as the aim of
the Venetian painters 'mere
elegance' (*Discourse IV*),
and he described all their art
as belonging to the
'ornamental' style, inferior to
the 'grand' style of the
Florentines, Romans and
Bolognese. But he singled
out Titian for praise, referring
to his 'senatorial dignity'. In
his own paintings, Reynolds
tried to emulate Venetian
colouring without
abandoning the elevated
aspects of the 'grand style'
(see M2).

Plate 4
Benjamin West PRA
(1738-1820)
The Death of Wolfe
1768   151 x 213 cm
National Gallery, Canada
Founder member and second
President of the Royal
Academy. West was a
successful painter of
allegorical and mythological
subjects. *The Death of
Wolfe* is, however, the first
scene from 'contemporary'
history which preserved the
scale, style and composition
of the grand manner while
introducing modern dress in
the participants (see M2).

Plate 5

Henry Fuseli RA
(1741–1825)
Lady Macbeth Seizing the Daggers
c. 1812   102 x 127 cm
Tate Gallery, London

Fuseli ranked 'the delineation of character' or 'drama' as second only to the epic in importance (*Lecture IV*). He embodied in his paintings a Burkean understanding of the effect of mystery and terror on the spectator (see M4). Fuseli's Shakespearean subjects are fully on the side of genius rather than tradition and an obedience to the rules (see M3).

Plate 6

Sir Peter Paul Rubens
(1577–1640) –
The Rape of the Sabines
1635 169 x 234 cm
National Gallery, London

Reynolds thought of
Rubens's paintings as
examples of the 'original or
characteristic style',
full of deficiencies
and lacking 'elegance of
mind', but making up for it
by 'the richness of his
composition, the luxuriant
harmony and brilliancy of
his colouring' and 'the
facility with which he
invented' (see M6 for
Ingres's comments on
Rubens).

Plate 7

Jacques Louis David
(1748-1825)
**The Intervention of the
Sabine Women**
1794-9   387 x 521 cm
Louvre, Paris

This suffers from many of the
defects of being a
programme painting,
designed to embody the
neo-classical doctrine of
emulating Greek and Roman
sculpture to the utmost. The
nudity of the participants
and the rigid, frieze-like
composition with the
selective, dramatic gestures
reveal an attempt to create a
wholly unreal classical world.
Stendhal's flippant censures
bear comparison with the
treatment afforded to Barry
several years earlier, when
his version of *The Death of
Wolfe* (1776) was ridiculed
for the nudity of its figures.

Plate 8

Gavin Hamilton (1723-98)
Priam Pleading with Achilles
for the Body of Hector
c. 1775   63 × 99 cm
Tate Gallery, London

This learned Scottish artist
lived most of his life in Rome,
where he made some
important archaeological
discoveries of antique
remains. The rigid formalism
and ascetic simplicity of his
paintings of Homeric subject
matter did almost as much as
Flaxman (see Plates 20 and
21) to associate the Homeric
epics with neo-classicism.
He came closer than any
other British artist to
anticipating the rigid
neo-classicism of the French
school under David and
Ingres (see Plates 7, 9 and
14).

Plate 9

Jean Auguste Dominique
Ingres (1780-1867)
Achilles Receiving the
Ambassadors of Agamemnon
1801 110 x 155 cm
Louvre, Paris

This was the painting which
won the youthful Ingres the
coveted *Prix de Rome*. The
subject is taken from the
Iliad and embodies many of
the principles of Flaxman's
engravings. This
uncompromising essay in
neo-classicism reflects the
Davidian, antiquarian wing
of the grand style. Almost all
the figures in the painting
are based directly on Roman
sculptures.

Plate 10

Sir Joshua Reynolds (1723-92)
Mrs Siddons as the Tragic Muse
1784   560 x 371 cm
Henry E. Huntingdon Library, California, USA

A perfect example of Reynolds taking his own advice on
how to elevate a portrait. Although the face is sharply characterized,
the setting, with its symbolic allusions, is as generalized as a
depiction of some figure from Greek or Roman mythology.

Plate 11

James Barry RA (1741-1806)
King Lear Weeping over the
Dead Body of Cordelia
1786-8   269 x 367 cm
Tate Gallery, London

This picture embodies many
of the elements of the
'sublime' in history painting –
the huge size of the canvas,
the Shakespearean subject
matter, the very powerful
expressions of the main
figure and the exaggerated
anatomical detail – which was
shared by Barry, Fuseli and
Blake (see M2 and M4).

Plate 12

Joseph Mallord William
Turner RA (1775-1851)
The Shipwreck
1805   171 x 241 cm
Tate Gallery, London

Like *The Death of Wolfe*,
this can be thought of as a
modern, or genre, epic. The
subject is taken from life, but
treated in so grand and
awe-inspiring a manner that
at first sight we appear to be
witnessing some terrible
mythological event, such as
The Deluge, or *The End of
the World*. Although the
subject of *The Shipwreck* is
not appropriate to grand art
as Reynolds defines it, the
treatment is (see M2).

Plate 13

Théodore Géricault
(1791-1824)

'The Raft of the Medusa
1819   491 x 716 cm
Louvre, Paris

Like *The Death of Wolfe*,
the subject is a contemporary
event, with strong political
overtones. The composition,
scale and style, moreover,
remove the painting from
mere reportage to
monumental epic
proportions. Poorly received
in Paris (see Ingres's views,
M6), its favourable reception
in London, when exhibited
there in 1820, reveals the
difference in attitude to
high art between France
and England.

Plate 14

Jean Auguste Dominique
Ingres (1780-1867)
The Apotheosis of Homer
1827 381 x 516 cm
Louvre, Paris

Designed as a ceiling for the
Salle Clarac in the Louvre,
this painting is a
statement of faith in the
great minds of literature.
Borrowing many of the
features of Raphael's
Parnassus, it also takes from
his *Marriage of Bolsena* the
introduction of more realistic
figures in the foreground,
such as Poussin and Molière,
who act as a link between
the earthly spectator and the
'semi-divine' personage such
as Raphael and Phidias on
the upper level (see M6).

Plate 15
Eugène Delacroix
(1798–1863)
The Death of Sardanapalus
1828   394 x 495 cm
Louvre, Paris

The canvas was not finished
in time for the 1827 Salon,
for which it was intended. It
was met by almost
universally hostile reviews
and Delacroix was ostracized
from official artistic circles
for many years as a result.
The horrific subject, based on
the story of Sardanapalus's
self-immolation, along with
the destruction of all his
servants and possessions,
was loosely based on a
tragedy of Byron's, and is the
quintessence of the sublime
(see M4). Delacroix was a
fervent admirer of Rubens
(see M6 for Ingres's
comments on Rubens).

Plate 16

Jean Baptiste Greuze
(1725-1805)
Filial Piety
1763   116 x 141 cm
The Hermitage, Leningrad
Greuze, like Wilkie,
specialized in genre painting,
but suffused pictures like
Filial Piety with the uplifting
moral tone which Diderot
so much admired (see M5j),
and which, in altered form,
was very important in the
work of David and his school.
Paintings like this in fact
anticipate much of the
neo-classical ethic, but not
its stylistic devotion to the
antique.

Plate 17

Sir David Wilkie RA
(1785-1841)
Distraining for Rent
1815   81 x 22 cm
The Countess of Swinton

Wilkie's genre painting was
very influential in turning
British art away from its lofty
ambitions (see M2k). Unlike
West, Turner or Martin,
Wilkie did not usually try to
elevate his everyday subjects
to sublime or epic
proportions.

Plate 18

William Blake (1757-1827)
'Los and his Spectre', from **Jerusalem**
1818
William Blake Trust and the Trianon Press

Plate 19

William Blake (1757-1827)
'Urizen in Chains', from **Book of Urizen**
1794

Plate 20 and Plate 21

John Flaxman RA
(1755-1826)
from his edition of Homer's
Iliad
1793
'Thetis Entreating Jupiter'
(Plate 5) and 'Otus and
Ephialtes Held the Chain
(Plate 11)

Flaxman's illustrations to
Homer's epics had an
immense influence in Europe.
They exemplify the absolute
paring away of detail, the
concentration on flowing line
as a means of expressing the
purest, most definitive forms.
Plate 20 was a direct influence
on Ingres who based his
Jupiter and Thetis on it.
Plate 21 helps us to see
why Blake admired Flaxman
so much.

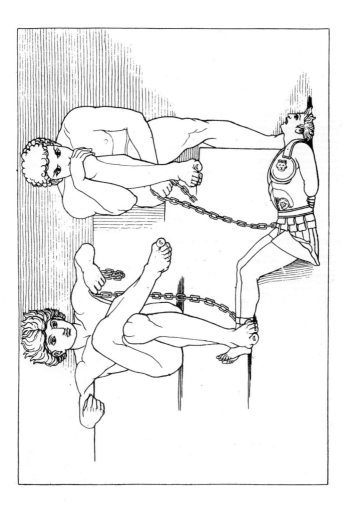

Plate 22

William Blake (1757-1827)
'The Ancient of Days', from **Europe, a Prophecy**
1794

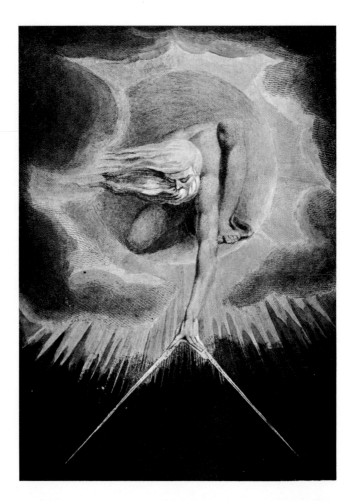

Plate 23
William Blake (1757-1827)
Frontispiece of **Book of Thel**
1789

Plate 24

John Martin (1789-1854)
The Bard
1817   213 x 160 cm
Laing Art Gallery, Newcastle

Martin learnt from Turner the art of creating unbelievably grand
landscapes, in which he set scenes from Biblical or historical legend.
In *The Bard*, the story, taken from ancient British history, is
subordinated to one grand gesture, the lone hero defying nature
and mankind. Martin used the immensity of nature to elevate his
paintings to the sublime.

among themselves, and to the distant objects; and when in any particular instance we cannot discover this connexion, we still presume it to exist. We may therefore consider the relation of CONTIGUITY as essential to that of causation; at least may suppose it such, according to the general opinion, till we can find proper occasion to clear up this matter, by examining what objects are or are not susceptible of juxtaposition and conjunction.

The second relation I shall observe as essential to causes and effects, is not so universally acknowledg'd, but is liable to some controversy. 'Tis that of PRIORITY of time in the cause before the effect.

Having thus discover'd or suppos'd the two relations of *contiguity* and *succession* to be essential to causes and effects, I find I am stopt short, and can proceed no farther in considering any single instance of cause and effect. Motion in one body is regarded upon impulse as the cause of motion in another. When we consider these objects with the utmost attention, we find only that one body approaches the other; and that the motion of it precedes that of the other, but without any sensible interval. 'Tis in vain to rack ourselves with *farther* thought and reflexion upon this subject. We can go no *farther* in considering this particular instance.

Shall we then rest contented with these two relations of contiguity and succession, as affording a compleat idea of causation? By no means. An object may be contiguous and prior to another, without being consider'd as its cause. There is a NECESSARY CONNEXION to be taken into consideration; and that relation is of much greater importance, than any of the other two above-mention'd.

Here again I turn the object on all sides, in order to discover the nature of this necessary connexion, and find the impression, or impressions, from which its idea may be deriv'd. When I cast my eye on the *known qualities* of objects, I immediately discover that the relation of cause and effect depends not in the least on *them*. When I consider their *relations*, I can find none but those of contiguity and succession; which I have already regarded as imperfect and unsatisfactory. Shall the despair of success make me assert, that I am here possest of an idea, which is not preceded by any similar impression? This wou'd be too strong a proof of levity and inconstancy; since the contrary principle has been already so firmly establish'd, as to admit of no farther doubt; at least, till we have more fully examin'd the present difficulty.

We must, therefore, proceed like those, who being in search of any thing that lies conceal'd from them, and not finding it in the place they expected, beat about all the neighbouring fields, without any certain view or design, in hopes their good fortune will at last guide them to what they search for. 'Tis necessary for us to leave the direct survey of this question concerning the nature of that *necessary connexion*, which enters into our idea of cause and effect; and endeavour to find some other questions, the examination of which will perhaps afford a hint, that may serve to clear up the present difficulty. Of these questions there occur two, which I shall proceed to examine, *viz*.

First, For what reason we pronounce it *necessary*, that every thing whose existence has a beginning, shou'd also have a cause?

Secondly, Why we conclude, that such particular causes must *necessarily* have such particular effects; and what is the nature of that *inference* we draw from the one to the other, and of the *belief* we repose in it?

To begin with the first question concerning the necessity of a cause: 'Tis a general maxim in philosophy, that *whatever begins to exist, must have a cause of existence*. This is commonly taken for granted in all reasonings, without any proof given or demanded. 'Tis suppos'd to be founded on intuition, and to be one of those maxims, which tho' they may be deny'd with the lips, 'tis impossible for men in their hearts really to doubt of. But if we examine this maxim by the idea of knowledge above-explain'd, we shall discover in it no mark of any such intuitive certainty; but on the contrary shall find, that 'tis of a nature quite foreign to that species of conviction.

All certainty arises from the comparison of ideas, and from the discovery of such relations as are unalterable, so long as the ideas continue the same. These relations are *resemblance, proportions in quantity and number, degrees of any quality, and contrariety*; none of which are imply'd in this proposition, *Whatever has a beginning has also a cause of existence*. That proposition therefore is not intuitively certain. At least any one, who wou'd assert it to be intuitively certain, must deny these to be the only infallible relations, and must find some other relation of that kind to be imply'd in it; which it will then be time enough to examine.

But here is an argument, which proves at once, that the foregoing proposition is neither intuitively nor demonstrably certain. We can never demonstrate the necessity of a cause to every new existence, or new modification of existence, without shewing at the same time the impossibility there is, that any thing can ever begin to exist without some productive principle; and where the latter proposition cannot be prov'd, we must despair of ever being able to prove the former. Now that the latter proposition is utterly incapable of a demonstrative proof, we may satisfy ourselves by considering, that as all distinct ideas are separable from each other, and as the ideas of cause and effect are evidently distinct, 'twill be easy for us to conceive any object to be non-existent this moment, and existent the next, without conjoining to it the distinct idea of a cause or productive principle. The separation, therefore, of the idea of a cause from that of a beginning of existence, is plainly possible for the imagination; and consequently the actual separation of these objects is so far possible, that it implies no contradiction nor absurdity; and is therefore incapable of being refuted by any reasoning from mere ideas; without which 'tis impossible to demonstrate the necessity of a cause.

Accordingly we shall find upon examination, that every demonstration, which has been produc'd for the necessity of a cause, is fallacious and sophistical.

Since it is not from knowledge or any scientific reasoning, that we derive the opinion of the necessity of a cause to every new production, that opinion must necessarily arise from observation and experience. The next question, then, shou'd naturally be, *how experience gives rise to such a principle?* But as I find it will be more convenient to sink this question in the following, *Why we conclude, that such particular causes must necessarily have such particular effects, and why we form an inference from one to another?* we shall make that the subject of our future enquiry. 'Twill, perhaps, be found in the end, that the same answer will serve for both questions.

'Tis easy to observe, that in tracing this relation, the inference we draw from cause to effect, is not deriv'd merely from a survey of these particular objects, and from such a penetration into their essences as may discover the dependance of the one upon the other. There is no object, which implies the existence of any other if we consider these objects in themselves, and never look beyond the ideas which we form of them. Such an inference wou'd amount to knowledge, and wou'd imply the absolute contradiction and impossibility of conceiving any thing different. But as all distinct ideas are separable, 'tis evident there can be no impossibility of that kind. When we pass from a present impression to the idea of any object, we might possibly have separated the idea from the impression, and have substituted any other idea in its room.

'Tis therefore by EXPERIENCE only, that we can infer the existence of one object from that of another. The nature of experience is this. We remember to have had frequent instances of the existence of one species of objects; and also remember, that the individuals of another species of objects have always attended them, and have existed in a regular order of contiguity and succession with regard to them. Thus we remember to have seen that species of object we call *flame*, and to have felt that species of sensation we call *heat*. We likewise call to mind their constant conjunction in all past instances. Without any farther ceremony, we call the one *cause* and the other *effect*, and infer the existence of the one from that of the other. In all those instances, from which we learn the conjunction of particular causes and effects, both the causes and effects have been perceiv'd by the senses, and are remember'd: But in all cases, wherein we reason concerning them, there is only one perceiv'd or remember'd, and the other is supply'd in conformity to our past experience.

Thus in advancing we have insensibly discover'd a new relation betwixt cause and effect, when we least expected it, and were entirely employ'd upon another subject. This relation is their CONSTANT CONJUNCTION. Contiguity and succession are not sufficient to make us pronounce any two objects to be cause and effect, unless we perceive, that these two relations are preserv'd in several instances. We may now see the advantage of quitting the direct survey of this relation, in order to discover the nature of that *necessary connexion*, which makes so essential a part of it. There are hopes, that by this means we may at last arrive at our propos'd end; tho' to tell the truth, this new-discover'd relation of a constant conjunction seems to advance us but very little in our way. For it implies no more than this, that like objects have always been plac'd in like relations of contiguity and succession; and it seems evident, at least at first sight, that by this means we can never discover any new idea, and can only multiply, but not enlarge the objects of our mind. It may be thought, that what we learn not from one object, we can never learn from a hundred, which are all of the same kind, and are perfectly resembling in every circumstance. As our senses shew us in one instance two bodies, or motions, or qualities in certain relations of succession and contiguity; so our memory presents us only with a multitude of instances, wherein we always find like bodies, motions, or qualities in like relations. From the mere repetition of any past impression, even to infinity, there never will arise any new original idea, such as that of a necessary connexion; and the number of impressions has in this case no more effect than if we confin'd ourselves to one only. But tho' this reasoning seems just and obvious; yet as it wou'd be folly to despair too soon, we shall continue the thread of our discourse; and having found, that after the discovery of the constant conjunction of any objects, we always draw an inference from one object to another, we shall now examine the nature of that inference, and of the transition from the impression to the idea. Perhaps 'twill appear in the end, that the necessary connexion depends on the inference, instead of the inference's depending on the necessary connexion.

Since it appears, that the transition from an impression present to the memory or senses to the idea of an object, which we call cause or effect, is founded on past *experience*, and on our remembrance of their *constant conjunction*, the next question is, Whether experience produces the idea by means of the understanding or of the imagination; whether we are determin'd by reason to make the transition, or by a certain association and relation of perceptions. Reason can never shew us the connexion of one object with another, tho' aided by experience, and the observation of their constant conjunction in all past instances. When the mind, therefore, passes from the idea or impression of one object to the idea or belief of another, it is not determin'd by reason, but by certain principles, which associate together the ideas of these objects, and unite them in the imagination. Had ideas no more union in the fancy than objects seem to have to the understanding, we cou'd never draw any inference from causes to effects, nor repose belief in any matter of fact. The inference, therefore, depends solely on the union of ideas. When ev'ry individual of any species of objects is found by experience to be constantly united with an individual of another species, the appearance of any new individual of either species naturally conveys the thought to its usual attendant. Thus because such a particular idea is commonly annex'd to such a particular word, nothing is requir'd but the hearing of that word to produce the correspondent idea; and 'twill scarce be possible for the mind, by its utmost efforts, to prevent that transition. In this case it is not absolutely necessary, that upon hearing such a particular sound, we shou'd reflect on any past experience, and consider what idea has been usually connected with the sound. The imagination of itself supplies the place of this reflection, and is so accustom'd to pass from the word to the idea, that it interposes not a moment's delay betwixt the hearing of the one, and the conception of the other.

Having thus explain'd the manner, *in which we reason beyond our immediate impressions, and conclude that such particular causes must have such particular effects*; we must now return upon our footsteps to examine that question, which first occur'd to us, and which we dropt in our way, *viz. What is our idea of necessity, when we say that two objects are necessarily connected together*. Upon this head I repeat what I have often had occasion to observe, that as we have no idea, that is not deriv'd from an impression, we must find some impression, that gives rise to this idea of necessity, if we assert we have really such an idea. In order to understand this I consider, in what objects necessity is commonly suppos'd to lie; and finding that it is always ascrib'd to causes and effects, I turn my eye to two objects suppos'd to be plac'd in that relation; and examine them in all the situations, of which they are susceptible. I immediately perceive, that they are *contiguous* in time and place, and that the object we call cause *precedes* the other we call effect. In no one instance can I go any farther, nor is it possible for me to discover any third relation betwixt these objects. I therefore enlarge my view to comprehend several instances; where I find like objects always existing in like relations of contiguity and succession. At first sight this seems to serve but little to my purpose. The reflection on several instances only repeats the same objects; and therefore can never give rise to a new idea. But upon farther enquiry I find, that the repetition is not in every particular the same, but produces a new impression, and by that means the idea, which I at present examine. For after a frequent repetition, I find, that upon the appearance of one of the objects, the mind is *determin'd* by custom to consider its usual attendant, and to consider it in a stronger light upon account of its relation to the first object. 'Tis this impression, then, or *determination*, which affords me the idea of necessity.

The idea of necessity arises from some impression. There is no impression convey'd by our senses, which can give rise to that idea. It must, therefore, be deriv'd from some internal impression, or impression of reflexion. There is no internal impression, which has any relation to the present business, but that propensity, which custom produces, to pass from an object to the idea of its usual attendant. This therefore is the essence of necessity. Upon the whole, necessity is something, that exists in the mind, not in objects; nor is it possible for us ever to form the most distant idea of it, consider'd as a quality in bodies. Either we have no idea of necessity, or necessity is nothing but that determination of the thought to pass from causes to effects and from effects to causes, according to their experienc'd union.

Thus as the necessity, which makes two times two equal to four, or three angles of a triangle equal to two right ones, lies only in the act of the understanding, by which we consider and compare these ideas; in like manner the necessity or power, which unites causes and effects, lies in the determination of the mind to pass from the one to the other. The efficacy or energy of causes is neither plac'd in the causes themselves, nor in the deity, nor in the concurrence of these two principles; but belongs entirely to the soul, which considers the union of two or more objects in all past instances. 'Tis here that the real power of causes is plac'd, along with their connexion and necessity.

'Tis now time to collect all the different parts of this reasoning, and by joining them together form an exact definition of the relation of cause and effect, which makes the subject of the present enquiry. This order wou'd not have been excusable, of first examining our inference from the relation before we had explain'd the relation itself, had it been possible to proceed in a different method. But as the nature of the relation depends so much on that of the inference, we have been oblig'd to advance in this seemingly preposterous manner, and make use of terms before we were able exactly to define them, or fix their meaning. We shall now correct this fault by giving a precise definition of cause and effect.

There may two definitions be given of this relation, which are only different, by their presenting a different view of the same object, and making us consider it either as a *philosophical* or as a *natural* relation; either as a comparison of two ideas, or as an association betwixt them. We may define a CAUSE to be 'An object precedent and contiguous to another, and where all the objects resembling the former are plac'd in like relations of precedency and contiguity to those objects, that resemble the latter.' If this definition be esteem'd defective, because drawn from objects foreign to the cause, we may substitute this other definition in its place, *viz.*, 'A CAUSE is an object precedent and contiguous to another, and so united with it, that the idea of the one determines the mind to form the idea of the other, and the impression of the one to form a more lively idea of the other.' Shou'd this definition also be rejected for the same reason, I know no other remedy, than that the persons, who express this delicacy should substitute a juster definition in its place. But for my part I must own my incapacity for such an undertaking. When I examine with the utmost accuracy those objects, which are commonly denominated causes and effects, I find, in considering a single instance, that the one object is precedent and contiguous to the other; and in inlarging my view to consider several instances, I find only, that like objects are constantly plac'd in like relations of succession and contiguity. Again, when I consider the influence of this constant conjunction, I perceive that such a relation can never be an object of reasoning, and can never operate upon the mind, but by means of custom, which determines the imagination to make a transition from the idea of one object to that of its usual attendant, and from the impression of one to a more lively idea of the other. We may now be able fully to overcome all that repugnance, which 'tis so natural for us to entertain against the foregoing reasoning, by which we endeavour'd to prove, that the necessity of a cause to every beginning of existence is not founded on any arguments either demonstrative or intuitive. Such an opinion will not appear strange after the foregoing definitions. If we define a cause to be *an object precedent and contiguous to another, and where all the objects resembling the former are plac'd in a like relation of priority and contiguity to those objects, that resemble the latter*; we may easily conceive, that there is no absolute nor metaphysical necessity, that every beginning of existence shou'd be attended with such an object. If we define a cause to be, *An object precedent and contiguous to another, and so united with it in the imagination, that the idea of the one determines the mind to form the idea of the other, and the impression of the one to form a more lively idea of the other*; we shall make still less difficulty of assenting to this opinion. Such an influence on the mind is in itself perfectly extraordinary and incomprehensible; nor can we be certain of its reality, but from experience and observation.

3 David Hume
Enquiries concerning the Human Understanding

from *Enquiries concerning the Human Understanding* 1748

There are no ideas, which occur in metaphysics, more obscure and uncertain, than those of *power, force, energy* or *necessary connexion*, of which it is every moment necessary for us to treat in all our disquisitions. We shall, therefore, endeavour, in this section, to fix, if possible, the precise meaning of these terms, and thereby remove some part of that obscurity, which is so much complained of in this species of philosophy.

It seems a proposition, which will not admit of much dispute, that all our ideas are nothing but copies of our impressions, or, in other words, that it is impossible for us to *think* of anything, which we have not antecedently *felt*, either by our external or internal senses.

To be fully acquainted, therefore, with the idea of power or necessary connexion, let us examine its impression; and in order to find the impression with greater certainty, let us search for it in all the sources, from which it may possibly be derived.

When we look about us towards external objects, and consider the operation of causes, we are never able, in a single instance, to discover any power or necessary connexion; any quality, which binds the effect to the cause, and renders the one an infallible consequence of the other. We only find, that the one does actually, in fact, follow the other. The impulse of one billiard-ball is attended with motion in the second. This is the whole that appears to the *outward* senses. The mind feels no sentiment or *inward* impression from this succession of objects: Consequently, there is not, in any single, particular instance of cause and effect, any thing which can suggest the idea of power or necessary connexion.

From the first appearance of an object, we never can conjecture what effect will result from it. But were the power or energy of any cause discoverable by the mind, we could foresee the effect, even without experience; and might, at first, pronounce with certainty concerning it, by mere dint of thought and reasoning.

In reality, there is no part of matter, that does ever, by its sensible qualities, discover any power or energy, or give us ground to imagine, that it could produce anything, or be followed by any other object, which we could denominate its effect. Solidity, extension, motion; these qualities are all complete in themselves, and never point out any other event which may result from them. The scenes of the universe are continually shifting, and one object follows another in an uninterrupted succession; but the power or force, which actuates the whole machine, is entirely concealed from us, and never discovers itself in any of the sensible qualities of body. We know, that, in fact, heat is a constant attendant of flame; but what is the connexion between them, we have no room so much as to conjecture or imagine. It is impossible, therefore, that the idea of power can be derived from the contemplation of bodies, in single instances of their operation; because no bodies ever discover any power, which can be the original of this idea.[1]

Since, therefore, external objects as they appear to the senses, give us no idea of power or necessary connexion, by their operation in particular instances, let us see, whether this idea be derived from reflection on the operations of our own minds, and be copied from any internal impression. It may be said, that we are every moment conscious of internal power; while we feel, that, by the simple command of our will, we can move the organs of our body, or direct the faculties of our mind. An act of volition produces motion in our limbs, or raises a new idea in our imagination. This influence of the will we know by consciousness. Hence we acquire the idea of power or energy; and are certain, that we ourselves and all other intelligent beings are possessed of power. This idea, then, is an idea of reflection, since it arises from reflecting on the operations of our own mind, and on the command which is exercised by will, both over the organs of the body and faculties of the soul.

We shall proceed to examine this pretension; and first with regard to the influence of volition over the organs of the body. This influence, we may observe, is a fact, which, like all other natural events, can be known only by experience, and can never be foreseen from any apparent energy or power in the cause, which connects it with the effect, and renders the one an infallible consequence of the other. The motion of our body follows upon the command of our will. Of this we are every moment conscious. But the means, by which this is effected; the energy, by which the will performs so extraordinary an operation; of this we are so far from being immediately conscious, that it must for ever escape our most diligent inquiry.

1. Mr Locke, in his chapter of power, says that, finding from experience, that there are several new productions in nature, and concluding that there must somewhere be a power capable of producing them, we arrive at last by this reasoning at the idea of power. But no reasoning can ever give us a new, original, simple idea; as this philosopher himself confesses. This, therefore, can never be the origin of that idea.

For *first*, is there any principle in all nature more mysterious than the union of soul with body; by which a supposed spiritual substance acquires such an influence over a material one, that the most refined thought is able to actuate the grossest matter? Were we empowered, by a secret wish, to remove mountains, or control the planets in their orbit; this extensive authority would not be more extraordinary, nor more beyond our comprehension. But if by consciousness we perceived any power or energy in the will, we must know this power; we must know its connexion with the effect; we must know the secret union of soul and body, and the nature of both these substances; by which the one is able to operate, in so many instances, upon the other.

Secondly, We are not able to move all the organs of the body with a like authority; though we cannot assign any reason besides experience, for so remarkable a difference between one and the other. Why has the will an influence over the tongue and fingers, not over the heart or liver? This question would never embarrass us, were we conscious of a power in the former case, not in the latter. We should then perceive, independent of experience, why the authority of will over the organs of the body is circumscribed within such particular limits. Being in that case fully acquainted with the power or force, by which it operates, we should also know, why its influence reaches precisely to such boundaries and no farther.

A man, suddenly struck with palsy in the leg or arm, or who had newly lost those members, frequently endeavours at first to move them, and employ them in their usual offices. Here he is as much conscious of power to command such limbs, as a man in perfect health is conscious of power to actuate any member which remains in its natural state and condition. But consciousness never deceives. Consequently, neither in the one case nor in the other, are we ever conscious of any power. We learn the influence of our will from experience alone. And experience only teaches us, how one event constantly follows another; without instructing us in the secret connexion, which binds them together, and renders them inseparable.

Thirdly, We learn from anatomy, that the immediate object of power in voluntary motion, is not the member itself which is moved, but certain muscles, and nerves, and animal spirits, and, perhaps, something still more minute and more unknown, through which the motion is successively propagated, ere it reach the member itself whose motion is the immediate object of volition. Can there be a more certain proof, that the power, by which this whole operation is performed, so far from being directly and fully known by an inward sentiment or conscious-ness, is, to the last degree mysterious and unintelligible? Here the mind wills a certain event: Immediately another event, unknown to ourselves, and totally different from the one in-tended, is produced: This event produces another, equally un-known: Till at last, through a long succession, the desired event is produced. But if the original power were felt, it must be known: Were it known, its effect also must be known; since all power is relative to its effect. And *vice versa*, if the effect be not known, the power cannot be known nor felt. How indeed can we be conscious of a power to move our limbs, when we have no such power; but only that to move certain animal spirits, which, though they produce at last the motion of our limbs, yet operate in such a manner as is wholly beyond our compre-hension?

We may, therefore, conclude from the whole, I hope, without any temerity, though with assurance; that our idea of power is not copied from any sentiment or consciousness of power within ourselves, when we give rise to animal motion, or apply our limbs to their power use and office. That their motion follows the command of the will is a matter of common experi-ence, like other natural events: But the power or energy by which this is effected, like that in other natural events, is un-known and inconceivable.

4 Immanuel Kant
Prolegomena

from *Prolegomena* 1783. Translated by P. G. Lucas, 1953

Since Locke's and Leibniz's essays, or rather since the beginning of metaphysics as far as the history of it reaches, no event has occurred which could have been more decisive in respect of the fate of this science than the attack which David Hume made on it. He brought no light into this kind of knowledge, but he struck a spark at which a light could well have been kindled, if it had found a receptive tinder and if the glow had been carefully kept up and increased.

Hume started in the main from a single but important concept in metaphysics, namely that of the *connection of cause and effect* (together with its consequential concepts of force and action etc.). He challenged Reason, who pretends to have conceived this concept in her womb, to give an account of herself and say with what right she thinks: that anything can be of such a nature, that if it is posited, something else must thereby also be posited necessarily; for that is what the concept of cause says. He proved irrefutably: that it is wholly impossible for reason to think such a conjunction *a priori* and out of concepts. For this conjunction contains necessity; but it is quite impossible to see how, because something is, something else must also necessarily be, and how therefore the concept of such an *a priori* connection can be introduced. From this he inferred that Reason completely deceives herself with this concept, in falsely taking it for her own child, whereas it is nothing but a bastard of the imagination fathered by experience. The imagination, having by experience brought certain representations under the law of association, passes off a subjective necessity arising out of this, namely custom, for an objective necessity from insight. From this he inferred: reason has no power to think such connections, not even only to think them universally, because its concepts would then be mere fictions, and all its ostensibly *a priori* knowledge is nothing but falsely stamped ordinary experiences; which is as much as to say that there is no metaphysics at all, and cannot be any.

I freely admit: it was David Hume's remark that first, many years ago, interrupted my dogmatic slumber and gave a completely different direction to my inquiries in the field of speculative philosophy. I was very far from listening to him in respect of his conclusions, which were merely the result of his not representing his problem to himself as a whole, and instead only lighting on part of it, which can give no information without taking the whole into account. When we begin from a thought well-grounded but not worked out which another has bequeathed to us, we may well hope through continued reflection to advance beyond the point reached by the sagacious man whom we have to thank for the first spark of this light.

So I tried first whether Hume's objection could not be represented universally, and I soon found that the concept of the connection of cause and effect is by no means the only one by which connections between things are thought *a priori* by the understanding; indeed that metaphysics consists of nothing else whatever. I tried to make certain of the number of these concepts, and when I had succeeded in doing this in the way I wished, namely from a single principle, I proceeded to the deduction of them. I was now assured that they are not, as Hume had feared, deduced from experience, but have their origin in pure understanding. This deduction, which seemed impossible to my sagacious predecessor, and had never even occurred to anyone except him, although everyone confidently used these concepts without asking on what their objective validity is grounded – this deduction, I say, was the most difficult thing that could ever be undertaken on behalf of metaphysics; and, worst of all, any metaphysics that there is anywhere at all could not give me the slightest help, because this deduction has first to establish the possibility of a metaphysics. Having succeeded in solving Hume's problem not merely in a special case, but with regard to the whole faculty of pure reason, I could take sure although still only slow steps towards determining at last the whole extent of pure reason, completely and according to universal principles, in its boundaries as well as in its content. This is what metaphysics needs in order to construct its system according to a sure plan.

But I fear that the *working out* of Hume's problem in its greatest possible extension (namely in the *Critique of Pure Reason*) may fare the same as the problem itself fared when it was first presented. It will be wrongly judged through not being understood; and it will not be understood because people will be willing to skim through the pages of the book but not think through it, and they will not want to spend this trouble on it because the work is dry, because it is obscure, because it is contrary to all ordinary ideas, and on top of that prolix. Now I admit that I do not expect to hear complaints from a philosopher about not being popular, entertaining and agreeable, when it is a matter of the very existence of a highly prized mode of knowledge, indispensable to humanity, which cannot be settled except according to the strictest rules of scholarly exactitude. This may eventually be followed by popularity, but can never begin with it. Yet as regards a certain obscurity deriving in part from the prolixity of the plan, which makes it difficult to survey the main points which are important for the inquiry: on this score the complaint is just, and I shall meet it with the present *Prolegomena*.

The former work, which exhibits the pure faculty of reason in its whole extent and boundaries, always remains the foundations to which the prolegomena refer as mere preliminary exercises; for that critique must exist as a science, systematic and complete to its smallest parts, before one can think of allowing metaphysics to make its appearance, or even have a remote hope of so doing.

We have long been used to seeing old worn-out modes of knowledge newly trimmed by being taken out of their former contexts and fitted out with a systematic dress according to a personal choice of cut, but with new titles; and the majority of readers will not anticipate anything else from the critique. But these prolegomena will give them the insight that it is a wholly new science which no one had previously even thought of, even the mere idea of which was unknown, and towards which nothing of all that has hitherto been done could be used, except the hint that Hume's doubt could give. He likewise suspected nothing of such a possible formal science but put his ship aground, to bring it into safety, on the shore of scepticism where it may lie and rot; instead of which what I want to do is to give it a pilot who will be able to sail the ship safely wherever he will, using sure principles of navigation drawn from knowledge of the globe, and equipped with a complete set of charts and a compass.

We must then first notice: that although all judgements of experience are empirical, i.e. have their ground in immediate sense perception, yet all empirical judgements are not conversely for that reason judgements of experience, but that in addition to the empirical and in general in addition to what is given to sensible intuition, special concepts which have their origin wholly *a priori* in pure understanding must still be added, under which every perception must first be subsumed before it can be changed into experience by their means.

Empirical judgements, so far as they have objective validity, are JUDGEMENTS OF EXPERIENCE; those which are only subjectively valid I call mere JUDGEMENTS OF PERCEPTION. The latter do not need a pure concept of the understanding but only the logical connection of perception in a thinking subject. The former on the other hand always need, in addition to the representations of sensible intuition, special concepts originally generated in the understanding, and it is these that make the judgement of experience objectively valid.

All our judgements are at first mere judgements of perception, they are valid only for us, i.e. for our subject, and only afterwards do we give them a new reference, namely to an object, and want the judgement to be valid for us at all times and equally for everybody; for if a judgement agrees with an object, all judgements about the same object must agree with one another, and thus the objective validity of the judgement of experience means nothing other than its necessary universal validity. And conversely if we find cause to hold a judgement to be necessarily universally valid (which never rests on perception but on the pure concept of the understanding under which the perception is subsumed) we must also hold it to be objective, i.e. that it expresses not merely a reference of the perception to a subject, but a quality of the object; for there would be no reason why the judgements of others should necessarily agree with mine if it were not for the unity of the object to which all refer, with which they agree and hence must also agree with one another.

Objective validity and necessary universal validity (for everyone) are therefore identical concepts, and although we do not know the object in itself, yet when we regard a judgement as universally valid and necessary we mean by this its objective validity. We know the object through this judgement (even if otherwise, as to what it may be like in itself, it remains unknown), through the universally valid and necessary connection of the given perceptions. This being the case for all objects of the senses, judgements of experience will take their objective validity not from immediate knowledge of the object (for this is impossible), but merely from the condition of the universal validity of empirical judgements, which, as has been said, never rests on empirical conditions or indeed on sensible conditions at all, but on a pure concept of the understanding. The object in itself always remains unknown; but when the connection of representations which are given to our sensibility by it is determined as universally valid by the concept of the understanding, the object is determined by this relation and the judgement is objective.

If one analyses all one's synthetic judgements so far as they are objectively valid, one finds that they never consist in mere intuitions which, as is commonly supposed, are merely connected in a judgement through comparison, but that they would be impossible if in addition to the concepts abstracted from intuition a pure concept of the understanding had not been added, under which these concepts have been subsumed and only then connected in an objectively valid judgement. For the reader who retains his long habit of taking experience for a merely empirical synthesis of perceptions and hence never thinks of the fact that it goes much further than perceptions reach, in that it gives universal validity to empirical judgements and needs for this a pure unity of the understanding preceding it *a priori*, I can do no more here, these being prolegomena, than to recommend him to heed well this difference between experience and a mere aggregate of perceptions, and to judge the mode of proof from this point of view.

This is now the place to dispose of the Humean doubt once and for all. He asserted, rightly, that we can in no way have insight by reason into the possibility of causality, i.e. of the reference of the existence of a thing to the existence of something else which is posited necessarily by the first. I add that we have equally little insight into the concept of subsistence, i.e. of the necessity that there must lie at the ground of existence of things a subject which cannot itself be a predicate of anything else, indeed that we can make for ourselves no concept of the possibility of such a thing (although we can point to examples of its use in experience); similarly that this same inconceivability touches the community of things, in that we can have no insight into how a consequence can be drawn from the state of one thing to the state of quite other things outside it, and reciprocally, and how substances, each one of which has its own separate existence, can be dependent on one another necessarily. None the less I am far from holding that these concepts are merely taken from experience and that the necessity which is represented in them is fictitious and mere illusion imposed on us by long habit; on the contrary I have shown adequately that these concepts and the principles drawn from them stand *a priori* before all experience and have their undoubted objective rightness, though admittedly only in respect of experience.

Hence the pure concepts of the understanding also have no meaning whatever if they try to leave objects of experience and to be referred to things in themselves (noumena). They serve as it were only to spell out appearances, so that they can be read as experience; the principles which arise from their reference to the world of the senses only serve our understanding for use in experience; beyond it they are arbitrary connections without objective reality, the possibility of which cannot be known *a priori*, nor their reference to objects confirmed by any example, or even made understandable, because all examples can only be taken from some possible experience, and the objects of those concepts can also be found nowhere else than in a possible experience.

This complete solution to the Humean problem, although it turns out contrary to the expectation of its originator, thus rescues their *a priori* origin for the pure concepts of the understanding, and their validity for the universal laws of nature, as laws of the understanding; but in such a way that it limits their use to experience only, because their possibility has its ground merely in the reference of the understanding to experience; not in such a way that they are deduced from experience but that experience is deduced from them, a completely reversed kind of connection which never occurred to Hume.

From this there flows the following result of all the foregoing researches: 'All synthetic principles *a priori* are nothing more than principles of possible experience' and can never be referred to things in themselves, but only to appearances as objects of experience. Hence pure mathematics as well as pure natural science can never bear on anything more than mere appearances, and can only represent either that which makes experience in general possible, or that which, as deduced from these principles, must always be capable of being represented in some possible experience.

5 Immanuel Kant
Critique of Pure Reason

from *Critique of Pure Reason* 1781 and 1787. Translated by N. K. Smith, 1964

Preface to Second Edition

Hitherto it has been assumed that all our knowledge must conform to objects. But all attempts to extend our knowledge of objects by establishing something in regard to them *a priori*, by means of concepts, have, on this assumption, ended in failure. We must therefore make trial whether we may not have more success in the tasks of metaphysics, if we suppose that objects must conform to our knowledge. This would agree better with what is desired, namely, that it should be possible to have knowledge of objects *a priori*, determining something in regard to them prior to their being given. We should then be proceeding precisely on the lines of Copernicus's primary hypothesis. Failing of satisfactory progress in explaining the movements of the heavenly bodies on the supposition that they all revolved round the spectator, he tried whether he might not have better success if he made the spectator to revolve and the stars to remain at rest. A similar experiment can be tried in metaphysics, as regards the *intuition* of objects. If intuition must conform to the constitution of the objects, I do not see how we could know anything of the latter *a priori*; but if the object (as object of the senses) must conform to the constitution of our faculty of intuition, I have no difficulty in conceiving such a possibility.

Since I cannot rest in these intuitions if they are to become known, but must relate them as representations to something as their object, and determine this latter through them, either I must assume that the *concepts*, by means of which I obtain this determination, conform to the object, or else I assume that the objects, or what is the same thing, that the *experience* in which alone, as given objects, they can be known, conform to the concepts. In the former case, I am again in the same perplexity as to how I can know anything *a priori* in regard to the objects. In the latter case the outlook is more hopeful. For experience is itself a species of knowledge which involves understanding; and understanding has rules which I must presuppose as being in me prior to objects being given to me, and therefore as being *a priori*. They find expression in *a priori* concepts to which all objects of experience necessarily conform, and with which they must agree. As regards objects which are thought solely through reason, and indeed as necessary, but which can never – at least not in the manner in which reason thinks them – be given in experience, the attempts at thinking them (for they must admit of being thought) will furnish an excellent touchstone of what we are adopting as our new method of thought, namely, that we can know *a priori* of things only what we ourselves put into them.

But, it will be asked, what sort of a treasure is this that we propose to bequeath to posterity? What is the value of the metaphysics that is alleged to be thus purified by criticism and established once for all? On a cursory view of the present work it may seem that its results are merely *negative*, warning us that we must never venture with speculative reason beyond the limits of experience. Such is in fact its primary use. But such teaching at once acquires a *positive* value when we recognize that the principles with which speculative reason ventures out beyond its proper limits do not in effect *extend* the employment of reason, but, as we find on closer scrutiny, inevitably *narrow* it. These principles properly belong [not to reason but] to sensibility, and when thus employed they threaten to make the bounds of sensibility coextensive with the real, and so to supplant reason in its pure (practical) employment. So far, therefore, as our critique limits speculative reason, it is indeed *negative*; but since it thereby removes an obstacle which stands in the way of the employment of practical reason, nay threatens to destroy it, it has in reality a *positive* and very important use. At least this is so, immediately we are convinced that there is an absolutely necessary *practical* employment of pure reason – the *moral* – in which it inevitably goes beyond the limits of sensibility. Though [practical] reason, in thus proceeding, requires no assistance from speculative reason, it must yet be assured against its opposition, that reason may not be brought into conflict with itself. To deny that the service which the critique renders is *positive* in character, would thus be like saying that the police are of no positive benefit, inasmuch as their main business is merely to prevent the violence of which citizens stand in mutual fear, in order that each may pursue his vocation in peace and security. That space and time are only forms of sensible intuition, and so only conditions of the existence of things as appearances; that, moreover, we have no concepts of understanding, and consequently no elements for the knowledge of things, save in so far as intuition can be given corresponding to these concepts; and that we can therefore have no knowledge of any object as thing in itself, but only in so far as it is an object of sensible intuition, that is, an appearance – all this is proved in the analytical part of the critique. Thus it does indeed follow that all possible speculative knowledge of reason is limited to mere objects of *experience*. But our further contention must also be duly borne in mind, namely, that though we cannot *know* these objects as things in themselves, we must yet be in position at least to *think* them as things in themselves;[1] otherwise we should be landed in the absurd conclusion that there can be appearance without anything that

---

1. To *know* an object I must be able to prove its possibility, either from its actuality as attested by experience, or *a priori* by means of reason. But I can *think* whatever I please, provided only that I do not contradict myself, that is, provided my concept is a possible thought. This suffices for the possibility of the concept, even though I may not be able to answer for there being, in the sum of all possibilities, an object corresponding to it. But something more is required before I can ascribe to such a concept objective validity, that is, real possibility; the former possibility is merely logical. This something more need not, however, be sought in the theoretical sources of knowledge; it may lie in those that are practical.

appears. Now let us suppose that the distinction, which our critique has shown to be necessary, between things as objects of experience and those same things as things in themselves, had not been made. In that case all things in general, as far as they are efficient causes, would be determined by the principle of causality, and consequently by the mechanism of nature. I could not, therefore, without palpable contradiction, say of one and the same being, for instance the human soul, that its will is free and yet is subject to natural necessity, that is, is not free. For I have taken the soul in both propositions *in one and the same sense*, namely as a thing in general, that is, as a thing in itself; and save by means of a preceding critique, could not have done otherwise. But if our critique is not in error in teaching that the object is to be taken *in a twofold sense*, namely as appearance and as thing in itself; if the deduction of the concepts of understanding is valid, and the principle of causality therefore applies only to things taken in the former sense, namely, in so far as they are objects of experience – these same objects, taken in the other sense, not being subject to the principle – then there is no contradiction in supposing that one and the same will is, in the appearance, that is, in its visible acts, necessarily subject to the law of nature, and so far *not free*, while yet, as belonging to a thing in itself, it is not subject to that law, and is therefore *free*. My soul, viewed from the latter standpoint, cannot indeed be known by means of speculative reason (and still less through empirical observation); and freedom as a property of a being to which I attribute effects in the sensible world, is therefore also not knowable in any such fashion. For I should then have to know such a being as determined in its existence, and yet as not determined in time which is impossible, since I cannot support my concept by any intuition. But though I cannot *know,* I can yet *think* freedom; that is to say, the representation of it is at least not self-contradictory, provided due account be taken of our critical distinction between the two modes of representation, the sensible and the intellectual, and of the resulting limitation of the pure concepts of understanding and of the principles which flow from them.

If we grant that morality necessarily presupposes freedom

(in the strictest sense) as a property of our will; if, that is to say, we grant that it yields practical principles – original principles, proper to our reason – as *a priori data* of reason, and that this would be absolutely impossible save on the assumption of freedom; and if at the same time we grant that speculative reason has proved that such freedom does not allow of being thought, then the former supposition – that made on behalf of morality – would have to give way to this other contention, the opposite of which involves a palpable contradiction. For since it is only on the assumption of freedom that the negation of morality contains any contradiction, freedom, and with it morality, would have to yield to the mechanism of nature.

Morality does not, indeed, require that freedom should be understood, but only that it should not contradict itself, and so should at least allow of being thought, and that as thus thought it should place no obstacle in the way of a free act (viewed in another relation) likewise conforming to the mechanism of nature. The doctrine of morality and the doctrine of nature may each, therefore, make good its position. This, however, is only possible in so far as criticism has previously established our unavoidable ignorance of things in themselves, and has limited all that we can theoretically *know* to mere appearances.

General Observations on Transcendental Aesthetic

To avoid all misapprehension, it is necessary to explain, as clearly as possible, what our view is regarding the fundamental constitution of sensible knowledge in general.

What we have meant to say is that all our intuition is nothing but the representation of appearance; that the things which we intuit are not in themselves what we intuit them as being, nor their relations so constituted in themselves as they appear to us, and that if the subject, or even only the subjective constitution of the senses in general, be removed, the whole constitution and all the relations of objects in space and time, nay space and time themselves, would vanish. As appearances, they cannot exist in themselves, but only in us. What objects may be in themselves, and apart from all this receptivity of our sensibility, remains completely unknown to us. We know nothing but our mode of perceiving them – a mode which is peculiar to us, and not necessarily shared in by every being, though, certainly, by every human being. Even if we could bring our intuition to the highest degree of clearness, we should not thereby come any nearer to the constitution of objects in themselves. We should still know only our mode of intuition, that is, our sensibility. We should, indeed, know it completely, but always only under the conditions of space and time – conditions which are originally inherent in the subject. What the objects may be in themselves would never become known to us even through the most enlightened knowledge of that which is alone given us, namely, their appearance.

We commonly distinguish in appearances that which is essentially inherent in their intuition and holds for sense in all human beings, from that which belongs to their intuition accidentally only, and is valid not in relation to sensibility in general but only in relation to a particular standpoint or to a peculiarity of structure in this or that sense. The former kind of knowledge is then declared to represent the object in itself, the latter its appearance only. But this distinction is merely empirical. If, as generally happens, we stop short at this point, and do not proceed, as we ought, to treat the empirical intuition as itself mere appearance, in which nothing that belongs to a thing in itself can be found, our transcendental distinction is lost. We then believe that we know things in themselves, and this in spite of the fact that in the world of sense, however deeply we inquire into its objects, we have to do with nothing but appearances. The rainbow in a sunny shower may be called a mere appearance, and the rain the thing in itself. This is correct, if the latter concept be taken in a merely physical sense. Rain will then be viewed only as that which, in all experience and in all its various positions relative to the senses, is determined thus, and not otherwise, in our intuition. But if we take this empirical object in its general character, and ask, without considering whether or not it is the same for all human sense, whether it represents an object in itself (and by that we cannot mean the drops of rain, for these are already, as appearances, empirical objects), the question as to the relation of the representation to the object at once becomes transcendental. We then realize that not only are the drops of rain mere appearances, but that even their round shape, nay even the space in which they fall, are nothing in themselves, but merely modifications or fundamental forms of our sensible intuition, and that the transcendental object remains unknown to us.

Principle of Succession in Time, in accordance with the Law of Causality

All alterations take place in conformity with the law of the connection of cause and effect.

Proof

The apprehension of the manifold of appearance is always successive. The representations of the parts follow upon one another. Whether they also follow one another in the object is a point which calls for further reflection, and which is not decided by the above statement. Everything, every representation even, in so far as we are conscious of it, may be entitled object. But it is a question for deeper inquiry what the word 'object' ought to signify in respect of appearances when these are viewed not in so far as they are (as representations) objects, but only in so far as they stand for an object. The appearances, in so far as they are objects of consciousness simply in virtue of being representations, are not in any way distinct from their apprehension, that is, from the reception in the synthesis of imagination; and we must therefore agree that the manifold of appearances is always generated in the mind successively. Now if appearances were things in themselves, then since we have to deal solely with our representations, we could never determine from the succession of the representations how their manifold may be connected in the object. How things may be in themselves, apart from the representations through which they affect us, is entirely outside our sphere of knowledge. In spite, however, of the fact that the appearances are not things in themselves, and yet are what alone can be given to us to know, in spite also of the fact that their representation in apprehension is always successive, I have to show what sort of a connection in time belongs to the manifold in the appearances themselves. For instance, the apprehension of the manifold in the appearance of a house which stands before me is successive. The question then arises, whether the manifold of the house is also in itself successive. This, however, is what no one will grant. Now immediately I unfold the transcendental meaning of my concepts of an object, I realize that the house is not a thing in itself, but only an appearance, that is, a representation, the transcendental object of which is unknown. What, then, am I to understand by the question: how the manifold may be connected in the appearance itself, which yet is nothing in itself? That which lies in the successive apprehension is here viewed as representation, while the appearance which is given to me, notwithstanding that it is nothing but the sum of these representations, is viewed as their object; and my concept, which I derive from the representations of apprehension, has to agree with it. Since truth consists in the agreement of knowledge with the object, it will at once be seen that we can here inquire only regarding the formal conditions of empirical truth, and that appearance, in contradistinction to the representations of apprehension, can be represented as an object distinct from them only if it stands under a rule which distinguishes it from every other apprehension and necessitates some one particular mode of connection of the manifold. The objective succession will therefore consist in that order of the manifold of appearance according to which, in *conformity with a rule*, the apprehension of that which happens follows upon the apprehension of that which precedes. Thus only can I be justified in asserting, not merely of my apprehension, but of appearance itself, that a succession is to be met with in it. This is only another way of saying that I cannot arrange the apprehension otherwise than in this very succession.

In conformity with such a rule there must lie in that which precedes an event the condition of a rule according to which this event invariably and necessarily follows. I cannot reverse this order, proceeding back from the event to determine through apprehension that which precedes. For appearance never goes back from the succeeding to the preceding point of time, though it does indeed stand in relation to *some* preceding point of time. The advance, on the other hand, from a given time to the determinate time that follows is a necessary advance. Therefore, since there certainly is something that follows [i.e. that is *apprehended* as following], I must refer it necessarily to something else which precedes it and upon which it follows in conformity with a rule, that is, of necessity. The event, as the conditioned, thus affords reliable evidence of some condition, and this condition is what determines the event.

Let us suppose that there is nothing antecedent to an event, upon which it must follow according to rule. All succession of perception would then be only in the apprehension, that is, would be merely subjective, and would never enable us to determine objectively which perceptions are those that really precede and which are those that follow. We should then have only a play of representations, relating to no object; that is to say, it would not be possible through our perception to distinguish one appearance from another as regards relations of time. For the succession in our apprehension would always be one and the same, and there would be nothing in the appearance which so determines it that a certain sequence is rendered objectively necessary. I could not then assert that two states follow upon one another in the [field of] appearance, but only that one apprehension follows upon the other. That is something merely subjective, determining no object; and may not, therefore, be regarded as knowledge of any object, not even of an object in the [field of] appearance.

If, then, we experience that something happens, we in so doing always presuppose that something precedes it, on which it follows according to a rule. Otherwise I should not say of the object that it follows. For mere succession in my apprehension, if there be no rule determining the succession in relation to something that precedes, does not justify me in assuming any succession in the object.

We have, then, to show, in the case under consideration, that we never, even in experience, ascribe succession (that is, the happening of some event which previously did not exist) to the object, and so distinguish it from subjective sequence in our apprehension, except when there is an underlying rule which compels us to observe this order of perceptions rather than any other; nay, that this compulsion is really what first makes possible the representation of a succession in the object.

We have representations in us, and can become conscious of them. But however far this consciousness may extend, and however careful and accurate it may be, they still remain mere representations, that is, inner determinations of our mind in this or that relation of time. How, then, does it come about that we posit an object for these representations, and so, in addition to their subjective reality, as modifications, ascribe to them some mysterious kind of objective reality. Objective meaning cannot consist in the relation to another representation (of that which we desire to entitle object), for in that case the question again arises, how this latter representation goes out beyond itself, acquiring objective meaning in addition to the subjective meaning which belongs to it as determination of the mental state. If we inquire what new character *relation to an object* confers upon our representations, what dignity they thereby acquire, we find that it results only in subjecting the representations to a rule, and so in necessitating us to connect them in some one specific manner. This rule, by which we determine something according to succession of time, is, that the condition under which an event invariably and necessarily follows is to be found in what precedes the event. Were I to posit the antecedent and the event were not to follow necessarily thereupon, I should have to regard the succession as a merely subjective play of my fancy; and if I still represented it to myself as something objective, I should have to call it a mere dream. Thus the relation of appearances (as possible perceptions) according to which the subsequent event, that which happens, is, as to its existence, necessarily determined in time by something preceding in conformity with a rule – in other words, the relation of cause to effect – is the condition of the objective validity of our empirical judgements, in respect of the series of perceptions, and so of their empirical truth; that is to say, it is the condition of experience. The principle of the causal relation in the sequence of appearances is therefore also valid of all objects of experience as being itself the ground of the possibility of such experience.

*Explanation of the Cosmological Idea of Freedom in its
Connection with Universal Natural Necessity*

Man is one of the appearances of the sensible world, and in so
far one of the natural causes the causality of which must stand
under empirical laws. Like all other things in nature, he must
have an empirical character. This character we come to know
through the powers and faculties which he reveals in his
actions. In lifeless, or merely animal, nature we find no ground
for thinking that any faculty is conditioned otherwise than in a
merely sensible manner. Man, however, who knows all the rest
of nature solely through the senses, knows himself also through
pure apperception; and this, indeed, in acts and inner determinations which he cannot regard as impressions of the senses. He
is thus to himself, on the one hand a phenomenon, and on the
other hand, in respect of certain faculties the action of which
cannot be ascribed to the receptivity of sensibility, a purely
intelligible object. We entitle these faculties understanding and
reason. The latter, in particular, we distinguish in a quite peculiar and especial way from all empirically conditioned powers.
For it views its objects exclusively in the light of ideas, and in
accordance with them determines the understanding, which then
proceeds to make an empirical use of its own similarly pure
concepts.

That our reason has causality, or that we at least represent
it to ourselves as having causality, is evident from the *impera-
tives* which in all matters of conduct we impose as rules upon
our active powers. '*Ought*' expresses a kind of necessity and of
connection with grounds which is found nowhere else in the
whole of nature. The understanding can know in nature only
what is, what has been, or what will be. We cannot say that
anything in nature *ought to be* other than what in all these
time-relations it actually is. When we have the course of nature
alone in view, '*ought*' has no meaning whatsoever. It is just as
absurd to ask what ought to happen in the natural world as to
ask what properties a circle ought to have. All that we are
justified in asking is: what happens in nature? what are the
properties of the circle?

This '*ought*' expresses a possible action the ground of which cannot be anything but a mere concept; whereas in the case of a merely natural action the ground must always be an appearance. The action to which the '*ought*' applies must indeed be possible under natural conditions. These conditions, however, do not play any part in determining the will itself, but only in determining the effect and its consequences in the [field of] appearance. No matter how many natural grounds or how many sensuous impulses may impel me to *will*, they can never give rise to the '*ought*', but only to a willing which, while very far from being necessary, is always conditioned; and the '*ought*' pronounced by reason confronts such willing with a limit and an end – nay more, forbids or authorizes it. Whether what is willed be an object of mere sensibility (the pleasant) or of pure reason (the good), reason will not give way to any ground which is empirically given. Reason does not here follow the order of things as they present themselves in appearance, but frames for itself with perfect spontaneity an order of its own according to ideas, to which it adapts the empirical conditions, and according to which it declares actions to be necessary, even although they have never taken place, and perhaps never will take place. And at the same time reason also presupposes that it can have causality in regard to all these actions, since otherwise no empirical effects could be expected from its ideas.

Now, in view of these considerations, let us take our stand, and regard it as at least possible for reason to have causality with respect to appearances. Reason though it be, it must none the less exhibit an empirical character. Since this empirical character must itself be discovered from the appearances which are its effect and from the rule to which experience shows them to conform, it follows that all the actions of men in the [field of] appearance are determined in conformity with the order of nature, by the empirical character and by the other causes which cooperate with that character; and if we could exhaustively investigate all the appearances of men's wills, there would not be found a single human action which we could not predict with certainty, and recognize as proceeding necessarily from its antecedent conditions. So far, then, as regards this empirical character there is no freedom; and yet it is only in the light of this character that man can be studied – if, that is to say, we are simply *observing*, and in the manner of anthropology seeking to institute a physiological investigation into the motive causes of his actions.

But when we consider these actions in their relation to reason – I do not mean speculative reason, by which we endeavour *to explain* their coming into being, but reason in so far as it is itself the cause *producing* them – if, that is to say, we compare them with [the standards of] reason in its *practical* bearing, we find a rule and order altogether different from the order of nature. For it may be that all that *has happened* in the course of nature, and in accordance with its empirical grounds must inevitably have happened, *ought not to have happened*. Sometimes, however, we find, or at least believe that we find, that the ideas of reason have in actual fact proved their causality in respect of the actions of men, as appearances; and that these actions have taken place, not because they were determined by empirical causes, but because they were determined by grounds of reason.

Granted, then, that reason may be asserted to have causality in respect of appearance, its action can still be said to be free, even although its empirical character (as a mode of sense) is completely and necessarily determined in all its detail. This empirical character is itself determined in the intelligible character (as a mode of thought).[2] The latter, however, we do not know; we can only indicate its nature by means of appearances; and these really yield an immediate knowledge only of the mode of sense, the empirical character. The action, in so far as it can be ascribed to a mode of thought as its cause, does not *follow* therefrom in accordance with empirical laws; that is to say, it is not *preceded* by the conditions of pure reason, but only by their effects in the [field of] appearance of inner sense. Pure reason, as a purely intelligible faculty, is not subject to the form of time, nor consequently to the conditions of succession in time.

2. The real morality of actions, their merit or guilt, even that of our own conduct, thus remains entirely hidden from us. Our imputations can refer only to the empirical character. How much of this character is ascribable to the pure effect of freedom, how much to mere nature, that is, to faults of temperament for which there is no responsibility, or to its happy constitution (*merito fortunae*), can never be determined; and upon it therefore no perfectly just judgements can be passed.

The causality of reason in its intelligible character does not, in producing an effect, *arise* or begin to be at a certain time. For in that case it would itself be subject to the natural law of appearances, in accordance with which causal series are determined in time; and its causality would then be nature, not freedom. Thus all that we are justified in saying is that, if reason can have causality in respect of appearances, it is a faculty *through* which the sensible condition of an empirical series of effects first begins. For the condition which lies in reason is not sensible, and therefore does not itself begin to be. And thus what we failed to find in any empirical series is disclosed as being possible, namely, that the condition of a successive series of events may itself be empirically unconditioned. For here the condition is *outside* the series of appearances (in the intelligible), and therefore is not subject to any sensible condition, and to no time-determination through an antecedent cause.

The same cause does, indeed, in another relation, belong to the series of appearances. Man is himself an appearance. His will has an empirical character, which is the empirical cause of all his actions. There is no condition determining man in accordance with this character which is not contained in the series of natural effects, or which is not subject to their law – the law according to which there can be no empirically unconditioned causality of that which happens in time. Therefore no given action (since it can be perceived only as appearance) can begin absolutely of itself. But of pure reason we cannot say that the state wherein the will is determined is preceded and itself determined by some other state. For since reason is not itself an appearance, and is not subject to any conditions of sensibility, it follows that even as regards its causality there is in it no time-sequence, and that the dynamical law of nature, which determines succession in time in accordance with rules, is not applicable to it.

Reason is the abiding condition of all those actions of the will under [the guise of] which man appears. Before ever they have happened, they are one and all predetermined in the empirical character. In respect of the intelligible character, of which the empirical character is the sensible schema, there can be no *before* and *after*; every action, irrespective of its relation in time to other appearances, is the immediate effect of the intelligible character of pure reason. Reason therefore acts freely; it is not dynamically determined in the chain of natural causes through either outer or inner grounds antecedent in time. This freedom ought not, therefore, to be conceived only negatively as independence of empirical conditions. The faculty of reason, so regarded, would cease to be a cause of appearances. It must also be described in positive terms, as the power of originating a series of events. In reason itself nothing begins; as unconditioned condition of every voluntary act, it admits of no conditions antecedent to itself in time. Its effect has, indeed, a beginning in the series of appearances, but never in this series an absolutely first beginning.

In order to illustrate this regulative principle of reason by an example of its empirical employment – not, however, to confirm it, for it is useless to endeavour to prove transcendental propositions by examples – let us take a voluntary action, for example, a malicious lie by which a certain confusion has been caused in society. First of all, we endeavour to discover the motives to which it has been due, and then, secondly, in the light of these, we proceed to determine how far the action and its consequences can be imputed to the offender. As regards the first question, we trace the empirical character of the action to its sources, finding these in defective education, bad company, in part also in the viciousness of a natural disposition insensitive to shame, in levity and thoughtlessness, not neglecting to take into account also the occasional causes that may have intervened. We proceed in this inquiry just as we should in ascertaining for a given natural effect the series of its determining causes. But although we believe that the action is thus determined, we none the less blame the agent, not indeed on account of his unhappy disposition, nor on account of the circumstances that have influenced him, nor even on account of his previous way of life; for we presuppose that we can leave out of consideration what this way of life may have been, that we can regard the past series of conditions as not having occurred and the act as being completely unconditioned by any preceding state, just as if the agent in and by himself began in this action an entirely new series of consequences. Our blame is based on a law of reason whereby we regard reason as a cause that irrespective of all the above-mentioned empirical conditions could have determined, and ought to have determined, the agent to act otherwise. This causality of reason we do not regard as only a cooperating agency, but as complete in itself, even when the sensuous impulses do not favour but are directly opposed to it; the action is ascribed to the agent's intelligible character; in the moment when he utters the lie, the guilt is entirely his. Reason, irrespective of all empirical conditions of the act, is completely free, and the lie is entirely due to its default.

Such imputation clearly shows that we consider reason to be unaffected by these sensible influences, and not liable to alteration. Its appearance – the modes in which it manifests itself in its effects – do alter; but in itself [so we consider] there is no preceding state determining the state that follows. That is to say, it does not belong to the series of sensible conditions which render appearances necessary in accordance with laws of nature. Reason is present in all the actions of men at all times and under all circumstances, and is always the same: but it is not itself in time, and does not fall into any new state in which it was not before. In respect to new states, it is *determining*, not *determinable*. We may not, therefore, ask why reason has not determined *itself* differently, but only why it has not through its causality determined the *appearances* differently. But to this question no answer is possible. For a different intelligible character would have given a different empirical character. When we say that in spite of his whole previous course of life the agent could have refrained from lying, this only means that the act is under the immediate power of reason, and that reason in its causality is not subject to any conditions of appearance or of time. Although difference of time makes a fundamental difference to appearances in their relations to one another – for appearances are not things in themselves and therefore not causes in themselves – it can make no difference to the relation in which the action stands to reason.

Thus in our judgements in regard to the causality of free actions, we can get as far as the intelligible cause, but not beyond it. We can know that it is free, that is, that it is determined independently of sensibility, and that in this way it may be the sensibly unconditioned condition of appearances. But to explain why in the given circumstances the intelligible character should give just these appearances and this empirical character transcends all the powers of our reason, indeed all its rights of questioning, just as if we were to ask why the transcendental object of our outer sensible intuition gives intuition in *space* only and not some other mode of intuition. But the problem which we have to solve does not require us to raise any such questions. Our problem was this only: whether freedom and natural necessity can exist without conflict in one and the same action: and this we have sufficiently answered. We have shown that since freedom may stand in relation to a quite different kind of conditions from those of natural necessity, the law of the latter does not affect the former, and that both may exist, independently of one another and without interfering with each other.

The reader should be careful to observe that in what has been said our intention has not been to establish the *reality* of freedom as one of the faculties which contain the cause of the appearances of our sensible world. For that inquiry, as it does not deal with concepts alone, would not have been transcendental. And further, it could not have been successful, since we can never infer from experience anything which cannot be thought in accordance with the laws of experience. It has not even been our intention to prove the *possibility* of freedom. For in this also we should not have succeeded, since we cannot from mere concepts *a priori* know the possibility of any real ground and its causality. Freedom is here being treated only as a transcendental idea whereby reason is led to think that it can begin the series of conditions in the [field of] appearance by means of the sensibly unconditioned, and so becomes involved in an antinomy with those very laws which it itself prescribes to the empirical employment of the understanding. What we have alone been able to show, and what we have alone been concerned to show, is that this antinomy rests on a sheer illusion, and that causality through freedom is at least *not incompatible with* nature.

6 W. H. Walsh
Categories

from 'Categories', *Kant-Studien* 1954

It has often been assumed that, apart from the relatively unimportant case of the violation of grammatical rules, there are only two ways in which a man can talk nonsense:

1. By saying something which patently conflicts with the well-attested findings of some recognized discipline or with what would be unquestionably accepted by common sense. This might be called material nonsense;
2. By breaking rules of logic and so producing statements which are logically impossible. Statements of this kind (the simplest examples would answer to the logical schema 'p.-p') might be said to be formally nonsensical.

I want to show that there are important cases of what we should all recognize to be nonsense which are omitted in this dichotomy. And I want to connect these cases with the investigations certain philosophers have conducted into categories, producing thereby (as I hope) a clearer account than these philosophers have themselves given of the function and status of categorial concepts and of what differentiates them from other concepts. Briefly, my thesis is that categorial concepts serve to mark off, at a basic level, what makes sense from what makes nonsense, and in so doing provide a framework inside which the construction of empirical concepts must proceed. This way of putting the matter has the advantage of making immediately apparent the difference in logical type between categories and the empirical concepts which can be said, in a sense, to fall under them, and so obviates a persistent misunderstanding according to which the former are taken as merely bigger and better versions of the latter, designating more fundamental characteristics and known in some superior way.

I hope to show further that the thesis that there are categories, and even that there must be some concepts of this nature, carries with it no unwelcome consequences of the rationalist type. It certainly implies a limitation on the range of empirical possibilities, but this limitation is not necessarily fixed and unchanging. The bounds of categorial sense and nonsense may even shift as empirical knowledge accumulates, though the way in which this happens will need careful scrutiny if the special status of categorial principles is to be preserved.

Let me begin by giving a couple of examples.

1. I am being driven by a friend in a motor-car when, without warning, the engine stops and the car comes to a standstill. I ask my friend what has happened. He replies that the car has stopped for no reason at all. I laugh politely at what I take to be his joke and wait for an explanation or for some activity on my friend's part to discover what has gone wrong; instead, he remains in his seat and neither says nor does anything more. Trying not to appear impolite, I presently ask my friend whether he knows much about motor-cars, the implication being that his failure to look for the cause of the breakdown must be explained by his just not knowing how to set about the job. He takes my point at once and tells me that it is not a question of knowledge or ignorance; there just was no reason for the stoppage. Puzzled, I ask him whether he means that it was a miracle, brought about by the intervention of what eighteenth-century writers called a 'particular providence'. Being philosophically sophisticated, he replies that to explain something as being due to an act of God is to give a reason, though not a natural reason, whereas what he said was that there was no reason for what occurred. At this point I lose my temper and tell him not to talk nonsense, for (I say) 'Things just don't happen for no reason at all'.

2. A calls on B at an awkward moment when B has dropped his collar stud and cannot find it. 'I had it in my hand a minute ago,' he tells his friend, 'so it can't be far off.' The search goes on for some time without success, until A suddenly asks B what makes him think the stud is there to be found. Controlling himself, B explains that he had the stud in his hand and was trying to do up his collar when it slipped from his fingers; that there are no holes in the floor; that the windows of the room are unusually high; and that if the stud had come to pieces he must certainly have come across some bit of it after looking for so long. 'Ah,' says A, 'but have you considered the possibility that it may have vanished without trace?' 'Vanished

without trace?' asks B : 'do you mean turned into gaseous form, gone off like a puff of smoke or something of that sort? Collar studs don't do things like that.' 'No, that isn't what I mean,' A assures him gravely; 'I mean literally vanished without trace, passed clean out of existence.' Words fail B at this point, but it is clear from the look he gives his friend that he takes him either to be making an ill-timed joke or to be talking downright nonsense, a proceeding which only his being a philosopher will excuse.

What sort of nonsense is talked by someone who asserts seriously that events sometimes happen for no reason at all or that things sometimes vanish without trace, passing clean out of existence?

Is it *formal* nonsense as defined above? There is a very strong temptation for philosophers to say that it is, for the contradictories of the statements in question are often formulated in terms of necessity ('There *must* always be a reason for whatever occurs,' 'Things just *cannot* vanish without trace'), and it is very common to identify necessary with analytic statements. Some philosophers, indeed, make the identification a matter of definition; they hold that the only necessary statements entitled to the description are those whose truth depends on logical considerations. Of this dogma no more need be said now than that the statements with which we are concerned seem *prima facie* to count against it, for there is nothing logically impossible in the notion of an event happening for no reason at all or of a thing vanishing without trace and passing clean out of existence. Of course we could, if we chose, make it a matter of definition that nothing should be *called* an event unless we believed it happened for a reason, and similarly in the other case; but it should be plain that this subterfuge will not solve the problem. There is an important difference between saying 'There are no events which happen for no reason at all' and saying 'There are no "events" which happen for no reason at all.' What we decide to call things makes no difference to what happens in the world.

Is, then, to make the statements in question to talk nonsense in the *material* sense? To many philosophers this would seem the only possible thing to say, once the thesis that it was formal nonsense had been considered and rejected. Yet it is at least clear that if I say, for instance, that things may perfectly well some-times go clean out of existence, vanishing without trace, I do not talk nonsense of the ordinary material sort. A man talks non-sense in the material sense, normally, if he fails to take account, or asserts the contradictory, of some obvious and well-established fact, or of some well-attested piece of theory; as for example if I say that you can put a kettle on the gas stove, light the gas and find after ten minutes that the water has not changed its tem-perature. We know perfectly well, as a matter of common ex-perience, that this is not how kettles behave when placed on lighted gas-stoves, and the politest thing we can say of someone who thinks that it is is that he has got his facts wrong. But in the examples given above mistakes of fact did not enter into the question. When my friend asserted that the car had stopped for no reason at all he was not putting forward an empirical hypo-thesis to the effect that this or that suggested explanation was false; he was asserting that there just was no explanation. It is true that if somebody said this sort of thing in real life he would be taken as asserting either that he did not know the explanation or that none of the obvious explanations for this kind of hap-pening would fit; but this is only because we should be unwill-ing to take him at his word. It would not be flattering to the man to suppose that he was talking such nonsense.

This point can perhaps be made clearer if we turn our atten-tion to the other example about a thing vanishing without trace. Of course there is a sense in which we regard it as perfectly sen-sible to say of something that it vanished without trace. Build-ings or features of the landscape can be obliterated without trace by a hurricane or the dropping of an atomic bomb; if fortunately few of us have personal experience of events of this sort, we know perfectly well that they occur. But of course we also know that the expression 'vanished without trace' is used somewhat loosely on these occasions, or rather is used with certain un-spoken reservations in mind. When the team of scientists res-ponsible for an atom-bomb experiment reports to its government that all the buildings on the island where the experiment took place vanished without trace, it is not meant that there is no answer to the question 'What became of them?' They along with many other solid-looking objects were vaporized by the heat of the explosion and scattered to the four winds. But buildings which vaporize and scatter to the four winds do not vanish without trace in an unqualified sense of the term; they merely leave no trace of themselves on the spot where they stood. What A suggested to B in my example was that the collar stud might have vanished without trace in an unqualified sense. That particular bit of matter might have gone clean out of existence, leaving no trace of itself in solid, liquid or gaseous form. If that had happened it would not be sense to ask the question what became of it, and this is what gives interest to the example for our purposes.

Hume in his essay on miracles mentions the case of an 'Indian' prince who refused to believe that water turned into ice in conditions of great cold (in Selby-Bigge (ed.), *Enquiry*, pp. 113–14). The position of someone who is incredulous about the report that solid buildings disappeared without trace when an atomic bomb was dropped is similar to that of this prince. Both have to learn that the boundaries of empirical possibility are not to be measured by any particular man's stock of empirical knowledge. Surprising as it may be, water turns into a solid in one set of circumstances and buildings vaporise in another. But however odd these events may seem to the unsophisticated, it would be even odder if water or buildings had vanished without trace, in the sense of having been not transmuted but annihilated. In fact, it would be another species of oddity altogether.

Doubts about the applicability on given occasions of questions like 'What was the reason for this?' and 'What became of that?' are not material doubts in the sense in which a doubt whether water will solidify if cooled is material. It is not facts or supposed facts which are challenged by such a doubt, but rather what I must call the framework of facts. The statements that nothing happens except for a reason and that nothing vanishes without trace in the unqualified sense of the phrase are, with the concepts which underlie them, of a higher logical order than are empirical statements and concepts; it is in terms of them that we present our empirical knowledge.[1] That is why any attempt to

1. This point seems to have escaped many critics. For an interesting recent instance see Mr G. J. Warnock's essay 'Every event has a cause' in *Essays in Logic and Language*, 2nd Series (Oxford University Press, 1955),

question them is felt to be far more serious than an attempt to question even a well-attested empirical truth. To discover that a statement we had believed to be materially true is false may come as a profound shock; but the shock is nothing like so great as would be that of discovering that there were events which occurred for no reason or things that went clean out of existence. Fortunately, we are not willing to let ourselves be readily exposed to the latter kind of shock: when the suggestion is made that we might here be in error, our instinct, as the examples show, is to repudiate it as absurd. And this reaction is a sound one, in so far as the statements in question serve to indicate bounds within which we can talk sense about the world. To ask whether it is sensible to observe what, in effect, functions as a rule for talking sensibly is not, on the face of it, a very sensible proceeding.

An alternative way of expressing what has just been said is this. If we were asked to write down as full a list as possible of true empirical statements, we should not (or ought not to) include the statements that nothing happens except for a reason and that nothing vanishes without trace in the sense of passing clean out of existence. These statements are rather presuppositions of empirical truths than empirical truths themselves. What is more (and this point is crucial), they are presuppositions of a very unusual kind. As Collingwood [2] made clear, every question has presuppositions in so far as asking the question implies (in the everyday, as opposed to the logician's, sense of the term) that something is true. Thus if I ask what is the name of the French Prime Minister I imply that someone is French Prime Minister. But most implications of this kind can be made the

---

A. G. N. Flew (ed.), pp. 95 ff. Warnock argues that the statement that every event has a cause, while not analytic, is empty of significance because it is of such a general character that there are no circumstances in which we should be justified in regarding it as false. To say that statements of this kind cannot be falsified is only to recognise that they are of a different logical character from everyday factual statements; but to go on and draw the conclusion that they are empty of significance is certainly not justified, for, as my examples show, we know very well what it would be like for such principles not to hold.

2. R. G. Collingwood, *An Essay on Metaphysics* (Oxford University Press, 1940), pp. 21 *et seq.*

subject of further inquiry: we can ask, e.g. whether it is in fact true that there is a Prime Minister of France. Presuppositions of this sort, which are themselves answers to further questions, are called by Collingwood 'relative presuppositions'. The distinguishing mark of such presuppositions as that which underlay my questions to my friend when the motor-car broke down, that there must be some reason for whatever happens, is that we cannot sensibly make them the subject of further questioning. There is no process by which we can establish them, comparable to the process by which we establish that there is (or is not) a Prime Minister of France. Hence, as Collingwood said, they are not 'relative' but 'absolute' presuppositions.

We need some convenient name for the class of statements of which the two statements in my examples are instances. Following Kant, I propose to call them 'categorial principles' and the concepts which underlie them 'categories'. And I shall say that the man who disregards or questions categorial principles is talking categorial nonsense.

My argument so far has been an argument from fact. I have taken it as true that, if someone suggests that something might happen without any reason for its happening, or that a thing might pass clean out of existence, vanishing without trace, the suggestion will be dismissed as nonsense. Examining the logical character of such assertions, I conclude that the nonsense in question is of a special kind. Now the question might be raised whether it is not only true that we can find statements which indicate the bounds of sense in the way in which I have said categorial principles do, but further that there must be statements of this kind. To put the question in terms which will perhaps make it more familiar, was Kant right in holding not only that *a priori* concepts function in human experience but further that they must do so – that there would be no such thing as experience unless they did?

Kant

from 'Kant', *A Critical History of Western Philosophy* 1964

Kant was a professor, and he wrote like a professor. The writings of some of his predecessors, of Descartes, for example, or Berkeley or Hume and perhaps even of Leibniz, are such that they can be read with enjoyment by ordinary men and – no doubt within limits – understood with comparative ease. In their way, they are contributions to literature as well as to philosophy. Not so with Kant. He sometimes expressed, with agreeable humility, a hopeless wish for the literary skill and force of Rousseau, but he was partly unable, and also partly unwilling, to give to his own writings a pleasing and perspicuous form. The bent of his mind was naturally, as well as by long training, academic, and besides this he firmly believed, on principle, in the value of aiming at *thoroughness* rather than elegance. As a result, his chief writings are formidably and unbendingly professional, elaborately schematic, ponderous with technical terms, and exceedingly laborious to read and to understand. This is due in part, of course, to the genuine difficulty of the problems with which Kant grappled. He really was, as he set himself to be, both thorough and profound. But it remains, one may feel, a misfortune in the history of philosophy that so powerful a thinker should have commanded so little art in conveying his thoughts.

Kant's highly professorial style both of thinking and writing is liable to give the impression that his interests were also narrowly academic. He is sometimes represented simply as debating the merits of, and seeking to mediate between, two rival philosophical schools – empiricism, regarded as culminating in Hume, and rationalism, as represented particularly by Leibniz. But the fact is that this particular debate, in which certainly Kant was greatly interested, emerged out of a problem of much deeper and more general concern. In this problem the at least apparent antagonists whose conflict Kant wished to bring to some conclusion were, on the one side, not Hume, but Newton, and on the other side, not Leibniz, but the essentials of morality and religion. This was not a domestic quarrel within the field of philosophy, a quarrel in which the general public had nothing at stake; it was a conflict, Kant thought, between far more formidable powers. It was an issue involving the deepest interests of every man. And it was, above all, the task of philosophy to come to terms with it.

It is not difficult to grasp in outline how Kant saw this conflict. In his early days he had both written and lectured on the physical science of his time, and it never occurred to him to question for a moment the solidity of its main conclusions. He disagreed with Newton on certain philosophical points but he believed that in general Newton and his great predecessors had undoubtedly laid hold of the key to the understanding of the natural world. The world was to be regarded as a mechanical system of bodies operating in accordance with mathematically formulated laws: to explain scientifically a natural occurrence was to produce a law or laws such that given the antecedent condition of the system, just that occurrence could be shown necessarily to have ensued. Perhaps no philosopher has accepted more wholeheartedly than Kant the essential rightness of the 'scientific world-view' – taking physics, understandably enough, as the ideal of a science, and Newton, again with good reason, as its ideal expositor.

But not only that; Kant thought also what Newton at least would not explicitly have claimed: that the gospel of science committed its devotees to the view that not only were their presuppositions and methods correct in their own field, but also that their scope and application could not be restricted. It must, he thought, be dismissed as unscientific to suppose that any limit might be reached in nature beyond which scientific inquiry could be pushed no further, or that there might be natural occurrences not susceptible to scientific explanation. Neither of these beliefs, he held, could properly be accepted by a thoroughgoing believer in scientific method, who must believe that that method could be applied at any point to answer any question, and that what could not be learned in this way could not be knowledge at all.

But if so, Kant thought that he discerned an inevitable conflict with many fundamental human convictions. The belief that God has created the world and shapes it for his purposes implies the admission that at least one happening – the act of creation – falls outside the order of nature and cannot be brought within the scope of any natural law. It implies that the course of nature cannot fully be understood in scientific terms alone. The very existence of God is not a scientifically demonstrable fact. It is a matter of even more immediate and evident concern that if we are to suppose, as we must, that human beings are responsible creatures who are morally answerable for what they do or omit to do, we have to suppose that they *can* act, or fail to act, as they choose and as their obligations demand of them. Yet can we suppose this if we are also to believe that all that occurs, occurs necessarily – that in just those conditions in which any event takes place, no other event *could* have taken place? It appears that if we accede to the claims of science to operate and formulate laws without bounds or restrictions, we may have to regard religious faiths as superstition and moral convictions as illusory. Yet how, except in a spirit of arbitrary dogmatism, can we say at what point scientific inquiry must end?

Since the time of Hobbes and Descartes, at least, it had been a primary interest of most philosophers to provide some kind of resolution of these apparent conflicts. A quite recent attempt, and perhaps the most ambitious of all, had been made by Leibniz.[1] Leibniz had persuaded himself that the view of the world presupposed in the system of Newtonian physics was, in its foundations, 'contrary to reason' although it 'satisfied the imagination'; therefore, he held, it could not be seriously put forward as the literal truth. Reason, he believed, could not accept 'atoms and the void'. To speak briefly, he then went on to devise a doctrine according to which the Newtonian view of the world might (with modifications) be accepted as a manner of speaking – that is, of recording what *appears* to be the case; while contrasted with this was to be the rationally acceptable,

1. Leibniz's writings, before the edition of 1768, were only fragmentarily available to Kant. He had been brought up on the versions put forth by Wolff and Baumgarten. His first thorough acquaintance with Leibniz's own work seems briefly to have revived his faith in metaphysical theory: but not, as we shall see, for long.

logically demonstrable account of what is *really* the case. There appears to be a world of material bodies in space and time, a world that can indeed be viewed as a mechanical system. What really exists is an infinite assemblage of immaterial, non-spatial, and even non-temporal *Monads*, created by, and in some sense subject to, the direction of God. In the apparent world there is rigorous causal determinism; in the real world of Monads there is no such thing. Yet God so orders the real and the apparent that no conflict arises at any point. The System of science holds true as an account of appearances; the truths of religion and morality apply in their different sphere, in God's creation as it really is. Finally, since God in creation must have chosen to create the best among the many worlds that He might have created, the world as it exists must be the best of all possible worlds.

Now it appears that Kant became gradually more and more dissatisfied with this and all similar attempts to solve his leading problem. Characteristically, such attempts consisted in trying to excogitate theories of what was really the case in such a way that the essential truths of morality and religion could be put forward as really (though sometimes in peculiar senses) true, while the rival corpus of scientific theory could be regarded as an account of mere *phenomena*, of the merely apparent. But in such undertakings Kant found great difficulties. For one thing, the alleged rational demonstrations of the true nature of reality were never conclusive and were sometimes definitely faulty. For another, whereas the allegedly merely 'apparent' truths of science formed a generally accepted, well attested, and steadily developing system, metaphysical theory had the look of a chaotic battlefield. It was a scene of incessant conflict, incessant disagreement, illusory victories and indecisive defeats in which nothing whatever could be taken as definitely established, and there appeared to be no prospect of any sure progress being made. Finally, was there not a manifest absurdity in seeking in this way for the foundations of morality and religion? No one's moral convictions could really be supposed to be dependent on the outcome of refined but chaotic metaphysical argument, and religious beliefs were already far more secure than the fragile metaphysical structures called in to support them.

For this complete lack of solid progress in metaphysics, two possible explanations might be considered. It might simply be the case that metaphysical problems were so extremely complicated and difficult that no one hitherto had been clever and pertinacious enough to solve them; if so, there would be nothing for it but dogged persistence, in the hope that the proper solutions would eventually be found. Alternatively, there might be something radically wrong with the procedures that had been followed, even perhaps with the very questions that had been posed. Metaphysicians might have been attempting, not merely the difficult, but actually the impossible. If so, it would not be surprising that nothing had been achieved; and moreover, it would be essential to desist forthwith from further attempts to go on in the same old way and instead to re-examine the nature of the whole undertaking. It was at this point that the influence of Hume was evidently decisive: 'David Hume, who can be said to have begun the assault on the claims of pure reason which made a thorough examination of them necessary.'

Through the prompting of Hume's arguments, Kant came to believe by the early 1770s that both schools among his predecessors – rationalists and empiricists alike – had accepted certain principles from which it *followed* that metaphysical theories must be illusory and impossible. The great merit of Hume – and Kant rated his merits very high – was that he had seen this to be so and had deliberately drawn the necessary conclusion. So long as these principles stood, the subject called philosophy must abandon the speculative ambitions of deductive metaphysics, must turn instead to 'the experimental method' and become what we might now regard as a satellite of empirical psychology and sociology. It was part of Hume's program to effect just this transformation.

It was in this way, then, that Kant was brought to the conviction that the fundamental question for a philosopher of his time must be the question of whether philosophy itself is a genuine subject: 'My purpose is to convince those who find it worth their while to occupy themselves with metaphysics: that it is absolutely necessary to suspend their work for the present, to regard everything that has happened hitherto as not having happened, and before all else first to raise the question: "whether such a thing as metaphysics is possible at all".' This is the essentially Kantian 'critical' question. And this question brings him to the starting point of his three great Critiques: *The Critique of Pure Reason* (1781), *The Critique of Practical Reason* (1788), and *The Critique of Judgement* (1790).

The Critique of Pure Reason

Let us ask, first, exactly why Kant supposed that the very possibility of metaphysics must be called into question. Here we may follow closely his own explanation.

One of the most striking passages in Hume's inquiries had been his investigation of the concept of causation. It is, as Hume and Kant agreed, generally supposed that when it is asserted that A causes B, what is meant thereby is that if A occurs, B *necessarily* ensues. A causal connection, one might say, is distinguished from a chance correlation or coincidence precisely as being necessary. Now Hume asked by what right we suppose, in such a case, that given the one occurrence, the other is necessary. Do we learn this by observation? No, for what we learn by observation is at best that when A occurs, B in fact does ensue; strictly, we learn only that in fact this *has been* the case. We do not learn that it always will be, still less that it is necessarily so. Do we then discern by reason that A and B are connected necessarily? No, for we are required by reason to accept as necessary only those propositions the contradictions of which are, or imply, impossibilities – that is, contradictions. But the denial of a causal statement is never a contradiction; although fire boils water, there is no contradiction in supposing that it should not. But if so, we have *no* right – we simply are not in a position – ever to assert that any pair of events is connected necessarily. When we do assert this we are mistaking, according to Hume, our own habitual, confident expectations for features of the world.

This argument rests, as Kant saw, on a general doctrine, which Hume indeed was anxious to insist upon generally. This is the doctrine that any true proposition is either a truth of reason, necessary in that its negation would be contradictory, or a truth of fact, established as such by observation or experiment and, even if certainly true, not necessarily true. On this dichotomy, Hume based (as did the logical positivists after him) the charge that 'divinity and school metaphysics' must be senseless and illusory. For these were not experimental sciences founded on empirical evidence; nor did they consist in the formal elaboration of theorems whose denials would be demonstrably contradictory. Yet there is, Hume held, no third possibility; hence, they must simply be dismissed as 'sophistry and illusion'.

Now Kant entirely agreed with Hume that if this dichotomy were valid and exhaustive, then there could be no such subject as metaphysics had been traditionally supposed to be. There would be only, on the one hand, empirical sciences, and, on the other, formal exercises in calculation. All necessary truths, all truths demonstrable *a priori*, would be on this view merely analytic: all synthetic truths, all assertions of matters of fact, would correspondingly be merely contingent. But the aim of the metaphysician was to formulate doctrines that would be both synthetic and demonstrable *a priori* – arrived at by reasoning but substantially true of the world; if so, he must either abandon his pursuits or show cause why Hume's dichotomy should not be accepted. He is called upon, before going on in the traditional style, to establish the credentials of his subject, which Hume challenged.

Kant himself, however dubious he may have been of the status and the claims of traditional metaphysics, was never seriously inclined to believe that Hume's dichotomy was in general tenable. He held that when he stated it, Hume had simply not realized the extent of the havoc that its acceptance would occasion. Certainly, in metaphysics there were supposed to occur propositions that were both synthetic and *a priori*; but in Kant's view such propositions certainly did occur also in some central parts of mathematics and of physical science. Thus, the weapon with which Hume sought to destroy 'school metaphysics' would, if effective, destroy at the same time mathematics and science – disciplines which, whatever may be the case with metaphysics, no sane man could be prepared to regard as mere 'sophistry and illusion'. The question with which Kant sets out, therefore, in his scrutiny of the credentials of metaphysics, is not the question whether there can be synthetic *a priori* propositions; for he is quite certain that there can be and are many such propositions. Rather, he asks how it is that we are in a position to assert them – what sorts of truths these are, and how they can be established. The three fields in which they are found or are alleged to be found, are mathematics, physical science and metaphysics. By asking exactly what it is in the first two fields that makes possible the assertion of synthetic *a priori* truths, Kant hopes to discover whether such truths can be established also in the third, and if so how. This three-stage inquiry is clearly reflected in the three main divisions of the first critique – the *Aesthetic*, the *Analytic* and the *Dialectic*.

It is now possible to summarize the general strategy of Kant's subsequent argument. It will be observed that it is marvellously neat, enormously ambitious, and, in the outcome, astringently paradoxical.

First, what sorts of things are synthetic *a priori* propositions? Kant's view may be briefly indicated as follows. In the course of human experience we find, whether by simple observation or by deliberate experiment, that certain events occur and certain features are present which it is possible and often easy to suppose might have been otherwise. Such things we record, of course, in *contingent* assertions; and it is evident that we can know such assertions to be true only if we have found that our experience does in fact comprise the events or the features alleged. In contrast with this, by examining the concepts we employ, we are able to state certain other propositions that we can see or show to be *necessarily* true in that their denial would involve conceptual or logical inconsistency; and here we have, of course, no need of empirical confirmation. But there is, Kant holds, a third class of propositions, whose existence none of his predecessors had explicitly recognized – certain propositions that must be true if human experience is to occur at all, propositions that state, in Kant's phrase, 'the conditions of the possibility of experience', or, as we might say, its fundamental defining characteristics. Now such propositions will not be analytic – for it is not analytic that any such thing as human experience does occur; the supposition that it does not implies no contradiction. But equally they will not be ordinarily contingent, for if the truth of a certain proposition is a condition of the very possibility of experience, there will clearly be no place for consulting the verdict of experience as to whether or not that proposition is true. On the assumption that any experience occurs at all, such a proposition could be asserted *a priori*. But if propositions of this class are not analytic and are not contingent, then they are precisely what Hume and the rest had rejected or ignored – namely, synthetic *a priori* propositions.

Kant's next point, a crucial one, can be expressed as follows. Such propositions, he says, say something about the world; but they are really based on something about ourselves. What the world is to us is the world as we experience it; our capacities for experience therefore impose a restriction on the *kind* of world that *our* world could be. If so, the question, 'what are the conditions of the possibility of experience?' is most illuminatingly approached, not primarily by asking 'what is necessarily true of the world that we experience?' but rather, 'what are the general conditions of any possible employment of our human faculties?' It is true, Kant says, that in detail 'our knowledge must conform to objects'; but it is also true that in general 'objects must conform to our knowledge'. That is: Any world of which we could have experience – and no other world could be a subject of significant discourse – must be such that the faculties we have could be employed in experience of it.

An objection may naturally occur to one at this point, which serves to bring out a distinction that for Kant is fundamental. Surely, one may think at first sight, it is quite fantastic to assert that 'objects must conform to our knowledge'; for how could it possibly be that the nature of our faculties should determine, or even influence in any way, what is the case in the world? Surely we are simply obliged to take the world as we find it: it would be a gross absurdity to suppose that it must somehow accommodate itself to our needs or our demands. Now, Kant feels the full force of this objection and to meet it he draws and insists upon a vital distinction between the world as it is *in itself* and as it *appears to us*. What exists, exists: its nature simply is what it is; with that, we ourselves can have nothing to do. It is, however, equally certain that what exists *appears* to human beings in a particular way, and is by them classified, interpreted, categorized and described in a particular manner. If our sense-organs had been radically different from what they are, certainly the world would have appeared to us as being radically different; if our languages and modes of thought had been utterly different, the descriptions of the world that we should have given would also have been different from those that we now give. Thus, though our faculties and capacities make no difference at all to the nature of what exists in itself, they do partly determine the character of the world as it appears; they determine the general form that it has; for whatever the world may be in itself, it appears to us in the way that it does because we are what we are. It is, then, with the world as appearance that Kant is concerned; it is objects as *phenomena* that must 'conform to our knowledge'. But this is not a cause for complaint or lamentation. For the desire to know, or even to talk, about the world as it is in itself is a desire without sense. It amounts to the desire to perceive without the employment of any particular mode of perception, to describe without the use of any particular descriptive vocabulary. In perception and thought we necessarily employ those faculties and propensities that we have; our subject-matter is, unavoidably, the world as it appears to one possessed of those faculties. In determining the general character – in Kant's phrase, the form – of this phenomenal world, it is thus with those faculties that we must be primarily concerned.

L Scientific Change

The excerpts relating to scientific change in this collection are
selected for their bearing on the correspondence material and are
not intended to be representative of scientific change in general.

The writings of William Paley were of enormous influence
in the nineteenth century, and the first chapter of his *Natural
Theology* was one of the most famous statements of the
argument from design in English literature. By contrast
Babbage was not concerned with the theological implications of
science, but rather with matters of practical organization; he
addressed himself to the perennial question : what can an
industrial nation do about the shortage of qualified scientists?

Apart from a short poem by Davy, the rest of the excerpts are
technical in nature. Priestley describes some of the experiments
which played a vital role in his study of combustion and
respiration, leading to a new understanding of the part played
by air in these processes. The work on nitrous oxide reported by
Davy is another illustration of the eighteenth century's
preoccupation with gases. But with the end of that century
chemistry became further transformed by a new alliance with
electricity : the new science of electrochemistry is introduced by
the man who virtually founded it – Humphry Davy.

Finally, we include an excerpt by the Cumberland Quaker
John Dalton in which chemistry is given an intellectual
framework that it has retained to this day – the theory of
chemical atomism.

C.R.

Further Reading

C. Babbage, *Reflections on the Decline of Science in England*, Gregg,
    1970. Facsimile reprint of Babbage's book of 1830.
I. B. Cohen and H. M. Jones, *Science Before Darwin*, Deutsch, 1963.
    An anthology of early nineteenth-century British scientific writing.
* Sir Harold Hartley, *Humphry Davy*, S.R. Publishers, 1971.

R. C. Olby (ed.) *Late Eighteenth Century European Scientists*, Pergamon, 1966. Includes short biographies of Lavoisier, Cavendish, Volta and the elder James Watt.

R. C. Olby (ed.), *Early Nineteenth Century European Scientists*, Pergamon, 1967. Includes short biographies of Davy and Berzelius.

C. A. Russell, *The History of Valency*, Leicester University Press, 1971. Chapter I is a broad survey of the European scientific scene in the early 1800s and refers particularly to Davy's work in chemistry.

Anne Treneer, *The Mercurial Chemist*, Methuen, 1963. Another biography of Davy, very readable but paying less attention to his science than the set book.

*Open University Set Book.

1 Joseph Priestley

On Dephlogisticated Air

from *Experiments and Observations on Different Kinds of Air*,
vol. 2   1775

The contents of this section will furnish a very striking illustration of the truth of a remark, which I have more than once made
in my philosophical writings, and which can hardly be too often
repeated, as it tends greatly to encourage philosophical investigations viz. that more is owing to what we call *chance*, that is,
philosophically speaking, to the observation of *events arising
from unknown causes*, than to any proper design, or preconceived *theory* in this business. This does not appear in the
works of those who write *synthetically* upon these subjects; but
would, I doubt not, appear very strikingly in those who are the
most celebrated for their philosophical acumen, did they write
analytically and ingenuously.

For my own part, I will frankly acknowledge, that, at the
commencement of the experiments recited in this section, I
was so far from having formed any hypothesis that led to the
discoveries I made in pursuing them, that they would have appeared very improbable to me had I been told of them; and
when the decisive facts did at length obtrude themselves upon
my notice, it was very slowly, and with great hesitation, that I
yielded to the evidence of my senses. And yet, when I reconsider the matter, and compare my last discoveries relating to
the constitution of the atmosphere with the first, I see the closest
and the easiest connexion in the world between them, so as to
wonder that I should not have been led immediately from the
one to the other. That this was not the case, I attribute to the
force of prejudice, which, unknown to ourselves, biasses not only
our *judgments*, properly so called, but even the perceptions of
our senses: for we may take a maxim so strongly for granted,
that the plainest evidence of sense will not intirely change, and
often hardly modify our persuasions; and the more ingenious a
man is, the more effectually he is entangled in his errors; his
ingenuity only helping him to deceive himself, by evading the
force of truth.

There are, I believe, very few maxims in philosophy that have laid firmer hold upon the mind, than that air, meaning atmospherical air (free from various foreign matters, which were always supposed to be dissolved, and intermixed with it) is *a simple elementary substance*, indestructible, and unalterable, at least as much so as water is supposed to be. In the course of my inquiries, I was, however, soon satisfied that atmospherical air is not an unalterable thing; for that the phlogiston with which it becomes loaded from bodies burning in it, and animals breathing it, and various other chemical processes, so far alters and depraves it, as to render it altogether unfit for inflammation, respiration, and other purposes to which it is subservient; and I had discovered that agitation in water, the process of vegetation, and probably other natural processes, by taking out the superfluous phlogiston, restore it to its original purity. But I own I had no idea of the possibility of going any farther in this way, and thereby procuring air purer than the best common air. I might, indeed, have naturally imagined that such would be air that should contain less phlogiston than the air of the atmosphere; but I had no idea that such a composition was possible.

It will be seen in my last publication, that, from the experiments which I made on the marine acid air, I was led to conclude, that common air consisted of some acid (and I naturally inclined to the acid that I was then operating upon) and phlogiston; because the union of this acid vapour and phlogiston made inflammable air; and inflammable air, by agitation in water, ceases to be inflammable, and becomes respirable. And though I could never make it quite so good as common air, I thought it very probable that vegetation, in more favourable circumstances than any in which I could apply it, or some other natural process, might render it more pure.

Upon this, which no person can say was an improbable supposition, was founded my conjecture, of volcanos having given birth to the atmosphere of this planet, supplying it with a permanent air, first inflammable, then deprived of its inflammability by agitation in water, and farther purified by vegetation.

Several of the known phenomena of the *nitrous acid* might have led me to think, that this was more proper for the constitution of the atmosphere than the marine acid: but my thoughts had got into a different train, and nothing but a series of observations, which I shall now distinctly relate, compelled me to adopt another hypothesis, and brought me, in a way of which I had then no idea, to the solution of the great problem, which my reader will perceive I have had in view ever since my discovery that the atmospherical air is alterable, and therefore that it is not an elementary substance, but a *composition* viz: what this composition is, or what is the thing *that we breathe*, and how is it to be made from its constituent principles.

At the time of my former publication, I was not possessed of a *burning lens* of any considerable force; and for want of one, I could not possibly make many of the experiments that I had projected, and which, in theory, appeared very promising. I had, indeed, a *mirror* of force sufficient for my purpose. But the nature of this instrument is such, that it cannot be applied, with effect, except upon substances that are capable of being suspended, or resting on a very slender support. It cannot be directed at all upon any substance in the form of *powder*, nor hardly upon any thing that requires to be put into a vessel of quicksilver; which appears to me to be the most accurate method of extracting air from a great variety of substances, as was explained in the Introduction to this volume. But having afterwards procured a lens of twelve inches diameter, and twenty inches focal distance, I proceeded with great alacrity to examine, by the help of it, what kind of air a great variety of substances, natural and factitious, would yield, putting them into vessels which I filled with quicksilver, and kept inverted in a bason of the same. Mr Warltire, a good chymist, and lecturer in natural philosophy, happening to be at that time in Calne, I explained my views to him, and was furnished by him with many substances, which I could not otherwise have procured.

With this apparatus, after a variety of other experiments, an account of which will be found in its proper place, on the 1 August 1774, I endeavoured to extract air from *mercurius calcinatus per se*; and I presently found that, by means of this lens, air was expelled from it very readily. Having got about three or four times as much as the bulk of my materials, I admitted water to it, and found that it was not imbibed by it. But what surprized me more than I can well express, was, that a candle burned in this air with a remarkably vigorous flame, very much like that enlarged flame with which a candle burns in nitrous air, exposed to iron or liver of sulphur; but as I had got nothing like this remarkable appearance from any kind of air besides this particular modification of nitrous air, and I knew no nitrous acid was used in the preparation of *mercurius calcinatus*, I was utterly at a loss how to account for it.

In this case, also, though I did not give sufficient attention to the circumstance at that time, the flame of the candle, beside being larger, burned with more splendor and heat than in that species of nitrous air; and a piece of red-hot wood sparkled in it, exactly like paper dipped in a solution of nitre, and it consumed very fast; an experiment which I had never thought of trying with nitrous air.

At the same time that I made the above mentioned experiment, I extracted a quantity of air, with the very same property, from the common *red precipitate*, which being produced by a solution of mercury in spirit of nitre, made me conclude that this peculiar property, being similar to that of the modification of nitrous air above mentioned, depended upon something being communicated to it by the nitrous acid; and since the *mercurius calcinatus* is produced by exposing mercury to a certain degree of heat, where common air has access to it, I likewise concluded that this substance had collected something of *nitre*, in that state of heat, from the atmosphere.

This, however, appearing to me much more extraordinary than it ought to have done, I entertained some suspicion that the *mercurius calcinatus*, on which I had made my experiments, being bought at a common apothecary's, might, in fact, be nothing more than red precipitate; though, had I been anything of a practical chymist, I could not have entertained any such suspicion. However, mentioning this suspicion to Mr Warltire, he furnished me with some that he had kept for a specimen of the preparation, and which, he told me, he could warrant to be genuine. This being treated in the same manner as the former, only by a longer continuance of heat, I extracted much more air from it than from the other.

This experiment might have satisfied any moderate sceptic: but, however, being at Paris in the October following, and knowing that there were several very eminent chymists in that place, I did not omit the opportunity, by means of my friend Mr Magellan, to get an ounce of *mercurius calcinatus* prepared by Mr Cadet, of the genuineness of which there could not possibly be any suspicion: and at the same time, I frequently mentioned my surprize at the kind of air which I had got from this preparation to Mr Lavoisier, Mr le Roy, and several other philosophers, who honoured me with their notice in that city; and who, I daresay, cannot fail to recollect the circumstance.

At the same time, I had no suspicion that the air which I had got from the *mercurius calcinatus* was even wholesome, so far was I from knowing what it was that I had really found; taking it for granted, that it was nothing more than such kind of air as I had brought nitrous air to be by the processes above mentioned; and in this air I have observed that a candle would burn sometimes quite naturally, and sometimes with a beautiful enlarged flame, and yet remain perfectly noxious.

At the same time that I had got the air above mentioned from *mercurius calcinatus* and the red precipitate, I had got the same kind from *red lead* or *minium*. In this process, that part of the minium on which the focus of the lens had fallen, turned yellow. One third of the air, in this experiment, was readily absorbed by water, but, in the remainder, a candle burned very strongly, and with a crackling noise.

That fixed air is contained in red lead I had observed before; for I had expelled it by the heat of a candle, and had found it to be very pure. I imagine it requires more heat than I then used to expel any of the other kind of air.

This experiment with *red lead* confirmed me more in my suspicion, that the *mercurius calcinatus* must get the property of yielding this kind of air from the atmosphere, the process by which that preparation, and this of red lead is made, being similar. As I never make the least secret of any thing that I observe, I mentioned this experiment also, as well as those with the *mercurius calcinatus*, and the red precipitate, to all my philosophical acquaintances at Paris, and elsewhere; having no idea, at that time, to what these remarkable facts would lead.

Presently after my return from abroad, I went to work upon the *mercurius calcinatus*, which I had procured from Mr Cadet;

and, with a very moderate degree of heat, I got from about one fourth of an ounce of it, an ounce-measure of air, which I observed to be not readily imbibed, either by the substance itself from which it had been expelled (for I suffered them to continue a long time together before I transferred the air to any other place) or by water, in which I suffered this air to stand a considerable time before I made any experiment upon it.

In this air, as I had expected, a candle burned with a vivid flame; but what I observed new at this time (19 Nov.), and which surprized me no less than the fact I had discovered before, was, that, whereas a few moments of agitation in water will deprive the modified nitrous air of its property of admitting a candle to burn in it; yet, after more than ten times as much agitation as would be sufficient to produce this alteration in the nitrous air, no sensible change was produced in this. A candle still burned in it with a strong flame; and it did not, in the least, diminish common air, which I have observed that nitrous air, in this state, in some measure, does.

But I was much more surprized, when, after two days, in which this air had continued in contact with water (by which it was diminished about one twentieth of its bulk) I agitated it violently in water about five minutes, and found that a candle still burned in it as well as in common air. The same degree of agitation would have made phlogisticated nitrous air fit for respiration indeed, but it would certainly have extinguished a candle.

These facts fully convinced me, that there must be a very material difference between the constitution of the air from *mercurius calcinatus*, and that of phlogisticated nitrous air, not withstanding their resemblance in some particulars. But though I did not doubt that the air from *mercurius calcinatus* was fit for respiration, after being agitated in water, as every kind of air without exception, on which I had tried the experiment, had been, I still did not suspect that it was respirable in the first instance; so far was I from having any idea of this air being, what it really was, much superior, in this respect, to the air of the atmosphere.

In this ignorance of the real nature of this kind of air, I continued from this time (November) to 1 March following; having, in the mean time, been intent upon my experiments on the vitriolic acid air above recited, and the various modifications of air produced by spirit of nitre. But in the course of this month, I not only ascertained the nature of this kind of air, though very gradually, but was led by it to the complete discovery of the constitution of the air we breathe.

Till this 1 March 1775, I had so little suspicion of the air from *mercurius calcinatus*, &c. being wholesome, that I had not even thought of applying to it the test of nitrous air; but thinking (as my reader must imagine I frequently must have done) on the candle burning in it after long agitation in water, it occurred to me at last to make the experiment; and putting one measure of nitrous air to two measures of this air, I found, not only that it was diminished, but that it was diminished quite as much as common air, and that the redness of the mixture was likewise equal to that of a similar mixture of nitrous and common air.

After this I had no doubt but that the air from *mercurius cal-cinatus* was fit for respiration, and that it had all the other pro-perties of genuine common air. But I did not take notice of what I might have observed, if I had not been so fully possessed by the notion of there being no air better than common air, that the redness was really deeper, and the diminution something greater than common air would have admitted.

Moreover, this advance in the way of truth, in reality, threw me back into error, making me give up the hypothesis I had first formed, viz. that the *mercurius calcinatus* had extracted spirit of nitre from the air; for I now concluded, that all the con-stituent parts of the air were equally, and in their proper propor-tion, imbibed in the preparation of this substance, and also in the process of making red lead. For at the same time that I made the above mentioned experiment on the air from *mercurius cal-cinatus*, I likewise observed that the air which I had extracted from red lead, after the fixed air was washed out of it, was of the same nature, being diminished by nitrous air like common air: but, at the same time, I was puzzled to find that air from the red precipitate was diminished in the same manner, though the pro-cess for making this substance is quite different from that of making the two others. But to this circumstance I happened not to give much attention.

I wish my reader be not quite tired with the frequent repetition of the word *surprize*, and others of similar import; but I must go on in that style a little longer. For the next day I was more surprized than ever I had been before, with finding that, after the above-mentioned mixture of nitrous air and the air from *mercurius calcinatus*, had stood all night, (in which time the whole diminution must have taken place; and, consequently, had it been common air, it must have been made perfectly noxious, and intirely unfit for respiration or inflammation) a candle burned in it, and even better than in common air.

I cannot, at this distance of time, recollect what it was that I had in view in making this experiment; but I know I had no expectation of the real issue of it. Having acquired a considerable degree of readiness in making experiments of this kind, a very slight and evanescent motive would be sufficient to induce me to do it. If, however, I had not happened, for some other purpose, to have had a lighted candle before me, I should probably never have made the trial; and the whole train of my future experiments relating to this kind of air might have been prevented.

Still, however, having no conception of the real cause of this phenomenon, I considered it as something very extraordinary; but as a property that was peculiar to air that was extracted from these substances, and *adventitious*; and I always spoke of the air to my acquaintance as being substantially the same thing with common air. I particularly remember my telling Dr Price, that I was myself perfectly satisfied of its being common air, as it appeared to be so by the test of nitrous air; though, for the satisfaction of others, I wanted a mouse to make the proof quite complete.

On the 8th of this month I procured a mouse, and put it into a glass vessel, containing two ounce-measures of the air from *mercurius calcinatus*. Had it been common air, a full-grown mouse, as this was, would have lived in it about a quarter of an hour. In this air, however, my mouse lived a full half hour; and though it was taken out seemingly dead, it appeared to have been only exceedingly chilled; for, upon being held to the fire, it presently revived, and appeared not to have received any harm from the experiment.

By this I was confirmed in my conclusion, that the air extracted from *mercurius calcinatus*, &c. was, *at least, as good* as common air; but I did not certainly conclude that it was any *better*; because, though one mouse would live only a quarter of an hour in a given quantity of air, I knew it was not impossible but that another mouse might have lived in it half an hour; so little accuracy is there in this method of ascertaining the goodness of air: and indeed I have never had recourse to it for my own satisfaction, since the discovery of that most ready, accurate, and elegant test that nitrous air furnishes. But in this case I had a view to publishing the most generally-satisfactory account of my experiments that the nature of the thing would admit of.

This experiment with the mouse, when I had reflected upon it some time, gave me so much suspicion that the air into which I had put it was better than common air, that I was induced, the day after, to apply the test of nitrous air to a small part of that very quantity of air which the mouse had breathed so long; so that, had it been common air, I was satisfied it must have been very nearly, if not altogether, as noxious as possible, so as not to be affected by nitrous air; when, to my surprize again, I found that though it had been breathed so long, it was still better than common air. For after mixing it with nitrous air, in the usual proportion of two to one, it was diminished in the proportion of $4\frac{1}{2}$ to $3\frac{1}{2}$; that is, the nitrous air had made it two ninths less than before, and this in a very short space of time; whereas I had never before found that, in the longest time, any common air was reduced more than one fifth of its bulk by any proportion of nitrous air, nor more than one fourth by any phlogistic process whatever. Thinking of this extraordinary fact upon my pillow, the next morning I put another measure of nitrous air to the same mixture, and, to my utter astonishment, found that it was farther diminished to almost one half of its original quantity. I then put a third measure to it; but this did not diminish it any farther: but, however, left it one measure less than it was even after the mouse had been taken out of it.

Being now fully satisfied that this air, even after the mouse had breathed it half an hour, was much better than common air; and having a quantity of it still left, sufficient for the experiment, viz. an ounce-measure and a half, I put the mouse into it; when

I observed that it seemed to feel no shock upon being put into it, evident signs of which would have been visible, if the air had not been very wholesome; but that it remained perfectly at its ease another full half hour, when I took it out quite lively and vigorous. Measuring the air the next day, I found it to be reduced from 1½ to ⅔ of an ounce-measure. And after this, if I remember well (for in my *register* of the day I only find it noted, that it was *considerably diminished* by nitrous air) it was nearly as good as common air. It was evident, indeed, from the mouse having been taken out quite vigorous, that the air could not have been rendered very noxious.

For my farther satisfaction I procured another mouse, and putting it into less than two ounce-measures of air extracted from *mercurius calcinatus* and air from red precipitate (which, having found them to be of the same quality, I had mixed together) it lived three quarters of an hour. But not having had the precaution to set the vessel in a warm place, I suspect that the mouse died of cold. However, as it had lived three times as long as it could probably have lived in the same quantity of common air, and I did not expect much accuracy from this kind of test, I did not think it necessary to make any more experiments with mice.

Being now fully satisfied of the superior goodness of this kind of air, I proceeded to measure that degree of purity, with as much accuracy as I could, by the test of nitrous air; and I began with putting one measure of nitrous air to two measures of this air, as if I had been examining common air; and now I observed that the diminution was evidently greater than common air would have suffered by the same treatment. A second measure of nitrous air reduced it to two thirds of its original quantity, and a third measure to one half. Suspecting that the diminution could not proceed much farther, I then added only half a measure of nitrous air, by which it was diminished still more; but not much, and another half measure made it more than half of its original quantity; so that, in this case, two measures of this air took more than two measures of nitrous air, and yet remained less than half of what it was. Five measures brought it pretty exactly to its original dimensions.

At the same time, air from the *red precipitate* was diminished in the same proportion as that from *mercurius calcinatus*, five measures of nitrous air being received by two measures of this without any increase of dimensions. Now as common air takes about one half of its bulk of nitrous air, before it begins to receive any addition to its dimensions from more nitrous air, and this air took more than four half-measures before it ceased to be diminished by more nitrous air, and even five half-measures made no addition to its original dimensions, I conclude that it was between four and five times as good as common air. It will be seen that I have since procured air better than this, even between five and six times as good as the best common air that I have ever met with.

Being now fully satisfied with respect to the *nature* of this new species of air, viz. that, being capable of taking more phlogiston from nitrous air, it therefore originally contains less of this principle; my next inquiry was, by what means it comes to be so pure, or philosophically speaking, to be so much *dephlogisticated*; and since the red lead yields the same kind of air with *mercurius calcinatus*, though mixed with fixed air, and is a much cheaper material, I proceeded to examine all the preparations of lead, made by heat in the open air, to see what kind of air they would yield, beginning with the *grey calx*, and ending with *litharge*.

The red lead which I used for this purpose yielded a considerable quantity of dephlogisticated air, and very little fixed air; but to what circumstance in the preparation of this lead, or in the keeping of it, this difference is owing, I cannot tell. I have frequently found a very remarkable difference between different specimens of red lead in this respect, as well as in the purity of the air which they contain. This difference, however, may arise in a great measure, from the care that is taken to extract the fixed air from it. In this experiment two measures of nitrous air being put to one measure of this air, reduced it to one third of what it was at first, and nearly three times its bulk of nitrous air made very little addition to its original dimensions; so that this air was exceedingly pure, and better than any that I had procured before.

The preparation called *massicot* (which is said to be a state between the grey calx and the red lead) also yielded a considerable quantity of air, of which about one half was fixed air, and the remainder was such, that when an equal quantity of nitrous air was put to it, it was something less than at first; so that this air was about twice as pure as common air.

I thought it something remarkable, that in the preparations of lead by heat, those before and after these two, viz. the red lead and *massicot*, yielded only fixed air. I would also observe, by the way, that a very small quantity of air was extracted from *lead ore* by the burning lens. The bulk of it was easily absorbed by water. The remainder was not affected by nitrous air, and it extinguished a candle.

I got a very little air by the same process from the *grey calx of lead*, of precisely the same quality with the former. That part of it which was not affected by nitrous air extinguished a candle, so that both of them may be said to have yielded fixed air, only with a larger portion than usual, of that part of it which does not unite with water.

Litharge (which is a state that succeeds the red lead) yielded air pretty readily; but this also was fixed air. That which was not absorbed by water, was not affected by nitrous air.

Much more than I had any opportunity of doing remains to be done, in order to ascertain upon what circumstances, in these preparations of lead, the quality of the air which they contain, depends. It can only be done by some person who shall carefully attend to the processes, so as to see himself in what manner they are made, and examine them in all their different states. I very much wished to have attempted something of this kind myself, but I found it impossible in my situation. However, I got Dr Higgins (who furnished me with several preparations that I could not easily have procured elsewhere) to make me a quantity of red lead, that I might, at least, try it when *fresh made*, and after keeping it some time in different circumstances; and though, by the help of this preparation, I did not do the thing that I expected, I did something else, much more considerable.

This fresh made red lead had a yellowish cast, and had in it several pieces intirely yellow. I tried it immediately, in the same manner in which I had made the preceding experiments, viz. with the burning lens in quicksilver, and found that it yielded very little air, and with great difficulty; requiring the application of a very intense heat. With an equal quantity of nitrous air, a part of this air was reduced to one half of its original bulk, and 3½ measures saturated it. The air, therefore, was very pure, and the quantity that it yielded being very small, it proved to be in a very favourable state for ascertaining on what circumstances its acquiring this air depended.

My object now was to bring this fresh made red lead, which yielded very little air, to that state in which other red lead had yielded a considerable quantity; and taking it, in a manner, for granted, in consequence of the reasoning intimated above, that red lead must imbibe from the atmosphere some kind of acid, in order to acquire that property, I took three separate half-ounces of this fresh made red lead, and moistened them till they made a kind of paste, with each of the three mineral acids, viz. the vitriolic, the marine, and the nitrous; and as I intended to make the experiments in a gun-barrel, lest the iron should be too much affected by them, I dried all these mixtures, till they were perfectly hard; then pulverizing them, I put them separately into my gun-barrel, filled up to the mouth with pounded flint, which I had found by trial to yield little, or no air when treated in this manner. I had also found that no quantity of air, sufficient to make an experiment, could be procured from an equal quantity of this red lead by this process.

Those portions of the red lead which had been moistened with the vitriolic and marine acids became white; but that which had been moistened with the nitrous acid, had acquired a deep brown colour. The mixtures with the nitrous and marine acids dried pretty readily, but that with the vitriolic acid was never perfectly dry; but a great part of it remained in the form of a softish paste.

Neither the vitriolic nor the marine acid mixtures gave the least air when treated in the manner above mentioned; but the moment that the composition into which the *nitrous* acid had entered became warm, air began to be produced; and I received the produce in quicksilver. About one ounce-measure was quite transparent, but presently after it became exceedingly red; and being satisfied that this redness was owing to the nitrous acid vapour having dissolved the quicksilver, I took no more than two ounce-measures in this way, but received all the remainder, which was almost two pints, in water. Far the greatest part of this was fixed air, being readily absorbed by water, and extinguishing a candle. There was, however, a considerable residuum, in which the flame of a candle burned with a crackling noise, from which I concluded that it was true dephlogisticated air.

In this experiment I had moistened the red lead with spirit of nitre several times, and had dried it again. When I repeated the experiment, I moistened it only once with the same acid, when I got from it not quite a pint of air; but it was almost all of the dephlogisticated kind, about five times as pure as common air. N.B. All the acids made a violent effervescence with the red lead.

Though there was a difference in the result of these experiments, which I shall consider hereafter, I was now convinced that it was the nitrous acid which the red lead had acquired from the air, and which had enabled it to yield the dephlogisticated air, agreeable to my original conjecture. Finding also, as will be seen in the following section, that the same kind of air is produced by moistening with the spirit of nitre any kind of earth that is free from phlogiston, and treating it as I had done the red lead in the last-mentioned experiment, there remained no doubt in my mind, but that *atmospherical air*, or the thing that we breathe, *consists of nitrous acid and earth*, with so much phlogiston as is necessary to its elasticity; and likewise so much more as it required to bring it from its state of perfect purity to the mean condition in which we find it.

For this purpose I tried, with success, *flowers of zinc, chalk, quick-lime, slacked-lime, tobacco-pipe clay, flint* and *Muscovy talck*, with other similar substances, which will be found to comprize all the kinds of earth that are essentially distinct from each other, according to their chymical properties. A particular account of the processes with these substances, I reserve for another section; thinking it sufficient in this to give a history of the discovery, and a general account of the nature of this dephlogisticated air, with this general inference from the experiment, respecting the constitution of the atmosphere.

I was the more confirmed in my idea of spirit of nitre and earth constituting respirable air, by finding, that when any of these matters, on which I had tried the experiment, had been treated in the manner above mentioned, and they had thereby yielded all the air that could be extracted from them by this process; yet when they had been moistened with fresh spirit of nitre, and were treated in the same manner as before, they would yield as much dephlogisticated air as at the first. This may be repeated till all the earthy matter be exhausted. It will be sufficient to recite one or two facts of this kind from my register.

April 18, I took the remains of the fresh made red lead, out of which a great quantity of dephlogisticated air had been extracted, and moistening about three quarters of an ounce of it a second time with spirit of nitre, I got from it about two pints of air, all of which was nearly six times as pure as common air. This air was generated very fast, and the glass tube through which it was transmitted was filled with red fumes; the nitrous acid, I suppose, prevailing in the composition of the air, but being absorbed by the water in which it was afterwards received.

In this, and many other processes, my reader will find a great variety in the purity of the air procured from the same substances. But this will not be wondered at, if it be considered that a small quantity of phlogistic matter, accidentally mixing with the ingredients for the composition of this air, depraves it. It will also be unavoidably depraved, in some measure, if the experiment be made in a gun-barrel, which I commonly made use of, when, as was generally the case, it was sufficiently exact for my purpose, on account of its being the easiest, and in many respects, the most commodious process.

The reason of this is, that if the produce of air be not very rapid, there will be time for the phlogiston to be disengaged from the iron itself, and to mix with the air. Accordingly I have seldom failed to find, that when I endeavoured to get all the air I possibly could from any quantity of materials, and received the produce at different times (as for my satisfaction I generally did) the last was inferior in purity to that which came first. Not unfrequently it was phlogisticated air; that is, air so charged with phlogiston, as to be perfectly noxious; and sometimes, as the reader will find in the next section, it was even nitrous air.

On the same account it frequently happened, that when I used a considerable degree of heat, the red lead which I used in these experiments would be changed into real lead, from which it was often very difficult to get the gun-barrel perfectly clear.

A good deal will also depend upon the ingredients which have been used in the gun-barrel in preceding experiments: for it is not easy to get such an instrument perfectly clean from all the matters that have been put into it: and though it may be presumed, in general, that every kind of air will be expelled from such ingredients by making the tube red-hot; yet matters containing much phlogiston, as charcoal, &c. will not part with it in consequence of the application of heat, unless there be at hand some other substance with which it may combine. Though, therefore, a gun-barrel, containing such small pieces of charcoal as cannot be easily wiped out of it, be kept for a long time in a red heat, and even with its mouth open; yet if it be of a considerable length, some part of the charcoal may remain unconsumed, and the effect of it will be found in the subsequent experiment. Of this I had the following very satisfactory proof.

Being desirous to shew some of my friends the actual production of dephlogisticated air, and having no other apparatus at hand, I had recourse to my gun-barrel; but apprized them, that having used it the day before to get air from charcoal, with which it had been filled for that purpose, though I had taken all the pains I could to get it all out, yet so much would probably remain, that I could not depend on the air I should get from it being dephlogisticated; but that it would probably be of an inferior quality, and perhaps even nitrous air. Accordingly, having put into it a mixture of spirit of nitre and red lead (being part of a quantity which I had often used before for the same purpose) dried, and pounded, I put it into the fire, and received the air in water.

The first produce, which was about a pint, was so far nitrous, that two measures of common air, and one of this, occupied the space of little more than two measures; that is, it was almost as strongly nitrous as that which is produced by the solution of metals in spirit of nitre. The second pint was very little different from common air, and the last produce was better still, being more than twice as good as common air. If, therefore, any person shall propose to make dephlogisticated air, in large quantities, he should have an apparatus appropriated to that purpose; and the greatest care should be taken to keep the instruments as clear as possible from all phlogistic matter, which is the very bane of purity with respect to air, they being exactly *plus* and *minus* to each other.

The hypothesis maintained in this section, viz. that atmospherical air consists of the nitrous acid and earth, suits exceedingly well with the facts relating to the production of nitre; for it is never generated but in the open air, and by exposing to it such kinds of earth as are known to have an affinity with the nitrous acid; so that by their union common nitre may be formed.

Hitherto it has been supposed by chymists, that this nitrous acid, by which common nitre is formed, exists in the atmosphere as an *extraneous substance*, like water, and a variety of other substances, which float in it, in the form of effluvia; but since there is no place in which nitre may not be made, it may, I think, with more probability be supposed, according to my hypothesis, that nitre is formed by a real *decomposition of the air itself*, the *bases* that are presented to it having, in such circumstances, a nearer affinity with the spirit of nitre than that kind of earth with which it is united in the atmosphere.

My theory also supplies an easy solution of what has always been a great difficulty with chymists, with respect to the *detonation of nitre*. The question is, what becomes of the nitrous acid in this case? The general, I believe the universal, opinion now is, that it is *destroyed*; that is, that the acid is properly decomposed, and resolved into its original elements, which Stahl supposed to be earth and water. On the other hand, I suppose that, though the common properties of the acid, as combined with water, disappear, it is only in consequence of its combination with some earthly or inflammable matter, with which it forms some of the many species of air, into the composition of which this wonderful acid enters. It may be common air, it may be dephlogisticated air, or it may be nitrous air, or some of the other kinds, of which an account will be given in a subsequent section. That it should really be the nitrous acid, though so much disguised by its union with earthy, or other matters, will not appear extraordinary to any person who shall consider how little the acid of vitriol is apparent in common sulphur.

With respect to *mercurius calcinatus*, and *red lead*, their red colour favours the supposition of their having extracted spirit of nitre from the air.

2 William Paley

Natural Theology

from *Natural Theology* 1802

State of the Argument

In crossing a heath, suppose I pitched my foot against a *stone*, and were asked how the stone came to be there; I might possibly answer, that, for any thing I knew to the contrary, it had lain there forever: nor would it perhaps be very easy to show the absurdity of this answer. But suppose I had found a *watch* on the ground, and it should be inquired how the watch happened to be in that place; I should hardly think of the answer which I had before given, that for any thing I knew, the watch might have always been there. Yet why should not this answer serve for the watch as well as for the stone? why is it not as admissible in the second case, as in the first? For this reason, and for no other, viz. that, when we come to inspect the watch, we perceive (what we could not discover in the stone) that its several parts are framed and put together for a purpose, e.g. that they are so formed and adjusted as to produce motion, and that motion so regulated as to point out the hour of the day; that, if the different parts had been differently shaped from what they are, of a different size from what they are, or placed after any other manner, or in any other order, than that in which they are placed, either no motion at all would have been carried on in the machine, or none which would have answered the use that is now served by it. To reckon up a few of the plainest of these parts, and of their offices, all tending to one result: — We see a cylindrical box containing a coiled elastic spring, which, by its endeavour to relax itself, turns round the box. We next observe a flexible chain (artificially wrought for the sake of flexure), communicating the action of the spring from the box to the fusee. We then find a series of wheels, the teeth of which catch in, and apply to, each other, conducting the motion from the fusee to the balance, and from the balance to the pointer; and at the same time, by the size and shape of those wheels, so regulating that motion, as to terminate in causing an index, by an equable and measured progression, to pass over a given space in a given time. We take notice that the wheels are made of brass in order to keep them from rust; the springs of steel, no other metal being so elastic; that over the face of the watch there is placed a glass, a material employed in no other part of the work, but in the room of which, if there had been any other than a transparent substance, the hour could not be seen without opening the case. This mechanism being observed (it requires indeed an examination of the instrument, and perhaps some previous knowledge of the subject, to perceive and understand it; but being once, as we have said, observed and understood), the inference, we think, is inevitable, that the watch must have had a maker: that there must have existed, at some time, and at some place or other, an artificer or artificers, who formed it for the purpose which we find it actually to answer; who comprehended its construction, and designed its use.

I Nor would it, I apprehend, weaken the conclusion, that we had never seen a watch made; that we had never known an artist capable of making one; that we were altogether incapable of executing such a piece of workmanship ourselves, or of understanding in what manner it was performed; all this being no more than what is true of some exquisite remains of ancient art, of some lost arts, and, to the generality of mankind, of the more curious productions of modern manufacture. Does one man in a million know how oval frames are turned? Ignorance of this kind exalts our opinion of the unseen and unknown artist's skill, if he be unseen and unknown, but raises no doubt in our minds of the existence and agency of such an artist, at some former time, and in some place or other. Nor can I perceive that it varies at all the inference, whether the question arise concerning a human agent, or concerning an agent of a different species, or an agent possessing, in some respects, a different nature.

II Neither, secondly, would it invalidate our conclusion, that the watch sometimes went wrong, or that it seldom went exactly right. The purpose of the machinery, the design, and the designer, might be evident, and in the case supposed would be evident, in whatever way we accounted for the irregularity of the movement, or whether we could account for it or not. It is not necessary that a machine be perfect, in order to show with what design it was made: still less necessary, where the only question is, whether it were made with any design at all.

III Nor, thirdly, would it bring any uncertainty into the argument, if there were a few parts of the watch, concerning which we could not discover, or had not yet discovered, in what manner they conduced to the general effect; or even some parts, concerning which we could not ascertain, whether they conduced to that effect in any manner whatever. For, as to the first branch of the case; if by the loss, or disorder, or decay of the parts in question, the movement of the watch were found in fact to be stopped, or disturbed, or retarded, no doubt would remain in our minds as to the utility or intention of these parts, although we should be unable to investigate the manner according to which, or the connexion by which, the ultimate effect depended upon their action or assistance; and the more complex is the machine, the more likely is this obscurity to arise. Then, as to the second thing supposed, namely, that there were parts which might be spared, without prejudice to the movement of the watch, and that we had proved this by experiment – these superfluous parts, even if we were completely assured that they were such, would not vacate the reasoning which we had instituted concerning other parts. The indication of contrivance remained, with respect to them, nearly as it was before.

IV Nor, fourthly, would any man in his senses think the existence of the watch, with its various machinery, accounted for, by being told that it was one out of possible combinations of material forms; that whatever he had found in the place where he found the watch, must have contained some internal configuration or other; and that this configuration might be the structure now exhibited, viz. of the works of a watch, as well as a different structure.

V Nor, fifthly, would it yield his inquiry more satisfaction to be answered, that there existed in things a principle of order, which had disposed the parts of the watch into their present form and situation. He never knew a watch made by the principle of order; nor can he even form to himself an idea of what is meant by a principle of order distinct from the intelligence of the watch-maker.

VI Sixthly, he would be surprised to hear that the mechanism of the watch was no proof of contrivance, only a motive to induce the mind to think so.

VII And not less surprised to be informed, that the watch in his hand was nothing more than the result of the laws of *metallic* nature. It is a perversion of language to assign any law, as the efficient, operative cause of any thing. A law presupposes an agent; this is only the mode, according to which an agent proceeds; it implies a power; for it is the order, according to which that power acts. Without this agent, without this power, which are both distinct from itself, the *law* does nothing; is nothing. The expression, 'the law of metallic nature', may sound strange and harsh to a philosophic ear; but it seems quite as justifiable as some others which are more familiar to him, such as 'the law of vegetable nature', 'the law of animal nature', or indeed as 'the law of nature' in general, when assigned as the cause of phenomena, in exclusion of agency and power; or when it is substituted into the place of these.

VIII Neither, lastly, would our observer be driven out of his conclusion, or from his confidence in its truth, by being told that he knew nothing at all about the matter. He knows enough for his argument: he knows the utility of the end: he knows the subserviency and adaptation of the means to the end. These points being known, his ignorance of other points, his doubts concerning other points, affect not the certainty of his reasoning. The consciousness of knowing little, need not beget a distrust of that which he does know.
(Chapter 1)

Of The Elements

When we come to the elements, we take leave of our mechanics; because we come to those things, of the organization of which, if they be organized, we are confessedly ignorant. This ignorance is implied by their name. To say the truth, our investigations are stopped long before we arrive at this point. But then it is for our comfort to find, that a knowledge of the constitution of the elements is not necessary for us. For instance, as Addison has well observed, 'we know *water* sufficiently, when we know how to boil, how to freeze, how to evaporate, how to make it fresh, how to make it run or spout out in what quantity and direction we please, without knowing what water is.' The observation of this excellent writer has more propriety in it now, than it had at the time it was made: for the constitution, and the constituent parts of water, appear in some measure to have been lately discovered; yet it does not, I think, appear, that we can make any better or greater use of water since the discovery, than we did before it.

We can never think of the elements, without reflecting upon the number of distinct uses which are *consolidated* in the same substance. The *air* supplies the lungs, supports fire, conveys sound, reflects light, diffuses smells, gives rain, wafts ships, bears up birds. Ἐξ ὕδατος τα παντα : water, besides maintaining its own inhabitants, is the universal nourisher of plants, and through them, of terrestrial animals; is the basis of their juices and fluids; dilutes their food; quenches their thirst; floats their burdens. *Fire* warms, dissolves, enlightens; is the great promoter of vegetation and life, if not necessary to the support of both.

We might enlarge, to almost any length we pleased, upon each of these uses; but it appears to me almost sufficient to state them. The few remarks, which I judge it necessary to add, are as follows:

I Air is essentially different from earth. There appears to be no necessity for an atmosphere's investing our globe; yet it does invest it; and we see how many, how various, and how important are the purposes which it answers to every order of animated, not to say of organized beings, which are placed upon the terrestrial surface. I think that every one of these uses will be understood upon the first mention of them, except it be that of *reflecting* light, which may be explained thus. If I had the power of seeing only by means of rays coming directly from the sun, whenever I turn my back upon the luminary, I should find myself in darkness. If I had the power of seeing by reflected light, yet by means only of light reflected from solid masses, these masses would shine, indeed, and glisten, but it would be in the dark. The hemisphere, the sky, the world, could only be *illuminated*, as it is illuminated, by the light of the sun being from all sides, and in every direction, reflected to the eye by particles, as numerous, as thickly scattered, and as widely diffused, as are those of the air.

Another general quality of the atmosphere is the power of evaporating fluids. The adjustment of this quality to our use is seen in its action upon the sea. In the sea, water and salt are mixed together most intimately; yet the atmosphere raises the water, and leaves the salt. Pure and fresh as drops of rain descend, they are collected from brine. If evaporation be solution (which seems to be probable), then the air dissolves the water, and not the salt. Upon whatever it be founded, the distinction is critical; so much so, that when we attempt to imitate the process by art, we must regulate our distillation with great care and nicety, or, together with the water, we get the bitterness, or, at least the distastefulness, of the marine substance: and after all, it is owing to this original elective power in the air, that we can effect the separation which we wish, by any art or means whatever.

By evaporation, water is carried up into the air; by the converse of evaporation, it falls down upon the earth. And how does it fall? Not by the clouds being all at once re-converted into water, and descending like a sheet; not in rushing down in columns from a spout; but in moderate drops, as from a colander. Our watering-pots are made to imitate showers of rain. Yet, *a priori*, I should have thought either of the two former methods more likely to have taken place than the last.

By respiration, flame, putrefaction, air is rendered unfit for the support of animal life. By the constant operation of these corrupting principles, the whole atmosphere, if there were no restoring causes, would come at length to be deprived of its necessary degree of purity. Some of these causes seem to have been discovered, and their efficacy ascertained by experiment. And so far as the discovery has proceeded, it opens to us a beautiful and a wonderful economy. *Vegetation* proves to be one of them. A sprig of mint, corked up with a small portion of foul air placed in the light, renders it again capable of supporting life or flame. Here, therefore, is a constant circulation of benefits maintained between the two great provinces of organized nature. The plant purifies what the animal has poisoned; in return, the contaminated air is more ordinarily nutritious to the plant. *Agitation with water* turns out to be another of these restoratives. The foulest air, shaken in a bottle with water for a sufficient length of time recovers a degree of its purity. Here then again, allowing for the scale upon which nature works, we see the salutary effects of *storms* and *tempests*. The yesty waves, which confound the heaven and the sea, are doing the very thing which was done in the bottle. Nothing can be of greater importance to the living creation than the salubrity of their atmosphere. It ought to reconcile us, therefore, to these agitations of the elements, of which we sometimes deplore the consequences, to know, that they tend powerfully to restore to the air that purity, which so many causes are constantly impairing.

II In water, what ought not a little to be admired, are those negative qualities which constitute its *purity*. Had it been vinous, or oleaginous, or acid; had the sea been filled, or the rivers flowed, with wine or milk; fish, constituted as they are, must have died; plants, constituted as they are, would have withered; the lives of animals which feed upon plants must have perished. Its very *insipidity*, which is one of those negative qualities, renders it the best of all menstrua. Having no taste of its own, it becomes the sincere vehicle of every other. Had there been a taste in water, be it what it might, it would have infected every thing we ate or drank with an importunate repetition of the same flavour.

Another thing in this element, not less to be admired, is the constant *round* which it travels; and by which, without suffering either adulteration or waste, it is continually offering itself to the wants of the habitable globe. From the sea are exhaled those vapours which form the clouds; these clouds descend in showers, which, penetrating into the crevices of the hills, supply springs; which springs flow in little streams into the valleys; and there, uniting, become rivers; which rivers, in return, feed the ocean. So there is an incessant circulation of the same fluid; and not one drop probably more or less now than there was at the creation. A particle of water takes its departure from the surface of the sea, in order to fulfil certain important offices to the earth; and, having executed the service which was assigned to it, returns to the bosom which it left.

Some have thought, that we have too much water upon the globe, the sea occupying above three quarters of its whole surface. But the expanse of ocean, immense as it is, may be no more than sufficient to fertilize the earth. Or, independently of this reason, I know not why the sea may not have as good a right to its place as the land. It may proportionably support as many inhabitants; minister to as large an aggregate of enjoyment. The land only affords a habitable surface; the sea is habitable to a great depth.

III Of fire, we have said that it *dissolves*. The only idea probably which this term raised in the reader's mind, was that of fire melting metals, resins, and some other substances, fluxing ores, running glass, and assisting us in many of our operations, chymical or culinary. Now these are only uses of an occasional kind, and give us a very imperfect notion of what fire does for us. The grand importance of this dissolving power, the great office indeed of fire in the economy of nature, is keeping things in a state of solution, that is to say, in a state of fluidity. Were it not for the presence of heat, or of a certain degree of it, all fluids would be frozen. The ocean itself would be a quarry of ice; universal nature stiff and dead.

We see, therefore, that the elements bear not only a strict relation to the constitution of organized bodies, but a relation to each other. Water could not perform its office to the earth without air; nor exist, as water, without fire.

IV Of light (whether we regard it as of the same substance with fire, or as a different substance), it is altogether superfluous to expatiate upon the use. No man disputes it. The observations, therefore, which I shall offer, respect that little which we seem to know of its constitution.

Light travels from the sun at the rate of twelve millions of miles in a minute. Urged by such a velocity, with what *force* must its particles drive against (I will not say the eye, the tenderest of animal substances, but) every substance, animate or inanimate, which stands in its way! It might seem to be a force sufficient to shatter to atoms the hardest bodies.

How then is this effect, the consequence of such prodigious velocity, guarded against? By a proportionable *minuteness* of the particles of which light is composed. It is impossible for the human mind to imagine to itself any thing so small as a particle of light. But this extreme axility, though difficult to conceive, it is easy to prove. A drop of tallow expended in the wick of a farthing candle, shall send forth rays sufficient to fill a hemisphere of a mile diameter; and to fill it so full of these rays, that an aperture not larger than the pupil of an eye wherever it be placed within the hemisphere, shall be sure to receive some of them. What floods of light are continually poured from the sun we cannot estimate; but the immensity of the sphere which is filled with its particles, even if it reached no farther than the orbit of the earth, we can in some sort compute; and we have reason to believe, that throughout this whole region, the particles of light lie, in latitude at least, near to one another. The spissitude of the sun's rays at the earth is such, that the number which falls upon a burning-glass of an inch diameter, is sufficient, when concentrated, to set wood on fire.

The tenuity and the velocity of particles of light, as ascertained by separate observations, may be said to be proportioned to each other; both surpassing our utmost stretch of comprehension; but proportioned. And it is this proportion alone which converts a tremendous element into a welcome visitor.

It has been observed to me by a learned friend, as having often struck his mind, that if light had been made by a common artist, it would have been of one uniform *colour*: whereas by its present composition, we have that variety of colours which is of such infinite use to us for the distinguishing of objects; which adds so much to the beauty of the earth, and augments the stock of our innocent pleasures.

With which may be joined another reflection, viz. that, considering light as compounded of rays of seven different colours (of which there can be no doubt, because it can be resolved into these rays by simply passing it through a prism), the constituent parts must be well mixed and blended together, to produce a

fluid, so clear and colourless as a beam of light is when received
from the sun.
(Chapter 21)

3 Humphry Davy
*On some New Phenomena of Chemical Changes
produced by Electricity*

in *Philosophical Transactions*, vol. 98   1808

I Introduction

In the Bakerian Lecture which I had the honour of presenting
to the Royal Society last year, I described a number of decom-
positions and chemical changes produced in substances of known
composition by electricity, and I ventured to conclude from the
general principles on which the phenomena were capable of
being explained, that the new methods of investigation promised
to lead to a more intimate knowledge than had hitherto been
obtained, concerning the true elements of bodies.

This conjecture, then sanctioned only by strong analogies, I
am now happy to be able to support by some conclusive facts.
In the course of a laborious experimental application of the
powers of electro-chemical analysis, to bodies which have appeared simple when examined by common chemical agents, or
which at least have never been decomposed, it has been my
good fortune to obtain new and singular results.

Such of the series of experiments as are in a tolerably mature
state, and capable of being arranged in a connected order, I shall
detail in the following sections, particularly those which demonstrate the decomposition and composition of the fixed alkalies,
and the production of the new and extraordinary bodies which
constitute their bases.

In speaking of novel methods of investigation, I shall not
fear to be minute. When the common means of chemical research
have been employed, I shall mention only results. A historical
detail of the progress of the investigation, of all the difficulties
that occurred, and of the manner in which they were overcome,
and of all the manipulations employed, would far exceed the
limits assigned to this Lecture. It is proper to state, however,

that when general facts are mentioned, they are such only as have been deduced from processes carefully performed and often repeated.

II On the Methods used for the Decomposition of the fixed Alkalies

The researches I had made on the decomposition of acids, and of alkaline and earthy neutral compounds, proved that the powers of electrical decomposition were proportional to the strength of the opposite electricities in the circuit, and to the conducting power and degree of concentration of the materials employed.

In the first attempts that I made on the decomposition of the fixed alkalies, I acted upon aqueous solutions of potash and soda, saturated at common temperatures, by the highest electrical power I could command, and which was produced by a combination of Voltaic batteries belonging to the Royal Institution, containing 24 plates of copper and zinc of 12 inches square, 100 plates of 6 inches, and 150 of 4 inches square, charged with solutions of alum and nitrous acid; but in these cases, though there was a high intensity of action, the water of the solutions alone was affected, and hydrogen and oxygen disengaged with the production of much heat and violent effervescence.

The presence of water appearing thus to prevent any decomposition, I used potash in igneous fusion. By means of a stream of oxygen gas from a gasometer applied to the flame of a spirit lamp, which was thrown on a platina spoon containing potash, this alkali was kept for some minutes in a strong red heat, and in a state of perfect fluidity. The spoon was preserved in communication with the positive side of the battery of the power of 100 of 6 inches, highly charged; and the connection from the negative side was made by a platina wire.

By this arrangement some brilliant phenomena were produced. The potash appeared a conductor in a high degree, and as long as the communication was preserved, a most intense light was exhibited at the negative wire, and a column of flame, which seemed to be owing to the development of combustible matter, arose from the point of contact.

When the order was changed, so that the platina spoon was made negative, a vivid and constant light appeared at the opposite point: there was no effect of inflammation round it; but aëriform globules, which inflamed in the atmosphere, rose through the potash.

The platina, as might have been expected, was considerably acted upon; and in the cases when it had been negative, in the highest degree.

The alkali was apparently dry in this experiment; and it seemed probable that the inflammable matter arose from its decomposition. The residual potash was unaltered; it contained indeed a number of dark grey metallic particles, but these proved to be derived from the platina.

I tried several experiments on the electrization of potash rendered fluid by heat, with the hopes of being able to collect the combustible matter, but without success; and I only attained my object, by employing electricity as the common agent for fusion and decomposition.

Though potash, perfectly dried by ignition, is a non-conductor, yet it is rendered a conductor, by a very slight addition of moisture, which does not perceptibly destroy its aggregation; and in this state it readily fuses and decomposes by strong electrical powers.

A small piece of pure potash, which had been exposed for a few seconds to the atmosphere, so as to give conducting power to the surface, was placed upon an insulated disc of platina, connected with the negative side of the battery of the power of 250 of 6 and 4, in a state of intense activity; and a platina wire, communicating with the positive side, was brought in contact with the upper surface of the alkali. The whole apparatus was in the open atmosphere.

Under these circumstances a vivid action was soon observed to take place. The potash began to fuse at both its points of electrization. There was a violent effervescence at the upper surface; at the lower, or negative surface, there was no liberation of elastic fluid; but small globules having a high metallic lustre, and being precisely similar in visible characters to quicksilver, appeared, some of which burnt with explosion and bright flame, as soon as they were formed, and others remained, and were merely tarnished, and finally covered by a white film which formed on their surfaces.

These globules, numerous experiments soon shewed to be the substance I was in search of, and a peculiar inflammable principle the basis of potash. I found that the platina was in no way connected with the result, except as the medium for exhibiting the electrical powers of decomposition; and a substance of the same kind was produced when pieces of copper, silver, gold, plumbago, or even charcoal were employed for completing the circuit.

The phenomenon was independent of the presence of air; I found that it took place when the alkali was in the vacuum of an exhausted receiver.

The substance was likewise produced from potash fused by means of a lamp, in glass tubes confined by mercury, and furnished with hermetically inserted platina wires by which the electrical action was transmitted. But this operation could not be carried on for any considerable time; the glass was rapidly dissolved by the action of the alkali, and this substance soon penetrated through the body of the tube.

Soda, when acted upon in the same manner as potash, exhibited an analogous result: but the decomposition demanded greater intensity of action in the batteries, or the alkali was required to be in much thinner and smaller pieces. With the battery of 100 of 6 inches in full activity I obtained good results from pieces of potash weighing from 40 to 70 grains, and of a thickness which made the distance of the electrified metallic surfaces nearly a quarter of an inch; but with a similar power it was impossible to produce the effects of decomposition on pieces of soda of more than 15 or 20 grains in weight, and that only when the distance between the wires was about 1/8 or 1/10 of an inch.

The substance produced from potash remained fluid at the temperature of the atmosphere at the time of its production; that from soda, which was fluid in the degree of heat of the alkali during its formation, became solid on cooling, and appeared having the lustre of silver.

When the power of 250 was used, with a very high charge for the decomposition of soda, the globules often burnt at the moment of their formation, and sometimes violently exploded and separated into smaller globules, which flew with great velocity through the air in a state of vivid combustion, producing a beautiful effect of continued jets of fire.

4 Humphry Davy

Researches on Nitrous Oxide

from *Researches, Chemical and Philosophical, chiefly concerning Nitrous Oxide, or Dephlogisticated Nitrous Air, and its Respiration* 1800. Reprinted in John Davy (ed.), *Collected Works*, vol. 3, 1839

In consequence of the discovery of the respirability and extraordinary effects of nitrous oxide, or the dephlogisticated nitrous gas of Dr Priestley, made in April 1799, in a manner to be particularly described hereafter, I was induced to carry on the following investigation concerning its composition, properties, combinations, and mode of operation on living beings.

In the course of this investigation, I have met with many difficulties; some arising from the novel and obscure nature of the subject, and others from a want of coincidence in the observations of different experimentalists on the properties and mode of production of the gas. By extending my researches to the different substances connected with nitrous oxide; nitrous acid, nitrous gas and ammonia; and by multiplying the comparisons of facts, I have succeeded in removing the greater number of those difficulties, and have been enabled to give a tolerably clear history of the combinations of oxygen and nitrogen.

By employing both analysis and synthesis whenever these methods were equally applicable, and comparing experiments made under different circumstances, I have endeavoured to guard against sources of error; but I cannot flatter myself that I have altogether avoided them. The physical sciences are almost wholly dependent on the minute observation and comparison of properties of things not immediately obvious to the senses; and from the difficulty of discovering every possible mode of examination, and from the modification of perceptions by the state of feeling, it appears nearly impossible that all the relations of a series of phenomena can be discovered by a single investigation, particularly when these relations are complicated, and many of the agents unknown. Fortunately for the active and progressive nature of the human mind, even experimental research is only a method of approximation to truth.

In the arrangement of facts, I have been guided as much as possible by obvious and simple analogies only. Hence I have seldom entered into theoretical discussions, particularly concerning light, heat, and other agents, which are known only by isolated effects.

Early experience has taught me the folly of hasty generalization. We are ignorant of the laws of corpuscular motion; and an immense mass of minute observations concerning the more complicated chemical changes must be collected, probably before we shall be able to ascertain even whether we are capable of discovering them. Chemistry in its present state, is simply a partial history of phenomena, consisting of many series more or less extensive of accurately connected facts.

With the most important of these series, the arrangement of the combinations of oxygen or the antiphlogistic theory discovered by Lavoisier, the chemical details in this work are capable of being connected.

In the present state of science, it will be unnecessary to enter into discussions concerning the importance of investigations relating to the properties of physiological agents, and the changes effected in them during their operation. By means of such investigations, we arrive nearer towards that point from which we shall be able to view what is within the reach of discovery, and what must for ever remain unknown to us, in the phenomena of organic life. They are of immediate utility, by enabling us to extend our analogies so as to investigate the properties of untried substances, with greater accuracy and probability of success.

Effects Produced by the Respiration of Different Gases

Having observed in my experiments upon venous blood, that nitrous gas rendered that fluid of a purple tinge, very like the colour generated in it by nitrous oxide; and finding no painful effects produced by the application of nitrous gas to the bare muscular fibre, I began to imagine that this gas might be breathed with impunity, provided it were possible in any way to free the lungs of common air before inspiration, so as to prevent the formation of nitrous acid.

On this supposition, during a fit of enthusiasm produced by the respiration of nitrous oxide, I resolved to endeavour to breathe nitrous gas.

One hundred and fourteen cubic inches of nitrous gas were introduced into the large mercurial air-holder; two small silk bags of the capacity of seven quarts were filled with nitrous oxide.

After a forced exhaustion of my lungs, my nose being accurately closed, I made three inspirations and expirations of nitrous oxide in one of the bags, to free my lungs as much as possible from atmospheric oxygen; then, after a full expiration of the nitrous oxide, I transferred my mouth from the mouth-piece of the bag to that of the air-holder, and turning the stop-cock, attempted to inspire the nitrous gas. In passing through my mouth and fauces, it tasted astringent and highly disagreeable; it occasioned a sense of burning in the throat, and produced a spasm of the epiglottis so painful as to oblige me to desist instantly from attempts to inspire it. After moving my lips from the mouth-piece, when I opened them to inspire common air, aëriform nitrous acid was instantly formed in my mouth, which burnt the tongue and palate, injured the teeth, and produced an inflammation of the mucous membrane which lasted some hours.

As after the respiration of nitrous oxide in the experiments in the last Research, a small portion of the residual atmospheric air remained in the lungs, mingled with the gas, after forced expiration; it is most probable that a minute portion of nitrous acid was formed in this experiment, when the nitrous gas was taken into the mouth and fauces, which might produce its stimulating properties. If so, perhaps I owe my life to the circumstance; for supposing I had taken an inspiration of nitrous gas, and even that it had produced no positive effects, it is highly improbable, that by breathing nitrous oxide, I should have freed my lungs from it, so as to have prevented the formation of nitrous acid when I again inspired common air. I never design again to attempt so rash an experiment.

In the beginning of September I often respired nitrous oxide mingled with different proportions of common air or oxygen. The effects produced by the diluted gas were much less violent than those produced by pure nitrous oxide. They were generally pleasant: the thrilling was not often perceived, but a sense of exhilaration was almost constant.

Between September and the end of October, I made but few experiments on respiration, almost the whole of my time being devoted to chemical experiments on the production and analysis of nitrous oxide.

At this period my health being somewhat injured by the constant labour of experimenting, and the perpetual inhalation of the acid vapours of the laboratory, I went into Cornwall; where new associations of ideas and feelings, common exercise, a pure atmosphere, luxurious diet and moderate indulgence in wine, in a month restored me to health and vigour.

27 November; immediately after my return, being fatigued by a long journey, I respired nine quarts of nitrous oxide, having been precisely thirty-three days without breathing any. The feelings were different from those I had experienced in former experiments. After the first six or seven inspirations, I gradually began to lose the perception of external things, and a vivid and intense recollection of some former experiments passed through my mind, so that I called out *what an amazing concatenation of ideas!* I had no pleasurable feeling whatever, I used no muscular motion, nor did I feel any disposition to it; after a minute, when I made a note of the experiment, all the uncommon sensations had vanished; they were succeeded by a slight soreness in one of the arms and in the leg: in three minutes these affections likewise disappeared.

From this experiment I was inclined to suppose that my newly acquired health had diminished my susceptibility to the effects of the gas. About ten days after, however, I had an opportunity of proving the fallacy of this supposition.

Immediately after a journey of 126 miles, in which I had no sleep the preceding night, being much exhausted, I respired seven quarts of gas for near three minutes. It produced the usual pleasurable effects, and slight muscular motion. I continued exhilarated for some minutes afterwards: but in half an hour found myself more nor less exhausted than before the experiment. I had a great propensity to sleep.

I repeated the experiment four or five times in the following week, with similar effects. My susceptibility was certainly not diminished. I even thought that I was more affected than formerly by equal doses.

Though, except in one instance, when indeed the gas was impure, I had experienced no decisive exhaustion after excitement from nitrous oxide, yet still I was far from being satisfied that it was unanalogous to stimulants in general. No experiment had been made in which the excitement from nitrous oxide had been kept up for so great a length of time and carried to so great an extent as that in which it is uniformly succeeded by excessive debility under the agency of other powers.

It occurred to me, that supposing nitrous oxide to be a stimulant of the common class, it would follow that the debility produced in consequence of excessive stimulation by a known agent, ought to be *increased* after excitement from nitrous oxide.

To ascertain whether this was the case, I made, on 23 December, at four p.m. the following experiment. I drank a bottle of wine in large draughts in less than eight minutes. Whilst I was drinking, I perceived a sense of fulness in the head, and throbbing of the arteries, not unanalogous to that produced in the first stage of nitrous oxide excitement. After I had finished the bottle, this fulness increased, the objects around me became dazzling, the power of distinct articulation was lost, and I was unable to walk steadily. At this moment the sensations were rather pleasurable than otherwise, the sense of fulness in the head soon however increased so as to become painful, and in less than an hour I sunk into a state of insensibility.

In this situation I must have remained for two hours or two hours and a half.

I was awakened by head-ache and painful nausea. The nausea continued even after the contents of the stomach had been ejected. The pain in the head every minute increased; I was neither feverish nor thirsty; my bodily and mental debility were excessive, and the pulse feeble and quick.

In this state I breathed for near a minute and a half five quarts of gas, which was brought to me by the operator for nitrous oxide; but as it produced no sensations whatever, and apparently rather increased my debility, I am almost convinced that it was from some accident, either common air, or very impure nitrous oxide.

Immediately after this trial, I respired 12 quarts of oxygen for nearly four minutes. It produced no alterations in my sensations at the time; but immediately after I imagined that I was a little exhilarated.

The head-ache and debility still however continuing with violence, I examined some nitrous oxide which had been prepared in the morning, and finding it very pure, respired seven quarts of it for two minutes and half.

I was unconscious of head-ache after the third inspiration; the usual pleasurable thrilling was produced, voluntary power was destroyed, and vivid ideas rapidly passed through my mind; I made strides across the room, and continued for some minutes much exhilarated. Immediately after the exhilaration had disappeared, I felt a slight return of the head-ache; it was connected with transient nausea. After two minutes, when a small quantity of acidified wine had been thrown from the stomach, both the nausea and head-ache disappeared; but langour and depression not very different in degree from those existing before the experiment, succeeded. They, however, gradually went off before bed time. I slept sound the whole of the night except for a few minutes, during which I was kept awake by a trifling head-ache. In the morning, I had no longer any debility. No head-ache or giddiness came on after I had arisen, and my appetite was very great.

This experiment proved, that debility from intoxication was not increased by excitement from nitrous oxide. The head-ache and depression, it is probable, would have continued longer if it had not been administered. Is it not likely that the slight nausea following the effects of the gas was produced by new excitability given to the stomach?

To ascertain with certainty, whether the most extensive action of nitrous oxide compatible with life, was capable of producing debility, I resolved to breathe the gas for such a time and in such quantities, as to produce excitement equal in duration and superior in intensity to that occasioned by high intoxication from opium or alcohol.

To habituate myself to the excitement, and to carry it on gradually, on 26 December, I was inclosed in an air-tight breathing-box, of the capacity of about 9 cubic feet and half, in the presence of Dr Kinglake.

After I had taken a situation in which I could by means of a curved thermometer inserted under the arm, and a stop-watch, ascertain the alterations in my pulse and animal heat, 20 quarts of nitrous oxide were thrown into the box.

For three minutes I experienced no alteration in my sensations, though immediately after the introduction of the nitrous oxide the smell and taste of it were very evident.

In four minutes I began to feel a slight glow in the cheeks, and a generally diffused warmth over the chest, though the temperature of the box was not quite 50°. I had neglected to feel my pulse before I went in; at this time it was 104 and hard, the animal heat was 98°. In ten minutes the animal heat was near 99°, in a quarter of an hour 99.5°, when the pulse was 102, and fuller than before.

At this period 20 quarts more of nitrous oxide were thrown into the box, and well mingled with the mass of air by agitation.

In 25 minutes the animal heat was 100°, pulse 124. In 30 minutes, 20 quarts more of gas were introduced.

My sensations were now pleasant; I had a generally diffused warmth without the slightest moisture of the skin, a sense of exhilaration similar to that produced by a small dose of wine, and a disposition to muscular motion and to merriment.

In three quarters of an hour the pulse was 104, and animal heat not quite 99.5°, the temperature of the chamber was 64°. The pleasurable feelings continued to increase, the pulse became fuller and slower, till in about an hour it was 88, when the animal heat was 99°.

Twenty quarts more of air were admitted. I had now a great disposition to laugh; luminous points seemed frequently to pass before my eyes, my hearing was certainly more acute, and I felt a pleasant lightness and power of exertion in my muscles. In a short time the symptoms became stationary; breathing was rather oppressed, and on account of the great desire of action, rest was painful.

I now came out of the box, having been in precisely an hour and quarter.

The moment after, I began to respire 20 quarts of unmingled nitrous oxide. A thrilling, extending from the chest to the extremities, was almost immediately produced. I felt a sense of tangible extension highly pleasurable in every limb; my visible impressions were dazzling, and apparently magnified, I heard distinctly every sound in the room, and was perfectly aware of my situation. By degrees, as the pleasurable sensations increased, I lost all connection with eternal things; trains of vivid visible images rapidly passed through my mind, and were connected with words in such a manner, as to produce perceptions perfectly novel. I existed in a world of newly connected and newly modified ideas. I theorised – I imagined that I made discoveries. When I was awakened from this semi-delirious trance by Dr Kinglake, who took the bag from my mouth, indignation and pride were the first feelings produced by the sight of the persons about me. My emotions were enthusiastic and sublime; and for a minute I walked round the room, perfectly regardless of what was said to me. As I recovered my former state of mind, I felt an inclination to communicate the discoveries I had made during the experiment. I endeavoured to recall the ideas, they were feeble and indistinct; one collection of terms, however, presented itself: and with the most intense belief and prophetic manner, I exclaimed to Dr Kinglake, *'Nothing exists but thoughts! – the universe is composed of impressions, ideas, pleasures and pains!'*

About three minutes and half only had elapsed during this experiment, though the time as measured by the relative vividness of the recollected ideas, appeared to me much longer.

Not more than half of the nitrous oxide was consumed. After a minute, before the thrilling of the extremities had disappeared, I breathed the remainder. Similar sensations were again produced; I was quickly thrown into the pleasurable trance, and continued in it longer than before. For many minutes after the experiment, I experienced the thrilling in the extremities, the exhilaration continued nearly two hours. For a much longer time I experienced the mild enjoyment before described connected with indolence; no depression or feebleness followed. I ate my dinner with great appetite and found myself lively and disposed to action immediately after. I passed the evening in executing experiments. At night I found myself unusually cheerful and active; and the hours between eleven and two, were spent in copying the foregoing detail from the common-place book, and in arranging the experiments. In bed I enjoyed profound repose. When I awoke in the morning, it was with consciousness of pleasurable existence, and this consciousness more or less continued through the day.

5 Humphry Davy

A Discourse Introductory to a Course of Lectures on Chemistry 1802

in John Davy (ed.), *Collected Works*, vol. 2 1839

Chemistry is that part of natural philosophy which relates to those intimate actions of bodies upon each other, by which their appearances are altered, and their individuality destroyed.

This science has for its objects all the substances found upon our globe. It relates not only to the minute alterations in the external world, which are daily coming under the cognizance of our senses, and which in consequence, are incapable of affecting the imagination, but likewise to the great changes, and convulsions in nature, which, occurring but seldom, excite our curiosity, or awaken our astonishment.

The phænomena of combustion, of the solution of different substances in water, of the agencies of fire; the production of rain, hail, and snow, and the conversion of dead matter into living matter by vegetable organs, all belong to chemistry; and, in their various and apparently capricious appearances, can be accurately explained only by an acquaintance with the fundamental and general chemical principles.

Chemistry, considered as a systematic arrangement of facts, is of later origin than most of the other sciences; yet certain of its processes and operations have been always more or less connected with them; and, lately, by furnishing new instruments and powers of investigation, it has greatly contributed to increase their perfection, and to extend their applications.

Mechanical philosophy, regarded as the science of the motions of the masses of matter, in its theories and practices, is, to a certain extent, dependent upon chemical laws. How in fact can the mechanic calculate with accuracy upon the powers of solids, fluids, or gases, in communicating motion to each other, unless he is previously acquainted with their particular chemical affinities, or propensities to remain disunited, or to combine? It is to chemistry that he is indebted for the knowledge of the nature and properties of the substances he employs; and he is obliged to that science for the artificial production of the most powerful and most useful of his agents.

Natural history and chemistry are attached to each other by very intimate ties. For while the first of these sciences treats of the general external properties of bodies, the last unfolds their internal constitution and ascertains their intimate nature. Natural history examines the beings and substances of the external world, chiefly in their permanent and unchanging forms; whereas chemistry by studying them in the laws of their alterations, developes and explains their active powers and the particular exertions of those powers.

It is only in consequence of chemical discoveries that that part of natural history which relates to mineral substances has assumed the form of a science. Mineralogy, at a period not very distant from the present, consisted merely of a collection of terms badly arranged, according to certain vague external properties of substances. It is now founded upon a beautiful and methodical classification; and that chiefly in consequence of the comparison of the intimate composition of the bodies it represents with their obvious forms and appearances. The mind of the mineralogist is no longer perplexed by endeavours to discover the loose and varying analogies between the colours, the shapes, and the weights of different substances. By means of the new method of analysis, he is furnished with instruments of investigation immediately applicable, and capable of producing uniform and accurate results.

Even botany and zoology as branches of natural history, though independent of chemistry as to their primary classification, yet are related to it so far as they treat of the constitution and functions of vegetables and animals. How dependent in fact upon chemical processes are the nourishment and growth of organized beings; their various alterations of form, their constant production of new substances, and finally their death and decomposition, in which nature seems to take unto herself those elements and constituent principles, which for a while she had lent to a superior agent as the organs and instruments of the spirit of life!

And in pursuing this view of the subject, medicine and physiology, those sciences which connect the preservation of the health of the human being with the abstruse philosophy of organized nature, will be found to have derived from chemistry most of their practical applications, and many of the analogies which have contributed to give to their scattered facts order and systematic arrangement. The art of preparing those substances which operate powerfully upon animal bodies, and which according to their different modes of exhibition are either efficient remedies or active poisons, is purely chemical. Indeed the want of an acquaintance with scientific principles in the processes of pharmacy has often been productive of dangerous consequences; and the study of the simple and unvarying agencies of dead matter ought surely to precede investigations concerning the mysterious and complicated powers of life. Knowing very little of the laws of his own existence, man has nevertheless derived some useful information from researches concerning the nature of respiration; and the composition and properties of animal organs even in their dead state. And if the connection of chemistry with physiology has given rise to some visionary and seductive theories; yet even this circumstance has been useful to the public mind in exciting it by doubt, and in leading it to new investigations. A reproach, to a certain degree just, has been thrown upon those doctrines known by the name of the chemical physiology; for in the applications of them, speculative philosophers have been guided rather by the analogies of words than of facts. Instead of slowly endeavouring to lift up the veil concealing the wonderful phænomena of living nature; full of ardent imaginations, they have vainly and presumptuously attempted to tear it asunder.

Though astronomy in its sublime views, and its mathematical principles, is far removed from chemistry, yet to this science it is indebted for many of its instruments of experiments. The progress of the astronomer has been in some measure commensurate with that of the chemical artist, who, indeed, by his perfection of the materials used for the astronomical apparatus, has afforded to the investigating philosopher the means of tracing the revolutions of the planets, and of penetrating into space, so as to discover the forms and appearances of the distant parts of the universe.

It would be unnecessary to pursue this subject to a greater extent. Fortunately for man, all the different parts of the human mind are possessed of certain harmonious relations; and it is even difficult to draw the line of distinction between the sciences; for as they have for their objects only dead and living nature, and as they consist of expressions of facts more or less analogous, they must all be possessed of certain ties of connection, and of certain dependencies on each other. The man of true genius who studies science in consequence of its application, – pointing out to himself a definite end, will make use of all the instruments of investigation which are necessary for his purposes; and in the search of discovery, he will rather pursue the plans of his own mind than be limited by the artificial divisions of language. Following extensive views, he will combine together mechanical, chemical, and physiological knowledge, whenever this combination may be essential; in consequence his facts will be connected together by simple and obvious analogies, and in studying one class of phænomena more particularly, he will not neglect its relations to other classes.

But chemistry is not valuable simply in its connections with the sciences, some of which are speculative and remote from our habitual passions and desires; it applies to most of the processes and operations of common life; to those processes on which we depend for the gratification of our wants, and which in consequence of their perfection and extension by means of scientific principles, have become the sources of the most refined enjoyments and delicate pleasures of civilized society.

Agriculture, to which we owe our means of subsistence, is an art intimately connected with chemical science. For though the common soil of the earth will produce vegetable food, yet it can only be made to produce it in the greatest quantity, and of the best quality, in consequence of the adoption of methods of cultivation dependent upon scientific principles. The knowledge of the composition of soils, of the food of vegetables, of the modes in which their products must be treated, so as to become fit for the nourishment of animals, is essential to the cultivation of land; and his exertions are profitable and useful to society, in proportion as he is more of a chemical philosopher. Since, indeed, this truth has been understood, and since the importance of agriculture has been generally felt, the character of the agriculturist has become more dignified and more refined. No longer a mere machine of labour, he has learned to think and to reason. He is aware of his usefulness to his fellow-men; and he is become at once the friend of nature and the friend of society.

The working of metals is a branch of technical chemistry; and it would be a sublime though a difficult task to ascertain the effects of this art upon the progress of the human mind. It has afforded to man the powers of defence against savage animals; it has enabled him to cultivate the ground, to build houses, cities, and ships, and to model much of the surface of the earth after his own imaginations of beauty. It has furnished instruments connected not only with his sublime enjoyments, but likewise with his crimes and his miseries; it has enabled him to oppress and destroy, to conquer and protect.

The arts of bleaching and dyeing, which the habits and fashions of society have made important are purely chemical. To destroy and produce colours, to define the causes of the changes they undergo, and to exhibit the modes in which they may be rendered durable, demand an intimate acquaintance with chemistry. The artist who merely labours with his hands, is obliged to theory for his discovery of the most useful of his practices; and permanent and brilliant ornamental colours which rival the most beautiful tints of nature, are artificially composed from their elements by means of human inventions.

Tanning and the preparation of leather are chemical processes, which, though extremely simple, are of great importance to society. The modes of impregnating skin with the tanning principle of the vegetable kingdom, so as to render it strong and insoluble in water, and the methods of preparing it for this impregnation have been reduced to scientific principles. And if the improvements resulting from new investigations have not been uniformly adopted by manufacturers, it appears to be owing rather to the difficulty occurring in inducing workmen to form new habits, to a want of certain explanations of the minutiæ of the operations, and perhaps in some measure to the common prejudice against novelties, than to any defect in the general theory of the art as laid down by chemical philosophers, and demonstrated by their experiments.

But amongst the chemical arts, few perhaps are more important than those of porcelain and glass making. To them we owe many of those elegant vessels and utensils which have contributed to the health and delicacy of civilized nations. They have furnished instruments of experiments for most of the sciences, and consequently have become the remote causes of some of the discoveries made in those sciences. Without instruments of glass, the gases could never have been discovered, or their combinations ascertained; the minute forms and appearances of natural objects could not have been investigated; and, lastly, the sublime researches of the moderns concerning heat and light would have been wholly lost to us.

This subject might be much enlarged upon; for it is difficult to examine any of our common operations or labours without finding them more or less connected with chemistry. By means of this science man has employed almost all the substances in nature either for the satisfaction of his wants or the gratification of his luxuries. Not contented with what is found upon the surface of the earth, he has penetrated into her bosom, and has even searched the bottom of the ocean for the purpose of allaying the restlessness of his desires, or of extending and increasing his power. He is to a certain extent ruler of all the elements that surround him; and he is capable of using not only common matter according to his will and inclinations, but likewise of subjecting to his purposes the ethereal principles of heat and light.

By his inventions they are elicited from the atmosphere; and under his control they become, according to circumstances, instruments of comfort and enjoyment, or of terror and destruction.

To be able indeed to form an accurate estimate of the effects of chemical philosophy, and the arts and sciences connected with it, upon the human mind, we ought to examine the history of society, to trace the progress of improvement, or more immediately to compare the uncultivated savage with the being of science and civilization.

Man, in what is called a state of nature, is a creature of almost pure sensation. Called into activity only by positive wants, his life is passed either in satisfying the cravings of the common appetites, or in apathy, or in slumber. Living only in moments he calculates but little on futurity. He has no vivid feelings of hope, or thoughts of permanent and powerful action. And unable to discover causes, he is either harassed by superstitious dreams, or quietly and passively submissive to the mercy of nature and the elements. How different is man informed through the beneficence of the Deity, by science and the arts! Knowing his wants, and being able to provide for them, he is capable of anticipating future enjoyments, and of connecting hope with an infinite variety of ideas. He is in some measure independent of chance or accident for his pleasures. Science has given to him an acquaintance with the different relations of the parts of the external world; and more than that, it has bestowed upon him powers which may be almost called creative; which have enabled him to modify and change the beings surrounding him, and by his experiments to interrogate nature with power, not simply as a scholar, passive and seeking only to understand her operations, but rather as a master, active with his own instruments.

But, though improved and instructed by the sciences, we must not rest contented with what has been done; it is necessary that we should likewise do. Our enjoyment of the fruits of the labours of former times should be rather an enjoyment of activity than of indolence; and, instead of passively admiring, we ought to admire with that feeling which leads to emulation.

Science has done much for man, but it is capable of doing

still more; its sources of improvement are not yet exhausted; the benefits that it has conferred ought to excite our hopes of its capability of conferring new benefits; and in considering the progressiveness of our nature, we may reasonably look forward to a state of greater cultivation and happiness than that we at present enjoy.

As a branch of sublime philosophy, chemistry is far from being perfect. It consists of a number of collections of facts connected together by different relations; but as yet it is not furnished with a precise and beautiful theory. Though we can perceive, develope, and even produce, by means of our instruments of experiment, an almost infinite variety of minute phænomena, yet we are incapable of determining the general laws by which they are governed; and in attempting to define them, we are lost in obscure, though sublime imaginations concerning unknown agencies. That they may be discovered, however, there is every reason to believe. And who would not be ambitious of becoming acquainted with the most profound secrets of nature, of ascertaining her hidden operations, and of exhibiting to men that system of knowledge which relates so intimately to their own physical and moral constitution?

The future is composed merely of images of the past, connected in new arrangements by analogy, and modified by the circumstances and feelings of the moment; our hopes are founded upon our experience; and in reasoning concerning what may be accomplished, we ought not only to consider the immense field of research yet unexplored, but likewise to examine the latest operations of the human mind, and to ascertain the degree of its strength and activity.

At the beginning of the seventeenth century very little was known concerning the philosophy of the intimate actions of bodies on each other; and before this time, vague ideas, superstitious notions, and inaccurate practices, were the only effects of the first efforts of the mind to establish the foundations of chemistry. Men either were astonished and deluded by their first inventions so as to become visionaries, and to institute researches after imaginary things, or they employed them as instruments for astonishing and deluding others, influenced by their dearest passions and interests, by ambition, or the love of money. Hence agencies on each other he becomes capable of predicting effects; in modifying these effects he gains activity; and science becomes the parent of the strength and independence of his faculties.

The appearances of the greater number of natural objects are originally delightful to us, and they become still more so, when the laws by which they are governed are known, and when they are associated with ideas of order and utility. The study of nature, therefore, in her various operations must be always more or less connected with the love of the beautiful and sublime; and in consequence of the extent and indefiniteness of the views it presents to us, it is eminently calculated to gratify and keep alive the more powerful passions and ambitions of the soul, which, delighting in the anticipation of enjoyment, is never satisfied with knowledge; and which is as it were nourished by futurity, and rendered strong by hope.

In common society, to men collected in great cities, who are wearied by the constant recurrence of similar artificial pursuits and objects, and who are in need of sources of permanent attachment, the cultivation of chemistry and the physical sciences may be eminently beneficial. For in all their applications they exhibit an almost infinite variety of effects connected with a simplicity of design. They demonstrate that every being is intended for some definite end or purpose. They attach feelings of importance even to inanimate objects; and they furnish to the mind means of obtaining enjoyment unconnected with the labour or misery of others.

To the man of business, or of mechanical employment, the pursuit of experimental research may afford a simple pleasure, unconnected with the gratification of unnecessary wants, and leading to such an expansion of the faculties of the mind as must give to it dignity and power. To the refined and fashionable classes of society it may become a source of consolation and of happiness, in those moments of solitude, when the common habits and passions of the world are considered with indifference. It may destroy diseases of the imagination, owing to too deep a sensibility; and it may attach the affections to objects, permanent, important, and intimately related to the interests of the human species. Even to persons of powerful minds, who are connected with society by literary, political, or moral relations,

arose the dreams of alchemy concerning the philosopher's stone, and the elixir of life. Hence, for a long while the other metals were destroyed or rendered useless by experiments designed to transmute them into gold; and for a long while the means of obtaining earthly immortality were sought for amidst the unhealthy vapours of the laboratory. These views of things have passed away, and a new science has gradually arisen. The dim and uncertain twilight of discovery, which gave to objects false or indefinite appearances, has been succeeded by the steady light of truth, which has shown the external world in its distinct forms, and in its true relations to human powers. The composition of the atmosphere, and the properties of the gases, have been ascertained; the phænomena of electricity have been developed; the lightnings have been taken from the clouds; and lastly, a new influence has been discovered, which has enabled man to produce from combinations of dead matter effects which were formerly occasioned only by animal organs.

The human mind has been lately active and powerful; but there is very little reason for believing that the period of its greatest strength is passed; or even that it has attained its adult state. We find in all its exertions not only the health and vigour, but likewise the awkwardness of youth. It has gained new powers and faculties; but it is as yet incapable of using them with readiness and efficacy. Its desires are beyond its abilities; its different parts and organs are not firmly knit together, and they seldom act in perfect unity.

Unless any great physical changes should take place upon the globe, the permanency of the arts and sciences is rendered certain, in consequence of the diffusion of knowledge by means of the invention of printing; and those words which are the immutable instruments of thought, are become the constant and widely-diffused nourishment of the mind, the preservers of its health and energy. Individuals, in consequence of interested motives or false views, may check for a time the progress of knowledge; moral causes may produce a momentary slumber of the public spirit; the adoption of wild and dangerous theories, by ambitious or deluded men, may throw a temporary opprobrium on literature; but the influence of true philosophy will never be despised; the germs of improvement are sown in minds even where they are not perceived, and sooner or later the spring-time of their growth must arrive.

In reasoning concerning the future hopes of the human species, we may look forward with confidence to a state of society in which the different orders and classes of men will contribute more effectually to the support of each other than they have hitherto done. This state indeed seems to be approaching fast; for in consequence of the multiplication of the means of instruction, the man of science and the manufacturer are daily becoming more nearly assimilated to each other. The artist who formerly affected to despise scientific principles, because he was incapable of perceiving the advantages of them, is now so far enlightened, as to favour the adoption of new processes in his art, whenever they are evidently connected with a diminution of labour. And the increase of projectors, even to too great an extent, demonstrates the enthusiasm of the public mind in its search after improvement. The arts and sciences also are in a high degree cultivated, and patronized by the rich and privileged orders. The guardians of civilization and of refinement, the most powerful and respected part of society, are daily growing more attentive to the realities of life; and, giving up many of their unnecessary enjoyments in consequence of the desire to be useful, are becoming the friends and protectors of the labouring part of the community. The unequal division of property and of labour, the difference of rank and condition amongst mankind, are the sources of power in civilized life, its moving causes, and even its very soul; and in considering and hoping that the human species is capable of becoming more enlightened and more happy, we can only expect that the great whole of society should be ultimately connected together by means of knowledge and the useful arts; that they should act as the children of one great parent, with one determinate end, so that no power may be rendered useless, no exertions thrown away. In this view we do not look to distant ages, or amuse ourselves with brilliant, though delusive dreams concerning the infinite improveability of man, the annihilation of labour, disease, and even death. But we reason by analogy from simple facts. We consider only a state of human progression arising out of its present condition. We look for a time that we may reasonably

expect, for a bright day of which we already behold the dawn.

So far our considerations have been general; so far we have examined chemistry chiefly with regard to its great agency upon the improvement of society, as connected with the increasing perfection of the different branches of natural philosophy and the arts. At present it remains for us only to investigate the effects of the study of this science upon particular minds, and to ascertain its powers of increasing that happiness which arises out of the private feelings and interests of individuals.

The quantity of pleasure which we are capable of experiencing in life appears to be in a great measure connected with the number of independent sources of enjoyment in our possession. And though one great object of desire, connected with great exertions, must more or less employ the most powerful faculties of the soul; yet a certain variety of trains of feeling and of ideas is essential to its health and permanent activity. In considering the relations of the pursuit of chemistry to this part of our nature, we cannot but perceive that the contemplation of the various phænomena in the external world is eminently fitted for giving a permanent and placid enjoyment to the mind. For the relations of these phænomena are perpetually changing; and consequently they are uniformly obliging us to alter our modes of thinking. Also the theories that represent them are only approximations to truth; and they do not fetter the mind by giving to it implicit confidence, but are rather the instruments that it employs for the purpose of gaining new ideas.

A certain portion of physical knowledge is essential to our existence; and all efficient exertion is founded upon an accurate and minute acquaintance with the properties of the different objects surrounding us. The germ of power indeed is native; but it can only be nourished by the forms of the external world. The food of the imagination is supplied by the senses, and all ideas existing in the human mind are representations of parts of nature accurately delineated by memory, or tinged with the glow of passion, and formed into new combinations by fancy. In this view researches concerning the phænomena of corpuscular action may be said to be almost natural to the mind, and to arise out of its instinctive feelings. The objects that are nearest to man are the first to occupy his attention: from considering their

an acquaintance with the science that represents the operations of nature cannot be wholly useless. It must strengthen their habits of minute discrimination; and by obliging them to use a language representing simple facts, may tend to destroy the influence of terms connected only with feeling. The man who has been accustomed to study natural objects philosophically, to be perpetually guarding against the delusions of the fancy, will not readily be induced to multiply words so as to forget things. From observing in the relations of inanimate things fitness and utility, he will reason with deeper reverence concerning beings possessing life; and perceiving in all the phenomena of the universe the designs of a perfect intelligence, he will be averse to the turbulence and passion of hasty innovations, and will uniformly appear as the friend of tranquillity and order.

6 Humphry Davy
The Sacred Stream of Science   c. 1799

from John Davy (ed.), *Collected Works*, vol. I. 1839

Many days have pass'd,
Beloved scene, since last my wet eyes saw
The moonbeams gild thy whitely-foaming waves.
Ambitious then, confiding in her powers,
Spurning the prison, – onward flew my soul,
To mingle with her kindred; – in the breeze
That wafts upon its wings futurity,
To hear the voice of praise; – and not in vain
Have these high hopes existed, – not in vain
The dew of labour has oppress'd my brow,
On which the rose of pleasure never glow'd;
For I have tasted of that sacred stream
Of science, whose delicious water flows
From Nature's bosom. I have felt the warmth,
The gentle influence of congenial souls,
Whose kindred hopes have cheer'd me; who have taught
My irritable spirit how to bear
Injustice; who have given

New plumes of rapture to my soaring wing
When ruffled with the sudden breath of storms,
Here, through the trembling moonshine of the grove,
My earliest lays were wafted by the breeze, –
And here my kindling spirit learn'd to trace
The mystic laws from whose high energy
The moving atoms, in eternal change,
Still rise to animation.
Beloved rocks! thou ocean white with mist,
Once more with joy I view thee;
Once more ye live upon my humid eyes;
Once more ye waken in my throbbing breast
The sympathies of nature. Now I go
Once more to visit my remember'd home,
With heartfelt rapture, – there to mingle tears
Of purest love, – to feel the ecstatic glow
Of warm affection, and again to view
The rosy light that shone upon my youth.

7 John Dalton
On the Constitution of Bodies

from *A New System of Chemical Philosophy* 1808

There are three distinctions in the kinds of bodies, or three
states, which have more especially claimed the attention of
philosophical chemists; namely, those which are marked
by the terms *elastic fluids, liquids,* and *solids.* A very familiar
instance is exhibited to us in water, of a body, which, in certain
circumstances, is capable of assuming all the three states. In
steam we recognise a perfectly elastic fluid, in water, a perfect
liquid, and in ice a complete solid. These observations have
tacitly led to the conclusion which seems universally adopted,
that all bodies of sensible magnitude, whether liquid or solid,
are constituted of a vast number of extremely small particles, or
atoms of matter bound together by a force of attraction, which is
more or less powerful according to circumstances, and which as

it endeavours to prevent their separation, is very properly called in that view, *attraction of cohesion*; but as it collects them from a dispersed state (as from steam into water) it is called, *attraction of aggregation*, or more simply, *affinity*. Whatever names it may go by, they still signify one and the same power. It is not my design to call in question this conclusion, which appears completely satisfactory; but to shew that we have hitherto made no use of it, and that the consequence of the neglect, has been a very obscure view of chemical agency, which is daily growing more so in proportion to the new lights attempted to be thrown upon it.

The opinions I more particularly allude to, are those of Berthollet on the Laws of chemical affinity; such as that chemical agency is proportional to the mass, and that in all chemical unions, there exist insensible gradations in the proportions of the constituent principles. The inconsistence of these opinions, both with reason and observation, cannot, I think, fail to strike every one who takes a proper view of the phenomena.

Whether the ultimate particles of a body, such as water, are all alike, that is, of the same figure, weight, &c. is a question of some importance. From what is known, we have no reason to apprehend a diversity in these particulars: if it does exist in water, it must equally exist in the elements constituting water, namely, hydrogen and oxygen. Now it is scarcely possible to conceive how the aggregates of dissimilar particles should be so uniformly the same. If some of the particles of water were heavier than others, if a parcel of the liquid on any occasion were constituted principally of these heavier particles, it must be supposed to affect the specific gravity of the mass, a circumstance not known. Similar observations may be made on other substances. Therefore we may conclude that *the ultimate particles of all homogeneous bodies are perfectly alike in weight, figure, &c.* In other words, every particle of water is like every other particle of water; every particle of hydrogen is like every other particle of hydrogen, &c.

Besides the force of attraction, which, in one character or another, belongs universally to ponderable bodies, we find another force that is likewise universal, or acts upon all matter which comes under our cognisance, namely, a *force of repulsion*. This is now generally, and I think properly, ascribed to the agency of heat. An atmosphere of this subtile fluid constantly surrounds the atoms of all bodies, and prevents them from being drawn into actual contact. This appears to be satisfactorily proved by the observation, that the bulk of a body may be diminished by abstracting some of its heat: but from what has been stated in the last section, it should seem that enlargement and diminution of bulk depend perhaps more on the arrangement, than on the size of the ultimate particles. Be this as it may, we cannot avoid inferring from the preceding doctrine on heat, and particularly from the section on the natural zero of temperature, that solid bodies, such as ice, contain a large portion, perhaps 4/5 of the heat which the same are found to contain in an elastic state, as steam.

On the Constitution of Pure Elastic Fluids

A pure elastic fluid is one, the constituent particles of which are all alike, or in no way distinguishable. Steam, or aqueous vapour, hydrogenous gas, oxygenous gas, azotic gas, and several others are of this kind. These fluids are constituted of particles possessing very diffuse atmospheres of heat, the capacity or bulk of the atmosphere being often one or two thousand times that of the particle in a liquid or solid form. Whatever therefore may be the shape or figure of the solid atom abstractedly, when surrounded by such an atmosphere it must be globular; but as all the globules in any small given volume are subject to the same pressure, they must be equal in bulk, and will therefore be arranged in horizontal strata, like a pile of shot. A volume of elastic fluid is found to expand whenever the pressure is taken off. This proves that the repulsion exceeds the attraction in such case. The absolute attraction and repulsion of the particles of an elastic fluid, we have no means of estimating, though we can have little doubt but that the contemporary energy of both is great; but the excess of the repulsive energy above the attractive can be estimated, and the law of increase and diminution be ascertained in many cases. Thus in steam, the density may be taken at 1/1728 that of water; consequently each particle of steam has 12 times the diameter that one of water has, and must press upon 144 particles of a watery surface; but the pressure upon each is equivalent to that of a column of water of 34 feet; therefore the excess of the elastic force in a particle of steam is equal to the weight of a column of particles of water, whose height is $34 \times 144 = 4896$ feet. And further, this elastic force decreases as the distance of the particles increases. With respect to steam and other elastic fluids then, the force of cohesion is entirely counteracted by that of repulsion, and the only force which is efficacious to move the particles is the excess of the repulsion above the attraction. Thus, if the attraction be as 10 and the repulsion as 12, the effective repulsive force is as 2. It appears then, that an elastic fluid, so far from requiring any force to separate its particles, it always requires a force to retain them in their situation, or to prevent their separation.

A vessel full of any pure elastic fluid presents to the imagination a picture like one full of small shot. The globules are all of the same size; but the particles of the fluid differ from those of the shot, in that they are constituted of an exceedingly small central atom of solid matter, which is surrounded by an atmosphere of heat, of great density next the atom, but gradually growing rarer according to some power of the distance; whereas those of the shot are globules, uniformly hard throughout, and surrounded with atmospheres of heat of no comparative magnitude.

It is known from experience, that the force of a mass of elastic fluid is directly as the density. Whence is derived the law already mentioned, that the repulsive power of each particle is inversely as its diameter. That is, the *apparent* repulsive power, if we may so speak; for the real or absolute force of repulsion is not known, as long as we remain ignorant of the attractive force. When we expand any volume of elastic fluid, its particles are enlarged, without any material change in the quantity of their heat; it follows then, that the density of the atmospheres of heat must fluctuate with the pressure. Thus, suppose a measure of air were expanded into 8 measures; then, because the diameters of the elastic particles are as the cube root of the space, the distances of the particles would be twice as great as before, and the elastic atmospheres would occupy nearly 8 times the space they did before, with nearly the same quantity of heat: whence we see that these atmospheres must be diminished in density in nearly the same ratio as the mass of elastic fluid.

Some elastic fluids, as hydrogen, oxygen, &c. resist any pressure that has yet been applied to them. In such then it is evident the repulsive force of heat is more than a match for the affinity of the particles, and the external pressure united. To what extent this would continue we cannot say; but from analogy we might apprehend that a still greater pressure would succeed in giving the attractive force the superiority, when the elastic fluid would become a liquid or solid. In other elastic fluids, as steam, upon the application of compression to a certain degree, the elasticity apparently ceases altogether, and the particles collect in small drops of liquid, and fall down. This phenomenon requires explanation.

From the very abrupt transition of steam from a volume of 1700 to that of 1, without any material increase of pressure, one would be inclined to think that the condensation of it was owing to the *breaking* of a spring, rather than to the *curbing* of one. The last however I believe is the fact. The condensation arises from the action of affinity becoming superior to that of heat, by which the latter is overruled, but not weakened. As the approximation of the particles takes place, their repulsion increases from the condensation of the heat, but their affinity increases, it should seem, in a still greater ratio, till the approximation has attained a certain degree, when an equilibrium between those two powers takes place, and the liquid, water, is the result. That this is the true explanation we may learn from what has been stated; wherein it is shewn that the heat given off by the condensation of steam, is in all probability no more than would be given off by any permanently elastic fluid, could it be mechanically condensed into the like volume, and is moreover a small portion of the whole heat previously in combination. As far then as the heat is concerned in this phenomenon, the circumstances would be the same, whether the approximation of the particles was the effect of affinity, or of external mechanical force.

The constitution of a liquid, as water, must then be conceived to be that of an aggregate of particles, exercising in a most powerful manner the forces of attraction and repulsion, but nearly in an equal degree. – Of this more in the sequel.

On the Constitution of Mixed Elastic Fluids

When two or more elastic fluids, whose particles do not unite chemically upon mixture, are brought together, one measure of each, they occupy the space of two measures, but become uniformly diffused through each other, and remain so, whatever may be their specific gravities. The fact admits of no doubt; but explanations have been given in various ways, and none of them completely satisfactory. As the subject is one of primary importance in forming a system of chemical principles, we must enter somewhat more fully into the discussion.

Dr Priestley was one of the earliest to notice the fact: it naturally struck him with surprise, that two elastic fluids, having apparently no affinity for each other, should not arrange themselves according to their specific gravities, as liquids do in like circumstances. Though he found this was not the case after the elastic fluids had once been thoroughly mixed, yet he suggests it as probable, that if two of such fluids could be exposed to each other without agitation, the one specifically heavier would retain its lower situation. He does not so much as hint at such gases being retained in a mixed state by affinity. With regard to his suggestion of two gases being carefully exposed to each other without agitation, I made a series of experiments expressly to determine the question, the results of which are given in the *Manch. Memoirs*, vol. 1, *new series*. From these it seems to be decided that gases always intermingle and gradually diffuse themselves amongst each other, if exposed ever so carefully; but it requires a considerable time to produce a complete intermixture, when the surface of communication is small. This time may vary from a minute, to a day or more, according to the quantity of the gases and the freedom of communication.

When or by whom the notion of mixed gases being held together by chemical affinity was first propagated, I do not know; but it seems probable that the notion of water being dissolved in air, led to that of air being dissolved in air. – Philosophers found that water gradually disappeared or evaporated in air, and increased its elasticity; but steam at a low temperature was known to be unable to overcome the resistance of the air, therefore the agency of affinity was necessary to account for the effect. In the permanently elastic fluids indeed, this agency did not seem to be so much wanted, as they are all able to support themselves; but the diffusion through each other was a circumstance which did not admit of an easy solution any other way. In regard to the solution of water in air, it was natural to suppose, nay, one might almost have been satisfied without the aid of experiment, that the different gases would have had different affinities for water, and that the quantities of water dissolved in like circumstances would have varied according to the nature of the gas. Saussure found however that there was no difference in this respect in the solvent powers of carbonic acid, hydrogen gas, and common air. — It might be expected that at least the *density* of the gas would have some influence upon its solvent powers, that air of half density would take half the water, or the quantity of water would diminish in some proportion to the density; but even here again we are disappointed; whatever be the rarefaction, if water be present, the vapour produces the same elasticity, and the hygrometer finally settles at extreme moisture, as in air of common density in like circumstances. These facts are sufficient to create extreme difficulty in the conception how any principle of affinity or *cohesion* between air and water can be the agent. It is truly astonishing that the same quantity of vapour should cohere to *one* particle of air in a given space, as to *one thousand* in the same space. But the wonder does not cease here; a torricellian vacuum dissolves water; and in this instance we have vapour existing independently of air at all temperatures; what makes it still more remarkable is, the vapour in such vacuum is precisely the same in quantity and force as in the like volume of any kind of air of extreme moisture.

These and other considerations which occurred to me some years ago, were sufficient to make me altogether abandon the hypothesis of air dissolving water, and to explain the phenomena some other way, or to acknowledge they were inexplicable. In the autumn of 1801, I hit upon an idea which seemed to be exactly calculated to explain the phenomena of vapour; it gave rise to a great variety of experiments upon which a series of essays were founded, which were read before the Literary and Philosophical Society of Manchester, and published in the 5th Vol. of their memoirs, 1802.

The distinguishing feature of the new theory was, that the particles of one gas are not elastic or repulsive in regard to the particles of another gas, but only to the particles of their own kind. Consequently when a vessel contains a mixture of two such elastic fluids, each acts independently upon the vessel, with its proper elasticity, just as if the other were absent, whilst no mutual action between the fluids themselves is observed. This position most effectually provided for the existence of vapour of any temperature in the atmosphere, because it could have nothing but its own weight to support; and it was perfectly obvious why neither more nor less vapour could exist in air of extreme moisture, than in a vacuum of the same temperature. So far then the great object of the theory was attained. The law of the condensation of vapour in the atmosphere by cold, was evidently the same on this scheme, as that of the condensation of pure steam, and experience was found to confirm the conclusion at all temperatures. The only thing now wanting to completely establish the independent existence of aqueous vapour in the atmosphere, was the conformity of other liquids to water, in regard to the diffusion and condensation of their vapour. This was found to take place in several liquids, and particularly in sulphuric ether, one which was most likely to shew any anomaly to advantage if it existed, on account of the great change of expansibility in its vapour at ordinary temperatures. The existence of vapour in the atmosphere and its occasional condensation were thus accounted for; but another question remained, how does it rise from a surface of water subject to the pressure of the atmosphere? The consideration of this made no part of the essays above mentioned, it being apprehended, that if the other two points could be obtained by any theory, this third too, would, in the sequel, be accomplished.

On Chemical Synthesis

When any body exists in the elastic state, its ultimate particles are separated from each other to a much greater distance than in any other state; each particle occupies the centre of a comparatively large sphere, and supports its dignity by keeping all the rest, which by their gravity, or otherwise are disposed to encroach up to it, at a respectful distance. When we attempt to conceive the *number* of particles in an atmosphere, it is somewhat like attempting to conceive the number of stars in the universe; we are confounded with the thought. But if we limit the subject, by taking a given volume of any gas, we seem persuaded that, let the divisions be ever so minute, the number of particles must be finite; just as in a given space of the universe, the number of stars and planets cannot be infinite.

Chemical analysis and synthesis go no farther than to the separation of particles one from another, and to their reunion. No new creation or destruction of matter is within the reach of chemical agency. We might as well attempt to introduce a new planet into the solar system, or to annihilate one already in existence, as to create or destroy a particle of hydrogen. All the changes we can produce, consist in separating particles that are in a state of cohesion or combination, and joining those that were previously at a distance.

In all chemical investigations, it has justly been considered an important object to ascertain the relative *weights* of the simples which constitute a compound. But unfortunately the enquiry has terminated here; whereas from the relative weights in the mass, the relative weights of the ultimate particles or atoms of the bodies might have been inferred, from which their number and weight in various other compounds would appear, in order to assist and to guide future investigations, and to correct their results. Now it is one great object of this work, to shew the importance and advantage of ascertaining *the relative weights of the ultimate particles, both of simple and compound bodies, the number of simple elementary particles which constitute one compound particle, and the number of less compound particles which enter into the formation of one more compound particle.*

If there are two bodies, A and B, which are disposed to combine, the following is the order in which the combinations may take place, beginning with the most simple: namely,

1 atom of A + 1 atom of B = 1 atom of C, binary.
1 atom of A + 2 atoms of B = 1 atom of D, ternary.
2 atoms of A + 1 atom of B = 1 atom of E, ternary.
1 atom of A + 3 atoms of B = 1 atom of F, quaternary.
3 atoms of A + 1 atom of B = 1 atom of G, quaternary.
&c. &c.

The following general rules may be adopted as guides in all our investigations respecting chemical synthesis.

1st. When only one combination of two bodies can be obtained, it must be presumed to be a *binary* one, unless some cause appear to the contrary.

2nd. When two combinations are observed, they must be presumed to be a *binary* and a *ternary*.

3rd. When three combinations are obtained, we may expect one to be a *binary*, and the other two *ternary*.

4th. When four combinations are observed, we should expect one *binary*, two *ternary*, and one *quaternary*, &c.

5th. A *binary* compound should always be specifically heavier than the mere mixture of its two ingredients.

6th. A *ternary* compound should be specifically heavier than the mixture of a binary and a simple, which would, if combined, constitute it; &c.

7th. The above rules and observations equally apply, when two bodies, such as C and D, D and E, &c. are combined.

From the application of these rules, to the chemical facts already well ascertained, we deduce the following conclusions; 1st. That water is a binary compound of hydrogen and oxygen, and the relative weights of the two elementary atoms are as 1 : 7, nearly; 2nd. That ammonia is a binary compound of hydrogen and azote, and the relative weights of the two atoms are as 1 : 5, nearly; 3rd. That nitrous gas is a binary compound of azote and oxygen, the atoms of which weigh 5 and 7 respectively; that nitric acid is a binary or ternary compound according as it is derived, and consists of one atom of azote and two of oxygen, together weighing 19; that nitrous oxide is a compound similar to nitric acid, and consists of one atom of oxygen and two of azote, weighing 17; that nitrous acid is a binary compound of nitric acid and nitrous gas, weighing 31; that oxynitric acid is a binary compound of nitric acid and oxygen, weighing 26; 4th. That carbonic oxide is a binary compound, consisting of one atom of charcoal, and one of oxygen, together weighing nearly 12; that carbonic acid is a ternary compound, (but sometimes binary) consisting of one atom of charcoal, and two of oxygen, weighing 19; &c. &c. In all these cases the weights are expressed in atoms of hydrogen, each of which is denoted by unity.

In the sequel, the facts and experiments from which these conclusions are derived, will be detailed; as well as a great variety of others from which are inferred the constitution and weight of the ultimate particles of the principal acids, the alkalis, the earths, the metals, the metallic oxides and sulphurets, the long train of neutral salts, and in short, all the chemical compounds which have hitherto obtained a tolerably good analysis. Several of the conclusions will be supported by original experiments.

From the novelty as well as importance of the ideas suggested in this chapter, it is deemed expedient to give plates, exhibiting the mode of combination in some of the more simple cases. A specimen of these accompanies this first part. The elements or atoms of such bodies as are conceived at present to be simple, are denoted by a small circle, with some distinctive mark; and the combinations consist in the juxta-position of two or more of these; when three or more particles of elastic fluids are combined together in one, it is to be supposed that the particles of the same kind repel each other, and therefore take their stations accordingly.

Enough has been given to shew the method; it will be quite unnecessary to devise characters and combinations of them to exhibit to view in this way all the subjects that come under investigation; nor is it necessary to insist upon the accuracy of all these compounds, both in number and weight; the principle will be entered into more particularly hereafter, as far as respects the individual results. It is not to be understood that all those articles marked as simple substances, are necessarily such by the theory; they are only necessarily of such weights. Soda and Potash, such as they are found in combination with acids, are 28 and 42 respectively in weight; but according to Mr Davy's very important discoveries, they are metallic oxides; the former then must be considered as composed of an atom of metal, 21, and one of oxygen, 7; and the latter, of an atom of metal, 35, and one of oxygen, 7. Or, soda contains 75 per cent metal and 25 oxygen; potash, 83.3 metal and 16.7 oxygen. It is particularly remarkable, that according to the above-mentioned gentleman's essay on the Decomposition and Composition of the fixed alkalies, in the Philosophical Transactions (a copy of which essay he has just favoured me with) it appears that 'the largest quantity of oxygen indicated by these experiments was, for potash 17, and for soda, 26 parts in 100, and the smallest 13 and 19'.

Explanation of the Plate
This plate contains the arbitrary marks or signs chosen to represent the several chemical elements or ultimate particles.

1. Hydrog. its rel. weight 1
2. Azote 5
3. Carbon or charcoal 5
4. Oxygen 7
5. Phosphorous 9
6. Sulphur 13
7. Magnesia 20
8. Lime 23
9. Soda 28
10. Potash 42
11. Strontites 46
12. Barytes 68
13. Iron 38
14. Zinc 56
15. Copper 56
16. Lead 95
17. Silver 100
18. Platina 100
19. Gold 140
20. Mercury 167
21. An atom of water or steam, composed of 1 of oxygen and 1 of hydrogen, retained in physical contact by a strong affinity, and supposed to be surrounded by a common atmosphere of heat; its relative weight = 8
22. An atom of ammonia, composed of 1 of azote and 1 of hydrogen 6
23. An atom of nitrous gas, composed of 1 of azote and 1 of oxygen 12
24. An atom of olefiant gas, composed of 1 of carbone and 1 of hydrogen 6
25. An atom of carbonic oxide composed of 1 of carbone and 1 of oxygen 12

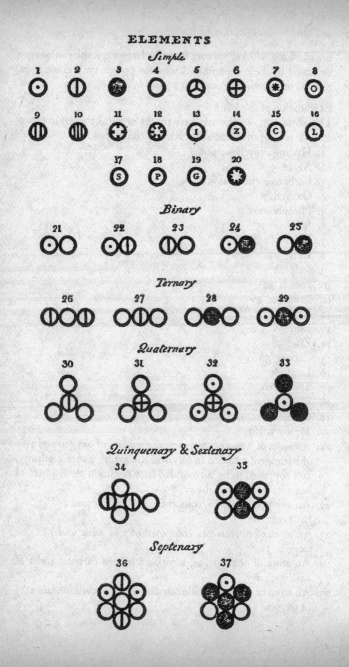

26. An atom of nitrous oxide, 2 azote + 1 oxygen 17
27. An atom of nitric acid, 1 azote + 2 oxygen 19
28. An atom of carbonic acid, 1 carbone + 2 oxygen 19
29. An atom of carburetted hydrogen, 1 carbone + 2 hydrogen 7
30. An atom of oxynitric acid, 1 azote + 3 oxygen 26
31. An atom of sulphuric acid, 1 sulphur + 3 oxygen 34
32. An atom of sulphuretted hydrogen, 1 sulphur + 3 hydrogen 16
33. An atom of alcohol, 3 carbone + 1 hydrogen 16
34. An atom of nitrous acid, 1 nitric acid + 1 nitrous gas 31
35. An atom of acetous acid, 2 carbone + 2 water 26
36. An atom of nitrate of ammonia, 1 nitric acid + 1 ammonia + 1 water 33
37. An atom of sugar, 1 alcohol + 1 carbonic acid 35

8 Charles Babbage
Suggestions for the Advancement of Science in England

from *Reflections on the Decline of Science in England
and on Some of its Causes* 1830

Section 1

*Of the Necessity that Members of the Royal Society should
express their Opinions*

One of the causes which has contributed to the success of the
party, is to be found in the great reluctance with which many of
those whose names added lustre to the Society expressed their
opinions, and the little firmness with which they maintained
their objections. How many times have those whose activity was
additionally stimulated by their interest, proposed measures
which a few words might have checked; whilst the names of
those whose culpable silence thus permitted the project to be
matured, were immediately afterwards cited by their grateful
coadjutors, as having sanctioned that which in their hearts they
knew to be a job.

Even in the few cases which have passed the limits of such

forbearance, when the subject has been debated in the Council, more than one, more than two instances are known, where subsequent circumstances have occurred, which proved, with the most irresistible moral evidence, that members have spoken on one side of the question, and have voted on the contrary.

This reluctance to oppose that which is disapproved, has been too extensively and too fatally prevalent for the interests of the Royal Society. It may partly be attributed to that reserved and retiring disposition, which frequently marks the man of real knowledge, as strongly as an officious interference and flippant manner do the charlatan, or the trader in science. Some portion of it is due to that improper deference which was long paid to every dictum of the President, and much of it to that natural indisposition to take trouble on any point in which a man's own interest is not immediately concerned. It is to be hoped, for the credit of that learned body, that no anticipation of the next feast of St Andrew[1] ever influenced the taciturnity of their disposition.

Section 2
Of Biennial Presidents

The days in which the Royal Society can have much influence in science seem long past; nor does it appear a matter of great importance who conduct its mismanaged affairs. Perpetual presidents have been tried until the Society has become disgusted with dictators. If any reform should be attempted, it might perhaps be deserving consideration whether the practice of several of the younger institutions might not be worthy of imitation, and

---

1. It may be necessary to inform those who are not members of the Royal Society, that this is the day on which those Fellows who choose, meet at Somerset House, to register the names of the Council and Officers the President has been pleased to appoint for the ensuing year; and who afterwards dine together, for the purpose of praising each other over wine, which, until within these few years, was *paid* for out of the *funds* of the Society. This abuse was attacked by an enterprising reformer, and of course defended by the coterie. It was, however, given up as *too bad*. The public may form some idea of the feeling which prevails in the Council, when they are informed that this practice was defended by one of the officers of the Society, on the ground that, if abolished, *the Assistant Secretary would lose his per centage on the tavern bills.*

the office of President be continued only during two sessions. There may be some inconveniences attending this arrangement; but the advantages are conspicuous, both in the Astronomical and Geological Societies. Each President is ambitious of rendering the period of his reign remarkable for some improvement in the Society over which he presides; and the sacrifice of time which is made by the officers of those Societies, would become impossible if it were required to be continued for a much longer period. Another circumstance of considerable importance is, that the personal character of the President is less impressed on the Society; and, supposing any injudicious alterations to be made, it is much less difficult to correct them.

Section 3
Of the Influence of the Colleges of Physicians and Surgeons in the Royal Society.

The honour of belonging to the Royal Society is much sought after by medical men, as contributing to the success of their professional efforts, and two consequences result from it. In the first place, the pages of the *Transactions of the Royal Society* occasionally contain medical papers of very moderate merit; and, in the second, the preponderance of the medical interest introduces into the Society some of the jealousies of that profession. On the other hand, medicine is intimately connected with many sciences, and its professors are usually too much occupied in their practice to exert themselves, except upon great occasions.

Section 4
Of the Influence of the Royal Institution on the Royal Society.

The Royal Institution was founded for the cultivation of the more popular and elementary branches of scientific knowledge, and has risen, partly from the splendid discoveries of Davy, and partly from the decline of the Royal Society, to a more prominent station than it would otherwise have occupied in the science of England. Its general effects in diffusing knowledge among the more educated classes of the metropolis, have been, and continue to be, valuable. Its influence, however, in the government of the Royal Society, is by no means attended with similar advantages, and has justly been viewed with considerable jealousy by many of the Fellows of that body. It may be stated, without disparagement to the Royal Institution, that the scientific qualifications necessary for its officers, however respectable, are not quite of that high order which ought to be required for those of the Royal Society, if the latter body were in a state of vigour.

The Royal Institution interest has always been sufficient to appoint one of the Secretaries of the Royal Society; and at the present moment they have appointed two. In a short time, unless some effectual check is put to this, we shall find them nominating the President and the rest of the officers. It is certainly not consistent with the dignity of the Royal Society thus to allow its offices to be given away as the rewards of services rendered to other institutions. The only effectual way to put a stop to this increasing interest would be, to declare that no manager or officer of the Royal Institution should ever, at the *same time*, hold office in the Royal Society.

The use the Members of the Royal Institution endeavour to make of their power in the Council of the Royal Society is exemplified in the minutes of the Council of 11 March 1830, which may be consulted with advantage by those who doubt.

Section 5
Of the Transactions of the Royal Society.

The *Transactions of the Royal Society*, unlike those of most foreign academies, contain nothing relating to the history of the Society. The volumes contain merely those papers communicated to the Society in the preceding year which the Council have selected for printing, a meteorological register, and a notice of the award of the annual medals, without any list of the Council and officers of the Society, by whom that selection and that award have been made.

Before I proceed to criticise this state of things, I will mention one point on which I am glad to be able to bestow on the Royal Society the highest praise. I refer to the extreme regularity with which the volumes of the *Transactions* are published. The appearance of the half-volumes at intervals of six months, insures for any communication almost immediate publicity; whilst the shortness of the time between its reception and publication, is a guarantee to the public that the whole of the paper was really communicated at the time it bears date. To this may also be added, the rarity of any alterations made previously to the printing, a circumstance which ought to be imitated, as well as admired, by other societies. There may, indeed, be some, perhaps the Geological, in which the task is more difficult, from the nature of the subject. The sooner, however, all societies can reduce themselves to this rule, of rarely allowing any thing but a few verbal corrections to papers that are placed in their hands, the better it will be for their own reputation, and for the interests of science.

It has been, and continues to be, a subject of deep regret, that the first scientific academy in Europe, the Institute of France, should be thus negligent in the regularity of its publications; and it is the more to be regretted, that it should be years in arrear, from the circumstance, that the memoirs admitted into their collection are usually of the highest merit. I know some of their most active members have wished it were otherwise; I would urge them to put a stop to a practice, which, whilst it has no advantages to recommend it, is unjust to those who contribute, and is only calculated to produce conflicting claims, equally injurious to science, and to the reputation of that body, whose negligence may have given rise to them.[2]

One of the inconveniences arising from having no historical portion in the volumes of the Royal Society is, that not only the public, but our own members are almost entirely ignorant of all its affairs. With a means of giving considerable publicity (by the circulation of above 800 copies of the *Transactions*) to whatever we wish to have made known to our members or to the world, will it be credited, that no notice was taken in our volume for 1826, of the foundation of two Royal medals, nor of the conditions under which they were to be distributed.[3] That in 1828,

2. Mr Herschel, speaking of a paper of Fresnel's, observes – 'This memoir was read to the Institute, 7 October 1816; a supplement was received, 19 January 1818; M. Arago's report on it was read, 4 June 1821 : and while every optical philosopher in Europe has been impatiently expecting its appearance for seven years, it lies as yet unpublished, and is only known to us by meagre notices in a periodical journal.' *Mr Herschel's Treasure on Light*, p. 533. – *Encyclopædia Metropolitana*.

3. That the Council refrained from having their first award of those medals thus communicated, is rather creditable to them, and proves that they had a becoming feeling respecting their former errors.

when a new fund, called the donation fund, was established, and through the liberality of Dr Wollaston and Mr Davies Gilbert, it was endowed by them with the respective sums of 2,000l. and 1,000l. 3 per cents; no notice of such fact appears in our *Transactions* for 1829. Other gentlemen have contributed; and if it is desirable to possess such a fund, it is surely of importance to inform the non-attending, which is by far the largest part of the Society, that it exists; and that we are grateful to those by whom it has been founded and augmented. Neither did the *Philosophical Transactions* inform our absent members, that they could purchase the President's Discourses at the trade-price.

The list of the Officers, Council, and Members of the Royal Society is printed annually; yet, who ever saw it bound up with the *Philosophical Transactions*, to which it is intended to be attached? I never met with a single copy of that work so completed, not even the one in our own library. It is extremely desirable that the Society should know the names of their Council; and whilst it would in some measure contribute to prevent the President from placing incompetent persons upon it, it would also afford some check, although perhaps but a slight one, on the distribution of the medals. When I have urged the expediency of the practice, I have been answered by excuses, that the list could not be made up in time for the volume. If this is true, of the first part, they might appear with the second; and even if this were impracticable, the plan of prefixing them to the volume of the succeeding year, would be preferable to that of omitting them altogether. The true reason, however, appeared at last. It was objected to the plan, that by the present arrangement, the porter of the Royal Society took round the list to those members resident in London, and got from some of them a remuneration, in the shape of a Christmas-box;[4] and this would be lost, if the time of printing were changed. Such are the paltry interests to which those of the Royal Society are made to bow.

Another point on which information ought to be given in each volume, is the conditions on which the distribution of the Society's medals are made. It is true that these are, or ought to

4. During the printing of this chapter, a friend, on whom I had called, complained that the porter of the Royal Society had demanded half-a-crown for leaving the list.

be, printed with the Statutes of the Society; but that volume is only in the hands of members, and it is for the credit of the medals themselves, that the laws which regulate their award should be widely known, in order that persons, not members of the Society, might enter into competition for them.

Information relative to the admissions and deaths amongst the Society would also be interesting; a list of the names of those whom the Society had lost, and of those members who had been added to its ranks each year, would find a proper place in the historical pages which ought to be given with each volume of our *Transactions*.

The want of a distinction between the working members of the Society, and those who merely honour it with their patronage, renders many arrangements, which would be advantageous to science, in some cases, injudicious, and in other instances, almost impossible.

Collections of Observations which are from time to time given to the Society, may be of such a nature, that but few of the members are interested in them. In such cases, the expense of printing above 800 copies may reasonably induce the Council to decline printing them altogether; whereas, if they had any means of discrimination for distributing them, they might be quite willing to incur the expense of printing 250. Other cases may occur, in which great advantage would accrue, if the principle were once admitted. Government, the Universities, public bodies, and even individuals might, in some cases, be disposed to present to the Royal Society a limited number of copies of their works, if they knew that they were likely to be placed in the hands of persons who would use them. Fifty or a hundred additional copies might, in some cases, not be objected to on the ground of expense, when seven or eight hundred would be quite out of the question.

Let us suppose twenty copies of a description of some new chemical process to be placed at the disposal of the Royal Society by any public body; it will not surely be contended that they ought all to remain on the Society's shelves. Yet, with our present rules, that would be the case. If, however, the list of the Members of the Society were read over to the Council, and the names of those gentlemen known to be conversant with chemical science were written down; then, if nineteen copies of the work were given to those nineteen persons on this list, who had contributed most to the *Transactions* of the Society, they would in all probability be placed in the fittest hands.

Complete sets of the *Philosophical Transactions* have now become extremely bulky; it might be well worth our consideration, whether the knowledge of the many valuable papers they contain would not be much spread, by publishing the abstracts of them which have been read at the ordinary meetings of the Society. Perhaps two or three volumes octavo, would contain all that has been done in this way during the last century.

Another circumstance, which would contribute much to the order of the proceedings of the Council, would be to have a distinct list made out of all the statutes and orders of the Council relating to each particular subject.

Thus the President, by having at one view before him all that had ever been decreed on the question under consideration, would be much better able to prevent inconsistent resolutions, and to save the time of the Council from being wasted by unnecessary discussions.

Section 6
Order of Merit

Amongst the various proposals for encouraging science, the institution of an order of merit has been suggested. It is somewhat singular, that whilst in most of the other kingdoms [5] of Europe, such orders exist for the purpose of rewarding, by honorary distinctions, the improvers of the arts of life, or successful discoverers in science, nothing of the kind has been established in England.

Our orders of knighthood are favourable only to military distinction. It has been urged, as an argument for such institu-

5. At the great meeting of the Philosophers at Berlin, in 1828, of which an account is given in the Appendix; the respect in which Berzelius, Oersted, Gauss, and Humboldt were held in their respective countries was apparent in the orders bestowed on them by the Sovereigns of Sweden, of Denmark, of Hanover, and of Prussia; and there were present many other philosophers, whose decorations sufficiently attested the respect in which science was held in the countries from which they came.

tions, that they are a cheap mode of rewarding science, whilst, on the other hand, it has been objected, that they would diminish the value of such honorary distinctions by making them common. The latter objection is of little weight, because the numbers who pursue science are few, and, probably, will long continue so. It would also be easily avoided, by restricting the number of the order or of the class, if it were to form a peculiar class of another order. Another objection, however, appears to me to possess far greater weight; and, however strong the disposition of the Government might be (if such an order existed) to fill it properly, I do not believe that, in the present state of public opinion respecting science, it could be done, and, in all probability, it would be filled up through the channels of patronage, and by mere jobbers in science.

Another proposal, of a similar kind, has also been talked of, one which it may appear almost ridiculous to suggest in England, but which would be considered so in no other country. It is, to ennoble some of the greatest scientific benefactors of their country. Not to mention political causes, the ranks of the nobility are constantly recruited from the army, the navy, and the bar; why should not the family of that man, whose name is imperishably connected with the steam-engine, be enrolled amongst the nobility of his country? In utility and profit, not merely to that country, but to the human race, his deeds may proudly claim comparison even with the most splendid of those achieved by classes so rich in glorious recollections. An objection, in most cases fatal to such a course, arises from the impolicy of conferring a title, unless a considerable fortune exists to support it; a circumstance very rarely occurring to the philosopher. It might in some measure be removed, by creating such titles only for life. But here, again, until there existed some knowledge of science amongst the higher classes, and a sound state of public opinion relative to science, the execution of the plan could only be injurious.

Section 7
Of the Union of Scientific Societies

This idea has occurred to several persons, as likely to lead to considerable advantages to science. If the various scientific societies could unite in the occupation of one large building, considerable economy would result from the union. By properly arranging their evenings of meeting, one meeting-room only need be required. The libraries might either be united or arranged in adjoining rooms; and such a system would greatly facilitate the inquiries of scientific persons.

Whether it would be possible to reunite in any way the different societies to the Royal Society, might be a delicate question; but although, on some accounts, desirable, that event is not necessary for the purpose of their having a common residence.

The Medico-Botanical Society might, perhaps, from sympathy, be the first to which the Royal Society would apply; and by a proper interchange of diplomas,[6] the two societies might be inoculated with each other. But even here some tact would be required; the Medico-Botanical is a little particular about the purity of its written documents, and lately attributed blame to one of its officers for some slight tampering with them, a degree of illiberality which the Council of the Royal Society are far from imitating.

The Geological and the Astronomical Societies nourish no feelings of resentment to the parent institution for their early persecution; and though they have no inducement to seek, would scarcely refuse any union which might be generally advantageous to science.

6. A thing well understood by the *initiated*, both at *home* and *abroad*.

M High Art

The most important single assumption on which eighteenth-century artists and writers based their theory of art was that there was a standard of taste to which people could refer in judging works of art. This assumption was far more credible then than now, since there was almost universal agreement that some authors and artists of the past, such as Homer, Phidias, Raphael and Michelangelo, had reached something very close to perfection.

The main issues at stake in most of these extracts concern the strength of tradition – how to live up to the art of the past. Most artists would have agreed with Reynolds that the artist must learn from the past by minutely studying the works of the great masters, by learning the rules embodied in them, by using material actually taken from them, and by emulating their style. The wonderful benefits of this tradition must not be lost, and any attempts to exploit novelty, individual genius or originality should be regarded with the greatest suspicion. This, eventually, is the stand taken by those who supported high art and the grand style derived from Raphael and Michelangelo.

Reaction to such attempts to elevate art in England were varied. The most important objection was to the idea that the mind could not generate pure inspiration of itself, without recourse to sense experience. Other important objections centred on the idea that genius and originality might be considered virtues in themselves, instead of being regarded with suspicion, as Reynolds had suggested.

In making this selection I have not tried to throw light on the stylistic phenomenon of Neo-classicism, but rather to pick out some of the more widely shared beliefs which coloured the way most artists and critics thought about art, while trying to show how these beliefs were beginning to be challenged and modified. It is as revealing to see how Reynolds and Fuseli adapted their Academic views to suit their personal taste, as it is to see how Blake rejected the whole framework, while still seeing himself in the great tradition of art stemming from Michelangelo.

The pictures illustrated in the plates cannot be considered as a commentary to the extracts so much as a self-contained confrontation of different kinds of painting, embodying some of the peculiarities and features mentioned in the extracts.

T.B.

Further Reading

It is suggested that these extracts should be read in conjunction with two other collections of source material for this period, both available in paperback.

* Lorenz Eitner, *Neoclassicism and Romanticism 1750–1850*, vol. 1, Prentice-Hall, 1970, which is particularly valuable for the reprinting of most of Reynolds's *Discourse III*.

Elizabeth Gilmore Holt, *From the Classicists to the Impressionists, A Documentary History of Art and Architecture in the 19th century*, Doubleday, 1966.

* Open University Set Book.

1 The Standard of Taste
(a) Edmund Burke

There is a Standard of Taste; any Sensible Man can
Attain it

from 'On Taste', *A Philosophical Enquiry into the Origin of our
Ideas on the Sublime and the Beautiful*, 2nd edn   1759

But to cut off all pretence for cavilling, I mean by the word Taste
no more than that faculty, or those faculties, of the mind
which are affected with, or which form a judgement of the
works of imagination and the elegant arts. This is, I think, the
most general idea of that word, and what is the least connected
with any particular theory. And my point in this inquiry is to
find whether there are any principles, on which the imagination
is affected, so common to all, so grounded and certain, as to
supply the means of reasoning satisfactorily about them. And
such principles of Taste, I fancy there are; however paradoxical
it may seem to those, who on a superficial view imagine, that
there is so great a diversity of Tastes both in kind and degree,
that nothing can be more indeterminate.

All the natural powers in man, which I know, that are conversant about external objects, are the Senses; the Imagination;
and the Judgement. And first with regard to the senses. We do
and we must suppose, that as the conformation of their organs
are nearly, or altogether the same in all men, so the manner of
perceiving external objects is in all men the same, or with little
difference. We are satisfied that what appears to be light to one
eye, appears light to another; that what seems sweet to one
palate, is sweet to another; that what is dark and bitter to this
man, is likewise dark and bitter to that; and we conclude in the
same manner of great and little, hard and soft, hot and cold,
rough and smooth; and indeed of all the natural qualities and
affections of bodies. If we suffer ourselves to imagine, that their
senses present to different men different images of things, this
sceptical proceeding will make every sort of reasoning on every
subject vain and frivolous, even that sceptical reasoning itself,
which had persuaded us to entertain a doubt concerning the
agreement of our perceptions. But as there will be very little

doubt that bodies present similar images to the whole species, it must necessarily be allowed, that the pleasures and the pains which every object excites in one man, it must raise in all mankind, whilst it operates naturally, simply, and by its proper powers only; for if we deny this, we must imagine, that the same cause operating in the same manner, and on subjects of the same kind, will produce different effects, which would be highly absurd. Let us first consider this point in the sense of Taste, and rather as the faculty in question has taken its name from that sense. All men are agreed to call vinegar sour, honey sweet, and aloes bitter; and as they are all agreed in finding these qualities in those objects, they do not in the least differ concerning their effects with regard to pleasure and pain. They all concur in calling sweetness pleasant, and sourness and bitterness unpleasant. [...]

But should any man be found who declares, that to him tobacco has a taste like sugar, and that he cannot distinguish between milk and vinegar; or that tobacco and vinegar are sweet, milk bitter, and sugar sour, we immediately conclude that the organs of this man are out of order, and that his palate is utterly vitiated. We are as far from conferring with such a person upon Tastes, as from reasoning concerning the relations of quantity with one who should deny that all the parts together were equal to the whole. We do not call a man of this kind wrong in his notions, but absolutely mad. This agreement of mankind is not confined to the Taste solely. The principle of pleasure derived from sight is the same in all. Light is more pleasing than darkness. Summer, when the earth is clad in green, when the heavens are serene and bright, is more agreeable than winter, when every thing makes a different appearance. I never remember that any thing beautiful, whether a man, a beast, a bird, or a plant, was ever shewn, though it were to an hundred people, that they did not all immediately agree that it was beautiful, though some might have thought that it fell short of their expectations or that other things were still finer. I believe no man thinks a goose to be more beautiful than a swan, or imagines that what they call a Friezland hen excels a peacock. It must be observed too, that the pleasures of the sight are not near so complicated, and confused, and altered by unnatural habits and associations, as the pleasures of Taste are; because the pleasures of the sight more commonly acquiesce in themselves; and are not so often altered by considerations which are independent of the sight itself. [...]

The cause of a wrong Taste is a defect of judgement. And this may arise from a natural weakness of understanding (in whatever the strength of that faculty may consist) or, which is much more commonly the case, it may arise from a want of proper and well-directed exercise, which alone can make it strong and ready. Besides that ignorance, inattention, prejudice, rashness, levity, obstinacy, in short, all those vices which pervert the judgement in other matters, prejudice it no less in this its more refined and elegant province. These causes produce different opinions upon every thing which is an object of the understanding without inducing us to suppose, that there are no settled principles of reason. And indeed on the whole one may observe, that there is rather less difference upon matters of Taste among mankind, than upon most of those which depend upon the naked reason; and that men are far better agreed on the excellence of a description in Virgil, than on the truth or falsehood of a theory of Aristotle.

(b) David Hume

Only a few Wise and Sensitive Critics acquire Good Taste; they can overcome Personal and Social Defects

from 'Of the Standard of Taste', *Four Dissertations* 1757

Every work of art has also a certain end or purpose for which it is calculated; and is to be deemed more or less perfect, as it is more or less fitted to attain this end. The object of eloquence is to persuade, of history to instruct, of poetry to please, by means of the passions and the imagination. These ends we must carry constantly in our view when we peruse any performance; and we must be able to judge how far the means employed are adapted to their respective purposes. Besides, every kind of composition, even the most poetical, is nothing but a chain of propositions and reasonings; not always, indeed, the justest and

most exact, but still plausible and specious, however disguised by
the colouring of the imagination. The persons introduced in
tragedy and epic poetry must be represented as reasoning, and
thinking, and concluding, and acting, suitably to their character and circumstances; and without judgement, as well as taste
and invention, a poet can never hope to succeed in so delicate
an undertaking. Not to mention, that the same excellence of
faculties which contributes to the improvement of reason, the
same clearness of conception, the same exactness of distinction,
the same vivacity of apprehension, are essential to the operations
of true taste, and are its infallible concomitants. It seldom or
never happens, that a man of sense, who has experience in any
art, cannot judge of its beauty; and it is no less rare to meet with
a man who has a just taste without a sound understanding.

Thus, though the principles of taste be universal, and nearly,
if not entirely, the same in all men; yet few are qualified to give
judgement on any work of art, or establish their own sentiment
as the standard of beauty. The organs of internal sensation are
seldom so perfect as to allow the general principles their full
play, and produce a feeling correspondent to those principles.
They either labour under some defect, or are vitiated by some
disorder; and by that means excite a sentiment, which may be
pronounced erroneous. When the critic has no delicacy,[1] he
judges without any distinction, and is only affected by the grosser and more palpable qualities of the object: the finer touches
pass unnoticed and disregarded. Where he is not aided by practice, his verdict is attended with confusion and hesitation.
Where no comparison has been employed, the most frivolous
beauties, such as rather merit the name of defects, are the object
of his admiration. Where he lies under the influence of prejudice,
all his natural sentiments are perverted. Where good sense is
wanting, he is not qualified to discern the beauties of design
and reasoning, which are the highest and most excellent. Under
some or other of these imperfections, the generality of men
labour; and hence a true judge in the finer arts is observed, even

---

[1.] Hume defines delicacy as follows: 'Where the organs are so fine as
to allow nothing to escape them, and at the same time so exact as to perceive every ingredient in the composition, this we call delicacy of taste!'
(Of the Standard of Taste).

during the most polished ages, to be so rare a character: strong sense, united to delicate sentiment, improved by practice, perfected by comparison, and cleared of all prejudice, can alone entitle critics to this valuable character; and the joint verdict of such, wherever they are to be found, is the true standard of taste and beauty. But where are such critics to be found? By what marks are they to be known? How distinguish them from pretenders? These questions are embarrassing; and seem to throw us back into the same uncertainty from which, during the course of this Essay, we have endeavoured to extricate ourselves.

But, in reality, the difficulty of finding, even in particulars, the standard of taste, is not so great as it is represented. Though in speculation we may readily avow a certain criterion in science, and deny it in sentiment, the matter is found in practice to be much more hard to ascertain in the former case than in the latter. Theories of abstract philosophy,[2] systems of profound theology, have prevailed during one age: in a successive period these have been universally exploded: the absurdity has been detected: other theories and systems have supplied their place, which again gave place to their successors: and nothing has been experienced more liable to the revolutions of chance and fashion than these pretended decisions of science. The case is not the same with the beauties of eloquence and poetry. Just expressions of passion and nature are sure, after a little time, to gain public applause, which they maintain for ever. Aristotle, and Plato, and Epicurus, and Descartes, may successively yield to each other: but Terence and Virgil maintain an universal, undisputed empire over the minds of men. The abstract philosophy of Cicero has lost its credit: the vehemence of his oratory is still the object of our admiration. [...] But notwithstanding all our endeavours to fix a standard of taste, and reconcile the discordant apprehensions of men, there still remain two sources of variation, which are not sufficient indeed to confound all the boundaries of beauty and deformity, but will often serve to produce a difference in the degrees of our approbation or blame. The one is the different humours of particular men; the other, the particular manners and opinions of our age and country.

[2.] By 'abstract philosophy' we would now mean 'mathematics and science'.

The general principles of taste are uniform in human nature: where men vary in their judgements, some defect or perversion in the faculties may commonly be remarked; proceeding either from prejudice, from want of practice, or want of delicacy: and there is just reason for approving one taste, and condemning another. But where there is such a diversity in the internal frame or external situation as is entirely blameless on both sides, and leaves no room to give one the preference above the other; in that case a certain degree of diversity in judgement is unavoidable, and we seek in vain for a standard, by which we can reconcile the contrary sentiments.

A young man, whose passions are warm, will be more sensibly touched with amorous and tender images, than a man more advanced in years, who takes pleasure in wise, philosophical reflections, concerning the conduct of life, and moderation of the passions. At twenty, Ovid may be the favourite author, Horace at forty, and perhaps Tacitus at fifty. Vainly would we, in such cases, endeavour to enter into the sentiments of others, and divest ourselves of those propensities which are natural to us. We choose our favourite author as we do our friend, from a conformity of humour and disposition. Mirth or passion, sentiment or reflection; whichever of these most predominates in our temper, it gives us a peculiar sympathy with the writer who resembles us.

One person is more pleased with the sublime, another with the tender, a third with raillery. One has a strong sensibility to blemishes, and is extremely studious of correctness; another has a more lively feeling of beauties, and pardons twenty absurdities and defects for one elevated or pathetic stroke. The ear of this man is entirely turned towards conciseness and energy; that man is delighted with a copious, rich, and harmonious expression. Simplicity is affected by one; ornament by another. Comedy, tragedy, satire, odes, have each its partisans, who prefer that particular species of writing to all others. It is plainly an error in a critic, to confine his approbation to one species or style of writing, and condemn all the rest. But it is almost impossible not to feel a predilection for that which suits our particular turn and disposition. Such performances are innocent and unavoidable, and can never reasonably be the object of dispute, because there is no standard by which they can be decided.

For a like reason, we are more pleased, in the course of our reading, with pictures and characters that resemble objects which are found in our own age and country, than with those which describe a different set of customs. [...]

For this reason, comedy is not easily transferred from one age or nation to another. A Frenchman or Englishman is not pleased with *Andria* of Terence, or *Clitia* of Machiavel; where the fine lady, upon whom all the play turns, never once appears to the spectators, but is always kept behind the scenes, suitably to the reserved humour of the ancient Greeks and modern Italians. A man of learning and reflection can make allowance for these peculiarities of manners; but a common audience can never divest themselves so far of their usual ideas and sentiments, as to relish pictures which nowise resemble them.

(c) Sir Joshua Reynolds
Everyone's Mind is pretty well Alike; we must check our Judgements by the Authority of History

from *Discourse VII*   1776³

I shall now say something on that part of *taste*, which, as I have hinted to you before, does not belong so much to the external form of things, but is addressed to the mind, and depends on its original frame, or, to use the expression, the organization of the soul; I mean the imagination and the passions. The principles of these are as invariable as the former, and are to be known and reasoned upon in the same manner, by an appeal to common sense deciding upon the common feelings of mankind. This sense, and these feelings, appear to me of equal authority, and equally conclusive. Now this appeal implies a general uniformity and agreement in the minds of men. It would be else

[3.] The dates given for Reynolds's *Discourses* refer to the original delivery of the lectures at the Royal Academy. The text in each case is the revised one of the 1797 edition.

an idle and vain endeavour to establish rules of art; it would be pursuing a phantom to attempt to move affections with which we were entirely unacquainted. We have no reason to suspect there is a greater difference between our minds than between our forms; of which, though there are no two alike, yet there is a general similitude that goes through the whole race of mankind; and those who have cultivated their taste can distinguish what is beautiful or deformed, or, in other words, what agrees with or deviates from the general idea of nature, in one case, as well as in the other. The internal fabrick of our minds, as well as the external form of our bodies, being nearly uniform; it seems then to follow of course, that as the imagination is incapable of producing any thing originally of itself, and can only vary and combine those ideas with which it is furnished by means of the senses,[4] there will be necessarily an agreement in the imaginations as in the senses of men. There being this agreement, it follows, that in all cases, in our lightest amusements, as well as in our most serious actions and engagements of life, we must regulate our affections of every kind by that of others. The well-disciplined mind acknowledges this authority, and submits its own opinion to the publick voice. It is from knowing what are the general feelings and passions of mankind, that we acquire a true idea of what imagination is; though it appears as if we had nothing to do but to consult our own particular sensations, and these were sufficient to ensure us from all error and mistake. [...]

He therefore who is acquainted with the works which have pleased different ages and different countries, and has formed his opinion on them, has more materials, and more means of knowing what is analogous to the mind of man, than he who is conversant only with the works of his own age or country. What has pleased, and continues to please, is likely to please again: hence are derived the rules of art, and on this immoveable foundation they must ever stand. [...]

We will take it for granted, that reason is something invari-

[4.] This is a key eighteenth-century concept, an axiom in the British empiricist tradition of Locke, Hume and Berkeley. Blake was one of the people who bitterly attacked it.

able[5] and fixed in the nature of things; and without endeavouring to go back to an account of first principles, which for ever will elude our search, we will conclude, that whatever goes under the name of taste, which we can fairly bring under the dominion of reason, must be considered as equally exempt from change. [...] The arts would lie open for ever to caprice and casualty, if those who are to judge of their excellencies had no settled principles by which they are to regulate their decisions, and the merit or defect of performances were to be determined by unguided fancy.[6]

(d) Sir Joshua Reynolds
Reasoned Judgement must not be Over-Simplified

from *Discourse XIII* 1786

All theories which attempt to direct or to control the Art, upon any principles falsely called rational, which we form to ourselves upon a supposition of what ought in reason to be the end or means of Art, independent of the known first effect produced by objects on the imagination, must be false and delusive. For though it may appear bold to say it, the imagination[7] is here the residence of truth. If the imagination be affected, the reasoning is erroneous, because the end is not obtained; the effect itself being the test, and the only test, of the truth and efficacy of the means.

There is in the commerce of life, as in Art, a sagacity which is far from being contradictory to right reason, and is superior to any occasional exercise of that faculty, which supersedes it;

[5.] Blake attacks this basic eighteenth-century premiss: 'Reason, or A Ratio of All we have Known, is not the Same it shall be when we know More; he therefore takes a Falsehood for granted to set out with.' He inserted marginal comments (like this one) in the first eight of Reynolds's *Discourses* about 1808. His copy of the *Discourses* is in the British Museum.

[6.] Blake commented: 'He may as well say that if Man does not lay down settled Principles, The Sun will not rise in a Morning' (annotations to Reynolds's *Discourses*).

[7.] But Reynolds does not mean by 'imagination' what one might suppose (see p. 441).

and does not wait for the slow progress of deduction, but goes at once, by what appears a kind of intuition, to the conclusion. A man endowed with this faculty, feels and acknowledges the truth though it is not always in his power, perhaps, to give a reason for it; because he cannot recollect and bring before him all the materials that gave birth to his opinion; for very many and very intricate considerations may unite to form the principle, even of small and minute parts, involved in, or dependent on, a great system of things: though these in process of time are forgotten, the right impression still remains fixed in his mind.

This impression is the result of the accumulated experience of our whole life, and has been collected, we do not always know how, or when. But this mass of collective observation, however acquired, ought to prevail over that reason, which however powerfully exerted on any particular occasion, will probably comprehend but a partial view of the subject; and our conduct in life as well as in the Arts, is, or ought to be, generally governed by this habitual reason: it is our happiness that we are enabled to draw on such funds. If we were obliged to enter into a theoretical deliberation on every occasion, before we act, life would be at a stand, and Art would be impracticable.

2 The 'Grand Style' of Painting
(a) Sir Joshua Reynolds
The 'Grand Style' and its Subject Matter[8]

from *Discourse IV* 1771

The value and rank of every art is in proportion to the mental labour employed in it, or the mental pleasure produced by it. As this principle is observed or neglected, our profession becomes either a liberal art, or a mechanical trade. In the hands of one man it makes the highest pretensions, as it is addressed to the noblest faculties: in those of another it is reduced to a mere matter of ornament; and the painter has but the humble province of furnishing our apartments with elegance.

[8.] Reynolds defined his concept of the 'grand style' at length in his third *Discourse*, largely reprinted in Lorenz Eitner, *Neoclassicism and Romanticism* (Prentice-Hall, 1970).

This exertion of mind, which is the only circumstance that truly ennobles our Art, makes the great distinction between the Roman and Venetian schools.[9] I have formerly observed, that perfect form is produced by leaving out particularities, and retaining only general ideas: I shall now endeavour to shew that this principle, which I have proved to be metaphysically just, extends itself to every part of the Art; that it gives what is called the *grand style*, to Invention, to Composition, to Expression, and even to Colouring and Drapery.

Invention in Painting does not imply the invention of the subject; for that is commonly supplied by the Poet or Historian. With respect to the choice, no subject can be proper that is not generally interesting. It ought to be either some eminent instance of heroick action, or heroick suffering. There must be something either in the action, or in the object, in which men are universally concerned, and which powerfully strikes upon the publick sympathy.

Strictly speaking, indeed, no subject can be of universal, hardly can it be of general, concern; but there are events and characters so popularly known in those countries where our Art is in request, that they may be considered as sufficiently general for all our purposes. Such are the great events of Greek and Roman fable and history,[10] which early education, and the usual course of reading, have made familiar and interesting to all Europe, without being degraded by the vulgarism of ordinary life in any country. Such too are the capital subjects of scripture history, which, besides their general notoriety, become venerable by their connection with our religion.

As it is required that the subject selected should be a general one, it is no less necessary that it should be kept unembarrassed with whatever may any way serve to divide the attention of the

[9.] In the 1771 edition, Reynolds included the following passage after 'Venetian schools': 'and gives the superiority to the painter of History over all others of our profession. No part of his work is produced but by an effort of the mind; there is no object which he can set before him as a perfect model; there is none which he can venture minutely to imitate, and to transfer with all its beauties and blemishes into his great design.'

[10.] The most respected source was Homer (see Plates 8, 9, 14, 20 and 21), but Shakespeare, Milton and Dante were increasingly admired, for their powerful 'sublimity' (see Plates 5 and 11).

spectator. Whenever a story is related, every man forms a picture in his mind of the action and expression of the persons employed. The power of representing this mental picture on canvass is what we call Invention in a Painter. And as in the conception of this ideal picture, the mind does not enter into the minute peculiarities of the dress, furniture, or scene of action; so when the Painter comes to represent it, he contrives those little necessary concomitant circumstances in such a manner, that they shall strike the spectator no more than they did himself in his first conception of the story.

(b) Sir Joshua Reynolds
The Genius of the Great Individualist can excuse some Irregularity

from *Discourse V*   1772

Such is the great style, as it appears in those who possessed it at its height: in this, search after novelty, in conception or in treating the subject, has no place.

But there is another style, which, though inferior to the former, has still great merit, because it shews that those who cultivated it were men of lively and vigorous imagination. This, which may be called the original or characteristical style, being less referred to any true archetype existing either in general or particular nature, must be supported by the painter's consistency in the principles which he has assumed, and in the union and harmony of the whole design. [...]

The faults or defects of some men seem to become them, when they appear to be the natural growth, and of a piece with the rest of their character. A faithful picture of a mind, though it be not of the most elevated kind, though it be irregular, wild, and incorrect, yet if it be marked with that spirit and firmness which characterises works of genius, will claim attention,[11] and be more striking than a combination of excellencies that do not seem to unite well together; or we may say, than a work that possesses even all excellencies, but those in a moderate degree.

[11.] Among the artists cited by Reynolds as having their qualities, is Rubens (see Plate 6).

(c) James Barry

British Art has been devoted to Trivial Subjects; History
Painting on a Grand Scale is what is Needed

from *An Enquiry into the Real and the Imaginary Obstructions
to the Acquisition of the Arts in England* 1774

Being attached to little things, we come naturally to admire and
over-rate the little men who succeed in them; one admirer
builds upon the admiration of another, until this mole-hill grows
up into a mountain and bounds our prospect. [...]

The study of history, large and of a noble character, is what
should have led the way in all things. [...] The excellence and
power of the art would never have been felt, and the Vatican
would have wanted its fame, if Michael Angelo and Raffael
had painted only pigmy figures, and upon scraps of canvass:
but their employers were men of too great minds to require
such an absurdity, such a maiming of art. [...] History painting
and sculpture should be the main views of every people desirous
of gaining honour by the arts. These are the tests by which the
national character will be tried in after ages, and by which it has
been, and is now,[12] tried by the natives of other countries.

(d) William Blake

How Blake saw his Art: the 'Grand Style' of Florence
and Rome versus the 'Blotting and Blurring' of the
Venetian and Flemish

from 'A descriptive Catalogue of Blake's Exhibition, at No. 28,
corner of Broad-street Golden Square. Printed 1809'[13]

THE grand style of Art restored; in FRESCO, or Water-colour
Painting, and England protected from the too just imputation

[12.] Barry is referring to suggestions made by Winckelmann and the
Abbé du Bois, that the cold northern climate, physical and intellectual, was
unpropitious for the development of artistic genius.

[13.] The Exhibition contained nine tempera paintings and seven draw-
ings. The tempera seems to have decayed badly so that it is difficult to judge
their original effect. At the time, the exhibition was a complete failure,
attracting almost no attention.

of being the Seat and Protectress of bad (that is blotting and blurring) Art. In this Exhibition will be seen real Art, as it was left us by *Raphael* and *Albert Durer*, *Michael Angelo*, and *Julio Romano*; stripped from the Ignorances of *Rubens* and *Rembrandt*, *Titian* and *Corregio*.

(e) James Barry
The Ideal of Art

from 'On Design' (Second lecture at the Royal Academy)   1783

Thus, young gentlemen, I have to the best of my power, endeavoured to direct your attention to the important essentials of that comprehensive design, upon which the becoming dignity of your art does absolutely depend. It is in the Design, and in that only, that men can recognize those operations of imagination and judgement, which constitute the *ideal of art*, and shew its high lineage, as the offspring of philosophy, and the sister of poetry.

This ideal of design has for its object *general* and *perfect*, and not individual, imperfect nature. It is extended to all the parts of the art, to ideal forms respecting beauty and propriety of character, to the ideal in the composition of the story, fable, or subject, purged of all dead, uninteresting, impertinent circumstances, to the ideal in colouring and the conduct of light and shade, respecting the happy choice and adaptation of peculiar tones or tints, the degrees of strength, tenderness, union or variety seizing upon and uniting all those transitory though happy accidental effects and graces, which may be extended to the most unimportant things, even to the folds of drapery.

(f) James Barry
The Scope of Art and Poetry is 'To raise Ideas in the Mind'

from *An Enquiry into the Real and the Imaginary Obstructions to the Acquisition of the Arts in England* 1774

All writers of character who have employed their thoughts upon the productions of genius, are universally agreed, that the essence and ground-work of poetry and painting is in every respect the same; and Aristotle's Poetics and Horace's Epistle to the Pisos, will be found just as essentially applicable to painting as to poetry. There is necessary in both, the same glowing enthusiastic fancy to go in search of materials, and the same cool judgement is necessary in combining them. They collect from the same objects, and the same result or abstract picture must be formed in the mind of each, as they are equally to be addressed to the same passions in the hearer or spectator. The scope and design of both is to raise ideas in the mind, of such great virtues and great actions, as are best calculated to move, to delight, and to instruct. In short, according to Simonides's excellent proverb, 'painting is silent poetry, and poetry is a speaking picture'.

(g) Henry Fuseli
The Hierarchy of Subject Matter

from *Lecture IV* 1805

To begin with advantageous subjects [immediately above the scenes of vulgar life, of animals, and common landscape], the simple representation of actions purely human appears to be as nearly related to the art as to ourselves; their effect is immediate; they want no explanation; from them, therefore, we begin our scale. The next step leads us to pure historic subjects, singly or in a series; beyond these the delineation of character, or, properly speaking, the drama, invites; immediately above this we place the epic with its mythologic, allegoric and symbolic branches.

(h) Henry Fuseli
Why the Antique provides a Necessary Example for Artists

from *Lecture VII* 1810

What was it that the Academy intended by making the Antique the basis of your studies? What, but to lead you to the sources of Form; to initiate you in the true elements of human essence; to enable you to judge at your transition from the marble to life what was substance and possession to the individual, and what excrescence and want, what homogenous, what discordant, what deformity, what beauty. It intended, by making you acquainted with a variety of figures, to qualify you for classing them according to character and function; ... in short, to supply by its stores, as far as time and circumstances permitted, what the *public* granted to the artists of Greece.

(j) Sir Joshua Reynolds
Apology for Portrait Painters

from *Discourse IV* 1771

It may be asserted, that the great style is always more or less contaminated by any meaner mixture. But it happens in a few instances, that the lower may be improved by borrowing from the grand. Thus if a portrait-painter [14] is desirous to raise and improve his subject, he has no other means than by approaching it to a general idea. He leaves out all the minute breaks and peculiarities in the face, and changes the dress from a temporary fashion to one more permanent, which has annexed to it no ideas of meanness from its being familiar to us. But if an exact resemblance of an individual be considered as the sole object to be aimed at, the portrait-painter will be apt to lose more than he gains by the acquired dignity taken from general nature. It is

[14.] Blake comments, rather harshly: 'Folly! Of what consequence is it to the Arts what a Portrait Painter does?' (annotations to Reynolds's *Discourses*).

very difficult to ennoble the character of a countenance but at the expense of the likeness, which is what is most generally required by such as sit to the painter.[15]

(k) Allan Cunningham
A Critical Summary of the Campaign to revive High Art

from the Introduction to *Pilkington's Dictionary of Painters* 1840

Reynolds lectured, Barry stormed, West toiled, and Fuseli drew supernatural, and Hilton natural shapes, in support and praise of the grand style; but all would not do. The heart of the country was not with them: more familiar subjects, and, we must add, less lofty, were demanded – subjects in which the beau-ideal, like light on a landscape, dawned rather than shone, and which more closely addressed our natural passions and sympathies. Our painters have yielded at last to the taste which they could not control: pictures of a moderate dimension are now numerous, which embody bright passages from our poets; incidents from domestic life [see Plate 17]; daring acts by sea and land [see Plate 12]; landscapes, on which even the cold moist light of our isle loves to shine; and the likenesses of men whose talents are an honour to their country. In all these, reality seems to be more desired than the poetic; and in scenes from either history or fiction, the actors are expected to appear in the garb and look which were theirs in life. This forbids Art, in high works, to paint the mind rather than the form and outer shell of things; and excludes the grand poetic principle, on which the sublimities of Greece and Italy are founded – that the noblest mind is lodged in the most perfect body.

[15.] Barry, in a footnote to his Sixth Lecture: 'His [Reynolds's] portrait of Mrs Siddons (Plate 10) is, both for the ideal and executive, the finest picture of the kind, perhaps, in the world, indeed it is something more than a portrait. . . .'

3 Genius and Tradition
(a) Sir Joshua Reynolds
Genius is less Important than being Conversant with the
Invention of Others

from *Discourse VI* 1774

Genius is supposed to be a power of producing excellencies,
which are out of the reach of the rules of art; a power which no
precepts can teach, and which no industry can acquire. [...]

When the arts were in their infancy, the power of merely
drawing the likeness of any object, was considered as one of its
greatest efforts. The common people, ignorant of the principles
of art, talk the same language, even to this day. But when it was
found that every man could be taught to do this, and a great
deal more, merely by the observance of certain precepts; the
name of Genius then shifted its application, and was given
only to him who added the peculiar character of the object he
represented; to him who had invention, expression, grace, or
dignity; in short, those qualities, or excellencies, the power of
producing which, could not *then* be taught by any known and
promulgated rules. [...]

We are very sure that the beauty of form, the expression of
the passions, the art of composition, even the power of giving a
general air of grandeur to a work, is at present very much under
the dominion of rules. These excellencies were, heretofore,
considered merely as the effects of genius; and justly, if genius
is not taken for inspiration, but as the effect of close observation and experience.

He who first made any of these observations, and digested
them, so as to form an invariable principle for himself to work
by, had that merit, but probably no one went very far at once;
and generally, the first who gave the hint, did not know how to
pursue it steadily, and methodically; at least not in the beginning. He himself worked on it, and improved it; others worked
more, and improved further; until the secret was discovered,
and the practice made as general, as refined practice can be
made. How many more principles may be fixed and ascertained,
we cannot tell; but as criticism is likely to go hand in hand with

the art which is its subject, we may venture to say, that as that art shall advance, its powers will be still more and more fixed by rules.[16] But by whatever strides criticism may gain ground, we need be under no apprehension, that invention will ever be annihilated, or subdued; or intellectual energy be brought entirely within the restraint of written law. Genius will still have room enough to expatiate, and keep always at the same distance from narrow comprehension and mechanical performance.

What we now call Genius begins, not where rules abstractedly taken, end; but where known vulgar and trite rules have no longer any place. It must of necessity be, that even works of Genius, like every other effect, as they must have their cause, must likewise have their rules. [...]

The mind is but a barren soil; a soil which is soon exhausted, and will produce no crop, or only one, unless it be continually fertilized and enriched with foreign matter.[17] [...] Invention is one of the great marks of genius; but if we consult experience, we shall find, that it is by being conversant with the inventions of others, that we learn to invent; as by reading the thoughts of others we learn to think. [...] The greatest natural genius cannot subsist on its own stock: he who resolves never to ransack any mind but his own, will be soon reduced, from mere barrenness, to the poorest of all imitations; he will be obliged to imitate himself, and to repeat what he has before often repeated. When we know the subject designed by such men, it will never be difficult to guess what kind of work is to be produced.

It is vain for painters or poets to endeavour to invent without materials on which the mind may work, and from which in-

[16.] Blake attacks Reynolds's progressive view of art history: 'If Art was Progressive We should have had Mich. Angelos & Rafaels to Succeed & to improve upon each other. But it is not so. Genius dies with its Possessor & comes not again till Another is Born with it' (annotations to Reynolds's *Discourses*).

[17.] This is a crucial statement, and one with considerable reason behind it, but for Blake it seems almost blasphemous: 'The mind that could have produced this Sentence must have been a Pitiful, a Pitiable Imbecility. I always thought the Human Mind was the most Prolific of All Things & Inexhaustible. I certainly do Thank God that I am not like Reynolds' (annotations to Reynolds's *Discourses*).

vention must originate. Nothing can come of nothing.[18] [...] To find excellencies, however dispersed, to discover beauties, however concealed by the multitude of defects with which they are surrounded, can be the work only of him, who having a mind always alive to his art, has extended his views to all ages and to all schools; and has acquired from that comprehensive mass which he has thus gathered to himself, a well-digested and perfect idea of his art, to which every thing is referred. Like a sovereign judge and arbiter of art, he is possessed of that presiding power which separates and attracts every excellence from every school, selects both from what is great, and what is little; brings home knowledge from the East and from the West; making the universe tributary towards furnishing his mind and enriching his works with originality, and variety of inventions.

(b) Sir Joshua Reynolds
Imitation as Distinct from Copying

from *Discourse II*   1769

I consider general copying as a delusive kind of industry; the Student satisfies himself with the appearance of doing something; he falls into the dangerous habit of imitating without selecting, and of labouring without any determinate object; as it requires no effort of the mind, he sleeps over his work; and those powers of invention and composition which ought particularly to be called out, and put in action, lie torpid, and lose their energy for want of exercise. [...]

But as mere enthusiasm[19] will carry you but a little way, let me recommend a practice that may be equivalent to and will

[18.] Again, Blake attacks this suggestion that ideas must spring from experience: 'Is the Mind Nothing?' (annotations to Reynolds's *Discourses*).
[19.] Blake sees this whole passage as another example of Reynolds's adherence to the empiricist tradition of Bacon, Newton and Locke: 'Meer Enthusiasm is the All in All! Bacon's Philosophy has Ruin'd England. Bacon is only Epicurus over again.' And in pencil he wrote: 'Damn the Fool' (annotations to Reynolds's *Discourses*).

perhaps more efficaciously contribute to your advancement, than even the verbal corrections of those masters themselves, could they be obtained. What I would propose is, that you should enter into a kind of competition, by painting a similar subject, and making a companion to any picture that you consider as a model. After you have finished your work, place it near the model, and compare them carefully together. You will then not only see, but feel your own deficiencies more sensibly than by precepts, or any other means of instruction. The true principles of painting will mingle with your thoughts. Ideas thus fixed by sensible objects, will be certain and definitive; and sinking deep into the mind, will not only be more just, but more lasting than those presented to you by precepts only; which will always be fleeing, variable, and undetermined.

(c) Sir Joshua Reynolds

Conclusions on how a Student learns from the Masters

from *Discourse VI* 1774

Study therefore the great works of the great masters, for ever. Study as nearly as you can, in the order, in the manner, and on the principles on which they studied. Study nature attentively, but always with those masters in your company; consider them as models which you are to imitate, and at the same time as rivals with whom you are to contend.

(d) Sir Joshua Reynolds

The Aim of the Student, in learning the Principle of Art, is to learn to see Nature as the Old Masters did

from *Discourse XII* 1784

The art of seeing Nature, or in other words, the art of using Models, is in reality the great object, the point to which all our studies are directed. As for the power of being able to do tolerably well, from practice alone, let it be valued according to its worth. But I do not see in what manner it can be sufficient for the production of correct, excellent, and finished Pictures. Works deserving this character never were produced, nor ever will arise, from memory alone; and I will venture to say, that an Artist who brings to his work a mind tolerably furnished with the general principles of Art, and a taste formed upon the works of good Artists, in short who knows in what excellence consists, will with the assistance of Models which we will likewise suppose he has learnt the art of using, be an over-match for the greatest Painter that ever lived who should be debarred such advantages.

(e) Sir Joshua Reynolds

Art, like Poetry, seeks to stimulate the Mind, not copy Nature in all its Details

from *Discourse XIII*   1786

So far is Art from being derived from, or having any immediate intercourse with, particular nature as its model, that there are many Arts that set out with a professed deviation from it. This is certainly not so exactly true in regard to Painting and Sculpture. Our elements are laid in gross common nature, an exact imitation of what is before us: but when we advance to the higher state, we consider this power of imitation, though first in the order of acquisition, as by no means the highest in the scale of perfection.

Poetry addresses itself to the same faculties and the same dispositions as Painting, though by different means. The object of both is to accommodate itself to all the natural propensities and inclinations of the mind. The very existence of Poetry depends on the licence it assumes of deviating from actual nature, in order to gratify natural propensities by other means, which are found by experience full as capable of affording such gratification. It sets out with a language in the highest degree artificial, a construction of measured words, such as never is, nor ever was used by man. Let this measure be what it may, whether hexameter or any other metre used in Latin or Greek – or Rhyme, or blank Verse varied with pauses and accents, in modern languages – they are all equally removed from nature, and equally a violation of common speech. When this artificial mode has been established as the vehicle of sentiment, there is another principle in the human mind, to which the work must be referred, which still renders it more artificial, carries it still further from common nature, and deviates only to render it more perfect. That principle is the sense of congruity, coherence, and consistency, which is a real existing principle in man; and it must be gratified. Therefore having once adopted a style and a measure not found in common discourse, it is required that the sentiments also should be in the same proportion elevated above common nature, from the necessity of there being an agreement of the parts among themselves, that one uniform whole may be produced.

(f) Sir Joshua Reynolds

If Students are to learn from the Art of the Past,
a National Collection of Art must be freely Available

from *Discourse I* 1769

The principal advantage of an Academy is, that, beside furnishing able men to direct the Student, it will be a repository for the great examples of the Art. These are the materials on which Genius is to work, and without which the strongest intellect may be fruitlessly or deviously employed. By studying these authentick models, that idea of excellence which is the result of the accumulated experience of past ages, may be at once acquired; and the tardy and obstructed progress of our predecessors may teach us a shorter and easier way. The Student receives, at one glance, the principles which many Artists have spent their whole lives in ascertaining; and, satisfied with their effect, is spared the painful investigation by which they came to be known and fixed. How many men of great natural abilities have been lost to this nation, for want of these advantages! They never had an opportunity of seeing those masterly efforts of genius, which at once kindle the whole soul, and force it into sudden and irresistible approbation.[20]

(g) William Blake

Blake's Summary of his Views on Reynolds's Attitude to Imitation

from annotations to Reynolds's *Discourses* c. 1808

After having been a Fool, a Student is to amass a Stock of Ideas, &, knowing himself to be a Fool, he is to assume the Right to put other Men's ideas into his Foolery.

(h) Henry Fuseli

Mediocrity in many Jobs has a Social Purpose; there is no Place for it in Art

from *Lecture X* 1825

Neither Poetry nor Painting spring from the necessities of society, or furnish necessaries to life; offsprings of fancy, leisure and lofty contemplation, organs of religion and government, ornaments of society, and too often mere charms of the senses and instruments of luxury, they derive their excellence from novelty, degree and polish. What none indispensably want, all may wish for, but few only are able to procure, acquires its value from some exclusive quality, founded on intrinsic, or some conventional merit, and that, or an equal substitute, mediocrity cannot reach : hence by suffering it to invade the province of genius and talent, we rob the plough, the shop, the loom, the school, perhaps the desk and pulpit of a thousand useful hands. A good mechanic, a trusty labourer, an honest tradesman, are beings more important, of greater use to society, and better sup-

[20.] It is clearly important for Reynolds's philosophy that students and artists should have examples of 'these authentick models' for imitation and self-improvement. Not until 1824, however, was a collection of art made publicly available, with the establishment of the National Gallery.

porters of the state, than any artist or poet of mediocrity. When I therefore say that it is the duty of the Academy to deter rather than to delude, I am not afraid of having advanced a paradox hostile to the progress of real Art. The capacities that time will disclose, genius and talents, cannot be deterred by the exposition of difficulties, and it is the interest of society that all else should.

(j) Jean Auguste Dominique Ingres
The Greeks have made Progress or Novelty Irrelevant

from *Pensées et Ecrits du Peintre* 1947.[21] Translated by Tim Benton

I'm sick of people coming up with this ridiculous maxim: 'We must have novelty, we must keep up with the times, everything has changed and is changing.' All that's pure sophistry. Does nature change, do light and air change, have the passions of man's heart changed since Homer's day? 'We must keep up with the times.' But what if the times are mistaken? Am I to do wrong just because my neighbour does? Just because you hold virtue and beauty in contempt, am I to spurn them too, do I have to follow your lead?

Once upon a time there was on this earth a little corner of land, called Greece, where under a matchless sky, among a people uniquely gifted with an intellectual grasp of things, the arts and literature came to reflect the natural world like a second sun, for all peoples and generations to see.

Homer was the first to concentrate refined, natural beauty into his poetry, just as God created life by organizing it out of chaos. He [Homer] has taught humanity once and for all, he has demonstrated the principles of beauty and given examples.

[21.] A posthumous collection of essays attributed to him.

(k) Eugène Delacroix

Real Genius will Always find something New to Say

from *Journal* 1893. Translated by Tim Benton

Yesterday, Friday 14 May 1824

You can add one more to the list of those souls who have seen
nature in their own particular way. What all these great minds
painted was new to them [then] and you will paint them new
once again. When they painted, it was their souls which they
depicted, and now it's your soul which clamours for its turn.
And why should one frustrate its call? Is its claim more ridiculous than the appeal for sleep that your limbs make when
they're tired, along with your whole body? The world has mis-
used you, but it will treat everyone else as badly. Those very
people who claim that all has been done, all has been discovered,
they too will greet you as a new force and will then shut the
door behind you, and once again they'll say, 'It's all been said
before.' Just as men who are enfeebled by old age think that it is
nature which is rotting away, so it is with men of a crude mentality, who have absolutely nothing to say about what has been
said before; they think that nature only allowed one set of
people, and only at the beginning of time at that, to have anything new and startling to say. In the days of those immortal
souls, what needed saying was apparent to all their contemporaries too, and yet very few were moved to seize the new
and rush to set it down so as to rob posterity of the harvest.
Novelty is in the heart of he who creates, not in the nature being painted. The modesty of any writer will always prevent him
from ranking himself among the great souls of whom he is
writing. He always addresses himself, or so people think, to one
of these luminaries, whoever they are whom nature . . .

You know that the new is always to be found, so point it
out to them in places they have ignored. Make them understand that they never really heard the nightingale before, or beheld the spectacle of the limitless ocean, or any of those things
which their addled senses couldn't stretch themselves to perceive, unless you took the trouble to feel it for them first. Don't

let the means of expression worry you. If you refine your soul, it'll find the way and time for revealing itself, in a language which will be worth every bit of this man's hemistiches, or that man's prose. 'What,' they reply, 'You're truly original, but your inspiration only catches fire in reading Byron or Dante, etc.? These transports which you take to be the mark of creative ability, why, they merely reveal the desire to imitate!' No, not at all. In fact they [Byron and Dante] haven't said a hundredth of what there is to say; in any one of the things they touch on, there is more material for the innovating genius to work on than ... and that nature has stored up for the great minds to come, more that is new to say about her creations, than created things.

27 March 1824

Interesting discussion at Leblond's about the genius of outstanding men. Dimier thought that great passions were the source of genius. I think it's imagination alone, or, what comes to the same thing, that delicacy of the organs which causes one to perceive what others cannot, and which makes one see in a different way. I said that even when the great passions were linked to imagination, they lead to a corrupting of the soul, etc. Dufresne said something very sensible, that what made a man really remarkable was a completely personal and unique way of seeing things. He extended this to great generals etc., in fact to great geniuses of all kinds. Therefore, great souls can be bound by no rules: these can only be of use to people whose only talent is acquired. The proof of this is, that you can't translate this faculty. He said: 'What a lot of reflexion goes into making a single expressive head, a hundred times more than solving any problem, and yet, basically, it must simply be an intuitive gift, since you can't analyse what it is he's thinking about.' It strikes me, now, that my soul is never so inspired to creation as when it sees a mediocre expression of a theme which interests me.

(I) Eugène Delacroix
The Language of the Soul
from *Journal* 1893. Translated by Tim Benton

8 October 1822

I have something in me which is often stronger than my body, which is often buoyed up by it. There are some people who are influenced minimally by their inner selves. With me, it's the strongest part. Without it I would go under, but it will devour me too (I suppose I'm talking about the imagination, which masters me and leads me by the hand).

When you have discovered some weakness in you, instead of pretending it isn't there, or confusing the issue, drop your artificial pose and correct yourself. If only the soul had just the body to contend with! But the soul too has evil leanings, and a part of it, a tiny though most spiritual part, must forever be ceaselessly fighting the other part. All the bodily passions are contemptible, but those vicious ones in the soul are the real cancers: envy, etc. Slothfulness is so contemptible, it must belong to both.

When I've made a beautiful painting, I haven't expressed an idea. That's what they say; they're so simple-minded. They strip painting of all its advantages. In order to be understood, the writer has to put almost everything down, but in painting, you can construct a sort of mysterious bridge between the souls of the people in the picture and that of the spectator. He sees only the exterior forms, but his thoughts relate to the inner being, that real kind of thinking shared by all men. Some people give substance to these thoughts by writing them down, but this misrepresents their essentially elusive quality. And indeed, insensitive people are more moved by literature than by music or painting. The painter's art is all the more intimately appreciated by man's sensibility, for being apparently materialistic, for in this art, as in nature, part is frankly devoted to the finite, part to the infinite, so that the soul can find itself inwardly inspired by objects which are perceived through the senses alone.

(m) Stendhal
Modernity is All

from the preface to his salon criticism   1824. Translated by
Tim Benton

In 1789, a man [David] refused to copy his predecessors slavishly
and discovered a new way of imitating nature. The plaudits of
a captious and critical age proclaimed him great. Immediately, a
mob of imitators rushed to follow in his footsteps. Instead of
looking to nature or antiquity for the forms and expressions of
the ideas which would give the greatest satisfaction to their contemporaries, they copied David's paintings instead. And they are
astonished when we critics make fun of them. [...]

We are about to witness a revolution in the arts. Great paintings made up of thirty nude figures copied from antique statues,
and turgid tragedies in five acts, and in verse too; these performances are, no doubt, highly respectable. But, whatever you
may say, they're beginning to be a bore. If the *Sabine Women*
[see Plate 7] was exhibited today, one would feel that their
figures were sterile, that in any country it is just ridiculous to
march off to fight without any clothes on. 'But that's how it's
done in the antique reliefs!' cry the classicist painters, those who
swear by David and who cannot speak three words without
mentioning *style*. But what do I care about the antique reliefs?
Let us try to make good modern pictures. The Greeks liked
nakedness, but we, why we never see it, and what's more, it dis-
gusts us. [...] My aim is to encourage every spectator to delve
into his own soul, to work out his own way of feeling so that he
comes to make his own judgement by himself. The way he sees
will be based on his own character, his tastes, his dominant
passions, assuming that he has any passions, for unfortunately
these are indispensable for judging art.

4 The Sublime and the Beautiful
(a) Edmund Burke

The Sublime is based on the Ideas of Pain and Danger

from *A Philosophical Enquiry into the Origin of our Ideas on the Sublime and the Beautiful* 1759

Of the passions which belong to SELF-PRESERVATION

Most of the ideas which are capable of making a powerful impression on the mind, whether simply of Pain or Pleasure, or of the modifications of those, may be reduced very nearly to these two heads, *self-preservation* and *society*; to the ends of one or the other of which all our passions are calculated to answer. The passions which concern self-preservation, turn mostly on *pain* or *danger*. The ideas of *pain*, *sickness*, and *death*, fill the mind with strong emotions of horror; but *life* and *health*, though they put us in a capacity of being affected with pleasure, they make no such impresssion by the simple enjoyment. The passions therefore which are conversant about the preservation of the individual, turn chiefly on *pain* and *danger*, and they are the most powerful of all the passions. [...]

Of the SUBLIME

Whatever is fitted in any sort to excite the ideas of pain, and danger, that is to say, whatever is in any sort terrible, or is conversant about terrible objects, or operates in a manner analogous to terror, is a source of the *sublime*; that is, it is productive of the strongest emotion which the mind is capable of feeling [see Plates 5 and 11]. I say the strongest emotion, because I am satisfied the ideas of pain are much more powerful than those which enter on the part of pleasure. Without all doubt, the torments which we may be made to suffer, are much greater in their effect on the body and mind, than any pleasures which the most learned voluptuary could suggest, or than the liveliest imagination, and the most sound and exquisitely sensible body could enjoy. [...]

Chuse a day on which to represent the most sublime and affecting tragedy we have; appoint the most favourite actors;

spare no cost upon the scenes and decorations; unite the greatest efforts of poetry, painting and music; and when you have collected your audience, just at the moment when their minds are erect with expectation, let it be reported that a state criminal of high rank is on the point of being executed in the adjoining square; in a moment the emptiness of the theatre would demonstrate the comparative weakness of the imitative arts, and proclaim the triumph of the real sympathy. I believe that this notion of our having a simple pain in the reality, yet a delight in the representation, arises from hence, that we do not sufficiently distinguish what we would by no means chuse to do, from what we should be eager enough to see if it was once done. We delight in seeing things, which so far from doing, our heartiest wishes would be to see redressed. [...]

But art can never give the rules that make an art. This is, I believe, the reason why artists in general, and poets principally, have been confined in so narrow a circle; they have been rather imitators of one another than of nature; and this with so faithful an uniformity, and to so remote an antiquity, that it is hard to say who gave the first model. Critics follow them, and therefore can do little as guides. I can judge but poorly of any thing whilst I measure it by no other standard than itself. The true standard of the arts is in every man's power; and an easy observation of the most common, sometimes of the meanest things in nature, will give the truest lights, where the greatest sagacity and industry that slights such observation, must leave us in the dark, or what is worse, amuse and mislead us by false lights. [...]

Of BEAUTY

The passion which belongs to generation, merely as such, is lust only; this is evident in brutes, whose passions are more unmixed, and which pursue their purposes more directly than ours. The only distinction they observe with regard to their mates, is that of sex. [...] But man, who is a creature adapted to a greater variety and intricacy of relation, connects with the general passion, the idea of some *social* qualities, which direct and heighten the appetite which he has in common with all other animals; and as he is not designed like them to live at large, it is fit that he should have something to create a preference, and fix his choice; and this in general should be some sensible quality; as no other can so quickly, so powerfully, or so surely produce its effect. The object therefore of this mixed passion which we call love, is the *beauty* of the *sex*.[22] Men are carried to the sex in general, as it is the sex, and by the common law of nature; but they are attached to particulars by personal *beauty*. [...]

Perfection not the cause of B E A U T Y

There is another notion current, pretty closely allied to the former; that *Perfection* is the constituent cause of beauty. This opinion has been made to extend much further than to sensible objects. But in these, so far is perfection, considered as such, from being the cause of beauty; that this quality, where it is highest in the female sex, almost always carries with it an idea of weakness and imperfection. Women are very sensible of this; for which reason, they learn to lisp, to totter in their walk, to counterfeit weakness, and even sickness. In all this, they are guided by nature. Beauty in distress is much the most affecting beauty. Blushing has little less power; and modesty in general, which is a tacit allowance of imperfection, is itself considered as an amiable quality, and certainly heightens every other that is so. I know, it is in every body's mouth, that we ought to love perfection. This is to me a sufficient proof, that it is not the proper object of love. Who ever said, we *ought* to love a fine woman, or even any of these beautiful animals, which please us? Here to be affected, there is no need of the concurrence of our will. [...]

The real cause of B E A U T Y

Having endeavoured to shew what beauty is not, it remains that we should examine, at least with equal attention, in what it really consists. Beauty is a thing much too affecting not to depend upon some positive qualities. And, since it is no creature of our reason, since it strikes us without any reference to use, and even where no use at all can be discerned, since the order and method of nature is generally very different from our measure

[22.] By 'the *sex*', Burke means the female sex.

and proportions, we must conclude that beauty is, for the greater part, some quality in bodies, acting mechanically upon the human mind by the intervention of the senses. [...]

There is a wide difference between admiration and love. The sublime, which is the cause of the former, always dwells on great objects, and terrible; the latter on small ones, and pleasing; we submit to what we admire, but we love what submits to us; in one case we are forced, in the other we are flattered into compliance. [...]

Recapitulation

On the whole, the qualities of beauty, as they are merely sensible qualities, are the following. First, to be comparatively small. Secondly, to be smooth. Thirdly, to have a variety in the direction of the parts; but fourthly, to have those parts not angular, but melted as it were into each other. Fifthly, to be of a delicate frame, without any remarkable appearance of strength. Sixthly, to have its colours clear and bright; but not very strong and glaring. Seventhly, or if it should have any glaring colour, to have it diversfied with others. These are, I believe, the properties on which beauty depends; properties that operate by nature, and are less liable to be altered by caprice, or confounded by a diversity of tastes, than any others.

(b) Stendhal
Intense Fear at Physical Danger likened to Michelangelo's Paintings

from *Histoire de la Peinture en Italie* 1817. Translated by Tim Benton

During our wretched retreat from Russia, we used to be frequently and suddenly awoken in the middle of the pitch black night, by a violent volley of gunfire, which seemed to be getting closer every minute. When this happened, we had to draw on every ounce of will we possessed; we were in the presence of destiny, no longer interested in any material matters, but quite ready to try to snatch life from death. Seeing Michelangelo's paintings brought this almost forgotten feeling straight back to me.

(c) Charles Nodier
The Imagination prefers the Bizarre to the Perfect

from *Mélanges de Littérature et de Critique* 1820
Translated by Tim Benton

The imagination is so fond of lies, that it prefers a frightening illusion to the painting of a charming but natural truth. This is the last resort of human minds tired with commonplace feelings; we call it the romantic style. It has a strange poetry which is nonetheless perfectly attuned to the moral attitude of our society, to the needs of a blasé generation which clamours for sensation at any price. The ideal of the primitive bards, like that of the classical poets who were their elegant imitators, was based on all that is perfect in our nature while romantic poetry springs from our agony and despair. This isn't a fault in our art, but a necessary consequence of the advances made by our progressive society.

5 Morality and the Social Order
(a) Sir Joshua Reynolds
The true Judge of Paintings must not only be Wise, he must be Virtuous

from *Discourse VII* 1776

It has been often observed, that the good and virtuous man alone can acquire this true or just relish even of works of art. This opinion will not appear entirely without foundation, when we consider that the same habit of mind which is acquired by our search after truth in the more serious duties of life, is only transferred to the pursuit of lighter amusements. The same disposition, the same desire to find something steady, substantial, and durable, on which the mind can lean as it were, and rest with safety, actuates us in both cases. The subject only is changed. We pursue the same method in our search after the idea of beauty and perfection in each; of virtue, by looking forwards beyond ourselves to society, and to the whole; of arts, by extending our views in the same manner to all ages and all times.

(b) Sir Joshua Reynolds
On Morality in Artists

from *Discourse I*   1769

When we read the lives of the most eminent Painters, every page informs us that no part of their time was spent in dissipation.

(c) William Blake
Blake's Reaction

from Annotations to Reynolds's *Discourses*

The Lives of Painters say that Rafael dies of Dissipation. Idleness is one Thing & Dissipation Another. He who has Nothing to Dissipate Cannot Dissipate; the Weak Man may be Virtuous Enough, but will Never be an artist. Painters are noted for being Dissipated and Wild.

(d) Sir Joshua Reynolds
Morality is Active, not Passive

from *Discourse VIII*   1778

It is in art as in morals: no character would inspire us with an enthusiastick admiration of his virtue, if that virtue consisted only in an absence of vice; something more is required; a man must do more than merely his duty, to be a hero.

(e) Sir Joshua Reynolds

Good Art is Intellectual and imparts Virtue; it is
Beneficial to Society

from *Discourse IX* 1780

The Art which we profess has beauty for its object; this it is our
business to discover and to express; but the beauty of which we
are in quest is general and intellectual; it is an idea that subsists
only in the mind; the sight never beheld it, nor has the hand
expressed it: it is an idea residing in the breast of the artist,
which he is always labouring to impart, and which he dies at
last without imparting; but which he is yet so far able to communicate, as to raise the thoughts, and extend the views of the
spectator; and which, by a succession of art, may be so far diffused, that its effects may extend themselves imperceptibly into
publick benefits, and be among the means of bestowing on
whole nations refinement of taste: which, if it does not lead
directly to purity of manners, obviates at least their greatest
depravation, by disentangling the mind from appetite, and
conducting the thoughts through successive stages of excellence,
till that contemplation of universal rectitude and harmony
which began by Taste, may, as it is exalted and refined, conclude
in Virtue.

(f) William Blake

Public Patronage has Ruined Art, the Great Artist must
exist in Isolation

from 'Public Address' in his Note-Book *c*. 1810

The wretched State of the Arts in this Country & in Europe,
originating in the wretched State of Political Science, which is
the Science of Sciences, Demands a firm & determinate conduct
on the part of Artists to Resist the Contemptible Counter Arts
Established by such contemptible Politicians as Louis XIV &
originally set on foot by Venetian Picture traders, Music traders
& Rhime traders, to the destruction of all true art as it is this

Day. To recover Art has been the business of my life to the Florentine Original & if possible to go beyond that Original; this I thought the only pursuit worthy of a Man. To Imitate I abhor. I obstinately adhere to the true Style of Art such as Michael Angelo, Rafael, Jul. Rom., Alb. Durer left it, [the Art of Invention, not of Imitation. Imagination is My World; this world of Dross is beneath my Notice & beneath the Notice of the Public.] [23] I demand therefore of the Amateurs of Art the Encouragement which is my due; if they continue to refuse, theirs is the loss, not mine, & theirs is the Contempt of Posterity. I have Enough in the Approbation of fellow labourers; this is my glory & exceeding great reward. I go on & nothing can hinder my course:

and in Melodius Accents I
will sit me down & Cry, I, I.

(g) William Blake
On Greece and Rome

from *On Virgil* [24]   *c.* 1820

Sacred Truth has pronounced that Greece & Rome, as Babylon & Egypt, so far from being parents of Arts & Sciences as they pretend, were destroyers of all Art. Homer, Virgil & Ovid confirm this opinion & make us reverence The Word of God, the only light of antiquity that remains unperverted by War. Virgil in the Eneid, Book VI, line 848, says, 'Let others study Art: Rome has somewhat better to do, namely War & Dominion.'

Rome & Greece swept Art into their maw & destroy'd it; a Warlike State never can produce Art. It will Rob & Plunder & accumulate into one place, & Translate & Copy & Buy & Sell & Criticise, but not Make. Grecian is Mathematic Form: Gothic is Living Form, Mathematic Form is Eternal in the Reasoning Memory: Living Form is Eternal Existence.

[23.] The passage in square brackets was deleted from Blake's original manuscript.

[24.] *On Virgil* is a didactic essay which Blake wrote and etched *c.* 1820 for distribution among his friends.

(h) Henry Fuseli
Was Greek Poetry and Art so Moral?

from a review of Bromley's 'Philosophical and Critical History of the Fine Arts', *Analytical Review*, vol. 16   July 1793

Surely none will deny that the activity of the mind is best employed when directed to the benefit of society; but to assert that the ancients thought so in the choice of subjects for painting and sculpture, is either not to know, or to pervert facts. [...] What were the subjects, of the greatest number of subjects, perpetuated by their genius? Images of superstition; gods and demi-gods of that ferocious age to which our author has refused the very knowledge of the word virtue; monuments of national pride; tyrants deified for trampling on humanity; incentives for refinement in vice, or dignified trifles. [...] It is ludicrous to give a consequence to the arts which they can never possess. Their moral usefulness is at best accidental and negative. It is their greatest praise to furnish the most innocent amusement for those nations to whom luxury is become as necessary as existence, and amongst whom alone they can rear themselves to any degree of eminence.

(j) Denis Diderot
Moral Painting means Providing a 'Moral Experience'

from 'The Salon of 1763', in the manuscript journal
Correspondance Littéraire Philosophique et Critique.
Translated by Tim Benton

This Greuze, he's really my painter ... I'll begin with his picture of *Filial Piety*, a better title for which would be, *The Reward for Imparting a Good Education*. For a start, I like this kind of picture: moral painting. Well, isn't it true that artists have devoted all their efforts to depicting debauchery and vice long enough? Shouldn't we be pleased that at long last they are beginning to use dramatic poetry to move us, to teach us, to improve us and lead us into virtue? Courage, Greuze, my friend, put morality into your pictures, and do it like this. On your deathbed, you'll be able to think back on your career without feeling ashamed of any of your pictures. Weren't you at the side of that young girl who looked at your *Paralytic*[25] and cried out impetuously, 'Dear God, how he moves me! but if I look any longer, I think I'm going to cry!' And that little girl, wasn't she mine? I would have recognized her by that exclamation. When I saw this eloquent and touching old man I too felt my heart melt, and my eyes prickling with tears. [...] It would be very strange if this artist didn't excel in his art.

He has a soul, he is sensitive, he loves his art and he spares no effort in preparing his pictures, going to every length and expense to find the models he wants. If he sees a head which strikes him in the street he would gladly fall to his knees and beseech the owner to come with him to his studio.

6 Ingres: The Faith of a Believer in Ideal Beauty
(a) Jean Auguste Dominique Ingres
Aphorisms Attributed to Ingres by his Pupils[26]

from *Pensées et Ecrits due Peintre* 1947
Translated by Tim Benton

The general public finds pleasure instinctively only in the lower forms of art, in painting as in poetry and music. The most sublime achievements of art have no effect on uncultivated minds. A rare and delicate taste comes only from education and experience. We do not have it at birth, but must develop it in ourselves, just as we must make our own decision as to whether we will accept society and its conventions and laws.

Can we ever have too much love for, or reverence towards, supreme beauty? Among all the most beautiful flowers, can any match the rose; and of all the birds of the air, what can compare with the eagle of Jupiter? Similarly, is there anything to equal

[25.] A reference to the dying man in 'Filial Piety' (see Plate 16).
[26.] These have been grouped together to show how the various aspects of Ingres's beliefs relate to each other.

the works of Homer, a statue by Phidias, a picture by Raphael, a lyric tragedy by Glück, a quintet or a sonata by Haydn? Surely, nothing is more beautiful than these things, and therefore more worth having.

I shall put up a sign over the studio door, 'School of Drawing', and I will produce painters.

The integrity of art rests in drawing.

I have at least this small merit, that I know the path we must take, and this is it: we must approach as close to antiquity as we can. For what's antiquity but nature herself, the intimate understanding and complete expression, philosophically, of the beauty of form?

Homer is the archetype and model of all beauty, in art as in literature.

Rubens has a bit of the butcher in him. Raw flesh colours his thoughts and his compositions remind you of a butcher's shop.

The Flemish and Dutch schools have their own kind of merit, I admit. I fancy I can appreciate their kind of beauty as well as anyone. But for goodness' sake, let us keep a sense of proportion. Let us not make the mistake, in our admiration for, say, Rembrandt, of comparing him and his kind with the immortal Raphael, and the Italian school, for that would be blasphemy.

It's about time we got rid of all those execution scenes, those auto-da-fé subjects and their like, once and for all. Are these subjects appropriate for painting, for healthy, moral painting? Is this what we're supposed to admire; are we supposed actually to like this kind of horror? I'm not suggesting that we should forbid all expressions of pity or terror, just that I wish they could be handled as Aeschylus, Sophocles or Euripides would have treated them in their art. What I don't want is this Medusa,[27] these scenes of carnage, which show us not men, but corpses, which represent only ugly, horrible things. I won't have anything to do with any of it. Art must consist of beauty alone and it must teach us only beauty.

[27.] Géricault's 'The Raft of the Medusa', exhibited in the Salon of 1819 (Plate 13).

On your knees and study nature.

You must be religious in your attitude towards your art. Don't think you'll ever make anything good, or even moderately good, unless your soul is inspired. If you're to grasp the beautiful, you must reach out for the sublime. Look neither to right nor left, above all don't look down; your gaze must be on the infinite, instead of peering down, like pigs rooting around in the mud.

In order to impart truth, we must please. You don't catch flies with vinegar, but with sugar and honey.

Every time you fail to show proper respect towards nature, every time you dare to insult her in your work, you're kicking your mother in the belly.

Love truth; you'll find that it is beautiful, provided that you have the perception to see and feel it. So I'm asking you to train your eyes to see well, with discernment. You may say, 'But this leg is just ugly,' and there may be some truth in that, but I say, 'See through my eyes and you will find it beautiful'.

N Stendhal

Stendhal (1783–1842), whose real name was Henri Beyle, lived through the French Revolution, served Napoleon, and in the days of the restoration of the Bourbon monarchy remained Jacobin and anti-clerical in his sympathies. The two articles reprinted were written for English periodicals and give an idea of Stendhal's attitudes to restoration France. The two passages from Jacques Droz's *Europe Between the Revolutions* (1967) provide useful illumination by a modern historian of the French society which forms the setting of Stendhal's *Scarlet and Black*.

A.K.

Further Reading

For those who read French the two chief recommendations are:

Henri Martineau, *Le Coeur de Stendhal*, Albin Michel, 1952–3.
Henri Martineau, *L'Oeuvre de Stendhal*, Albin Michel, 1951.
Maurice Bardèche, *Stendhal Romancier*, La Table Ronde, 1947.

In English, or translated into English:

* Stendhal, *Scarlet and Black*, Penguin, 1967.
F. W. J. Hemmings, *Stendhal, A Study of his Novels*, Oxford University Press, 1964.
M. Turnell, *The Novel in France*, Hamish Hamilton, 1950, pp. 123–208.
V. Brombert (ed.), *Stendhal, A Collection of Critical Essays*, Prentice-Hall, 1962.
H. Levin, *The Gates of Horn*, Oxford University Press, 1966, pp. 84–149.
E. Auerbach, *Mimesis*, Berne, 1946. Translated by W. R. Trask, Princeton University Press, 1953.
G. Lukàcs, *Studies in European Realism*, Hillway, 1950, pp. 65–85.

* Open University Set Book.

1 Stendhal

The Revolution in Literature and the Reaction in Philosophy

from G. Strickland (ed.), *Selected Journalism from the English Reviews by Stendhal* 1959

In France we have four distinct classes of men in politics and literature; first, the triflers of the reign of Louis XVI, who were twenty years of age in 1788; secondly, the revolutionaries, who were only twenty in 1793; thirdly, the Bonapartists, who were fifteen years old in 1800, and who, from 1800 to 1814, were imbued with the love of military glory by reading the Emperor's bulletins; and fourthly, the young men, who, since 1815 and the second restoration of the Bourbons, have been educated for the Church, under the influence of the Jesuits. Many of the sons of our noblest and wealthiest families are educated by the Jesuits at St Acheul, near Amiens, and other similar colleges. Under such tuition they become what is known as men of the world and acquire the great art of serving their own interests by flattering the men in power. The Jesuit colleges have certainly produced many able men; but the youths who now leave them with the reputation of excellent classical scholars, are sometimes unable to understand the simplest school books, and completely incompetent when it comes to construing a page of Horace or Tacitus. The young students of St Acheul have the manners and opinions of the old men who were moving in society twenty years before the Revolution.

Napoleon checked the progress of literature from 1800 until 1814. He bribed men of letters with sinecures and pensions, because he stood in awe of them. The last chapters of the Memoirs of the Duke de Rovigo contain an account of the corruption of M. Esménard, a writer who obtained credit for a certain literary talent during the Empire. It was Napoleon who instructed the Academy to elect M. de Chateaubriand. His object was to have a claim on the gratitude of every man of talent. From the treatment suffered by Mme de Staël's *De l'Allemagne,* however, it is easy to guess the fate that was to be expected by a writer who ventured to express his opinions with any honesty. The restrictions to which authorship was subjected from 1800 to 1814 are sufficient evidence that the Revolution had not had time to extend its influence to literature. The need to defend French territory against the combined sovereigns of Europe occupied our whole attention between 1792 and 1800. Since the return of the Bourbons, the tyranny exercised by the nobles during the reaction of 1816, and the various political manoeuvres which have led to the election of the prudent and reasonable chamber of 1828, have taken the place of all other subjects of interest. However, a great literary revolution is about to take place. Only one department seems to show no promise of rising above mediocrity, namely, metaphysics and logic. MM. Cousin and Royer-Collard (the President of the Chamber of 1828) have set out to abolish the truths established by Locke, Condillac, Tracy, Cabanis and Bentham, and, instead of argument, prefer to send us to the poetic reveries of Plato. The majority of young men, educated under the imperial régime between 1800 and 1814, despise Condillac and admire M. Royer-Collard. The political reputation, and the honour of being President of the Elective Chamber, have enhanced his popularity, and materially helped the reveries of Plato to triumph over the truths of Locke and De Tracy. These circumstances clearly explain the offence that has been taken in certain quarters at Dr Broussais' ingenious work, *De l'Irritation et de la Folie*, which, as I mentioned in one of my former letters is a bold attack upon Plato.

It is for the reasons here given that the great literary revolution which is about to take place in France, from where it will spread over the whole Continent, will not extend to philosophy (that is, to logic and metaphysics) but will be confined to literature alone. The names of Racine and Shakespeare will be watchwords in the conflict; and the question will be which of these two great poets is henceforth to be the model for dramatic composition.

2 Stendhal

The Misfortunes of a Nobleman Under the Restoration

from G. Strickland (ed.), *Selected Journalism from the English Reviews by Stendhal* 1959

It is difficult in England to conceive any idea of the great sensation that has been produced in France by M. de Montlosier's denunciation of the Jesuits. To understand its proper significance you will have to compare the situation of one of your wealthy landowners residing on his country estate and that of a Frenchman of equal means, a peer of France, if you prefer, who spends eight months of the year in his chateau in Burgundy. The Englishman is a Justice of the Peace, and is highly respected by the parson of the parish who hopes to get a living from him. He is sheriff of the county, or else an intimate friend of the sheriff, who will take good care not to offend him, still less to interfere in his business. The English squire is perhaps unacquainted with the bishop of the diocese in which he resides; but at all events the bishop will do nothing to cause him inconvenience or harm. If the road leading to his house needs making up, he complains to the parish officers, and, if necessary, gives orders for its repair. If he wishes to shoot a partridge he takes his gun, and far from being interfered with in his sport, will more often be guilty of disturbing his neighbours. The fact is that the English squire is a king on his own estate while the French landowner, on retiring to his, becomes a slave and feels his slavery in a hundred different ways. You can have no idea of the state of affairs which has prevailed in France over the last three years, ever since the Jesuits, that is, have been given the power of appointing the various officials who tyrannise over the landowners. If our Burgundian gentleman steps out with a gun in his hand, the constable of the district, known as the *garde champêtre*, who has a salary of about two hundred francs a year, comes up and orders him to show his licence for carrying arms. This licence has to be purchased every year from the Prefect. The *garde champêtre* may be a particularly ill-humoured individual, or he may have received a hint from the priest to give the landowner as much trouble as possible. He may therefore insist that the licence is out of order and take him before the Mayor. The Mayor, who is afraid of offending the priest, writes to the Sub-Prefect; the Sub-Prefect, who also has no desire to offend the priest, writes to the Prefect. The Prefect, who knows that the Bishop can get him dismissed, writes to the Minister of the Interior (M. de Corbière), who never replies. Thus it is that, as the entire power is left in the hands of the *garde champêtre*, he can, if the priest so desires, simply confiscate the gentleman's gun. If he resists, the gendarmerie wait on him next morning, and the Court of the First Instance, glad of an opportunity, not just but legal, of fining a man who is no favourite with the Bishop, is not slow in pronouncing judgement against him. Thus it is that the gentleman of property is obliged to pay court to the priest and mayor of the village, to the *garde champêtre*, and the gendarmeries, in fact to all who have it in their power to cause him trouble. But the matter does not end here. He must also take care to keep in good humour all the religious devotees who live under the protection of the priest. Now compare this life with that of a Devonshire squire of five thousand a year, living on his estate. His unfortunate French equivalent, if he wishes to cut down half a dozen trees in his own grounds, must write to the Prefect for permission, and he, in turn, must write to Paris for authority to grant the permission. You will find in Baron Dupin's work on England, and in M. Fiévée's *Lettres Administratives*, a humorous description of the seventeen letters which must be written by the Sub-Prefect, the Prefect and the Minister of the Interior, before our Burgundian gentleman can cut down six trees growing on his own estate. If he wishes to re-inforce the banks, build the smallest bridge or alter the course in the slightest way of a river or stream flowing through his grounds, he is once again obliged to write seven or eight letters to Paris. If the Prefect wishes to be particularly unhelpful, he may allow an interval of three months to elapse between each of these letters.

All this was vexatious enough in 1816; but consider how the tyranny under which the landed proprietors suffer has increased since 1822, ever since the Jesuits, that is, have obtained the right to appoint officials. It is they who appoint the *garde champêtre*, the Justice of the Peace, the officers of the gendarmerie, the

Mayor, the priest and the Sub-Prefect, all of whom have an influence which is oppressively felt by an unfortunate gentleman who has left Paris to spend eight months of the year on his estates. Why should the Jesuits take so much trouble to secure the appointment of the six functionaries I have just indicated, unless it is in order to control the activities of the landowner and use him to further their own ends? The result of their influence is that, if he is a member of the Council General of his department, he is obliged to vote additional emoluments to the Bishop, to follow the missionary processions, to support the priests in their persecution of peasants who like to dance on feast days, and submit to many other obligations of a similar nature.

Now, you are certainly aware that all the present French priests are young peasants, all more or less imbued, unfortunately, with a spirit of fanaticism. They come from seminaries established by the Jesuits, in which they are taught the doctrines of the famous M. de Maistre, a writer who may, at this moment, be regarded as the French St Paul. M. de Maistre declares that all persons in authority, even the King, are subject to the authority of the Pope. Twenty bulls with papal signatures maintain the same pretension. Leo XII protects the *Giornale Ecclesiastico*, which is printed in Rome and which preaches the same doctrine. Everything, therefore, in the Jesuit scheme of things is consistent and well ordered. Our unfortunate Burgundian gentleman is led from one submission to another, until eventually perhaps he becomes a *short-robed Jesuit* like M. de Pusieux, minister under Louis XV and the uncle of Mme de Genlis. (See the *Mémoires de Mme de Genlis*, vol. 2.) His only two means of escape in fact are: 1. To become a short-robed Jesuit; 2. To take refuge in Paris. Paris is, in fact, the only part of France in which there is any liberty at all.

Let us suppose that he has spirit enough to resist becoming a Jesuit. Sooner or later, persecuted by the vexations of the holy fathers, he will leave Burgundy and come to Paris in order to give vent to his impotent rage. What can a single man do, however, even if he is a millionaire and a peer of France, against a society so powerful and with so many adherents? He can do precisely nothing. Imagine his pleasure, nevertheless, if on arriving in Paris, he finds that a man of courage like M. de

Montlosier is uttering the very denunciation which he so longs to hear. His pleasure naturally increases when he realizes that M. de Montlosier has insisted that the Royal Court of Paris should come to an explanation concerning the privileges and functions of the Order of St Ignatius. Every Royal Court in the kingdom imitates the Royal Court of Paris, while the Courts of the First Instance imitate in their turn the Royal Court of the district. Our landowner therefore begins to cherish the hope of at last obtaining something like justice if he should bring an action against a Court of the First Instance; or if ever he should complain of some vexation caused him by the Mayor or by the young priest of his parish.

To denounce the Jesuits in 1826 is, in France, nothing more or less than to demand a complete change in the internal administration of the country. It is therefore a great mistake on the part of the *Times*, which has so great an influence on public opinion in England, to ridicule the denunciations which are being uttered against the various congregations of Jesuits. In every town there are three congregations, each as well organized as any regiment in the army:

1st, there is the congregation of the gentry. In Paris, M. Ferdinand de Berthier commands the one hundred and eight Jesuits of the short robe, who are members of the Chamber of Deputies. The late Duke Mathieu de Montmorency was colonel-general of all the short-robed Jesuits in France.

2nd, the congregation known as the *Bonnes Etudes*. This society is employed in seducing and crimping students of law and medicine between the ages of seventeen and twenty-one.

3rd, the congregation of the common people, whose business is to seduce servants and employ them as spies upon their masters.

The *Times* had treated with misplaced derision the denunciation which a man of courage published this month against the *Congrégation des Bonnes Etudes*. I shall therefore bring to your recollection a number of facts to justify my previous assertions. To offer one example of the fanaticism of the young priests formed by the influence of M. de Maistre and the Abbé de

La Mennais, you may recall the case of the young priest in the neighbourhood of Lyons, who was acquitted by a Court of the First Instance. It was proved that this priest had climbed up a tree in pursuit of a musician who had been playing to a group of peasants. These peasants had met, after the church service, to dance together before returning home. The priest had finally knocked the unfortunate musician from his seat in the tree. Every day the newspapers relate something of the kind. I have quoted this last example because it rests on judicial proof. Those who find the story hard to believe may find an account of the trial in the *Gazette des Tribunaux*, an excellent newspaper which I recommend to all Englishmen who wish to become acquainted with the true state of French society.

A counsellor of the Royal Court of Grenoble died about two years ago. He was one of the leading figures in the *Congrégation des Bonnes Etudes* and a number of papers found in his desk bearing the signatures of persons of the highest rank were subsequently published. Those who are sceptical of what I am saying will do well to read these truly curious papers. Grenoble is one of the towns most attached to the Charter, and consequently most feared by the Government. The Jesuits have therefore been making every effort to influence the minds of the young law students of the town. What remains to be legally proved is the seduction of servants. Cases of this kind are notoriously public, though no one has yet instituted actions against the offenders. I have read a number of letters on the subject written by English Protestant families residing in France. There is not perhaps a single respectable man in the country who has not, at some time or another, detected attempts to seduce his servants, and to persuade them to report to one of the local priests everything that goes on in their master's house.

There still remains one objection which may naturally occur to the mind of a disinterested foreigner, not thoroughly acquainted with the present state of French society. He may possibly imagine that the liberals themselves wish to exercise a tyrannical authority over those Frenchmen who choose to become Jesuits. This is by no means the case. All we demand is that we should enjoy the same degree of liberty enjoyed by the Jesuits, with the connivance of the Government. Some years ago the Duke de Broglie and several other distinguished men formed a society called the *Society for the Liberty of the Press*. The police suppressed it because it met on certain days and in a number exceeding twenty.

Such meetings were prohibited by a tyrannical law of Bonaparte's, a law which, though abolished by the Charter, still continues to be enforced. At the present moment, the King's ministers apply it to the liberals and not to the Jesuits. All we ask is to be treated in the same way. Let us be permitted to have our congregations, too, and soon there will be no dangerous meetings in France. No meetings are dangerous in England because all are legal.

The Government permits the Jesuits to go about the streets armed, though this is an offence for anyone else. The *Times*, however, seems to have no idea that such things can happen. I am perfectly aware that an English newspaper is written for English readers but when speaking of a country not more than twenty miles from its own shores, it would be as well if it were to be a little less in the wrong, and if it were not to call black white, and white black.

As to the attacks that have been made on the Jesuits during the past year, you may be sure that what their antagonists desire is a total change in the internal administration of the country. The Jesuits are our masters everywhere except in Paris, and one must either pay them homage or be exposed to their vexations. Do not blame me for making an incursion into the realm of politics. In speaking of the Jesuits, I have merely given you an outline of the conversation of polite society during the months of August and September. It seems that the Government has to some extent deserted them, and we have talked of nothing else.

If you go to the trouble of consulting that excellent work the *Journal de la Librairie*, edited by M. Beuchot, which gives the titles of all the works published in Paris, you will find that the vast majority consists of publications by the disciples of Loyola or by their enemies. During the last six months, the number of purely literary works has been falling off. Take, for instance, number 63 of the *Journal de la Librairie* (9 August 1826). There you will find announced: *Nouvelles Etrennes Spirituelles*, *in-24, La Journeé du Chrétien, in-24, Réflections sur la Religion, Lettres d'un Anglican à un Gallican, Les Jésuites Athées, ou la France en danger, Le Catholicisme Primitif* and *La Réfutation de l'opinion de M. l'Abbé de la Mennais sur la Puissance Spirituelle des Papes.* All these works are advertised in a single page of M. Beuchot's journal, and from this you may judge the number of more or less absurd pamphlets to which the disputes concerning the legal status of the Jesuits have given rise.

If the Jesuits were to form a purely religious association, like the various sects of your Methodists, Quakers or Swedenborgians, we should have nothing to say against them. We would merely insist that the Government allow them complete liberty. What they have done, however, is to place under their control *gardes champêtres*, mayors, parish priests, sub-prefects, prefects and judges, whom they have the power even to appoint in office. These officials render our lives impossible unless we submit to the Jesuits in everything. M. de Villèle's own private secretary is a Jesuit and he has been seeking to get rid of him for the past two years. When a Prime Minister, who is also a man of talent, finds himself as hampered as this, what can the private citizen who has taken refuge in Paris hope to do? He merely spends his time cursing St Ignatius and his disciples and reading all the pamphlets, which are of varying degrees of absurdity, for and against the Congregation. I hope that your readers will now be able to form some idea of the cunning and intricate machinery which at the present moment makes the influence of the Jesuits felt in every corner of France.

3 Jacques Droz
Liberalism and the Bourgeoisie

from 'Liberalism and the Bourgeoisie', *Europe Between the Revolutions, 1815–48* 1967. Translated by R. Baldick

The period 1815–1848 was characterized, in all countries of Europe, by the steady rise of the bourgeoisie. A human type was to appear, whom literature has popularized under the name of Joseph Prudhomme, César Birotteau or Podsnap, who prided himself on his respectability and good manners, and even, despite his fear of the common people, on a certain humanitarian idealism, yet who has been constantly denounced as hypocritically scrupulous, devoid of all artistic sensibility, and ridiculous in his self-satisfaction. This was a type we can recognize in the portrait of the founder of the *Journal des Débats*, the elder Bertin, whom Ingres has seated squarely in his armchair, his hands resting firmly on his knees, and his gaze magnificent in its assurance. The great writers who have depicted the bourgeoisie in the first half of the nineteenth century have been struck by the contrast between, on the one hand, that passion for money and that ambition to climb the social ladder which endowed the bourgeoisie with a conquering character, and on the other hand a ridiculous vanity, a strict, narrow conformity, and a mistrust of anything new which confined it to a sort of mediocrity from which it was powerless to escape.

In every state in Europe the pattern of development was the same: everywhere money assigned a place to the individual inside the bourgeoisie and in relation to it. True, there was no comparison to be made between the English middle class about 1830, a class which was already imprinting its character on England, and the few individuals who ran factories in Russia. The former were men who were already applying to the political problems, over which they had control after 1832, the methods which had brought them success in the economic sphere; men whose desire for independence and whose highly developed will-power had endowed them with an individualistic character; men in whom a sense of realism and business experience had strengthened the utilitarian instinct of their race. The Russians, on the other hand, were a small group of merchant-manufacturers, sprung from the class of peasant serfs, often remaining serfs themselves in spite of being in control of a factory labour force, and only after years of work succeeding in buying their freedom, as well as the factory in which they had toiled. Between these two extremes, there was, of course, the greatest variety of types, depending on the degree to which the economy had developed; but in a country like Germany, where the economy had been making great strides since 1835, the change from the hierarchy of the pre-revolutionary states to a class system founded on work and wealth was a long way from being complete in 1848; outside the Rhineland, where the influence of French legislation had had its effect, it was very difficult to find any sign of a Third Estate ready to become that 'totality' to which Sieyès had referred in 1789; and even then, these contractors, factory-owners, businessmen or bankers were nearly all of Calvinist origin. Friedrich Engels observed that in the middle of the century it was impossible to make any comparison between the impotent, poverty-stricken German *Bürger* and the powerful bourgeois of the western states. 'Its lack of numbers and above all its dispersion,' he wrote, 'would prevent the German middle class from acquiring that political supremacy which the English middle class had possessed since 1688 and which the French bourgeoisie had won in 1789.'

It was in France that the rise of the bourgeoisie was most spectacular. It was there that it distinguished itself most clearly in relation to the aristocracy from which it had seized power in the 1830 Revolution, and to the 'common people' from which it felt separated by its wealth and its occupations. The July Monarchy can be regarded as the most typical example of a régime in which money became the basic factor of social discrimination. It is therefore the formation of this French middle class that we shall consider first of all.

Under the Restoration (1815–1830), the rise of the bourgeoisie was still taking place. In the society of that time, still very close to that of the Ancien Régime, everyone was trying to climb the social ladder, by means of work and patronage; the artisan aspired to set up in business on his own; the petty bourgeois, who sent his daughters to a convent school and his sons to a private school where they were given an exclusively classical education, dreamt of their obtaining a fine match, a solicitor's practice, a barrister's gown, or best of all a public office. For the power of the civil service, inherited from the empire, caused a rush for the bureaucratic professions, on account of the authority, respect and security which went with them : a career in the civil service came to be regarded as the chief means of social betterment. But there were also a great many petty bourgeois who laboriously worked their way up in business; the number of registered tradesmen rose from 847,000 in 1817 to 1,163,000 in 1830. The dream of every shop-keeper who was a member of the National Guard, paying for his uniform and his equipment, was to fulfil the property qualifica-tion for the franchise, and thus enter the 'pays légal', some-thing which made him a 'notability' enjoying local prestige. The bourgeoisie used its savings to buy land, which it leased out in return for payment in money or kind, or else to buy house property: a new social type appeared, the landlord who let out flats in tenements. But so far it was rare for money to be in-vested in companies or industrial undertakings, for the risk was regarded as too great.

For this bourgeoisie Paris had a real fascination. The dullness of provincial life, in which the hard-working money-grubbing middle class seemed to be enslaved to conformist public opinion and obsessed with fierce petty intrigues, contrasted with the capital, which attracted not only the working class but also the more ambitious elements of the provincial bourgeoisie, such as Balzac's hero Rastignac, who as he first set foot on Parisian soil exclaimed: 'It's between the two of us now, Paris!' Thiers, an ambitious young journalist from Aix-en-Provence, would be helped to enter the drawing-rooms and the newspaper world by Talleyrand, whose sarcastic smile paid knowledgeable tribute to his frenzied *arrivisme*. All the provinces of France contributed to this rejuvenation of the capital, the consequences of which could only be favourable: there was nothing stiff or stuffy about the Parisian bourgeois milieu, where the desire to climb the social ladder was general. To force one's way into the different bourgeois circles of the capital did in fact call for a great deal of talent, ability and courage, and there were count-less cases of exclusion and failure. But there can be no doubt that the drift from the provinces gave much of its character to the Parisian bourgeoisie; 55 per cent of the electors registered in Paris between 1815 and 1830 were emigrants; among tradesmen and civil servants the proportion was above 60 per cent; it was slightly lower for the liberal professions and the unemployed.

This Parisian bourgeoisie, at the time of the July Mon-archy, was a long way from offering a homogeneous appearance; it was divided into an infinite number of groups, whose interests, aspirations, standards of living and degrees of prosperity were profoundly different, if not opposed. Right at the top there was a limited élite, the *haute bourgeoisie*, a small minority of rich men which tended to merge into the landed aristocracy; lower down was the *bonne bourgeoisie*, which included some of the notabilities, more down to earth than the *haute bourgeoisie*, but resembling them in their wealth and occupations, and the bulk of the liberal professions and the business world; then came the *moyenne bourgeoisie*, largely consisting of the shopkeepers of Paris; and finally there was the *bourgeoisie populaire*, which was rather hard to distinguish from the common people, except by its occupations, which were not of a manual character. Between these various groups, the frontiers were vague and the exchanges constant; the bourgeois categories overlapped, as someone remarked, 'like the tiles of a roof', and there were countless links between the different layers. So far there was no segregation of districts in the capital, of the kind which is so marked in nearly every great modern metropolis.

However, the new feature of the 1830s was the establishment of the supremacy of the *haute bourgeoisie*. Naturally exclusive, it had no wish to be absorbed into a social order it considered out of date, and it succeeded in creating a new hierarchy; an aristocracy of money, office and responsibility, which in its turn tended to become an aristocracy of birth. These bourgeois were able to base their supremacy on a threefold power, economic, political and social; in other words, by means of money, by which they obtained political position enabling them to favour their own interests by legislation, and to mould public opinion as they wished. They were the 'great notabilities' of the July Monarchy, the representatives of those 'bourgeois dynasties' which for a long time would turn power into a profitable monopoly under the banner of Orleanism. At the height of their success they appeared as a meritocracy consisting of individuals with a sense of innovation and a love of power, but without magnanimity or nobility of character; individuals who pursued their objectives with unimaginable ruthlessness, and who showed themselves to be incapable of subordinating their personal aims to the general interest, as was evidenced by the economic policy of the July Monarchy.

The 1830 Revolution thus substituted the *grande bourgeosie* for the aristocracy as the principal governing class of the country. With the 1830s, the industrial revolution brought to the fore a series of phenomena – mechanization, industrialization on a large scale, and concentration –which were doubtless not new, but which had a new amplitude, and which would stamp their character on the society and the economy then emerging in France. Admittedly this transformation was only in its early stages under Louis-Philippe; and it would not be until after the middle of the nineteenth century that the keynote of the French economy would be really capitalistic. All the same, as early as the period 1830–1850, it became clear that the first effect of the country's economic development would be to enrich the *grande bourgeoisie* more than the other classes. Among the various sources of income, the upper middle class would retain control of those likely to give the best return.

On the other hand, the landed aristocracy became a 'declining class' in France after 1830. Many noblemen retired to their estates and gradually became *'émigrés* inside their country and their century'. True, this political abstention could in certain cases be accompanied by a strengthening of their influence on their peasants in so far as they taught them new agricultural techniques and allowed them to join in their enterprises; but for one Forbin-Janson or one Duc de Montmorency-Laval, scores of heirs to large landed fortunes abandoned all interest in the development of their estates and confined themselves to dissipating the family heritage in their Faubourg Saint-German mansions or simply in the nearest town. The breaking-up of the great landed estates continued: a process which, during the Restoration, had already caused considerable concern to the Ultra party and to those who, like Balzac, dreaded the economic and social consequences of such a development. However, this decadence had not reached its conclusion in 1848: at the end of the July Monarchy, the aristocracy still represented a force to be reckoned with in many parts of France –in the west of course, but also in Provence, in the south of the Massif Central, and in the regions of the Parisian basin notable for large estates.

The fact remains that the *grande bourgeoisie* was the 'conquering' or 'rising' class. But this term comprised a great many different categories. At the summit was the *grande bourgeoisie* of the business world, whose strength and cohesion were reinforced by the rapid development of industry and trade: the upstarts of finance and banking, like Laffitte, Gouin, Hottinger and Mallet, or leading manufacturers such as Delessert and Casimir Pèrier – the latter a native of Dauphiné, enriched by both industry and banking, who combined his famous political career with the offices of Governor of the Bank of France and President of the Anzin Mining Company. It was in the drawing-rooms of the Chaussée d'Antin that most of the politicians of the régime gathered together, and the bonds between the business world and the July Monarchy were tightened. In the provinces, merchants and ship-builders, enriched by the development of sea-borne trade, reigned over the society of Marseilles, Le Havre and Bordeaux. In the manufacturing regions, large-scale industrial development was often the work of self-made men, such as those who founded at this period the great undertakings in Dauphiné. This upper middle class also included the great industrial dynasties: the Wendels in Lorraine, the Peugeots and the Japys in the Montbéliard region, and the great families of Mulhouse, the Miegs, Dollfuses and Schlumbergers.

However, this *grande bourgeoisie* of the business world did not make up the whole of the governing class. In the middle of the nineteenth century, land still remained the principal source of wealth. Income from land formed a great part of the fortune of many manufacturers or financiers: to be convinced of this, one has only to study the electoral registers giving the taxes paid by each elector, and their nature: the landed proprietors far outclass the owners of small factories or modest businesses. Finally, it was common practice for these rich landed proprietors to add to their ground rents the income from a liberal profession or a public office: if the notabilities in Paris included lawyers and university professors (such as Guizot), in the provinces it was the magistrates who played an essential role, as did the notaries, the chief advisers and bankers to the peasant masses.

On the other hand, this *grande bourgeoisie*, which was the principal beneficiary of economic change, was careful to keep its distance from the *moyenne* and *petite bourgeoisie*. The latter had joyfully welcomed the 1830 Revolution and had made up the bulk of the National Guard, that essential bulwark of the régime. But they had never been accepted by the governing classes and their bitterness, sustained by the systematic refusal of any reform of the franchise, finally resulted in their turning against the régime. Moreover, social advancement became increasingly infrequent, the closer one came to 1848: the richer bourgeois tended to close their ranks as their positions were consolidated, and by the end of Louis-Philippe's reign it was difficult for a man of humble birth to get to the top of the social ladder. All the same, it would be incorrect to see the *grande bourgeoisie* as a monopolistic class whose large-scale undertakings ruined the small businesses and workshops of France. In fact, the movement towards concentration was only beginning before 1848. What was striking was rather the frenzied individualism of every kind of bourgeois confronting each other inside one and the same social group: the existence of coteries engaged in a fight to the death. The sense of class was sustained only by the desire to keep the common people outside the quarrels of the bourgeoisie.

The rise of the bourgeoisie was matched by a certain concept of the world known as liberalism, which in the last analysis was simply the expression of its economic and political interests. The bourgeoisie, while industrial development was enabling it to increase its income slowly but surely, declared itself to be satisfied with the normal operation of supply and demand. Unaffected by the growing misery of the masses, it contented itself with preaching charity, thrift and celibacy; besides, it believed that technical advances would make possible a progressive improvement in general well-being. As for forms of government, the best was that which least disturbed the bourgeois in his accumulation of wealth. In short, the bourgeois considered the state as the guardian of freedom; its function was confined to the protection of individual interests; it had no business to interfere in economic relations, still less in the organization of society; its role was entirely negative.

Not that the advocates of the *laisser faire, laisser passer* policy were all necessarily 'optimists'. Economists such as Malthus and Ricardo no longer believed, as did Adam Smith and the physiocrats, in a spontaneous order due to the kindness of Providence, and the free play of individual liberty. On the contrary, they discerned disturbing conflicts explained by economic laws; but since these laws were ineluctable, there was nothing to do but regret them and bow before them. The pessimistic Malthus observed that the population of the world was increasing faster than its subsistence, and that mankind was advancing towards famine; but to deal with this state of affairs, all that he proposed (putting aside the natural operation of epidemics, famines and wars) was voluntary birth control and conjugal chastity, firmly opposing any measure of assistance and any state interference in social matters. 'The common people,' he wrote, 'must regard themselves as being themselves the principal cause of their misfortunes.' As for Ricardo, he formulated the theory of differential ground rent, showing that ground rent would tend to increase on account of the rising cost of farming land newly put under cultivation, while the price of food would also rise to the detriment of the masses, whose wages would remain at the minimum required for subsistence. But according to him, this regrettable situation could not be changed by state legislation; the only way of combating this rise in ground rent was to allow foreign corn to enter Britain freely, especially from younger nations with lower production costs.

The position of the French representatives of the classical school seemed more logical, for they were liberals and advocates of State abstention in economic affairs because they considered that everything was for the best in the best of all possible worlds. J. B. Say, an admirer of England, a country that had inspired his *Traité d'Économie Politique* as early as 1803, a manufacturer, a professor of political economics and a man of the left in his political sympathies, who had consistently defended mechanization and exalted the role of the contractor, gave pride of place in his economic theories to the mechanism of the market: according to him, there was no reason to fear that markets would ever be choked for any length of time by economic activity,

for 'goods are exchanged for goods'. Money was simply an intermediary which one accepted only to get rid of it straight away.
Goods found openings on a reciprocal basis; a country which
manufactured one object created the possibility of buying another. The greater the variety of goods produced, the easier it
would be to sell them. There could not be any general crisis
of overproduction. At the very most, some partial crisis of overproduction might occur when the productive services had been
badly organized; but these crises would be only temporary, provided that trade remained free, and provided that the working of
prices enabled contractors to know what was in demand and
what they should manufacture. An even more radical figure,
the economist Bastiat, whose advocacy of free trade brought him
into conflict with political circles under the July Monarchy,
believed that he could discern a pre-established harmony in the
economic world, and gave his principal work the characteristic
title: *Les Harmonies Économiques*: 'It is not simply the
celestial organization which reveals God's wisdom and shows his
glory.' This was because Bastiat, like Charles Dunoyer, denied
that poverty was on the increase: a poverty, incidentally, which
they considered inseparable from civilization, like a necessary
evil, because it 'gave encouragement to the difficult virtues' of
economy and continence.

The accuracy of these opinions was scarcely questioned under
the July Monarchy by the theoreticians of political economy, the
elder Blanqui, Pellegrino Rossi and Wolowski. In England, the
middle class, strongly influenced by the utilitarian philosophy
and the doctrine of the happiness of the greatest number which
Jeremy Bentham had inculcated into it during the preceding
generation, and to which the electoral reforms of 1832 had given
a place among the governing classes, now followed the guidance
of McCulloch and Nassau Senior. McCulloch and Senior argued
that irresistible natural forces doomed any sort of social
intevention to failure and, while they had to accept in principle
assistance to the poor, hoped that it would be organized in such
a way as to make it unacceptable.

4 Jacques Droz

The Constitutional Monarchy in France

from 'The Constitutional Monarchy in France', *Europe Between the Revolutions, 1815–48* 1967. Translated by R. Baldick

The constitutional Charter of 1814 had created a system which was a compromise with the society born of the revolution and the Empire, and kept unaltered its essential institutions, from the Civil Code and the Concordat to the sale of *biens nationaux*, the university, and the Napoleonic administrative system. Thus the Restoration had been neither judicial nor social, but purely dynastic in character.

The Charter 'granted' by the King established in France a régime inspired by the British. There were three powers: the king, who initiated, sanctioned and enforced laws, convoked the Chambers annually, and could dissolve the elected Chamber; the peers, nominated by the king on a hereditary basis, with no limit on numbers; and the deputies of the departments, aged over forty and paying 1000 francs in direct taxation, chosen by electors aged at least thirty and paying 300 francs in direct taxation – about 90,000 electors in all, who made up the *pays légal*. English customs were introduced into the system imposed on Parliament: an annual vote on the budget, a 'civil list' voted to the king by Chambers, a speech from the throne at the opening of the parliamentary session, and an address from the Chamber in reply to that speech. Secret in the Senate and public in the Palais-Bourbon, the parliamentary sittings often gave rise to impassioned debates, and the Tribune of the Chamber helped to carry out the political education of the nation. Gaps in the Charter left unanswered important questions which dominated public life after 1815. Had the ministers any responsibility to parliament other than a 'penal' responsibility for 'acts of treason or peculation'? In accordance with what electoral law were the deputies to be elected? How was the press to be controlled? It was according to the reply given to these questions that the political parties were gradually formed.

As it happened, the régime was installed in an atmosphere of civil war. True, Talleyrand's ministry, in which the most active figure was Pasquier, the Minister of Justice, urged the Prefects to follow a policy of appeasement; but it came up against violent passions. Although the king had promised an amnesty in his Cambrai declaration, a policy of proscription was initiated: nineteen generals were court-martialled. Immediately after the Battle of Waterloo, reprisals against the Bonapartists began in the valley of the Rhône and in Marseilles. Once the Restoration was an accomplished fact, an epidemic of acts of vengeance broke out – at Avignon, where Brune was killed, at Nîmes, where the massacres were extended to the Protestants, and at Toulouse, where the Verdets put General Ramel to death. The government proved itself, if not inert, at least impotent: Fouché, the Minister of Police, was dismissed. It was in the midst of this 'White Terror' that the elections took place, for which the electoral colleges of the Empire were used, with the addition of Royalist notabilities. The result was the so-called *Chambre introuvable*, bristling with hatred for the Revolution; and the Duc de Richelieu, who succeeded Talleyrand in September 1815, formed a government of a more reactionary complexion. It put through a series of emergency laws, suspending individual freedom, punishing seditious crimes, and setting up *cours prévotales*, half military, half civil courts, from whose decisions there was no appeal: this was the 'Legal Terror'. Its principal victim was Marshal Ney, who was sentenced to death by the peers. As for the administration, it encouraged widespread repression. Thanks to the activity of secret societies such as the *Association bretonne*, the *Association royale du Midi*, and the *Francs-régénérés*, the whole of France bowed down under the Terror. Reactions such as Didier's anti-Bourbon conspiracy at Grenoble were insignificant.

However, this situation finally began to cause some anxiety to Louis XVIII's advisers, as well as to certain foreign ambassadors, such as Pozzo di Borgo, who represented Russia in Paris. The Chamber soon found itself at odds with the ministry. The conflict between the two powers turned on the electoral question, which, by a curious paradox, the Chamber wished to settle by fixing the franchise qualification at 50 francs, in order to rally the electors to its side. In opposition to the ministry, which upheld the royal prerogative, the deputies stood up for the parliamentary system, which they saw as destined to give the Chamber control of the administration. This was calculated to annoy Louis XVIII, who was extremely sensitive on the subject of his prerogatives. Decazes, the Minister of Police, persuaded him to dissolve the *Chambre introuvable*; and the electors showed their approval of this attitude in October 1816, by returning to Parliament a majority in favour of the ministers.

It was after these elections that a real public life began. Three parties gradually made their appearance, though without setting up recognized organizations as in England. Moreover, the distinction between them came out more often under the pressure of events than as a result of preconceived ideas, more through negative reflexes than on the basis of a positive programme.

The first to take shape was the Ultra-Royalist party, as its opponents called it. Its supporters described themselves as 'pure royalists', seeking to contrast in this way their unswerving loyalty with the dubious devotion of the men of the Revolution and the Empire, tardy adherents to the monarchy which they intended, so they claimed, to adapt to the new ideas. The Hundred Days had shown the Ultra party the dangers of this policy of compromise. They intended not so much to go back to the Ancien Régime, as has been said too often, but to found a new monarchical and religious order, based on the ideas which had come to fruition during the emigration and which the Catholic and Romantic revival in France had developed. 'France,' wrote Chateaubriand, 'wants all the freedoms and all the institutions brought about by time, the change in manners, and the progress of understanding, but with everything which has not perished of the old monarchy, with the eternal principles of justice and morality. ... France wants the political and material interests created by time and consecrated by the Charter, but it wants neither the principles nor the men who have brought about our misfortunes.' However, this comparatively moderate position adopted by Chateaubriand, who in *De La Monarchie selon la Charte* (1816), as well as in *Le Conservateur*, stressed the impossibility of a complete return to the past, was outstripped by the Ultra press, which, giving prominence to the ideas of the Vicomte de Bonald, advocated in *La Gazette de France, La Quotidienne*, later *Le Drapeau Blanc*, and Fiévée's

Correspondance politique et administrative, the close alliance of throne and altar. The party's principal asset, its great hope and its leader, was the King's own brother, the Comte d'Artois, who gathered around him the men of the *Pavillon de Marsan*, the Baron de Vitrolles, Jules de Polignac, and the Comte de Bruges: a real 'secret government' with considerable facilities at its disposal. As the Comte d'Artois had been appointed Colonel of the National Guard of the entire kingdom, with the right to choose his officers, it had been possible to exclude from that militia all who were opposed to their ideas and to make it an internal army at the service of their party. Finally, the secret society of the *Chevaliers de la Foi*, created to fight the Empire, and more or less put to sleep during the first Restoration, had come to life again to combat the Talleyrand-Fouché Ministry and its Orleanist schemes. Another royalist secret society, that of the *Francs-Régénérés*, was formed at this time by dissident freemasons, and competed with the Masonic movement for a while, but had only an ephemeral existence. It was the *Chevaliers de la Foi* who maintained the remarkable cohesion of the deputies of the Ultra-Royalist party in the Palais-Bourbon. 'The party stood up, sat down, spoke and kept silent like a single man,' said Molé. Tactics were decided upon in secret committee, and instructions were then given to the uninitiated in meetings which were held at the house of the deputy Piet, an individual whose insignificance protected him from jealousy. The real parliamentary leaders were the Comte de Villèle, a former mayor of Toulouse, who in the *Chambre introuvable* had shown himself to be an indefatigable debater and a cunning tactician, and who had considerable financial and administrative ability; his friend the lawyer Corbière, the deputy for Rennes, and in the Chamber of Peers, Mathieu de Montmorency, Polignac and also Chateaubriand. Many of these leaders were also members of the Supreme Council of the *Chevaliers de la Foi*. The chief supporters of the Ultra party were to be found in the bishoprics, seminaries and presbyteries, as well as in the country seats of the south and west of France; its electors were the great landed proprietors, but also the merchants of the big ports such as Marseilles, who had particularly suffered from the blockade; and through the activities of the clergy its influence was widely exerted on the peasantry and certain trade guilds.

The 'Constitutional' party was born of a reaction against the excesses of the Ultra party, just as the latter had come from a reaction against the policy of compromise of the first Restoration; the 1816 elections gave it consistency by grouping behind the ministry all those who repudiated the methods and principles which had inspired the White Terror. Such a negative programme obviously left room for a great many shades of opinion, and this party never had the practical cohesion or the doctrinal unity of its opponents. The right wing of the party was represented in the ministry by the Duc de Richelieu and Lainé, who had less distaste for the theories of the Ultras, than for their methods; and the left wing by a small group of intellectuals, the *doctrinaires*, namely Jordan, Guizot, Barante, the Comte de Serre, the young Duc de Broglie, and Charles de Rémusat, who all recognized the influence of the philosopher Royer-Collard. In point of fact, they were tools in the hands of the Minister of Police, then of the Interior, Élie Decazes, the son of a Libourne notary, and a high official of the Empire who had come over to the Bourbons. Decazes was a clever politician, without any beliefs or principles, but who, by reporting the secrets and the gossip of the *cabinet noir* to the king, had managed to make himself indispensable, and who moreover knew all the currents of public opinion. The Constitutional party, whose supporters included an important section of the aristocracy and liberal upper middle class, had *Le Moniteur* as its principal organ, but intellectual circles preferred to read *Le Journal Général de France*, inspired by Royer-Collard, as well as the *Archives philosophiques, politiques et littéraires*.

The party of the Independents took shape and distinguished itself from the Constitutional party during the summer of 1817. This name concealed all the enemies of the regime, who however had not declared their true loyalties: Republicans, Bonapartists and Orleanists. After the 1817 elections they formed an 'anti-ministerial' group with Casimir Périer, Dupont de l'Eure, and the banker Laffitte, who were joined by Lafayette, Manuel and finally Benjamin Constant. These various figures made up a 'guiding committee', opposed to the *Pavillon de Marsan* and the supreme council of the *Chevaliers de la Foi*,

which corresponded with affiliated members and electoral committees in all the provinces; its programme was very close to that
of the Masonic movement, of which most of the Independents
were dignitaries; it was even more anti-clerical than anti-
monarchist. The Bonapartists, by joining the party and gaining
increasing influence in it, introduced into it a note of military
nationalism and of revenge against the 1815 treaties, as well as
a tendency to resort to violent methods foreign to the liberal
spirit. The brain of the party was Benjamin Constant, its figure-
head Lafayette, its financial backer Laffitte. Its press was constantly censored, and survived only by becoming positively
Protean: a single editorial team brought out in succession a
series of papers with different names, which were no sooner
published than they were suppressed; thus the year 1818 alone
saw fifty-six independent papers come and go. The best known,
because they lasted, were to be *Le Constitutionnel, Le Journal
du Commerce*, and finally the review *La Minerve* which, thanks
to Benjamin Constant, was probably the finest product of
French journalism under the Restoration.

The political history of the Restoration was characterized
by two separate periods: an attempt at constitutional government which lasted from 1816 to 1820 and an Ultra period,
more marked under Charles X than under Louis XVIII, which
culminated in the 1830 Revolution.

After forming his ministry following the elections, the Duc
de Richelieu tried to win the support of the middle classes for
the regime. He put through the electoral law of February 1817 –
the so-called *Loi Lainé* – which laid down that elections should
be held at the chief town of each department and on the basis
of a vote for several deputies out of a list, a system which favoured the liberals; he settled the financial question by starting
a sinking fund to repay the national debt; and he allowed
Marshal Gouvion-Saint-Cyr, the Minister of War, to reorganize
the army in accordance with the law of 12 March 1818, which
enacted recruiting by voluntary enlistment and ballot (with provision for substitution), and contained rules for officer promotion
designed to prevent arbitrary appointments. However, the progress made by the Liberals in the elections of September 1817
and October 1818 ended up by alarming him: he obtained the

resignation of the ministry, in order to bring right-wing elements into it; but the demands of the Ultras made this solution impossible, and the Dessoles-Decazes Ministry, formed in December 1818, moved in fact further and further left. After having Guizot appointed director general of departmental and communal administration, the Cabinet dismissed the Ultra prefects, and then carried out a purge of the principal state institutions. Wishing to make public life more open, it put through the *Loi de Serre* – named after the Keeper of the Seals – which abolished censorship and preliminary authorization, prescribed trial by jury for press offences, and stipulated that caution-money should be the only obligation placed on the founders of newspapers: whence, for a short period, the remarkable rise of the liberal press. Decazes was planning a complete reform of the administration and of criminal law, as well as constitutional organization of ministerial responsibility. But the successes obtained by the left in the 1819 elections (typified by the election of the regicide Abbé Grégoire at Grenoble) led him to take his government further to the right, and even to review the electoral law. The murder of the Duc de Berry by a republican workman, Louvel (February 1820), a murder committed in the hope of putting an end to the dynasty, forced Decazes to resign and opened the way for a long period of Ultra reaction.

The Duc de Richelieu, who succeeded Decazes, suspended individual freedom and freedom of the press, and changed the electoral law, so that there was a double vote, in both arrondissement and department, the latter vote being reserved for the more heavily taxed electors (June 1820). Put into application straight away, this law brought an Ultra majority to the Chamber. Richelieu, who had thought he would be able to govern with the help of the right, but without a right-wing programme, soon found himself overwhelmed by the demands of the Ultras, represented in the government by Corbière and Villèle: in December 1821 he had to resign, having lost the support of Louis XVIII.

The opposition, deprived of its legal weapons, then moved in the direction of revolutionary action. Liberal deputies, republican university students grouped together in the *Loge des Amis de la Vérité*, and Bonapartist officers on half pay (although it is true that not all half-pay officers automatically became enemies of the regime), had already planned an insurrection under the tricolour flag for 20 August 1820; but it was discovered even before it could break out. The next year, they grouped together in the Carbonari, a secret society copied from the Italian *Carbonaria*, whose basic unit was the private or communal *vente* consisting of ten members, so that the members of the different *ventes* did not know one another and communicated only through their delegates – a cellular arrangement which was essential to foil infiltration by the police. Each member entered into four engagements: to observe secrecy, to pay a monthly contribution, to have weapons ready at all times, and to obey the orders of the *Haute Vente*. A powerful force in Paris, around Mulhouse and Lyons, and in the west where it was linked with the *Chevaliers de la Liberté*, the Carbonari were in favour of overthrowing the Bourbons and convoking a constituent assembly. If Lafayette, Manuel and Dupont de L'Eure controlled the supreme *vente*, which itself headed a centralized hierarchical organization, the young members, students and officers, formed the really active element. Hopes of a general revolutionary movement throughout Europe led in 1821 and 1822 to a whole series of risings, at Belfort, Saumur, La Rochelle and Colmar. The most sensational event was the trial of the four sergeants of La Rochelle, whose execution did more harm to the Restoration even than Ney's execution. Repression, as well as internal disagreements, resulted at the end of 1822 in the dissolution of the Carbonari. In fact, it had never had more than about 40,000 members and had never succeeded in penetrating the working class.

The fears aroused by these movements favoured the reactionaries, who held the Villèle-Corbière Ministry in their power. Villèle, a talented administrator who had continued the policy of financial reform begun by Corvetto and Louis, organized the State accountancy system, arranged the voting on the budget by sections and ministries, and made parliamentary control of public expenditure a permanent reality, he was much less at ease in the political sphere – 'He never sees the lofty side of things,' Pasquier said of him – where he was the tool of the Ultra party, whose excesses he tried in vain to control. The Press Law of 1822 restored censorship, created a number of arbitrary offences, and substituted trial by summary jurisdiction for trial by jury: which accounts for the rapid decline of the left-wing press. After the dissolution of the Chamber, new Ultra-Royalist elections (resulting in the *Chambre retrouvée*) and the accession of Charles X, who was both less intelligent and less prudent than his brother, there was no longer anything to obstruct the political and religious programme of the right. In the religious sphere, the university, under its Grand Master, Mgr Frayssinous, was brought under the influence of the clergy; the government closed its eyes to the little seminaries, which had become in fact secondary schools; as for the alliance between church and state, it was consecrated not only by the coronation – which evoked paeans of enthusiasm from Romantics such as Lamartine and Hugo, but was ridiculed by the liberal and Voltairean songwriter Béranger – but also by the passing of two laws, one authorizing the government to restore by ordinance the religious communities of women, the other punishing the profanation of sacred objects with hard labour or death: a 'sacrilege law' which would concentrate liberal hostility to the 'priest party' and help to develop that anti-clericalism which would be one of the principal causes of the fall of the Bourbons. In the political sphere, the so-called 'law of the milliard *émigrés*' authorized the payment of indemnities to those *émigrés* whose property had been sold as *biens nationaux* by means of a conversion of government stock which fell most heavily on the bourgeoisie (April 1823). On the other hand, the law restoring certain rights of primogeniture was rejected by the peers (April 1826); while the Press Law, introduced by Peyronnet, the Keeper of the Seals, described as a measure 'of justice and love' and intended to gag the opposition press, was withdrawn by the Ministry to escape a hostile vote (April 1827).

Villèle's government was shaken by the defection of the extreme right (the so-called *Pointus*), supported by Chateaubriand, who had been refused the Ministry of Foreign Affairs, and by *Le Journal des Débats*, edited by the Bertin brothers. As for the liberal opposition, it occasionally disguised itself behind a Gallican mask, and found itself supported in 1826 by a *Mémoire à consulter* written by a nobleman from Auvergne called the Comte de Montlosier. This work, which denounced the Congregation, the Jesuits, Ultramontanism and the missionary zeal of the priesthood, created a confusion, which lasted a long time, between the very active but much reduced group of the *Chevaliers de la Foi*, and a huge secret society which, under the name of the Congregation, was alleged to be plotting the destruction of the Charter in order to found a theocracy, to control all public offices, and to dominate the court, the ministries, Parliament and the public services. A great many magistrates and a few members of the Chamber of Peers urged the government to enforce the law against the Jesuits. On the left, the new liberal generation, which had abandoned its clandestine airs, now read *Le Globe*, which provided it with a philosophic doctrine. After demonstrations by the National Guard, which was disbanded in April 1827 – a step which further antagonized important sections of the Parisian bourgeoisie – Villèle, the object of concerted attacks, set up a censorship office in the Ministry of the Interior, and pronounced the dissolution of the Chamber (November 1827). But the government came up against well organized opposition, due partly to Chateaubriand's *Société des Amis de la Presse*, and partly to Guizot's *Société 'Aide-toi, le Ciel t'aidera'* which re-established relations between Paris and the provinces by means of a pamphlet campaign, and checked the electoral registers: in many constituencies the right-wing and left-wing opposition presented common lists of candidates. The election resulted in a defeat for Villèle, whose government had long been regarded as moribund, and who resigned in January 1828.

Was Martignac, who kept the Ministry of the Interior for himself in the new cabinet, capable of governing? His task would be all the more difficult in that, in a hybrid cabinet, he enjoyed neither the confidence of the King nor a definite majority in the Chamber. He was personally in favour of a conciliatory policy, allowed Guizot and Cousin to resume their lecture courses, and accepted proposed changes to the Press Law. He took up a position against the 'Priest party', by issuing an ordinance forbidding the Jesuits to teach, and by limiting the number of pupils in each seminary, though not without arousing lively opposition among the bishops. He then tried, by administrative reform, to obtain the election of municipal and general councils, without weakening the central authority. In fact, 'a shamefaced Villèle', he satisfied nobody. After he had suffered a parliamentary reverse, the King asked him for his resignation (August 1829).

The programme of Prince Jules de Polignac, a personal friend of the king, who succeeded Martignac, was to establish a constitutional and aristocratic regime rather similar to the one which existed in England. But by appointing Bourmont to the Ministry of War and La Bourdonnais to the Ministry of the Interior (with their associations with Coblentz and Waterloo), he immediately aroused a strong current of opposition in the country, where he was extremely unpopular. A Republican party now appeared with Armand Marrast's newspaper *La Tribune*; others envisaged an Orleanist solution, which was advocated by the *Le National*. This paper was produced under the inspiration of Talleyrand by Thiers, Mignet and Armand Carrel, who tried to spread the idea that the constitutional regime which the nation desired was incompatible with the maintenance on the throne of the elder branch of the Bourbons; all the people had to do, they said, was to imitate what the English had done in 1688. Political discontent was aggravated by the unrest created, since 1827, by the intensification of the economic crisis. In some circles there was talk of refusing to pay taxes.

Faced with this situation, the Ministry was divided and powerless, but it acted all the more threateningly for that: on 2 March 1830, the speech from the throne hinted at the possibility of a fresh dissolution. When the Chamber showed its lack of confidence with a reply, signed by 221 deputies, which raised the question of ministerial responsibility, it was first prorogued, then dissolved (16 May). In spite of the capture of Algiers which took place in the midst of all this, and in spite of the personal intervention of the King who implied that an opposition vote would be an offence, the July elections, carefully prepared for by the *Société 'Aide-toi, le Ciel t'aidera'*, were a liberal triumph: 274 members of the opposition were returned. However, the situation was not yet desperate for the monarchy: the opposition deputies were quite prepared to spare the King's feelings; moreover, as well-to-do bourgeois they were scarcely ready to open the flood-gates to a lower-class movement, and some of them even approached Polignac suggesting that he should take them into his Cabinet.

But the King, in his feudal simplicity, thought only of fighting, convinced that his just cause would eventually triumph. The government, invoking Article 14 of the Charter, which authorized it to issue what regulations and ordinances it considered necessary for the enforcement of the law and the safety of the state, signed four ordinances on 24 July, which had in fact been drawn up before the election results had come in. They provided for the suspension of freedom of the press, the dissolution of the Chamber, changes in the electoral law to take into account only land tax and property tax, and the calling of new elections. Resistance was organized, not among the deputies, but among the journalists, the first to be affected by the royal decisions, especially at the offices of *Le National*, where Thiers drew up a protest (26 July). Popular agitation, helped by the closing of the workshops, was rapidly taken in hand by the Republicans (Cavaignac, Bastide, Marrast, Arago and Trelat). On the 27th, Marmont, the commandant of the troops in Paris, was still in control of the situation; but on the 28th, trying to take the offensive against the barricades which had been put up, he lost the eastern districts and fell back on the Tuileries; on the 29th, with the Louvre surrounded, he gave the order for retreat. But in the meantime the deputies had intervened, alarmed at the strength of the popular movement. On the 29th, at Guizot's suggestion, they appointed Lafayette commandant of the Municipal Guard and set up a municipal commission of five members. They did not believe yet that the regime was doomed, and their only concern was to bring the insurrection under control. It was on the 30th that, faced with growing Republican agitation – which the tardy formation of a Mortemart cabinet at Saint-Cloud and the withdrawal of the ordinances had been unable to stem – they rallied to the candidature of the Duc d'Orleans, proposed by Thiers and supported by the banker Laffitte: they saw in him a means of avoiding a republic. After coming to an agreement with the peers, they offered Louis-Philippe the post of Lieutenant-General of the Kingdom. On the 31st, the latter appeared beside Lafayette on the balcony of the Hôtel de Ville, was acclaimed by the people, and promised to surround his throne with 'republican institutions': the insurrection died down, while Charles X left Saint-Cloud for Rambouillet, abdicating on 2 August in favour of his grandson, the Duc de Bordeaux. In point of fact, the liberal deputies had cheated the Republicans of their revolution. Really the Revolution was in no way inevitable: in the course of those July days, the deputies rallied to the Orleanist solution only because it limited as far as possible the consequences of a rising which had begun and developed outside their control.

O Religious Changes

The religious thought of the period is marked by the evangelical revival. This was in no small measure the work of the Wesleys, who were, it should be remembered, loyal members of the Church of England. By the end of the century the spotlight turns to the small group known as the Clapham Sect, whose Agamemnon was William Wilberforce. In the background were clerics like Isaac Milner, John Newton (friend to William Cowper, the poet), Charles Simeon and John Venn. The evangelicals were for the most part Tory in politics (Wilberforce was a close friend of Pitt), though with a strongly independent streak. They did not seek radical changes in society. They tried to make the rich more generous employers of the poor and the poor more honest servants of the rich. Their religion was a personal devotion to a personal Saviour, a religion of faith, not of works. But, although they did not believe in works without faith, they equally knew that faith without works is dead. Their faith had its outcome in works. And although they disavowed a political religion they found that their religion drove them to political action. The evangelicals have to their credit one of the great political reforms of all time, the abolition of the slave trade. ('Well, Henry,' said Wilberforce to Thornton, 'what shall we abolish next?') In this connection we should not forget the practical good sense which founded a settlement for freed slaves at Freetown in Sierra Leone. Also, their work in education, through Raikes's Sunday schools, and, in a different way through Wesley's organization of Methodism with responsibility laid on local stewards, contributed to the advance of democracy in the nineteenth century.

J.F.

Further Reading

G. E. Harrison, *Son to Susanna*, 1937.
B. Martin, *An Ancient Mariner*, Epworth Press, 1960.
R. Coupland, *Wilberforce*, Collins, 1945.
*E. M. Howse, *Saints in Politics*, University of Toronto Press, 1952. Allen & Unwin, 1971.

*Open University Set Book.

1 Alexander Knox
Character of John Wesley

from Robert Southey, *Life of John Wesley* 1820

Character of John Wesley. It will hardly be denied that even in this frail and corrupted world, we sometimes meet persons who, in their very mien and aspect, as well as in the whole habit of life, manifest such a stamp and signature of virtue as to make our judgement of them a matter of intuition, rather than a result of continued examination. I never met a human being who came more perfectly within this description than John Wesley. It was impossible to converse with him, I might say, to look at him, without being persuaded, not only that his heart and mind were animated with the purest and most exalted goodness, but that the instinctive bent of his nature accorded so congenially with his Christian principles, as to give a pledge for his practical consistency in which it was impossible not to place confidence.

In estimating John Wesley, I am not conscious of partiality. For his singularities, as a public teacher, I had no predilection. I loved and revered him for his cheerful piety, his resistless amiability, and his perfect superiority to every vulgar feeling and selfish motive. But I was not blind to his weaknesses, nor to the important defects and liabilities of his religious system. Still, the more deeply I have reflected, the more disposed have I have been to regard him as an instrument of Providence for most valuable purposes; and, whatever may have been his misconceptions in intellect, or his errors in conduct, my conviction is that he never consciously swerved from what he considered his 'heavenly calling'.

2 John Wesley

Scheme of Self-Examination

from Robert Southey, *Life of John Wesley* 1820

Love of God and Simplicity; means of which are
Prayer and Meditation
Have I been simple and recollected in every thing I said or did?
Have I? 1. Been *simple* in every thing, i.e. looked upon God as
my good, my pattern, my one desire, my disposer, parent of
good; acted wholly for him; bounded my views with the
present action or hour? 2. *Recollected*? i.e. Has this simple view
been distinct and uninterrupted? Have I done any thing without
a previous perception of its being the will of God? or without
a perception of its being an exercise or a means of the virtue
of the day? Have I said any thing without it?

2. Have I prayed with fervour? At going in and out of
church? In the church? Morning and evening in private? Monday, Wednesday, and Friday, with my friends? At rising?
Before lying down? On Saturday noon? All the time I was
engaged in exterior work? In private? Before I went into the
place of public or private prayer, for help therein? Have I,
wherever I was, gone to church morning and evening, unless
for necessary mercy? and spent from one hour to three in private?
Have I in private prayer frequently stopt short, and observed
what fervour? Have I repeated it over and over, till I adverted
to every word? Have I at the beginning of every prayer or
paragraph owned, I cannot pray? Have I paused before I concluded in His name, and adverted to my Saviour now inter-
ceding for me at the right hand of God and offering up these
prayers?

3. Have I daily used ejaculations? i.e. Have I every hour
prayed for humility, faith, hope, love, and the particular virtue
of the day? Considered with *whom* I was the last hour, *what* I
did, and *how*? With regard to recollection, love of man,
humility, self-denial, resignation, and thankfulness? Considered the next hour in the same respects, offered all I do to my
Redeemer, begged His assistance in every particular, and com-
mended my soul to His keeping? Have I done this deliberately,

(not in haste,) seriously, (not doing any thing else the while,) and fervently as I could?

4. Have I duly prayed for the virtue of the day? i.e. Have I prayed for it at going out and coming in? Deliberately, seriously, fervently?

5. Have I used a collect at nine, twelve, and three; and grace before and after eating? Aloud at my own room, deliberately, seriously, fervently?

6. Have I duly meditated? Every day, unless for necessary mercy? 1. From six, etc., to prayers? 2. From four to five, what was particular in the providence of this day? How ought the virtue of the day to have been exerted upon it? How did it fall short? (Here faults.) 3. On Sunday, from six to seven with Kempis? from three to four on redemption, or God's attributes? Wednesday and Friday from twelve to one on the Passion? After ending a book, on what I had marked in it?

Love of Man

1st. Have I been zealous to do and active in doing good? i.e. 1. Have I embraced every probable opportunity of doing good, and preventing, removing, or lessening evil?

2. Have I pursued it with my might?

3. Have I thought any thing too dear to part with, to serve my neighbour?

4. Have I spent an hour at least every day in speaking to some one or other?

5. Have I given any one up till he *expressly* renounçed me?

6. Have I, before I spoke to any, learned, as far as I could, his temper, way of thinking, past life, and peculiar hindrances, internal and external? Fixed the point to be aimed at? Then the means to it?

7. Have I, in speaking, proposed the motives, then the difficulties, then balanced them, then exhorted him to consider both calmly and deeply, and to pray earnestly for help?

8. Have I, in speaking to a stranger, explained what religion is not, (not negative, not external,) and what is it; (a recovery of the image of God;) searched at what step in it he stops, and what makes him stop there? Exhorted and directed him?

9. Have I persuaded all I could to attend public prayers,

sermons, and sacraments? And in general to obey the laws of the Church Universal, the Church of *England*, the State, the University, and their respective Colleges?

10. Have I, when taxed with any act of obedience, avowed it, and turned the attack with sweetness and firmness?

11. Have I disputed upon any practical point, unless it was to be practised just then?

12. Have I, in disputing, (1.) desired my opponent to define the terms of the question: to limit it: what he grants, what denies: (2.) delayed speaking my opinion; let him explain and prove his: then insinuated and pressed objections?

13. Have I, after every visit, asked him who went with me, Did I say any thing wrong?

14. Have I, when any one asked advice, directed and exhorted him with all my power?

2dly. Have I rejoiced with and for my neighbour in virtue or pleasure? Grieved with him in pain, for him in sin?

3rdly. Have I received his infirmities with pity not anger?

4thly. Have I thought or spoke unkindly of or to him? Have I revealed any evil of any one, unless it was necessary to some particular good I had in view? Have I then done it with all the tenderness of phrase and manner consistent with that end? Have I any way appeared to approve them that did otherwise?

5thly. Has good-will been, and appeared to be, the spring of all my actions towards others?

6thly. Have I duly used intercession? 1. Before, 2. After speaking to any? 3. For my friends on Sunday? 4. For my pupils on Monday? 5. For those who have particularly desired it, on Wednesday and Friday? 6. For the family in which I am every day?

3 John Wesley
The Rabble

from the *Journal* of John Wesley   19 March 1742

Friday, 19 March 1742 – I rode once more to Pensford, at the earnest request of several serious people. The place where they desired me to preach was a little green spot near the town. But I had no sooner begun, than a great company of rabble, hired (as we afterwards found) for that purpose, came furiously upon us, bringing a bull which they had been baiting and now drove in among the people. But the beast was wiser than his drivers, and continually ran either on one side of us or the other, while we quietly sang praise to God and prayer for about an hour. The poor wretches finding themselves disappointed, at length seized upon the bull, now weak and tired after being so long torn and beaten both by dogs and men, and by main strength partly dragged and partly thrust him in among the people. When they had forced their way to the little table on which I stood, they strove several times to throw it down by thrusting the helpless beast against it, who of himself stirred no more than a log of wood. I once or twice put aside his head with my hand, that the blood might not drop upon my clothes, intending to go on as soon as the hurry should be a little over. But the table falling down, some of our friends caught me in their arms and carried me right away on their shoulders, while the rabble wreaked their vengeance on the table which they tore bit from bit. We went a little way off, where I finished my discourse without any noise or interruption.

4 John Wesley
The Rules of a Helper

from Robert Southey, *Life of John Wesley* 1820

1. Be diligent. Never be unemployed a moment: never be triflingly employed. Never while away time; neither spend any more time at any place than is strictly necessary.

2. Be serious. Let your motto be, Holiness to the Lord. Avoid all lightness, jesting, and foolish talking.

3. Converse sparingly and cautiously with women; particularly with young women in private.

4. Take no step towards marriage without first acquainting us with your design.

5. Believe evil of no one; unless you see it done, take heed

how you credit it. Put the best construction on everything: you know the judge is always supposed to be on the prisoner's side.

6. Speak evil of no one; else *your* word, especially, would eat as doth a canker. Keep your thoughts within your own breast, till you come to the person concerned.

5 John Wesley
Letter to William Wilberforce

reprinted in R. H. Murray, *Group Movements throughout the Ages* 1935

My Dear Sir,
   Unless Divine power has raised you up to be an Athanasius *contra mundum*, I see not how you can go through your glorious enterprise, in opposing that execrable villainy (i.e. the slave trade) which is the scandal of religion, of England, and of human nature. Unless God has raised you up for this very thing, you will be worn out by the opposition of men and devils; but if God be for you who can be against you? Are all of them stronger than God? Oh! be not weary in well-doing. Go on in the name of God, and in the power of His might, till even American slavery, the vilest that ever saw the sun, shall vanish away before it. That He who has guided you from your youth up, may continue to strengthen you in this and all things, is the prayer of, dear sir, your affectionate servant,

John Wesley.

6 Charles Wesley
Wrestling Jacob

from T. Ingram and D. Newton (eds.), *Hymns as Poetry* 1956

Come, O Thou Traveller unknown,
   Whom still I hold, but cannot see,
My Company before is gone,

And I am left alone with Thee,
With Thee all Night I mean to stay,
And wrestle till the Break of Day.

I need not tell Thee who I am,
　My Misery, or Sin declare,
Thyself hast call'd me by my Name,
　Look on Thy Hands, and read it there,
But who, I ask Thee, who art Thou,
Tell me Thy Name, and tell me now?

In vain Thou strugglest to get free,
　I never will unloose my Hold:
Art Thou the Man that died for me?
　The Secret of Thy Love unfold;
Wrestling I will not let Thee go,
Till I Thy Name, Thy Nature know.

Wilt Thou not yet to me reveal
　Thy new, unutterable Name?
Tell me, I still beseech Thee, tell,
　To know it Now Resolv'd I am;
Wrestling I will not let Thee go,
Till I Thy Name, Thy Nature know.

'Tis all in vain to hold Thy Tongue,
　Or touch the Hollow of my Thigh:
Though every Sinew be unstrung,
　Out of my Arms Thou shalt not fly;
Wrestling I will not let Thee go,
Till I Thy Name, Thy Nature know.

What tho' my shrinking Flesh complain,
　And murmur to contend so long,
I rise superior to my Pain,
　When I am weak then I am strong,
And when my All of Strength shall fail,
I shall with the G o D-man prevail.

My Strength is gone, my Nature dies,
 I sink beneath Thy weighty Hand,
Faint to revive, and fall to rise;
 I fall, and yet by Faith I stand,
I stand, and will not let Thee go,
Till I Thy Name, Thy Nature know.

Yield to me Now – for I am weak;
 But confident in Self-despair:
Speak to my Heart, in Blessings speak,
 Be conquer'd by my Instant Prayer,
Speak, or Thou never hence shalt move,
And tell me, if Thy Name is L o v e.

'Tis Love, 'tis Love! Thou diedst for Me,
 I hear Thy Whisper in my Heart.
The Morning breaks, the Shadows flee:
 Pure U n i v e r s a l L o v e Thou art,
To me, to All Thy Bowels move,
Thy Nature, and Thy Name is L o v e.

My Prayer hath Power with G o d; the Grace
 Unspeakable I now receive,
Thro' Faith I see Thee Face to Face,
 I see Thee Face to Face, and live:
In vain I have not wept, and strove,
Thy Nature, and Thy Name is L o v e.

I know Thee, Saviour, who Thou art,
 J e s u s the feeble Sinner's Friend;
Nor wilt Thou with the Night depart,
 But stay, and love me to the End;
Thy Mercies never shall remove,
Thy Nature, and Thy Name is L o v e.

The Sun of Righteousness on Me
 Hath rose with Healing in his Wings,
Wither'd my Nature's Strength; from Thee

My Soul it's Life and Succour brings,
My Help is all laid up above;
Thy Nature, and Thy Name is L o v e.

    Contented now upon my Thigh
    I halt, till Life's short Journey end;
All Helplessness, all Weakness I,
    On Thee alone for Strength depend,
Nor have I Power, from Thee, to move;
Thy Nature, and Thy Name is L o v e.

    Lame as I am, I take the Prey,
    Hell, Earth, and Sin with Ease o'ercome;
I leap for Joy, pursue my Way,
    And as a bounding Hart fly home,
Thro' all Eternity to prove
Thy Nature, and Thy Name is L o v e.

7 Sydney Smith
The Unpopularity of Sermons

from *The Works of the Reverend Sydney Smith* 1839

To this cause of the unpopularity of sermons may be added the extremely ungraceful manner in which they are delivered. The English, generally remarkable for doing very good things in a very bad manner, seem to have reserved the maturity and plenitude of their awkwardness for the pulpit. A clergyman clings to his velvet cushion with either hand, keeps his eye riveted upon his book, speaks of the ecstasies of joy and fear with a voice and a face which indicate neither, and pinions his body and soul into the same attitude of limb and thought, for fear of being called theatrical and affected. The most intrepid veteran of us all dares no more than wipe his face with his cambric sudarium; if, by mischance, his hand slip from its orthodox gripe of the velvet, he draws it back as from liquid brimstone, or the caustic iron of the law, and atones for this indecorum by fresh inflexibility and more rigorous sameness. Is it wonder, then, that every semi-delirious sectary who pours forth his animated nonsense with the genuine look and voice of passion should gesticulate away the congregation of the most profound and learned divine of the Established Church, and in two Sundays preach him bare to the very sexton? Why are we natural everywhere but in the pulpit? No man expresses warm and animated feelings anywhere else with his mouth alone, but with his whole body; he articulates with every limb, and talks from head to foot with a thousand voices. Why this holoplexia on sacred occasions alone? Why call in the aid of paralysis to piety? Is it a rule of oratory to balance the style against the subject, and to handle the most sublime truths in the dullest language and the driest manner? Is sin to be taken from men, as Eve was from Adam, by casting them into a deep slumber? Or from what possible perversion of common sense are we all to look like field-preachers in Zembla, holy lumps of ice, numbed into quiescence, and stagnation, and mumbling?

8 Bishop Beilby Porteous
Charge to the Clergy

from *A Charge Delivered to the Clergy of the Diocese of London in 1798 and 1799* 1799

You may remember that when we last assembled in this place, I thought it my duty to set before you the state of religion in foreign countries, the rapid progress which *infidelity* had for some years past been making on the Continent, and the effects which this might naturally be expected to produce in our own island.[1]

I then stated to you, merely on the grounds of what had occurred to my own mind, in perusing the writings of the most celebrated philosophers (as they were pleased to stile themselves) in different parts of Europe, that there appeared to me to be a regular SYSTEM AND SCHOOL OF INFIDELITY established

1. Charge in 1794.

amongst them, and that their grand object evidently was to extirpate Christianity from the earth, and to establish Theism at least, if not Atheism in its room. At that time, however, I was not, I confess, aware (and few people I believe in this country were) how deep the foundations of this system were laid, and how widely the principles and the projects of these adventurers were diffused. It now appears from undoubted evidence, collected from the most authentic sources, and produced about the same time by two different authors, of different countries and different religions, and writing without the least concert or communication with each other,[2] that there has in fact subsisted in the heart of Europe, certain sects of men, distinguished by various fanciful names and various mysterious rites and ceremonies, but all concurring in one common object, namely, the gradual overthrow not merely of all religion, but of all civil government and all social order throughout the whole Christian world. This design they had been carrying on with incredible industry and perseverance in various ways for a long course of years; some openly attacking the great bulwarks of morality and religion, others secretly and silently undermining their foundations, till at length the explosion burst out instantaneously on one devoted country; and the full effects of its concentrated force were felt at once in the total subversion of a great empire, and the extirpation of the national faith.

It was hardly possible that such a convulsion as this, such a public and formal renunciation of Christianity, should take place in a country so near our own, without communicating some sensations of the shock which tore that country in pieces, to this kingdom. And in fact we know that similar attempts have been made here to shake our belief in revelation; that our religion has been represented as a gross imposture, and a scandalous imposition on the credulity of mankind; that even the sacred writings themselves have been reviled and ridiculed without the smallest regard to decency and to truth; that every effort has been made to contaminate the principles, and extinguish the faith of all ranks of people, but especially of the middling and the lower classes, by arguments brought down to the level of their understandings; by bold assertions, by coarse buffoonery,

2. Barruel and Robison.

by unblushing falsehoods, by language the most impious and blasphemous that ever insulted the religion of any Christian country.

But, thanks be to God, the effects of all this fury and malignity, have been much less formidable and less extensive than could have been expected. A few men of unsettled minds or weak understandings, may have been gained over to the cause of infidelity, but the bulk of the people, though rudely and roughly assailed, have stood firm and unmoved. This has probably been owing to various causes, to the natural good sense, the sound judgement, and steady character of the people of this land; to the over-ruling influence of the Holy Spirit upon their hearts; to the purity in which Christianity is here professed and taught; to the excellent liturgy we have constantly in our hands to direct and animate our devotions; to the masterly defences of scripture and of revelation which have lately issued from the press;[3] and I may add also, I trust, to the vigilance and attention of the parochial clergy, each in their respective departments. But to whatever causes the preservation of our people from the contagion of infidelity may hitherto be ascribed, we must not be too secure: the danger is not over, nor the hope of finally accomplishing their purpose abandoned by our enemies. They are still active and alert, still enterprizing, and intent upon their great object. In so righteous a cause they are deterred by no difficulties, they are discouraged by no defeats. Unabating perseverance, unconquerable hatred, and eternal enmity to the name of Christ, are their ruling principles. Whether there are in this country any of the sect called Illuminati, and other infidel mystics, that have been so long diffusing vice and atheism over the rest of Europe, I do not undertake to say; but that there are *societies* amongst us, instituted for the very purpose of propagating infidelity and profligacy through the island, more especially among the lower classes of the people, I can have no doubt. Publications of the most impious and indecent nature, have, *I know*, been distributed, with infinite activity and industry, not only in the metropolis and its neighbourhood, and in large manufacturing towns, but in little obscure villages in the remotest parts of

3. More particularly those of Dr Paley and the Bishop of Llandaff.

the kingdom; nay, they have even found their way into the very bowels of the earth, among the miners of Cornwall and the colliers of Newcastle, some of whom are said to have sold their bibles in order to purchase the *Age of Reason*. This very extensive circulation of such Tracts from one end of the kingdom to the other, cannot be the work of a few unconnected individuals; it must be the combined effort of a considerable body of men, united together for the purpose of corrupting the morals, and perverting the principles of the people, and contributing each their share of labour and expense to so honourable and meritorious an undertaking. [...]

You must lay before your people, with plainness and with force, the great fundamental doctrines of the gospel; you must shew them to themselves, you must tell them plainly and honestly what they are and what they ought to be; you must convince them that they are frail, corrupt, and fallen creatures; that man, since he came out of the hands of his Creator, has contracted a radical taint, which has miserably vitiated his moral frame; that the remedy, the only remedy, for this great, this inveterate disease of the soul, is to be found in the gospel; in the application of the means there pointed out for the recovery of what we have lost; in the renovation of the heart and life by its doctrines and its precepts; in the illumination of the understanding, in the sanctification of the soul, in the aid given to the infirmities of our nature, by the heavenly influences of the holy spirit; and, above all, in the sacrifice made for all mankind upon the cross by our Redeemer, and in humble reliance on that sacrifice for pardon and acceptance. These are the great evangelical doctrines which must be pressed repeatedly, with devout and solemn earnestness, on the minds of your hearers, which can alone speak to their consciences, their affections, and their hearts; can alone awaken them to a just sense of their condition, and convince them of the absolute necessity of sincere repentance, of a vital faith in Christ, and a uniform obedience to his laws.

In addition to all this, you must frequently represent to them the infinite importance of their spiritual concerns; the extreme, the contemptible insignificance of every thing this world has to offer in comparison of their eternal interests; the awful lesson which these turbulent and disastrous times hold out to them of the precarious nature of all worldly splendour, all worldly glory, all worldly happiness. [...]

Our interests are essentially interwoven with those of the state, and if that perish, we must all perish with it. It is not merely the revenue allotted to us by the state, it is not the honours, the emoluments, the advantages, which some of us happen to possess, that are at stake; these are, comparatively speaking, trivial things: it is something much more valuable than all these for which we are now contending. It is that freedom which we all equally enjoy; it is those laws from which we all equally derive security and protection; it is that unrivalled constitution, both in church and state, which is the glory of this country and the envy of every other; it is, in fine, the religion of that God whom we all worship, and of that Redeemer from whom we all look for salvation. These, and every thing else that is dear and valuable to us as men, as Britons, as Christians, as ministers of the gospel, we must (should our enemies succeed in their attempts against us) be content to part with. [...]

Yes, my brethren, we *will* indulge the consolatory hope, that this island, which has been so often marked as the object of God's peculiar care and favour, which has been distinguished by a religion, by a constitution, by a degree of security and freedom superior to that of every other nation under heaven, will not now, in its utmost need, be deserted by its Almighty Friend and Protector. We *will* cherish the belief that there is some degree of felicity still in store for us; that the illustrious part we have been so long appointed to act on the great theatre of the world, is not yet accomplished; but that this happy country is reserved to be a chosen remnant from a desolated world; to be the last refuge of the afflicted and distressed, the asylum of liberty, the guardian of morality, the bulwark of Christianity, and an impregnable barrier against that dreadful torrent which has deluged all the rest of Europe; but to which, when it approaches these shores, the great Ruler of the universe will I trust say, in the sublime and irresistible language of Omnipotence, 'HITHERTO SHALT THOU COME, BUT NO FURTHER: AND HERE SHALL THY PROUD WAVES BE STAYED.' Job, xxxviii, 11.

9 George Crabbe
The Vicar

from 'The Vicar', *The Works of the Reverend George Crabbe*, vol. 2   1823

Now rests our Vicar. They who knew him best,
Proclaim his life t' have been entirely rest;
Free from all evils which disturb his mind,
Whom studies vex and controversies blind.
   The rich approved, – of them in awe he stood;
The poor admired, – they all believed him good;
The old and serious of his habits spoke;
The frank and youthful loved his pleasant joke;
Mothers approved a safe contented guest,
And daughters one who back'd each small request:
In him his flock found nothing to condemn;
Him sectaries liked, – he never troubled them;
No trifles fail'd his yielding mind to please,
And all his passions sunk in early ease;
Nor one so old has left this world of sin,
More like the being that he enter'd in.

To what famed college we our Vicar owe,
To what fair county, let historians show:
Few now remember when the mild young man,
Ruddy and fair, his Sunday-task began;
Few live to speak of that soft soothing look
He cast around, as he prepared his book;
It was a kind of supplicating smile,
But nothing hopeless of applause, the while;
And when he finish'd, his corrected pride
Felt the desert, and yet the praise denied.
Thus he his race began, and to the end
His constant care was, no man to offend;
No haughty virtues stirr'd his peaceful mind,
Nor urged the priest to leave the flock behind;
He was his Master's soldier, but not one
To lead an army of his martyrs on:
Fear was his ruling passion.

The Puritan

from 'The Frank Courtship', *The Works of the Reverend
George Crabbe*, vol. 3   1823

Grave Jonas Kindred, Sybil Kindred's sire,
Was six feet high, and look'd six inches higher;
Erect, morose, determined, solemn, slow,
Who knew the man, could never cease to know;
His faithful spouse, when Jonas was not by,
Had a firm presence and a steady eye;
But with her husband dropp'd her look and tone,
And Jonas ruled unquestion'd and alone.

He read, and oft would quote the sacred words,
How pious husbands of their wives were lords;
Sarah called Abraham lord! and who could be,
So Jonas thought, a greater man than he?
Himself he view'd with undisguised respect,
And never pardon'd freedom or neglect.

They had one daughter, and this favourite child
Had oft the father of his spleen beguiled;
Soothed by attention from her early years,
She gain'd all wishes by her smiles or tears:
But Sybil then was in that playful time,
When contradiction is not held a crime:
When parents yield their children idle praise
For faults corrected in their after days.

Peace in the sober house of Jonas dwelt,
Where each his duty and his station felt:
Yet not that peace some favour'd mortals find,
In equal views and harmony of mind;
Not the soft peace that blesses those who love,
Where all with one consent in union move;
But it was that which one superior will
Commands, by making all inferiors still;
Who bids all murmurs, all objections cease,
And with imperious voice announces – Peace!

    They were, to wit, a remnant of that crew,
Who, as their foes maintain, their sovereign slew;
An independent race, precise, correct,
Who ever married in the kindred sect:
No son or daughter of their order wed
A friend to England's king who lost his head;
Cromwell was still their saint, and when they met,
They mourn'd that saints [1] were not our rulers yet.

    Fix'd were their habits; they arose betimes,
Then pray'd their hour, and sang their party-rhymes:
Their meals were plenteous, regular, and plain;
The trade of Jonas brought him constant gain;
Vender of hops and malt, of coals and corn —
And, like his father, he was merchant born:
Neat was their house; each table, chair, and stool,
Stood in its place, or moving moved by rule;
No lively print or picture graced the room:
A plain brown paper lent its decent gloom;
But here the eye, in glancing round, survey'd
A small recess that seem'd for china made;
Such pleasing pictures seem'd this pencill'd ware,
That few would search for nobler objects there —
Yet, turn'd by chosen friends, and there appear'd
His stern, strong features, whom they all revered;
For there in lofty air was seen to stand
The bold protector of the conquer'd land;
Drawn in that look with which he wept and swore,
Turn'd out the members, and made fast the door,
Ridding the house of every knave and drone,
Forced, though it grieved his soul, to rule alone.
The stern still smile each friend approving gave,
Then turn'd the view, and all again were grave.

    There stood a clock, though small the owner's need,
For habit told when all things should proceed;
Few their amusements, but when friends appear'd,

   1. This appellation is here used not ironically, nor with malignity; but it is taken merely to designate a morosely devout people, with peculiar austerity of manners.

They with the world's distress their spirits cheer'd;
The nation's guilt, that would not long endure
The reign of men so modest and so pure:
Their town was large, and seldom pass'd a day
But some had fail'd, and others gone astray;
Clerks had absconded, wives eloped, girls flown
To Gretna-Green, or sons rebellious grown;
Quarrels and fires arose; – and it was plain
The times were bad; the saints had ceased to reign!
A few yet lived to languish and to mourn
For good old manners never to return.

11 William Carey
The Glorious Door

from *Enquiry into the Obligations of Christians to use
Means for Converting the Heathens* 1792

Some controversies which have long perplexed and divided the
Church, are more clearly stated than ever; there are calls to
preach the Gospel in many places where it has not been usually
published; yea, a glorious door is opened, and is likely to be
opened wider and wider, by the spread of civil and religious
liberty, accompanied also by a diminution of the spirit of popery;
a noble effort has been made to abolish the inhuman Slave
Trade. [. . .] These are events that ought not to be overlooked;
they are not to be reckoned small things.

12 Thomas Fowell Buxton
Newgate Prison before and after Elizabeth Fry's work

from *An Inquiry whether Crime and Misery are produced or
prevented by our present System of Prison Discipline* 1818

About four years ago, Mrs Fry was induced to visit Newgate,
by the representations of its state made by some persons of the
Society of Friends.

She found the female side in a situation which no language can describe. Nearly *three hundred women*, sent there for every gradation of crime, some untried, and some under sentence of death, were crowded together in the two wards and two cells, which are now quite appropriated to the untried, and which are found quite inadequate to contain even this diminished number with any tolerable convenience. Here they saw their friends, and kept their multitudes of children; and they had no other place for cooking, washing, eating and sleeping.

They all slept on the floor; at times one hundred and twenty in one ward, without so much as a mat for bedding; and many of them were very nearly naked. She saw them openly drinking spirits; and her ears were offended by the most dreadful imprecations. Every thing was filthy to excess, and the smell was quite disgusting. Every one, even the Governor, was reluctant to go amongst them. He persuaded her to leave her watch in the office, telling her that his presence would not prevent its being torn from her! She saw enough to convince her that every thing bad was going on. In short, in giving me this account, she repeatedly said 'All I tell thee, is a faint picture of the reality; the filth, the closeness of the rooms, the ferocious manners and expressions of the women towards each other, and the abandoned wickedness which everything bespoke, are quite indescribable!' [...]

Many of these knew Newgate; had visited it a few months before, and had not forgotten the painful impressions made by a scene exhibiting, perhaps, the very utmost limits, of misery and guilt. – They now saw, what, without exaggeration may be called a transformation. Riot, licentiousness, and filth, exchanged for order, sobriety, and comparative neatness in the chamber, the apparel, and the persons of the prisoners. They saw no more an assemblage of abandoned and shameless creatures, half-naked and half-drunk, rather demanding, than requesting charity. The prison no more resounded with obscenity, and imprecations, and licentious songs; and to use the coarse, but the just, expression of one who knew the prison well, 'this hell upon earth' already exhibited the appearance of an industrious manufactory, or a well-regulated family.

13 William Cowper
Letter to Lady Hesketh

reprinted in Robert Southey, *The Life and Works of William Cowper* 1835

The Lodge, 16 Feb. 1788

I have now three letters of yours, my dearest cousin, before me, all written in the space of a week, and must be indeed insensible of kindness, did I not feel yours on this occasion. I cannot describe to you, neither could you comprehend it if I should, the manner in which my mind is sometimes impressed with melancholy on particular subjects. Your late silence was such a subject. I heard, saw, and felt a thousand terrible things which had no real existence, and was haunted by them night and day, till they at last extorted from me the doleful epistle, which I have since wished had been burned before I sent it. But the cloud has passed, and as far as you are concerned, my heart is once more at rest.

Before you gave me the hint, I had once or twice, as I lay on my bed, watching the break of day, ruminated on the subject which, in your last but one, you recommend to me.

Slavery, or a release from slavery, such as the poor negroes have endured, or perhaps both these topics together, appeared to me a theme so important at the present juncture, and at the same time susceptible of poetical management, that I more than once perceived myself ready to start in that career, could I have allowed myself to desert Homer for so long a time as it would have cost me to do them justice.

While I was pondering these things, the public prints informed me that Miss More was on the point of publication, having actually finished what I had not yet begun. The sight of her advertisement convinced me that my best course would be that to which I felt myself most inclined, – to persevere, without turning aside to attend to any other call, however alluring, in the business I have in hand.

It occurred to me likewise, that I have already borne my testimony in favour of my black brethren; and that I was one of the earliest, if not the first, of those who have in the present day expressed their detestation of the diabolical traffic in question.

On all these accounts I judged it best to be silent, and especially because I cannot doubt that some effectual measures will now be taken to alleviate the miseries of their condition, the whole nation being in possession of the case, and it being impossible also to allege an argument in behalf of man-merchandise, that can deserve a hearing. I shall be glad to see Hannah More's poem; she is a favourite writer with me, and has more nerve and energy both in her thoughts and language than half the he rhymers in the kingdom. The Thoughts on the Manners of the Great will likewise be most acceptable. I want to learn as much of the world as I can, but to acquire that learning at a distance; and a book with such a title promises fair to serve the purpose effectually.

I recommend it to you, my dear, by all means to embrace the fair occasion, and to put yourself in the way of being squeezed and incommoded a few hours, for the sake of hearing and seeing what you will never have an opportunity to see and hear hereafter, – the trial of a man who has been greater and more feared than the great Mogul himself. Whatever we are at home, we certainly have been tyrants in the East; and if these men have, as they are charged, rioted in the miseries of the innocent, and dealt death to the guiltless with an unsparing hand, may they receive a retribution that shall in future make all governors and judges of ours, in those distant regions, tremble! While I speak thus, I equally wish them acquitted. They were both my schoolfellows, and for Hastings I had a particular value. Farewell.

W. C.

14 William Cowper
Letter to John Newton

reprinted in Robert Southey, *The Life and Works of William Cowper* 1835

Weston, 19 Feb. 1788.

My Dear Friend,

I have much to thank you for. In the first place for your Sermon; in which you have addressed your brethren with all the delicacy and fidelity that were due both to their character and your own. If they were not impressed by it, it must be because, like the rabbies of old, they are less impressible than others. Such I suppose they are, and will be, so long as doctorship and clerical honours of every degree shall have a tendency to make unenlightened simpletons imagine themselves the only interpreters of God. In the next place, for your thoughts on the Slave Trade; in which there is such evidence of conscientious candour and moderation as will make it, I doubt not, to all prudent persons the most satisfactory publication on the subject. It is a subject on which I can ruminate till I feel myself lost in mazes of speculation, never to be unravelled. Could I suppose that the cruel hardships under which millions of that unhappy race have lived and died, were only preparatory to a deliverance to be wrought for them hereafter, like that of Israel out of Egypt, my reasonings would cease, and I should at once acquiesce in a dispensation, severe indeed for a time, but leading to invaluable and everlasting mercies. But there is no room, Scripture affords no warrant for any such expectations. A question then presents itself which I cannot help asking, though conscious that it ought to be suppressed. Is it to be esteemed a sufficient vindication of divine justice, if these miserable creatures, tormented as they have been from generation to generation, shall at last receive some relief, some abatement of their woes, shall not be treated absolutely as brutes for the future? The thousands of them who have already passed into an eternal state, hopeless of any thing better than they found in this life, what is to become of them? Is it essential to the perfection of a plan concerted by infinite wisdom, that such wretches should exist at all, who from the beginning of their being, through all its endless duration, can experience nothing for which they should say, It is good for us that we were created? These reasonings, and such as these engage me often, and more intensely than I wish them to do, when the case of the poor Negroes occurs to me. I know that the difficulty, if it cannot be solved, may be severed, and that the answer to which it lies open is this or somewhat like it, – God is sovereign: All are his, and he may do what he will with his own: What passes upon this grain of sand, which we call the earth, is trivial when considered with reference to those purposes that have the universe for their object. And lastly – All these things will be accounted for and explained hereafter. An answer like this would have satisfied me once, when I was myself happy; – for I have frequently thought that the happy are easily reconciled to the woes of the miserable. But in the school of affliction I have learned to cavil and to question; and finding myself in my own case reduced frequently to the necessity of accounting for my own lot by the means of an uncontrolable sovereignty which gives no account of its matters, am apt to discover, what appear to me, tremendous effects of the same sovereignty in the case of others. Then I feel – I will not tell you what – and yet I must – a wish that I had never been, a wonder that I am, and an ardent but hopeless desire not to be. Thus have I written to you my whole heart on a subject which I thought to have touched only, and to have left it. But the pen once in my hand, I am no longer master of my own intentions.

To make you some small amends, (the best I can at present,) after having thanked you in the third place, for a basket of most excellent fish, (halibut and lobsters,) I will subjoin some stanzas in the mortuary style, composed at the request of the clerk of All-Saints' parish, Northampton. They were printed at the foot of his Bill of Mortality, published at Christmas last. Some time in November the said clerk was introduced to me one morning before breakfast. Being asked his business, he told me that he wanted verses, and should be much obliged to me if I would furnish them. I replied, that in Northampton there must be many poets, because poets abound every where, and because the newspaper printed there was seldom destitute of a copy. I then mentioned in particular his namesake, Mr Cox the statuary, who to my knowledge often wooes the Muse, and not without some cause to boast of his success. To which he answered – What you say, Sir, is true. But Mr Cox is a gentleman of much reading, and the people of our town do not well understand him. He has written for me, but nine in ten of us were stone-blind to his meaning. Finding that he had an answer to all that I could urge, and particularly affected by the eulogium implied in his last, I suffered myself to be persuaded.

We are truly sorry to be informed, as we were by Mr Bull, that Mrs Newton is so much indisposed. Our affectionate remembrances and best wishes attend you both.

Yours most sincerely, my dear friend,
Wm. Cowper.

15 William Cowper
Sweet Meat has Sour Sauce

from Robert Southey, *The Life and Works of William Cowper* 1835

A trader I am to the African shore,
But since that my trading is like to be o'er,
I'll sing you a song that you ne'er heard before,
                    Which nobody can deny, deny,
                    Which nobody can deny.

When I first heard the news it gave me a shock,
Much like what they call an electrical knock,
And now I am going to sell off my stock,
                    Which nobody, &c.

'Tis a curious assortment of dainty regales,
To tickle the Negroes with when the ship sails,
Fine chains for the neck, and a cat with nine tails,
                    Which nobody, &c.

Here's supple-jack plenty, and store of rat-tan,
That will wind itself round the sides of a man,

As close as a hoop round a bucket or can,
          Which nobody, &c.

Here's padlocks and bolts, and screws for the thumbs,
That squeeze them so lovingly till the blood comes,
They sweeten the temper like comfits or plums,
          Which nobody, &c.

When a Negro his head from his victuals withdraws,
And clenches his teeth and thrusts out his paws,
Here's a notable engine to open his jaws,
          Which nobody, &c.

Thus going to market, we kindly prepare
A pretty black cargo of African ware,
For what they must meet with when they get there,
          Which nobody, &c.

'Twould do your heart good to see 'em below,
Lie flat on their backs all the way as we go,
Like sprats on a gridiron, scores in a row,
          Which nobody, &c.

But ah! if in vain I have studied an art
So gainful to me, all boasting apart,
I think it will break my compassionate heart,
          Which nobody, &c.

For oh! how it enters my soul like an awl!
This pity, which some people self-pity call,
Is sure the most heart-piercing pity of all,
          Which nobody, &c.

So this is my song, as I told you before;
Come, buy off my stock, for I must no more
Carry Caesars and Pompeys to Sugar-cane shore,
          Which nobody can deny, deny,
          Which nobody can deny.

16 William Cowper

Walking with God

from T. Ingram and D. Newton (eds.), *Hymns as Poetry*   1956

Oh! for a closer walk with GOD,
   A calm and heavenly frame;
A light to shine upon the road
   That leads me to the Lamb!

Where is the blessedness I knew
   When first I saw the LORD?
Where is the soul-refreshing view
   Of JESUS, and his word?

What peaceful hours I once enjoy'd!
   How sweet their mem'ry still!
But they have left an aching void,
   The world can never fill.

Return, O holy Dove, return,
   Sweet messenger of rest;
I hate the sins that made thee mourn,
   And drove thee from my breast.

The dearest idol I have known,
   Whate'er that idol be;
Help me to tear it from thy throne,
   And worship only thee.

So shall my walk be close with GOD,
   Calm and serene my frame;
So purer light shall mark the road
   That leads me to the Lamb.

17 John Newton
The Name of Jesus

from T. Ingram and D. Newton (eds.), *Hymns as Poetry*   1956

How sweet the name of JESUS sounds
    In a believer's ear?
It soothes his sorrows, heals his wounds,
    And drives away his fear.

It makes the wounded spirit whole,
    And calms the troubled breast;
'Tis Manna to the hungry soul,
    And to the weary rest.

Dear name! the rock on which I build,
    My shield and hiding place;
My never-failing treas'ry fill'd
    With boundless stores of grace.

By thee my pray'rs acceptance gain,
    Altho' with sin defil'd;
Satan accuses me in vain,
    And I am own'd a child.

JESUS! my Shepherd, Husband, Friend,
    My Prophet, Priest, and King;
My LORD, my Life, my Way, my End,
    Accept the praise I bring.

Weak is the effort of my heart,
    And cold my warmest thought;
But when I see thee as thou art,
    I'll praise thee as I ought.

'Till then I would thy love proclaim
    With every fleeting breath;
And may the music of thy name
    Refresh my soul in death.

18 John Newton
The New Birth

from 'The New Birth', Nathaniel Micklem (ed.),
A Book of Personal Religion 1938

There is a certain important change takes place in the heart, by
the operation of the Spirit of God, before the soundest and most
orthodox sentiments can have their proper influence upon us.
This work, or change, the Scripture describes by various names,
each of which is designed to teach us the marvellous effects it
produces, and the almighty power by which it is produced. It is
sometimes called a new-birth, sometimes a new creature or new
creation, sometimes the causing light to shine out of darkness,
sometimes the opening the eyes of the blind, sometimes the
raising the dead to life. Till a person has experienced this
change, he will be at a loss to form a right conception of it : but
it means, not being proselyted to an opinion, but receiving a
principle of divine life and light in the soul. [. . .]

At length he begins to *feel* the inward depravity, which he
had before owned as an opinion; a sense of sin and guilt cut
him out new work. Here reasoning will stand him in no stead.
This is a painful change of mind; but it prepares the way for a
blessing. It silences some objections better than a thousand arguments, it cuts the comb of his own wisdom and attainments, it
makes him weary of work for life, and teaches him, in God's
due time, the meaning of that text, 'To him that worketh not,
but believeth in him who justifieth the ungodly, his faith is
counted for righteousness.' Then he learns that scriptural faith
is a very different thing from a rational assent to the gospel, –
that it is the immediate gift of God, the operation of God, that
Christ is not only the object, but the author and finisher of faith,
and that faith is not so properly a part of that obedience we owe
to God, as an inestimable benefit we receive from him for
Christ's sake, which is the medium of our justification and the
principle by which we are united to Christ (as the branch to
the vine).

The jailor was certainly a Christian when baptised, as you
observe. He trembled; he cried out, 'What must I do to be

saved?' Paul did not bid him amend his life, but believe in the Lord Jesus. He believed, and rejoiced. But the Lord blessed the Apostle's words to produce in him that saving faith which filled him with joy and peace. It was, as I observed before, something more than an assent to the proposition that Jesus is the Christ, a resting in him for forgiveness and acceptance and a cleaving to him in love. No other faith will purify the heart, work by love, and overcome the world.

19 John Newton
Utterance of the Heart

from *Cardiphonia, or the Utterance of the Heart in the course of a Real Correspondence* 1781

A

It remains therefore a truth, in defiance of all the cavils of the ignorant, that the holy Spirit does influence the hearts of all the children of God, or in other words, they are inspired, not with new revelations, but with grace and wisdom to understand, apply and feed upon the great things already revealed in the scriptures, without which the scriptures are as useless as spectacles to the blind. Were it not so, when we become acquainted with the poverty, ignorance and wickedness of our hearts, we must sit down in utter despair of being ever able to think a good thought, to offer a single petition aright in prayer, or to take one safe step in the path of life. But now we may be content with our proper weakness, since the power and spirit of Christ are engaged to rest upon us; and while we are preserved in a single dependance upon this help, though unable of ourselves to do any thing, we shall find an ability to do every thing that our circumstances and duty call for. What is weaker than a worm? Yet the Lord's worms shall, in his strength, thresh the mountains, and make the hills as chaff. But this life of faith, this living and acting by a power above our own, is an inexplicable mystery, till experience makes it plain. I have often wondered that St Paul has obtained so much quarter at the hands of some people, as to pass with them for a man of sense. For surely the greatest part of his writings, must be to the last degree absurd and unintelligible upon their principles. How many contradictions must they find, for instance, if they give any attention to what they read, in that one passage, Gal. ii. 20. I am crucified with Christ, nevertheless I live; yet not I, but Christ liveth in me; and the life which I now live in the flesh, I live by faith in the Son of God, who loved me and gave himself for me.

B

Though there is a principle of consciousness, and a determination of the will, sufficient to denominate our thoughts and performances our own, yet I believe mankind in general, are more under an invisible agency than they apprehend. The Lord, immediately from himself, and perhaps by the ministry of his holy Angels, guides, prompts, restrains or warns his people. So there undoubtedly is what I may call a *black inspiration*, the influence of the evil spirits who work in the hearts of the disobedient, and not only excite their wills, but assist their faculties, and qualify as well as incline them to be more assiduously wicked, and more extensively mischievous, than they could be of themselves. I consider Voltaire, for instance, and many writers of the same stamp, to be little more than secretaries and amanuenses of one who has unspeakably more wit and adroitness in promoting infidelity and immorality, than they of themselves can justly pretend to. They have, for a while, the credit (if I may so call it) of the fund from whence they draw; but the world little imagines who is the real and original author of that philosophy and poetry, of those fine turns and sprightly inventions, which are so generally admired. Perhaps many, now applauded for their genius, would have been comparatively dolts, had they not been engaged in a cause which Satan has so much interest in supporting.

C

In the first place, I beg you to be upon your guard against a reasoning spirit. Search the Scriptures; and where you can find a plain rule or warrant for any practice, go boldly on; and be not discouraged because you may not be clearly able to answer or reconcile every difficulty, that may either occur to your own mind or be put in your way by others. Our hearts are very dark and narrow, and the very root of all apostacy is a proud disposition to question the necessity or propriety of divine appointments. But the child-like simplicity of faith is to follow God without reasoning; taking it for granted a thing must be right if he directs it, and charging all seeming inconsistencies to the account of our own ignorance.

D

I hope the good people at Bristol, and every where else, are praying for our sinful, distracted land, in this dark day. The Lord is angry, the sword is drawn, and I am afraid nothing but the spirit of wrestling prayer can prevail for the returning it into the scabbard. Could things have proceeded to these extremities, except the Lord had withdrawn his salutary blessing from both sides? It is a time of prayer. We see the beginning of trouble, but who can foresee the possible consequences? The fire is kindled, but how far it may spread those who are above may perhaps know better than we. I meddle not with the disputes of party, nor concern myself with any political maxims, but such as are laid down in scripture. There I read that righteousness exalteth a nation, and that sin is the reproach, and if persisted in, the ruin, of any people. Some people are startled at the enormous sum of our national debt: they who understand spiritual arithmetic may be well startled, if they sit down and compute the debt of national sin. Imprimis, infidelity: item, contempt of the Gospel: item, the profligacy of manners: item, perjury: item, the cry of blood, the blood of thousands, perhaps millions, from the East Indies. It would take sheets, yea quires, to draw out the particulars under each of these heads, and then much would remain untold. What can we answer, when the Lord saith, Shall not I visit for these things? Shall not my soul be avenged on such a nation as this? Since we received the news of the first hostilities in America, we have had an additional prayer meeting. Could I hear that professors in general, instead of wasting their breath in censuring men and measures, were plying the throne of grace, I should still hope for a respite. Poor New England! once the glory of the earth, now likely to be visited with fire and sword. They have left their first love, and the Lord is sorely contending with them. Yet surely their sins as a people are not to be compared with ours. I am just so much affected with these things as to know, that I am not affected enough. Oh! my spirit is sadly cold and insensible, or I should lay them to heart in a different manner: yet I endeavour to give the alarm as far as I can. There is one political maxim which comforts me, *the Lord reigns*. His hand guides the storm, and he knows them that are his, how to protect, support and deliver them. He will take care of his own cause, yea, he will extend his kingdom, even by these formidable methods. Men have one thing in view, he has another, and his counsel shall stand.

E

An experimental knowledge of Jesus, as the deliverer from *sin* and *wrath*, and the author of eternal life and salvation to all who are enabled to believe, is a sufficient ground for union of heart: in this point all who are taught of God are of one mind. But an eager fighting for or against those points which are usually made the subjects of controversy tends to nourish pride and evil tempers in ourselves, and to alienate our hearts from those we hope to spend an eternity with. In heaven we shall neither be Dissenters, Moravians, nor Methodists; neither Calvinists nor Arminians; but followers of the Lamb, and children of the kingdom. There we shall hear the voice of war no more.

F

Last Sunday a young man died here of extreme old age at 25. He laboured hard to ruin a good constitution, and unhappily succeeded; yet amused himself with the hopes of recovery almost to the last. We have a sad knot of such poor creatures in this place, who labour to stifle each other's convictions, and to ruin themselves and associates, soul and body. How industriously is Satan served! I was formerly one of his most active undertempters. Not content with running the broad way myself, I was indefatigable in enticing others; and had my influence been equal to my wishes, I would have carried all the human race with me. And doubtless some have perished, to whose destruction I was greatly instrumental, by tempting them to sin, and by poisoning and hardening them with principles of infidelity: and yet I was spared. When I think of the most with whom I spent my unhappy days of ignorance, I am ready to say, I only am escaped alive to tell thee. Surely I have not half the activity and zeal in the service of him, who snatched me as a brand out of the burning, as I had in the service of his enemy. Then the whole stream of my endeavours and affections went one way; now my best desires are continually crossed, counteracted and spoiled, by the sin which dwelleth in me: then the tide of a corrupt nature bore me along; now I have to strive and swim against it. The Lord cut me short of opportunities, and placed me where I could do but little mischief; but had my abilities and occasions been equal to my heart, I should have been a Voltaire and a Tiberius in one character, a monster of prophaneness and licentiousness. O to grace how great a debtor! A common drunkard or profligate is a petty sinner to what I was. I had the ambition of a Caesar or an Alexander, and wanted to rank in wickedness among the foremost of the human race. When you have read this, praise the Lord for his mercy to the chief of sinners, and pray that I may have grace to be faithful.

20 John Newton
Thoughts upon the African Slave Trade

from *Thoughts upon the African Slave Trade*　1788

Usually, about two-thirds of a cargo of Slaves are males. When a hundred and fifty or two hundred stout men, torn from their native land, many of whom never saw the sea, much less a ship, till a short space before they are embarked; who have, probably, the same natural prejudice against a white man, as we have against a black; and who often bring with them an apprehension that they are bought to be eaten: I say, when thus circumstanced, it is not to be expected that they will, tamely, resign themselves to their situation. It is always taken for granted, that they will attempt to gain their liberty, if possible. Accordingly, as we dare not trust them, we receive them on board, from the first, as enemies: and before their number exceeds, perhaps, ten or fifteen, they are all put in irons; in most ships, two and two together. And frequently, they are not thus confined, as they might, most conveniently, stand or move, the right hand and foot of one to the left of the other; but across, that is, the hand and foot of each on the same side, whether right or left, are fettered together: so that they cannot move, either hand or foot, but with great caution, and with perfect consent. Thus they must sit, walk and lie, for many months, (sometimes for nine or ten,) without any mitigation or relief, unless they are sick.

In the night they are confined below, in the day-time (if the weather be fine) they are upon deck; and as they are brought up, by pairs, a chain is put through a ring upon their irons, and this is likewise locked down to the ring-bolts, which are fastened at certain intervals upon the deck. These, and other precautions, are no more than necessary; especially, as while the number of Slaves increases, that of the people, who are to guard them, is diminished, by sickness, or death, or by being absent in the boats: so that, sometimes, not ten men can be mustered, to watch, night and day, over two hundred, besides having all the other business of the ship to attend.

That these precautions are so often effectual, is much more to be wondered at, than that they sometimes fail. One unguarded hour, or minute, is sufficient to give the Slaves the opportunity they are always waiting for. An attempt to rise upon the ship's company, brings on instantaneous and horrid war; for, when they are once in motion, they are desperate; and where they do not conquer, they are seldom quelled without much mischief and blood-shed, on both sides.

Sometimes, when the Slaves are ripe for an insurrection, one of them will impeach the affair; and then necessity, and the state policy, of these small, but most absolute governments, enforce maxims directly contrary to the nature of things. The traitor to the cause of liberty is caressed, rewarded, and deemed an honest fellow. The patriots, who formed and animated the plan, if they can be found out, must be treated as villains, and punished, to intimidate the rest. These punishments, in their nature and degree, depend upon the sovereign will of the Captain. Some are content with inflicting such moderate punishment, as may suffice for an example. But unlimited power, instigated by revenge, and where the heart, by a long familiarity with the sufferings of Slaves, is become callous, and insensible to the pleadings of humanity, is terrible.

I have seen them sentenced to unmerciful whippings, continued till the poor creatures have not had power to groan under their misery, and hardly a sign of life has remained. I have seen them agonizing for hours, I believe, for days together, under the torture of the thumb-screws; a dreadful engine, which, if the screw be turned by an unrelenting hand, can give intolerable anguish. There have been instances in which cruelty has proceeded still further; but, as I hope they are few, and I can mention but one, from my own knowledge, I shall but mention it.

I have often heard a Captain, who has been long since dead, boast of his conduct in a former voyage, when his Slaves attempted to rise upon him. After he had suppressed the insurrection, he sat in judgement upon the insurgents; and not only, in cold blood, adjudged several of them, I know not how many, to die, but studied, with no small attention, how to make death as excruciating to them as possible. For my reader's sake, I suppress the recital of particulars.

Surely, it must be allowed, that they who are long conversant with such scenes as these, are liable to imbibe a spirit of ferociousness, and savage insensibility, of which human nature, depraved as it is, is not, ordinarily, capable. If these things be true, the reader will admit the possibility of a fact, that was in current report, when I was upon the coast, and the truth of which, though I cannot now authenticate it, I have no reason to doubt.

A Mate of a ship, in a long-boat, purchased a young woman, with a fine child, of about a year old, in her arms. In the night, the child cried much, and disturbed his sleep. He rose up in great anger, and swore, that if the child did not cease making such a noise, he would presently silence it. The child continued to cry. At length he rose up a second time, tore the child from the mother, and threw it into the sea. The child was soon silenced indeed, but it was not so easy to pacify the woman: she was too valuable to be thrown overboard, and he was obliged to bear the sound of her lamentations, till he could put her on board his ship.

I am persuaded, that every tender mother, who feasts her eyes and her mind, when she contemplates the infant in her arms, will commiserate with the poor Africans. – But why do I speak of one child, when we have heard and read a melancholy story, too notoriously true to admit of contradiction, of more than a hundred grown slaves, thrown into the sea, at one time, from on board a ship when fresh water was scarce; to fix the loss upon the Underwriters, which otherwise, had they died on board, must have fallen upon the Owners of the vessel. These instances are specimens of the spirit produced, by the African Trade, in men, who, once, were no more destitute of the milk of human kindness, than ourselves.

Hitherto, I have considered the condition of the Men Slaves only. From the Women, there is no danger of insurrection, and they are carefully kept from the men; I mean, from the Black men. But – In what I have to offer, on this head, I am far from including every ship. I speak not of what is universally, but of what is too commonly, and, I am afraid, too generally, prevalent.

I have already observed, that the Captain of an African ship, while upon the coast, is absolute in his command; and if he be humane, vigilant, and determined, he has it in his power to protect the miserable; for scarcely any thing can be done, on board the ship, without his permission, or connivance. But this power is, too seldom, exerted in favour of the poor Woman Slaves.

When we hear of a town taken by storm, and given up to the ravages of an enraged and licentious army, of wild and unprincipled Cossacks, perhaps no part of the distress affects a feeling mind more, than the treatment to which the Women are exposed. But the enormities frequently committed, in an African ship, though equally flagrant, are little known *here*, and are considered, *there*, only as matters of course. When the Women and Girls are taken on board a ship, naked, trembling, terrified, perhaps almost exhausted with cold, fatigue and hunger, they are often exposed to the wanton rudeness of white Savages. The poor creatures cannot understand the language they hear, but the looks and manner of the speakers, are sufficiently intelligible. In imagination, the prey is divided, upon the spot, and only reserved till opportunity offers. Where resistance, or refusal, would be utterly in vain, even the sollicitation of consent is seldom thought of. But I forbear. – This is not a subject for declamation. Facts like these, so certain, and so numerous, speak for themselves. Surely, if the advocates for the Slave Trade attempt to plead for it, before the Wives and Daughters of our happy land, or before those who have Wives or Daughters of their own, they must lose their cause.

Perhaps some hard-hearted pleader may suggest, that such treatment would indeed be cruel, in Europe; but the African Women are Negroes, Savages, who have no idea of the nicer sensations which obtain among civilized people. I dare contradict them in the strongest terms. I have lived long, and conversed much, amongst these supposed Savages. I have often slept in their towns, in a house filled with goods for trade, with no person in the house but myself, and with no other door than a mat; in that security, which no man in his senses would expect, in this civilized nation, especially in this metropolis, without the precaution of having strong doors, strongly locked and bolted. And with regard to the women, in Sherbro, where I was most acquainted, I have seen many instances of modesty, and even delicacy, which would not disgrace an English woman. Yet, such is the treatment which I have known permitted, if not encouraged, in many of our ships – they have been abandoned, without restraint, to the lawless will of the first comer.

Accustomed thus to despise, insult, and injure the Slaves on board, it may be expected that the conduct of many of our people to the Natives, with whom they trade, is, as far as circumstances admit, very similar; and it is so. They are considered as a people to be robbed and spoiled, with impunity. Every art is employed to deceive, and wrong them. And he who has most address, in this way, has most to boast of.

Not an article, that is, capable of diminution or adulteration, is delivered genuine, or entire. The spirits are lowered by water. False heads are put into the kegs that contain the gunpowder; so that, though the keg appears large, there is no more powder in it, than in a much smaller. The linen and cotton cloths are opened, and two or three yards, according to the length of the piece, cut off, not from the end, but out of the middle, where it is not so readily noticed.

The Natives are cheated, in the number, weight, measure, or quality, of what they purchase, in every possible way. And, by habit and emulation, a marvellous dexterity is acquired in these practices. And thus the Natives, in their turn, in proportion to their commerce with the Europeans, and (I am sorry to add) particularly with the English, become jealous, insidious and revengeful. [...]

For, with a few exceptions, the English and the Africans, reciprocally, consider each other as consummate villains, who are always watching opportunities to do mischief. In short, we have, I fear too deservedly, a very unfavourable character upon the Coast. When I have charged a Black with unfairness and dishonesty, he has answered, if able to clear himself, with an air of disdain, 'What! do you think I am a White Man?'

Such is the nature, such are the concomitants, of the Slave Trade; and such is the school in which many thousands of our Seamen are brought up. Can we then wonder at that impatience of subordination, and that disposition to mutiny, amongst them, which has been, of late, so loudly complained of, and so severely felt? Will not sound policy suggest, the necessity, of some expedient here? Or can sound policy suggest any, effectual, expedient, but the total suppression of a Trade, which, like a poisonous root, diffuses its malignity into every branch?

With our ships, the great object is, to be full. When the ship is there, it is thought desirable, she should take as many as possible. The cargo of a vessel of a hundred tons, or little more, is calculated to purchase from two hundred and twenty to two hundred and fifty Slaves. Their lodging-rooms below the deck, which are three, (for the men, the boys, and the women,) besides a place for the sick, are sometimes more than five feet high, and sometimes less, and this height is divided towards the middle, for the Slaves lie in two rows, one above the other, on each side of the ship, close to each other, like books upon a shelf. I have known them so close, that the shelf would not, easily, contain one more.

And I have known a white man sent down, among the men, to lay them in these rows to the greatest advantage, so that as little space as possible might be lost. Let it be observed, that the poor creatures, thus cramped for want of room, are likewise in irons, for the most part both hands and feet, and two together, which makes it difficult for them to turn or move, to attempt either to rise or to lie down, without hurting themselves, or each other. Nor is the motion of the ship, especially her heeling, or stoop on one side, when under sail, to be omitted; for this, as they lie athwart, or across the ship, adds to the uncomfortableness of their lodging, especially to those who lie on the leeward, or leaning, side of the vessel.

Dire is the tossing, deep the groans.

The heat and the smell of these rooms, when the weather will not admit of the Slaves being brought upon deck, and of having their rooms cleaned every day, would be, almost, insupportable, to a person not accustomed to them. If the Slaves and their rooms can be constantly aired, and they are not detained too long on board, perhaps there are not many die; but the contrary is often their lot. They are kept down, by the weather, to breathe a hot and corrupted air, sometimes for a week: this, added to the galling of their irons, and the despondency which seizes their spirits, when thus confined, soon becomes fatal. And every morning, perhaps, more instances than one are found, of the living and the dead, like the Captives of Mezentius, fastened together.

Epidemical fevers and fluxes, which fill the ship with noisome and noxious effluvia, often break out, infect the Seamen likewise, and the Oppressors, and the Oppressed, fall by the same stroke. I believe, nearly one half of the Slaves on board, have, sometimes, died; and that the loss of a third part, in these circumstances, is not unusual. The ship, in which I was Mate, left the Coast with Two Hundred and Eighteen Slaves on board; and though we were not much affected by epidemical disorders, I find, by my journal of that voyage, (now before me,) that we buried Sixty-two on our passage to South-Carolina, exclusive of those which died before we left the Coast, of which I have no account.

I believe, upon an average between the more healthy, and the more sickly voyages, and including all contingencies, One Fourth of the whole purchase may be allotted to the article of Mortality. That is, if the English ships purchase *Sixty Thousand* Slaves annually, upon the whole extent of the Coast, the annual loss of lives cannot be much less than *Fifteen Thousand*.

I have apprized the reader, that I write from memory, after

an interval of more than thirty years. But at the same time, I believe, many things which I saw, heard and felt, upon the Coast of Africa, are so deeply engraven in my memory, that I can hardly forget, or greatly mistake them, while I am capable of remembering any thing. I am certainly not guilty of wilful misrepresentation. And, upon the whole, I dare appeal to the Great Searcher of hearts, in whose presence I write, and before whom I, and my readers, must all shortly appear, that (with the restrictions and exceptions I have made) I have advanced nothing, but what, to the best of my judgement and conscience, is true.

21 Nicholas Cresswell

Slavery in the West Indies

from *The Journal of Nicholas Cresswell, 1774-7* 1924

Tuesday 13 September 1774
Went ashore and saw a Cargo of Slaves land. One of the most shocking sights I ever saw. About 400 Men, Women, and Children, brought from their native Country, deprived of their liberty, and themselves and posterity become the property of cruel strangers without a probability of ever enjoying the Blessings of Freedom again, or a right of complaining, be their sufferings never so great. The idea is horrid and the practice unjust. They were all naked, except a small piece of blue cloth about a foot broad to cover their nakedness, and appear much dejected. [...]

Friday 16 September 1774
The British nation famed for humanity suffers it to be tarnished by their Creolian subjects – the Cruelty exercised upon the Negroes is at once shocking to humanity and a disgrace to human nature. For the most trifling faults, sometimes for mere whims of their Masters, these poor wretches are tied up and whipped most unmercifully. I have seen them tied up and flogged with a twisted piece of Cowskin till there was very little signs of Life. [...] Some of them die under the severity of these barbarities, others whose spirits are too great to submit to the

insults and abuses they receive put an end to their own lives. If a person kills a slave he only pays his value as a fine. It is not a hanging matter. Certainly these poor beings meet with some better place on the other side of the Grave, for they have a hell on earth. It appears they are sensible of this, if one may judge from their behaviour at their funerals. Instead of weeping and wailing, they dance and sing and appear to be the happiest mortals on earth.

22 William Wilberforce
Erroneous Notion of Religion

from *A Practical View of the Prevailing Religious System of Professed Christians in the Higher and Middle Classes in this Country, contrasted with Real Christianity* 1797

A

Hence it is that so little sense of responsibility seems attached to the possession of high rank, or splendid abilities, or affluent fortunes, or other means or instruments of usefulness. The instructive admonitions, 'give an account of thy stewardship', – 'occupy till I come'; are forgotten. Or if it be acknowledged by some men of larger views than ordinary, that a reference is to be had to some principle superior to that of our own gratification, it is, at best, to the good of society, or to the welfare of our families: and even then the obligations resulting from these relations are seldom enforced on us by any higher sanctions than those of family comfort, and of worldly interest or estimating. Besides, what multitudes of persons are there, people without families, in private stations, or of a retired turn. to whom they are scarcely held to apply! and what multitudes of cases to which it would be thought unnecessary scrupulosity to extend them! Accordingly we find *in fact*, that the generality of mankind among the higher order, in the formation of their schemes, in the selection of their studies, in the choice of their place of residence, in the employment and distribution of their time, in their thoughts, conversation, and amusements, are considered as being at liberty, if there be no actual vice, to consult in the main their own gratification.

Thus the generous and wakeful spirit of Christian Benevolence, seeking and finding everywhere occasions for its exercise, is exploded, and a system of *decent selfishness* is avowedly established in its stead; a system scarcely more to be abjured for its impiety, than to be abhorred for its cold insensibility to the opportunities of diffusing happiness. 'Have we no families, or are they provided for? Are we wealthy, and bred to no profession? Are we young and lively, and in the gaiety and vigour of youth? Surely we may be allowed to take our pleasure. We neglect no duty, we live in no vice, we do nobody any harm, and have a right to amuse ourselves. We have nothing better to do; we wish we had; our time hangs heavy on our hands for want of it.'

Yet thus life rolls away with too many of us in a course of 'shapeless idleness'. Its recreations constitute its chief business. Watering-places – the sports of the field – cards! never-failing cards! – the assembly – the theatre – all contribute their aid – amusements are multiplied, and combined and varied, 'to fill up the void of a listless and languid life'; and by the judicious use of these different resources, there is often a kind of sober settled plan of domestic dissipation, in which with all imaginable decency year after year wears away in unprofitable vacancy. Even old age often finds us pacing in the same round of amusements, which our early youth had tracked out. Meanwhile, being conscious that we are not giving into any flagrant vice, perhaps that we are guilty of no irregularity, and, it may be, that we are not neglecting the offices of Religion, we persuade ourselves that we need not be uneasy. In the main we do not fall below the general standard of morals, of the class and station to which we belong; we may therefore allow ourselves to glide down the stream without apprehension of the consequences.

A very erroneous notion appears to prevail concerning the true nature of Religion. Religion, agreeably to what has been already stated, (the importance of the subject will excuse repetition) may be considered as the implantation of a vigorous and active principle; it is seated in the heart, where its authority is recognized as supreme, whence by degrees it expels whatever is opposed to it, and where it gradually brings all the affections and desires under its complete control and regulation.

But though the heart be its special residence, it may be said to possess in a degree the ubiquity of its Divine Author. Every endeavour and pursuit must acknowledge its presence; and whatever receives not its sacred stamp, is to be condemned as inherently defective, and is to be at once relinquished. It is like the principle of vitality, which, animating every part, lives throughout the whole of the human body, and communicates its kindly influence to the smallest and remotest fibres of the frame. But the notion of Religion entertained by many among us seems altogether different. They begin indeed, in submission to her clear prohibitions, by fencing off the field of human action, a certain district, which, though it in many parts bear fruits on which they cast a longing eye, they cannot but confess to be forbidden ground. They next assign to Religion a portion, larger or smaller according to whatever may be their circumstances and views, in which however she is to possess merely a qualified jurisdiction; and having so done, they conceive that without let or hindrance they have a right to range at will all over the spacious remainder. Religion can claim only a stated proportion of their thoughts, their time, their fortune, and influence; and of these, or perhaps of any of them, if they make her any thing of a liberal allowance, she may well be satisfied: the rest is now their own to do what they will with; they have paid their tythes, say rather their composition, the demands of the Church are satisfied, and they may surely be permitted to enjoy what she has left without molestation or interference.

It is scarcely possible to state too strongly the mischief which results from this fundamental error. At the same time its consequences are so natural and obvious, that one would think it scarcely possible not to foresee that they must infallibly follow. The greatest part of human actions is considered as indifferent. If men are not chargeable with actual vices, and are decent in the discharge of their religious duties; if they do not stray into the forbidden ground, if they respect the rights of the conceded allotment, what more can be expected from them? Instead of keeping at a distance from *all sin*, in which alone consists our safety, they will be apt not to care how near they approach what they conceive to be the boundary line; if they have not actually passed it, there is no harm done, it is no trespass. Thus the free and active spirit of Religion is 'cribbed and hemmed in'; she is checked in her disposition to expand her territory, and enlarge the circle of her influence. She must keep to her prescribed confines, and every attempt to extend them will be resisted as an encroachment. [...]

B

The Parlous Condition of the Nation

Can there, then, be a doubt, whither tends the path in which we are travelling, and whither at length it must conduct us? If any should hesitate, let them take a lesson from experience. In a neighbouring country, several of the same causes have been in action; and they have at length produced their full effect; manners corrupted; morals depraved, dissipation predominant, above all, Religion discredited, and infidelity, grown into repute and fashion,[1] terminating in the public disavowal of every religious principle which had been used to attract the veneration of mankind: the representatives of a whole nation publicly witnessing, not only without horror, but without the smallest disapprobation, an open unqualified denial of the very existence of God; and at length, as a body, withdrawing their allegiance from the Majesty of Heaven.

I might here enlarge with pleasure on the unrivalled excellence, in this very view, of the constitution under which we live in this happy country; and point out how, more perhaps than any which ever existed upon earth, it is so framed, as to provide at the same time for keeping up a due degree of public spirit, and yet for preserving unimpaired the quietness, and comfort, and charities of private life; how it even extracts from selfishness itself many of the advantages which, under less happily constructed forms of government, public spirit only can supply. But such a political discussion, however grateful to a British mind, would here be out of place. It is rather our business to remark, how much Christianity in every way sets herself in direct hos-

1. What is here stated must be acknowledged by all, be their political opinions concerning French events what they may; and it makes no difference in the writer's view of the subject, whether the state of morals was or was not, quite, or nearly, as bad, before the French Revolution.

tility to selfishness, the mortal distemper of political communities; and consequently, how their welfare must be inseparable from her prevalence. It might indeed be almost stated as the main object and chief concern of Christianity to root out our natural selfishness, to rectify the false standard which it imposes on us, and to bring us not only to a just estimate of ourselves, and of all around us, but to a due impression also of the various claims and obligations resulting from the different relations in which we stand. Benevolence, enlarged, vigorous, operative benevolence, is her master-principle. Moderation in temporal pursuits and enjoyments, comparative indifference to the issue of worldly projects, diligence in the discharge of personal and civil duties, resignation to the will of God, and patience under all the dispensations of his providence, are among her daily lessons. Humility is one of the essential qualities which her precepts most directly and strongly enjoin, and which all her various doctrines tend to call forth and cultivate; and humility lays the deepest and surest grounds for benevolence. In whatever class or order of society Christianity prevails, she sets herself to rectify the particular faults, or, if we would speak more distinctly, to counteract the particular mode of selfishness to which that class is liable. Affluence she teaches to be liberal and beneficent; authority, to bear its faculties with meekness, and to consider the various cares and obligations belonging to its elevated station as being conditions on which that station is conferred. Thus, softening the glare of wealth, and moderating the insolence of power, she renders the inequalities of the social state less galling to the lower orders, whom also she instructs in their turn, to be diligent, humble, patient: reminding them that their more lowly path has been allotted to them by the hand of God; that it is their part faithfully to discharge its duties, and contentedly to bear its inconveniences; that the present state of things is very short; that the objects about which worldly men conflict so eagerly, are not worth the contest; that the peace of mind, which Religion offers indiscriminately to all ranks, affords more true satisfaction than all the expensive pleasures which are beyond the poor man's reach; that in this view the poor have the advantage; that, if their superiors enjoy more abundant comforts, they are also exposed to many temptations from which the inferior classes are happily exempted; that 'having food and raiment, they should be therewith content,' since their situation in life, with all its evils, is better than they have deserved at the hand of God; and finally, that all human distinctions will soon be done away, and the true followers of Christ will all, as children of the same Father, be alike admitted to the possession of the same heavenly inheritance. Such are the blessed effects of Christianity on the temporal well-being of political communities.

Let him, then, who wishes well to his country, no longer hesitate what course of conduct to pursue. The question now is not, in what liberties he might warrantably indulge himself in another situation? but, what are the restraints on himself which the exigencies of the present times render it advisable for him to impose? Circumstanced as we now are, it is more than ever obvious, that *the best man is the truest patriot*.

Nor is it only by their personal conduct (though this mode will always be the most efficacious) that men of authority and influence may promote the cause of good morals. Let them in their several stations encourage virtue, and discountenance vice, in others. Let them enforce the laws by which the wisdom of our forefathers has guarded against the grosser infractions of morals; and congratulate themselves, that in a leading situation on the bench of justice there is placed a man, who, to his honour be it spoken, is well disposed to assist their efforts.[2] Let them favour and take part in any plans which may be formed for the advancement of morality. Above all things, let them endeavour to instruct and improve the rising generation; that, if it be possible, an antidote may be provided for the malignity of that venom which is storing up in a neighbouring country. This has long been to my mind the most formidable feature of the present state of things in France; where, it is to be feared, a brood of moral vipers, as it were, is now hatching, which, when they shall have attained to their mischievous maturity, will go forth to poison the world. But fruitless will be all attempts to sustain, much more to revive, the fainting cause of morals, unless you can in some degree restore the prevalence of Evangelical Christianity. It is in morals as in physics; unless the source of prac-

2. It is a gratification to the writer's personal, as well as public, feelings, to pay this tribute of respect to the character of Lord Chief Justice KENYON.

tical principles be elevated, it will be in vain to attempt to make them flow on a high level in their future course. You may force them for a while into some constrained position, but they will soon drop to their natural point of depression. By all therefore who are studious of their country's welfare, more particularly by all who desire to support our ecclesiastical establishment, every effort should be used to revive the Christianity of our better days. [...]

C

The Place of the Affections in Religion

The objection of our Opponent, that by insisting on the obligation of making our blessed Saviour the object of our affections, we are degrading our religious services, and are substituting a set of mere feelings in place of the worship of the understanding, is an objection which deserves our most serious consideration. If it be just, it is decisive; for ours must be unquestionably 'a reasonable service' (Rom. ii, 1).

The Objector must mean, either that these affections are unreasonable in themselves, or that they are misplaced in Religion. He can scarcely, however, intend that the affections are in their own nature unreasonable. To suppose him to maintain this position, were to suppose him ignorant of what every schoolboy knows of the mechanism of the human mind. We shall therefore take it for granted, that this cannot be his meaning, and proceed to examine the latter part of the alternative. Here also it may either be intended, that the affections are misplaced in Religion, *generally*, or that our blessed Saviour is not the proper object of them.

This notion of the affections being out of place in Religion, is indeed an opinion which appears to be generally prevalent. The affections are regarded as the strong holds of enthusiasm. It is therefore judged most expedient to act, as prudent generals are used to do, when they raze the fortress, or spike the cannon, which are likely to fall into the hands of an enemy. Mankind are apt to be the dupes of misapplied terms; and the progress of the persuasion now in question, has been considerably aided by an abuse of language, not sufficiently checked in its first advances, whereby that species of Religion which is opposite to the warm and affectionate kind, has been suffered, almost without disturbance, to usurp to itself the epithet of *rational*. But let not this claim be too hastily admitted. Let the position in question be thoroughly and impartially discussed, and it will appear, if I mistake not, to be a gross and pernicious error.

23 William Hazlitt
Character of Wilberforce

from *The Spirit of the Age* 1825

Mr Wilberforce is a less perfect character in his way. He acts from mixed motives. He would willingly serve two masters, God and Mammon. He is a person of many excellent and admirable qualifications, but he has made a mistake in wishing to reconcile those that are incompatible. He has a most winning eloquence, specious, persuasive, familiar, silver-tongued, is amiable, charitable, conscientious, pious, loyal, humane, tractable to power, accessible to popularity, honouring the king, and no less charmed with the homage of his fellow-citizens. 'What lacks he then?' Nothing but an economy of good parts. By aiming at too much, he has spoiled all, and neutralised what might have been an estimable character, distinguished by signal services to mankind. A man must take his choice not only between virtue and vice, but between different virtues. Otherwise, he will not gain his own approbation, or secure the respect of others. The graces and accomplishments of private life mar the man of business and the statesman. There is a severity, a sternness, a self-denial, and a painful sense of duty required in the one, which ill befits the softness and sweetness which should characterize the other. Loyalty, patriotism, friendship, humanity, are all virtues; but may they not sometimes clash? By being unwilling to forego the praise due to any, we may forfeit the reputation of all; and instead of uniting the suffrages of the whole world in our favour, we may end in becoming a sort of bye-word for affectation, cant, hollow professions, trimming, fickleness, and effeminate imbecility. It is best to choose and act up to some one leading character, as it is best to have some settled profession or regular pursuit in life.

We can readily believe that Mr Wilberforce's first object and principle of action is to do what he thinks right: his next (and that we fear is of almost equal weight with the first) is to do what will be thought so by other people. He is always at a game of *hawk and buzzard* between these two: his 'conscience will not budge', unless the world goes with it. He does not seem greatly to dread the denunciation in Scripture, but rather to court it — 'Woe unto you, when all men shall speak well of you!' We suspect he is not quite easy in his mind, because West-India planters and Guinea traders do not join in his praise. His ears are not strongly enough tuned to drink in the execrations of the spoiler and the oppressor as the sweetest music. It is not enough that one half of the human species (the images of God carved in ebony, as old Fuller calls them) shout his name as a champion and a saviour through vast burning zones, and moisten their parched lips with the gush of gratitude for deliverance from chains — he must have a Prime-Minister drink his health at a Cabinet-dinner for aiding to rivet on those of his country and of Europe! He goes hand and heart along with Government in all their notions of legitimacy and political aggrandizement, in the hope that they will leave him a sort of *no-man's ground* of humanity in the Great Desert, where his reputation for benevolence and public spirit may spring up and flourish, till its head touches the clouds, and it stretches out its branches to the farthest part of the earth. He has no mercy on those who claim a property in negro-slaves as so much live-stock on their estates; the country rings with the applause of his wit, his eloquence, and his indignant appeals to common sense and humanity on this subject — but not a word has he to say, not a whisper does he breathe against the claim set up by the Despots of the Earth over their Continental subjects, but does every thing in his power to confirm and sanction it! He must give no offence. Mr Wilberforce's humanity will go all lengths that it can with safety and discretion: but it is not to be supposed that it should lose him his seat for Yorkshire, the smile of Majesty, or the countenance of the loyal and pious. He is anxious to do all the good he can without hurting himself or his fair fame. His conscience and his character compound matters very amicably. He rather patronises honesty than is a martyr to it. His patriotism, his philanthropy are not so ill-bred, as to quarrel with his loyalty or to banish him from the first circles. He preaches vital Christianity to untutored savages; and tolerates its worst abuses in civilized states. He thus shews his respect for religion without offending the clergy, or circumscribing the sphere of his usefulness. There is in all this an appearance of a good deal of cant and tricking. His patriotism may be accused of being servile; his humanity ostentatious; his loyalty conditional; his religion a mixture of fashion and fanaticism. 'Out upon such half-faced fellowship!' Mr Wilberforce has the pride of being familiar with the great; the vanity of being popular; the conceit of an approving conscience. He is coy in his approaches to power; his public spirit is, in a manner, *under the rose*. He thus reaps the credit of independence, without the obloquy; and secures the advantages of servility, without incurring any obligations. He has two strings to his bow: he by no means neglects his worldly interests, while he expects a bright reversion in the skies. Mr Wilberforce is far from being a hypocrite; but he is, we think, as fine a specimen of *moral equivocation* as can well be conceived. A hypocrite is one who is the very reverse of, or who despises the character he pretends to be: Mr Wilberforce would be all that he pretends to be, and he is it in fact, as far as words, plausible theories, good inclinations, and easy services go, but not in heart and soul, or so as to give up the appearance of any one of his pretensions to preserve the reality of any other. He carefully chooses his ground to fight the battles of loyalty, religion, and humanity, and it is such as is always safe and advantageous to himself! This is perhaps hardly fair, and it is of dangerous or doubtful tendency. Lord Eldon, for instance, is known to be a thorough-paced ministerialist: his opinion is only that of his party. But Mr Wilberforce is not a party-man. He is the more looked up to on this account, but not with sufficient reason. By tampering with different temptations and personal projects, he has all the air of the most perfect independence, and gains a character for impartiality and candour, when he is only striking a balance in his mind between the *éclat* of differing from a Minister on some 'vantage ground, and the risk or odium that may attend it. He carries all the weight of his artificial popularity over to the Government on vital points and hard-run questions; while they, in return, lend him a little of the gilding of court-favour to set off his disinterested philanthropy and tramontane enthusiasm. As a leader or a follower, he makes an odd jumble of interests. By virtue of religious sympathy, he has brought the Saints over to the side of the abolition of Negro slavery. This his adversaries think hard and stealing a march upon them. What have the SAINTS to do with freedom or reform of any kind? — Mr Wilberforce's style of speaking is not quite *parliamentary*, it is halfway between that and *evangelical*. He is altogether a *double-entendre*: the very tone of his voice is a *double-entendre*. It winds, and undulates, and glides up and down on texts of Scripture, and scraps from Paley, and trite sophistry, and pathetic appeals to his hearers in a faltering, inprogressive, sidelong way, like those birds of weak wing, that are borne from their strait-forward course

By every little breath that under heaven is blown.

Something of this fluctuating, time-serving principle was visible even in the great question of the Abolition of the Slave Trade. He was, at one time, half inclined to surrender it into Mr Pitt's dilatory hands, and seemed to think the gloss of novelty was gone from it, and the gaudy colouring of popularity sunk into the *sable* ground from which it rose! It was, however, persisted in and carried to a triumphant conclusion. Mr Wilberforce said too little on this occasion of one, compared with whom he was but the frontispiece to that great chapter in the history of the world — the mask, the varnishing, and painting — the man that effected it by Herculean labours of body, and equally gigantic labours of mind was Clarkson, the true Apostle of human Redemption on that occasion, and who, it is remarkable, resembles in his person and lineaments more than one of the Apostles in the *Cartoons* of Raphael. He deserves to be added to the Twelve![1]

1. After all, the best as well as most amusing comment on the character just described was that made by Sheridan, who being picked up in no very creditable plight by the watch, and asked rather roughly who he was, made answer — 'I am Mr Wilberforce!' The guardians of the night conducted him home with all the honours due to Grace and Nature.

Dinah Morris's Sermon

from *Adam Bede* 1859

'Take off the bridle and give him a drink, ostler,' said the traveller to the lad in a smock-frock, who had come out of the yard at the sound of the horse's hoofs.

'Why, what's up in your pretty village, landlord?' he continued, getting down. 'There seems to be quite a stir.'

'It's a Methodis preaching, sir; it's been gev hout as a young woman's a-going to preach on the Green,' answered Mr Casson, in a treble and wheezy voice, with a slightly mincing accent. 'Will you please to step in, sir, an' tek some think?'

'No, I must be getting on to Rosseter. I only want a drink for my horse. And what does your parson say, I wonder, to a young woman preaching just under his nose?'

'Parson Irwine, sir, doesn't live here; he lives at Brox'on, over the hill there. The parsonage here's a tumbled-down place, sir, not fit for gentry to live in. He comes here to preach of a Sunday afternoon, sir, an' puts up his hoss here. It's a grey cob, sir, an' he sets great store by't. He's allays put up his hoss here, sir, iver since before I hed the Donnithorne Arms. I'm not this countryman, you may tell, by my tongue, sir. They're cur'ous talkers i' this country, sir; the gentry's hard work to hunderstand 'em. I was brought hup among the gentry, sir, an' got the turn o' their tongue when I was a bye. Why, what do you think the folks here says for 'hevn't you?' – the gentry, you know, says, "hevn't you" – well, the people about here says "hanna yey." It's what they call the dileck as is spoke hereabout, sir. That's what I've heard Squire Donnithorne say many a time; it's the dileck, says he.'

'Ay, ay,' said the stranger, smiling. 'I know it very well. But you've not got many Methodists about here, surely – in this agricultural spot? I should have thought there would hardly be such a thing as a Methodist to be found about here. You're all farmers, aren't you? The Methodists can seldom lay much hold on *them*.'

'Why, sir, there's a pretty lot o' workmen round about, sir.

There's Mester Burge as owns the timber-yard over there, he underteks a good bit o' building an' repairs. An' there's the stone-pits not far off. There's plenty of emply i' this country-side, sir. An' there's a fine batch o' Methodisses at Treddles'on – that's the market-town about three mile off – you'll maybe ha' come through it, sir. There's pretty nigh a score of 'em on the Green now, as come from there. That's where our people gets it from, though there's only two men of 'em in all Hay-slope: that's Will Maskery, the wheelwright, and Seth Bede, a young man as works at the carpenterin'.'

'The preacher comes from Treddleston, then, does she?'

'Nay, sir, she comes out o' Stonyshire, pretty nigh thirty mile off. But she's a-visitin' hereabout at Mester Poyser's at the Hall Farm – it's them barns an' big walnut trees, right away to the left, sir. She's own niece to Poyser's wife, an' they'll be fine an' vexed at her for making a fool of herself i' that way. But I've heared as there's no holding these Methodisses when the mag-git's once got i' their head: many of 'em goes stark starin' mad wi' their religion. Though this young woman's quiet enough to look at, by what I can make out; I've not seen her myself.'

The stronger curiosity of the women had drawn them quite to the edge of the Green, where they could examine more close-ly the Quaker-like costume and odd deportment of the female Methodists. Underneath the maple there was a small cart which had been brought from the wheelwright's to serve as a pulpit, and round this a couple of benches and a few chairs had been placed. Some of the Methodists were resting on these, with their eyes closed, as if wrapt in prayer or meditation. Others chose to continue standing, and had turned their faces towards the villagers with a look of melancholy compassion, which was highly amusing to Bessy Granage, the blacksmith's buxom daughter, known to her neighbours as Chad's Bess, who won-dered 'why the folks war a-makin' faces a that'ns'. Chad's Bess was the object of peculiar compassion, because her hair, being turned back under a cap which was set at the top of her head, exposed to view an ornament of which she was much prouder than of her red cheeks, namely, a pair of large round ear-rings with false garnets in them, ornaments contemned not only by the Methodists, but by her own cousin and namesake Timothy's

Bess, who, with much cousinly feeling, often wished 'them ear-rings' might come to good. . . .

'Here! gie him here to me, Jim,' said Chad Cranage; 'I'll tie him up an' shoe him as I do th' hosses. Well, Mester Casson,' he continued, as that personage sauntered up towards the group of men, 'how are ye t' naight? Are ye coom t' help groon? They say folks allays groon when they're hearkenin' to th' Methodys, as if they war bad i' th' inside. I mane to groon as loud as your cow did th' other naight, an' then the praicher 'ull think I'm i' th' raight way.'

'I'd advise you not to be up to no nonsense, Chad,' said Mr Casson, with some dignity; 'Poyser wouldn't like to hear as his wife's niece was treated any ways disrespectful, for all he mayn't be fond of her taking on herself to preach.'

'Ay, an' she's a pleasant-looked un too,' said Wiry Ben. 'I'll stick up for the pretty women preachin'; I know they'd per-suade me over a deal sooner nor th' ugly men. I shouldna won-der if I turn Methody afore the night's out, an' begin to coort the preacher, like Seth Bede.'

'Why, Seth's looking rether too high, I should think,' said Mr Casson. 'This woman's kin wouldn't like her to demean her-self to a common carpenter.'

'Tchu!' said Ben, with a long treble intonation, 'what's folks's kin got to do wi't? – Not a chip. Poyser's wife may turn her nose up an' forget bygones, but this Dinah Morris, they tell me, 's as poor as iver she was – works at a mill, an's much ado to keep hersen. A strappin' young carpenter as is a ready-made Methody, like Seth, wouldna be a bad match for her. Why, Poysers make as big a fuss wi' Adam Bede as if he war a nevvy o' their own.'

'Idle talk! idle talk!' said Mr Joshua Rann. 'Adam an' Seth's two men; you wunna fit them two wi' the same last.'

'Maybe,' said Wiry Ben, contemptuously, 'but Seth's the lad for me, though he war a Methody twice o'er. I'm fair beat wi' Seth, for I've been teazin' him iver sin' we've been workin' to-gether, an' he bears me no more malice nor a lamb. An' he's a stout-hearted feller too, for when we saw the old tree all a-fire a-comin' across the fields one night, an' we thought as it war a boguy, Seth made no more ado, but he up to't as bold as a constable. Why, there he comes out o' Will Maskery's; an' there's Will hisself, lookin' as meek as if he couldna knock a nail o' the head for fear o' hurtin't. An' there's the pretty preacher-woman! My eye, she's got her bonnet off. I mun go a bit nearer.'

Several of the men followed Ben's lead, and the traveller pushed his horse on to the Green, as Dinah walked rather quickly, and in advance of her companions, towards the cart under the maple-tree. While she was near Seth's tall figure, she looked short, but when she had mounted the cart, and was away from all comparison, she seemed above the middle height of woman, though in reality she did not exceed it – an effect which was due to the slimness of her figure, and the simple line of her black stuff dress. The stranger was struck with surprise as he saw her approach and mount the cart – surprise, not so much at the feminine delicacy of her appearance, as at the total absence of self-consciousness in her demeanour. He had made up his mind to see her advance with a measured step, and a demure solemnity of countenance; he had felt sure that her face would be mantled with the smile of conscious saintship, or else charged with denunciatory bitterness. He knew but two types of Methodist – the ecstatic and the bilious. But Dinah walked as simply as if she were going to market, and seemed as unconscious of her outward appearance as a little boy: there was no blush, no tremulousness, which said, 'I know you think me a pretty woman, too young to preach'; no casting up or down of the eyelids, no compression of the lips, no attitude of the arms, that said, 'But you must think of me as a saint.' She held no book in her ungloved hands, but let them hang down lightly crossed before her, as she stood and turned her grey eyes on the people. There was no keenness in the eyes; they seemed rather to be shedding love than making observations; they had the liquid look which tells that the mind is full of what it has to give out, rather than impressed by external objects. She stood with her left hand towards the descending sun, and leafy boughs screened her from its rays; but in this sober light the delicate colouring of her face seemed to gather a calm vividness, like flowers at evening. It was a small oval face, of a uniform transparent whiteness, with an egg-like line of cheek and chin, a full but firm mouth, a delicate nostril, and a low perpendicular brow, surmounted by a rising arch of parting between smooth locks of pale reddish hair. The hair was drawn straight back behind the ears and covered, except for an inch or two, above the brow, by a net Quaker cap. The eyebrows, of the same colour as the hair were perfectly horizontal and firmly pencilled; the eyelashes, though no darker, were long and abundant; nothing was left blurred or unfinished. It was one of those faces that make one think of white flowers with light touches of colour on their pure petals. The eyes had no peculiar beauty, beyond that of expression; they looked so simple, so candid, so gravely loving, that no accusing scowl, no light sneer could help melting away before their glance. Joshua Rann gave a long cough, as if he were clearing his throat in order to come to a new understanding with himself; Chad Cranage lifted up his leather skull-cap and scratched his head; and Wiry Ben wondered how Seth had the pluck to think of courting her.

'A sweet woman,' the stranger said to himself, 'but surely nature never meant her for a preacher.'

Perhaps he was one of those who think that nature has theatrical properties, and, with the considerate view of facilitating art and psychology, 'makes up' her characters, so that there may be no mistake about them. But Dinah began to speak.

'Dear friends,' she said, in a clear but not loud voice, 'let us pray for a blessing.'

She closed her eyes, and hanging her head down a little, continued in the same moderate tone, as if speaking to some one quite near her:

'Saviour of sinners! when a poor woman, laden with sins, went out to the well to draw water, she found Thee sitting at the well. She knew Thee not; she had not sought Thee; her mind was dark; her life was unholy. But Thou didst speak to her, Thou didst teach her, Thou didst show her that her life lay open before Thee, and yet Thou wast ready to give her that blessing which she had never sought. Jesus! Thou art in the midst of us, and Thou knowest all men: if there is any here like that poor woman – if their minds are dark, their lives unholy – if they have come out not seeking Thee, not desiring to be taught; deal with them according to the free mercy which Thou didst show to her. Speak to them, Lord; open their ears to my message; bring their sins to their minds, and make them thirst for that salvation which Thou art ready to give.

'Lord! Thou art with Thy people still: they see Thee in the night-watches, and their hearts burn within them as Thou talkest with them by the way. And Thou art near to those who have not known Thee: open their eyes that they may see Thee – see Thee weeping over them, and saying "Ye will not come unto me that ye might have life" – see Thee hanging on the cross and saying, "Father, forgive them, for they know not what they do" – see Thee as Thou wilt come again in Thy glory to judge them at the last. Amen.'

Dinah opened her eyes again and paused, looking at the group of villagers, who were now gathered rather more closely on her right hand.

'Dear friends,' she began, raising her voice a little, 'you have all of you been to church, and I think you must have heard the clergyman read these words: "The Spirit of the Lord is upon me, because he hath anointed me to preach the gospel to the poor." Jesus Christ spoke those words – he said he came *to preach the Gospel to the poor*: I don't know whether you ever thought about those words much; but I will tell you when I remember first hearing them. It was on just such a sort of evening as this, when I was a little girl, and my aunt as brought me up, took me to hear a good man preach out of doors, just as we are here. I remember his face well: he was a very old man, and had very long white hair; his voice was very soft and beautiful, not like any voice I had ever heard before. I was a little girl, and scarcely knew anything, and this old man seemed to me such a different sort of a man from anybody I had ever seen before, that I thought he had perhaps come down from the sky to preach to us, and I said, "Aunt, will he go back to the sky tonight, like the picture in the Bible?"

'That man of God was Mr Wesley, who spent his life in doing what our blessed Lord did – preaching the Gospel to the poor – and he entered into his rest eight years ago. I came to know more about him years after, but I was a foolish thoughtless child then, and I remembered only one thing he told us in his sermon. He told us as "Gospel" meant "good news". The Gospel, you know, is what the Bible tells us about God.

'Think of that now! Jesus Christ did really come down from heaven, as I, like a silly child, thought Mr Wesley did; and what he came down for, was to tell good news about God to the poor. Why, you and me, dear friends, are poor. We have been brought up in poor cottages, and have been reared on oat-cake, and lived coarse; and we haven't been to school much, nor read books, and we don't know much about anything but what happens just round us. We are just the sort of people that want to hear good news. For when anybody's well off, they don't much mind about hearing news from distant parts; but if a poor man or woman's in trouble and has hard work to make out a living, they like to have a letter to tell 'em they've got a friend as will help 'em. To be sure, we can't help knowing something about God, even if we've never heard the Gospel, the good news that our Saviour brought us. For we know everything comes from God: don't you say almost every day, "This and that will happen, please God;" and "We shall begin to cut the grass soon, please God to send us a little more sunshine"? We know very well we are altogether in the hands of God: we didn't bring ourselves into the world, we can't keep ourselves alive while we're sleeping; the daylight, and the wind, and the corn, and the cows to give us milk – everything we have comes from God. And he gave us our souls, and put love between parents and children, and husband and wife. But is that as much as we want to know about God? We see he is great and mighty, and can do what he will: we are lost, as if we was struggling in great waters, when we try to think of him.

'But perhaps doubts come into your mind like this: Can God take much notice of us poor people? Perhaps he only made the world for the great and the wise and the rich. It doesn't cost him much to give us our little handful of victual and bit of clothing; but how do we know he cares for us any more than we care for the worms and things in the garden, so as we rear our carrots and onions? Will God take care of us when we die? and has he any comfort for us when we are lame and sick and helpless? Perhaps, too, he is angry with us; else why does the blight come, and the bad harvests, and the fever, and all sorts of pain and trouble? For our life is full of trouble, and if God sends us good, he seems to send bad too. How is it? how is it?

'Ah! dear friends, we are in sad want of good news about God; and what does other good news signify if we haven't that? For everything else comes to an end, and when we die we leave it all. But God lasts when everything else is gone. What shall we do if he is not our friend?'

Then Dinah told how the good news had been brought, and how the mind of God towards the poor had been made manifest in the life of Jesus, dwelling on its lowliness and its acts of mercy.

'So you see, dear friends,' she went on, 'Jesus spent his time almost all in doing good to poor people; he preached out of doors to them, and he made friends of poor workmen, and taught them and took pains with them. Not but what he did good to the rich too, for he was full of love to all men, only he saw as the poor were more in want of his help. So he cured the lame and the sick and the blind, and he worked miracles, to feed the hungry, because, he said, he was sorry for them; and he was very kind to the little children, and comforted those who had lost their friends: and he spoke very tenderly to poor sinners that were sorry for their sins.

'Ah! wouldn't you love such a man if you saw him – if he was here in this village? What a kind heart he must have! What a friend he would be to go to in trouble! How pleasant it must be to be taught by him.

'Well, dear friends, who *was* this man? Was he only a good man – a very good man, and no more – like our dear Mr Wesley, who has been taken from us? ... He was the Son of God – "in the image of the Father", the Bible says; that means, just like God, who is the beginning and end of all things – the God we want to know about. So then, all the love that Jesus showed to the poor is the same love that God has for us. We can understand what Jesus felt, because he came in a body like ours, and spoke words such as we speak to each other. We were afraid to think what God was before – the God who made the world and the sky and the thunder and lightning. We could never see him; we could only see the things he had made; and some of these things was very terrible, so as we might well tremble when we thought of him. But our blessed Saviour has showed us what God is in a way us poor ignorant people can understand; he has showed us what God's heart is, what are his feelings towards us.

'But let us see a little more about what Jesus came on earth for. Another time he said, "I came to seek and to save that which was lost", and another time, "I came not to call the righteous but sinners to repentance."

'The *lost*! ... *Sinners*! ... Ah! dear friends, does that mean you and me?'

Hitherto the traveller had been chained to the spot against his will by the charm of Dinah's mellow treble tones, which had a variety of modulation like that of a fine instrument touched with the unconscious skill of musical instinct. The simple things she said seemed like novelties, as a melody strikes us with a new feeling when we hear it sung by the pure voice of a boyish chorister; the quiet depth of conviction with which she spoke seemed in itself an evidence for the truth of her message. He saw that she had thoroughly arrested her hearers. The villagers had pressed nearer to her, and there was no longer anything but grave attention on all faces. She spoke slowly, though quite fluently, often pausing after a question, or before any transition of ideas. There was no change of attitude, no gesture; the effect of her speech was produced entirely by the inflections of her voice, and when she came to the question, 'Will God take care of us when we die?' she uttered it in such a tone of plaintive appeal that the tears came into some of the hardest eyes. The stranger had ceased to doubt, as he had done at the first glance, that she could fix the attention of her rougher hearers, but still he wondered whether she could have that power of rousing their more violent emotions, which must surely be a necessary seal of her vocation as a Methodist preacher, until she came to the words, 'Lost! – Sinners!' when there was a great change in her voice and manner. She had made a long pause before the exclamation, and the pause seemed to be filled by agitating thoughts that showed themselves in her features. Her pale face became paler; the circles under her eyes deepened, as they do when tears half gather without falling; and the mild loving eyes took an expression of appalled pity, as if she had suddenly discerned a destroying angel hovering over the heads of the people. Her voice became deep and muffled, but there was still no gesture. Nothing could be less like the ordinary type of the Ranter than Dinah. She was not preaching as she heard others preach, but speaking directly from her own emotions, and under the inspiration of her own simple faith.

But now she had entered into a new current of feeling. Her manner became less calm, her utterance more rapid and agitated, as she tried to bring home to the people their guilt, their wilful darkness, their state of disobedience to God – as she dwelt on the hatefulness of sin, the Divine holiness, and the sufferings of the Saviour, by which a way had been opened for their salvation. At last it seemed as if, in her yearning desire to reclaim the lost sheep, she could not be satisfied by addressing her hearers as a body. She appealed first to one and then to another, beseeching them with tears to turn to God while there was yet time; painting to them the desolation of their souls, lost in sin, feeding on the husks of this miserable world, far away from God their Father; and then the love of the Saviour, who was waiting and watching for their return.

There was many a responsive sigh and groan from her fellow-Methodists, but the village mind does not easily take fire, and a little smouldering vague anxiety, that might easily die out again, was the utmost effect Dinah's preaching had wrought in them at present. Yet no one had retired, except the children and 'old Feyther Taft', who being too deaf to catch many words, had some time ago gone back to his ingle-nook. Wiry Ben was feeling very uncomfortable, and almost wishing he had not come to hear Dinah; he thought what she said would haunt him somehow. Yet he couldn't help liking to look at her and listen to her, though he dreaded every moment that she would fix her eyes on him, and address him in particular. She had already addressed Sandy Jim, who was now holding the baby to relieve his wife, and the big soft-hearted man had rubbed away some tears with his fist, with a confused intention of being a better fellow, going less to the Holly Bush down by the Stone-pits, and cleaning himself more regularly of a Sunday.

In front of Sandy Jim stood Chad's Bess, who had shown an unwonted quietude and fixity of attention ever since Dinah had begun to speak. Not that the matter of the discourse had arrested her at once, for she was lost in a puzzling speculation as to what pleasure and satisfaction there could be in life to a young woman who wore a cap like Dinah's. Giving up this inquiry in despair, she took to studying Dinah's nose, eyes, mouth, and hair, and wondering whether it was better to have such a sort of pale face as that, or fat red cheeks and round black eyes like her own. But gradually the influence of the general gravity told upon her, and she became conscious of what Dinah was saying. The gentle tones, the loving persuasion, did not touch her, but when the more severe appeals came she began to be frightened. Poor Bessy had always been considered a naughty girl; she was conscious of it; if it was necessary to be very good, it was clear she must be in a bad way. She couldn't find her places at church as Sally Rann could; she had often been tittering when she 'curcheyed' to Mr Irwine; and these religious deficiencies were accompanied by a corresponding slackness in the minor morals, for Bessy belonged unquestionably to that unsoaped, lazy class of feminine characters with whom you may venture to 'eat an egg, an apple, or a nut'. All this she was generally conscious of, and hitherto had not been greatly ashamed of it. But now she began to feel very much as if the constable had come to take her up and carry her before the justice for some undefined offence. She had a terrified sense that God, whom she had always thought of as very far off, was very near to her, and that Jesus was close by looking at her, though she could not see him. For Dinah had that belief in visible manifestations of Jesus, which is common among the Methodists, and she communicated it irresistibly to her hearers: she made them feel that he was among them bodily, and might at any moment show himself to them in some way that would strike anguish and penitence into their hearts.

'See!' she exclaimed, turning to the left, with her eyes fixed on a point above the heads of the people – 'see where our blessed Lord stands and weeps, and stretches out his arms towards you. Hear what he says: "How often would I have gathered you as a hen gathereth her chickens under her wings, and ye would not!" ... and ye would not,' she repeated, in a tone of pleading reproach, turning her eyes on the people again. 'See the print of the nails on his dear hands and feet. It is your sins that made them! Ah! how pale and worn he looks! He has gone through all that great agony in the garden, when his soul was exceeding sorrowful even unto death, and the great drops of sweat fell like blood to the ground. They spat upon him and buffeted him, they scourged him, they mocked him, they laid the heavy cross on his bruised shoulders. Then they nailed him up. Ah! what pain! His lips are parched with thirst, and they mock him still in this great agony; yet with those parched lips he prays for them, "Father, forgive them, for they know not what they do." Then a horror of great darkness fell upon him, and he felt what sinners feel when they are for ever shut out from God. That was the last drop in the cup of bitterness. "My God, my God!" he cries, "why hast Thou forsaken me?"

'All this he bore for you! For you – and you never think of him; for you – and you turn your backs on him; you don't care what he has gone through for you. Yet he is not weary of toiling for you: he has risen from the dead, he is praying for you at the right hand of God – "Father, forgive them, for they know not what they do." And he is upon this earth too; he is among us; he is there close to you now; I see his wounded body and his look of love.'

Here Dinah turned to Bessy Cranage, whose bonny youth and evident vanity had touched her with pity.

'Poor child! poor child! He is beseeching you, and you don't listen to him. You think of ear-rings and fine gowns and caps, and you never think of the Saviour who died to save your precious soul. Your cheeks will be shrivelled one day, your hair will be grey, your poor body will be thin and tottering! Then you will begin to feel that your soul is not saved; then you will have to stand before God dressed in your sins, in your evil tempers and vain thoughts. And Jesus, who stands ready to help you now, won't help you then: because you won't have him to be your Saviour, he will be your judge. Now he looks at you with love and mercy, and says, "Come to me that you may have life"; then he will turn away from you, and say, "Depart from me into everlasting fire!"'

Poor Bessy's wide-open black eyes began to fill with tears, her great red cheeks and lips became quite pale, and her face was distorted like a little child's before a burst of crying.

'Ah! poor blind child!' Dinah went on, 'think if it should happen to you as it once happened to a servant of God in the days of her vanity. *She* thought of her lace caps, and saved all her money to buy 'em; she thought nothing about how she might get a clean heart and a right spirit, she only wanted to have better lace than other girls. And one day when she put her new cap on and looked in the glass, she saw a bleeding Face crowned with thorns. That face is looking at you now,' – here Dinah pointed to a spot close in front of Bessy. – 'Ah! tear off those follies! cast them away from you, as if they were sting-ing adders. They *are* stinging you – they are poisoning your soul – they are dragging you down into a dark bottomless pit, where you will sink for ever, and for ever, and for ever, further away from light and God.'

Bessy could bear it no longer: a great terror was upon her, and wrenching her ear-rings from her ears, she threw them down before her, sobbing aloud. Her father, Chad, frightened lest he should be 'laid hold on' too, this impression on the rebel-lious Bess striking him as nothing less than a miracle, walked hastily away, and began to work at his anvil by way of reassur-ing himself. 'Folks mun ha' hoss-shoes, praichin' or no praichin': the divil canna lay hould o' me for that,' he muttered to himself.

But now Dinah began to tell of the joys that were in store for the penitent, and to describe in her simple way the divine peace and love with which the soul of the believer is filled – how the sense of God's love turns poverty into riches, and satisfies the soul, so that no uneasy desire vexes it, no fear alarms it: how, at last, the very temptation to sin is extinguished, and heaven is begun upon earth, because no cloud passes between the soul and God, who is its eternal sun.

'Dear friends,' she said at last, 'brothers and sisters, whom I love as those for whom my Lord has died, believe me, I know what this great blessedness is; and because I know it, I want you to have it too. I am poor, like you: I have to get my living with my hands; but no lord nor lady can be so happy as me, if they haven't got the love of God in their souls. Think what it is – not to hate anything but sin; to be full of love to every crea-ture; to be frightened at nothing; to be sure that all things will turn to good; not to mind pain, because it is our Father's will; to know that nothing – no, not if the earth was to be burnt up, or the waters come and drown us – nothing could part us from God who loves us, and who fills our souls with peace and joy, because we are sure that whatever he wills is holy, just, and good.

'Dear friends, come and take this blessedness; it is offered to you; it is the good news that Jesus came to preach to the poor. It is not like the riches of this world, so that the more one gets the less the rest can have. God is without end; his love is without end –

Its streams the whole creation reach,
So plenteous is the store;
Enough for all, enough for each,
Enough for evermore.'

Dinah had been speaking at least an hour, and the reddening light of the parting day seemed to give a solemn emphasis to her closing words. The stranger, who had been interested in the course of her sermon, as if it had been the development of a drama – for there is this sort of fascination in all sincere unpremeditated eloquence, which opens to one the inward drama of the speaker's emotions – now turned his horse aside, and pursued his way, while Dinah said, 'Let us sing a little, dear friends;' and as he was still winding down the slope, the voices of the Methodists reached him, rising and falling in that strange blending of exultation and sadness which belongs to the cadence of a hymn.

P Shelley

P. B. Shelley (1792–1822) wrote *A Defence of Poetry* in 1821,
his immediate object being to reply to T. L. Peacock's essay
The Four Ages of Poetry. But the interest of the *Defence* is
far wider than this particular controversy. It is one of the
great Romantic manifestoes of literature.

A.K.

1 Percy Bysshe Shelley
A Defence of Poetry

from *A Defence of Poetry* 1821

I

According to one mode of regarding those two classes of mental action, which are called reason and imagination, the former may be considered as mind contemplating the relations borne by one thought to another, however produced; and the latter, as mind acting upon those thoughts so as to colour them with its own light, and composing from them, as from elements, other thoughts, each containing within itself the principle of its own integrity. The one is the τὸ ποιεῖν, or the principle of synthesis, and has for its objects those forms which are common to universal nature and existence itself; the other is the τὸ λογίζειν or principle of analysis, and its action regards the relations of things, simply as relations; considering thoughts, not in their integral unity, but as the algebraical representations which conduct to certain general results. Reason is the enumeration of quantities already known; imagination is the perception of the value of those quantities, both separately and as a whole. Reason respects the differences, and imagination the similitudes of things. Reason is to the imagination as the instrument to the agent, as the body to the spirit, as the shadow to the substance.

Poetry, in a general sense, may be defined to be 'the expression of the imagination': and poetry is connate with the origin of man. Man is an instrument over which a series of external and internal impressions are driven, like the alternations of an ever-changing wind over an Aeolian lyre, which move it by their motion to ever-changing melody. But there is a principle within the human being, and perhaps within all sentient beings, which acts otherwise than in the lyre, and produces not melody alone, but harmony, by an internal adjustment of the sounds or motions thus excited to the impressions which excite them. It is as if the lyre could accommodate its chords to the motions of that which strikes them, in a determined proportion of sound; even as the musician can accommodate his voice to the sound of the lyre. A child at play by itself will express its delight by its voice and motions; and every inflexion of tone and every gesture will bear exact relation to a corresponding antitype in the pleasurable impressions which awakened it; it will be the reflected image of that impression; and as the lyre trembles and sounds after the wind has died away, so the child seeks, by prolonging in its voice and motions the duration of the effect, to prolong also a consciousness of the cause. In relation to the objects which delight a child, these expressions are, what poetry is to higher objects. The savage (for the savage is to ages what a child is to years) expresses the emotions produced in him by surrounding objects in a similar manner; and language and gesture, together with plastic or pictorial imitation, become the image of the combined effect of those objects, and of his apprehension of them. Man in society, with all his passions and his pleasures, next becomes the object of the passions and pleasures of man; an additional class of emotions produces an augmented treasure of expressions; and language, gesture, and the imitative arts, become at once the repesentation and the medium, the pencil and the picture, the chisel and the statue, the chord and the harmony. The social sympathies, or those laws from which, as from its elements, society results, begin to develop themselves from the moment that two human beings coexist; the future is contained within the present, as the plant within the seed; and equality, diversity, unity, contrast, mutual dependence, become the principles alone capable of affording the motives according to which the will of a social being is determined to action, inasmuch as he is social; and constitute pleasure in sensation, virtue in sentiment, beauty in art, truth in reasoning, and love in the intercourse of kind. Hence men, even in the infancy of society, observe a certain order in their words and actions, distinct from that of the objects and the impressions represented by them, all expression being subject to the laws of that from which it proceeds. But let us dismiss those more general considerations which might involve an inquiry into the principles of society itself, and restrict our view to the manner in which the imagination is expressed upon its forms.

In the youth of the world, men dance and sing and imitate natural objects, observing in these actions, as in all others, a certain rhythm or order. And, although all men observe a similar, they observe not the same order, in the motions of the dance, in the melody of the song, in the combinations of language, in the series of their imitations of natural objects. For there is a certain order or rhythm belonging to each of these classes of mimetic representation, from which the hearer and the spectator receive an intenser and purer pleasure than from any other: the sense of an approximation to this order has been called taste by modern writers. Every man in the infancy of art observes an order which approximates more or less closely to that from which this highest delight results: but the diversity is not sufficiently marked, as that its gradations should be sensible, except in those instances where the predominance of this faculty of approximation to the beautiful (for so we may be permitted to name the relation between this highest pleasure and its cause) is very great. Those in whom it exists in excess are poets, in the most universal sense of the word; and the pleasure resulting from the manner in which they express the influence of society or nature upon their own minds, communicates itself to others, and gathers a sort of reduplication from that community. Their language is vitally metaphorical; that is, it marks the before unapprehended relations of things and perpetuates their apprehension, until the words which represent them become, through time, signs for portions or classes of thoughts instead of pictures of integral thoughts; and then if no new poets should arise to create afresh the associations which have been thus disorganized, language will be dead to all the nobler purposes of human intercourse. These similitudes or relations are finely said by Lord Bacon to be 'the same footsteps of nature impressed upon the various subjects of the world'; and he considers the faculty which perceives them as the storehouse of axioms common to all knowledge. In the infancy of society every author is necessarily a poet, because language itself is poetry; and to be a poet is to apprehend the true and the beautiful, in a word, the good which exists in the relation, subsisting, first between existence and perception, and secondly between perception and expression. Every original language near to its source is in itself the chaos of a cyclic poem: the copiousness of lexicography and the distinctions of grammar are the works of a later age, and are merely the catalogue and the form of the creations of poetry.

But poets, or those who imagine and express this indestructible order, are not only the authors of language and of music, of the dance, and architecture, and statuary, and painting; they are the institutors of laws, and the founders of civil society, and the inventors of the arts of life, and the teachers who draw into a certain propinquity with the beautiful and the true, that partial apprehension of the agencies of the invisible world which is called religion. Hence all original religions are allegorical, or susceptible of allegory, and, like Janus, have a double face of false and true. Poets, according to the circumstances of the age and nation in which they appeared, were called, in the earlier epochs of the world, legislators, or prophets: a poet essentially comprises and unites both these characters. For he not only beholds intensely the present as it is, and discovers those laws according to which present things ought to be ordered, but he beholds the future in the present, and his thoughts are the germs of the flower and the fruit of latest time. Not that I assert poets to be prophets in the gross sense of the word, or that they can foretell the form as surely as they foreknow the spirit of events: such is the pretence of superstition, which would make poetry an attribute of prophecy, rather than prophecy an attribute of poetry. A poet participates in the eternal, the infinite, and the one; as far as relates to his conceptions, time and place and number are not. The grammatical forms which express the moods of time, and the difference of persons, and the distinction of place, are convertible with respect to the highest poetry without injuring it as poetry; and the choruses of Aeschylus, and the book of *Job*, and Dante's *Paradise*, would afford, more than any other writings, examples of this fact, if the limits of this essay did not forbid citation. The creations of sculpture, painting, and music, are illustrations still more decisive.

Language, colour, form, and religious and civil habits of action, are all the instruments and materials of poetry; they may be called poetry by that figure of speech which considers the effect as a synonym of the cause. But poetry in a more restricted sense expresses those arrangements of language, and especially metrical language, which are created by that imperial faculty, whose throne is curtained within the invisible nature of man.

And this springs from the nature itself of language, which is a more direct representation of the actions and passions of our internal being, and is susceptible of more various and delicate combinations, than colour, form, or motion, and is more plastic and obedient to the control of that faculty of which it is the creation. For language is arbitrarily produced by the imagination, and has relation to thoughts alone; but all other materials, instruments, and conditions of art, have relations among each other, which limit and interpose between conception and expression. The former is as a mirror which reflects, the latter as a cloud which enfeebles, the light of which both are mediums of communication. Hence the fame of sculptors, painters, and musicians, although the intrinsic powers of the great masters of these arts may yield in no degree to that of those who have employed language as the hieroglyphic of their thoughts, has never equalled that of poets in the restricted sense of the term; as two performers of equal skill will produce unequal effects from a guitar and a harp. The fame of legislators and founders of religions, so long as their institutions last, alone seems to exceed that of poets in the restricted sense; but it can scarcely be a question, whether, if we deduct the celebrity which their flattery of the gross opinions of the vulgar usually conciliates, together with that which belonged to them in their higher character of poets, any excess will remain. [. . .]

The whole objection, however, of the immorality of poetry rests upon a misconception of the manner in which poetry acts to produce the moral improvement of man. Ethical science arranges the elements which poetry has created, and propounds schemes and proposes examples of civil and domestic life: nor is it for want of admirable doctrines that men hate, and despise, and censure, and deceive, and subjugate one another. But poetry acts in another and diviner manner. It awakens and enlarges the mind itself by rendering it the receptacle of a thousand unapprehended combinations of thought. Poetry lifts the veil from the hidden beauty of the world, and makes familiar objects be as if they were not familiar; it reproduces all that it represents, and the impersonations clothed in its Elysian light stand thenceforward in the minds of those who have once contemplated them, as memorials of that gentle and exalted content which extends itself over all thoughts and actions with which it co-exists. The great secret of morals is love; or a going out of our nature, and an identification of ourselves with the beautiful which exists in thought, action, or person, not our own. A man, to be greatly good, must imagine intensely and comprehensively; he must put himself in the place of another and of many others; the pains and pleasures of his species must become his own. The great instrument of moral good is the imagination; and poetry administers to the effect by acting upon the cause. Poetry enlarges the circumference of the imagination by replenishing it with thoughts of ever new delight, which have the power of attracting and assimilating to their own nature all other thoughts, and which form new intervals and interstices whose void for ever craves fresh food. Poetry strengthens the faculty which is the organ of the moral nature of man in the same manner as exercise strengthens a limb.

II

But poets have been challenged to resign the civic crown to reasoners and mechanists, on another plea. It is admitted that the exercise of the imagination is most delightful, but it is alleged that that of reason is more useful. Let us examine as the grounds of this distinction, what is here meant by utility. Pleasure or good, in a general sense, is that which the consciousness of a sensitive and intelligent being seeks, and in which, when found, it acquiesces. There are two kinds of pleasure, one durable, universal and permanent; the other transitory and particular. Utility may either express the means of producing the former or the latter. In the former sense, whatever strengthens and purifies the affections, enlarges the imagination, and adds spirit to sense, is useful. But a narrower meaning may be assigned to the word utility, confining it to express that which banishes the importunity of the wants of our animal nature, the surrounding men with security of life, the dispersing the grosser delusions of superstition, and the conciliating such a degree of mutual forbearance among men as may consist with the motives of personal advantage.

Undoubtedly the promoters of utility, in this limited sense, have their appointed office in society. They follow the footsteps of poets, and copy the sketches of their creations into the book of common life. They make space and give time. Their exertions are of the highest value, so long as they confine their administration of the concerns of the inferior powers of our nature within the limits due to the superior ones. But whilst the sceptic destroys gross superstitions, let him spare to deface, as some of the French writers have defaced, the eternal truths charactered upon the imaginations of men. Whilst the mechanist abridges, and the political economist combines labour, let them beware that their speculations, for want of correspondence with those first principles which belong to the imagination, do not tend, as they have in modern England, to exasperate at once the extremes of luxury and want. They have exemplified the saying, 'To him that hath, more shall be given; and from him that hath not, the little that he hath shall be taken away'. The rich have become richer, and the poor have become poorer; and the vessel of the state is driven between the Scylla and Charybdis of anarchy and despotism. Such are the effects which must ever flow from an unmitigated exercise of the calculating faculty.

It is difficult to define pleasure in its highest sense; the definition involving a number of apparent paradoxes. For, from an inexplicable defect of harmony in the constitution of human nature, the pain of the inferior is frequently connected with the pleasures of the superior portions of our being. Sorrow, terror, anguish, despair itself, are often the chosen expressions of an approximation to the highest good. Our sympathy in tragic fiction depends on this principle; tragedy delights by affording a shadow of the pleasure which exists in pain. This is the source also of the melancholy which is inseparable from the sweetest melody. The pleasure that is in sorrow is sweeter than the pleasure of pleasure itself. And hence the saying, 'It is better to go to the house of mourning, than to the house of mirth'. Not that this highest species of pleasure is necessarily linked with pain. The delight of love and friendship, the ecstasy of the admiration of nature, the joy of the perception and still more of the creation of poetry, is often wholly unalloyed.

The production and assurance of pleasure in this highest sense is true utility. Those who produce and preserve this pleasure are poets or poetical philosophers.

The exertions of Locke, Hume, Gibbon, Voltaire, Rousseau[1] and their disciples, in favour of oppressed and deluded humanity, are entitled to the gratitude of mankind. Yet it is easy to calculate the degree of moral and intellectual improvement which the world would have exhibited, had they never lived. A little more nonsense would have been talked for a century or two; and perhaps a few more men, women, and children, burnt as heretics. We might not at this moment have been congratulating each other on the abolition of the Inquisition in Spain. But it exceeds all imagination to conceive what would have been the moral condition of the world if neither Dante, Petrarch, Boccaccio, Chaucer, Shakespeare, Calderon, Lord Bacon, nor Milton, had ever existed; if Raphael and Michael Angelo had never been born; if the Hebrew poetry had never been translated; if a revival of the study of Greek literature had never taken place; if no monuments of ancient sculpture had been handed down to us; and if the poetry of the religion of the ancient world had been extinguished together with its belief. The human mind could never, except by the intervention of these excitements, have been awakened to the invention of the grosser sciences, and that application of analytical reasoning to the aberrations of society, which it is now attempted to exalt over the direct expression of the inventive and creative faculty itself.

We have more moral, political and historical wisdom, than we know how to reduce into practice; we have more scientific and economical knowledge than can be accommodated to the just distribution of the produce which it multiplies. The poetry in these systems of thought, is concealed by the accumulation of facts and calculating processes. There is no want of knowledge respecting what is wisest and best in morals, government, and political economy, or at least, what is wiser and better than what men now practise and endure. But we let '*I dare not* wait upon *I would*, like the poor cat in the adage'. We want the creative faculty to imagine that which we know; we want the generous impulse to act that which we imagine; we want the poetry of life: our calculations have outrun conception; we have eaten more than we can digest. The cultivation of those

1. Although Rousseau has been thus classed, he was essentially a poet. The others, even Voltaire, were mere reasoners.

sciences which have enlarged the limits of the empire of man over the external world, has, for want of the poetical faculty, proportionally circumscribed those of the internal world; and man, having enslaved the elements, remains himself a slave. To what but a cultivation of the mechanical arts in a degree disproportioned to the presence of the creative faculty, which is the basis of all knowledge, is to be attributed the abuse of all invention for abridging and combining labour, to the exasperation of the inequality of mankind? From what other cause has it arisen that the discoveries which should have lightened, have added a weight to the curse imposed on Adam? Poetry, and the principle of Self, of which money is the visible incarnation, are the God and Mammon of the world.

The functions of the poetical faculty are twofold; by one it creates new materials of knowledge and power and pleasure; by the other it engenders in the mind a desire to reproduce and arrange them according to a certain rhythm and order which may be called the beautiful and the good. The cultivation of poetry is never more to be desired than at periods when, from an excess of the selfish and calculating principle, the accumulation of the materials of external life exceed the quantity of the power of assimilating them to the internal laws of human nature. The body has then become too unwieldy for that which animates it.

Poetry is indeed something divine. It is at once the centre and circumference of knowledge; it is that which comprehends all science, and that to which all science must be referred. It is at the same time the root and blossom of all other systems of thought; it is that from which all spring, and that which adorns all; and that which, if blighted, denies the fruit and the seed, and withholds from the barren world the nourishment and the succession of the scions of the tree of life. It is the perfect and consummate surface and bloom of all things: it is as the odour and the colour of the rose to the texture of the elements which compose it, as the form and splendour of unfaded beauty to the secrets of anatomy and corruption. What were virtue, love, patriotism, friendship – what were the scenery of this beautiful universe which we inhabit; what were our consolations on this side of the grave –and what were our aspirations beyond it, if poetry did not ascend to bring light and fire from those eternal regions where the owl-winged faculty of calculation dare not ever soar? Poetry is not like reasoning, a power to be exerted according to the determination of the will. A man cannot say, 'I will compose poetry.' The greatest poet even cannot say it; for the mind in creation is as a fading coal, which some invisible influence, like an inconstant wind, awakens to transitory brightness; this power arises from within, like the colour of a flower which fades and changes as it is developed, and the conscious portions of our natures are unprophetic either of its approach or its departure. Could this influence be durable in its original purity and force, it is impossible to predict the greatness of the results; but when composition begins, inspiration is already on the decline, and the most glorious poetry that has ever been communicated to the world is probably a feeble shadow of the original conceptions of the poet. I appeal to the greatest poets of the present day, whether it is not an error to assert that the finest passages of poetry are produced by labour and study. The toil and the delay recommended by critics can be justly interpreted to mean no more than a careful observation of the inspired moments, and an artificial connexion of the spaces between their suggestions by the intertexture of conventional expressions; a necessity only imposed by the limitedness of the poetical faculty itself; for Milton conceived the *Paradise Lost* as a whole before he executed it in portions. We have his own authority also for the muse having 'dictated' to him the 'unpremeditated song'. And let this be an answer to those who would allege the fifty-six various readings of the first line of the *Orlando Furioso*. Compositions so produced are to poetry what mosaic is to painting. This instinct and intuition of the poetical faculty is still more observable in the plastic and pictorial arts; a great statue or picture grows under the power of the artist as a child in the mother's womb; and the very mind which directs the hands in formation is incapable of accounting to itself for the origin, the gradations, or the media of the process.

Poetry is the record of the best and happiest moments of the happiest and best minds. We are aware of evanescent visitations of thought and feeling sometimes associated with place or person, sometimes regarding our own mind alone, and always arising unforeseen and departing unbidden, but elevating and delightful beyond all expression: so that even in the desire and regret they leave, there cannot but be pleasure, participating as it does in the nature of its object. It is as it were the interpenetration of a diviner nature through our own; but its footsteps are like those of a wind over the sea, which the coming calm erases, and whose traces remain only, as on the wrinkled sand which paves it. These and corresponding conditions of being are experienced principally by those of the most delicate sensibility and the most enlarged imagination; and the state of mind produced by them is at war with every base desire. The enthusiasm of virtue, love, patriotism, and friendship, is essentially linked with such emotions; and whilst they last, self appears as what it is, an atom to a universe. Poets are not only subject to these experiences as spirits of the most refined organization, but they can colour all that they combine with the evanescent hues of this ethereal world; a word, a trait in the representation of a scene or a passion, will touch the enchanted chord, and reanimate, in those who have ever experienced these emotions, the sleeping, the cold, the buried image of the past. Poetry thus makes immortal all that is best and most beautiful in the world; it arrests the vanishing apparitions which haunt the interlunations of life, and veiling them, or in language or in form, sends them forth among mankind, bearing sweet news of kindred joy to those with whom their sisters abide — abide, because there is no portal of expression from the caverns of the spirit which they inhabit into the universe of things. Poetry redeems from decay the visitations of the divinity in man.

Poetry turns all things to loveliness; it exalts the beauty of that which is most beautiful, and it adds beauty to that which is most deformed; it marries exultation and horror, grief and pleasure, eternity and change; it subdues to union under its light yoke all irreconcilable things. It transmutes all that it touches, and every form moving within the radiance of its presence is changed by wondrous sympathy to an incarnation of the spirit which it breathes: its secret alchemy turns to potable gold the poisonous waters which flow from death through life; it strips the veil of familiarity from the world, and lays bare the naked and sleeping beauty, which is the spirit of its form.

Notes on Authors

Charles Babbage (1792–1871)
A Cambridge mathematician who invented the mechanical computer. He was an uninhibited and perceptive critic of the contemporary scene, and his reflections on the declining fortunes of science and technology led to (amongst other things) the formation of the British Association.

Augustin Barruel (fl. 1798)
French priest, trained as a Jesuit, one of the earliest emigrés during the French Revolution. His *Memoirs Illustrating the History of Jacobinism* were published in Hamburg in 1798 and present the classic formulation of the conspiratorial theory of the causes of the French Revolution.

James Barry (1741–1806)
This acute, abrasive Irishman applied his considerable energy single-mindedly to the vocation of immortalizing himself and English art. Elected to the Royal Academy in 1773 and Professor of Painting in 1782, he made so many enemies that he was expelled not only from his chair but from the Academy itself. He consistently failed to obtain private patronage. His main work was a mammoth single-handed decoration of the great room of the Society of Arts with six huge moral allegories, which took him seven years to complete. He died in poverty, pathologically convinced of persecution by society, a martyr to high art (see Plate 11).

William Blake (1757–1827)
Blake earned his living as an engraver, with some subsidiary income from his marvellous hand-printed illustrated poems (see Plates 18, 19, 22 and 23). He knew a surprisingly large number of artists in official circles, such as John Flaxman (1755–1826) (see

Plates 20 and 21) and Henry Fuseli (see Plate 5), many of whose ideas he shared, applying to them, however, his own individual-istic and passionate enthusiasm.

William Cullen Bryant (1794–1878)
One of the first real American poets. He started in law but turned to journalism and became editor of the *New York Even-ing Post*. 'The Embargo', an attack on Jefferson's policies, is a remarkable achievement for a young teenager. His best-known poem 'Thanatopsis' shows a romantic attitude to nature.

Edmund Burke (1729–97)
Born in Dublin, the son of a Protestant attorney, in 1729. Educated at Trinity College Dublin, he entered the Middle Temple in London in 1750. He entered Parliament in 1765. Burke was one of the principal supporters of the American colo-nists in Parliament during the War of Independence but was a most violent critic of the Revolution in France; the former revolt he believed was founded on legality, the French Revolution how-ever was illegal. His *Reflections on the Revolution in France* were acknowledged as the principal statement of counter-revo-lution in Europe during the 1790s. Burke was also extremely in-fluential for his occasional contributions to art criticism and theory. He was an intimate of Reynolds and Dr Johnson, and his patronage of James Barry was crucial in the latter's early years.

Sir Thomas Fowell Buxton (1746–1845)
Buxton was not a Quaker but married into the Gurney family and was brother-in-law to Elizabeth Fry. He was for some time a Member of Parliament but lost his seat because he refused to use bribery. He succeeded Wilberforce as leader of the anti-slavery party and played a major part in the campaign for the abolition of slavery.

Joan Derck Van der Capellen tot de Pol (fl. 1781)
A Dutch nobleman who was an opponent of the established order in the United Provinces and the ruling house of Orange. Capellen corresponded with parliamentary reformers in Eng-

land and with leaders of the American Revolution; his *Appeal to the Dutch People*, published anonymously in 1781, has been called the first piece of writing in which anyone ever spoke to the Dutch people as a national unit.

William Carey (1761–1834)

Carey was a Northamptonshire cobbler who was brought up an Anglican and became a Baptist. His advocacy led to the forming of the Baptist Missionary Society, and he is rightly regarded as the pioneer of the modern missionary movement. He himself served in India, and was responsible for the abolition of suttee (the death of a widow at her husband's funeral).

Marie-Joseph Chénier (1764–1811)

A brother of the great French poet André Chénier. He wrote several revolutionary and patriotic songs and was also a playwright.

William Cowper (1731–1800)

A man whose intensity of feeling unbalanced him and who suffered through much of his life from fits of insanity; he called himself a 'stricken deer'. His profession was law, his interest poetry, classical in structure, romantic in feeling. With John Newton he collaborated in *Olney Hymns*; two or three of his own contributions are classics of devotion.

George Crabbe (1754–1832)

Grew up in Suffolk, began working in the field of medicine, but turned to the church and to literature. As a poet he stands out for the honesty of his pictures of country life and the craftsmanship of his verse.

Nicholas Cresswell (fl. 1774)

Author of a journal covering the years 1774 to 1777, including a voyage from Virginia to Barbados, with a vivid account of the practice of slavery.

François Crouzet

A contemporary French economist.

Allan Cunningham (1784–1842)

A native of Dumfriesshire who was at first a stonemason and subsequently secretary to Francis Chantrey, the sculptor. Among his publications was *Lives of the most eminent British Painters, Sculptors, and Architects*, 1829–33.

John Dalton (1766–1844)

Cumberland-born chemist whose greatest achievement was to found the modern chemical atomic theory (in Manchester, in the early 1800s). He worked also on meteorology and colour-blindness.

Sir Humphry Davy (1778–1829)

Cornishman with no scientific training who attained the Presidency of the Royal Society. His reputation as a chemist was established by his work on nitrous oxide at Bristol and consolidated by his massive achievements at the Royal Institution, London. Here he discovered potassium and sodium and founded the new science of electrochemistry. His miners' safety-lamp was invented in 1815.

Eugène Delacroix (1798–1863)

He was an admirer of Géricault, posing for one of the figures in *The Raft of the Medusa* (see Plate 13). His three important early paintings: *Dante and Virgil* (1822), *The Massacre of Chios* (1824) and *The Death of Sardanapalus* (1827) (see Plate 15) formed a watershed in French painting. His *Journal*, a highly intimate but methodical record of his life and thoughts about art was first published in 1893, from the manuscript in the possession of the University of Paris.

Denis Diderot (1713–84)

One of the most important of the 'philosophes', Diderot edited the *Encyclopédie* from 1746–66 and during this time became interested in making the theatre more morally instructive, writing two moral bourgeois plays, which were not very successful. He employed much the same approach in his art criticism. His 'Salons' were important examples of philosophical art criticism, and were circulated through Grimm's *Correspondence littéraire* to an exclusive but tiny clique of aristocratic subscribers.

Jacques Droz
A contemporary French historian. The excerpts in this volume are from his book *Europe Between the Revolutions 1815–1848*, published in translation as part of the *Fontana History of Europe*.

George Eliot (1819–80)
Pen-name of Mary Ann Evans, the last of the great nineteenth-century women novelists. She had a strict Evangelical upbringing, but became a free-thinker; this did not prevent her from writing an imaginatively sympathetic picture of the Methodists in *Adam Bede* (1849). She lived with George Henry Lewes, who was separated from his own wife; he encouraged her literary work. *Middlemarch* (1872) remains one of the greatest English novels.

Henry Fuseli (1741–1825)
Born in Switzerland and widely travelled on the continent, Fuseli was well read in a wide range of European literature. Elected to the Royal Academy in 1790, after a late conversion to painting and several years studying from the antique in Rome (1770–78), he was widely liked as a witty and picturesque character. His most important paintings illustrate wild and bizarre scenes from Milton and Shakespeare, strangely at variance with his rather orthodox teaching at the Academy as Lecturer in Painting (see Plate 5).

Oliver Goldsmith (1730–74)
Goldsmith was a friend of Dr Johnson who said that he adorned whatever he touched. Apart from his classic poem 'The Dissected Village' he is remembered as the author of *She Stoops to Conquer* and *The Vicar of Wakefield*.

William Hazlitt (1778–1830)
Son of a Unitarian minister, he was a difficult man, moody but beloved by his friends. He became a notable critic and essayist, pungent, outspoken, stimulatory.

David Hume (1711–76)

The great Scottish empiricist philosopher and historian is now most admired for his *Treatise of Human Nature* (1739–40) in which he took Locke's empiricism to its logical conclusions, in scepticism and subjectivism, but this work was largely misunderstood during his lifetime. His essays were more influential, particularly those on political theory, ethics and aesthetics. He published *An Enquiry Concerning the Human Understanding* (under the title *Philosophical Essays Concerning the Human Understanding*) in 1748. He knew and was admired by many of the French *philosophes*, including d'Alembert and Diderot.

Jean Auguste Dominique Ingres (1780–1867)

The star pupil of David's school, Ingres spent much of his life in Italy (1806–24 and 1834–41). Although highly successful during most of his life, and loaded with honours, Ingres was deeply hurt by any hostile criticism and his attitude hardened into a wilfully possessive glorification of the beautiful, defined as a mastery of composition and form along the lines of the Greeks and Raphael. In his art, however, there is a streak of extraordinarily obsessive imagination which has helped to maintain his reputation (see Plates 9 and 14).

Washington Irving (1783–1859)

He was born in New York, and rose to eminence in the diplomatic service, but his fame rests on his writings. *The History of New York*, allegedly by a Dutch scholar Diedrich Knickerbocker, was published in 1809 when he was only twenty-six, and is wittily satirical; it contains a clever caricature of Jefferson. His voluminous biography of George Washington is almost unreadable now, but 'Rip Van Winkle' and 'The Legend of Sleepy Hollow' live on.

Thomas Jefferson (1743–1826)

Third President of the United States, Jefferson was a man of many parts; his house 'Monticello' in Virginia shows his taste as an architect and his ingenuity as an inventor. He wanted to be remembered as author of the Declaration of Independence, of the Statute of Virginia for religious freedom, and Father of the University of Virginia.

Immanuel Kant (1724–1804)
Born in East Prussia; his magnum opus, *The Critique of Pure Reason*, was published in 1781. He tried to remove misunderstandings by restating the main argument in the *Prolegomena to Any Future Metaphysics* of 1783, and by rewriting some of the central sections of the *Critique* for a second edition in 1787. Later works included *The Critique of Practical Reason* (1790), *Religion within the Bounds of Mere Reason* (1793) and *Metaphysic of Morals* (1797).

Alexander Knox (1757–1831)
A descendant of the great John Knox he was himself a High Church Anglican, and at the same time a close friend of John Wesley.

John Locke (1632–1704)
Locke was a leading member of the school of philosophy known as 'British Empiricism'. His two most important works are the *Essay Concerning Human Understanding* (1689) and the *Two Treatises of Government* (1690).

Thomas Mann (1875–1955)
German novelist and critic, he left Germany for America with the rise of the Nazis. *Buddenbrooks*, *Tonio Kröger*, *The Magic Mountain* and *Doctor Faustus* are among the high points of an outstanding achievement. He won the Nobel Prize in 1929.

John Newton (1725–1807)
After an adventurous career at sea he was converted to a deeply personal Christianity. He became ordained and served at Olney in Northamptonshire where he was associated with William Cowper, and at St Mary Woolnoth, London. He was a persuasive preacher and magnificent hymn-writer, and vigorous campaigner against the slave-trade in which he had at one time shared.

Charles Nodier (1780–1844)
Author of a chain of highly popular romantic novels, beginning in 1818, Nodier is also crucial to the literary romantic movement

in France for bringing together in social gatherings at his house, Victor Hugo, Alfred de Vigny and others during the 1820s.

Tom Paine (1737–1809)

Born in Thetford, Norfolk in 1737. After a disastrous early life he took ship for the American colonies in 1744 where he began a new career as a journalist. *Common Sense* was published in 1776, the first public demand for independence from Britain; it enjoyed a phenomenal success. During the 1790s Paine was back in Europe mixing in revolutionary circles; the *Rights of Man* was first published in England, Part One in March 1791, Part Two in February 1792, ostensibly as a reply to Burke's *Reflections on the Revolution in France*.

William Paley (1743–1805)

Cambridge theologian and Archdeacon of Carlisle noted for his powerful pre-Benthamite advocacy of utilitarianism and his attempts to confound atheism by arguments derived from natural phenomena. His *Natural Theology* and his *Evidences* were prescribed reading in some universities well into the twentieth century.

Robert R. Palmer

A contemporary American historian.

Beilby Porteous (1731–1808)

One of nineteen children. In his younger days a distinguished scholar. He became Bishop of Chester in 1776, of London in 1787. He helped the rise of the evangelicals while opposing some of their views. He was a great supporter of the abolition of slavery, and of the missionary movement.

Joseph Priestley (1773–1804)

Nonconformist minister whose forthright political and religious views led to the destruction of his home in the Birmingham riots of 1791. A prolific writer, he was also one of the greatest experimental chemists of the eighteenth century, discovering 'more new and curious substances' than anyone before him, and anticipating Lavoisier in his isolation of pure oxygen.

Sir Joshua Reynolds (1723–92)
Following three years in Italy (1749–52), Reynolds became the foremost portraitist in England, employing the sensuous Venetian colouring which he greatly admired, while trying to introduce a more serious tone in his art (see Plate 10). He was unanimously chosen by the founder members of the Royal Academy as their first President, for which he was knighted in 1768. His highly influential writings are noted for their masterly summing up of the most important eighteenth-century views on art, combined with a sensitivity towards individual genius which was prophetic of later developments.

John Robison (fl. 1790)
Scots chemist of considerable repute at Edinburgh University during the 1790s. He had mixed in Masonic circles in St Petersburg during the 1770s and claimed in his *Proofs of a Conspiracy* that from this period in his life he gleaned much of his information on the Masonic conspiracy to revolutionize the world.

Jean-Jacques Rousseau (1712–78)
Born in Geneva in 1712, he was the son of a watchmaker. After a wandering early life, vividly described in the opening Books of his *Confessions*, he established himself in Paris during the 1740s, writing operas and ballets and contributing to Diderot's *Encyclopédie*, a project which brought together the leading French intellectuals and *philosophes*. His own subsequent writings on social and political topics, and especially *The Social Contract* (1762) profoundly influenced political thinking during and after the French Revolution; while his discursive novels *La Nouvelle Héloïse* and *Émile* became formative influences on the literature of Romanticism. He died near Paris in 1778.

Percy Bysshe Shelley (1792–1822)
Wrote *A Defence of Poetry* in 1821. Its immediate purpose was to reply to an essay by T. L. Peacock.

Emmanuel Joseph Sieyès (fl. 1789)
At the beginning of the French Revolution Sieyès was Canon of Chartres. He was a deputy for the Third Estate at the Estates

General in 1789; three years later he had given up the priesthood and was a deputy to the National Convention. When asked in later life what he did during the Terror he is said to have replied, 'I survived.' In 1799 he aided Napoleon in his seizure of power, but served in relative obscurity during the Empire.

Sydney Smith (1771–1845)

One of the greatest of all wits, a fact which kept him from ecclesiastical preferment; he described his career as a contradiction of Newton's law, because levity prevented him from rising, whereas more gravity would have helped him to rise. He founded the influential *Edinburgh Review*, distrusted emotional extremism, supported Catholic emancipation and the Reform Bill.

Stendhal (1783–1842)

The *nom de plume* of Marie Henri Beyle. Stendhal served in Napoleon's armies and held a position of some importance during the traumatic retreat from Russia, an experience which haunted him throughout his life. Most famous for his novels (particularly *Scarlet and Black*), Stendhal was also an influential and trenchant art critic. His *Histoire de la Peinture en Italie* (1817) and his literary criticisms of the French Academy exhibitions, the 'Salons', are important for the stress he placed on modernity and originality in art. He also wrote articles interpreting restoration France for contempory English Periodicals, which were first published in English.

William Makepeace Thackeray (1811–63)

Born in India, educated in England, he became an art student in Paris, then turned to journalism and literature. His best-known book remains *Vanity Fair* (1847–8); apart from his longer novels he made many worthy contributions to *Punch* and other journals.

J. F. Vonck (fl. 1789)

A Belgian lawyer, the son of a wealthy farmer. Vonck was a leader of the resistance to the Emperor Joseph II in the Austrian Netherlands; he organized a revolution there by conspiratorial methods and was leader of the extremist democratic party seeking widespread internal changes in the country during the brief period of the collapse of Austrian rule in 1789.

W. H. Walsh and G. J. Warnock

Present-day British philosophers.

Charles Wesley (1707–88)

Younger brother to John, Charles shared many of the same experiences. He is one of England's two great hymn-writers (the other being Isaac Watts), writing over 5500 in all, including the universally known 'Hark! the herald angels sing' and 'Love divine, all loves excelling'. His hymns are eminently singable and masterpieces of theology and devotion.

John Wesley (1703–91)

Educated at Oxford, where he gathered round him a group of 'Methodists'. He went on a missionary journey to Georgia, where his outspoken opposition to slavery and alcohol led to bitter opposition. He had a profound religious experience in 1728 which sent him out to preach in the highways and by-ways. In the next fifty-three years he travelled 224,000 miles, mostly on horseback and preached 40,000 sermons. He wanted to remain a loyal Anglican but hostility forced him to work outside the established church.

William Wilberforce (1759–1833)

MP for Hull from 1780. Converted to Evangelical Christianity by John Newton, who prevented him from taking orders so that he could give a Christian lead in Parliament. Wilberforce was a leading member of the Clapham Sect and a major fighter for the abolition of slavery. In other ways he appears as a worthy but conservative moralist.

William Wordsworth (1770–1850)

He is primarily regarded for his celebration of the permanent values of Nature. But as a young man he was an ardent sympathizer with republican movements, and although he quickly became disillusioned with politics, his poetry until the end of his life reflects his feeling for the poor, and for the spiritual poverty of contemporary life. What is printed here amplifies the selection we have chosen for the Course: *The Poetry of Wordsworth*, ed. T. Crehan, University of London Press, 1965.

Sources

A Worldwide Revolution?

1   R. R. Palmer, 'The World Revolution of the West, 1763–1801', from *Political Science Quarterly*, vol. 64, 1954.

2   Abbé Augustin Barruel, *Memoirs Illustrating the History of Jacobinism*, 4 vols., 1798, translated by the Hon. Robert Clifford, London, 1798.

3   John Robison, *Proofs of a Conspiracy against all the Religions and Governments of Europe*, Edinburgh, 1798.

B The American Revolution

1, 2, 5, 7, 8, 9 H. S. Commager (ed.), *Documents of American History*, New York, Appleton-Century-Crofts, 1963.

3   Thomas Paine, *Common Sense*, Philadelphia, 1776.

4   Carl L. Becker, *The Declaration of Independence*, New York, Knopf, 1942.

6   Philip S. Foner (ed.), *Basic Writings of Thomas Jefferson*, New York, Wiley, 1944.

C Disturbances before the French Revolution

1, 2, 3, 4 Jacques Godechot (ed.), *La Pensée révolutionnaire en France et en Europe, 1780–99*, Paris, 1964. C1 is a modern translation from R. C. Bridges, P. Dukes, J. D. Hargreaves and W. Scott (eds.), *Nations and Empires: Documents on the History of Europe and on its Relations with the World since 1648*, London, Macmillan, 1969. C2, C3 and C4 are translated by Clive Emsley.

5   The *Annual Register*, 1780.

D   The French Revolution

1   Abbé Sieyès, *What is the Third Estate?*, 1789,
    translated by M. Blondel, London, Pall Mall Press,
    1963.

2   Translation published in Thomas Paine,
    Rights of Man, Part I, London, 1791. Harmonds-
    worth, Penguin, 1969.

3, 4   Walter Markov and Albert Soboul (eds.), *Die
    Sansculotten von Paris*, East Berlin, 1957. Extracts
    translated by Clive Emsley.

5, 6   Recorded on 'Chants Révolutionnaires' issued by
    Le Chant du Monde, Paris, No. LD 45-3001/EP
    45 3001/EP YEG-45-557.

E   The English Reaction

1   Edmund Burke, *Reflections on the Revolution in
    France*, London, 1790. Harmondsworth, Penguin,
    1969.

2   Thomas Paine, *Rights of Man*, London, 1791
    and 1792. Harmondsworth, Penguin, 1969.

3   Minute Book of the London Corresponding
    Society, Place Papers, British Museum, Add.
    MSS. 27812.

4, 5   R. W. Postgate (ed.), *Revolution from 1789-1906*,
    New York, Harper & Row, 1962.

F   Economic Changes

1   F. Crouzet, 'England and France in the
    eighteenth century: a comparative analysis of
    two economic growths', from R. W. Hartwell
    (ed.), *The Causes of the Industrial Revolution*
    translated by J. Sondheimer, London, Methuen,
    1967.

G   Thomas Jefferson

1, 2, 10   H. S. Commager (ed.), *Documents of American History*, New York, Appleton-Century-Crofts, 1963.

3   P. L. Ford (ed.), *The Writings of Thomas Jefferson*, vol. 3, New York, 1894.

4, 5, 6, 7, 8, 9   Merrill D. Peterson, *Thomas Jefferson and the New Nation*, New York, Oxford University Press, 1970.

11   William Cullen Bryant, *The Embargo*, Boston, 1809.

12, 13   Philip S. Foner (ed.), *Basic Writings of Thomas Jefferson*, New York, Wiley, 1944.

14   Washington Irving, *Knickerbocker's History of New York*, New York, 1812.

15   Saul K. Padover, *Jefferson*, Mentor Books, 1942.

H   Rousseau and Goethe

1   Jean-Jacques Rousseau, *Du Contrat Social*, 1762, translated and with an introduction by G. D. H. Cole as *The Social Contract* and *Discourses*, London, Dent, 1913.

2   Jean-Jacques Rousseau, *Émile*, 1762, translated by Barbara Foxley, London, Dent, 1911.

3   Thomas Mann, *Essays*, 1918, translated by H. T. Lowe-Porter, New York, Knopf, 1918.

4   W. M. Thackeray, *Miscellanies*, vol. 1, London, 1855.

J   William Wordsworth

1, 2   William Wordsworth, *The Prelude*, 1805–6. E. de Selincourt (ed.), 1933. Revised edition, Helen Darbishire, London, Oxford University Press, 1959.

3   Alexander Grosart (ed.), *The Prose Works of William Wordsworth*, 3 vols., London, 1876.

4, 5, 6, 9, 10   William Wordsworth and Samuel Coleridge,
                 Lyrical Ballads, 1798, 1800 and 1802. R. L. Brett
                 and A. R. Jones (eds.), London, Methuen, 1963.

7, 8, 11   William Wordsworth, *Poetical Works*, Thomas
                 Hutchinson (ed.), London, 1904. Revised edition,
                 E. de Selincourt (ed.), London, Oxford University
                 Press, 1967.

12   Austin Dobson (ed.), *Poetical Works of Oliver
                 Goldsmith*, London, 1908.

13   A. J. Carlyle and R. M. Carlyle (eds.), *Poetical
                 Works of George Crabbe*, London, 1908. Howard
                 Mills (ed.), *Tales, 1812 and Other Selected
                 Poems*, Cambridge, Cambridge University Press,
                 1967.

14   William Hazlitt, *The Spirit of the Age*, London,
                 1825.

K   *Philosophy*

1   John Locke, *An Essay concerning Human
    Understanding*, London, 1690. A. S. Pringle-
    Pattison (ed.), London, Oxford University Press,
    1924, (abridged).

2   David Hume, *A Treatise of Human Nature*,
    London, 1739. L. A. Selby-Bigge (ed.), Oxford,
    Clarendon Press, 1888, reprinted, London,
    Oxford University Press, 1967, 3 vols., with an
    analytical index.

3   David Hume, *Enquiries concerning the Human
    Understanding and concerning the Principles of
    Morals*, London, 1748. L. A. Selby-Bigge (ed.),
    Oxford, Clarendon Press, 2nd edition, 1962
    (reprinted from the 1777 edition).

4   Immanuel Kant, *Prolegomena*, translated by
    P. G. Lucas, Manchester, Manchester University
    Press, 1953.

5   Immanuel Kant, *Critique of Pure Reason*,

translated by N. K. Smith, London, Macmillan, 1964.

6   W. H. Walsh, 'Categories', from *Kant-Studien*, Band 45, 1954, Kölner Universitäts Verlag.
R. P. Wolff (ed.), *Kant*, New York, Doubleday, 1967.

7   G. J. Warnock, 'Kant', D. J. O'Connor (ed.), *A Critical History of Western Philosophy*, New York, Free Press, 1964.

L   Scientific Change

1   Joseph Priestley, *Experiments and Observations on Different Kinds of Air*, vol. 2, London, 1775. Reprinted as Alembic Club Reprint No. 7, Edinburgh, 1894.

2   William Paley, *Natural Theology*, 1802, London, 18th edition, 1819.

3   Humphry Davy, 'On some new phenomena of chemical changes produced by electricity', from *Philosophical Transactions*, 1808, vol. 98. Reprinted in vol. 5 of *Collected Works*, London, 1840.

4   Humphry Davy, *Researches, Chemical and Philosophical, chiefly concerning Nitrous Oxide, or Dephlogisticated Nitrous Air, and its Respiration*, Bristol, 1800. Reprinted in vol. 3 of *Collected Works*, London, 1839.

5   Humphry Davy, 'A Discourse Introductory to a Course of Lectures on Chemistry', delivered January 1802. Reprinted in vol. 2 of *Collected Works*, London, 1839.

6   Humphry Davy, *Collected Works*, London, 1839.

7   John Dalton, *A New System of Chemical Philosophy*, Manchester, 1808.

8   Charles Babbage, *Reflections on the Decline of Science in England and on Some of its Causes*, London, 1830. London, Gregg International Publishers, 1969.

M High Art

1a, 4a Edmund Burke, *A Philosophical Enquiry into the Origin of our Ideas on the Sublime and the Beautiful*, London, 1757, second edition, 1759. J. T. Boulton (ed.), London, Routledge & Kegan Paul, 1958.

1b David Hume, *Four Dissertations*, London, 1757. Reprinted in John W. Lenz (ed.), *Of the Standard of Taste and Other Essays*, Indianapolis, Bobbs-Merrill, 1965.

1c, d Joshua Reynolds, *Discourses Delivered at the*
2a, b, j *Royal Academy*, London, 1820. Reprinted in
3a-f *Discourses on Art*, Robert R. Wark (ed.), San
5a, b, d, e Marino, California, Henry E. Huntingdon Library, 1959.

2c, f James Barry, *An Enquiry into the Real and the Imaginary Obstructions to the Acquisition of the Arts in England*, London, 1774.

2d, 3g Geoffrey Keynes (ed.), *Blake, Complete Writings*
5c, f, g *with Variant Readings*, London, Oxford University Press, 1966.

2e James Barry, *The Works of James Barry Esquire*, London, 1809.

2g, h Eudo C. Mason (ed.), *The Mind of Henry Fuseli*,
3h, 5h London, Routledge & Kegan Paul Limited, 1951.

2k *Pilkington's Dictionary of Painters*, London, 1840.

3j Jean Auguste Dominique Ingres, *Pensées et Ecrits*
6 *du Peintre*, Geneva, 1947. Extracts translated by Tim Benton.

3k, l Eugène Delacroix, *Journal*, Paris, 1893. Extracts translated by Tim Benton. Reprinted in Hubert Wellington (ed.), *The Journal of Eugène Delacroix*, translated by Lucy Norton, London, Phaidon Press, 1951.

3m Juliusz Starzynski (ed.), *Stendhal: du Romantisme dans les Arts*, Paris, Hermann, 1966. Extract translated by Tim Benton.

4b   Stendhal, *Histoire de la Peinture en Italie*, Paris, 1817. Extract translated by Tim Benton.

4c   Charles Nodier, *Mélanges de Littérature et de Critique*, Paris, 1820. Extract translated by Tim Benton. Reprinted in Guy Michaud and Ph. van Tiegheim (eds.), *Nodier: Le Romantisme*, Paris, Classiques Hachette, 1952.

5j   Jean Seznec and Jean Adhemar (eds.), *Diderot's Salons*, 4 vols., Oxford University Press, Clarendon Press, 1957–67. Extract translated by Tim Benton.

N   Stendhal

1, 2   Geoffrey Strickland (ed.), *Selected Journalism from the English Reviews by Stendhal*, London, Calder & Boyars, 1959.

3, 4   Jacques Droz, *Europe Between the Revolutions, 1815–48*, translated by R. Baldick, London, Fontana, 1967.

O   Religious Changes

1, 2, 4   Robert Southey, *Life of John Wesley*, London, 1820.

3, 12, 21   T. Charles Edwards and B. Richardson, *They Saw It Happen*, Oxford, Blackwell, 1958.

5   R. H. Murray, *Group Movements throughout the Ages*, London, Hodder & Stoughton, 1935.

6, 16, 17   Tom Ingram and Douglas Newton (eds.), *Hymns as Poetry*, London, Constable, 1956.

7   Sydney Smith, *The Works of the Reverend Sydney Smith*, London, 1839.

8   Bishop Beilby Porteous, *A Charge Delivered to the Clergy of the Diocese of London in 1798 and 1799*, London, 1799.

9, 10   George Crabbe, *The Works of the Reverend George Crabbe*, vols. 2 and 3, London, 1823.

11	William Carey, *Enquiry into the Obligations of Christians to use Means for Converting the Heathens*, Leicester, 1792.
13, 14, 15	Robert Southey, *The Life and Works of William Cowper*, London, 1835.
18	Nathaniel Micklem (ed.), *A Book of Personal Religion*, London, 1938.
19	John Newton, *Cardiphonia, or the Utterance of the Heart in the course of a Real Correspondence*, London, 1781.
20	John Newton, *Thoughts upon the African Slave Trade*, London, 1788.
21	P. T. Charles Edwards and B. Richardson (eds.), *The Journal of Nicholas Cresswell*, 1774–7, Blackwell, 1924.
22	William Wilberforce, *A Practical View of the Prevailing Religious System of Professed Christians in the Higher and Middle Classes in this Country, contrasted with Real Christianity*, London, 1797.
23	William Hazlitt, *The Spirit of the Age*, London, 1825.
24	George Eliot, *Adam Bede*, Edinburgh, 1859.

P   Shelley

| 1 | Edmund P. Jones (ed.), *English Critical Essays (Nineteenth Century)*, London, Oxford University Press, 1916. |

Acknowledgements

Permission to reproduce the documents in this volume is acknowledged to the following sources:

A1 *Political Science Quarterly*

C1 St Martin's Press, Inc., New York, Macmillan Company of Canada, and Macmillan, London and Basingstoke

D1 Pall Mall Press Ltd

F1 F. Crouzet, *Annales: Economies, Sociétés, Civilisations*, and Methuen & Co. Ltd

H1 J. M. Dent & Sons Ltd, and E. P. Dutton & Co. Inc.

H2 J. M. Dent & Sons Ltd, and E. P. Dutton & Co. Inc.

H3 Secker & Warburg Ltd, and Random House Inc.

K4 Manchester University Press

K5 St Martin's Press, Inc., New York, Macmillan Company of Canada, and Macmillan, London and Basingstoke

K6 Macmillan, London and Basingstoke

K7 Macmillan Co.

N1 Calder and Boyars Ltd

N2 Calder and Boyars Ltd

N3 Collins

N4 Collins

Index

Extracts in this book are indicated by
bold page references

Index